ART OF
EFFECTIVE ENGLISH WRITING
WITH
AURAL AND ORAL SKILLS
(FOR STUDENTS OF ICSE)

ART OF
EFFECTIVE ENGLISH WRITING
WITH
AURAL AND ORAL SKILLS
(FOR STUDENTS OF ICSE)

ESSAYS (Argumentative, Descriptive, Topical & Outline of Essays)
PICTURE COMPOSITION • LETTERS (Personal & Official)
PROVERBS & IDIOMS • Synonymous Words & Phrases
Words Likely to be Confused • Comprehension and Summary Writing
Functional Grammar • Latest ICSE Question Papers (Fully Solved)

MEENA SINGH
Former Senior English Teacher
Loreto Convent, Lucknow (U.P.)
The Gandhi Memorial International School
JAKARTA - INDONESIA

and

O.P. SINGH

S. CHAND
PUBLISHING
empowering minds

S. CHAND & COMPANY PVT. LTD.
(AN ISO 9001 : 2008 COMPANY)
RAM NAGAR, NEW DELHI-110 055

S. CHAND & COMPANY PVT. LTD.

(An ISO 9001 : 2008 Company)

Head Office: 7361, RAM NAGAR, NEW DELHI - 110 055
Phone: 23672080-81-82, 9899107446, 9911310888
Fax: 91-11-23677446
Shop at: **schandgroup.com**; e-mail: **info@schandgroup.com**

S. CHAND
PUBLISHING
empowering minds

Branches :
AHMEDABAD : 1st Floor, Heritage, Near Gujarat Vidhyapeeth, Ashram Road, **Ahmedabad** - 380 014,
Ph: 27541965, 27542369, ahmedabad@schandgroup.com
BENGALURU : No. 6, Ahuja Chambers, 1st Cross, Kumara Krupa Road, **Bengaluru** - 560 001,
Ph: 22268048, 22354008, bangalore@schandgroup.com
BHOPAL : Bajaj Tower, Plot No. 2&3, Lala Lajpat Rai Colony, Raisen Road, **Bhopal** - 462 011,
Ph: 4274723, 4209587. bhopal@schandgroup.com
CHANDIGARH : S.C.O. 2419-20, First Floor, Sector - 22-C (Near Aroma Hotel), **Chandigarh** -160 022,
Ph: 2725443, 2725446, chandigarh@schandgroup.com
CHENNAI : No.1, Whites Road, Opposite Express Avenue, Royapettah, **Chennai** - 600014
Ph. 28410027, 28410058, chennai@schandgroup.com
COIMBATORE : 1790, Trichy Road, LGB Colony, Ramanathapuram, **Coimbatore** -6410045,
Ph: 2323620, 4217136 coimbatore@schandgroup.com **(Marketing Office)**
CUTTACK : 1st Floor, Bhartia Tower, Badambadi, **Cuttack** - 753 009, Ph: 2332580; 2332581,
cuttack@schandgroup.com
DEHRADUN : 1st Floor, 20, New Road, Near Dwarka Store, **Dehradun** - 248 001,
Ph: 2711101, 2710861, dehradun@schandgroup.com
GUWAHATI : Dilip Commercial (Ist floor), M.N. Road, Pan Bazar, **Guwahati** - 781 001,
Ph: 2738811, 2735640 guwahati@schandgroup.com
HALDWANI : Bhatt Colony, Talli Bamori, Mukhani, **Haldwani** -263139 **(Marketing Office)** Mob. 09452294
HYDERABAD : Padma Plaza, H.No. 3-4-630, Opp. Ratna College, Narayanaguda, **Hyderabad** - 500 029,
Ph: 27550194, 27550195, hyderabad@schandgroup.com
JAIPUR : 1st Floor, Nand Plaza, Hawa Sadak, Ajmer Road, **Jaipur** - 302 006,
Ph: 2219175, 2219176, jaipur@schandgroup.com
JALANDHAR : Mai Hiran Gate, **Jalandhar** - 144 008, Ph: 2401630, 5000630, jalandhar@schandgroup.com
KOCHI : Kachapilly Square, Mullassery Canal Road, Ernakulam, **Kochi** - 682 011,
Ph: 2378740, 2378207-08, cochin@schandgroup.com
KOLKATA : 285/J, Bipin Bihari Ganguli Street, **Kolkata** - 700 012, Ph: 22367459, 22373914,
kolkata@schandgroup.com
LUCKNOW : Mahabeer Market, 25 Gwynne Road, Aminabad, **Lucknow** - 226 018, Ph: 4076971, 4026̄7
4065646, 4027188, lucknow@schandgroup.com
MUMBAI : Blackie House, IInd Floor, 103/5, Walchand Hirachand Marg, Opp. G.P.O., **Mumbai** - 400
Ph: 22690881, 22610885, mumbai@schandgroup.com
NAGPUR : Karnal Bagh, Near Model Mill Chowk, **Nagpur** - 440 032, Ph: 2720523, 2777666
nagpur@schandgroup.com
PATNA : 104, Citicentre Ashok, Mahima Palace , Govind Mitra Road, **Patna** - 800 004, Ph: 2300489,
2302100, patna@schandgroup.com
PUNE : Sadguru Enclave, Ground floor, Survey No. 114/3, Plot no. 8 Alandi Road ,
Vishrantwadi **Pune** – 411015 Ph: 64017298 pune@schandgroup.com
RAIPUR : Kailash Residency, Plot No. 4B, Bottle House Road, Shankar Nagar, **Raipur** - 492 007,
Ph: 2443142,Mb. : 09981200834, raipur@schandgroup.com **(Marketing Office)**
RANCHI : Shanti Deep Tower, Opp.Hotel Maharaja, Radium Road, **Ranchi**-834001
Mob. 09430246440 ranchi@schandgroup.com
SILIGURI : 122, Raja Ram Mohan Roy Road, East Vivekanandapally, P.O., Siliguri, **Siliguri**-734001,
Dist., Jalpaiguri, (W.B.) Ph. 0353-2520750 **(Marketing Office)** siliguri@schandgroup.com
VISAKHAPATNAM: No. 49-54-15/53/8, Plot No. 7, 1st Floor, Opp. Radhakrishna Towers,
Seethammadhara North Extn., **Visakhapatnam** - 530 013, Ph-2782609 (M) 09440100555,
visakhapatnam@schandgroup.com **(Marketing Office)**

First Edition 2002
Subsequent Editions and Reprints 2002, 2003, 2004, 2005 (Twice), 2006, 2007, 2008 (Twice) 2009 (Twice), 2011 (Twice), 2012; Fourth Revised Edition 2013
Reprint 2014 (with Question Paper 2013)
Reprint 2014
ISBN : 81-219-2130-9   **Code : 11E 784**

PRINTED IN INDIA
By Nirja Publishers & Printers Pvt. Ltd., 54/3/2, Jindal Paddy Compound, Kashipur Road, Rudrapur-263153, Uttarakhand and published by S. Chand & Company Pvt. Ltd., 7361, Ram Nagar, New Delhi -110 055.

Preface to the Fourth Revised Edition

The Council of Indian School Certificate Examination New Delhi, has made changes in the English language syllabus for ICSE examinations, from the year 2012 onwards. This necessitated revision of the book. Besides updating the book, a new section on listening (aural) and speaking (oral skills) has been added. This now forms an integral part of the internal assessment process, for English language examination for class IX and X.

Specific changes in the new edition are :

- A NEW section on LISTENING (AURAL) AND SPEAKING (ORAL) SKILLS with internal assessment syllabus, guidelines for examination and exercises for practice.

- Recent Essays and Letters Section with latest essays and letters.

- Comprehension and grammar section

- LATEST SOLVED ICSE QUESTION PAPERS.

The above changes would augment the language skills of the students, to face the ICSE examination with confidence.

Any suggestions for further improvement of the book are most welcome.

Meena Singh
O.P.Singh

Preface to the Second Revised Edition

There was an immediate need to revise our book **'Art of Effective English Writing'** so as confirm to recent changes in the syllabus of ICSE for the year 2008 onwards.

Besides adding new composition addressing a variety of subject in the essays and the letter section . We have added a **NEW GRAMMAR SECTION** keeping the syllabus in view. Besides this the **MODEL TEST PAPERS** and the **SOLVED ICSE QUESTION PAPERS** have been updated to make it more useful and relevant.

We are indeed grateful to the comments and valued suggestion we have received from numerous students and teachers across the country. We have tried to incorporate their suggestion in this book. However we would welcome your comments to further improve on the same.

MEENA SINGH
O.P. SINGH

Acknowledgements

We are indebted to a number of personalities who have at various stages helped and motivated us to bring out this book .We would also like to thank Mr. Naveen Joshi, Executive Vice-President, S. Chand & Company Ltd. for the encouragement, Ms Jaya Singh and Soumya Singh for computer assistance and last but not the least our dear father Shri Kalika Singh to whom we dedicate this book.

MEENA SINGH
O.P. SINGH

AIMS:

1. To develop and integrate the use of the four language skills, i.e. listening, speaking, reading and writing for the purpose of effective communication.
2. To develop a functional understanding of the grammar, structure and idiom of the language.
3. To develop the capacity to read efficiently and access information effectively.
4. To develop an appreciation of good literature.
5. To experience, through literature, the thoughts and feelings of the people of the world.

The paper will be of two hours duration.

Paper 1 : **English Language**	*80 Marks*
Internal assessment	*20 Marks*

PAPER 1 -- ENGLISH LANGUAGE
(Two hours) - 80 marks

Four questions will be set, all of which will be compulsory.

Question 1: Candidates will be required to write a composition from a choice of subjects which will test their ability to: organise, describe, narrate, report, explain, persuade or argue, present ideas coherently, compare and contrast ideas and arrive at conclusions, present relevant arguments and use correct style and format. The subjects will be varied and may be suggested by language or by other stimuli such as pictures. The subjects will be so chosen so as to allow the candidates to draw on first hand experience or to stimulate their imagination.

With one subject, a number of suggestions about the content of the composition will be given, but the use of the suggestions will be optional and a candidate will be free to treat the subject in any way that he/she chooses.

The organisation of subject matter, syntax, punctuation, correctness of grammatical constructions and spelling will be expected to be appropriate to the mode of treatment required by the subject.

Question 2: Candidates will have to write a letter from a choice of two subjects requiring either a formal or an informal mode of treatment. Suggestions regarding the content of the letter may be given. The layout of the letter with address, introduction, conclusion, etc., will form part of the assessment. Candidates will be expected to be familiar with the use of appropriate salutation, format and style for letters.

Question 3: An unseen passage of prose of about 500 words will be given. Uncommon items of vocabulary, or structure will be avoided. One question will be set to test vocabulary. Candidates will be required to show that they understand the words/phrases in the context in which they have been used. A number of questions requiring short answers will also be asked on the passage. These questions will test the candidates' ability to understand the explicit content and organisation of the passage and to infer information, intentions and attitudes from it.

The last question will consist of a summary that will test the candidates' ability to distinguish main ideas from supporting details and to extract salient points to re-express them in the form of a summary. Candidates will be given clear indications of what they are to summarise and of the length of the summary.

Question 4: There will be a number of short answer questions to test the candidates' knowledge of functional grammar, structure and usage of the language. All the items in this question will be compulsory. They will consist of sentence completion, multiple choice or other short answer type of questions.

INTERNAL ASSESSMENT – SYLLABUS
LISTENING (AURAL) AND SPEAKING (ORAL) SKILLS
For ICSE Examinations in and after 2012
Paper 1 English Language

1. Schools will prepare, conduct and record assessments of the **Listening and Speaking Skills** of candidates as follows

   Class IX: Three assessments in the course of the year.

   Class X: Two assessments in the course of the year.

2. **Pattern of assessment.**

   (*a*) **Listening Skills.**

   A passage of about 300 words is read aloud by the examiner twice. The first time at normal reading speed (About 110 words a minute) and the next time at a slower speed. Candidates may make brief notes during the reading. They then answer an objective type test based on the passage on the paper provided.

   The recommended number of candidates at a sitting is 30.

   (*b*) **Speaking Skills.**

   Each candidate is required to make an oral presentation of about two minutes, which will be followed by a discussion on the subject by the examiner, for about three minutes.

   Subject for presentation may include narrating an experience, providing a description, giving direction how to make or operate something, expressing an opinion, giving a report, relating an anecdote, or commenting on a current event.

   A candidate may refer to brief notes in the course of the presentation but reading or excessive dependence on notes will be penalized.

   It is recommended that the candidates be given an hour for preparation of their subject for presentation and that they may be given a choice of subject, on a common paper.

   Evaluation.

   The assessment will be conducted jointly by the subject teacher and the external examiner who will each assess the candidates (The External Examiner may be a teacher nominated by the Head of the School who could be from the faculty **but not teaching the subject in the section / class**. For example, a teacher of English of Class VIII may be deputed to be an External Examiner for Class X).

   Award of Marks

   Listening Skills: 10 marks

   Speaking Skills: 10 marks.

   The total marks obtained out of 20 are to be sent to the Council by the Head of the School. The Head of the School will be responsible for the entry of marks on the mark sheet provided by the council.

Schools are required to maintain a record of all assessments conducted in **Listening and Speaking Skills** for candidates of class IX and X. These include copies of the assessment tests, topics for presentation and marks awarded. The record will be maintained for a period of two months after the ICSE (10) examinations of the candidates concerned.

Internal Assessment in English Language. Guidelines for marking with grades –Aural Assignment for class IX and X

Grade	Understanding/Comprehension Main Idea, Central Theme	Recall	Vocabulary	Centext/Correlation to Other Areas	Marks
I	The candidate accurately understands the central idea of the passage as well as the relevant points in the selected passage/talk	The candidate recalls all the important points made (written/verbal)	The candidate uses appropriate and correct vocabulary while recalling the points made.	The candidate clearly understands the context and can widely correlate the passage to the other areas.	3
II	The candidate gives ideas farily close to the central/main idea of the passage as well as understands some of the relevant points heard in the selected passage/talk.	The candidate recalls some of the important points made (written/verbal).	The candidate uses correct but simple vocabulary while recalling the points made.	The candidate can moderately understand the context of the passage and can moderately correlate the passage to the other areas.	2
III	The candidate cannot fully comprehend the passage and gives only a few ideas related to the central theme of the passage	The candidate recalls very few of the important points made (written/verbal).	The candidate makes various errors in vocabulary while recalling the points made.	The candidate can only faintly understand the context of the passage and relate it to the other areas.	1
IV	The candidate is neither able to understand the central/main idea of the passage; nor able to understand relevant points heard in the passage/talk.	The candidate is unable to recall the important points made (written/verbal)	The candidate uses incorrect vocabulary while recalling the points made	The candidate is uable to understand the context of the passage and is unable to correlate the passage to the other areas.	0

Internal Assessment in English Language. Guidelines for marking with grades –Oral assignment for class IX and X

Grade	Fluency of language	Subject matter	Organization	Vocabulary/ Delivery	Understand-ing	Gestures	Marks
I	Speaks with fluency and has full operational command over the language.	Matter is relevant, rich in content and original	Content is well sequenced and well organized	Uses appropriate vocabulary and pronounces words correctly	While speaking, the candidate emphasizes the important points	Uses natural and spontaneous gestures that are not out of place.	3
II	The candidate speaks with fairly good fluency and has reasonable operational command of the language.	Subject matter is mostly relevant, consisting of few original ideas	The content is satisfactorily sequenced and well organized	The candidate pronounces most words correctly and uses simple vocabulary	While speaking, the candidate emphasizes most important points.	Uses some natural gestures	2
III	The candidate speaks with poor fluency and does not communicate except for the most basic information.	The subject matter is irrelevant and lacks originality	The subject content is very poor and lacks organisational structure	The candidate pronounces many words incorrectly and uses inappropriate vocabulary	While speaking, the candidate emphasizes some important points.	Uses very few natural gestures	1
IV	The candidate cannot communicate even the most basic information	The subject matter is negligible	The subject content comprises of mere words with no structured sentences.	The candidate is unable to correctly pronounce most words and has a limited vocabulary	While speaking, the candidate is unable to emphasize important points.	Uses no natural gestures	0

Contents

SECTION - A. RECENT ESSAYS

SECTION - B. ESSAYS

Views Including Argumentative

(*xvii*)

SECTION G. PROVERBS, IDIOMS
SYNONYMOUS WORDS AND CONFUSING WORDS

SECTION H. COMPREHENSION AND SUMMARY WRITING

SECTION I. GRAMMAR

IMPORTANCE OF WRITING GOOD COMPOSITION

Writing a good composition is just like creating a piece of good Art. Just as any budding artist goes about perfecting his art, following some basic ground rules. Similarly a budding writer goes about refining his art, by writing different types of composition. This Art is not difficult to perfect and once the methodology is understood, one derives a great sense of satisfaction, which stands one in good stead throughout life. In the case of students especially those preparing for ICSE English language Paper 1, writing a composition of 350 to 400 words in essay, and a letter is the most important part of the paper. The objective of this question is, to test the ability of the examinee, in writing well-organised clear and accurate English.

The Art of effective English writing

English is a typical language. It is not uncommon to find, that people who are good at spoken English, not able to express themselves in writing. The reason is that, they do not visualise and write to a plan. For a composition to be meaningful, it is not necessary that it should be written in superfluous language, with big difficult words. What is required is, that the same should be written to a plan, with a line of continuity and should express the feelings of the writer in plain simple English.

Therefore, for a composition (essay or letter) to be meaningful we must observe the following basic rule:

- Write to a plan.
- Ensure a line of continuity throughout the composition.
- Avoid use of high-flown language.
- A good introduction and conclusion are an essential pre-requisite.

Besides the above some other valuable guidelines are —

The presentation of material should be orderly and coherent

This specifically means, that you have to take some time in thinking what you are going to write about. You must therefore read the topic carefully, and determine what it is about (Please do not hazard a guess). As we all know a good composition must have a good beginning (introduction), a body and a conclusion. The Introduction should arouse interest and attract attention, while the conclusion should satisfy it. There are a number of ways by which you can make your composition instantly appealing.

(a) **Suggested ways to begin or conclude a composition** .
- Begin or end with a quotation which is appropriate to the subject.
- Pose a question.
- Make a factual statement that is supported by statistical facts and figures.
- Define the problem.
- Describe the scene (in case of a descriptive composition)
- Make a strong statement.
- State an anecdote that is related to the subject.

Having decided on how you are to begin and conclude your composition you must plan the rest of your composition as given in the next page.

1

(b) Write to a plan

Arrange your ideas in a proper, orderly sequence, with each paragraph dwelling on a central idea, which can be located in a sentence or two. The rest of the paragraph is but an expansion of this central idea. Weave your sentences so that they flow smoothly, and are linked to one another without any jarring effect. This can be done by judiciously using appropriate linking words. Similarly, the paragraphs should also be linked to one another, with each idea meshing into the other, to make the composition interesting (for more on this see what to write and how to generate ideas).

(c) Add variety to your sentences

Short monotonous sentences make the composition drab and boring. It is therefore important, to vary the pattern of the sentences, to make them expressive and lively. This can be done in a variety of ways. Thus for example the following idea can be expressed in many different ways :

He went to sleep after returning home from office.
On returning home from office, he went to sleep.
Having returned from office he went to sleep, etc.

(d) Smooth flow of sentences by the use of effective transitional words and phrases (linkers)

Transitional words and phrases are used to connect the sentences, so that they flow smoothly from one to the next, and are coherent. Such words also called Linkers. They link the sense of one sentence, or paragraph to another. Some of the most common transitional words are, consequently, however, afterwards, furthermore, notwithstanding, nevertheless, etc.

(e) Optimum length of the composition

Try to limit your composition to 350 to 400 words which would be about three hand written pages . A composition of optimum size would be one, which does justice to the topic by dwelling on each relevant point. This is so for a short composition, would limit the expression and evolution of ideas, while a long composition may lead to digression from the point, and also increase the likelihood of committing careless mistakes. Care should be taken in adhering to the above optimum limits. Avoid wasting precious time in counting the number of words.

General accuracy of spelling, punctuation and grammar

It is but natural, that you will make careless mistakes, as you are writing under pressure. You must therefore correct the same, by editing your composition, for which you must spare five minutes of your time. Some of the most common mistakes, which students generally make, are

Errors of Tense example: He comes to see me yesterday
Wrong sentence construction example: He was getting late for the party, he hurried.
Misuse of words (Vocabulary) example: The teacher eulogized him for his misdeed
Wrong spelling
Omission or wrong use of prepositions
Punctuation errors
Wrong use of idioms
Wrong use of pronouns example: She had told him that he would be coming late.
Errors of agreement and number example: All the children have come in uniform

Use of appropriate style

There are broadly six types of essay composition. Each has its own distinct style and flavour. They can sometimes even be combined to give a natural feel and flavour to your writing. Thus a narrative composition can be made richer, by adding an element of description. Similarly adding an element of narration, can enliven a descriptive passage.   (See the different types of essays)

Some Do's and Don'ts on writing a good composition

Do's

- Write on a topic with which you are familiar.
- Write on a topic on which you have enough matter and which interests you.
- Write on a topic in which you can show originality.
- Write to the point on the subject, don't waiver from the theme.
- Do quote from the literary works of great authors, to make your introduction and conclusion interesting.
- Remember an introduction should arouse interest and the conclusion should satisfy it.
- Use plain and simple English, with good punctuation and grammar.
- A good vocabulary is an asset worth having, which helps in conveying the precise thought.
- Be logical in expressing your view, without being unduly offensive.
- Revise your essay after writing the last sentence.

Don'ts

- Write on a topic on which you do not have complete knowledge of facts.
- Write memorised material, especially when it may appear to be out of context.
- Use word which are ambiguous, or the meaning of which is not known to you.
- Use long confusing sentences.
- Be repetitive in the use of words or phrases.

What to write and how to go about it?

Having chosen a topic based on the guidelines given above, one should first of all list out all ideas, which come to mind pertaining to the subject. After having made out an exhaustive list, one should go about arranging them in a proper sequence, making out points and sub points, ensuring that there is continuity of thought. The next step is to express each point effectively. This ensures that you write to a plan, without being repetitive. Such a composition is instantly appealing to the examiner, as he is quickly able to access the examinees capability. This is specially so in a composition, in which one is required to give one's view for, or against a particular statement.

Suggested Guidelines.

- Choose a Topic.
- List out all ideas that come to mind.
- Organise them in a proper sequence making out points and sub points.
- Express each point effectively.
- Conclude.
- Revise.

How to generate Ideas?

To generate good ideas, is the crux of the problem and many a student of English language, find this a major stumbling block. The more original the ideas, the more different would be your composition, from the general run of the mill stuff. However for this, one has to have a habit of extensive reading of books and newspapers. The readers are encouraged to inculcate this habit.

There are, however, some basic guidelines, which can be followed for generation of ideas. Just as one cannot take the same medicines for different ailment, similarly for different type of topics, different approach is required.

Given below are the different types of Essays and the suggested guidelines to generate idea for each. Students shall find them helpful initially and in course of time; they shall be able to improve upon them on their own.

Type of Essay	Type of approach
Narrative Essays	By replying to questions as Where, When, Why, How, Who and What approach?
Descriptive Essays	By responding to senses of sight, smell, taste, touch and hearing
Argumentative Essays	Arguments based on Historical, Personal, Social, Economic, Religious and Psychological factors
Topical or reflective Essays	Logic based on Historical, Personal, Social, Economic Religious and Psychological factors.

How to organise Ideas?

Having listed down all the ideas that come to mind, based on the above approach. The next step is to organise them into a proper sequence. In this process some ideas may have to be discarded, as they do not fit into the sequence. In order to help you organise them, you could use any of the following sequence, depending on the subject of the composition.

Time related	Giving a sequence of events in a chronological order.
People related	Giving an account of different types of people and their activity.
Logic related	Stating of ideas in their logical sequence.

Having understood how to generate ideas and organise them, it would now be appropriate to differentiate the different types of essays. This identification would help you to judge, whether you know enough of the subject before attempting it. You can also present the same more effectively, by using the method suitable for such a type of essay.

Types of Essays

Essays can be divided into five types. Their different types and method of presentation are as given below:

1. Narrative essays

As the name suggests, it is the narration of a story or an event that has happened. This could be a real or an imaginary event, like an accident, festival, social function, street incident, a journey or a natural disaster.

Methodology

1. Keep to the chronological order in which the events have happened. However, you can at times create special emphasis, by using a flashback (events happened earlier) before coming to the present.
2. Arrest the attention of the reader beginning with a bang.
3. Create the right atmosphere or the scene by dwelling on the place, time and season
4. Introduce the characters with a brief character sketch.
5. Use dialogues to make it lively, interesting and also to break the monotony.
6. If writing a story remember that it must have a good plot and convey something to the reader. This if not explicitly expressed should suggest it between the lines.

2. Descriptive Essays

Essays of this type describe some place, person or thing which could be real or imaginary. The objective being, to convey to the reader, a vivid and realistic account of what you are visualising. Thus just as a painter uses colours to recreate a scene, you have to use appropriate words presented in a beautiful style for the same purpose. Typical examples of such essays are:

Character sketches of people.

Description of a book, film or a program.

Methodology

1. Dwell on the significant details of the place like the surroundings, the weather, time, etc. Use all your five senses, namely your sense of sight, smell, taste, touch and hearing. This shall add depth to your composition and also help in the vivid picturisation of the subject.
2. Start with the general and proceed to the specific detail.
3. Use comparison, simile and metaphors for making the details distinct.
4. Be imaginative and original in your presentation.

3. Argumentative Essays

These are essays that are argumentative in nature, where the writer arrives at a conclusion by logical reasoning. This would require due consideration to various aspects of the subject, so as to convince the reader to the writer's point of view. It requires a good knowledge of the subject, so that strong and weak points of both sides of the arguments are known. This helps in presenting one's views either for or against the subject, by highlighting the strong points and attacking the opponents weak points.

Methodology

1. Jot down all the points under the heads 'for' or 'against' the subject.
2. Decide whether you are going to write 'for' or 'against' the subject matter, if so specified in the question. In case you are to discuss or give the advantages and disadvantages, then you shall have to give both the aspects of the subject.
3. In the introduction, begin with a brief lead into the subject by stating its importance, relevance, etc.
4. In the body of the composition, refute your opponent's arguments point by point. This may be supplemented by practical or historical evidence, to substantiate your point so as to make it more convincing.
5. Plan your composition, so that you are able to justify your point of view, reserving your strong points or arguments towards the end.
6. Conclude with your well thought out personal view, based on a clear reasoning.

4. Topical or reflective essays

Essays of this type are reflective or thoughts on some topic, which are of an abstract nature for example:

Topics based on social, political or domestic issues like education, poverty, democracy, etc.

Qualities, habits (friendship, patriotism, disciple, love, etc.).

Methodology

1. In the introduction, begin by explaining or defining the subject and its relevance.
2. Justify your point of view by historical, personal, social, religious and psychological factors.
3. Conclude by putting forth your balanced point of view.

5.   Expository Essays

Essays of this type are an exposition, or an explanation of subjects like how things work. It is an elucidation of the operating process, that is in the form of instructions. They require a logical step-by-step approach of presentation. Examples of such essays could be.

How to organise a birthday party

How to prepare a particular dish, etc.

6.   The Short Story

This is difficult to attempt in the 35 minutes available, unless one has very good command on the language, and the ability to weave a unique plot, having no resemblance to a story encountered elsewhere.

Methodology

1.   Build a story around the theme or title if given. In case you have to begin or end your story with a particular sentence, evolve a theme or plot so that the sentence fits naturally, and does not appear to be artificially imposed.
2.   Write the story in the third person, for writing in the first person is more difficult (unless specifically instructed as in case of composition of reflective or introspective nature).
3.   Character sketch of the main protagonist (central character)
4.   Graphically create the atmosphere that relates to the story, for example a mystery story could dwell on creaking doors, rattling windows, or piercing cry to heighten the tension, etc.
5.   A gradual builds up to the climax.

A surprise ending, which   stimulates the readers mind.

Illustrated Examples

In order to make the reader adept in this, we have selected some essay topics, which have been asked in the ICSE Examination in the last few years. As you shall observe, the above methodology of first listing out the points and then writing elaborately on them, has been demonstrated for each of these essays. The examples are for the purpose of illustration only and the students are advised to experiment on the same. For this purpose we have given below, some assignments, which the student are requested to attempt on their own. This shall give them confidence.

QUOTABLE QUOTATIONS

Likely Subject	Quotations	Author
Act now	Trust no future, howe'er pleasant Let the dead Past bury its dead! Act – act in the living Present! Heart within, and God o'erhead!	H.W. Longfellow
Adversity	Sweet are the uses of adversity Which like the toad, ugly and venomous. Wears yet a precious jewel on his head; (As you like it)	William Shakespeare
Adversity	Prosperity is the blessing of the old testament; adversity is the blessing of the new.	Francis Bacon
Adversity	Prosperity doth best discover vice, but adversity best discover virtue.	Francis Bacon
Advice	Advice is seldom welcome; and those who want it the most always want it the least.	Earl of Chesterfield
Age	Crabbed age and youth cannot live together; Youth is full of pleasance, age is full of care. (Poems)	William Shakespeare
Ambition	Ambition should be made of sterner stuff. (Julius Caesar)	William Shakespeare
Ambition	That lowliness is young ambition's ladder, Whereto the climber upward turns his face; But when he once attains the upmost round , He than unto the ladder turns his back, Looks in the clouds, scorning the base degrees By which he did ascend. (Julius Caesar)	William Shakespeare
Ambitious	As Caesar loved me, I weep for him; as he was fortunate, I rejoice at it; as he was valiant, I honour him, but as he was ambitious, I slew him... Who is there so base that would be a bondman? If any speak, for him have I offended. (Julius Caesar)	William Shakespeare
Antagonist	He that wrestles with us strengthens our nerves, and sharpens our skill. Our antagonist is our helper.	Edmund Burke
Ballot	The ballot is stronger than the bullet.	Abraham Lincoln
Beauty	Remember that the most beautiful things in the world are the most useless; peacock and lilies for instance	John Ruskin
Beauty	A thing of beauty is a joy forever. Its loveliness increases; it will never, Pass into nothingness.	John Keats
Beauty	"Beauty is truth, truth beauty." That is all Ye knows on earth, and all ye need to know.	John Keats
Beauty	Beauty provoketh fools sooner than gold.	William Shakespeare
Beauty	Beauty is in the eyes of the beholder.	Margaret Hangerford

Book	Who kills a man kills a reasonable creature, Gods image; but he who destroys a good book. Kills reason itself, kills the image of God, as it were in the eye.	John Milton
Book	A good book is the precious lifeblood of a master spirit, embalmed and treasured up on purpose to a life beyond life.	John Milton
Book	A good book is the best of friends, the same today and forever.	Martin Tupper
Book	Some books are to be tasted, others to be swallowed and some few to be chewed and digested	Francis Bacon
Borrower	Neither a borrower nor a lender be; For loan oft loses both itself and friend. (Hamlet)	William Shakespeare
Brevity	Brevity is the soul of wit. (Hamlet)	William Shakespeare
Character	But I am constant as the northern star Of whose true fixed and resting quality There is no fellow in the firmament. (Julius Caesar)	William Shakespeare
Character (Test)	Men have a touchstone whereby to try gold, but gold is the touchstone whereby to try men.	Thomas Fuller
Child	The child is father of the man, And I would wish my days to be Bound each to each by natural piety.	William Wordsworth
Childhood	I have had playmates, I have had companions In my days of childhood, in my joyful schooldays All, all are gone, the old familiar faces	Charles Lamb
Circumstances	Man is not the creature of circumstances. Circumstances are the creatures of man.	
Communism	From each according to his abilities To each according to his needs.	Karl Marx
Cowards	Cowards die many times before their death's; The valiant never taste of death but once. (Julius Caesar)	William Shakespeare
Credulity	Credulity is the man's weakness but the Childs strength.	Charles Lamb
Crown /Power	Uneasy lies the head that wears the crown. (Henry 1V)	William Shakespeare
Death	For that which is born death is certain, and for the dead birth is certain. Therefore grieve not over that which is unavoidable.	Bhagavad-Gita
Death	In this world nothing can be said to be certain, except death and taxes.	Benjamin Franklin
Death	All that live must die Passing through nature to eternity (Hamlet)	William Shakespeare
Death	A man can die but once; we owe God a death. (Henry IV)	William Shakespeare
Death	When beggars die there are no comets seen; The heavens themselves blaze forth the death of princes. (Julius Caesar)	William Shakespeare
Death	Death is one of two things, Either it is annihilation or the dead have no consciousness of anything; or as we are told, it is really a change; a migration of the soul from this p⌐ ⌐ to another.	Socrates

Death	We thanked with brief thanksgiving Whatever God may be, That no man lives forever, That dead men rise up never, That even the weariest river, Winds somewhere safe to sea.	A.C. Swinburne
Death/Fate	The glories of our blood and state Are shadows not substantial things There is no armour against fate Death lays his icy hands on kings Sceptre and crown Must tumble down And in the dust be equal made With the poor crooked scythe and spade.	Jame Shirley
Deeds	We live in deeds, not years; in thoughts, nor breaths In feeling, not in figures on a dial We should count time by heartthrobs. He most lives Who thinks most-feels the noblest-acts the best	P. J. Bailey
Deeds	For sweetest things turn sourest by their deeds; Lilies and fester smell far worse than weeds. (Poems)	William Shakespeare
Deeds (Good)	The evil that men do lives after them. The good is oft interred with their bones. (Julius Caesar)	William Shakespeare
Deeds (Good)	How far that little candle throws his beams! So shines a good deed in a naughty world. (Merchant of Venice)	William Shakespeare
Democracy	A perfect democracy the most shameless thing in the world.	Edmund Burke
Democracy	Government of the people, by the people, and for the people, shall not perish from the earth.	Abraham Lincoln
Democracy	You can fool all the people some of the time, and some of the people all the time, but you cannot fool all the people all the time.	Abraham Lincoln
Democracy	Democracy substitutes election by the incompetent many for appointment by the corrupt few.	G. Bernard Shaw
Destiny	I claim not to have controlled events, but confess plainly that events have controlled me.	Abraham Lincoln
Destiny	But yesterday the word of Caesar might Have stood against the world; now lies he there, And non so poor to do him reverence. (Julius Caesar)	William Shakespeare
Destiny	There is a tide in the affairs of men, Which taken at the flood, leads on to fortune; Omitted all the voyage of their life Is bound in shallows and in miseries. (Julius Caesar)	William Shakespeare
Devil	The devil can cite Scripture for his purpose (Merchant of Venice)	William Shakespeare
Dictators	Dictators ride to and fro upon tigers, which they dare not dismount. And the tigers are getting hungry.	Winston Churchill

Diplomat	A diplomat is a man who always remembers a woman's birthday but never remembers her age.	Robert Frost
Discretion	The better part of valour is discretion. (Henry IV)	William Shakespeare
Duty	I slept and dreamt that life was beauty I woke and found that life was duty.	Anonymous
Duty	The woods are lovely, dark and deep But I have promises to keep. And miles to go before I sleep.	Robert Frost
Education	T'is education form the common mind Just as the twig is bent, the tree's inclined.	Alexander Pope
Education	Education make a people easy to lead, but difficult to drive; easy to govern but impossible to enslave.	Lord Biougham
Fools	For fools rush in where angels fear to tread.	Alexander Pope
Forgive	To err is human, to forgive is divine.	Alexander Pope
Friend	I shot an arrow into the air It fell to earth I know not where And the song from beginning to end I found again in the heart of a friend.	H.W. Longfellow
Friend	Forsake not an old friend, for the new is not comparable to him. A new friend is as new wine; when it is old, thou shall drink it with pleasure.	Anonymous
Friend	A faithful friend is a medicine of life.	Anonymous
Friend	Some great misfortune to potend, No enemy can match a friend.	Jonathan Swift
Genius	Genius is one percent inspiration and ninety nine percent perspiration.	Anonymous
Glories	Glories like glow-worms, afar off shine bright, But looked to near, have neither heat nor light.	John Webster
God	God moves in a mysterious way, He wonders to perform; He plants his footsteps in the sea, And rides upon the storm.	William Cowper
God	Judge not the lord by feeble sense, But trust him for his grace; Behind a frowning providence, He hides a smiling face.	William Cowper
God	In the beginning God created the heaven and the earth, And God said, Let there be light; and there was light. So God created man in his own image, in the image of God he him; male and female created he then	Bible
Government	Every nation has the government that it deserves.	Anonymous
Government	No government can be long secure without a formidable opposition.	Benjamin Disraaeli
Greed	The love of money is the root of all evil.	Timothy
Guilt	Will all great Neptune's ocean wash this blood Clean from my hand? No, this my hand will rather The multitudinous seas incarnadine, Make the green one red. (Macbeth)	William Shakespeare
Imperfect (Beauty)	Roses have thorns, and silver fountains mud; Clouds and eclipses stain both moon and sun. (Poems)	William Shakespeare

Jealousy	O! beware, my lord, of jealousy, It is the green eyed monster which doth mock The meat it feeds on. (Othello)	William Shakespeare
Kindness	Little deeds of kindness, little words of love Help to make earth happy, like the heaven above.	Julia Carney
Labour(fruits)	No gain, no palm, no thorn, no throne; No gall, no glory; no cross, no crown	William Penn
Law	Laws grind the poor, and rich men rule the law	Oliver Goldsmith
Life	Tell me not in mournful numbers Life is but an empty dream For the soul is dead and slumbers And things are not what they seem.	H. W. Longfellow
Life	Life is real! Life is earnest! And the grave is not its goal. Dust thou art, to dust returnest Was not spoken of the soul.	H. W. Longfellow
Life	Life is brief - a little hope, a little dream and then goodnight.	Leon Montenaaeken
Life	This life at best is as an inn And we the passengers	James Howell
Little Neglect	A little neglect may breed mischief...for want of a nail the shoe was lost; for want of a shoe the horse was lost; and for want of a horse the rider was lost.	Benjamin Franklin
Little Things	Little drops of water, little grain of sand Make the mighty ocean, and the pleasant land So the little minutes, humble may though be Make the mighty ages of eternity.	Julia Carney
Man (Patriotic)	Breathes there the man with soul so dead Who never to himself hath said? This is my own, my native land!	Sir Walter Scott
Man (Positive thinking)	Life's battle don't always go To the stronger or faster man, But sooner or later the man who wins Is the man who thinks he can	H. W. Longfellow
Man (Good)	Bad men live to eat and drink, whereas good men eat and drink in order to live.	Socrates
Man (Good)	Nothing can harm a good man, either in life or death.	Socrates
Man (Honest)	An honest man's the noblest work of God.	Alexander Pope
Man (Patriotic)	Never in the field of human conflict was so much owed by so many to so few.	Winston Churchill
Manners	A gentle mind by gentle deeds is known, For a man by nothing is so well bewrayed, As by his manners.	Edmund Spenser
Men (Great)	The height by great men reached and kept. Were not attained by sudden flight. But, they while their companion slept. Were toiling upwards in the night.	H. W. Longfellow
Men (Great)	Lives of great men all remind us We can make our lives sublime	

	And, departing, leave behind us Footprints on the sands of time.	H. W. Longfellow
Men (Great)	Be not afraid of greatness; some men are born great, some achieve greatness and some have greatness thrust upon them. (Twelfth Night)	William Shakespeare
Men (Great)	No great men live in vain. The history of the world is but the biography of great men.	Thomas Carlyle
Mercy	The quality of mercy is not strained It droppeth as the gentle rain from heaven Upon the place beneath; It is twice blessed; It blesseth him that gives and him that takes. (Merchant of Venice)	William Shakespeare
Mind	The mind is its own place and in itself can make a heaven of hell, a hell of heaven.	John Milton
Miser	They are as sick that surfeit with too much, as they that starve with nothing. (Merchant of Venice)	William Shakespeare
Misery	Misery acquaints a man with strange bedfellows. (Tempest)	William Shakespeare
Mother	The hand that rocks the cradle Is the hand that rules the world.	W. R. Wallace
Name	What's in a name? that which we call a rose By any other name would smell as sweet. (Romeo and Juliet)	William Shakespeare
Nature	Accuse not nature, she hath done her part; Do thou but thine.	John Milton
Nature	All are but parts of one stupendous whole, Whose body nature is, and God the soul.	Alexander Pope
Nature	For men may come and men may go. But I go on for ever.	Lord Tennyson
Nature	I wandered lonely as a cloud That floats on high o'er vales and hills, When all at once I saw a crowd. A host of golden daffodils	William Wordsworth
Nature	My heart leaps up when I behold A rainbow in the sky.	William Wordsworth
Nature	The world is too much with us; late and soon, Getting and spending, we lay waste our power; Little we see in Nature that is ours;	William Wordsworth
Nature/(Solitude)	Continuous as the stars that shine And twinkle on the milky way Ten thousand saw I at a glance Tossing their head in sprightly dance... They flash upon that inward eye Which is the bliss of solitude.	William Wordsworth
News	When a dog bites a man that is not news, but when a man bites a dog that is news.	Charles A. Dana
Newspapers	Newspapers always excite curiosity. No one ever lays one down without a feeling of disappointment.	Charles Lamb
Oblivion	Full many a flower is born to blush unseen And waste its sweetness on the desert air.	Thomas Gray

Patience	Though the mills of God grind slowly, yet they grind exceeding small; Though with patience He stands waiting, with exactness grinds He all.	H. W. Longfellow
Patriotism	Happy the man whose wish and care. A few paternal acres abound, Content to breathe his native air In his own ground.	Alexander Pope
Peace	Peace hath her victories No less renown than war. For what can war, but endless war still breed?	John Milton
Politics	He knows nothing; and he thinks he knows everything That points clearly to a political career.	G. Bernard Shaw
Power	Power tends to corrupt, and absolute power tends to corrupt absolutely. Great men are almost always bad men.	Lord Aston
Power	The greater the power ,the more dangerous the abuse.	Edmund Burke
Progress	The reasonable man adopts himself to the world; the unreasonable one persist in trying to adapt the world to himself. Therefore all progress depends on the unreasonable man.	G. Bernard Shaw
Propaganda/ Greater Lie	The greater masses of the people ..will more easily fall victims to a great lie than to a small one.	Adolf Hitler
Read	Read not to contradict and confute nor to believe and take for granted, nor to find talk and discourse, but to weigh and consider.	Francis Bacon
Reading	Reading maketh a full man; conference a ready man; and writing an exact man	Francis Bacon
Reign	Better to reign in hell than serve in heaven	John Milton
Religion	Man is by his constitution a religious animal	Edmund Burke
Religion	Men will wrangle for religion; write for it; fight for it; anything but –live for it.	Charles Colton
Religion	There is only one religion though there are a hundred versions of it.	G. Bernard Shaw
Religion	We have just enough religion to make us hate, but not enough to make us love one another.	Jonathan Swift
Religion	Educate men without religion and you make them but clever devils.	Arthur Wellesley
Remedies	Extreme remedies are most appropriate for extreme diseases.	Hippocrates
Reputation	Reputation, reputation, reputation! O! I have lost my reputation, I have lost the immortal part of myself, and what remains is bestial (Othello)	William Shakespeare
Reputation	But he that filches from me my good name Robs me of that which not enriches him, And makes me poor indeed. (Othello)	William Shakespeare
Superstition	Superstition is the religion of feeble minds	Edmund Burke
Thought	There is nothing either good or bad. But thinking makes it so. (Hamlet)	William Shakespeare

Thoughts	My words fly up, my thoughts remain below; Words without thought never to heaven go. (Hamlet)	William Shakespeare
Travel	Travel in the younger sort, is a part of education; in the elder a part of experience.	Francis Bacon
Triumph	Not in the clamour of crowded street Not in the shouts of plaudits of the throng. But in ourselves, are triumph and defeats.	H. W. Longfellow
Truth	He who considers this (Self) as a slayer or he who thinks that this (Self) is slain, neither of these know the Truth. For it does not slay, nor is it slain	Bhagavad-Gita
Unity	Yes we must indeed, hang together or, most assuredly, we shall all hang separately.	Benjamin Franklin
Virtue	There is however, a limit at which forbearance ceases to be a virtue.	Edmund Burke
Virtue	Virtue may be assailed. But never hurt. Surprised by unjust force, but not enthralled.	John Milton
Virtues	Men's evil manners live in brass; their virtues We write in water. (Henry VIII)	William Shakespeare
Wealth (Harmful)	Superfluity comes sooner by white hair, But competence lives longer. (Merchant of Venice)	William Shakespeare
Wealth	If we command our wealth, we shall be rich and free, if our wealth commands us, we are poor indeed	Edmund Burke
Wisdom/Knowledge	Knowledge comes but wisdom lingers.	Lord Tennyson
Woman	A man is as old as he's feeling A woman is as old as she looks	Mortimer Collins
Words	Words are like leaves; and where they most abound Much fruit of sense beneath is rarely found.	Alexander Pope
World/Stage	All the world a stage, And all the men and women merely players; They have their exits and entrances; And one man in his time plays many parts. (As you like it)	William Shakespeare
Writing	True ease in writing comes from art, not chance. As those move easiest who have learnt to dance	Alexander Pope
Youth	His best companions, innocence and health; And his best riches ignorance and wealth. How happy he who crowns in shades like these A Youth of labour with an age of ease.	Oliver Goldsmith

Recent Essays

'Money causes more harm than good.' Express your views either for or against the statement.

(ICSE 2012)

- Introduction:- Money is the cause of most of the problems that plague modern society.
- Money has an intoxicating effect that goes into the head of it's beholder, making them arrogant, selfish and hallucinate in self-glory and pride.
- Money is the cause of discord in families and causes serious ailments.
- There is no denying the fact that 'Money makes the mare go.' However being unduly obsessed with it, leads to corruption and crime, causing stress, ailments and unhappiness.
- Money brings with it fair weather friends, sycophants, scheming relatives professional rivals. Need to be on guard thereby making life uneasy and unpleasant.
- Conclusion:- Money is essential to live. It is important to maintain the right balance for as we all know, 'Money can't buy happiness, but neither can poverty.'

"They are sick that surfeit with too much, as they that starve with nothing," said William Shakespeare in his play 'Merchant of Venice.' This very aptly brings out the role of money in our lives. Excessive money and wealth brings with it problems of security and mental tension, while not having any reduces one to penury, making life miserable and not worth living. This is for in today's materialistic world, we have assigned a monetary value to everything. Thus in the words of Somerset Maugham," Money is like a sixth sense without which you cannot make complete use of the other five." However even today, money is not the end all and be all of our existence, for it cannot buy happiness, true love, friends, good health and peace. It is the cause of most of the problems that plague modern society.

There is no denying the fact that money brings with it prosperity, which has a psychological and social dimension. Psychological for the security, self-confidence and a sense of accomplishment it gives to the beholder, along with the increase in social and political status. It has an intoxicating effect that goes into the head of it's beholder, making them arrogant, selfish and insensitive to others around them. Often so great is the intoxication especially in the neo rich, that they begin to hallucinate in self-glory and pride.

Money has also been the root cause of most of the problems that plague the society. Dispute over it have been known to be a major cause of discord in families, making even siblings sworn enemies. Its acquisition by others in the family or circle of friends, gives rise to baser and negative emotions like jealousy, enmity and hatred. In the endless pursuit of money, people become unhappy, tense, inviting serious ailments like blood pressure, diabetes, that lead to more deadly diseases like heart attack, brain hemorrhage and others.

Despite the dubious role that money plays in our life, there is no denying the fact that, 'Money makes the mare go.' This is for it is the biggest and the most effective motivator. Ordinary men have become great and wealthy in its pursuit. The rags to riches stories of Dirubhai Ambani, Steve Jobs, Bill Gates and numerous others, bear testimony to it's important role as a motivator. Human progress can to a large extent be attributed to one's desire to acquire money and wealth. However being unduly obsessed with money, leads one to indulge in corrupt practices and crimes. This invariably lead to punishment, causing stress, ailments and unhappiness.

Surfeit of money brings with it many fair weather friends sycophants, and scheming relatives. Besides them there are personal and professional rivals against whom one has to be constantly on guard, making life uneasy and unpleasant.

Money is essential to live. Nevertheless it's endless pursuit, does one more harm than good. This is for happiness, love of dear one's, true friend, and good health, that are essential to live a wholesome life, are not a purchasable commodity. It is therefore essential to maintain the right balance, for as we all know, 'Money can't buy happiness, but neither can poverty.'

Modes of communication are constantly changing. What are some of these changes? Say which one change you like best and why ?

(ICSE 2012)

- Introduction:- Man being a social animal evolved different modes of communication from sign language to words, letters, telephone and the telegraph.
- The advent of the twenty first century, paved the way for the internet. The World Wide Web made communication possible instantly.
- Telephones made way for mobiles. These come loaded with value added features and are the best way to stay connected with your near and dear one's.
- The integration of the Internet in the mobile, is undoubtedly the best change ever to have taken place. This now enables me to use my dead time to more effective use.
- Conclusion:- Our insatiable need to communicate has led to constant change in our mode of communication, the best being the advent of mobile phones. Life today is unimaginable without it.

'Man is by nature a social animal,' said the Greek philosopher Aristotle. This attribute made him constantly explore different and more effective ways to communicate with fellow humans. Thus what may have started as a sign language, gradually transformed to words and sentences, by which one could communicate one's ideas and thoughts. His endeavour to reach out to the vast multitude of people across the globe, lead him to make inventions like the telephone and the telegraph. These till the twentieth century were powerful and effective means of communication by which he could reach out to people all over the world. They were however too slow and cumbersome to meet his insatiable desire.

However with the advent of the twenty first century, there came a dramatic and revolutionary change in our mode of communication. The vast multitude of communication satellites and the arrival of computer, paved the way for the internet. This provided easy and instant connectivity to communicate with anyone across the globe. The World Wide Web through networking sites like Face book, Twitter, and Google, reduced the world to a global village, where anyone can communicate his views or seek any information on pressing a key on a computer. Besides communicating one can also visually interact with others, using web cams and microphones. Thus what took hours or even weeks has now become possible instantly.

Telephones that used cables has now made way for mobiles. This small gadgetry using wireless medium, has revolutionized communication. Being extremely light and portable, and coming loaded with value added features like camera, audio and video recording, music, and many others, are now indispensable for youth like me. They are undoubtedly the easiest and most effective way to stay connected with your near and dear one's

The integration of the Internet in the mobile, is undoubtedly the best change ever to have taken place in the field of telecommunication. This feature in my mobile now enables me to use my dead time (time spent in travelling or at leisure) to best use. I can now access any information on the net for my project work anytime, find my way about the city, or interact with my friends and relatives without using a computer or the hassle of visiting a cyber café.

Our insatiable need to communicate has led to constant change in our mode of communication, ever since the dawn of civilization. Out of all the changes the best change ever to happen was the advent of the mobile phone. This has become my most valuable and trusted companion, without which life is unimaginable.

Private tuitions are a necessary evil. Give your views either for or against the statement.

(ICSE 2011)

- Introduction- Need for private tuition in the age of cut-throat competition.
- Why it is a Necessary Evil?
    Evil because it is at the expense of childhood.
    Schools have become commercial institutions
    Parents do not have time and cannot help.
- How it is advantageous?
    Augments school learning by clarifying abstract concepts
    Greater interaction and motivation improves learning.
- Conclusion- Private tuition plays an important role in shaping the future of children.

The cut-throat competition for qualifying in competitive examinations or even getting admission in good colleges has pushed students to new limits. This has led to the meteoric rise in the demand for private tuitions, with children as young as six years going for personalised coaching. The popularity of private tuition can be attributed to the declining standards of teaching and instruction in schools, especially government schools.

Unhealthy as it seems, private tuitions cannot be dispensed with. Unhealthy because in the rat race for acquiring knowledge, children have lost their childhood. After spending six to seven hours in school and another couple of hours in tuition, the child has just no time in indulging in playing, daydreaming and other activities associated with childhood.

Schools that were once considered to be the temple of learning, have now become commercial institutions. The high student to teacher ratio in school, makes it impossible for teachers to give personalised attention to students. There is also dearth of quality teachers, to explain the difficult concepts and lack of creative teaching methods, to address different need of students. Furthermore teachers are inaccessible in school and students fear reprimand on approaching them to clarify their doubts. The picture in Government or rural schools is even more alarming, for teacher absenteeism is quite common. Thus even in rural areas students are forced to go for private tuition.

The students cannot turn to their parents for help, as they do not have the time, or are not equipped to help at home. The parents thus have no option but to send their wards for private tuitions.

Private tuition are in a way advantageous, for besides augmenting learning in school, they help in clarifying abstract concepts and solving difficult problem of students. This is for the tutor is more friendly and accessible and the student can look up to him without fear of being scolded. The interactive method of teaching is more comprehendible and lasting. It also inculcate in the student the importance of time management, for besides school homework they have to allocate some time for tuition and not waste it in unhealthy pursuits. Private tutors thus help to motivate students to study hard, and often guide and mentor them in their academic pursuit.

The popularity of private tuition is indeed a direct fallout of and testament to the inefficient system of education in the country, where there is a premium on academic excellence. This evil may have affected the childhood of children. Nevertheless it has helped shape their future careers, by making them good professionals in their chosen field.

> ## Children's Day is celebrated in your school every year. Write what you particularly liked about this year's celebration. What did you learn from the efforts of those who planned and organised the function? How did you express your gratitude to them?

(ICSE 2011)

- Introduction – Children's day celebrated to commemorate the memory of Pandit Jawaharlal Nehru.
- Going to school was like going on a picnic.
- Greeted by teachers
- Play staged by teachers
- Learning the importance of hard work and team work done by the teachers.
- Conclusion- Resolved to express my gratitude by respecting and obeying them.

On the 14 th of November we celebrate Children's Day in school. This day is celebrated to commemorate the memory of Pundit Jawaharlal Nehru, his birth anniversary. He loved children, who fondly called him 'Chacha Nehru'.

Going to school on this day was great fun. It was like going to a picnic, wearing casual dress instead of school uniform and the hefty school bag. Banners and welcome arches wishing ' Happy Children's Day' greeted us, as we made our way to the school auditorium.

It was indeed a pleasant experience, for unlike other days, we found the teachers and staff being extra indulgent towards us. The Principal greeted us and informed that the teachers had organized a special program for us.

The first program slated was a play titled 'Alice in Wonderland'. It was staged by teachers of the primary section, dwelling on the transformation of the child in the wonderland of a school. It was interesting to see teachers behaving like small kids. This was followed by a hilarious comedy aptly titled, 'Three idiots'. It was a satire on the students of the senior section, dwelling on the innovative excuses for not doing their homework and making fun of teachers behind their back. To know that the teachers knew it all, was surprising, yet a pleasant experience. There was a deafening roar of applause as the curtains came down. We clapped and shouted our hearts out. The play was a welcome departure from the usual song and dance program of previous years and hence was appreciated by everyone.

The school Captain thanked the teachers on behalf of the students, for taking extra pains in make this occasion memorable. The teachers distributed chocolates to the students and the program finally concluded.

It was good to see the humorous side of teachers, who generally appear very serious and somber. Yet they were able to put up such a magnificent performance, spoke volumes about their hard work and team effort. Indeed one and one makes eleven, for working in a group we can do wonders.

The Children's day may have come to a close, but the respect for my teachers grew multifold that day. We can never repay them for what they do for us. I however resolved to respect and obey them, for this is the least I can do to express my gratitude for them.

Think of a time when you achieved a personal goal.
Say why the goal was important to you and how you achieved it.
Describe how you felt on achieving it.

(ICSE 2010)

Learning something new can be a very scary experience. One of the most difficult things, I have ever had to do when I was in class six, was to learn cycling. I was mortally afraid of falling and injuring myself. I watched my friends with disdain as they cycled to school, while I trudged along with my school bag on my shoulder. Occasionally a friend would give me a lift on his bicycle. This would make me feel even more lowly and awkward. One day I finally decided to learn this important skill and requested my father to help me.

New situations always made me a bit nervous and my first cycling lesson was no exception. Early Sunday morning when everyone was fast asleep, I crept out of bed, put on my full sleeves shirt and full trouser, to protect me from injury. As I wheeled out my brother's bicycle on to the driveway, my father called out to me. He was glossing over the newspaper, which he put aside as he came towards me. We steadily made our way to the park adjacent to our house.

Reaching the park, he made me sit on the cycle holding the seat from behind. My legs barely touched the lower pedal. Then followed a stream of instructions like "Hold the handle straight", "Look straight ahead", "Don't stop peddling, etc". He gave an initial push to the cycle from behind. I found these coordinated instructions quite difficult to follow, and soon I was down on my knees, with the cycle over me. However the strong grip of my father had softened the fall and I escaped with minor bruises. But my father was patient. He encouraged me saying "Good, keep it up Sumit". This boosted my confidence. I was up on my feet. Holding the handle of the cycle firmly, I pushed the pedal down with my legs, at the same time trying to retain my upright position. The very presence of my father had boosted my confidence no end. In about an hour's time, I learnt to coordinate the movements, as my father ran behind holding the seat of the cycle.

The next day we repeated the entire exercise, completing one round of the park. During the second round I felt more free and easy, as I feverishly pushed the pedals. To my surprise I found my father smiling and waving out to me standing right in front of me. He had intentionally let go of my seat after the first round. I had indeed mastered the skill of cycling. It was a wonderful free feeling – like flying. From that day onwards, it became my hobby and later fetched me the states championship trophy in college.

Learning to cycle was not easy for me. However my persistence paid off. Now whenever I am faced with a new challenge, I am not nervous. This is for I know, that as I practice my skills would get better. This has made me more confident and bold. It is indeed a wonderful feeling when you achieve a goal you have set for yourself.

'More lessons are learnt on the sports field than in the classroom'.
Express your views either for or against this statement.

(ICSE 2010)

To take the above statement "More lessons are learnt on the sports field than in the classroom", literally would be a great fallacy especially for students. This is for the primary activity of a student is to study and acquire knowledge. He can effectively do this only through lessons learnt in the classroom.

The giant strides in the field of science and technology was possible only through persistent effort of scholars and scientists. Their thirst for knowledge through lessons learnt   in the class-rooms has made our lives more comfortable and luxurious. Similarly the lessons that we learn in the classrooms would help us shape our future career and life. In this age of cutthroat competition, a difference of one mark in academics can make the difference between success and failure - at times changing our very lives. Our academic achievements not only help in passing competitive examinations, but also mould our personality and future.

Undoubtedly there are lessons to be learnt in the sports field too. Lessons like the virtues of discipline, hard work, perseverance sportsmanship and teamwork. These too are important lessons that one must learn in life. They teach us to be magnanimous in victory and sporting in defeat. Nevertheless, these lessons and attributes can also be acquired by engaging in other activities, like indulging in one's hobby, playing indoor games like cards, carom, etc.

History is proof of great scholars and reformers not known for their sporting skills, like Mahatma Gandhi, Pandit Jawaharlal Nehru, Mother Teresa and many others, who transformed society. We have also before us the great achievement of differently abled scientist Stephan Hawking and social reformer Helen Keller. Being physically handicapped they never played in the sports field - yet their achievement would put ordinary mortals to shame.

At best the lesson one learns in the sports field could help in improving one's skill in a particular sport. This . could be important for an aspiring sportsman and women, who have chosen to excel in a particular sport. It could also help others in staying physically fit and be a good source of recreation.

Thus for students more lessons are learn in the classrooms then in the sports fields. This is for classrooms are meant for serious study, while activities in the sports field can at best help recreate and augment our learning.

A school carnival or fete is a great occasion for fun with friends. Describe one such event in your school.

(ICSE 2010)

An occasion looked forward to by most of us is the school fete. This is usually held in October, before the onset of winters. This year our school organized a fete on Saturday the 10th of October. Feverish preparation began a fortnight before the event. Each class was asked to set up a stall of their choice. Contributions from the students were collected, and invitations sent out to the parents, requesting them to join the festivity with their friends and relatives.

The day turned out to be cloudy. By midday the Sun peeped through the clouds that hung heavy in the sky. The clouds threatened to play spoilsport, but thankfully a westerly breeze blew them steadily away, bringing much cheer to our dampened spirits.

Excited voices and shouts of glee from my friends greeted me, as I made my way to the big playfield. Numerous colourful stalls had been set up around the playfield. In the center of the field, was an orchestra belting out the latest musical hits.

It was exciting to see students manning the stalls, selling assorted items from raffle tickets, to ring a gift, hoop la, target practice. There was a huge giant wheel for small children who were shouting with delight as the wheel went up and down. There were also stalls of eatables selling snacks, chowmein, cakes, chocolates and beverages like tea and coffee. The students seemed to have matured overnight. They were working like true businessmen, accounting for cash and stocks. The eatable stalls were however the most crowded and noisy. The occasional cackle of the loud-speaker broke the revelry to make an announcement.

A friendly tap on my shoulder made me turn around "Hi Siddhant,' said Rohit as he caught my hand and escorted me to his stall selling raffle tickets. He persuaded me to buy one. I reluctantly parted with a ten rupee note in exchange for the ticket, which I carelessly shove in my pocket. Thereafter I had a gala time with my friends eating chowmein and ice cream, till we had run out of money. Just as I was about to depart, the microphone cackled to life, announcing the number of the lucky winner in the lucky draw. I pulled out the crumbled ticket from my pocket. - Lo and behold ! I had struck the jackpot. In a trance I walked up to the podium, to collect my prize.

Soon the program concluded. The Principal Father Rodriquez announced that the fete had garnered a collection of ₹ 20,000 which would be donated to the Chief Minister's Relief Fund. Thereafter all boundaries began to crumble, as teachers and students danced to the music of the orchestra. I too joined in the fun and merrymaking. Later in the evening I trudged home with my prize, which shall always remind me of the wonderful time I spent in the school fete.

Recall a time in your life when you were certain about something but were later proved terribly wrong.

(ICSE 2009)

I have always been scary of numbers and that precisely was the reason for my poor score in Mathematics. . This has been my Achilles heel, for in spite of doing well in all subjects, my poor performance in Math's always let me down.

I therefore devised a strategy to overcome my weakness. I somehow had a strong conviction, that teachers gave hints of important questions to students taking tuition from them. Since my parents did not share this conviction. I befriended Mohan, who was taking tuition in Math's from my class teacher. Showering him with chocolates and gifts, I soon became one of his best friends.

With the final exams around the corner. I finally decided to put my strategy to work. I broached the subject subtly, seeking hints of important questions given to him by the teacher. He was taken aback, but denied any such hints. I kept pestering him to ask the teacher, to which he finally agreed.

A day before the exams, I went over to his place and jotted down all the important questions, specified by the teacher .I spent the night memorizing the answers to the questions. By morning I felt reasonably pleased with myself, for I had at last found the solution to my problem. In the examination hall I confidently surveyed the surroundings. The sight of boys nervously flicking pages of books amused me. A little later as the bell rang the examination commenced.

I stared at the question paper in disbelief.- Lo and behold ! It was an entirely different paper, with different set of questions for which I was totally unprepared. My mouth turned dry and my limbs felt weak and numb. With considerable effort, I tried to gain composure, but in vain. The invigilator noticed my discomfort and enquired if I was well. She sent me to the dispensary, where after taking a tranquilizer I was advised rest.

Needless to mention, I got a big zero in maths and consequently was not promoted. It was indeed a heavy price I paid, for realizing an old age adage " Success is ninety nine percent perspiration and one percent inspiration".

"The use of mobile phones has lowered active social life and has become an addiction". Express your views for or against the statement.

(ICSE 2009)

Mobile phones undoubtedly, are one of the most spectacular developments, ever to have taken place in the field of telecommunication. They offer the easiest and simplest way to stay connected, with your near and dear one's, thus augmenting and invigorating our social life. However on the contrary, they have actually lowered active social life, and have become an addiction to the youth of today.

The young generation is enamoured by this latest gadgetry, for it undisputedly offer many advantages, like added convenience, greater personal security, (being able to access help in an emergency) and the ability to use dead time, (time spent in traveling or in leisure) to best use. It is however these conveniences that actually erode our social life.

The urge to stay connected with our own circle of friend and relatives has made us a social outcast in the society in which we live. It is quite common to find groups of youngsters sitting together in a place talking on phone to people far away, unmindful of the presence of others. Thus we are more concerned and connected to people far away, than to those immediately around us. This dissuades us in cultivating new friendship, in the mistaken belief that we are more secure by staying connected to our known circle of friend's. This virtual networking, actually weakens our social life.

The convenience of utilizing 'dead time' also affect us socially. Business executives and professionals are the worst sufferers, for being compelled to be on duty, round the clock There is thus no leisure for them for they can be called for work whenever the need arises. This not only affects their social life, but also their family life. On certain occasions like meeting a friend, attending an important meeting, praying or attending a funeral, the melodious ringing of the mobile phone becomes a real nuisance. On such occasions people do not join in, but impose themselves on us, which causes social embarrassment.

The mobile phones have caught the imagination of the youth as they now come loaded with features like GPS, Internet access, FM radio, games, Camera, etc. They are so much engrossed with their phones, that it has now become an addiction. According to psychiatrist, this habit cause compulsive disorders and threatens to be one of the biggest non-drug addiction in the 21st century. It totally isolates the victim from society, ruining them economically, due to the heavy bills they run up, and eventually leading to criminal activity. Mobile addict tend to neglect obligations like work or study, eventually drifting away from friends. Being victim of low self-esteem, they have problems of developing social relations, and are more comfortable in the virtual world. They feel insecure without their phones. Switching off their phones for sometime causes anxiety, irritability, sleeplessness and even shivering and digestive problems. Besides the addictive influence, it also poses serious health hazard to the frequent user.

Undoubtedly mobile phones have made our lives more safe and comfortable. Nevertheless it has definitely lowered our active social life and made us its addict.

The waiting room at a railway station presents a wonderful opportunity to observe human behaviour. Describe an experience when you were early for a train and had to spend some time in the waiting room with different kind of people

(ICSE 2009)

"Train number 2229 from Lucknow to New Delhi is late by one and half hour and shall now be coming at 11.30 PM". This loud and crisp announcement greeted me, as I entered the railway station with my strolley in two. I shrugged my shoulders in despair and proceeded to the first class waiting room .My wish of having a good night sleep, so as to be fresh for the interview the next day, lay in shreds.

Walking into the waiting room, which was the size of a small auditorium, with steel armchairs lined up on all the sides. In the center were two large tables, on which four young men lay fast asleep, with their bags and briefcases tucked under their heads. On one side of the room at shoulder height was a TV monitor   displaying the status of trains.

Looking for a place to park myself, I noticed a chair vacant in the extreme corner of the room. No sooner had I seated myself, a man wearing a dark blue shirt, limped towards me with clutches in his hand. He held out a small register . Chewing tobacco he murmured "Please write your name and ticket number in the register." The strong smell of tobacco nauseated me. I quickly did his bidding, sparing myself the agony of putting up with him for long. Putting the strolley under my seat, I thankfully stretched out on the steel armchair preparing for the long wait.

Glancing around, I saw a middle aged couple seated next to me. The man with a receding hairline and bushy moustache, smiled, as I looked his way.

" Going to Delhi".

" Yes " I replied.

"Same here".

The ice being broken, he gave vent to his feelings on the working of the Indian railways and their pathetic record of punctuality. Being weary I just nodded in approval. His wife seated beside him, nudged him to silence, pointing to the passengers sleeping around us.

Relieved, I shut my eyes to take a small nap. I had hardly fallen asleep when a loud thud awoke me. I opened my eyes to see a man who was sleeping on the table before me lying on the floor. The briefcase lay open, with its contents spilling out on the floor. His face was contorted with pain as he tried to stand up. I rushed to help him and made him sit on my chair. He thanked me profusely, as I packed his belongings in his briefcase.

A little later I was pleased to hear the announcement of Lucknow Mail coming on platform number one. I pulled the strolley from under the seat and waving to the couple, who had also scrambled to catch the train, walked out of the waiting room.

"No other subject taught in school is as important as Moral Science". Express your views either for or against this statement.

(ICSE 2008)

- Introduction - Moral Science basically is a well-structured study of books, by which moral values are imparted, thus making us proper human beings .
- Other subjects can be of use only after one is a proper civilized person.
- Moral Science moulds our character, personality and enables us to differentiate between good and evil.
- Examples of intellectual and successful people bringing disgrace to themselves and the nation by their immoral deeds.
- Education and advancement in any field without good moral values and character bring about chaos and ruin. Example of   Germany under Adolf Hitler.
- Conclusion - Moral science   is the basic building block of our character and hence its importance over other subjects taught in school.

No other subject taught in school is as important as Moral Science. This is for only after we become proper human beings, can we aspire to become an engineer, doctor or a lawyer. It is thus the first basic step in education at school, where through a well-structured study of books, moral values are imparted. Being secular in character valuable insight is provided on all religions through stories.

This is not to suggest that all the other subjects taught in school are irrelevant. Subjects like Science, History, Geography, Maths, and Language, etc. are also important. However they can only be of use after one has become a proper civilized person. This is the basic objective of teaching moral science in school, and hence its importance over other subjects.

Moral Science not only helps us in imbibing good moral values, but also enables us to differentiate between good and evil. It moulds our character, personality, and equips us with good etiquettes and manners making our lives happy and wholesome.

This is for what use to the society would be a doctor, engineer, or for that matter any person bereft of moral values. Such persons no matter how good they are in their profession would be a threat to the society. There are numerous examples of intellectual and successful people bringing disgrace to themselves and the nation by their immoral deeds. The latest being the high profile doctors who stole kidneys from unsuspecting poor people for monetary gains. Such people may have been good in academics, but their scant regard for moral values, because of lack of moral science, ultimately proved to be their nemesis.

Education and advancement in any field without good moral values and character bring about chaos and ruin. There are innumerable examples from history that bear testimony to this fact. Germany under Adolf Hitler advanced and progressed considerably. However his misplaced notion of the superiority of the German race and the profound hatred for the Jews brought his country to ruins. The world would have been spared the scourge of the Second World War, when millions perished, had Adolf Hitler in his childhood got proper instructions in Moral Science.

Moral science thus undoubtedly is the basic building block of our character and hence its importance over other subjects taught in school. It not only benefits the individual, but also the society at large, making the world a better place to live in.

Elements of Western Culture have had a very influential role on cultures of the world. How are these elements different from those of Indian culture? What according to you, should we as Indians adopt from the west to make life more meaningful.

(ICSE 2008)

- Introduction - Colonization by the European powers resulted in western culture influencing different cultures of the world.
- How is western culture different from Indian culture

    Western culture is individual oriented resulting in nuclear families while Indian culture is family oriented

    It is more self-centered and materialistic. .

    It is flexible and practical with few customs and traditions while Indian culture is the oldest, caters to different religions and spiritually oriented

    It is open and exhibitionist in nature resulting in immoral social conduct, not approved in the Indian society

- Good things we can adopt from the west

    Issues like gender equality, human rights and progressive outlook to life.

- Conclusion -Western culture is versatile, individualistic but also progressive and self-dependent. Need to imbibe these good thing without forgetting our culture and values

The rapid colonization of different parts of the world by the European powers in the last two centuries resulted in elements of the western culture influencing different cultures of countries under their rule. The British also considerably influenced Indian culture as they ruled the country for well over two centuries.

Western culture is primarily individual oriented resulting in nuclear families with fewer kinship bonds. It is thus common to find 18-year teenagers moving out from their parent's home to stay on their own. On the other hand Indian culture is more family oriented with strong family and kinship ties. Unfortunate this fad of nuclear families is fast catching up in India, where such families are on the rise especially in metros. This is however more on account of economic reasons rather than social or cultural. The family values, ethos, and the respects that we have for our elders, differentiate us from other cultures of the world.

The individualistic and self-centered character of western culture is primarily on account of the society being highly materialistic, attaching a lot of importance to wealth, power and success. On the other hand we in India attach a lot of importance to customs and family values than material gains.

Western culture being flexible and practical has fewer customs and traditions to be followed. While our culture is the oldest, richest and the most diverse of all cultures in the world. This is for we have different religious and social customs in different parts of the country that bind us into a large family. We thus offer a unique example of unity in diversity to the world. Such customs enrich our lives, making the individual and the society more pleasant and peaceful. It is indeed a paradox that while we are adopting western lifestyle, the people in the west are looking up to India for peace and salvation. They flock to India in search of peace through meditation and yoga.

The western culture being open and exhibitionist in nature, has led to immoral social conduct. This is reflected in their clothes, mannerism and behavior. The Indian society does not approve such immoral conduct. However with the onslaught of western TV programs, beamed through satellite, a cultural invasion is gradually taking place. The Indian society has also been influenced with the impact being more discernable in the metros.

This is not to suggest, that there is nothing good in western culture, which we In India cannot adopt. There are many important issues like gender equality, human rights and progressive outlook to life, which we can adopt from the west. This will make our life more meaningful and also develop the society and the nation.

Western culture is no doubt more versatile and individualistic in nature. Nevertheless it has taught us to be progressive and self-dependent. We should however not blindly adopt it with all its ills. We have a tradition of imbibing the good thing from others, without forgetting our culture and values.

Cinema, both entertains and educates the masses. Express your views either for or against this statement.

(ICSE 2007)

- Introduction- Cinema, both entertains and educates the masses, for it mirrors our social values.
- Offers an affordable mean of entertainment catering to a variety of tastes, interest and moods.
- Powerful tool for education through audio-visual medium. Pictures like Gandhi, Saheed Bhagat Singh and Mugla-e-Azam promote brotherhood, communal harmony and nationalism.

- A powerful tool for social change, by awakening public conscience against social malpractices, like unsociability, sati pratha, dowry, child labour and corruption.
- Excellent medium of propaganda used by government to promote social harmony and health care.
- Unscrupulous persons exploit it for personal gains, showing scenes of sex and violence, that corrupt youth, and the society.
- Conclusion- As conclusive proof, the government has a Film Division for production and distribution of pictures, to the general public.

Cinema today has come a long way from the early days of 'silent pictures'. The true to life sets, dramatic screen plays, photographic techniques, acting histrionics, and their portrayal on a 70 mm screen, with digital sound effect, in plush multiplexes, have made cinema an ideal medium for entertainment and education. Because of its close affinity to the people, it mirrors their social values and ethos. It shows us the true picture of life. The evils of society, are vividly portrayed on screen, making it a powerful medium for social change.

There is no disputing the fact, that cinema offers an easy, and affordable means of entertainment to the masses. After a day of hard work, they are able to escape from the tension and worries of life. To others it is an escape from boredom. The true to life portrayal of characters, provoke our emotions, moving us to tears, laughter, thrill or even shock. They thus cater to a variety of our tastes, interest and moods.

It is also a very powerful tool for education. The audio-visual mode of presentation leaves an indelible on our memory and makes learning a pleasant experience. This is for we get to see, and hear about different people, places, and customs leading to a better understanding and assimilation of ideas and knowledge. It gives life like reality to the dead pages of history, by bringing to life the heroes of the past. Thus pictures like Gandhi, Saheed Bhagat Singh and Mugla-e-Azam give valuable insight about these great people, their struggle, aspirations, and ideology. Such pictures promote brotherhood, communal harmony and nationalism, by reminding us of our rich cultural heritage.

Cinema is a very powerful tool for social change as it effectively reflects the evil prevailing in the society. The effective portrayal of social malpractices like unsociability, sati pratha, dowry, child labour and corruption pricks our conscience.

It is also an excellent medium of propaganda. The advertisements and endorsements help in promoting the sale of goods and services. The government also uses it, to promote social harmony and health care. Thus documentaries creating awareness for prevention of Aids, Polio and other information to benefit the society, are effectively dissipated through this medium. The fashion industry owes its genesis and growth, to cinema. It sets the fashion trends for the youth, who imitate the dresses and hairstyles of popular film stars.

The popularity of this media, has led to some unscrupulous mandarins of cinema, exploiting it for personal gains. Thus unwarranted scenes of sex and violence, are displayed, to draw the crowd which fetch them the moolah. They contend that these are essential for a film to be realistic and viable. This is indeed a very frivolous and irresponsible argument, for such acts corrupt the youth, and the society. They resort to such tactics, to cover up the weak story line, lack of creativity, and direction. This has been amply proved, by the resounding success of good film, that do not resort to such cheap gimmickry. The censor board plays an important role in censoring film that are in bad taste.

Realizing the significant role of Cinema in entertainment and education. The government has setup a separate unit, the Film Division, under the Ministry of Information and Broadcasting. The Films Division helps in the production and distribution of good pictures, to the general public. This itself is ample proof of the significant role played by cinema in entertainment and education.

Siblings often grow up side by side in families; yet have very different life experiences. If you have one or more siblings and feel that your lives have differed significantly, write an essay explaining the reasons and the effects of such differences.

(ICSE 2007)

- Introduction- Man is the only creation of God, endowed with a unique individuality,
- Different in physical attributes.
- Different hobbies , interests.
- Greater life experiences making her confident, and knowledgeable.
- Conclusion- Distinctly different tastes, habits, and life experiences, but bound by strong family ties, that would become stronger as life goes by.

Man is perhaps the only creation of God, endowed with a unique individuality, different from any other man. It is because of this we differ in looks, colour, attitude, behaviour, likes and dislikes and personality traits, though born in the same family. It is thus quite natural for siblings, to have different life experiences, especially if they are not of the same gender.

I have a sister who is eight years my senior. She is elegant and beautiful, quite different to my stout and robust self. Being industrious by nature, she is either busy in studies, or doing needle work, which is her hobby. I am on the other hand quite carefree, and fun loving. My studies are confined to course books and newspapers. Staying at home is a taboo.

As regard hobbies, we are poles apart. While she likes cooking delicacies, reading novels and chatting, I like to go out with my friends for a movie or play cricket in the park close by. I enjoy the company of friends and cousins, and occasionally go out to stay with them, during weekends. We play cricket, football and if we have to stay indoors, then there is nothing better than computer games. This is however not to suggest, that my sister has no friends. She goes out to watch movies with them, and when they came home, they seem to only laugh and gossip.

Being elder to me, she treats me like a kid, lecturing me on what I should, or should not do. This at times drives me wild, and we have our usual tiffs. Unfortunately for me, my parents take her side and I am left puffing and fuming. However the animosity is short lived. We are back to teasing each other, to the dismay of our parents.

As for life experiences, she has greater exposure, being elder to me. She has traveled to many cities, studied in different schools, because of my father's frequent transfers. She has been to different places like Dehradoon, Srinagar, Delhi, etc., while I have only visited some of the places and studied in only one school. This exposure has made her very confident, and knowledgeable.

Being sincere and hard working, she burnt the midnight oil, while preparing for the Common Admission Test to IIM's. Her good marks enabled her to get admission in a prestigious college. I on the other hand am not very serious with my studies, and am constantly being lectured to mend my ways.

Being the youngest in the family, I have been pampered, making me carefree and fun loving. This is now going to change. With my sister away to college, I would now have to shoulder greater responsibility and become serious with my studies.

Though being siblings, we are distinctly different in tastes, habits, and life experiences. Nevertheless we are bound by strong family ties. These would further strengthen, as life goes by.

Recall a remarkable event of social importance in your city or locality. Give a little of its background, the event as it occurred, and its, impact on the lives of people.

(ICSE 2007)

- Introduction- Inauguration of the Lohia Hospital by the C. M. of U.P.
- The Lohia Hospital in Gomti Nagar, equipped with sophisticated medical equipments, and best doctors.
- The scene on the day of inauguration.
- Conclusion - Event of social importance, as it would mitigate the suffering of the sick and poor patients.

I recall being rudely awakened one fine morning, by a loud announcement being made by a man moving in a rickshaw. Straining my ears, I realized that he was inviting the public to the inauguration of the Lohia Hospital by the honorable Chief Minister of U.P, Mr. Mulayam Singh Yadav. The inauguration was scheduled to take place on the 10th of October at 11 a.m.

The Lohia Hospital a brain child of the Chief Minister, had been coming up in Gomti Nagar, a prestigious colony of Lucknow for quite sometime. Located on the main road, it offered good connectivity to people coming from various parts of the city, and adjoining districts. The massive hospital had been equipped with the most sophisticated medical equipments, and had some of the best doctors from renown institutions. The hospital would fulfill a long standing demand of the residents of the locality, for there was no government hospital, within a radius of 10 km.

Being curious about the facility offered at the hospital, and also to have a glimpse of the honourable Chief Minister, I decided to attend the event, which was to unfold very close to my house. I reached there well before the event commenced, and found the roads swamped by cars with red and blue beacon lights, and a large number of security personnel's. The flower decked gate led to a huge pandal, in which were seated thousands of spectators. The dais had bright coloured curtains, with numerous mikes on the table. On one side of the dais, was the press gallery, on which were seated a large number of journalists from the print and electronic media.

At sharp 11 a.m. Dr. A. Narain, Head of the hospital announce the arrival of the chief guest. I and the spectators rose to see the doughty Chief Minister being escorted to the dais, amidst dazzling flash light of the cameras. There was the welcome address, and presentation of bouquet, to the chief guest, after which he was invited to address the gathering. In his brief address the chief guest exhorted the doctors, to fulfill the aspirations of the people, by providing quality health care facilities to them. Dr. Narain then invited the C.M. to unveil the plaque, to formally dedicate the hospital to the public. Amidst showering of petals, he unveiled the plaque, and the function finally came to an end.

This was a remarkable event of social importance for the residents of the locality, who were till now dependent on private hospitals and nursing homes for health care facilities. This super specialist hospital would mitigate the suffering of the poor, and also provide specialized treatment to patients, who need not go to far off places.

The Computer will soon replace the Book. Express your views either for or against this statement.

(ICSE 2006)

- Introduction –The computer can never replace a book.
- A book provides the most cost effective means for spreading literacy, portable and handy.
- Reading a book does not cause any physical discomfort or eye strain.
    High degree of respectability in the written word.
    Develops our power of expression and personality.
- It is the source of a wealth of knowledge on a particular subject.
- Conclusion- The computer can never replace a book, either now or in the near future, for the convenience and conviction offered by a book, can never be possible through a computer .

A good book in the words of John Milton "Is the precious lifeblood of a master spirit, embalmed and treasured up to a purpose to a life beyond life". The thoughts and ideas contained in a book are immortal like Tulsidas's Ram Charitra Manas, Ved Vyas Mahabharata ,The Bible and many other religious and literary works like Shakespeare's play, etc. On the other hand a computer is but a machine, that at best can visually display the contents of a specific book. To think that a computer would one day replace a book, is indeed unthinkable and far fetched .

A book provides the most cost effective means for spreading education and literacy, for it is available at a fraction of the cost of a computer. Moreover being extremely portable and handy, it is not dependent on any external factors like availability of power supply, software and space that are an essential prerequisite for a computer .To go through the contents of a book, the two basic ingredients required are time and inclination .It can be read at any time of the day or night, and anywhere, like while traveling or even while dozing of to sleep.

Reading a book does not cause any physical discomfort or eye strain, while the same cannot be said for while reading the contents of a computer .We are all aware of the hazards of back pain and eye strain ,caused by long stretch of viewing a computer screen. Another factor in favour of the book, is the general high degree of respectability and faith commanded by the written word. Thus while we may see or hear event on our computer terminal, there is nothing better than to confirm the same from a newspaper or a book .Besides helping in spreading education to the masses, a book plays an important role in developing our power of expression, and the generation of new ideas and thoughts, which help in moulding our personality.

A book is the source of a wealth of knowledge on a particular subject, offering no diversion or distraction . While a computer offers multiple uses like serious reading, entertainment, games or news. This at times leads to distraction of our mind, and consequently hinders the acquisition of knowledge.

The computer thus can never replace a book, either now or in the near future. This is for the convenience and conviction offered by a book, can never be possible through a computer. More over, being a machine, it is liable to breakdown and error , factors that are non-existent while reading a book

India has always believed in the value of the family. Discuss the changes, both good and bad, that have resulted from the break-up of the traditional Indian joint family.

(ICSE 2006)

- Introduction- The value of the family has been deeply ingrained in the Indian society.
- Breakup of the joint family due to economic factors, and the corrupting influence of the western society.
- Positive impact is the kindling of the spirit of enterprise in the people.
  End of the internal squabbles inherent in a joint family.
- Negative impact is the loss of security and protection offered in a joint family.
- Conclusion- The break-up of the joint family system may be due to economic and social compulsions. But we must preserve the rich family values, and strengthen the kinship bonds.

The value of the family has been deeply ingrained in the Indian society over the ages .This is for, we have been fed with mythological epics like the Ramayan and the Mahabharata, very early in life . While the Ramayan vividly portrays the duties of a son towards his father , mother , brothers, sisters and wife, the Mahabharata exhorts us to fight for justice and rights .It was this rich family value and cultural heritage, that found reflection in the Indian joint family system .

However like everything, this too has been corrupted by the evil influence of western society The present generation aping the west is becoming highly materialistic and this is leading to the break-up of the joint family system. Further with the exponential growth in the population, people were compelled to migrate to towns and cities in search for employment. This is for the meager land holdings can not support their livelihood .

A positive impact of this break-up has been the kindling of the spirit of enterprise in people, who till now were conditioned to conform to the decisions of the family head or Karta the sole decision maker. We know of numerous rags to riches stories of people, who leaving the safety of their hearth and home in the villages, carved a niche for themselves in the cities and towns, on their own merit. With the emergence of the nuclear family system in the cities the society has became more broad based and open. This transformation has led to the crumbling of the boundaries of caste and creed, making it more human and hospitable.

Another positive impact has been the end of the internal squabbles and unpleasantness, that are inherent in a joint family. The clash of individual personalities, aspirations and egos, at times led to tension and ill-will in the family.

Not withstanding the above, the break- up of the joint family system, has taken away the umbrella of security and protection from the individual. Thus one can no longer seek protection, advice, or support from elders, in time of crisis. Further the emotional bonds of the family have also been weakened by distance and time, so much so that near cousins often meet as strangers. This lack of emotional bonding has given rise to psychological problems for the youth, resulting in more case of suicide, and socially unacceptable behaviour.

The break-up of the Indian joint family system may be due to economic and social compulsions. However we must preserve the rich family values, and strengthen the kinship bonds , by greater interaction showing respect to elders, and love to our family members. It is for these family values that differentiate us from others in the universe.

You are a spectator at a cricket match. Trouble erupts suddenly in the stadium and you witness a riot among the crowd. Give a vivid description of the scene.

(ICSE 2006)

- Introduction- Crucial match being played at the Feroze Shah Kotla ground in Delhi for the 'Champion's Trophy' between India and Pakistan.
- Pakistan won the toss and chose to bat, putting up a massive total.
- Indian response was disastrous and the crowd became violent. Order was restored.
- Conclusion- The last few overs proved to be the turning point, and led to India winning the match.

Waving the Indian tricolour I and my friends shouted " we want four" to Mahendra Singh Dhoni and Irfan Pathan batting with the score reading a dismal 184 for 8 ,with just 2 overs remaining and trailing a good 36 runs behind the Pakistan score of 220 for 6. This was a crucial match being played at the Feroze Shah Kotla ground in Delhi for the 'Champion's Trophy'.

Earlier in the day, the Pakistani captain Inzimam ul Haq had won the toss and opted to bat, on a wicket that was green and promised to be full of runs. How right his decision was became evident, with the steady flow of runs. The captain himself leading from the front by remaining unbeaten with 110 runs.

The Indian response to this mammoth total was disastrous, with the front order batting crumbling to the pace of Shoaib Akhtar. With certain defeat staring in the face, the tension in the crowd became palpable, and increased as the run rate per over mounted .Unhappy with the slow scoring a section of the crowd started raising slogans and hurling bottles into the field. This was objected to by others, and soon a melee ensued. In the free for all that followed, people ran helter skelter for cover. Women and children caught in the stampede cried out for help. There was utter confusion in the stadium for well over fifteen minutes. By then the local administration swung into action and the police used mild force to quell the rioters. The match was halted, and the organizers appealed to the audience to remain calm and maintain order, for the match to continue. They reminded the spectators , that such unsporting behaviour would bring a bad name to the city. In the mean time the police rounded up the mischief mongers, and herded them out of the stadium. The injured were provided first aid by the doctors and paramedical staff, while those seriously injured were carried away on stretchers . With some semblance of order, the umpires decided to continue the match.

Taking a cue from our motivating gesture, the crowd too joined in and the stadium reverberated with slogan "we want four". In the very first ball of Shoaib Akhtar's last over M.S. Dhoni responded with a four .This was followed by two consecutive fours and a six, in an over that yielded twenty runs, and proved to be the turning point of the match. With victory in sight, the crowd became ecstatic, and started bursting crackers and beating drums. However with sixteen runs still remaining in just six balls, victory seemed quite elusive . There was pin drop silence as the over progressed, with just ten runs coming of the first five balls. As the last ball was bowled to Dhoni, he valiantly lofted the ball over long on. A fielder ran after it, and to the dismay of the crowd, took a brilliant catch just as his outstretched leg crossed the boundary rope. The third umpires decision was called for, and with the light blinking green bedlam broke loose in the stadium. The crowd went berserk with joy and happiness. I and my friend returned home jubilant at India's victory, and with a realization "Uncertainty thy name is Cricket".

'The commercialization of festivals has eroded their real significance.' Express your views either for or against this statement.

(ICSE 2005)

- Introduction - Pious occasions of festivals degenerated to only merrymaking, due to commercialisation.
- Market man use such occasions to promote products before festivals like Deepawali, and Christmas.
- Religious rites and customs have undergone a sea change.
- It is playing havoc with our culture for dance forms like the 'Dandia' have degenerated to disco.
- Effect of modernity and Information Technology has diluted the essence of festivals as we now sent e-mails, or cards to our friends and relatives rather than meeting them.
- Conclusion- Need for us to pray and introspect, while celebrating festivals, for this can only enrich us spiritually and mentally.

'Man is by constitution a religious animal' said the great scholar Edmund Burke. This is for religion makes him more loving, humane and sociable. Every religion has festivals, which are basically occasions of celebrations, to commemorate a special occasion. Thus festivals which were pious occasions, usually associated with religious ceremonies and merry making, have now degenerated to only merrymaking, due to their commercialisation.

It is indeed unfortunate, to see clever market man usurping such pious occasions, to enrich themselves. They launch new range of products, garments, fashion accessories and even luxury items like cars, well before the onset of festivals like Deepawali, and Christmas. Their advertisements and discount schemes create an urge to splurge, thus propping up their sales. They induce us to purchase costly presents for our friends, relatives and children. Gone is the joy, love and compassion that one experienced during such festive occasions.

The religious rites and customs observed in celebrating festivals, have also undergone a sea change. Thus for example we now use decorative lights instead of the traditional diyas burnt with ghee during Deewali. This was a symbolic welcome to lord Rama on his return to Ayodhya after defeating the demon king Ravana. Similarly at Christmas the carol singing and the hymns have now been replaced with Christmas ball, and other forms of merry making.

The commercialization of festivals, is also playing havoc with our culture, as is evident during the Navratri festival. This festival which stretches over a period of nine days devotees dance 'dandia' to please the Goddess Durga. This dance has now degenerated to 'Dandiya Ras' with filmy songs giving it the form of a disco. The western influence on it is so profound, that the true essence of pleasing the Goddess Durga, is completely forgotten.

Modernity and the Information Technology revolution has also contributed in diluting the essence of festivals. This is for we now sent e-mails, or just a card to our friends and relatives on such occasions. So great is the pressure of time on us, that we do not have the energy, or the inclination to visit our near and dear ones, to celebrate the festivals that comes once a year. On the contrary we love to go shopping at Deewali Melas, Christmas sale or other functions usually associated with commercialization of such festivals.

Thus festivals have now been reduced to celebrations and merry making only. Man has succeeded by his ingenuity, to convert such pious occasions, to enrich himself materially. There is however an urgent need for us to pray and introspect, while celebrating our festivals, for this can only enrich us spiritually and mentally.

You have returned to your city after spending five years in a foreign country. The city has changed during your absence. Describe the changes that have affected the life of people in the city. Give your personal views regarding the changes.

(ICSE 2005)

- Introduction- No place like home.
- Speedy clearance at airport ,spectacular progress in telecommunication.
- Impressed by the brightly lit roads and flyovers.
- Signs of prosperity and changing lifestyle.
- Conclusion - I decided to stay back home.

'Mid pleasures and palaces though we may roam.

Be it ever so humble, there's no place like home' said John Howard Payne. These words echoed to me as my aircraft touched down at Indira Gandhi International Airport Delhi. Hastily unhooking my seat belt I climbed down the stairs. This was the great moment I had been looking forward to in the last five years of my stay in London, for higher studies.

I was indeed surprised with the efficiency shown by the airport authorities, for in about ten minutes flat, I was walking through the green channel to be with my parents. After exchanging pleasantries, I spoke on their mobile to my brother and sisters in Bombay and Chennai. It was indeed thrilling to experience the speedy progress made at home in telecommunication. Distance did not seen to matter any longer.

As the taxi sped towards my home in Gurgaon, a sleepy town on the outskirts of Delhi. I was pleasantly surprised to see the broad brightly lit roads with a number of flyovers shortening the journey. We reached home without facing any traffic jam, a normal feature in the past.

At home I found my friends waiting for me, after the usual greetings, we decided to go out for dinner. Climbing into their shiny cars, that signified prosperity, we sped off to hotel Holiday Inn. Even at this unearthly hour around midnight, we found the roads alive with traffic flowing smoothly. The Disco 'cellar' at the hotel was overflowing with people enjoying themselves. I learnt from my friends that such places now abound in the city, thanks to the change in lifestyle and work culture of the people. The booming economy, and the BPO revolution, had indeed transformed my sleepy hometown into a growing metropolis. Celebrations over we return home at the break of dawn.

I was by now weary with sleep. Tossing and turning on my bed I could not but appreciate the spectacular changes that had taken place at home. Comforts that I was accustomed to, during my stay abroad, had also now become available here. I decided to stay back home, never to return to the cold environs of London, before dozing off to sleep.

Essays

Views Including Argumentative

"Teenagers today are more worldly wise than their parents". Express your views for or against the statement.

(ICSE 2004)

- Introduction –Disagree with the above statement.
- Parents are a better judge of human character than teenagers.
- Teenagers may have more information which is no substitute for experience of their parents.
- Teenagers are enthusiastic and optimistic. While parents by nature are seasoned and cautious. They know the virtue of patience and tolerance.
- Teenagers follow the dictate of their heart, while parents take decisions on merit, using their mind.
- Conclusion - Teenagers are not more worldly wise than their parents. They lack experience, and wisdom which comes with age.

Agreeing with this statement would amount to casting aspersions on the wisdom of parents, to which all teenagers looked up to. The teenagers knowledge maybe significantly more on a particular subject, but with respect to being worldly wise, they are far behind their parents. This is for parents have knowledge blended with years of experience. This makes them more worldly wise than the teenagers, who are on the threshold of life.

Years of experiencing the many ups and downs of life make parents a better judge of human character and nature. They can therefore judge people more accurately and are not waved by superficial factors. On the other hand teenagers are swayed by superficial, irrelevant factors which may just be a facade and far away from reality.

The information explosion in the print and electronic media, may give more information to teenagers. This however cannot make them more worldly wise then their parents. Their knowledge obtained from such sources are primarily confined to what they have seen, heard or read. The parents on the other hand can better use this knowledge, blending it with their personal experiences in life. It is because of this we find teenagers looking up to their parents for advice, in important decisions relating to their work or career.

Moreover teenagers being young are more enthusiastic and optimistic by nature. This is for they have seen the brighter side of life only, being protected from its harsh realities by their parents. They are therefore prone to taking decisions in a haste. Parents on the other hand, being seasoned and cautious, make more rational decisions, for they take a balanced view of things. They know the virtue of patience and tolerance, and are therefore in a better position to evaluate options more logically and practically, before arriving at a firm decision. There advise is thus more practical and useful.

Besides being optimistic and rash, the teenagers have a tendency to follow the dictates of the heart, rather then their mind. They are easily moved by superficial considerations like colour, looks or aesthetic appeal. On the other hand parents take decisions on merit, with sound time tested logic, using their mind. They are therefore less prone to error. It is because of this we find successful teenagers like models, actors seeking the advise of parents, in matters concerning their career or future. On the other hand, we have numerous instances of teenagers ruining their lives, in the misconception of being more worldly wise than their parents.

Thus teenagers even today are not more worldly wise than their parents. They lack experience, and wisdom which comes with age. These attributes are possessed by the parents in ample measure. Teenagers therefore must make proper use of this invaluable resource to enrich their lives.

ASSIGNMENTS

- Should parents exercise control over teenagers? Give your views for or against the statement.
- Students should wear school uniform in school. Give your views for or against the statement.
- Should polythene bags be banned. Give your views for or against the statement.

Animals should not be used for drug development or medical research. Express your views either for or against this statement.

(ICSE 2003)

- Introduction – Using animals for drug development or medical research is unjustifiable on moral, ethical and social grounds.
- Men has no right to destroy, what we cannot create
- Colossal wastage of precious life by students
- This callous attitude to life is reflected in the growing incidence of violence in the society.
- Because of this many species of animals have become extinct, endangering the ecological balance of nature
- Conclusion - We should ban the use of animals for drug development and medical research.

"He prayeth well who loveth well"

Both man and bird and beast said Collridge, bringing out the importance of showing benevolence and compassion to animals, as we do for fellow beings. This is because like us, animals also experience pain and suffering. They too are as much God's creation, as man himself. Hence to use them as guinea pigs, for drug- development or medical research, is totally uncalled for. It is not only unnatural, but also unjustifiable on moral, ethical and social grounds.

Man has from times immemorial, exploited animals to serve his ends. They have been used for making his life comfortable by catering to his various needs. It is therefore against the basic tenets of morality to perpetuate pain and suffering on these poor creatures, such as pigs, dogs, frogs, etc., on the pretext of facilitating medical research. This is for we have no right to destroy, what we cannot create. The life of an animal is also precious and invaluable, as the life of man. Destroying them in this manner, is but trampling on their basic right to live.

Often, people advocate the use of animals for medical research, on the grounds of expedience for the larger benefit to mankind. Can such an absurd logic justify the daily extermination of millions of frogs, birds, etc, by school and college students, to make them aware of the basic metabolic system? We all know, that only a miniscule number of students, actually pursue a career in medicine or pharmacology. The majority migrate to other fields like commerce and arts. What a colossal waste of precious animal lives sacrificed at the alter of the above premise, with no benefits accruing to mankind!

Such senseless killing of animals, must make us hang our heads in shame. It shows our complete insensitivity towards them. At the same time, killing them in such a wanton manner, makes us cruel and uncaring for life, even towards our own fellow human beings. This callous attitude to life is reflected in the growing incidence of violence in the society, especially among the youth.

We have over centuries used animals to enrich our lives. This, however, does not give us the right to sacrifice their lives, in the wanton manner as is being done today. Our senseless acts in the past, have already made many species of animals extinct, and has dangerously altered the ecological balance of nature. We can only advocate the above to our own peril.

The need of the hour is to develop advanced technology, to simulate the various life processes, for drug development or medical research. We should only in special cases use animals for the above. This would minimise our interference with Nature, and at the same time respect the animals, right to live.

To prevent further degradation to the envoirnment, we should ban the use of animals for drug development and medical research. This will make our universe a better place to live, with less pain and suffering, to all living being, be it man or beast.

ASSIGNMENTS

- Wars are necessary evil. Discuss.
- Perfects and Monitors in classes should be elected and not appointed. Discuss.
- It is better to be a fool than a rogue. Give your views.

Man and Women should have equal rights. Give your views for or against the statement.

(ICSE 2002)

- Introduction- Agree with the statement
    Ideology propounded by great revolutionaries like Voltaire, Karl Marx and our own Mahatma Gandhi
- Women play a complementary role in the life of men.
    Nature has gifted them special attributes for the human race to grow and prosper.
    They are the fulcrums around which the family revolves
- Intellectually they are the same or even better than men.
    They are venturing into fields like aviation, defense and even space.
- Their well-acknowledged contribution in the field of education and healthcare
    As a teacher, doctor or a nurse
- They comprise fifty percent of the human population, contributing the same percentage to the GDP.
    Realising this the developed and developing countries have given them equal rights.
    Countries which have denied equal rights to them, are backward both technological and socially.
- Conclusion- Undoubtedly, men and women should have equal rights in all respects.
    This would enrich society, and help in the growth and development of the country.

"Behind every successful man there is a women." All great men in their autobiographies have acknowledged this fact. Indeed it is inconceivable to deny them equal rights in the society. After all they are also human beings, endowed with the same mental, emotional and physical faculties possessed by men. This realisation dawned on us after two centuries of revolutionary social and political struggle. Great revolutionaries like Voltaire, Karl Marx and our own Mahatma Gandhi inspired the masses with their ideology of freedom, justice and equality. Their ideology paved the way for a more equitable and socially benevolent political order, eventually leading to democracy. Under this political dispensation, equal right including the right to adult franchise was guaranteed to all irrespective of sex, religion, caste or creed. Thus in this age of enlightenment to deny equal right to women, would be like adopting an ostrich like approach, oblivious of the present realities and their contribution to society.

Women today play a complementary and important role in the life of men. Nature has gifted them with special attributes, so that the human race would continue to grow and prosper. Thus while men have been endowed with virile strength, women are endowed with humane sensibilities and emotion like love, compassion, and caring. These are extremely vital for the upbringing of the future generation, who are the hope of tomorrow. They are the fulcrums around which the family and our lives revolve. Thus as a wife, mother or sister they play an indispensable part in the life of men.

Intellectually they have also time and again shown, that they are second to none. A cursory glance at the high school or secondary school results, confirm a higher pass out percentage of girls than boys. They are thus blessed with the same or even better mental and intellectual power than men. We today find more and more women, working shoulder to shoulder with their male counterparts. They are even venturing into new fields that were till recently considered to be the exclusive domain of males, like aviation, defence and even space.

Their contribution in the field of education and healthcare is a well-acknowledged fact. "The hand that rocks the cradle rules the world." Thus as a mother, she inculcates spiritual and moral values in the child. Outside home, she moulds the destiny of the children as teacher, counselor and guide. As doctors, nurses or a social worker, she provides health care facilities to the community. Their contributions are indeed invaluable for the well-being, growth and economic development of society and the country.

Quantitatively too they comprise about fifty percent of the human population and also contribute the same percentage to the GDP of the country. Taking note of their invaluable contribution, the developed and developing countries have accorded women their rightful place in society, by giving them equal rights in all respects. Thus they not only have the right to vote, but also have the same right to property, education and work, as enjoyed by men. This has resulted in their emancipation, and consequently a renaissance in the society, making it more progressive and modern. On the contrary, countries which have denied equal rights to them continue to be backward in all spheres, including technological and social. We therefore find women in most Muslim countries suffering from oppressive customs like purdah and polygamy, with no right to vote or inheritance.

Undoubtedly, men and women should have equal rights in all respects .The need of the hour is not to question this reality, but to devise ways and means to ameliorate their lot. We should provide them proper educational and vocational facilities, so that they can grow and develop to their optimum potential. This would enrich the society, and lead to greater growth and development of the country.

ASSIGNMENTS

- Military training should be made compulsory in schools. Give your views for or against the statement.
- There is no role of religion in politics. Give your views for or against the statement.

There are three kinds of people in the world–the wills, the won'ts and the can'ts. The first accomplish everything, the second oppose everything, and the third fail in everything. By giving reasons or referring to some incidents, state in which category you fall.

(ICSE 2001)

- Introduction-Agree with the statement.
- Man has done the impossible by sheer will power
    Meeting challenge is the essence of life.
    Examples from history
- Qualities which put me in the category of 'Wills'
    Optimistic outlook to life and opportunities
    Never say die attitude
    Value time
    Self motivation and desire to excel
- Conclusion. We must not only wish and aspire for something, but also work with resolve for achieving it, for 'God helps those who help themselves'

There is much truth in the above adage, which describes the types of human being in the world "The wills, the won'ts and the can'ts. The first accomplish everything, the second oppose everything and the third fail in everything." Man is a creature basically six feet tall, but he has been able to conquer space and the majestic height of the imposing mountains. He is relentlessly in the pursuit of breaking new grounds, not on account of his physical prowess, but because of his resolve and will power. We all possess this, to a lesser or greater extent. However great souls have been known to exercise this to achieve the impossible, while lesser mortals in its absence lead an ignoble existence. This is so for men with a wavering mind and feeble will, cannot succeed in life as Victor Hugo rightly said, "People do not lack strength, they lack the will."

It is in meeting challenges and facing our adversary that we improve ourselves. "He that wrestles with us strengthens our nerves, and sharpens our skills. Our antagonist is our helper," said Edmund Burke. Meeting challenges is the essence of life. We would not be privy to such spectacular developments, had our great predecessors, not overcome   challenges posed to them by nature. There is in fact nothing impossible to achieve and Napoleon rightly said, "The word impossible exists in the dictionary of fools".

The history of mankind is replete with instances of how ordinary people achieve great things, by dint of their will power. The pioneers of aviation the Wright brothers, had their limbs broken, but they did finally succeed in achieving their dream of flying Such heroes are my ideals, and place me firmly in the category of the 'Wills'.

To me life is a challenge to be faced boldly and optimistically. It is this attitude, which makes me see an opportunity even in a difficult situation. The words of Disraeli inspire me when he said "Success is the child of audacity, mould it by opportunity."

The never say die attitude, impels me to take on the toughest of challenges, for I know that my efforts will not be in vain. The thought of failure does not daunt me, for I believe it is a stepping stone to success. I have confidence in myself and am convinced that my perseverance will sooner or later bear fruit.

I know the value of time for as they say, "procrastination is the thief of time". Thus time once gone can never be recuperated. Therefore I believe to "Act–act in the living present! Heart within, and God overhead!"

The desire to excel, gives me the self-motivation to face new challenges, that life throws at me. This spirit of competition, propels me to accomplish great things in life and place me resolutely in the class of the wills.

We must therefore not only wish and aspire for something, but also work with resolve for achieving it, for 'God helps those who help themselves'. The won'ts and the can'ts, have no place in the highly competitive world of today. As it is rightly said, "Great souls have will, feeble one's have only wishes." and wishes we know lead nowhere.

ASSIGNMENTS

- 'Fortune favours the brave'. Give your views. You may refer to some instance to elaborate your view.
- Right to employment should be made a fundamental right. Give your views for or against the statement.

Which in your opinion is more important a healthy body or a healthy mind. Give relevant arguments to support your opinion.

(ICSE 2000)

- Introduction—A healthy mind is more important.
- It enables us to differentiate between good and bad.
- It is more lasting and grows with age.
- Increases with sharing, and makes us powerful.
- Influences our lives and those around us with examples of Mahatma Gandhi and Helen Keller.
- Affects our personality.
- Conclusion—An essential prerequisite.

Man is the only creature in the entire universe blessed with a body and a mind. It is this, which makes him the crown of creation. While a healthy body is necessary, but in the absence of a healthy mind, he is no longer a human being, but is more akin to an animal. Thus in my opinion a healthy mind is more important than a healthy body. This is but echoed by William Shakespeare when he said, "For sweetest things turn sourest by their deeds, Lilies that fester smell far worse than weeds".

Not only does it make us a proper human being, but also enables us to differentiate between what is good or bad, virtuous and evil. So significant is its contribution, that without it we cannot lead a happy life.

While the body is subject to ageing the mind is not. Thus a healthy person may with passage of time, grow old with age. On the other hand, the mental faculty of a person not only increases with age, but he becomes more mature, wiser and experienced. People come to him for advice and guidance.

Unlike the body it is unaffected by fatigue and overwork, on the contrary the more we use it the more perfect it becomes. It enables us to imbibe knowledge, which we can use for our own betterment, or for the welfare of the society. For as we all know "Knowledge is power". This power if used judiciously, can make us advance in our life. It is, therefore, not uncommon to find people of a frail constitution, managing the destiny of their countries. They hold sway over millions of otherwise well-bodied people.

Thus we can also to a great extent influence the life of people around us. At times so powerful is the impact, that we had Mahatma Gandhi who despite his frail constitution led the entire country to wage a war for independence. His unique approach of using the weapon of non-violence and truth shook the mighty British Empire. They were in mortal fear of this frail, semi clad fakir as they called him and had to at last concede independence. Similarly we had Helen Keller, though being mute and dumb since birth, she led a normal life. This was by sheer dint of her will power endowed to her by a healthy mind. Thus she became a source of inspiration for even able bodied men and women. It is hence evident, that a healthy mind, can more than makes up for a frail or even a challenged body.

So all pervading is its impact on our lives, that it moulds our personality by making us more humane, loving, compassionate and caring. Thus endearing us to the people and the society. A healthy body on the other hand is of no use, if it lacks a good personality. This is for people remember us by our deeds and not by our looks.

This reminds us of what John Ruskin said, "Remember that the most beautiful things are the most useless, Peacocks and lilies for instance." Thus a healthy mind is not only more important, but an essential prerequisite for us to lead a normal happy life.

ASSIGNMENTS

- "For sweetest things turn sourest by their deeds, Lilies that fester smell far worse than weeds." Discuss

- "The mind is in its place and in itself can make a heaven of hell, a hell of heaven." (Milton) Discuss.

"Cigarette smoking in public places should be banned" Give your views for or against this statement.

(ICSE 1999)

- Introduction—Agree with the statement.
- Reasons for smoking.
- Harmful effects of smoking.
- Infringement on the fundamental right of others.
- Banned in advanced countries showing favourable results.
- Conclusion—Immediate need to ban smoking in public places.

It is common knowledge that smoking cigarettes is injurious to health. It harms the smoker, and also endangers the lives of others around him, through passive smoking. Do we have this right to harm others, and ourselves by our irresponsible behaviour? Definitely not. Therefore, in all propriety smoking cigarettes in public places should be banned altogether.

Cigarette smoking is a gift of modern times and has become fashionable nowdays. Many psychologists have done detailed statistical studies, to investigate why people smoke? Their findings are indeed shocking. The reasons given by smokers indicate, that it is habit forming, increases concentration, helps in killing time and to be in fashion.

These are but purely psychological reasons without any concrete benefit. On the other hand, specific medical studies have confirmed a direct linkage between Nicotine, that is present in tobacco and the high incidence of Heart attack and Cancer in smokers and even passive smokers. These are dreadful diseases and at times prove fatal. The fortunate few, who manage to survive its clutches through expensive surgery and medication remain scarred for life. They ultimately have to quit smoking and have to adopt a very strict and somber lifestyle if they want to live. We thus have no moral right to smoke, for smoking exposes us and the innocent public to the vagaries of this scourge. Someone rightly said, "You smoke we choke".

Smoking in public places is also an infringement on the fundamental right of our fellow citizens, for it violates their right to live. Our protagonist may argue, that banning smoking would violate the fundamental right of the individual. This is untrue, as no one has the right to endanger his own life, what to talk of others around him.

It is this realisation, that has forced many advanced countries like USA and UK to ban smoking in public. The immediate fallout of this has been, a drastic fall in the incidence of cases of heart attack, which is reported to have reduced by 30 to 40 percent. There is therefore no reason as to why, the same should not be done in India.

The consequences of smoking are indeed very grave and hence there is an immediate need to ban smoking in public .The public opinion should be built in this favour and if required, the law-makers of the country should enact laws, whereby smoking in public places is effectively banned.

ASSIGNMENTS

- Consumption of alcoholic beverages in public places should be banned. Give your views for or against.
- 'Drug abuse among students calls for an effective ban'. Discuss the problem and what need to be done.

"Tradition is an obstacle to progress"
Give your views for or against the statement

(ICSE 1999)

- Introduction — What is tradition?
- Importance of tradition in our lives.
- Tradition helps in progress.
- Historical evidence in support of the above.
- Different types of tradition.
- Conclusion — A virtue that guides our lives.

> "Theirs not to make reply,
> Theirs not to reason why,
> Theirs but to do and die,"

said Lord Tennyson about the noble tradition of discipline in the patriotic fighting forces across the world. The word tradition, however means, unwritten beliefs and customs handed down from generation to generation, which we all knowingly or unknowingly adhere to in our daily lives. It is the emotional fabric, which binds us to our forefathers and makes us distinct from one another. In fact some of the finest moments in our lives are, when we uphold the traditions of our family, clan or country. Men have laid down their lives for upholding noble traditions and have become immortal and great.

Such is the noble role and significance of tradition in our lives, that it can never become an obstacle in progress. It lays down guidelines for simple and even complex decision-making and leaves us free to utilize our time more effectively. Take for example the complex decision of marriage. If there is a tradition of marriage within the same or related clan, then the decision is far easier and easily acceptable. Its advantages are well seen in the Indian society, where there is a tradition of arranged marriages. This has proved to be more successful than love marriages in the west, with fewer cases of divorces and broken homes. It also has a lot of emotional and ornamental value, which is practised very proudly by our armed forces. Some of these traditions have been passed down from the British Army, take for example the pulling of jeep by fellow officers on the retirement of a senior officer, or the ceremonial parade, flag hoisting, etc. These are all fine traditions that should be maintained at all cost.

Tradition in fact is a stimulant to progress. We do not have to worry about how to do mundane or even very important things, as there is a set custom or procedure to do it. In fact it is a scientific approach to life, where the final outcome is assured, without having to experiment. We are emotionally and physiologically at peace, which enables us to focus our complete energy for advancement and progress of self as well as the society at large.

The tradition of holding the flag high in the face of adversary, has made many small men immortal and great. These men did not think twice, before laying down their lives upholding this tradition. Their act of bravery, has at times changed the course of battle and even History.

Not all traditions are good. There is need for rethinking and weeding out some traditions like untouchability, child marriages and dowry, etc., which have no place in the modern society. We are today more educated and enlightened to differentiate between good and bad. It should be our endeavour to promote good and weed out the bad tradition, in keeping with the times.

Following tradition, therefore, guides our lives and saves us from the many pitfalls and dangers. It is a virtue, which helps us lead a happy and progressive life.

ASSIGNMENTS

- Tradition has no place in modern society. Give your views on the same.
- The role of tradition in our lives.
- Tradition and the Indian youth.

Of all the subjects you are studying at present which one do you think would be most useful to you in future and why?

(ICSE 1999)

- Introduction — Need for so many subjects for study.
- Their relevance.
- The subject of my choice.
- How it would be useful to me in future.
- Conclusion.

The multiplicity of subjects that we have to study bewilders me. I do sometimes wonder the utility of studying Shakespeare in English Literature, History, Geography, Social Studies, etc. There are a host of other subjects, which have probably no use in our later lives .One could understand, if we were to study about the History and Geography of our country. What is perplexing however, is that we have to learn the history and geography of different countries and continents, that we shall probably never even see in our lives.

Though valid, this hypothesis is far from the truth. All the subjects are equally relevant, to have a holistic view of things in our later lives, irrespective of the subject that we are specialising in. Thus it is equally important for a doctor to know, why and how seasonal variations take place. Similarly the historian should have elementary knowledge of the human body, so that he can take proper care of his health.

Out of all the subjects I am studying, I have a special liking for Science, for not only is it interesting but also systematic and logical. Chemistry and Physics are tough no doubt, but quite engrossing. Biology is the most interesting of the three. It dwells on aspects directly concerning us. We get to know the functions of different organs like heart, liver and kidney. We also learn how to avoid dreadful diseases like malaria, chickenpox, dysentery, etc. In the unfortunate event of our affliction with these diseases, we also know their malady. Besides this, we pick up knowledge of hygiene that is important for us in our later lives. Though I have a special liking for Biology, but as all the three subjects are in the science stream, my single preference is but Science. The reason for my choice is but obvious. It would be of tremendous use to me in realising my ambition of becoming a doctor, a profession which is noble and respectable.

In order to study medicine, I would need to have a thorough knowledge of Science, which would encompass Biology, Chemistry and Physics. This would enable me to pass the Pre medical competitive examination, held every year for selecting students for pursuing medical studies in the various medical colleges in the state. Lakhs of students appear in this examination for a few thousand seats only. Hence there is very stiff competition for each seat.

This does not deter me, for I am not studying out of compulsion or force, but studying for the love of the subject. Moreover, I know that "Life's battle don't always go. To the stronger or the fastest man. But sooner or later the man who wins. Is the man who thinks he can " as said by H.W. Longfellow.

ASSIGNMENT

- Of all the games you played at school, which according to you would be most useful to you in future and why?

Set out briefly but clearly the arguments for or against animals being used in public and street performance.

(ICSE 1998)

- Introduction — Against the statement. (should not be used)
- Animals subjected to cruelty while training.
- Role of animals in our lives.
- Banning of the same in advanced countries, role of SPCA in eradication of this evil.
- Conclusion — Evil practice should be banned.

Use of animals in public, or in street performance, should be condemned by one and all. This is not only barbaric, but also goes against the laws of nature. Animals just like human beings are born free and have just as much right to live their lives, as we have. It is indeed very painful to see, man exploit these animals to fulfill his greed for wealth. In his own self-interest, he subjugates them for his aggrandisement. In my opinion this is an evil practice that should be done away with immediately.

Animals like monkeys, snakes, elephants, bears, etc., are captured from their natural surroundings and then subjected to inhuman torture in the process of their training. This is done so that they can perform completely unnatural tricks, which can be later encashed from the public for profit. The training schedules are at times so stringent that quite a few perish in the process. Those that survive the ordeal, are just not their normal self. The animals in captivity gradually lose their natural instinct. The effect of the artificial surroundings and diet is so profound, that it also has an adverse affect on their health and life span.

Like the Homosepians, animals too have an important role to play in the universe. It would be difficult to imagine our world without them. In fact scientist will authenticate the fact that without some of these animals, the food cycle itself would not be complete. Consequently life on earth itself could be endangered. The Almighty God has bestowed man with intellect, so that he is able to utilise the resources of nature. This he effectively does, by harnessing the natural and the animal resources, so as to make his life comfortable. However, exploiting animals just for the sake of his delight is an unpardonable sin, which he must avoid.

The realisation of this has dawned on some of the advanced countries like America and the United Kingdom, who have banned use of animals in public and for street performance. This issue has been taken up by many Non Government Organisations, including the SPCA (Society for the prevention of Cruelty to Animals). The results of their efforts are not encouraging yet. This is so because, it is still the source of livelihood for some people.

What is therefore required, is public education and awareness of the ill effects of this practice. This can be done by creating strong public opinion, for which the Government as well as the NGO's should rise to the occasion. If required, laws should also be enacted, so that this cruelty perpetuated on animals is stopped forthwith. This is a noble cause, for it is our moral duty to preserve the earth and its species for our children.

ASSIGNMENT

- 'Animals are happy in Zoo's and free from the dangers of the jungle'. Give your views for or against.

Give an account of the ways in which advertising has affected modern life.

(ICSE 1997)

Or

Role of Advertising in our lives

- Introduction — What is advertising and the different medias?
- Importance of advertising in daily life.
- Affect in business and commerce.
- Improves quality of life, effect on education, health and entertainment.
- Negative aspects of Advertising.
- Conclusion — Contributes to our economic growth.

Advertising in the simplest term means, giving publicity to goods and services, so as to create awareness. This is a fine art man has perfected over the years, though the type and form of advertising has undergone a phenomenal change. While our ancestors relied on word of mouth advertising, it has today taken on different forms like advertising through press, (newspaper's and magazines), electronic media (radio and TV), outdoor media and most recently through the internet. These are far more effective and have a greater reach.

The affect of advertising on our daily lives is all pervasive. There is no part of our lives unaffected by the onslaught of advertising. The finest of the product would not find a market and would rot in the go-down, unless it is properly advertised. Not only has it contributed to our economic growth, but has also helped in the field of health care, entertainment and education . It has proved to be an effective tool for the spread of knowledge and has contributed vastly to improving the quality of our daily lives.

Advertising has changed the very style and concept of doing business, making it more scientific and enhancing its scope. Consumers can be induced to buy a particular product by effective advertising. It has also opened up new horizons and removed all form of geographic, language and social barriers.

Not only has it affected the way we do business but it has also made a profound effect on the educational, health, entertainment and even political activity. We are today subjected to bombardment through various media, on the types of educational avenues open, the type of nutrition to give to children or the sick. The types of clothes that are in fashion and the different movies or plays in town. It is off late also being increasingly used in the political sphere. We find most political parties and even candidates, carrying out well-researched advertisement campaign, to boost or acquire an image, which is crucial for victory. In fact so widespread is its use and so significant is its contribution, that some business houses earmark a major percentage of their annual expenditure to this head alone.

Just as a tool is as good as the intention of the user, hence hereto we see that if used for ulterior motives, it can have a very corrupting influence on the younger generation. In recent times, we are seeing multinationals resorting to excessive advertising, that is leading to promotion of an alien lifestyle, different to our ethos. It can also aid in deception, by promoting unworthy products, by playing on psychological aspirations of the consumer.

So profound is the effect of advertising in our modern life, that it is inconceivable to imagine life without it. Not only has it contributed to our economic growth, but has also helped in the field of health care, entertainment and education. In fact it has proved to be an effective tool for the spread of knowledge and has contributed vastly to improving the quality of modern life.

ASSIGNMENTS

- There is too much advertising in today's world and it should be curtailed. Give your view for or against the statement.
- Advertising promotes Consumerism. Discuss.
- Advertisement of alcoholic beverages and cigarettes have a corrupting influence on youth and hence should be banned. Give your view for or against the statement.

The Advantages and Disadvantages of being young.

(ICSE 1997)

- Introduction — What is youth?
- Advantages of Youth
    Mentally and physically at its peak and more adaptable
    No prejudice and optimistic
    Forever enthusiastic and daring.
- Disadvantages of youth
    Too much expected of them by parents and peer groups
    Too optimistic, Heart rules over mind
    Lacks experience and are hence misguided.
- Conclusion — Advantages far outweigh Disadvantages.

"His best companion, innocence and health. And his best riches ignorance and wealth. How happy he who crowns in shades like these. A youth of labour with an age of ease," said Oliver Goldsmith. This but vividly sums up what youth is all about. It is indeed sad, that this stage in our lives comes but only once, for what precedes it is childhood, which is spent in play and fun and what follows is old age and misery. Thus in a sense this is the prime of our lives.

Youth is indeed "age of ease" for they are mentally and physically in the pink of health. Their minds are fresh and hence more receptive to new ideas and thoughts. Physically too they have matured with all faculty functioning optimally. It is, therefore, the right age, for them to choose their future career, by selecting a specific course of study. This is why we find most competitive examinations targeting youth. Their physical attributes and adaptability to their new envoirnment, makes them ideal for recruitment to the defence services.

The innocence and the ignorance are but a blessing, for they suffer from no prejudice or doubts and thus their approach to life is positive and optimistic. This makes them highly enthusiastic and daring. Thus in time of an emergency, their enthusiasm can carry the day for them.

The youth of today are however not a happy lot, for despite their endowments, their peers and parents expect too much from them. This makes them stretch beyond their capacity , that at times leads to psychological disturbance and frustration. They have at times also been accused of using their heart, rather than brains, to decide on important matters concerning them. This makes them vulnerable to get easily misguided. Their inexperience and lack of worldly wisdom makes them a novice, when it comes to performing especially demanding work that calls for specialisation.

Notwithstanding these disadvantages, one still longs for one's youth to come back, for the wealth of youth is priceless indeed .We are reminded of William Shakespeare when he said "All the world a stage, And all men and women mere players: They have their exit and entrances: And one man in his time plays many parts." It is unfortunate, however, that in this play of life the part of youth has but no retake. We must, therefore, live the part truly and sincerely.

ASSIGNMENTS

- The advantages and disadvantages of childhood.
- The agony of old age.

There is no scope for adventure in this modern world. Give your views for or against the statement.

(ICSE 1997)

- Introduction — Agree with the statement.
- Medieval period was the period of Adventure.
- Adventure in the field of discovery.
- Adventure in Travel.
- Adventure in education, sports and entertainment.
- Conclusion — Modernity has made us lazy and less adventurous.

Man has always been fascinated by the mysteries of the unknown. It is the process of unveiling these mysteries that make him adventurous. Unfortunately for him there are fewer mysteries to unveil today. Life has indeed become very comfortable; consequently there is no scope for adventure in this modern world.

Adventure was manifest in all spheres of human life during the medieval times, when man lived on the strength of his physical prowess. This was the period when in his quest for supremacy, he waged great wars and made big conquests. There were many avenues for adventure in unveiling the mysteries of nature, in travel and sports.

It was also the age of discovery. Adventure was writ in the entire gamut of discoveries ranging from the invention of engines, train, aeroplane and even the discovery of new regions, tribes, planets, oceans and islands, etc. Compared to this, the avenues of adventure in the modern age are very limited. This is so because there are fewer discoveries being made today and those that are taking place are difficult for the common man to comprehend.

Travel has always been the best form of adventure. Travel by train car or aeroplanes can hardly be called adventurous .The journeys that used to take months and years on horseback are today accomplished in hours. Ordinary men had become immortal on their making new discoveries of countries and places like, Columbus discovering America and Vasco Da Gama discovering India.

In the field of education, sports and entertainment too, the advent of modernity has reduced the scope for adventure. We now study and play to make a career of it. Gone is the personal touch, which was the hallmark of education in the gurukuls. Manly sports like hunting and fighting wild animals have become extinct. We have today sporting events like cricket, football and indoor games, which by no stretch of imagination can be called adventurous.

The modern age in fact has made us lazy. The emphasis is more on the use of mental power than physical strength. We are today accustomed to having all amenities at the flick of a button. This is one of the primary reasons as to why, there is no scope for adventure in the modern world.

ASSIGNMENTS

- 'The world is yet uncivilised'. Give your views for or against the statement.
- Adventure in the modern world.

The Impact of modern entertainment on society, provide a balanced write-up of your views on the subject.

(ICSE 1996)

- Introduction — Entertainment it's importance.
- Vast avenues of entertainment leading to economic growth.
- Positive impact of entertainment in education, cultural and social life of individual and the society.
- Negative impact due to degradation of moral, leading to crime.
- Conclusion — Enriches society.

Man by nature is a gregarious animal. He loves to socialise, to entertain and be entertained. In fact it is rightfully said, "All work and no play make Jack a dull boy". Entertainment be it in any form like playing games, watching movies or going for a picnic, acts like a tonic in our lives. It gives the much needed change, so that life does not become a drudgery of routine. Social scientists have conclusively proved the positive impact of such relaxation, which enables one to get back to work with renewed vigor. It is on account of the favourable impact that it has on people, some progressive organisations encourage their employees to go on vacation, expedition, sightseeing, etc. This enriches the individual and consequently the society.

The last century has been a witness to a boom, in the various avenues of entertainment. We have come a long way from when; entertainment was confined to theatre and sports. Today there are various forms of entertainment, at our doorsteps like TV, cable TV, radio, internet, etc. Other forms of entertainment include cinema, sports, expedition and going on exotic vacations, etc. The vast avenues of entertainment have opened up enormous potential for growth and economic development of the society.

The tremendous boom in this area has made an immediate impact in the awareness level of youth today. They are better informed and knowledgeable than their predecessors. While the group activities like games and expeditions inculcate team spirit, develop social value and interpersonal skills, television and radio give a fillip to their awareness level. They also help in spreading, desirable cultural, social norms and values. The new millennium has seen the advent of a powerful medium of entertainment and education, through the Internet. This shall indeed prove to be a boon to students for self-development and career planning. The society in turn is more progressive and enjoys a higher standard of living than in the past.

The only disturbing aspect of this boom is the gradual degeneration of moral values in the society. This is due to the over exposure of violence and sex to impressionable minds. So great is the attraction of some media like Cinema, Television and now Internet that people get addicted to it. This is indeed very harmful as it distracts them from their work and studies, making them lead a life of a recluse. The most disastrous consequences of overindulgence are, when people try to emulate their role models in films and TV that ultimately leads them on to crime. It is not uncommon to see, many a budding career get snuffed out, even before it can bloom.

Notwithstanding the above, the importance and the role of entertainment in our lives cannot be diminished. Some restraint on the part of individual and effective controls by the government, can make this medium helpful in enriching the society and the lives of the individual immensely.

ASSIGNMENTS

- Leisure — its uses and abuses.
- New avenues of entertainment in the new millennium.

'Hobbies are a waste of time'.
Give your views for or against the statement.

(ICSE 1995)

- Introduction — Against the statement. What are hobbies?
- Need for hobbies and their role in our lives.
- Varied kinds of hobbies.
- Usefulness of hobbies in our daily lives.
- Conclusion — They are the essence of our lives.

"All work and no play makes Jack a dull boy." goes an old saying. Hobbies make up the "play" part in our lives, so that life becomes interesting and worth living. The genesis of the word Hobby, comes from a contraption of a wooden horse head tied onto a long stick. The child puts this between his legs and prances about, pretending to be riding a horse to the amusement of all. It, therefore, denotes something that one does which brings him joy and happiness. Such a thing can never be a waste of time for anyone.

Life is full of stress, the children are burdened with studies, the youth suffer from anxiety, the middle aged and the elderly from worldly and health worries. In this depressing scenario, a good hobby acts as a safety valve, releasing our mental and emotional stress .It has a stabilizing effect on our life and makes us more lively and happy. It lends variety to our life giving us motivation and inspiration to do great things effectively. We have heard of some people striking it rich and becoming millionaires overnight, through their hobby of collecting rare stamps and antiques. At times what starts as a hobby during childhood, blossoms into one's profession in later life.

There are many different kinds of hobbies, depending on ones interest and liking. Many take to collecting stamps (philately), antiques, photography, gardening, reading, painting, writing, rearing animals or even sporting activities as hunting, boating, fishing, etc. The list is endless, the underlying principle being, that it should be enjoyable to the person. In fact whiling away ones leisure time, in sleep or gossip is a criminal waste of time, that can be better utilised by indulging in one's hobby.

Hobbies channelise our excess energy to more productive areas .The youth of today are bubbling with energy and enthusiasm. This energy, if channelised in the right direction, through promotion of hobbies in schools and colleges, can help them become good citizens. On the other hand, if we do not harness this energy, it can lead to serious consequences for them, as well as the society. A good hobby is a God sent in our retired life, when we have no work to do. One who has not cultivated any hobby feels lost and life becomes an unending drudgery of routine.

Hobbies are an essence of one's life. It is therefore imperative, that we must inculcate and nurture this virtue, very early in our lives, so that we can enjoy its fruit, throughout our lives. The time spent in nurturing it, is time well spent.

ASSIGNMENT

- What is your Hobby and how does it help you in your life?

What you Like or Dislike about being a Teenager?

(ICSE 1992)

- Introduction — What I like about being a Teenager?
- You are taken seriously.
- Highly energetic.
- Youth and beauty are at its peak.
- Abundant freedom without worry .
- Opportunity to excel in chosen field.
- Conclusion — Comes but only once.

"His best companions, innocence and health;
And his best riches ignorance and wealth.
How happy he who crowns in shades like these
A youth of labour with an age of ease."

So said Oliver Goldsmith. Yes indeed a teenager has the best of both worlds. If you commit a mistake you are easily pardoned, for you are merely a child. On the other hand, you can throw tantrums if something is not to your liking. So much so that your views are solicited on subjects concerning the family. Well it is something akin to, enjoying the fruits of adulthood, without having to shoulder its responsibilities.

The best thing about being a teenager is, that elders including your parents and teachers take you seriously. Your individuality is respected and you are not taken for granted. While just a few years ago, you were shooed away to play when anything important was being discussed. Now you are called upon to participate and give your views on the same. This boosts the confidence and generates a feeling of self-esteem and importance.

One is bubbling with energy and euphoria. There is desire to pursue hobbies like outdoor and indoor games. Such is the fitness and enthusiasm of many a teenager, that we find them excelling in many sports. Some of them have even won laurels for themselves and their countries, by winning many an Olympic medal.

Youth and beauty are the hallmark of this age. One is more conscious about one's looks. While girls are the embodiment of beauty at "sweet sixteen", boys tend to emulate the eternal hero, symbolised as "tall, dark and handsome". To further accentuate this God gifted beauty fashion comes handy. This is the time when you can indulge in the latest fashions and fads and get noticed. It is, therefore, not uncommon to find many beauty queens in their teens.

There is a sense of complete freedom, bereft of any worries or responsibilities to shoulder. Making friends, socialising and indulging in one's hobby are the major pastime. Gone are the restrictions of childhood for you can live as you please.

However, everything is not "hunky-dory", for we have also to take major decisions, which have a profound effect on our lives. We have to compete for qualifying in various competitive examinations, to become a doctor, an engineer, or a lawyer. The mental level is at its peak and there is a keen desire to excel. This spirit of competition and challenge makes us extra energetic and ambitious. Gone are the daydreams of childhood, being replaced with living idols and icons that we try to emulate.

Given a choice, I would like to remain a teenager throughout my life. But alas! Just as 'time and tide waits for none', similarly this phase in life is also very short lived. However, the joys, sorrows and achievements of this period will constantly remind me of this stage in life, which unfortunately comes but once.

ASSIGNMENTS

- What do you think about modern fashion trends among teenagers, write your views on the same?
- Teenagers should be allowed more freedom. Give your views for or against.

'The Wealthy are not Happy'.
Give your views for or against the statement.

(ICSE 1993)

- Introduction — Agree, other aspects more important.
- Importance of wealth.
- Root cause of unhappiness.
- Historical examples.
- We can enrich our lives by social service.
- Conclusion — Real happiness comes by working for noble causes.

The wealthy are not happy and can never be so, as wealth is the root cause of their unhappiness. In fact it is a universal truth that a healthy man lives a much more happy and content life, than a man blessed with wealth. We are all aware of an old adage 'Health is wealth'. Thus we see that there are many things besides wealth, which can enrich us and help us lead a full and wholesome life.

The importance of earning money cannot be disputed in the present social environment. One just cannot visualise living a decent life without it. It would be a folly, however, if one attaches undue importance to money, for as we all know man-made money and not vice versa. Money is just one of the many components in a man's life, which can give him limited happiness.

Wealth is the root cause of his unhappiness. Some people are unhappy throughout their lives, in the pursuit of creating wealth, while the wealthy are unhappy in safeguarding their wealth. They spend sleepless nights worrying about it, for they are the target of the Government for evasion of income tax and the antisocial elements, who have an eye on their ill-gotten wealth. The threat is not only from external sources but also sometimes it is also from within the family, leading to estranged family relations, legal disputes and unhappiness.

The really happy people were those who had contributed to the society, like Mother Teresa, Mahatma Gandhi and William Shakespeare to name a few. None of them were wealthy during their lifetime, but their invaluable contribution in the field of Social Welfare and literature will continue to inspire generations.

Just as one should eat to live and not live to eat, similarly earning wealth should not be the ultimate of all human endeavour. We must realise, that we are fortunate in being the crown of creation. It should be our endeavour to leave our imprint in the society in which we live. This can be done by cherishing high ideals, values and a desire to contribute to the welfare of mankind, which can make our lives more richer, satisfying, complete and happy.

"Superfluity comes sooner by white hair while competency lives longer", said William Shakespeare in his play the 'Merchant of Venice'. Wealthy men indeed age faster with worry, while healthy competent men live longer. We must, therefore, have enough wealth, to enable us to lead a respectable life. Thereafter in order to be happy we should work for noble and social causes, so that we could 'leave our foot prints in the sands of time'.

ASSIGNMENTS
- 'Money can make you rich, but so can many other things'. Give your views for or against the statement.
- Make an impartial assessment of the statement 'Money is happiness'.
- 'It is better to be a fool than a rogue '. Give reasons why you agree or disagree with the statement.

"Success depends on opportunity and not on character". Express your views for or against the statement.

(ICSE 1990)

- Introduction — Against the statement.
- Success comes to one with character.
- The importance of character for success.
- Good character leads to good personality and success.
- Historical examples to the fact.
- Conclusion – Character is The Touchstone of sucess.

"So shines a good deed in a naughty world," said William Shakespeare, implying thereby that anything good stands out in this bad and selfish world. Similarly a person with a good character stands out among the crowd and is recognized as such. Success comes to him sooner than later, in his chosen field of activity without him having to wait for an opportunity.

A person with a good character is a gem to the society. The success that he achieves has the stamp of his character, therefore, more stable and lasting .On the contrary we find people today hankering for success. They are ready to do anything to seize the opportunity to become great. Such a success is very transitory and is likely to depart sooner or later.

Success has different connotations for different people. Accumulation of wealth could be a barometer of being successful for some, while for others it could be exercise of power, authority, knowledge or social status. We can aspire for success in any of the above spheres, but without the foundation of a good character, we may not be able to seize the opportunity when it comes our way. A characterless person even if he does get an opportunity, is bound to frit it away.

"Character maketh a man", such is its significance. A man without character is more akin to an animal that survives purely on instinct. While on the other hand, a person with good character has a good wholesome personality. He is appreciated for this virtue and gradually with this recognition, many opportunities for success come his way.

History is replete with examples of illustrious men, who on the strength of their character not only achieved success and became immortal themselves, but also changed the course of history. One such illustrious example is that of Mahatma Gandhi, who just by dint of his character was able to challenge the mighty British Empire. He did not have to look for an opportunity to come his way, but opportunity was thrust on him and he became immortal as the father of the nation.

This is virtue that stands us in good stead throughout our lives, for in the words of John Milton "Virtue may be assailed, But never hurt.

Surprised by unjust force, but not enthralled,"

The character is the touchstone of success. One must nurture this virtue very early in our lives to be successful, for as a saying goes, 'there is no shortcut to success.'

ASSIGNMENT

- 'The most important thing in life is to be successful'. Give reasons why you agree or disagree with the statement.

The best things in life are free.
Give your view for or against the statement.

(ICSE 1991)

- Introduction — Agree.
- For example — Nature.
- The love of parents, brothers or sisters.
- The encouragement from parents.
- The good time spent with friends.
- Conclusion — Life is brief we must make the most of it.

The best things in life are free. This is undoubtedly true for there is one vital aspect of life, that is nature and this is available in abundance, for each one of us for free. However, we are so much involved with ourselves and in our worldly pursuits that we fail to appreciate it. William Wordsworth has this to say, "The world is too much with us, late and soon. Getting and spending, we lay waste our power, little we see in Nature that is ours".

Thus, in Nature we have the lovely spring, the cold snowy winters, the beautiful rainbows, the soft moonlit night, the breath taking sights of the rising and setting sun. While in the mountains, the beauty of the hills, the wild flowers, the brooks and springs keep us spellbound. The roar of the mighty oceans on the seashores, accompanied by the swaying of the palm trees and the salubrious climate, are for every body to enjoy. Nature has thus bestowed the best of its treasures to us in abundance.

Besides nature, there are other aspects of our lives, that are very invaluable like the love, affection of our parents and near and dear one's. These are essential for us and we know that they just cannot be bought. The love of parents for their children or the love of a brother for his sister or vice -versa are lovely emotions. They make our lives worth living, for these are sentiments, which we just cannot do without.

The little words of encouragement and praises from our well-wishers or peers works wonders for us. They not only encourage us, but also make us feel happy. They do not require any induce-ment from us, nor has one to fish for compliments, but they by their spontaneity add flavour to our lives.

Our friends are another source of delight. Some of our best moments are spent in their com-pany. "A true friend is like a diamond, precious and rare, false friends are like autumn leaves lying everywhere". We have to be cautious in our choice of friends. Fair weathered friends are many and are with us in our good days. It is only in our bad days that a true friend stands by us. The friendship of such a true friend is priceless and not a purchasable commodity.

We all know that "Life is brief- a little hope, a little dream and then good night". In this short period we must therefore learn to enjoy life, for there are numerous good facets of life which are only for us free of cost. Only we have to appreciate and enjoy them.

ASSIGNMENTS

- Nothing in life is free. Discuss.
- "Getting and spending, we lay waste our power, little us see in Nature that is ours". Discuss.

'Should the Use of Polythene be Banned' Give your views for or against the statement.

- Introduction — Product of the last century.
- Uses of polythene.
- Harmful effects in daily life.
- Harmful effect on the environment.
- Need to ban the same.
- Conclusion — Effective ban needed to save environment.

Plastic was one of the most important inventions of the last century. Out of its various derivatives one form is polythene, made from hydrocarbons, which is a by-product of petroleum, an important energy fuel. It has great industrial and commercial use. However, its excessive use in recent times has threatened the environment. This is a cause of great concern to all of us.

Polythene finds use in a number of industrial products like toys, automotive parts, waterproof ware, etc. However, the most predominant form of its use in our daily life, is in the packaging industry. It is this extensive use in domestic, as well as industrial sector that is a cause of worry. One of the primary advantages for its increasing use is that it is durable and cheap. On account of this, it has virtually replaced the good old paper bags, which were more environment friendly.

It is the indestructible property of this product that has disastrous consequences. It cannot be destroyed, nor can it decay and decompose, like jute or paper or any organic material. The polythene bags are dumped on the streets and garbage bins which litter the roads. Unsuspecting animals eat them resulting in their untimely death. Some of these bags, find their way into the sewage and drainage systems of the city and choke them.

It is also one of the most hazardous material causing environmental pollution .The polythene bags that find their way into the river or the fields, pollute the riverbed and the soil by making it infertile. It makes the soil impermeable and consequently useless for growing crop. Such is the indestructible nature of this product, that it cannot be even burnt. Hence like a demon in the making, it continues to haunt our environment.

There is, therefore, immediate need for checking this menace before it acquires gigantic proportion. We should therefore start educating the people, on the harmful effects of using polythene, by organizing discussions and workshops. Moreover to put an immediate stop to this menace, we should ban the use of polythene in the packaging sector forthwith. This is so, because it is in this area that it is being grossly abused. If required, we should enact laws by proper legislation, so as to effectively deal with this threat. This is the least that we can do to ensure, that we leave a clean environment for our children, as had been inherited by us.

ASSIGNMENTS

- 'Environment Pollution is a cause of concern'. Give your views on the causes and remedies.
- Noise pollution a cause for concern. Discuss.

'Should Capital Punishment be abolished?'
Give your views for or against the statement.

- Introduction — What is Capital Punishment?
- Why it should not be abolished?
- Social reasons — Preserves Society from Undesirable elements.
- Psychological reasons — Enforces fear of Law.
- It is irrevocable punishment hence calls for greater care.
- Historical Reasons — Failure in countries where it has been abolished.
- Conclusion — Should not be abolished.

"An eye for an eye, a tooth for a tooth" is one of the oldest form of justice, which we all today know as Capital Punishment.This is the severest of punishment which can be given to a criminal, for indulging in a heinous crime. It entails death to the convict, either by hanging or in some advanced countries through the electric chair. In recent times there is a heated debate on this issue, which involves taking the life of an individual, a right that nobody has.

Modernity has brought with it many evils. The glorifying of violence and terrorism through print and electronic media, has cast an evil spell on the younger generation. The daily newspapers are replete with horrendous crimes, which are getting worse by the day. To keep this in check, there is need to make capital punishment more effective and stringent, rather than abolish it.

Though this form of punishment is inhuman and cruel, there is no other alternative but to enforce it. Just as one removes a rotten apple to save the basket full of apples, similarly we must get rid of the unwanted elements so that we can preserve the society.

The criminal laws today are much more humane, than they were centuries ago. During that period, one could have his hands amputated for stealing and death penalty was quite common for even small offences. The laws today are more lenient and complex and the ways of circumventing it has at times also been amply demonstrated. Hence to completely do away with capital punishment, would even remove the psychological fear in the minds of criminals, to deter them from criminal acts.

The only argument against capital punishment is that it is irrevocable. Justice is not in- fallible, and at times valuable lives have been lost due to its miscarriage. This calls for greater care and scientific investigation in awarding this form of punishment, rather than doing away with it altogether.

We have before us examples of countries like Italy and Holland, where the cases of murder and other heinous crimes have increased, consequent to abolishment of the death penalty. These countries are in the process of rethinking on the same. There is, therefore, no conceivable reason to abolish this form of punishment in India.

What is, therefore required, is not abolishment of capital punishment, but a thorough review of the present judicial system and a more scientific approach to investigation by the law enforcement agencies. Only by having a just and dynamic legal system, can the criminals be promptly brought to book. The death penalty should be awarded in the rarest of the rare case, as it is advisable to let a hundred criminals go scot free than to hang an innocent person.

ASSIGNMENT
- "Laws grind the poor and rich men rule the law". Discuss.

'If you would have Peace, prepare for War'.
Give your views for or against the statement.

- Introduction — Agree, Need of the hour.
- Practical examples in day-to-day life.
- Examples from history.
- Price for freedom we must be ready to pay.
- Positive effects — leads to technological advancement. Builds Nationalistic feeling.
- Conclusion – A proactive policy that has withstood the test of time.

"Prevention is better than cure' is a sound logic. Just as we take preventive measures so that we do not get afflicted with diseases, similarly if we want peace we must prepare for war. This is so for 'offence is the best form of defence'. War is indeed reprehensible for it leads to wanton destruction of life and property, but so is a disease which if allowed to spread, can be disastrous for life.

Even in our daily lives we see the manifestation of "might is right", which is the exploitation of the weak and poor by the rich and powerful. This does not mean that the weak should meekly give in to their dictat. They should unite and fight back for social justice, politically and economically. This will rid them of their exploitation and ensure harmony in the society.

History has also vindicated the above logic. Had we been properly armed, would China have dared to embark on its misadventure on our northern borders in 1962? Similar is the case with Tibet, which till date is under the yoke of Chinese Rule .We have also witnessed, over half a decade of cold war between America and Russia, which had at times threatened to flare up. It was only the defence preparedness of these countries, which restrained them from going to war, resulting in peace.

Preparing for war has a price, which a developing country like us can ill afford. But is there anything more valuable than freedom? This is the price we must pay for ensuring our freedom. Arguably there are international organisations like, UNO and it's Security Council, founded for enforcing peace. Their track record, however, is quite dismal. We have seen how they have miserably failed, to resolve issues in Vietnam and even in Kashmir, which is a cause for concern.

Shoring up our defence or war preparedness, has in fact been a major stimulus for technological and industrial advancement. Some of the new discoveries, for example laser weapons, were initially intended for defence. This technology has now been successfully used in Medical Science for surgery. Similarly quite a few technologies developed for defence are now in the forefront in the field of Medical Sciences and Health Care. This pursuit for excellence also makes us more nationalist and patriotic towards our country.

There is no denying the fact that war is evil and we agree with John Milton when he says, "Peace hath her victories, No less renown than war, for what can war but endless war still breed". There is, however, no viable alternative. The geopolitical scenario is such, that there is suspicion, mistrust and a feeling of inequality among nations. This occasionally manifests itself in flare-ups, that we can ill afford. The above proactive policy has withstood the test of time. It has proved to be the best way for ensuring peace.

ASSIGNMENTS

- "Peace hath her victories, No less renown than war, For what can war but endless war still breed". Give your views for or against the statement.
- "Nuclear deterrence is a mirage."Give your views for or against the statement.
- There is no justification for increasing defence expenditure for a developing country like India. Give your views for or against the statement.
- 'Offence is the best form of defence' Discuss.

"Our frorefathers were luckier than us".
Write your views for or against the statement.

- Introduction — Against the statement.
- More advanced in Political and Social field.
- More advanced in the field of Science and Technology.
- More knowledgeable about Nature and the Universe.
- Giant strides made in Medical Sciences and health care.
- More advance in Education.
- Conclusion — Our forefathers were less fortunate.

To say that our forefathers were luckier than us is a travesty of the truth. I do not subscribe to the above view and consider ourselves to be luckier in every sphere, be it social, political, economic, medical, educational or any field of human activity. The quality of life today, is far more superior to what our forefathers could have ever imagined.

In the political field, our forefathers suffered under the yoke of autocratic rulers with restriction on their human rights. We are today more fortunate in living in a democratic setup, where there is respect for human dignity and labour. Each one of us has some basic fundamental rights, which are guaranteed by the constitution of the country. Socially also we are far better of, for there is no caste or creed barrier, which made lives of socially backward people of yore worse than animals.

In the field of science and technology we have progressed by leaps and bounds. Our forefathers would have found it difficult to imagine, that simple things like rockets and aeroplanes would ever be possible one day. We can today travel from one end of the globe to the other end in a couple of hours, thanks to the jet supersonic engines. Even on-land transport is far more faster and comfortable, due to various mode of transport like cars, scooters, etc. We can update ourselves on the latest news through radio, television and can communicate with our friends on the other side of the globe in a flash of a second through telephone, satellite phones and the internet. Computers have made our lives far more richer and comfortable. The new millennium would see more advancement in the field of Information Technology, bridging the geographic and social distance of people across the world.

We are today more knowledgeable about the Universe and have explored far of planets like Moon and Mars, a feat which our forefathers could never have visualised. We can predict natural calamities through satellite imagery and also exploit our natural mineral resources through remote sensing satellites.

We have eradicated the scourge of plague, smallpox and other dreadful diseases from the face of the earth .The average life expectancy today is much more than our forefathers, thanks to the spectacular advancement made in Medical Sciences and Health Care.

Beside advancement in Medical Science, there has been all round spread of education that has transformed our lives and has made us more compassionate, humane and sociable. Our children have more avenues for good education, through well-equipped schools, colleges, universities and can aspire for lucrative careers within the country and even abroad.

Our forefathers were thus undoubtedly less fortunate than us and we must consider ourselves lucky to have been born in the 21st centaury. It is, therefore, our moral obligation, to ensure that our children too reap the rewards and enjoy a better life than we do .

ASSIGNMENT

- Our future generations would be luckier than us. Give your views for or against the statement.

The greater the power the more dangerous the abuse. Give your views for or against the statement.

- Introduction — Agree, The greater the power, the more dangerous the abuse.
- Examples from history.
- More in autocratic form of government.
- Need for having checks and balances.
- Conclusion – Need for accountability & Transparency to check abuse of power.

"The greater the power the more dangerous the abuse", said Edmund Burke. There is much truth in the statement. This but sums up what power can do to normal mortals. The feeling of power, that is a position of authority and status works like an intoxicant on people, going directly to their head. It makes them arrogant, proud, and audacious. They feel that they can get away with almost anything. This is what leads them to corruption, for there is no accountability for their action. It is only an exceptionally strong man, endowed with incorrigible character, who does not fall for the loaves and fishes of office.

History is repeated with example of how good men under its influence, not only became corrupt when they rose to power, but also played havoc with the destiny of their country. We have for example Adolf Hitler, who was an epitome of a patriot, but no sooner did he become Fuehrer, he let loose the scourge of war culminating into the Second World War. The war crimes that he perpetuated against Jews, shall forever be a blot on the history of mankind. Even in India, we had the Rajas and Maharajas enjoying absolute powers over their subjects, which made them corrupt and immoral.

History is witness to the fact that such people thrive more in an autocratic, or oligarchy form of government, where the head of the state has unbridled power. This abuse of power at times lead to general dissatisfaction, making the people revolt in mutiny. This is what we saw in Philippines and Uganda, where president Marcos and Idi Amin were overthrown in the uprising..

Thus, there is need for a proper check and balance on all people occupying positions of power and authority. There should also be stringent laws, facilitating early identification of corrupt officials and their legal indictment. This would serve as a deterrent for others not to harbour corrupt intensions.

There is no doubt whatsoever in the above statement that the greater the power the more dangerous the abuse. However, having in place a proper system, for ensuring accountability, can effectively check this. Such people should be adequately compensated, so that they do not adopt corrupt method for their own aggrandizement and are able to exercise their powers without fear and favour. Until we do the above, the words of Lord Aston will continue to haunt us for said he, "Power tends to corrupt and absolute power tends to corrupt absolutely. "

ASSIGNMENTS

- Corruption in public life.
- "Power tends to corrupt and absolute power tends to corrupt absolutely". Do you agree.

Environmental Pollution is a cause for concern. Provide a balanced write-up of your views on the subject.

- Introduction — What is environmental pollution?
- Causes of pollution — Industrial, Transportation, Population.
- Effects of pollution.
- Remedial measures.
- Conclusion – Menace if not checked has the potential to obliterate life on earth.

Environmental pollution is a cause for concern, not only for us but also for mankind as a whole. The last century has seen the rise of this menace assume gigantic proportions, so much so that it has cast its gloomy shadow on nature itself. The diminishing ozone ionosphere leading to global warming and the unpredictable seasonal variation, are some of the adverse effects of pollution that are threatening the environment in which we live.

Pollution is a by-product of the unprecedented Industrial revolution that we have seen in the last few decades .The establishment of large scale factories belching out smoke, fumes and chemically hazardous waste, has now started having a telling effect on the environment. This coupled with the unprecedented growth of automobiles and the ever-increasing human population, are some of the factors that are making environmental pollution a cause for concern.

The effects of pollution are all pervasive. An immediate fallout being the reduction in the oxygen content in the atmosphere, presence of potentially harmful gases causing asthma and even lung cancer, which at times proves fatal. The large-scale release of chemical wastes into the rivers and streams are the cause of dwindling aquatic life in the rivers and oceans. This also adversely affects the soil where river water is used for irrigation purposes. Some gases like chlorofluorocarbon (CFC) used in air conditioners and refrigerators, have been known to cause reduction of the protective ozone in the ionosphere. We have also before us the devastating consequences of the Union Carbide gas leak in Bhopal, that led to wanton destruction of life, when thousands perished and lakhs were rendered crippled for life. It has also been conclusively proved that global warming and unpredictability of seasons are some of its immediate fallouts.

The threat of environmental contamination looms large on the earth today. It no longer remains an individual or national concern, but is now a global problem, to be addressed internationally. As an immediate measure, environmentalist have suggested ban on use of potentially harmful chemicals/gases in industry and discharge of wastes only after proper treatment. The establishment of emission norms for vehicles and protecting the green cover in the form of forest and trees are some of the measures suggested. While the government is setting up enforcement and monitoring agencies for keeping this menace under check, it is also our responsibility to lend a helping hand in this monumental task.

It is common for us to curse nature, when it causes major devastation due to its unpredictability, but in the words of John Milton 'Accuse not Nature, she hath done her part. Do thou but thine'. This is something we owe to ourselves and to our future generations, for this evil if not kept under check, has the potential to obliterate life on the only planet known to nurture it.

ASSIGNMENTS

- Environmental pollution — causes and remedies.
- Sound pollution a cause for concern.

Student's indiscipline is a burning problem.
What according to you are its causes and remedies?

- Introduction — Indiscipline in students is against our cultural ethos.
- A burning problem.
- Causes — Pampering by parents, external influence,
                Politics and frustration,
- Remedies — Selective admission for higher education,
                Ban political influence,
                Qualified teachers and parent teacher interaction.
- Conclusion. — A grave problem needing immediate attention.

Student indiscipline is something alien to our cultural ethos. Our rich cultural history is proof of the high regard that students had for their teachers and the concern, the teacher had in turn for his students. Thus we all know how Eklavya sacrificed his thumb as an offering to his Guru Dronacharya, who had the welfare of his pupil Arjuna at heart. This bond has indeed been broken to shreds and it is this materialistic society, which is responsible for the present state of affair.

The problem has assumed gigantic proportions and threatens to vitiate and destroy the academic atmosphere of these institutions. It is quite common to see students resorting to strikes, boycotting examinations and even taking law into their own hands, for sometimes real, but quite often imaginary grievances. They behave more like industrial and political workers, rather than as students. To understand this metamorphosis; we shall have to examine the causes for this radical transformation.

Students today are a more pampered and doted lot by their parents. This makes them at times get unreasonable protection from them, thus distorting their value system of right or wrong, To add to this, we have excessive external influence of powerful people, to safeguard the interest of misguided elements. Thus making the task of enforcing discipline in the campus arduous.

To compound the problem further, we have influence of political parties, who use them as their political cadres. The political leaders of all hues instigate students to take to the streets to further their political causes. They thus use them as fodder to further their own political ambitions. This evil influence has politicalised the entire education spectrum, with teachers conspiring among themselves, students and the administration. The students are more often, used as pawns in their internal squabbles. This affects their studies, and with future prospects becoming dim, a sense of frustration sets in, which occasionally finds vent in violent outbursts.

There is, however, a malady for this ill, but it requires a strong resolve and a political will to address the problem, before it becomes unmanageable. As a first step there is need for a clear education policy, stressing more on vocational education. This will ensure that only serious students go for higher studies, while the non-serious ones can opt for vocational training. It will reduce the strength of students in colleges and universities and help in safeguarding the sanctity of these institutions. The vocational training at the same time will help other students, by preparing them better for life, taking care of their frustration.

The government should show the political will, in banning party politics by students and teachers, Moreover these educational institutions are the temples of learning and should at best be left to academicians. There should be minimum interference by administration or any other external authority.

There should also be periodic parent teacher's interaction, so that the parents are apprised of the performance of their wards .The last but the most important being the role of teachers. They should restrain from ungentlemanly acts, like going on strikes, practicing unfair means to accumulate wealth, etc. These are highly unbecoming qualities of a teacher. They should be a real Guru, in the true sense of the word, setting an example for the pupils to emulate.

This is the only panacea, which can help us to get rid of the indisciplined behaviour of students . It, however, calls for a determined effort on the part of all of us, to appreciate the gravity of the problem .We must rise above our narrow self, political interest and restore the sanctity of these educational institutions. This would make the students passing out from such hallowed portals, law abiding and disciplined citizens, worthy of being torch bearers to the nation.

ASSIGNMENT

- Students indiscipline it's causes. What do you think about it and how would you deal with it?

Joint family system has lost its value in the present day context. Give your views for or against the statement

- Introduction — Agree. What is joint family system and its advantages?
- It's irrelevance today because of economic reasons.
- Political and educational factors.
- Social factors.
- Conclusion — Out of tune with modern times.

Joint Family in the true sense means a group of people belonging to the same line of descent staying together as one unit. The genesis of this system dates back to the Aryan period, when the feudal system was prevalent. This provided an effective way to combat natural calamities and also safeguarded them from the onslaught of enemies'. It acted as an umbrella, shielding the old and the infirm, demonstrating the concept of 'strength in unity'. However, such a family system has outlived its use in the modern times.

Today this concept of a family system is neither plausible nor practical. The reasons for this are very obvious. With the increasing population, it is no longer viable to cultivate and subsist on the marginal landholding. People are therefore compelled to migrate to cities and towns seeking employment opportunities. Life in the cities are not conducive to a joint family system, where it is not economically viable to sustain a large family. Not only in cities this family system is also crumbling in the villages, as people get more ambitious and materialistic.

With the increasing education and awareness level of people, has come the desire to be independent. This is also in keeping with the democratic setup in the country, where everyone has an equal right. This is contrary to the concept of a joint family system that thrives on an authoritarian setup, where the 'Karta' or the family head takes all the decisions. It therefore, stunts the growth of young minds and acts like an impediment in their development. In an age where initiative and ideas command a premium such a family system is obsolete.

Socially too a joint family system is now impractical. The society has become one great family, where there is a tremendous opportunity for people from different caste and creeds to come together. The boundaries of caste and creed are fast crumbling, as we see more and more of inter caste marriages taking place. This is possible because of an open society, where there is complete freedom of thought and action. Moreover the internal squabbles and unpleasantness that are inherent in a joint family system, are unheard of in the nuclear family system. On the other hand it increases love and affection between family members, as 'absence makes the heart grow fonder'.

The joint family system notwithstanding its advantages is a misfit and has lost its relevance in the modern age. It is no longer possible to live in such a system which is completely out of tune with the time, when there is emphasis on excellence and not consensus.

ASSIGNMENTS

- Nuclear Family system the need of the hour. Give your views for or against.
- Life in the cities is not conducive to a joint family system. Do you agree?

'It is and will always be a Man's World.'
Give your views for or against the statement.

- Introduction — Agree.
- Prevalent since ages.
- Biological fact.
- Exist in society even today. (examples).
- Conclusion – Instead of competing they should complement each other.

Whether we like it or not and no matter what facts and figures we may quote, the fact remains that, "It is and will always be a man's world". There may be an occasional variant and exploits by exceptionally gifted women, but the crux of the matter always remains as above.

Ever since the dawn of civilization, man has showed his dominance over them, by the sheer magnitude of his physical prowess. This was the reason for such inhibitive customs, like the pardah system, dowry and the Sati practice which was a sheer manifestation of his hold over women .She played a crucial role in his life no doubt, as a mother, wife and daughter, but when it came to equal rights she virtually had none. This was so because men never wanted to make her an equal partner. Thus in all crucial matters pertaining to property, or ascendance to the throne, it was the son who inherited the property or the throne.

Even if we concede, that man may have usurped their rights by sheer brute force, but we still cannot deny the biological truth. The very conjecture of a man brings forth a picture of brawn, rough and muscular personality, whereas the women is the emblem of beauty, frail, soft and tender. Thus biologically too, they are quite distinct from one another and in fact complement each other. This is the reason why we graciously refer to the other, as the better halves.

This discrimination against women is even true today no matter how loudly we may proclaim to the contrary. Is it not a fact, that after marriage the girl has to adopt the surname of her spouse, and move in with him? Thus what little she had of her identity, is also lost after marriage. She is also denied her share in parental property. The male hegemony is more evident in Muslims, who are legally permitted to have four wives and have the liberty to divorce their wives, by mere uttering of the word 'Talaq' thrice .In some countries they have no right of franchise and, therefore, cannot cast their vote. Their evidence is also not acceptable in courts. All this is but to prove that, it was and it will be a man's world .

With the increase in literacy and awakening among women, this gap is bound to lessen, but the divide is so great that it seems nature also wills it this way. Thus instead of competing, it would be better if they complement each other and lead a wholesome life respecting each others rights and liberty.

ASSIGNMENTS

- Women's liberation is a myth. Discuss.
- There are certain professions from which women should be excluded. Discuss.

Democracy has lost its meaning in India
Or
Democracy in India is a Success or a Failure

Given your view on the statement.
- Introduction — What is Democracy?
- Practiced in India since ages, present Democracy based on the west.
- Discrepancies that have crept in due to divisive caste and creed feelings.
- Discrepancies on account of religious fundamentalism.
- Reason for the above.
- Conclusion — Need for a relook.

Democracy as rightly defined by Abraham Lincoln is 'Government of the people, for the people and by the people.' Thus the people have a major stake in the functioning of the government, which is a major reason for this system of government thriving in the world. Such a form of government is bound to succeed, as it owes its strength to the popular support of the people. India is in fact one of the largest democratic country in the world, a fact in which we pride ourselves. Is our pride justified?

This form of government is nothing new to us, in fact it is in our ethos. The form of collective decision making practiced in Gram Panchayats, dates back to times immemorial, when democratic practices were unheard of in the world. However, with our becoming independent, the architects of our constitution laid out the foundations of a truely democratic and secular country. They rightly visualised that a country as large as India, with a vast multitude of caste, creed and religion, could only thrive in a democracy setup, where the aspiration of the people could be effectively reflected. Keeping this in mind they framed our constitution, which has adopted all the good facets of the American and British constitution. In order that it truly reflect the aspirations of the people, provision of reservations were made for backward classes and communities, so that they could have an effective say in the governance of the country. Such provisions were made in every sphere like Education, Employment, Legislature and Parliament, so that all segment of the population enjoy the fruit of freedom without feeling alienated.

However, the lofty ideals that our leaders envisioned for getting Ram Rajya in the country, has been completely distorted. Instead of ensuring that the backward and downtrodden classes are brought into the mainstream, our political parties have in their own vested interest, divided the community on caste and creed lines, so as to feather their own nests. Thus we have parties championing the interest of different castes and communities, to the detriment of the national cause.

Contrary to the secular tenets of our constitution, we have seen a distinct rise in religious fundamentalism in the country. This is another play to gain power, by exploiting the religious feeling of the people. It portends a very dangerous future for us. Thus we find that instead of narrowing the gap, this has in fact been widened with each party playing to the gallery, for purely political reasons. The people are being treated as vote banks and all political and administrative decisions are taken, after considering the effect of the same on the vote bank. The consequences of this are already discernable, in the slackening of the pace of development and economic growth of the country.

Someone has rightly said 'the people get the government they deserve'. This applies to us too. The dismally low level of education and the correspondingly great disparity in their economic growth, makes such people gullible to the mechanisation of crafty politicians who have their own axe to grind. Such people act as fodder, on which the ambitions of politicians thrive. George Bernard Shaw rightly said that "Democracy substitutes election by the incompetent many, for appointment by the corrupt few." This is exactly what we are witnessing in India today, that raises serious doubts about its relevance.

There is no denying the fact that democracy is still the most successful form of government in the world today. There is, however, an urgent need for us to educate our masses and also have a relook at our constitution. The anomalies and distortions that have crept in over time inadvertently, should be set right. This is of crucial importance, if we really want democracy to succeed in India. For as Abraham Lincoln rightly said "You can fool all the people some of the time, and some of the people all the time, but you cannot fool all the people all the time."

ASSIGNMENTS

- Democracy is the best form of government. Give your views for or against the statement.
- "Democracy substitutes election by the incompetent many for appointment by the corrupt few." Give your views for or against the statement.

It is better to be born rich than talented.
Give your views for or against the statement.

- Introduction — It is better to be born talented. (Against)
- Talent is lasting, while riches are transitory.
- Talent is enjoyed by society and immortalises one while riches are individualistic.
- Talent cannot be inherited or acquired.
- Conclusion – Wealth brings worries which Talent males one happy and content.

'If Wishes were horses beggars would ride'. This is inconceivable as we can only wish to have been born rich or talented. However, if I were given a choice, I would have preferred to be born talented, for having a talent is more honourable, lasting and satisfying.

To be born talented is something very tangible, as it is inherent in you. It is something by which you are recognised and appreciated throughout your life. It cannot be lost, squandered or abused unlike riches which are quite transitory being there today and gone tomorrow. Moreover wealth tends to corrupt and drives us to vices. We also know that wealth declines if it is shared with others, such is not the case with talent. On the contrary it increases with use getting perfected. Thus, the more you use your talent the better it becomes.

Talent is a wealth that is bestowed on you, for giving joy and happiness to the society while riches are very individualistic. They can only be of use to you, or your near and dear ones. Talent brings with it name, fame and immortalises a person, the same cannot be said for riches. Thus, we have renowned statwarts in the sphere of literature, music and many other field who have become immortal by their talent. The likes of William Shakespeare, Premchand and Tansen are not born everyday. They by their talent, continue to inspire generations even after they are no more.

Talent is also more sublime, unlike riches it cannot be inherited or acquired by fair or foul means. It requires sincerity, dedication and rigorous discipline to nurture, so that it can blossom and spread its aroma in the society. This is by no way implying that talent cannot be acquired. We can acquire it, but there is some basic inclination that must be inborn. There is also no shortcut for acquiring talent. It is a long and torturous journey to the top, but once there, one is the monarch of all that he surveys. No amount of wealth can help in acquiring talent, for if that would be so, all rich people would have acquired talent. A talented person is never in want of money or fame these are in fact at his beck and call.

I would therefore choose to be born talented, for William Shakespeare rightly said in the Merchant of Venice "Superfluity comes sooner by white hair, but competence lives longer". Thus implying that wealth and riches brings with it many worries that turn our hairs grey. However, for people who are talented and competent, they have no such cause for worry and hence live a more happy and content life.

ASSIGNMENTS

- Talent cannot be acquired. Discuss.
- Geniuses are born not made.

Multinationals a boon or a curse for the country. Give reasons why you think so?

- Introduction — The present Socialistic pattern of economy is a misfit in the world today. Need for change.
- Proved by the disintegration of USSR and emergence of countries with free enterprise.
- Advantages of liberalisation, so as to facilitate entry of multinationals.
- Advantage to the society.
- Advantage to the country.
- Disadvantages, if any.
- Conclusion — Only panacea for accelerating the rate of growth and development.

The Socialistic form of government adopted by us after independence, was able to nurture the industrial development and safeguard the interest of the poor. It has however, been unable to provide the large-scale economic development that is crucial for us, so as to make the country strong and stable. This has resulted in stagnation of the rate of development and economic growth, due to lack of capital for investment. To this end , the entry of multinationals with capital and technology is to be welcomed.

The country is as strong as its economy. This has been amply demonstrated by the disintegration of the erstwhile communist superpower USSR, because of it being economically weak. While on the other hand, we have seen the emergence of the free enterprise economies of Japan and Germany, devastated by the Second World War.

Thus if India has to take its rightful place in the world order, it must be economically strong. This can only be possible, if besides being self-sufficient, we are also in a position to produce world-class products competing globally. This could be only possible, if the artificial protection to the domestic industries are removed. It would also require removal of the barriers to growth and development, that are an impediment in our growth. This would facilitate the entry of multinationals, bringing with them new technology and foreign capital, so crucial for our economy.

The advantages which would accrue to society, would be in making available quality products at competitive prices, by encouraging domestic companies to compete with multinational corporations. It would also check inefficiency in the public sector, which would be brought to the fore by competition .The influx of new capital and technology, would usher an industrial revolution, which is imperative for a developing country like India. We have already been witness to a mini revolution in the car industry, ever since the entry of multinational companies.

This would check effectively the corruption in the government and the industry, due to unnecessary checks and controls. It would also enable the government to spare more capital for. investment in infrastructure, health care and social security, which have been gravely neglected. The rapid industrialisation that it would bring about, would effectively tackle the insurmountable problem of unemployment and poverty.

Their entry could also spell initial problems. This could be on account of closure of some uncompetitive and unviable domestic companies, making a few jobless, who would need to be trained for redeployment. Nevertheless these sacrifices will have to be made.

The entry of multinationals is but a boon for the country, as it offers the only panacea, for the Herculean problems facing it. The availability of cheap skilled manpower and resources attract them to invest in India and we must therefore, welcome them with open arms.

ASSIGNMENTS

- Is the Socialistic pattern of economy still relevant for India? Give your views for or against the statement.
- Entry of Multinational companies is harmful for our trade and industry.

The advantages and disadvantages of co-education in Schools. Discuss

- Introduction.— What is co-education?
- Need for co-education?
- Advantages of co-education.
    - Improves moral standards and reduces absenteeism.
    - Makes all round personality development.
- Disadvantages of coeducation.
    - Distract students from studies, leads to romance.
    - Results in violence.
- Conclusion — Good for students and society.

Co-education in school, is the imparting of education to boys and girls together. This is prevalent in many institutions across the country, especially in colleges and universities. There is however, gradually an increasing trend towards co-education in schools, because of the advantages accruing from it.

It is the need of the hour, if women have to join the main stream and be equal partner in progress. Women in India like their counterparts in all developed countries like USA, UK and Canada have got equal rights, both personal and political. It is therefore, imperative for them, to liberate themselves from the age-old shackles of ignorance and backwardness, which is a result of their segregation. They therefore, have to ameliorate their lot, by educating themselves, through the various educational institutions available in the country. It would not be conceivable to have separate institutions for there are not many institutions, nor is there the financial resources required for establishing them. It is also not in the national interest to segregate the sexes, for imparting education. These children are the future of the country and it is essential, that they have a normal development. Co-education in school would enable them to become responsible citizen, offering numerous advantages to the students themselves.

Contrary to the fear of orthodox people, this improves the moral and social etiquettes of student to behave themselves in the presence of the other. Moreover, familiarity blunts the edge of curiosity, leading to a better understanding of each other. The school life becomes more interesting and charming, with lesser absenteeism. It also results in keen competition and opens up new horizons hitherto unknown to them.

This interaction also generates more self-confidence in them. They are thus better equipped to appreciate each other point of view ,which is very crucial for their all around development. It is but a known fact that students from such institutions are more genuine, frank and have a wholesome personality. They are neither mesmerized, nor over awed in female company, which makes them a class apart.

The most common argument against coeducation is, that it distracts students from their studies. This leads them to romance and heartbreaks, which at their tender age have disastrous consequences. This fear however is unwarranted, for such instances have been known to happen mostly, where students study in separate schools for boys or girls. It is the curiosity to know each other that drives them away from school and wrecks their lives.

Another charge leveled against it, is the growing incidence of violence in schools, for winning the affection of a fellow student. This indeed is a problem, which is on account of the hitherto policy of segregation of sexes. With increasing awareness, this evil which is not the exclusive preserve of coeducational institution, would also be effectively tackled.

Co-education in schools therefore, provides a unique opportunity for the students, for their all around development. It prepares them for their later lives, by making them better citizens. They can thus together strive for greater excellence, by improving themselves, as well as accelerating the pace of development of the country.

ASSIGNMENTS

- Is coeducation in schools desirable? Discuss.
- Boarding schools are better than Day schools. Give your views.

'Manners Maketh a Man'.
Give your views for or against the statement.

- Introduction — What are Manners?
- Importance of Manners in our lives and its effect on our reputation.
- Manners mould character.
- Imparted by parents at a very early age.
- Absence of manners affects personality, with examples.
- Conclusion — It plays a significant role in our lives.

"A gentleman by gentle deeds is known, for a man by nothing is more bewrayed. As by his manners", said Edmund Spencer. Manners do not only constitute mere outward behaviour, but also construes good conduct and morality. Thus it would be wrong to assume that manners constitute table manners, social etiquettes and salutations only. Any form of education, which does not cater to imparting moral training is incomplete, if it does not lead to a good moral character.

It is this character which gives him a 'reputation' by which he is known and recognised. The loss of which was deeply bemoaned by William Shakespeare in 'Othello', when he said "Reputation, reputation, reputation! O! I have lost my reputation, I have lost the immortal part of myself and what remains is bestial!"Such is the significance of our reputation or manners.

Manners are an essential prerequisite for a good character. This could be only possible if one has a wholesome education, that would enable him to differentiate between what is good or bad, noble or evil. Education should be such that one imbibes good virtues like honesty, truthfulness, compassion, and shuns bad habits and vices. In this our parents, teachers and peer groups have a very important role to play. These are attributes that are important for our future. A man without these qualities of head and heart, is but a savage.

This moral instruction starts very early in life, even before the child starts going to school. The parents are best equipped to impart him this moral education. They can not only preach, but also by percept inculcate good values in the child, whose tender mind gets suitably moulded by the environment at home.

This is the reason why we find people who have either lost their parents at an early age, or have had a disturbed childhood, severely wanting in some personality traits .We have with us the example of Hitler, who because of his troubled childhood and bad experiences with Jews, became such a tyrant in history .The background of most hardened criminals also reveals an unhappy and sad childhood, that affects their character and consequently their manners. They may adorn themselves with the most expensive of dresses, but their mannerism and actions, betray them for what they actually are.

Manners thus play a significant role in a man's life, without which he can never be a complete man, in the true sense of the word. This has been aptly summed up when we say, "Manners maketh a man."

ASSIGNMENTS

- "A gentleman by gentle deeds is known, for a man by nothing is more bewrayed. As by his manners" Discuss.
- Manners are a hindrance to our progress. Give your views for or against the statement.
- Good manners are a handicap in today's society. Give your views for or against the statement.

The advantages and disadvantages of living in a democratic society. Discuss.

- Introduction — What is a democratic society?
- Advantages of a democratic society
    All fundamental rights are secure.
    Regional and cultural aspirations are taken care of
    Feeling of participation.
- Disadvantages
    Minorities feel threatened.
    Energy wasted in discussion and debate.
- Most successful form of society.
- Conclusion — Hope of the future.

'Government of the people, for the people and by the people, shall not perish from the earth' said Abraham Lincoln. He was indeed very prophetic, for the democratic form of society in which people have a say in the working of the government, is bound to be successful. We have the privilege of being the citizens of one of the largest Democratic country in the world, a fact in which we take pride.

The basic advantage of living in a democratic society is, having absolute freedom to live one's life. There is freedom of speech, work, religion and owning property. Thus life is more secure and progressive. There is no interference of the state in such personal matters as religion, customs, that exist in an autocratic or communist society. The right of franchise enables one to elect the government of one's choice.

It truly caters to the regional aspirations of the people, so that their identity and individuality in terms of language, traditions, etc., are adequately safeguarded. The different cultural, social practices are encouraged and allowed to prosper, so there is no feeling of alienation and deprivation among any section of society. There are special concessions and privileges like reservation, extended to the backward classes, so that they can also join the mainstream of society.

It is this feeling of goodwill and participation in the government, that makes the citizens feel that they are the master of their own destiny. In fact it is an ideal system to cater to the needs of such a large and diverse society as ours. It exemplifies the concept of unity in diversity.

There are, however, many disadvantages plaguing this system. Some of them being real and some created as a bogey by narrow-minded political and religious leaders. The very concept of majority rule, drives a fear among the minorities. Thus real or even imaginary grievances are projected by so called sectarian leaders with an eye on votes, to garner more power and clout. This politics of appeasement and vote banks at times, result in strife and violence.

Besides this valuable time and energy is wasted in discussion, debate and forming of public opinion before, any major decision can be implemented. This at times not only leads to monetary losses, but also slows down the pace of economic development, which is very harmful for any developing country.

There is, however, no denying the fact that, it is still the most successful form of society in the world today. We have seen the fate of fascist, communist and the autocratic society in the last century. All of them have failed miserably to address the diverse aspiration of their people. They may have been able to usher in stupendous growth and development, like the USSR under the communist and Iran under the autocratic rule of the Shah. However, they broke up and gave way to factionism, or fundamentalism that is still tormenting the people.

Thus undoubtedly the democratic form of society is the hope of the future and we should nurture it with great care and respect. The anomalies which have inadvertently crept into the polity like casteism, regionalism, fundamentalism with an eye on the vote banks, should be done away with, before it is too late. For in the words of Abraham Lincoln, "You can fool all the people some of the time, and some of the people all the time, but you cannot fool all the people all the time".

ASSIGNMENTS

- The democratic society in India is a living example of unity in diversity. Discuss.
- 'Government of the people, for the people and by the people, shall not perish from the earth'. Write your views on the statement.

Corporal punishment should be abolished
Give your views for or against the statement.

- Introduction — Agree. What is Corporal Punishment?
- Effect on the school.
- Effect on the students
    Inhibits learning and initiative.
    Increases dropouts from school and often causes grievous injury.
    Affects personality development.
- Conclusion – Need to ban corporal punishment.

Corporal punishment is meted out to students at school by their teachers, for minor acts of indiscipline or misbehaviour. This is done by caning or spanking them in public, which is a retributive form of punishment. The objective being to deter others from committing the same mistake. This very concept and method of giving punishment, is not in conformity to what a school stands for.

A school is a temple of learning, where students go to acquire knowledge and to add to their mental acumen, rather than to be subjected to torture and humiliation. The school where this is practiced becomes a dignified prison, where all students are to follow set rules and procedures. The non-compliance of which would invite immediate retribution. Thus instead of looking forward to another day at school, students are happier staying away from it, defeating the very objective of a school.

It also inhibits their mental faculty, which gets clouded with fear and apprehension. Thus curtailing their natural urge for experimenting and learning through trial and error, that is so vital for the learning process. It also dampens his initiative, for there is the lurking fear of punishment, on committing a mistake. Thus he remains content in following rules, thereby curbing his creative talent to do things differently.

Quite seldom it has been observed, that it has a telling effect on the morale of the student, who no longer wish to go to school. Apart from the physical injury, the embarrassment that accompanies this form of punishment, has a profound effect on the psychology of the young pupil. He detests the school and its tormentors and quite often drops out of school. Thus not only does it kill his desire for acquiring knowledge, but changes the course of his life, by making him a criminal or an antisocial element. We also hear of instances, when a teacher in a fit of rage, beats his pupil resulting in his death.

It also has a crippling effect on his personality, which by the time he comes out of school, is in shreds. He is nervous, fearful and lacks confidence. He may be externally a perfect gentleman, but is severely wanting in initiative, creativity and self esteem. Such a person cannot make any positive contribution to society and will be a misfit.

There is, therefore, an urgent need to ban corporal punishment, for which if required laws should be framed. It is, however, encouraging to note, that quite a few institutions on their own have done away with this sort of punishment. The days of 'Spare the rod and spoil the child,'are indeed over. This is but a belated realisation of what Alexander Pope once said "T'is education from the common mind. Just as the twig is bent, the tree's inclined."

ASSIGNMENTS

- 'Spare the rod and spoil the child'. Give your views for or against the statement.
- Fear of punishment only enforces discipline. Give your views for or against the statement.

Child Labour should be banned.
Give your views for or against the statement.

- Introduction — Agree. It is evil should be banned.
- Childhood is for play, not for work.
- Reasons for it to be banned
    It exploits children physically and mentally.
    It affects their personality, forcing them to crime.
    Affects the society.
- Need to effectively ban.
- Conclusion – To make the ban effective they must has social security like food, shelter & Education.

"The child is the father of man," said William Wordsworth, for it is the experience of our childhood that cast their shadow on our future. This is the reason why children are imparted noble values and virtues, so that they can grow up to be good and responsible citizens of the country.By making them work in this tender age we are not only destroying their future, but also playing with the destiny of the country.

It is indeed unfortunate, that we find children being forced to work, to eke out a living. Thus the hands that should be used for study or play are used for hard manual work. Their gentle and impressionable minds, which ought to imbibe good and noble qualities, are exposed to the vagaries of the world. It is indeed a pity to see them toil and shoulder responsibilities, which are far more than their tender shoulders can bear. It is thus a childhood wasted, which but comes once in their lives.

They are weak and undemanding making them susceptible to exploitation. They are made to do menial and at times even hazardous work, without proper compensation. Thus it is normal to find them working in the agricultural sector and in the small factories making fireworks and chemicals. They often risk their lives just to keep their body and soul together. So tragic is their condition, that in the prime of youth, they are but a physical and mental wreck. Their frail body suffers from many ailments; making them appear old .Youth seems to have bypassed them altogether.

Their personality and attitudes reflect their survival instincts, which quite often take them to crime and other antisocial activities. The Chota Rajans, the Dawood Ibrahims and countless others, bear testimony to what deprivation of childhood can bring about. Thus instead of growing up to be law-abiding citizens, they become a threat to society.

Realising the gravity of the situation the government has banned child labour, making it an offence under law. It is, however, unfortunate to see, that it is not effectively enforced, as it should be. The reason could be, that while law has been made, there is no provision for the child, to cater to his basic needs like food and shelter. This therefore amounts to paying lip service to the evil, that continues to gnaw into the vitals of our society.

No ban can work, unless we can ensure that they are provided with food shelter and education. This would not only bring back their childhood, but also secure the future of the nation, whose citizens they would one day be. If the nation is to be spared, the likes of the mafia dons and criminals, it must effectively ban child labour, ensuring at the same time that no child goes to sleep hungry.

ASSIGNMENTS

- Exploitation of children as domestic help is an evil. Give your views for or against.
- 'The child is father of the man'. Do you agree and if so why give reasons?

Women in India are Under Privileged.
Give your views for or against the statement.

- Introduction — Agree.
- Prevalent since ages.
- Exist in society even today.
     Dowry and female infanticide.
     Social customs and practices.
- Conclusion — Immediate steps required to improve their lot.

Women in India are under privileged. Whether we like it or not and no matter what facts and figures we may quote, the fact remains that the fruits of development have not reached them in the measure that it should have. They constitute nearly one half of the population of the country and therefore, no real development can take place without their involvement and participation.

Ever since the dawn of civilization, man has showed his dominance over them, by the sheer magnitude of his physical prowess. This was the reason for such inhibitive customs, like the pardah system, dowry and the Sati practice which was a sheer manifestation of his hold over women .She played a crucial role in his life no doubt, as a mother, wife and daughter but when it came to equal rights she virtually had none. Thus in all crucial matters pertaining to property, or ascendance to the throne, it was the son who inherited the property or the throne.

It is indeed a matter of concern, that even after more than fifty years of independence, they continue to live an underprivileged existence, more like second-class citizen. We may have done away with the Sati and the Pardah system, but evils like dowry and female infanticide continue to thrive in our society, even in this age of enlightenment. A girl child is looked upon as a burden for her parents and her birth is seldom rejoiced .The discrimination starts from birth and continues right through their lives in their nutrition, education and upbringing.

The present social customs and practices also discriminate against her. Thus after marriage, she has to adopt the surname of her spouse and move in with him. What little she had of her identity, is also lost after marriage .She is also denied her share in parental property .The male hegemony is more evident in Muslims, who are legally permitted to have four wives and have the liberty to divorce their wives, by mere uttering of the word 'Talaq' thrice.

This discrimination does not auger well for the growth and development of the country. Immediate steps are called for ameliorating their lot, by providing them free education and ensuring their economic independence.This can be done by making reservation in jobs for them. The women's reservation bill in parliament, is a step in the right direction and would help women to have a say in affairs that concern them and the country.

ASSIGNMENTS

- Women's liberation is a myth. Discuss.
- There are certain professions from which women should be excluded. Discuss.

Should competitive examination be abolished?

- Introduction — What is competitive examination?
- Need for competitive examination.
- Arguments against competitive examination.

    It does not test candidates' suitability.

    Knowledge also not adequately tested.

    No means for assessing personality traits.

- Suggestion for change.
- Conclusion — Need to make it more humane and objective.

All examinations are but competitive in nature, as each candidate tries to secure the maximum marks. This is prevalent not only in studies, but in every sphere of human activity, as each one strives for excellence. It is the secret of our growth and development.

However, competitive examination is an examination of candidates for selection for jobs and assignments. This is, therefore, a selection process that uses the procedure of elimination, based on the applicant's performance in a written examination .The basis for selection being certain parameters of knowledge, traits and analytical reasoning, etc. The need for a selection process becomes all the more necessary, for while jobs are increasing by arithmetic progression, the number of applicants increases by geometric progression. Thus we find more number of applicants for fewer jobs, which make these examinations highly competitive. There is, therefore, need for a proper form of evaluation, whereby applicants can be objectively judged, for taking on particular assignments.

The case against the present form of examination is, that they are not infallible test of fitness and are highly subjective in nature. They may test a candidates knowledge on a certain subject, mental ability and awareness, but they cannot judge other essential traits necessary for a particular job. Take for example the Indian Civil Service Examination held for recruiting people to the Indian Administrative Service. Every year lakhs of candidates appear for the examination that is, designed to test their knowledge on certain subjects. This is oblivious to the fact, that there are more essential attributes required by a civil servant, like administrative ability, man management, tact, diplomacy and quick decision-making. Thus it acts like an imperfect sieve, through which candidates are selected subjectively and not objectively.

What is further distressing is that, candidates can pass such examinations by selective cramming. Thus it cannot be a real test of intelligence or knowledge. The knowledge so acquired is very superficial and hence easily forgotten. We know from practical life that students, who may have topped their examination in school, are not always very successful, while those who were mediocre excelled in life.

A major handicap of the system is that, there is scant regard for judging the candidate's personality, character and will power. These are essential attributes for any responsible position, especially for a civil servant. The inadequacy of the present system makes the whole exercise appear a big farce.

Though we may concede this system to be imperfect, there is, however, no alleviation for its malady. We all agree that there must be some sort of examination, but it is difficult to device a foolproof system. Perhaps the existing system could be augmented with group discussion, group tasks and personal interviews that would enable a more realistic and objective assessment of the candidates other valuable traits, besides knowledge. There could also be a provision for a small probation period, in which the applicant's suitability for a particular job could be judged.

As of now, there is no panacea for all the ills of the present competitive examination and hence it cannot be done away with. However, there is an urgent need for making them more objective and humane, so that they achieve the purpose for which they are intended.

ASSIGNMENTS

- The ills of the present examination system. State your views on the subject.
- Too many examinations are of little value. Discuss the statement.
- Examination work like an imperfect sieve. Discus the statement.

Pen is mightier than the sword.
Give your views for or against the statement

- Introduction — Agree with the statement, as pen ruled by mind while sword ruled by muscle.
- Pen of revolutionary writers create revolution, Some examples.
- Pen conquers the mind permanently, while sword conquers the body temporarily, some examples.
- Pen of saints and philosophers generate love, while sword generates animosity.
- Conclusion — The power wielded by the pens of writers and seges are but an image of God.

"Power flows from the barrel of a gun". History is witness to the plight of people, thrown into oblivion, as they believed in the above dictum. This is because the power of a pen is ruled by the mind, which is far mightier than a sword, ruled by the muscle. The sword may conquer the body, but it can never conquer the heart and mind of the person. There in lies the difference, for the conquest of the body is short-lived, while that of the heart is everlasting.

This is the reason why we find the great ideas and thoughts penned by great writers, behind all big revolutions. While the fiery slogan of liberty, equality and fraternity' put forth by Rousseau and Voltaire ignited the French revolution. Similarly Das Kapital authored by Karl Marx, fired the imagination of countries ushering in the communist revolution, that swept across Asia and Europe. These revolutionary thoughts expressed by writers in their books, continue to influence our lives. They are more resounding than the greatest of all military victories. Thus while the world still remembers such great writers with awe, it has thrown into oblivion great conquerors like Napoleon, Taimur and Hitler. In India we had seen the magic woven by the pen of Mahatma Gandhi. He wakened the Indian masses from their age-old slumber, to wage a fight for independence from the mighty British Empire.

The reason for this is obvious, we can subdue our opponents by use of force only temporarily. If we are able to influence his mind we can bring about a permanent transformation. The great emperor Ashoka realised this after the long and arduous battle of Kalinga. So moved was he by the teachings of Buddha, that he set forth spreading his message of love and compassion throughout Asia. It was because of this he was able to achieve greater glory and fame by winning the hearts of people, than by the use of his sword.

While the thought of great revolutionaries generate revolution, the writing of great sages and religious leaders influence our lives profoundly. The Ramayana and Geeta written by Valmiki and Vedvyas not only inspire us today, but shall continue to inspire generations till eternity. The great exploits of Rama and Arjuna would have faded away from memory, had it not been immortalised by them. So it is evident that the pen carries the sword, on its shoulder, for without it even the little impact that it has is transitory. This is the reason why even in war, we try to influence, the enemies mind through propaganda. The Nazis feared the leaflet raids more than the allied bombers in the Second World War. While the use of the sword brings with it such negative feelings like animosity, anger and hatred. The effect of the pen is much more humane and noble as it brings love, affection, peace and tranquility.

It is this, which made John Milton remark, "Who kills a man, kills a reasonable creature. God's image but he who destroys a good book. Kills reason itself, kills the image of God as it were in the eye". Thus the powers wielded by the pens of writers are but an image of God. They rule the mind and heart of people, while the sword can only conquer their body.

ASSIGNMENT

- "Power flows from the barrel of gun". Give your views for or against the statement.

The present education system has outlived its use.
Give your views for or against the statement.

- Introduction — Need and importance.
- Outdated system left as legacy by the British.
- Over-emphasis in awarding degrees.
- Highly subjective system encourages manipulation.
- Large-scale distribution of degrees leading to corruption.
- Conclusion – Need to replace with a system which lays more stress on character building and vocational Training

"T' is education form the common mind. Just as the twig is bent, the tree's inclined" said Alexander Pope. Such is the importance of education in our lives. Thus it is imperative for any government to ensure, that there is a proper education system for its youth who are the future of the nation. This should not only take care of the aspirations of the people, but also cater to the growth and economic development of the country. The present education system has failed on both counts and hence has outlived its use .

Unfortunately we in India have still persisted with the system devised by the British, that enabled them to rule over this hapless country for over two hundred years. This system ideally suited them to meet their requirement of clerks and assistants, who could implement the dictat of their white masters. Thus this system enabled a handful of imperialist forces, to hold hegemony over the entire subcontinent.

It is indeed a matter of shame, that even after more than half a century of our independence, we have still not been able to remove the shackles of this outdated system. This arrangement hence continues to produce, an army of graduates and postgraduates, who have no vocational training whatsoever, making them unemployable. Moreover with the economic liberlisation and the current thinking of downsizing the government, there would be fewer employment opportunities. The over emphasis on awarding degrees on a variety of subjects, from social sciences to music and dance is the root cause of disgruntlement in the youth today. Thus after spending considerable time and money, he does qualify for a degree, which is unable to fetch him a job, making the entire exercise irrelevant.

Apart from preparing him for gainful employment, it does not even prepare him for life. The overemphasis of passing through theoretical examination, at the end of the year, leads to highly subjective assessment of individual's true potential and in-depth knowledge. Thus we find students resorting to selective cramming, to obtain excellent grades in the examination. Those with more ingenuity and muscle power, are able to resorting to cheating and manipulating marks, reducing the system to a farce. This is but an irony, for instead of imbibing good values, it rewards those resorting to cheating and using unfair means.

The government's persistence for having graduation, as the minimum qualification for government jobs, has led to large-scale distribution of degrees. Some of which can be procured from dubious institutions. This leads to rampant corruption in the so-called universities that are the temple of learning. Thus making mockery of the system, that has indeed outlived its use.

It is therefore imperative, that as we enter the new millennium, we replace the structure with a more humane, objective, forward-looking system. Where there is more stress on character building and vocational training. A system where the youth not only grows up with a health personality, but also with wholesome knowledge for his own, as well as the nation's progress. .

ASSIGNMENT

- Examinations are a true test of knowledge. Give your views for or against the statement.

Should punishment be retributive or reformatory? Discuss

- Introduction — What is retributory punishment?
- Harmful effects of retributive punishment.
- Need for change to a reformatory form of punishment.
- Advantages of reformatory form of punishment.
- Conclusion — Reformatory punishment is more effective as it addresses the root cause.

'Give a dog a bad name and hang him,' this vividly is what retributive or avenging punishment is all about. Thus under such form of punishment, a criminal is severely punished, so that it serves as a deterrent for others to obey the law. The effect on the people is difficult to gauge, but the effect that it had on the criminal is evident. This was the type of punishment that existed until recent times, when the legal codes were severe and the penalties harsh, sometimes even savage. This was consciously done, so as to compel people to fear law. It was also felt that such criminals or people who broke the law, should be kept away from contaminating society, as if they were morally infectious cases.

Thus the state took upon itself the role of policing the society. The effect of this type of punishment on the criminal, who may have committed a small offence was disastrous .He was made to suffer brutalities in prison by unscrupulous warden's, who bullied them into submission. Punishment like flogging and solitary confinement, even denial of food and water were the order of the day. Being in the company of hardened criminals, he imbibed their skills and nursed a secret hatred for society. Thus he became more like a sullen animal, than a human being. After his term was over, he came out of prison a hardened and more potentially dangerous criminal. His animosity towards society further aggravated, when he found himself in a hostile world, where people shunned and looked down on him. Even if he made an effort for earning an honest living, he could not find any work, for no one was willing to employ a branded criminal. Exasperated he had no other option, but to take to crime on a much larger scale. Thus a small time offender, becomes a hardened criminal.

It was this negative aspect of punishment that led humanitarians to campaign for prison reforms. This has now started bearing fruit and over the years, we have steadily seen a quantum shift in the ideology of meting out punishment .The prison codes have been modified and savage penalties have been abolished. Prisoners today have human rights, which are duly respected. This has happened because of the growing conviction, that the legal form of punishment should be reformatory, rather than being merely punitive.

The reformatory form of punishment considers a convict a human being, who may have committed a crime but is likely to be modified and corrected, so that he becomes a good citizen. Thus in the case of imprisonment, where there is a loss of personal liberty for the criminal, the state sees this as an opportunity for reforming him. Thus today we find jails better equipped with television, libraries and vocational centers, where apart from formal education, vocational training is also given. This enables the convict to practice his vocation on completing his term of imprisonment. Thus a small offender is reformed to become a good citizen, contributing to society.

The result of reformatory form of punishment are very encouraging, for it addresses the root cause of the problem. This is also in line with what Mahatma Gandhi had once said, "Hate the sin, not the sinner."

ASSIGNMENTS

- Retributive punishment is the need of the hour to curb the growing incidence of crime. Give your views for or against the statement.
- Crime and punishment in the modern world.

Are betting and gambling national evils? Discuss.

- Introduction — What is betting and gambling?
- Evils of betting and gambling.
  - Addict's people.
  - Discourages work.
  - Leads to crime.
  - Generates rampant corruption.
- Conclusion – Need to make laws to curtail this menace.

Life itself is a big gamble, for we know not what the future holds. However, betting and gambling is, when we resort to playing for financial stakes in the hope of striking it rich. Thus in a way playing cards, or dealing in stocks and shares are all but a game of chance. Surely being independent citizens we do have a legitimate right to partake in this excitement, which is no evil on grounds of morality.

It is only when the not so well off and poor partake in this, by force of habit does it becomes an evil. This is so because quite often, their greed for wealth overcomes their reasoning, which leads to disastrous consequences. Thus while it may be a sport or a game of chance for the wealthy, it becomes an obsession for the poor, who resorts to it in the hope of becoming rich overnight.

This no longer remains a game of chance for him, it now becomes a habit. A person so addicted, finds it difficult to break away from it. It therefore becomes a vicious circle for him, where in spite of losing he keeps on at it, in the hope of covering up his losses. Such is its stranglehold on people, that it makes them not only financially, but also mentally bankrupt. We all know the ignominy that the Pandavas had to suffer, when they lost their wife Draupadi to the Kauravas in the game of dice.

It also changes the work culture of people so addicted. They no longer want to put in steady hard work. So gripped are they under the delusion of the 'get rich quick syndrome', that in course of time they are unfit for work.

The culmination of the above leads them to crime and violence. To satisfy their craving, they resort to theft and other criminal activities. This changes the course of their lives, leading them to conviction and consequently breaking up their homes.

The ramification of this evil, has also infiltrated the halo arena of sports, like football and cricket and almost about anything. Thus leaving a trail of corruption even at high places. We have been just witness to the betting and match fixing charges levied against reputed players, that have sullied the gentleman's game of cricket.

So widespread and deep rooted is this malice, that there is an immediate need to declare betting and gambling a national evil. We must also devise effective laws to curtail this menace, before it assumes gigantic proportions.

ASSIGNMENTS

- Betting in cricket should be banned. Give your views for or against the statement.
- Betting and Gambling should be banned. Discuss

It is better to be born a genius than talented. Discuss.

- Introduction — What is a genius and talent?
- Would like to be born a genius, as it is inborn while talent is acquired, examples.
- Genius can thrive in even an adverse environment.
- They are rare born after centuries, leaving a legacy for posterity some examples.
- Conclusion – Would like To be born a genius.

A Genius is not born everyday. They are as rare as the blue moon. The word genius implies very extraordinary or native powers, especially as displayed in original creations, discoveries and achievement. They are inborn and are independent of instruction or training. While talent on the other hand, is an ability with which we are blessed and can be acquired by learning or instruction. Thus while talent is a capacity to learn to do a thing well, genius is an inborn inspiration, that drives a man to do a thing with original excellence. Thus while a 'genius' does what it must, a talent does what it can.

Given a choice I would like to be born a genius, for imagine having to bestow something new and inspiring to mankind like Newton or William Shakespeare. They were indeed trailblazers in their respective fields and left behind a rich trail for others to dwell on . A talented person is also equally great but it is the originality that makes the difference. This is why we call the painting of Monalisa by Leonarda Da Vinci a work of genius. Though there have been equally good paintings by many a talented painters, but they do not command this distinction.

Geniuses have been known to thrive in all circumstances. Their genius has sparkled in the most unfavourable of environment. We have illustrious personalities like William Shakespeare, Mirza Galib, Tulsi Das and Munshi Premchand. They were born in acute poverty, but their genius raised them to the pinnacle of glory, making them immortal. They did not even have the privilege of a formal education, but the literary wealth that they bequeathed to us, makes even the so-called educated man blush with ignorance. Their language style and presentation are as original as during their times. So loaded are they with wisdom and truth, that they are as relevant today as they were then . A few of them like Mirza Galib, were even so unaware of their genius that had it not been for their patrons, who painstakingly compiled their collections, the world would have been that much poorer today.

They are therefore, God's gift to mankind and are born after centuries. They have illuminated our lives in varied fields, for example, we have Beethoven's in Music, Albert Einstein in Science and Mahatma Gandhi in Social Welfare. They, left behind a legacy so rich and varied, that it continues to inspire generations. Their works are the benchmarks, against which we ordinary mortals set about acquiring talent, basking in their reflected glory.

Thus I would also like to make some innovative contribution to society , rather than be reduced to a mere copy of the works of a true genius. This is by no means derogatory for talented people, who are also great men. But when it comes to a choice then why choose a replica, when you can have the unique. So a genius I would be, leaving behind for posterity, a malady to cure mankind of the ills of materialism. Propagating a new trail in Social engineering. Where there is no rich, no poor and no suffering.

ASSIGNMENTS

- Talent and Genius.
- "Genius does what it must, a talent does what it can" Discuss.
- Genius are born not made .Give your views for or against the statement.

"Education makes the people easy to lead, but difficult to drive, easy to govern, but impossible to enslave". Discuss.

- Introduction — What is education?
- The present scenario in the country.
- Effect on the people.
    - Awakens his mind.
    - Trains the intellect for logical reasoning.
    - Makes him cultured, civilised and humane.
- Effect on the nation.
    - Strengthens democracy.
- Conclusion — Urgent need of the hour.

"Education makes the people easy to lead, but difficult to drive, easy to govern, but impossible to enslave", so said Lord Brougham. This is entirely true, for without education a man is a shade better than an animal. Just as it is difficult to lead a flock of sheep, you can at best herd them around. Similarly without education man also behaves like a flock of sheep that can only be herded. After all why is this education so important for us? This can only be understood if we know what education stands for. The word education is derived from the Latin word meaning 'to draw out'. Thus true education is the drawing out of the mental faculties, that are so essential for leading a happy life.

The abysmally low level of education among the poor and the downtrodden, makes them vulnerable to economic and political exploitation. Though adequate provisions had been made in the constitution, to ensure their empowerment and participation. At the ground level it seems the fruits of this, have not percolated down to them. The main culprit for this being lack of education, which deprives them of their power to claim their right. Not only are they economically exploited by the landlords and traders, but politically also they fall easy prey to the mechanisation of crafty politicians. Their so-called messiah treat them as vote banks, for garnering power and clout for themselves, leaving them worse off. This problem can only be addressed by enlightening the masses, by imparting proper education. Thus enabling them to distinguish between good and bad.

The education of the masses would awaken their minds to the wonders and mysteries of the universe. This would free them from doubts, superstition and remove many social evils that are plaguing the society. It would train their intellect to reason logically and not to be carried away by false or illogical promises of politicians or power brokers. In short it would make them civilised, cultured and humane citizens of a proud country.

This would also auger well for the country, as it would strengthen democracy. The people would in the true sense be able to elect their leaders. They would be better able to appreciate national problems, thus strengthen the hands of the government, rather than be misguided by vested and selfish sectarian interest.

Education is the need of the hour if we have to safeguard our independence. We have just been witness to how a few thousand Englishmen, had ruled over this country for over two hundred years, for want of an educated population. We should not allow this to happen again. This can only be ensured by imparting proper education to the masses, so that they exercise their franchise without fear or favour. This would indeed make them master of their destiny.

ASSIGNMENTS

- Poverty and unemployment are the major problems facing the country. Write about any one suggesting what remedies might be effective.
- Unemployment is a major problem affecting the country. Suggest what remedies might be effective.

Students should not take Part in Politics.
Give your views for or against the statement.

- Introduction — Agree with the statement.
- Evil of politics, due to degeneration into party politics after independence because of :—
  Absence of ethics and morality.
  Politics instead of being associated with social service, is now a profession for earning money and corruption.
- Negative impact on students because of :—
  Their exploitation by political parties.
  Ruins their career and future prospects.
- Conclusion. — Should be banned.

A student is expected to devote his time and effort in studies, rather than involve himself in the rough and tumble of politics. Studies and politics are in fact diametrically opposite attributes and they are but incompatible. It is, however unfortunate, that the money and power attract the youth to it. This is for, in the words of G. Bernard Shaw, a person with political aspirations "knows nothing and he thinks he knows everything. That points clearly to a political career."

Politics is no longer a noble service that it used to be. It was associated with social service and a political worker was first and foremost a social worker, or reformer. During our struggle for independence it was these social workers, that spread Mahatma Gandhi's message throughout the length and breadth of the country. They were also in the forefront for unifying the country and reforming the society, by educating the public on the social evils like child marriage, untouchability, etc. Ever since independence the political party politics, has vitiated the political atmosphere of the country, with the morality and ethics touching an all time low. It is now a full-fledged profession, where the power and pelf of office turns one's fortune overnight, by resorting to corruption.

It is unfortunate to see the students being increasingly exploited by political parties, for their own selfish interest. They exploit the young blood, for their dirty work by using them to promote their divisive and casteist politics. At times they also exhort them to violence, for their perceived or drummed up grievances to get political mileage. Quite often many a promising youth's career is ruined, because of their mechanisation. This is a very dangerous sign, for the impressionable mind of the student can be easily led astray.

The students should, therefore, not take part in politics, which should infact be banned. The Political parties should behave responsibly and not involve students in their dirty work. They should desist from doing so, for it portends a great danger to the youth, who are the future of the country.

ASSIGNMENTS

- Students and Politics.
- Should students go on strikes. Discuss.

It is better to have brains than Beauty.
Give your views for or against the statement.

- Introduction — Agree, Beauty is but skin deep.
- Beauty is brief, while brains is lasting and grows with age.
- Beauty is superficial, while brain is all encompassing bringing out the beauty within.
- Beauty can enthrall us, while brains can be used for welfare of society.
- Impact of brains on our personality.
- Conclusion — Brain is essential for happiness.

"Remember that the most beautiful things in the world are the most useless, peacock and lilies for instance," said John Ruskin. It is better to have brain than beauty, that is not only useful for us but also for society. While physical beauty is purely visual, the beauty of the brain is all encompassing. It is, a known fact that "beauty is but skin-deep". Most beautiful people are but superficial, beneath their exterior countenance lies baser qualities of jealousy, wickedness, pride and arrogance.

What is worse, it is not even lasting, for it declines with age and time. Thus what is at its peak in youth withers out with age, so much so that it is unrecognisable in old age. Contrary to this, our brain and mental faculty improve and grows with age .We become wiser, more experienced and people look up to us for advice and direction.

Another important aspect of the brain is that it is all pervasive. It spreads its influence over us, in all that we do or say. Thus a person with a pleasing mental disposition, could leave a very satisfying influence on the people around him, for a long time. This in sharp contrast to beauty, which by its glamour can but razzle dazzle us, but for a moment. No sooner is it out of sight its impact is gone forever. Some beauty also lives in vain unnoticed and unsung, in the words of Thomas Gray, "For many a flower is born to blush unseen. And waste its freshness on the desert air'. A noble mind on the other hand brings out the beauty within. Thus we had such personalities like Mother Teresa and Mahatma Gandhi, who could by no stretch of imagination be called beautiful. However, their noble deeds and actions, which were the outcome of a noble mind, would inspire generations. People gratefully remember them as Mother and Mahatma respectively.

While beauty can but enthrall us for the present, the brain with its inspiration can reach out and influence the lives of countless people profoundly. This is exemplified in the life and travails of Florence Nightingale. She could also have lived a normal life of other girls of her age, but she chose to reach out to the injured and the suffering .The maiden with the lamp not only brightened the lives of those she came in contact with, but she blazed a new trail of the nursing profession.

The impact of our brain on our personality is but an acknowledged fact. This is the reason why even at national and international beauty pageants, an effort is made to gauge the intelligence of the participants by eliciting response to identical queries.

William Shakespeare acknowledged this when he, says, "For sweetest things turn sourest by their deeds, Lilies that fester smell far wore than weeds". This is in sharp contrast to the brain, which inspires us to do noble things. This not only make us happy but also spread happiness around for, "How far that little candle throws her beams. So shines a good deed in a naughty world".

ASSIGNMENTS

- Beauty is but skin deep. Discuss.
- "Remember that the most beautiful things in the world are the most useless, peacock and lilies for instance." Give your views.
- Beauty pageants are a vulgar display of body, give your views for or against the statement.

Prohibition is an infringement of our Fundamental Right. Give your views for or against the statement.

- Introduction — Agree, What is Prohibition?
- It is an Infringement of our fundamental right.
- Disadvantages of Prohibition:
    Leads to bootlegging and loss of life.
    Loss of revenue for the state.
- Conclusion — Best left to the public.

The word Prohibition owes its genesis from the word 'prohibit' which means ban. In this case, it is to ban the use of intoxicant beverages by the rule of law. In this age of enlightenment. it's imposition on the citizens, is but an infringement of their fundamental rights.

People advocate its imposition on grounds of morality and ethics, for according to them it addicts people to become drunkards. This brings about their , as well as their family to ruins. What they fail to realise, is that they should not ban something, for the sake of handful of people, who would anyway come to ruin for their weak will power. People drink for enjoyment, for overcoming weariness and for some, it is a matter of aping the Jones, so as to be in fashion. Alcoholic drinks have been known to be good for health, if taken within limits as confirmed by medical experts. It is also known to provide relief to people staying in cold climatic conditions. Enforcement of prohibition would indeed interfere with their private lives.

However, enforcing prohibition is easier said than done. It gives rise to a plethora of other problems like bootlegging, and trafficking in illicit liquor. While the former provides encouragement to antisocial elements and makes a mockery of the law, the latter gives rise to a parallel uncontrolled industry. This is far more dangerous, as there are numerous instances of these illicit breweries serving poisonous brew to the poor labourers, killing them in large numbers. Those that are spared death are maimed for life, either becoming blind or paralyzed.

The state in turn loses considerable revenue, in the form of excise duty and sales tax. This leads to resource crunch, adversely affecting the development and social welfare activities of the state. Such is the reliance of the state on this revenue, that quite a few states had as a result of popular sentiments imposed prohibition in their state, but after some time they had to roll back the same. A specific example being, the state of Andhra Pradesh, where after a brief stint of prohibition it was done away with.

It is thus of paramount importance that the public should be educated on the evils of excessive drinking .The glamour and macho illusions depicted in advertisements should be countered effectively. Finally respecting the fundamental right of an individual, it should be best left to his discretion.

ASSIGNMENTS

- Drinking of alcoholic beverages should be banned in public places. Discuss.
- The evil of drug abuse among students. What are the cause and suggest what remedies might be effective?

The programmes launched by the government for improving literacy in the country are a dismal failure. Write how and what you think should be done to remove illiteracy in the country.

- Introduction — The dismal scenario of literacy in the country.
- Reasons for this dismal performance.
  - Low priority given to the spread of literacy programs.
  - Absence of infrastructure.
  - Lack of good and motivated teachers.
- Drastic steps needed to accelerate the slow pace.
  - High priority to be given with more investment in schools and colleges.
  - Involvement of youth and NGO's.
- Advantages to the people and the nation.
- Conclusion — The only way to bring about Swaraj of Bapu's dream .

"Education makes the people easy to lead, but difficult to drive, easy to govern, but impossible to enslave," said Lord Biougham. This is true for any nation, but more so for us because of our size, diversity of customs and culture. It was the lack of education that was responsible for our enslavement to the British, for more than two centuries .The current strife and sectarian politics, is also a direct consequence of a gullible and misguided public. It is indeed a matter of shame, that even as we enter the new millennium, more than fifty percent of the population are still illiterate. This is despite our being the largest democracy in the world, for the last more than sixty years.

The dismal performance is on account of the low priority accorded to the spread of literacy programmes in the country .It has been observed, that though a lot of hue and cry has been made over the last few decades, for ensuring speedy education to the masses. However, the situation at the ground level remains unchanged. Every year a substantial proportion of the budget is allocated for this sector, but most of this goes to meet the administrative costs of the ongoing schemes only. Leaving very meagre resources for launching the new schemes in far off regions.

There is dearth of proper schools and those that exist, do not have good motivated teachers. This is on account of the abysmally low salaries paid to them, which do not attract the right talent. It is, therefore, obvious that something more drastic needs to be done in this field, so that all enjoy the fruits of literacy .The present system of providing formal /informal education needs to be reviewed and a high priority to be accorded to it. The government should allocate more financial resources for strengthening the existing schools with good teachers and establish new schools in far flung areas.

The college youth should also be deployed for this purpose, by making it obligatory for them to engage in imparting adult education, before awarding them degrees or jobs. The primary and secondary school teachers, could also be effectively deployed on an honorarium basis, using the present facilities of schools and colleges beyond normal hours. The government should also take the help of voluntary organisations, like Non Government Organisations in this important nation-building task.

The advantages that could accrue from this, could have long time repercussions for the citizens, as well as the country .The citizens would reap the benefits of the various welfare schemes of the government, making them self reliant and also escape exploitation by petty traders and politicians .The nation would also gain by having a wise and mature electorate, contributing to its economic development.

We have waited far too long, for realizing Bapu's dream of bringing "Swaraj" to the millions of Indians residing in the heart of India, which lies in the villages .The above would be a step in the right direction in realising his dream. It would also strengthen the nation, for a wise electorate would elect a good government for as they say, "The people get the government they deserve."

ASSIGNMENT

- Discuss in the Indian context " The people get the government they deserve."

DESCRIPTIVE ESSAYS

You have lived in your ancestral house since birth. The house is to be sold so that flats may be built. Narrate the circumstances that led to this decision and describe your feelings about moving out of the house.

(ICSE 2004)

- Introduction -When did it happen ?
- Why was it necessary to vacate our ancestral home ? Narrate the circumstances
- Description of the house
- The sweet memories associated with this house and the emotions and feeling on leaving it
- Packing of my belongings
- Conclusion –Bidding fare well to friends and my ancestral house, which was not just a home, but a temple of love for me.

"We shall have to leave home today," said my mother with tears in her eyes last Sunday, which was the saddest day of my life. I put down the toast of bread, which I was having for breakfast, unbelieving what I had heard. "Leaving Home ! But why Mummy?" I asked foolishly.

She then went on to recount the severe financial loss my father had been incurring in business of late. Loans had been taken against mortgage of our ancestral house to a financer, who was now pressing hard for return of his money. Being unable to repay the debt, there was no alternative but to vacate the house. The financer wanted to build multistoried flats on the prime piece of land, on which our house stood. I had sensed for some time that some trouble was brewing, for I often found my father and mother not quite their usual self. They seemed quite perturbed and restless. But things would become so serious, I had never imagined.

'Singh Villa' was indeed a prestigious property located in Lalbagh, very close to the posh Hazratganj market of Lucknow. It was brought by my grand father from an Englishman, in the year 1911. The architecture of the bungalow was typically European, with walls made of red sandstone, having a red tiled roof, atop which stood a tall chimney. The long driveway led to a big porch, beyond which was a verandah, opening into the drawing room. The huge doors and windows with ventilators near the ceiling, made the place very airy and fresh. From the high ceiling hung chandeliers and ceiling fans, that reminded one of the age gone by. Besides the drawing room, there were three other equally large rooms on the ground floor. My room on the first floor opened into a huge balcony. This had a commanding view of the adjoining park, where children from the neighbourhood came to play cricket. One could never feel lonely or bored, for there was so much activity around to watch.

The very thought of leaving this place made my heart sink. I had been born and brought up here, and could not fathom to live anywhere else. I had numerous friends in the neighborhood, with whom I had grown up. The thought that I would not be able to see or play with them, made me feel sad. Besides this, the precious memories of my grand father playing cricket with me in the lawns, made me suppress a sob. Unable to control my emotions, I clung to my mother crying inconsolably.

Realising that the news was harsh on me, she comforted me, assuring that this was just a temporary set back. "We would be moving to a smaller house in Gomti Nagar, and God willing happy days would come again," she said. I marveled at her courage, and resolved never to let go of my emotion again.

With a heavy heart, I set about packing my personal belongings, into two huge trunks. After I had finished my packing by late afternoon, we had a very quiet lunch. None of us, was willing to speak a word, for fear of betraying our feelings. I could see the sign of anguish on my father's face. It was indeed a very tough decision for him, but being a great fighter, he showed utmost restraint and self confidence. The packing of the furniture was over by evening, and we waited patiently for the truck to arrive.

Loading the last item on the truck, I bid farewell to my friends, who had come to see me off. I sat in the car and took a last glance at my ancestral house, which was not just a home, but a temple of love for me.

ASSIGNMENTS

- You have to leave your school where you studied from class 1. Narrate the circumstances that led to this decision and describe your feelings on leaving school.
- You were traveling by car which had a mechanical breakdown or accident making further travel by car impossible. Describe what happened and how you finally reached your destination.

Write about two deeds you have done one of which gave you immense joy and satisfaction while the other was a cause of deep regret.

(ICSE 2004)

- Introduction - We live in deeds not years.
- A good deed of helping a friend.
- An action that was the cause of regret.
- Conclusion - Our good deeds give us joy while our bad deeds cause deep regret. Neverthless we learn and benefit from them.

In the words of P.J. Bailey "we live in deeds not years, in thoughts nor breath. In feeling not figures on a dial". Thus our life is enriched by our good deeds, for which we are known and respected. It is of no consequence as to how long we live. Good deeds give us immense joy and satisfaction, while some of our actions are the cause of much regret and unhappiness.

I distinctly recall the day last summer, while going to school on my bicycle, I saw a huge crowd on the road side. Recognizing the bicycle of my friend Abhay lying on the road, I made way through the crowd, and found him lying in a pool of blood. He had apparently been knocked down by a speeding car. Quickly taken stock of the situation, I signaled a car to stop. Taking the help of the bystanders, I put Abhay in the car and sped towards the Civil hospital. Here he was immediately taken to the emergency ward. Due to the serious head injury, the doctors decided to go in for an emergency operation. They asked me to immediately arrange for blood of 'O' group, which was required for the operation. My blood group being the same, I volunteered and was immediately wheeled into the OT. While the blood transfusion was going on, I felt dizzy and dozed off. I opened my eyes to see Abhay's parents standing anxiously around me. Their eyes were brimming with tears, as they held my hand firmly. Fortunately for Abhay the operation was successful, and after a few months rest he was back to school. Ever since he has been my best friend.

While this deed gave me immense joy and satisfaction, I am however, filled with deep regret and shame, in recalling my first and last attempt at using unfair means in the examination. I was then in class VIII and detested the social science subject specially History. The date of birth and death of great men was something which I found hard to memorise. I thought of an easy way out, and wrote the same in a small piece of paper, which I concealed in my pencil box. I was caught in the act of taking a glimpse of this note, and was hauled up by the invigilator. The matter was reported to the Principal, and my parents were called to school. I was severely reprimanded for my conduct, and was let off with a stern warning. Even today, just thinking about it makes me feel awkward and embarrassed. I found myself unable to face my friends and colleagues. The understanding shown by my friend Abhay made me overcome this ignominy.

Thus I know from personal experience that while good deeds give us tremendous joy and satisfaction, the not so good deeds are the cause of deep regret. Nevertheless, they too help us in moulding our lives, for we also learn and benefit from them.

ASSIGNMENTS

- 'One lie leads to another' Relate an incident when you told a lie and went on to deeply regret it later.
- Write about two deeds you have done in school which gave you immense joy and satisfaction.

While on a picnic you and your friends decide to go sailing, unfortunately, your boat capsizes in a violent storm. However all of you manage to swim to safety. Give a vivid account of the incident.

(ICSE 2003)

- Introduction –When and where you went ?
- What happened ?
- Caught in a storm
- How you swam to safety ?
- Conclusion - a harrowing experience, that I shall never forget in my life.

The first showers of the monsoon signaled the end of our summer vacation. I along with my friends Soumya and Arti, decided to have a memorable picnic, before going back to our books. After much deliberation we finally settled to go to Saheed Smarak the very next day.

The sky was a little overcast, as we set out on our bicycles towards Saheed Smarak. The cool morning breeze was a welcome respite from the heat wave we had been facing lately. We hired a medium sized boat with a sail, for sailing on the river Gomti. The old boatman welcomed us aboard, and made us sit comfortably on the seats facing the rudder. With a mighty heave on the oars, he steered the boat gently into the river. Soon we were sailing in the middle of the river. The gentle breeze across the sails accelerated our pace. We shouted with joy, splashing the river water with our hands, and sang to our heart's content.

Suddenly the clouds darkened and the gentle breeze transformed into a violent storm. The strong dusty wind threatened to blow of the sail, making the boat rock violently. Gone was the bonhomie, as we all huddled to the corner of the boat in fright. The old boatman warned us against it, while struggling to bring down the sail. It was, however, too late. Before we could fathom the situation, a strong gust of wind made the boat capsize, right in the middle of the river.

We screamed in despair, as we were flung into the twirling water of the river. Gasping for breath I came to the surface, and flinging my arms in despair, clutched the bottom of the capsized boat. Soon Soumya, Arti and the old boatman, also joined in. We were all shocked, and on the verge of tears. Fortunately for us, we all knew how to swim, Leaving the boatman to tend to his boat, we began to swim towards the river bank, that seemed to be far away in the horizon.

To compound to our misery, it began to rain heavily, which obliterated our vision. In a couple of minutes we were thoroughly exhausted, and gasping for breath, but the end to our misery was still a distance away from us. Just then, I saw a fisherman's boat coming toward us. He hauled us on to the boat, and brought us to the river bank at the Saheed Smarak. We profusely thanked him for saving our lives.

We were all badly shaken, and scared by the close brush with death. Even today, just reminiscing about it makes my hairs stand on end. It was indeed a harrowing experience, that I shall never forget in my life.

ASSIGNMENTS

- Imagine you have been in a difficult or awkward situation . Write a composition describing it and how you got out of it.
- Suppose you are a fisherman or a scientist .Write an account of some of your experiences.

Looking back at the last ten years of your life, describe the events that have been significant in shaping your personality.

(ICSE 2003)

- Introduction - Events of the past portend the future
- Your own personal experiences
- Conclusion - influenced my personality, making me more sober, cautious, humble and God fearing

Events of the past portend the future, sometimes giving new direction to our life altogether. The humiliating experience of being thrown out of a train because of his colour, strengthened Mahatma Gandhi resolve to fight the British. The rest as we all know is history. Thus often unseemly incidents influence our life and personality.

Looking back at the last ten years of my life, I distinctly recall an incident when I was studying in class VI. That day I had gone to school on my brand new Hero cycle. I had embellished this first worldly possession of mine with new seat cover, chains cover, rear mirrors, etc. In my characteristic flamboyant style, I parked the cycle in the cycle stand, to the envy of my friends. After the school got over, I ran to collect it from the stand, but there was no trace of it. My heart skipped a beat, as I looked around fugitively, but it had just vanished into thin air. I lodged a report with the school authorities, who in turn called the police, but all in vain. I was reprimanded by all, including my parents, for my carelessness in not locking the cycle while parking. Even now, just thinking about this incident, embarrasses me no end. I had however learned the virtue of being careful and cautious. Gone was my flamboyance, making me more sober and fastidious.

The other incident happened about two years ago, when I fell severely ill. I was running high fever for nearly a month, which the doctors were unable to diagnose. All test for malaria, jaundice proved negative. The long hours of solitude in the hospital, made me restless and ill tempered. My mother consoled and prayed for me. Initially I ridiculed her for it, but her firm resolve and faith in the Almighty, finally moved me. She read the Ramayana, and the Mahabharata to me, which strengthened my resolve to fight the illness. It also gave me new insight into life, and strengthened my resolve to fight against odds. I found myself praying, -a thing I had never done till then. By the end of the month, I had finally recovered from the mysterious disease, which was later diagnosed to be meningitis. The days spent in the hospital, were indeed the most horrifying. The pain, suffering and solitude, made my life very miserable. I was however able to bear it all, because of my new found faith in God.

These two incidents were milestones in the last ten years of my life, which profoundly influenced my personality, making me more sober, cautious, humble and God fearing.

ASSIGNMENTS

- You had gone to a riverbank for a picnic along with your friends. You suddenly hear the shout of someone crying for help. Describe what happened thereafter.
- You are among the spectators watching a hockey match when suddenly it begins to rain. Describe the scene before during and after the rain.

Write a short story to illustrate the proverb, 'Knowledge is power'

(ICSE 2003)

"Vijay Bhaiya Zindabad. Jeet mubarak", shouted the motley crowd of people assembled at the stadium, to welcome their new leader, as he walked in to address them. A tall, lean, strikingly handsome man, dressed in spotless white chooridar pyjama kurta, walked up to the dais, raising his hands to acknowledge the greetings of the people. He was profusely garlanded by the elite of the town, who had come to honour their elected representative to the state assembly. His bosom friend Piyush, with tears in his eyes watched him from a distance. He still could not believe, that his modest and unassuming friend, had become a celebrity.

Vijay's trek to glory was not all that easy. After completing his schooling in the village Vijay went to Varanasi for higher education. He eventually completed his master's degree in agriculture from Banaras Hindu University. His friend Piyush however stayed back in the village, and took up a mundane job in the city nearby, Unlike other youths, Piyush returned to his native village, to put his knowledge to practical use, for the benefit of the villagers. Initially; all his friends and peers rebuked him for wasting his talent in the god forsaken village, instead of taking up a job in the city. Unperturbed by criticism, Vijay continued to work on his fann, applying his knowledge to improve the yield of his crops.

His scientific method of farming, soon caught the attention of the villagers. They came rushing to him, for advice on the type of crops to grow, and the ways to protect them from insects and pests. His willingness to help, and compassion for their well being, soon won their hearts. He became very popular, and gradually people started coming to him, to resolve their personal problems. Having gained their confidence, he formed self-help groups, comprising village youths, and with the help of an NGO developed a proper drainage system for the village.

To alleviate the problem of potable drinking water, he drew the attention of the district authorities, to install hand pumps in the densely populated parts of the village. His knowledge of science came in handy, to produce gober gas from cow dung. This became an alternate fuel for the oppressed housewives of the village .

Thus in a span of five years, he transformed the village into a small town having all the basic amenities of a city. His good work, soon caught the attention of the opposition party. Seeing a sure winner in him, they gave him a ticket to contest the election as their party candidate. The rest was indeed history, with Vijay emerging victorious in the elections This indeed illustrates the aptness of the proverb 'Knowledge is Power'.

ASSIGNMENTS

- Write a short story to illustrate the proverb , 'unity is strength'.
- Write a short story to illustrate the proverb , 'All that glitters is not gold'.
- Write a short story to illustrate the proverb , 'Power corrupts'.

'Society is influenced more by show than by substance'. Relate an incident from your experience, which brings out the truth of this statement.

(ICSE 2002)

- Introduction- In the materialistic society, there is just no place for plain speak or modesty. Blatantly resorted to in the corporate world for influencing people.
- Few examples
- Personal experience at the hands of a renowned event management group of Delhi
        Event titled ' Dance with the stars'.
        Blitzing of advertisements, promoting the program.
- What happened on the day of the event ?
        The tantalising wait for the stars
- The stars failed to make an appearance, What happened thereafter?
- Conclusion- Their advertisement campaign had carried me away which was the basic reason for my disappointment.

In today's highly materialistic society, there is just no place for plain speak or modesty .It is therefore quite common, to find friends and associates bragging about their royal or star connections, for impressing others. We find this being used more blatantly in the corporate world, for advertising their products or services. Many companies resort to gimmicks, just for getting noticed. They make tall claims about their products or services, which are not in conformity to what they offer.

Thus we find a manufacturer of a renowned brand of air conditioners, showing droplets of water freezing in a tap, so that the owner could sleep in peace in their TV advertisements. Similarly, we find star personalities from Bollywood or sports, endorsing products that have no association to their field. Thus we find film stars, extolling the virtues of a car, or a bearded celebrity, eulogizing a particular brand of shaving cream. They justify their actions as advertising gimmicks, for catching the attention of the consumer, in the highly competitive marketplace. No doubt this is all the more possible because, 'Society is influenced more by show than by substance'.

I had first hand experience of the truth of this statement during the Navratri festival last year. 'The Times' a renowned event management group of Delhi organised an event titled ' Dance with the stars'. The program was a Dandiya dance, in the lawns of a prestigious hotel of the city. Renowned stars like Aishwariya Rai, Urmila Matondkar, Raveena Tandon, Salman Khan and my favourite hero Hritik Roshan, were to attend. They launched this program with a blitzing of advertisements, in the print and the electronic media, heralding it as a never before event. Such was the hype created by their advertisements, that the tickets priced at Rs 1000/ each, got sold out on the very first day itself. I was with great difficulty able to manage a ticket for myself after waiting for two hours.

On the D-day, I put on my best attire, and proceeded regally to the main gate. A clutch of youngsters standing there for having a glimpse of the stars, watched me in envy. One lad actually offered me double the amount I had spent on the ticket, if I would part with it. I haughtily rejected his proposition, and ushered myself into the elite company. The show as with all such star studded programs began an hour late. The local orchestra 'Guys', tried their best to regale the crowd with some of the best pop music. The dancers with dandia in their hands, danced away well into the night, but there was no trace of the 'Stars'. Sonia the VJ of channel V, would time and again heighten the anxiety, by announcing that the stars were about to descend. This continued well past midnight, but there was just no trace of the promised stars.

At about half past twelve Sonia introduced the audience to Johnny Lever, Namrata and another starlet of Bollywood, stating that the others could not make it, because of other pressing engagements. It was a big letdown. The crowd grew restless and gave vent to their anger by booing and hooting the organisers. Normalcy returned with great difficulty as Johnny lever with his characteristic jokes made light of the situation. The three-hour program just lasted for an hour, after which the crowd just thinned out. I returned home feeling cheated to the core. I cursed myself for having spent a princely amount on an event, that was just no better than the jam sessions at school.

Indeed, my decision to participate was influenced more by more by show than by substance. Their advertisement campaign 'Dance with the stars' than the joy and gaiety of the dandiya ras had carried me away. This was the basic reason for my disappointment.

ASSIGNMENTS

- Relate an incident that brings out the truth in the statement 'Don't judge a book by its cover'.
- Describe some of your happy and sad moments of school life.

It was a long awaited climax to your period of training for the parachute regiment –the day of the first jump! Describe how you prepared yourself for the parachute drop, the drop itself, and your feeling after the event.

(ICSE 2002)

"Jump", barked the instructor, standing near the exit of the plane as it soared 10000 ft above sea level. My heart skipped a beat, as I nervously fidgeted my feet, trying to muster up courage. After an agonizing long minute, he glared furiously at me shouting, "Jump you fool, others are waiting for their turn". As if on cue I sidestepped, making way for Mohan standing just behind me to go ahead and jump. Mohan looked contemptuously at me, and with a grin ran towards the exit. He was off the plane in a jiffy.

It all appeared so simple, watching Mohan take the plunge. It was however not so, for the para jump was the climax of a month long training. This was a crucial part of the exercise of the parachute regiment of the NCC battalion that I had joined in school. The first week was spent in familiarising ourselves with the basic of air dynamics. This was followed by practical classes, where the nitty gritty of the parachutes were explained. We were also taught the technique of maneuvering the chute, taking into account the direction of the wind. This would later help us to land safely, away from trees and high rise buildings. The training program finally concluded with a special psychological session, in which we were mentally prepared to take the plunge. Our seasoned instructors gave us some very valuable advice, like – never to look down before you jump. Never to panic and lose one's cool while hurtling down space.

The para drop today, was the climax of the month long training, I had initially felt very confident. Yet here I was, afraid of taking the plunge, fumbling and nervous at the last minute. The question that dogged me-what if the chute failed to open? My legs seemed to quiver; as I glanced down from the nearby window. It was now that I remembered the advice of my instructor, "Never look down before you jump"

"Next", barked the instructor. I looked behind me, making way for the others, but there was no one. Steeling myself, I ran toward the exit, and leaped into space, with my eyes shut firmly, and a prayer on my lips. My heart literally jumped into my mouth, as I hurtled down space like a stone. The first few seconds were very agonizing, as I fidgeted with the buckle of the parachute to make it open. I felt a sudden tug as it opened, halting my speedy descent. After that it was smooth sailing, as I drifted into and out of the clouds, sailing over fields, meadows and orchards in the countryside. The sceneric beauty from the great height, was indeed breathtaking. I saw tall buildings which looked like match boxes, the serpentine roads on which plied cars and buses. Their size continued to increase as I descended. The descent took about fifteen minutes, and I enjoyed every moment of it. I could see my friends sailing in the vicinity, frantically waving out to me. I landed in a small field, a little distance away from our base camp with my legs firmly on the ground. Folding my parachute I clamoured up to Sumeet, who had also landed a little distance away from me. Together we jogged down to the camp, exchanging notes of our experiences.

It was overall a thrilling experience, that I shall never forget in my life. The very thought of the traumatizing seconds, just before and after the jump, even today makes my hairs stand on end. But then what is life without risk and adventure? The parachute jump did enhance my will power, and made me more self-confident .It added a new facet to my personality, which was hitherto unknown to me.

ASSIGNMENTS

- Relate an experience that you found thrilling in your life.
- You are to organise a farewell party for your class teacher. Describe in detail what arrangements you would make to make it a success

You have just interviewed a famous person at his/her residence. Write an account of the whole experience. You may include the following points.

(ICSE 2002)

Preparation for the interview – description of the person's home –A brief description of his / her achievements – What happened during the interview –his / her behaviour – general impressions.

Getting an opportunity to interview a politician is not easy, especially if they happen to be a celebrity like Mrs. Maneka Gandhi, the minister of state for statistics and programme implementation. Maneka better known for her single-minded crusade for upholding animal rights. My dogged persistence however paid off, as my request for an interview was finally accepted. Her personal assistant asked me to come on the 1 st of March 2002 at 9 AM sharp, cautioning me to be punctual. I started feeling apprehensive and nervous as the day approached. That morning I meticulously prepared for the interview, carefully choosing questions on her life and passion.

I reached 10 Ashoka Road; the official residence of the minister on the dot. The whitewashed building was like any other government bungalow. The security guard after checking my credentials allowed me in. I walked up the driveway, adjacent to which was a medium size lawn, fenced with green hedges. The garden was in full bloom, with a variety of flowers. At the far end of the driveway was a white kennel, from which emerged a ferocious looking Alsatian dog, who heralded my presence with his incessant barking.

I was quickly ushered into a big drawing room by a smart butler .The tastefully decorated room had huge oil paintings of famous painters, depicting the pain and agony of animals. The wall-to-wall carpeted room had elegant sofas and chairs. Huge mementos and awards both national and international adorned the showcase. I had barely settled down on a sofa, when Maneka walked up to me, greeting me with a namaste. She had a cheerful grin on her countenance, and sat next to me , enquiring about the purpose of my visit. I was sweating with nervousness, but her informal style and charisma made me more confident of my self. Her reply to a personal question caught me off guard. "I don't want to talk about myself. Let's talk about People for Animals instead." This I later learnt was the second stage of her campaign for animal rights, in which she sought greater participation of the common man. Thanks to her untiring effort, the first stage was already in an advanced stage of implementation. Some of the major victories to her credit are, the various legislation passed by parliament prohibiting the use of animals in circuses, selling birds in cages, and the dissection of animals by students. She however seemed unhappy with the pace of implementation of some of the schemes, and felt that a lot more needs to be done, to ameliorate the lot of animals. "The process had been slow but significant. We started with five people and a capital of Rs 1000/, now we have 160 centers, with about 250000 people working for us," said the minister with an element of pride. Besides this, she also has to her credit, the establishments of numerous hospitals and ambulance services for injured animals, in the various parts of the country.

Her achievements are indeed noteworthy, nevertheless she confesses "There's so much more to be done for animals, I have just made a beginning." This humble remark, speaks volumes of her sincerity of purpose, and the missionary zeal. Her vision for the future is to have an animal hospital in each city of the country, Inclusion of animal law as part of the law curriculum, and banning the slaughter of animals for exports.

She came across as a great visionary, with a clear objective and goal. Her concern for the poor mute animals, are indeed noble and worth emulating. In a world where people are busy lining their pockets. She is busy lining the nests of our feathered and furry friends.

ASSIGNMENTS

- If you were granted three wishes. What would you wish for and why?
- You have just interviewed a renown scientist at his/her residence. Write an account of the whole experience.

Describe a weekly market scene in your area. State why you like or do not like the scene.

(ICSE 2001)

- Introduction-Where and Why are they held ?
- Describe one such market
- State what you like or dislike about this market
- Conclusion -need to make them more organised and accessible.

Weekly markets are a common sight for most towns and villages of the country. These markets, are usually held in the periphery of towns, on one day of the week. They provide an excellent opportunity, for the people of the town and villages, to partake in the exchange process. Thus we find such markets having shops selling the health care and even cosmetics products, available in cities, side by side with agricultural products and farm produce, brought by the peasants from the surrounding villages. This provides a tremendous occasion for the people to savour the good thing of the town as well as villages.

Such a weekly market is held every Sunday in Chinhat very close to Gomtinagar where I live. On this day you find this market full of colour from dawn to dusk, with a lot of hustle and bustle, throughout the day. As you enter the market, located in a big field, adjacent the highway, you see a line of makeshift shops displaying their wares, ranging from toys to clothes, ready made garments and cosmetics. These shops are crowded with rural folks, specially women, busy in selecting the item of their choice, or haggling over the price of a particular product, that has caught their fancy.

Further down the road there is the food grain market, where farmers bring their produce to sell. Huge stockpiles of food grain of different variety are displayed, with the more vociferous of them hawking their wares, by quoting attractive prices. They are crowded with people selecting and comparing the produce, so as to strike a good bargain. This is the most crowded part of the market, with rickshaws, trolleys and coolies jostling their way.

On the other side, across the road, there is a merry go round and a small giant wheel. Children are enjoying themselves on the swings, while their parents are away shopping. The balloon man, the juggler and the snake charmer, have an appreciative audience and seem to be thoroughly enjoying themselves. There is much merrymaking and laughter, which gives the market the semblance of a fair rather than a market.

Further down the road there is a vegetable market, followed by a fish market. This is the dirtiest, and the most congested part of the market. However, you would find, farm fresh vegetables at very attractive prices. This is the favourite joint for people, who usually purchase in bulk. The high pitch sales talk, the price haggling, shouts and arguments ,predictably signify for what it actually is 'the fish market'.

I like such weekly markets, for they provide a very healthy interaction between the urban and the rural folks. They give the rural folks an opportunity to sell their produce directly to the customers thus improving their economic lot. The customers are also benefited by getting farm fresh products at fair prices. What I dislike about such markets are the unhygienic surroundings in which they are held which pose serious health hazards. The traffic congestion also dissuades city folks to shop there.

Thus they play an important role in promoting trade and industry, which is very vital for our economic development. There is however immediate need to make them more organised and accessible.

ASSIGNMENTS

- Relate an incident that brings out the truth in the statement 'The pen is mightier than the sword'.
- Describe a cattle market scene in your area. State why you like or do not like the scene.

You have been on a plane journey recently. While going through a cloud the plane develops engine trouble.
Describe what took place in the plane and how you were saved.

(ICSE 2000)

- When and why you had to fly?
- What happened during the flight?
- What followed when the captain made the announcement? (reactions of the co-passengers)
- What happened thereafter?
- How you were saved?

Traveling by air has always been a very difficult task for me. Since my childhood I had developed a fear for air travel. It was in the month of May last year, when on receiving a call from my mother, I had to rush to Bombay to be at the side of my seriously ill grandmother. Since there was no other mode of transport, I was compelled to take a flight from Delhi to Bombay in flight number IA 814.

When the flight took off, I was in mortal fear and held my breath fearing the worst. An old woman sitting beside me sensed my nervousness and tried to console me. In a moment we were air borne. I had a strange sensation of butterflies in my stomach, which made me uneasy. To divert my mind I settled down with a Sidney Sheldon novel, which kept me engrossed for about an hour. The old woman beside me broke the ice chatting about her family and children. She also laughed at her first experience of air travel, which now for her was a thing of the past. We were served refreshments by the airhostesses and had just about finished, when we felt a big jolt. The cup on the tray fell onto my lap splashing to the ground making it messy. As if in explanation the public address system came to life. "This is your captain speaking. The plane has entered into a thick cluster of clouds causing turbulence. One engine has developed a snag, which is being taken care of. Please do not panic and fasten your safety belts immediately. We shall overcome this problem shortly".

The panic button had inadvertently been pressed, for instead of inspiring confidence it caused great apprehension. I looked around to see fear stalking everyone's face. While some were whispering their doubts about the possibility of the plane running on the single engine, the others were busy tightening their belts and praying silently. The jolts and bumps increased our trauma. People were now clinging desperately to their seats and praying loudly. The old woman beside me was a mental wreck and I found myself consoling and reassuring her. Suddenly the plane was in a spin, losing considerable height instantly. This made me feel sick, I found some people vomiting. In this tense and nerve racking scenario, the public address system again crackled to life, "This is your captain speaking we have an emergency. The second engine of the plane has also developed a snag. We are now preparing for an emergency landing at Santa Cruz airport Bombay. Please don't panic. Follow all emergency instructions and you shall be safe". The message was short, but the impact was stunning. Though he sounded optimistic, the lurking danger of death appeared imminent.

We instinctively obeyed. There was a loud thud as the plane landed on its belly. It seemed as if all hell broke lose, with people trampling over each other to jump out though the emergency hatch. I found myself pushed through, after which I lost consciousness. When I opened my eyes, I found myself in a hospital with my parents beside me. Luckily for me, I had escaped unscratched and was immediately discharged. This ordeal not only overcame my fear for air travel, but also made me more self-confident.

ASSIGNMENT

- You have been on a train journey recently. Your bogie catches fire. Describe what took place in the compartment and how you were saved.

One of your parents has Influenced you considerably. Give details of the influence

(ICSE 2000)

- Introduction — The influence of parents.
- Influence of my mother because of :–
  Her industrious nature and qualities of head and heart.
  Love, compassion and sacrifice
  Will power and perseverance.
- Conclusion — My guide and mentor.

Blessed are we who have parents to look after and care for us. They are but an incarnation of God, for not only do they bring us into the world, but also care for us when we need them the most. They are there in our sorrow, mitigating our grief and jubilant in our joy, multiplying it manifold. We not only imbibe from them good virtues, but also learn to differentiate between good and evil. These leave an indelible impression on our minds and consciously or unconsciously influence our lives. Though I love both my parents, but I am greatly influenced by my mother.

So overwhelming is her influence that I am quite enamoured by her. My friends call me a 'mama's, boy but I couldn't care less. She is by nature very industrious and loving. She is up with the lark and after attending to all our needs she goes to work. In the evening despite being tired, she has ample time for all of us and is the last to rest. Her stellar qualities of head and heart have drawn me close to her. So large hearted and forgiving is her nature, that at times she has stood by me even when I was at fault. Nevertheless being stern enough, so that I do not repeat it again. It is on account of this understanding nature, that I share all my worries and apprehensions with her. No matter what I may have done, I know that I shall get a dispassionate and sound advice from her, without rebuke or retribution.

She is but an embodiment of love and compassion. So unselfish and dedicated is her love, that last summer when I was down with Typhoid, she would stay awake throughout the night a caring for me. She has influenced my outlook to life, that is something more than just becoming successful. I can thus appreciate the importance of the emotion of love and care, which makes us in the true sense a real human being.

Her will power and perseverance makes me proud of her. Despite her busy schedule, she persevered to complete her Ph.D., after having done her post graduation quite some time back. This was in the face of many odds, like insufficient time and my illness. She is but a living example of what we can achieve, if we have the will power and the perseverance.

I do not have to look elsewhere, or in history for my inspiration, for she is my mentor and my motivation. Her only advice to me is to be yourself and have a clear objective of what you want. There is nothing impossible, provided we strive towards it consistently, sooner or later success is but bound to follow. Thus in the words of H.W. Longfellow "Life's battle don't always go to the stronger or the fastest man, But sooner or later the man who wins .Is the man who thinks he can."

ASSIGNMENTS

- One of your teachers has influenced your life. Refer to relevant incidents or relate appropriate anecdotes to show how the action of your teacher has affected your life.
- One of your friends has influenced you considerably. Give details of the influence.

Write a story beginning with "I do not believe in Ghosts".

(ICSE 1999)

- When and how it happened?
- Fear of a ghost haunting.
- Aggravation of fear and apprehension.
- The painful wait for daybreak.
- Realisation of the cause of the strange happenings.

I do not believe in ghosts, but the tinkering of the cup and saucer placed on my study table was indeed mysterious. I had retired early to bed after a tiring day, for my parents had gone out of town. I had been jarred from my sleep on hearing a loud explosion. I woke up with a start and grasped for my torchlight, which I had kept under my pillow, for such an eventuality. Hesitatingly I called out loudly 'Who is there', simultaneously flashing my torch in all directions. I slowly crept towards the switchboard by now wide awake and alert. Reaching it, I switched on the light of the room and went around the house to find nothing amiss. I heaved a sigh of relief and sat on my bed, trying to fathom what could have caused the explosion. It was then that I noticed the strange clinking of the cup in the saucer. I sat up tense and worried. The tentacles of fear were gradually taking hold of me. I pinched myself to ascertain, if I was hallucinating. That was, however, not to be, for I was completely in my senses.

The tinkering stopped and I took a deep breath. The very thought of a ghost in my room made my heart palpitate fast, but my mind refused to accept the logic. I had read many scientific reports, which had dispelled the hypothesis of ghosts, but the films and serials portraying them as real and wicked, mystified them.

Sleep was by now miles away from me, as I decided to keep the lights on and be awake. As if to challenge my resolve, the curtain rod on my window came clanking down, along with the curtain. I sprang to my feet, rushing towards the window shouting 'Who is there? Who is there?' but to no avail. I was by now exasperated and hysteric with fear and apprehension. Glancing towards the wall clock, I saw the needle indicating two a.m. There was still three more hours for daybreak. I prayed fervently to God to get me through this ordeal and save me from the clutches of the ghost, which I was sure was haunting me.

The next three hours were indeed very painful, as I sat on my bed dosing on and off to sleep, occasionally waking up with a start. I was glad to see the day break and got up stretching my limbs which were by now sore. I went to the adjacent room to find splinter of glass strewn on the floor in one corner of the room, which were the remnants of a bulb that probably had caused the explosion.

I switched on the T.V. just as the news broadcast commenced. The newsreader began 'Lucknow experienced a mild earthquake measuring four to five in the Richter scale, leaving a trail of destruction ....'. The words of the announcer subsequently did not seem to register, as suddenly the mysterious happenings of the previous night dawned on me. I thanked God for his grace, in sparing me from the more disastrous consequence.

ASSIGNMENT

- Write a story with the following ending "When it was all over, it was well past midnight."

On a train journey you detect a bomb in the compartment, you help in evacuating and rescuing the passengers and in the confusion lost your baggage. Give a detailed account of your adventure.

(ICSE 1998)

- When it happened?
- How I discovered the bomb?
- Helping and rescuing passengers.
- Lost my baggage.
- Reach home safely.

It was in the month of December in the year 1991, when I boarded the Himgiri express from Jalandhar to Lucknow, after spending my Christmas vacation with my cousins. The train was dot on time and after depositing my luggage on my seat, I got down to bid farewell to them, for they had come to see me off.

At sharp nine p.m. the train departed and I thankfully stretched myself on my berth, after what otherwise was a very tiring day. The train was full to capacity. There was an old man and a child just opposite my berth. I later learned that they were also going to Lucknow, where the old man's son was working. With the usual exchange of pleasantries, I settled down to sleep. My purse accidentally fell through the berth and I hurriedly got up to retrieve it. It was while shifting the baggage, that I saw a metallic object lying in one corner under my berth. I collected my purse and rushed towards the ticket collector with the news of my discovery. I feared the presence of a bomb that was a common occurrence during the Khalistan movement. Soon there was an apprehensive crowd around my berth. No sooner had the conductor come, that the presence of the bomb was confirmed and people rushed towards the door to jump out. I caught hold of the alarm chain and pulled with all my might, after what seemed an eternity the train finally came to a halt.

The moment it halted, people trampled over each other in their haste to move out of the train, with whatever they could lay their hands on. I somehow also managed to get out of the train. By now the compartment had been separated from the train and people were searching for their near and dear ones. It was then, when Mr. Fared Ali sobbingly told me that his grandson was probably in the compartment. He pleaded with the passengers to help him retrieve the child. His plea, however, fell on deaf ears, as none were willing to enter the compartment that could just blow up about any moment. Seeing the old man's grief, I decided to venture into the compartment. Taking a powerful torch I peered in shouting, 'Salim, Salim'. My shouts were answered by a frail voice calling out for help. I saw him lying on the floor below one berth, grievously injured. Lugging him on my shoulder, I leapt towards the door, scrambling down the train. No sooner had I set my foot on the ground that the compartment literally blew up behind me. So strong was the impact that it flung us to the ground. We crawled to safety and were immediately hugged by the crowd. The old man with tears in his eyes fell on my feet, thanking me for what I had done.

I looked around for my baggage that I had left on the tracks, but to my dismay it just wasn't there. I desperately searched but all in vain. My tickets, purse everything was in the bag and I was at a loss as to what to do. Fared Ali patted me on my shoulders telling me not to worry, for he would take care.

By this time the relief train had come and we boarded it in the first light of dawn . We reached Lucknow twelve hours behind schedule, to receive a tumultuous welcome, by our friends and relatives who had gathered since morning, keenly awaiting our return.

ASSIGNMENTS

- Write a description of an uncomfortable journey imaginary or real, in which you are a central figure.
- You are returning home by train after an exciting visit abroad. Suddenly you wake up at night to discover that your suitcase containing costly articles has been stolen. Give a vivid account of your feelings at that time and the subsequent efforts you made to recover your suitcase. *ICSE 1989*

Rivers and Lakes are always interesting and commercially important to People who Live near them. Describe some of the ways in which people living close to a lake or a river use it to their advantage commercially and also for their relaxation and amusement all through the year.

(ICSE 1999)

- Introduction — Role of rivers and lakes in our lives
    - It is the lifeline for the people.
- Their important role in the spread of civilisation.
    - Historic examples being the Indus valley civilisation.
    - Worshipped by the Hindus, for their life giving role
- Their importance even today, for people living close to a lake or a river.
  An indispensable source of drinking water.
  Provides water for Irrigation and Horticulture.
  Provides a source of livelihood to the fishermen who fish in their water.
  Makes available water for industrial use by big factories.
  An invaluable source for entertainment. relaxation and a great tourist attraction.
- The apathy shown by people is a cause for concern because of :–
  Pollution of the rivers and lakes by dumping sewage.
  Dumping hazardous chemicals.
- Conclusion — They are the lifelines for the people staying close to them and hence their purity must be preserved.

Rivers and lakes have always played an important role in our lives, since times immemorial. It is on account of them that it has been possible to sustain life on the universe. They are and shall always remain the lifeline for the people, who dwell close to them.

It was because of their life-sustaining role, that we find all great civilisations existing on the banks of rivers. Thus we had the great Indus valley civilisation on the banks of the river Indus and the Egyptian civilisation on the banks of the river Nile. The people worshipped the rivers, while the Hindu mythology treating them as sacred. Their importance can be gauzed from the fact that, we call Egypt the gift of the river Nile, for had it not been for this river, the country would have been a vast desert.

Their importance has not diminished till this day, for they provide to the people living close by, with an indispensable source of drinking water throughout the year. Their water is used for irrigating the food grain and the horticulture crops, which provide food and vegetables. They thus provide people with the two most essential factors for sustaining life, that is food and water.

They are also the source of livelihood for the fishermen, who fish in their water. They thus provide the inhabitants, fish and other aquatic products to eat.

The rivers and lakes also play an important role in our economic development and progress. Large industries are set up near them, so that water that is required for the industrial process is available from them. They are also used to ferry goods from one place to the other by boats and steamers, which are an economical means of transport.

Their munificence does not end here, for they also provide an invaluable source of entertainment, relaxation and amusement. Thus people can revel in fishing, boating and engaging in various water sports like water surfing, motor boating, etc. In some places we find they are an important tourist attraction, as we see in the Dal lake in Srinagar .The Shikaras and Houseboats on this lake are a tourist delight and people from far and near flock to savour its beauty.

It is indeed very unfortunate; to see the very people for whom the rivers and lakes bestow so much, pollute their water with sewage, hazardous chemical and other biodegradable wastes. This renders their life giving water poisonous.

The rivers and the lakes are in the true sense lifeline for the people staying close to them. It is, therefore, our moral duty to ensure, that we do not contaminate this wonderful blessing bestowed on us and turn it into a curse, for ourselves as well as for our future generations.

You are sleeping in your bedroom. Someone knocks at your door. You wake up to see a boy who says he has come from outer space. Write an account of what he tells about his life in space.

— (ICSE 1998)

- Introduction — When and where?
- Watched a movie and then went to sleep.
- Knock on the door, enter man from Mars.
- Life on Mars.
- Unusual experience.

The night was cold, a thick fog hung outside, which I could see from my window. In the moonlight, the fog appeared like clouds descending on the earth. How I wished I could go out and be amongst the clouds, but here I was trying to catch some sleep, which was eluding me .My mother had just put me to bed wishing me sweet dreams, but sleep was miles away from me.

I paced the floor up and down, clutching the shawl to myself and switched on the Television to see if there was any interesting programme on the channel. The Movie 'Mars Attacks' 'was being aired, of which I had read good reviews in the press. It was an exciting movie about strange unpredictable creatures from Mars landing on earth. They were welcomed by the American public, to be later annihilated by a mere misunderstanding of releasing a pigeon, as a gesture of peace. The wanton destruction they brought about, ultimately to flee on hearing a typical classical music. The movie kept me spell bound. After it was over, I stretched myself on the bed and fell fast asleep.

There was a knock on my door, I woke up to see before me a strange looking boy, with two antenna like objects sticking out of his head over a hairy body. His owl like round eyes resembled the characters I had just seen from Mars. I screamed in fright, but he said something in an alien language and gesticulated with his hands, indicating that he meant no harm. I stared at him in disbelief unable to even scream. Sensing that I was frightened, he gave me a translator to put on my ears that would allow me to understand his language. I hesitatingly agreed and learnt that he indeed had come from Mars. He wanted to take me to his friends and show me his planet. I politely refused, telling him that I had my Math's exams the very next day and hence could not oblige. He extended his thin wiry like hand in friendship, but I was wary of him and chose to do namaste instead. Though he sounded friendly, I was scared for I knew not what would offend him.

He talked about life in Mars, telling me that it is much bigger than our planet earth, having its own solar system. They do not eat, for they survive on noble gases that are in abundance. Seeing that I was impressed, he continued to brag about the superiority of his race. I bore with it for quite some time. However, unable to take it any longer, I politely requested him to let me sleep, for I had to wake up early, to attend school.

He reacted with alacrity. Snatching the translator from my hand, he pointed his gun at me and in a flash I was in flames .I screamed with all my might "Help, Help, this boy from Mars has killed me." I suddenly felt a splash of cold water on my face. Opening my eyes I saw my mother peering down at me, "What's the matter son" said she. How relieved I was to realise, that it was all but a dream.

ASSIGNMENTS

- An interesting Dream.
- A frightening nightmare.

Write a story in which a suitcase, a photographer and a soldier play an important role.

(ICSE 1997)

- Introductory background (When).
- The incident (How). Arrival of the man with briefcase.
- Arrival of the soldier.
- Cause for alarm.
- Courage shown by the soldier.
- Conclusion — No dearth of patriots .

This story pertains to the period when terrorism in Punjab was at its peak. The people in the state lived under the shadow of terror, let loose by mercenaries from across the border. There were daily incidents of murder, bomb blast and other heinous crimes committed by these misguided elements. The people lived in constant fear for their lives and property. The police were constantly publishing photographs of dreaded terrorists and offering handsome rewards, to the person providing information for their capture dead or alive.

One fine day a clean-shaven, muscular built gentleman walked into the studio located in Civil Lines, the main commercial market of Hoshirapur, carrying a medium size suitcase. He requested the photographer for a passport size photograph, which he wanted to affix on his visa application. He told the photographer that he had to leave for Delhi the very next day and hence, the photograph would be required positively by late evening. He also requested him to keep his suitcase, as he had some urgent shopping to do prior to his departure for Delhi. The photographer was initially reluctant, but seeing a hundred rupee note thrusted into his pocket he agreed. He immediately set about taking the photograph and reassured him about the same being ready by six p.m.

No sooner had the strange gentleman left the shop, than the photograph's friend Col. A.K. Singh, a soldier in the Indian Army walked in, carrying the local daily newspaper. After the usual exchange of pleasantries, Col. Singh thrust the newspaper into his hands, expressing his anxiety over the deterioration of the law and order condition of the state. On the cover page was a photograph of a terrorist, whom the police suspected to be behind the latest spurt of terrorist activities. The photographer was taken aback, for the photograph bore a striking resemblance to the stranger who had just left the shop. He immediately told Col. Singh as to what had transpired.

Col. Singh heard him intently, after which he instructed him to call the local police immediately. The telephone lines were dead. It was then that the Colonel took charge. Fearing the worst, he instructed all the shopkeepers to immediately vacate the building. The word spread like wildfire and within no time the entire commercial center wore a deserted look, as everyone scampered for safety.

Col. Singh then very cautiously moved toward the suitcase and with deft fingers opened it. There was indeed a time bomb set of to explode within a minute. With trembling fingers he set about defusing the deadly device. Time seemed to stand still, as the timer in the device seemed to make a deafening sound as it ticked away. We all held our breath in apprehension. The device was defused and we heaved a sigh of relief. The police reinforcement had also come by now and they took the awesome briefcase into their custody. By now Col. Singh had become an instant hero, press photographer crowded him trying to record his picture and statement in their video cameras. The grateful residents offered him a cash reward for his exemplary bravery, which he politely declined for he had just done his duty.

The future of the country can never be in peril, till we have such soldiers who are ready to sacrifice theirs present, so that we can live a happy tomorrow.

ASSIGNMENTS

- Write a story in which a soldier, a child and a pet dog play an important part.   *ICSE 1991*
- A mysterious telephone call awakens you at night. Describe what it leads to.

You have represented your school in National Inter School Competition. Describe your excitement on being selected, the competition and the joy you felt at having brought honours to your school.

(ICSE 1996)

- Preparation for selection.
- Selection to the team.
- Qualifying in the finals.
- Performance in the finals.
- Presentation of awards.

I had for quite sometime been preparing myself, for the extempore debating competition to be held in our school. This was a prelude to selecting the team, which was to represent the school in the National Inter school competition being held at Vigyan Bhawan in New Delhi on 10th October. This competition was being held for the first time on a national level. Students from schools across the country would be participating, in various extra curricular activities like music, singing, dancing, dramatics, debating and quiz competition. Besides awarding individual performance, shields would also be awarded to schools sending the best team. It was therefore, a matter of pride, to represent the school at such an event.

It was with keen anticipation, that I counted the days for the debating competition. On the D-day, I was initially quite nervous with stage fright as my name was announced. It was an extempore debate, the topic of which would be known to me by a draw of lot. Fortunately for me, I had to speak on "The present education system has outlived its use". This subject being close to my heart I spoke for the motion, with thorough reasoning and conviction. The applause boosted my confidence. With bated breath, I waited for the result to be announced. My name was announced in the team that left me overjoyed. and speechless I was applauded by my friends and prepared to leave for the national competition beginning next week.

The national meet was indeed a gala affair, with teams from reputed colleges taking part. So enamoured was I by their high profile image, that initially I did feel uncomfortable. But as the preliminary round got over, I gained confidence and was finally selected to participate in the final round. This was to be held on the concluding day of the competition.

My heart skipped a beat, as I approach the stage to speak on a subject unknown to me till then. There had been other speakers before me and their applause sort of intimidated me. With shaking hands I opened the slip offered to me by the compere .The subject of the speech was, "Should students take part in extracurricular activities ". I was given three minutes to plan my speech, after which I had to speak extempore for ten minutes. Having participated in school events, I did have first hand knowledge on the subject. I used this to maximum advantage giving funny anecdotes and examples that caught the imagination of the audience. When I had finished, the tremendous round of applause was proof enough, of my having done a good job. My colleagues also congratulated me.

When the results were announced, it was a matter of satisfaction for me, that I was judged the best speaker. As I walked towards the dais, to receive the award from the Lt. Governor of Delhi, I was given a standing ovation by the crowd. Besides receiving the coveted award, our college also bagged the shield for the best debating team. . It was indeed a matter of pride for me for having won this award and also an honour for our college, to which we owe so much.

ASSIGNMENT

- You have to represent your school in an Inter school sports meet. Describe your excitement on being selected in the team, the competition and your feelings on having won laurels for your school.

There are several Humourous Incidents that occur in every Family. Describe one such event that you and your family found really amusing

(ICSE 1991)

Or
Describe one Embarrassing/Awkward Incident that you and your family found really amusing.

- Introduction.
- The incident, when, where and how?
- What happened? Why I was frightened?
- The rescue.
- Conclusion.

Yesterday while we all were sitting for dinner, I asked my elder brother to drop me to my friends place the next day. The aftermath of this statement was, a heated argument, in which he exclaimed with disgust, "I wish I had left you in that ditch, so that you would not trouble me now." What followed, was a deep stunning silence, after which we all burst out laughing.

The incident relates to what happened eight years ago. I had gone to attend the marriage of my cousin sister at Bareilly. All the children of our family had collected on this occasion, after a long period of time. So one day in the afternoon, we went to play cricket in the barren ground behind the house. On running after the ball, I saw it disappear near by. I looked around carefully and at last saw it deep down in a ditch. I thought I could collect it with my hand and therefore, lying down on the ground, I stretched my hand as far as possible. Slowly inching forward, I was just about reaching it, when lo and behold, to my horror I plunged head over heels into the ditch. Recovering from the shock, I sat down to survey my surroundings. My grief knew no bounds, when I saw that what I had thought to be a ball, was actually a hollow plastic shell.

I started screaming for help, but it seemed everyone had turn a deaf ear. The scene inside the ditch was fearful, with many spiders and lizards in it. My clothes were soiled and I was prespiring badly. As it was getting dark, I started getting terrified, at the thought of spending the night in this well of misery. All my efforts to get out of the well were in vain.

All of a sudden, I felt something crawling on my feet. Fearing the worst I decided not to move, for I had heard that snakes bite when distracted. However, I gathered courage and peeped down. To my utter relief I saw nothing but a leafy twig, entwined around my ankle. Just then, I heard the sound of my brother calling out to me, I also started shouting on top of my voice. After what seemed eternity, he was able to locate me and I could not hide my joy when I saw him peering down with the help of his torch. He helped me come out, with the rope, which he found nearby. I was weeping inconsolably, while he comforted me. We then returned home to the joy of the entire family.

Everyone was amazed to see me in that state. I ran towards my mother crying and she embraced me. After having a quick bath and putting on fresh clothes, I narrated the incident to all of them. At first they felt sorry for me, but then my cousins started teasing me saying, that I was better in the company of spiders and lizards in the well. Initially I was offended, but seeing that they were just pulling my leg, laughed heartedly. Reliving the incident sends a chill down my spine but at the same time tickles me no end.

ASSIGNMENT

- Describe one frightening incident that you and your family found really nightmarish.

Write a story on Two Old Women, a Small Child and an Aeroplane Playing an important role.

Or

Write a story titled 'The Hijacking'.

- Introductory background.
- When and where it happened?
- How it happened?
- The old ladies diverted attention of hijacker.
- Conclusion. Return to a hero's welcome.

I was returning to India after having completed my studies abroad. The yearning to meet my parents and friends grew with every passing minute as I boarded the plane. I heaved a sigh of relief as I was on the last lap of the journey. Vision of my near and dear ones flooded before me, as I settled down for the long flight.

Seated next to me was a boy who was about five years old, he was visiting his grandma in India and was travelling alone. Next to him were two old ladies in their late fifties, who despite their gray hair were bubbling with excitement and chattering excitely causing some distraction. No sooner had the plane taken off from London aerodrome, the boy jumped out of his seat removing his seat belt and started roaming about in the plane. He was very candid and spoke to every one in the plane. The old ladies called the boy and gave him two chocolates, he sat near them and answered all their questions with child like innocence. The air- hostess brought some snacks and tea, which was indeed very tempting. After having my refreshment, I settled down to complete a novel that I had brought with me. I had about completed my novel, when I heard the captain requesting passengers to fasten the safety belts, as we were about to land at Palam airport.

Just then a young man seated behind me got up and caught hold of the boy, placing a knife on his neck. He warned us to stick to our chairs. Entering the cockpit, he ordered the pilot not to land the plane and proceed to Kabul after refueling. Seeing the delicate situation, the pilot obeyed and requested the ground authorities to make arrangements for refueling. The hijacker demanded the immediate release of a hard-core terrorist from the Tihar jail in Delhi. The plane was by now hovering over the Delhi aerodrome and all the passengers were praying to God for their safety. As if this problem was not enough, the pilot announced that he had fuel for another twenty minutes only. The ground authorities requested the hijacker that they were considering his demands, but he must allow the plane to land safely. The hijacker was adamant and wanted the release of the terrorist, before he would allow the plane to land.

Suddenly one of the old ladies collapsed on the floor, seeing this the other lady shouted at the hijacker for having caused her a heart attack .The Hijacker's attention was momentarily diverted. Sensing this, a well-built young man sitting in the front aisle just near the hijacker, knocked the knife out of his hand. Pandemonium prevailed for a while, as the others pounced on the unarmed hijacker, freeing the boy in the process. He was overpowered and everybody heaved a sigh of relief.

I was surprised to see the old lady who had collapsed on the floor get up and hug her companion, with tears rolling down her cheeks. Their plan had worked. They were inundated with applause for their presence of mind .The plane finally landed at the airport and the hijacker was promptly arrested. We were all accorded a warm welcome from the motley crowd, which had gathered at the airport as news of the hijacking had spread. The child leaped into the open arms of his grandma, who hugged him lovingly. The two old ladies were the cynosure of all eyes and they seemed to be enjoying every bit of it. It was indeed a very eventful homecoming for all of us.

ASSIGNMENTS

- Write a short story titled 'The chase'.
- Give an account of a terrifying experience you had while trying to hitch a ride home one night.
- You see a man drop his wallet while getting into a taxi. You pick up the wallet — narrate what happens after that.
- Write a short story titled 'The Earthquake'. Your story ought to illustrate the fear, panic, chaos and destruction caused by such a disaster.   *ICSE 1984*

Write a short story titled 'What is Real?'

- Introduction — When and where?
- What happened?
- Unusual experience.
- Conclusion .Was it real?

It was a cool pleasant moonlight night in the month of March. The full moon was peeping through the branches of a tree adjacent to my window. The innumerable stars twinkling above added to the glamour of the night .The cool fresh breeze spread the aroma of spring flowers. How I wished I could go out and savour the heavenly sight, but here I was studying for my Math's exams. How I wished somebody could program my brains to absorb the insensitive formulae that I was desperately cramming. I leaned on my chair, closed my eyes and took a deep breath.

All of a sudden there was a loud knock on the door. I opened it standing before me was a strange looking man with two antenna like objects sticking out of his head over a hairy body. I screamed in fright but he said something in an alien language and gesticulated with his hands, indicating that he meant no harm. I stared at him in disbelief unable to even scream. Sensing that I was frightened, he gave me a trasnslator to put on my ears that would allow me to understand his language. I hesitatingly agreed and learnt that he wanted to take me to his friends and show me his planet. I politely refused, telling him that I had my Math's exams the very next day and had to prepare for it. His answer indeed surprised me, for he said that he would program my mind for the exam and I need not worry. This relieved me immediately of my anxiety and I prepared to go.

With a press of a button on his wrist, we were in his spaceship that was orbiting the earth to meet his friends. When I saw them, I couldn't help laughing because they looked so funny. Fortunately they did not mind my laughing and we became friends. I offered them some sweets that I had brought with me. After a long chat I suddenly looked out of the spaceship and saw my school, which reminded me of my exams. After what seemed like eternity, I returned home. Now it was time to say Good bye ! They shook my hands so vigorously that my arm ached terribly. I screamed and pulled away with all my might. Lo and behold! I found myself on the floor clutching my book and screaming incoherently. My mother came rushing in. I related all that had happened but she smiled and comforted me putting me to sleep. The next day was my exam. I did well (I think so). In the evening my teacher rang me up and asked me to meet her the next day.

When I went to meet my teacher she gave me my answer sheet and asked me to read it. aloud. I couldn't read a word, for it was in a language totally alien to me. But my handwriting was distinct. "What is this dear ?" she shouted indignantly. I went blank for a moment and the words that I finally uttered were "What? Have I written it ?" Needless to say I got a duck in the exam, but till today I cannot get over the weird experience. Was it real or just a dream?

ASSIGNMENT

- Write a story beginning with "I could not believe my eyes............."

Write a composition titled 'The Great Fraud'.
Or
The Betrayal

- Introduction — Brief background.
- My total involvement in the game.
- Disclosure of match fixing.
- Conclusion — The great fraud /betrayal perpetuated on the audience.

Hurrah! I shouted jumping with joy, as Ganguly scored the winning run in the first one-day international match played at Delhi, between South Africa and India. It had indeed been quite sometime, since India had scored a victory over South Africa. The three consecutive test matches which were lost, had dampened my cricketing spirit. This was indeed a moment of celebration and I along with my friends went on a celebrating spree, shouting, singing and bursting crackers late into the night.

The game of cricket completely mesmerises me, it is indeed a "Game of chance". In one moment, you are right on top of the game with a near certain win, while in the next you are down in the dumps. This is what appeals to me and makes my friends call me a 'cricketing maniac'. It is at its height during any test or one day series, when I prefer to stick to the T.V. watching each movement of the ball with great enthusiasm. This at times rubs on other members of the family, who join me in my exclamation of a century well made, or a shout of disgrunt on a foolish dismissal. These are the days when I do nothing but, 'eat, sleep and dream cricket'. The win in the first one-day test was indeed rejuvenating, this was followed by consecutive wins in the second and the third test under more palpitating conditions. Each ball or a stroke stopping many a heartbeat. It was in fact a clean sweep. We had won all the three one day test, in sharp contrast to our dismal performance in the test series against the same side. Indeed cricket was gentlemen's game of chance and once again India had emerged right on top of the game. There followed a lot of backslapping and applause, while we celebrated the return of the champions.

One day a small news clipping on the front page caught my attention "Cronje's link with Indian bookies'. I read it in utter disbelieve, there were allegations against Cronje, the South African captain, for his role in fixing matches through Indian bookies. My immediate reaction was, dismissing it as a humbug created by media. This was, however, not to be, for what followed was, concrete evidence, dramatic denials and ultimately confession by Cronje himself. This left me along with many other cricket enthusiasts shattered.

To think that our yells of joy and excitement were all in vain, is something that we cannot get over till date. We had indeed been cheated and betrayed. To further add insult to injury, there were explosive interviews given by Manoj Prabhakar in 'tahelka.com' and to media confirming our worst fears. We had indeed been betrayed for long. While the allegations and counter allegations will take some time to settle. One thing is certain, cricket will never be the same again at least for me, for no longer will my cheers be as loud, nor my enthusiasm as great.

ASSIGNMENT

- "They can who think they can". Relate an incident of your experience ,which brings out the truth of the statement.

Write a composition beginning with, "If only I had told the Truth.............."

- When and where the incident happened?
- How it happened?
- What followed thereafter?
- Meeting the demands.
- Regretting the lie. Conclusion.

If only I had told the truth my friend Sweta would have been alive today. I just cannot forget the fateful day last year, when Sweta and I went for our usual stroll in the park near by. It was approaching dusk and the park that normally was quite crowded wore a deserted look. Sensing something unusual we decided to return.

Just as we came out of the park a white Maruti van screeched to a halt and two men jumped out. While one of them caught hold of my friend, the other gagged me with a piece of cloth and tied my hands behind my back. Thrusting a piece of paper, he threatened that I would not see my friend alive, if I went to the police. Before I could gather my wits they were gone. I struggled for what seemed to me an eternity, before I could free myself with the help of a good samaritan. I then rushed home to inform my parents of the incident.

While we were heatedly debating over the ransom note of Rupees. two lakhs demanded by the kidnappers, the police patrol that was near by called me for recording my statement. On the insistence of Sweta's parents, I decided not to tell the truth. I told them that it was one of my friend's pranks, in which she had tied me up just to frighten me. This is one lie that I shall regret throughout my life.

I along with Sweta's father reached the dhaba on the highway, which was the appointed place with the ransom amount in a briefcase. It was six p.m. and the road was quite deserted, except for an occasional car or vehicle that passed by. Seeing us standing on the highway with a morose look on our face, an occasional driver inquired if we needed help, but we waved them off .Our anxiety grew with every passing minute. It was well over an hour from the time we had been informed. Growing restless, I decided to explore the surroundings. There was a small hut next to the dhaba, as if by intuition I walked towards it and peered inside. In the dim light of setting Sun, I could make out the silhouette of a girl lying on the cot. I instinctively called out to Sweta's father and he rushed in with a torch that he had brought with him.

My worst fears were confounded, when in the light of the torch, I recognized my friend who was no more. What followed thereafter is something I would like to forget, but nightmares are not easily forgotten. I still have a nagging feeling of guilt, that had I told the truth to the police, my friend Sweta would have been alive today.

ASSIGNMENTS

- Write a story beginning with, I felt the ground slipping beneath my feet...........
- Write a story titled 'Never Again'.

A day when everything went wrong in school

- Introduction.
- When and what happened?
- Major incident (What happened?).
- Other incidents.
- Conclusion.

A day in school is normally like any other day, but there is a day that we would like to forget, in which nothing right seemed to happen. Till today I have nightmares recalling the day and wish I do not have to relive the same again.

It was on the first of September last year and we were in the midst of our half yearly exams, that I got up an hour late. I was feeling quite dizzy, for I had gone to sleep late last night, after giving finishing touches to my preparation for the English Language test. The look at my alarm clock left me pale. I had just ten minutes to board the bus for school. I scrambled from bed and finished my daily chores in a jiffy. I had barely got dressed when the blaring horn of the bus sounded. Clutching my bag, I hounded out of the driveway but to my dismay the bus was nowhere in sight. Rushing back I entreated my father to drop me to school in his car. He grudgingly agreed, after giving me a pep talk on being so careless.

I reached school about twenty minutes late, being immediately ticked off by the monitor and asked to stay back after school as punishment. I took this in my stride, cursing my ill stars for the humiliation. On reaching my class I took my seat and settled down to face the test. The question paper left me dumbstruck. Was I hallucinating? I pinched myself to see whether I was in my senses. Yes I was. I glanced at my watch, it was indeed the first of September and the test slated was not English but Maths. The earth seemed to slip beneath me, as I tried to come to terms with this catastrophe. Maths itself was my Achilles heel, but to give a test without any preparation was indeed a nightmare. I however gathered my wits and began to attempt the questions with trembling hands.

After two hours the ordeal was finally over. I had visions of a sound whacking, which were in store for me. I was morose throughout the lunch recess and my friend Arvind comforted me, allaying my fears. As if this was not enough, I was punished for not bringing the science book and was asked to stand outside class. I heaved a sigh of relief on hearing the toll of the school bell. But alas! I had to stay back for detention, which meant catching a public bus to reach home.

The bus journey home was an altogether shattering experience. I had first hand experience of how sardines must feel, being so tightly packed. It is now over a year, but I have still illusions of this nightmare of that day when everything went wrong in school. Recalling it sends a shiver down my spine.

ASSIGNMENTS

- Write a description of the happiest day in your life.
- Write about the unhappiest day of your life.

Write an original story about a man, whose doctor has given him three months to live

- Introduction — Death the ultimate truth.
- Story background.
- What happens after doctors advise?
- What else happens?
- Conclusion.

"This life at best is as inn and we the passengers", said James Howell. It is quite evident from this saying that death is the ultimate of all human activities and is a universal truth .The learned man being aware of this are not scared of death. However, life becomes miserable for a normal person, who is aware of the time duration for which he is going to live.

This is what happened to Richard Brown, a middle class widower who worked in the municipal office of a town. He had no one to care for him, as he had no children and his beloved wife had also left for her heavenly abode some ten years ago. Richard as I knew him, was a man of strong character with a soft and gentle disposition. He was popular with the children of the neighbourhood, with whom he used to play in the evening or on weekends. The children of the area called him Richi Uncle. However, age was catching up on him and he no longer was as agile nor energetic to play cricket with them. One day on the suggestion of a local lad, Richard went to see the doctor to enquire of his ailment. The doctor after a medical examination asked him to carry out a few tests including blood test, sugar test and various other pathological examinations, before he could make a final diagnosis.

A week elapsed and on the appointed day, Richard set forth to collect his pathological report. The doctor on seeing the report turned morose and with a sympathetic tone told him, that he was suffering from blood cancer that was in the terminal stage. So grave and hopeless was his condition that he had only three months to live. This unexpected piece of bad news came as a shock to him, for he had just reconciled from the grief of losing his wife. He was very anguished and spent sleepless nights mulling over his fate. He just could not fathom as to why God was so unkind to him. But time is a great healer and in course of time he reconciled to his fate. Bowing to the wishes of God almighty that knows best, he donated all his worldly possessions including moveable and immovable property as charity to the local orphanage of the town. He also took retirement from his job and devoted himself to the service of the poor and the education of the children in his neighbourhood.

Two months passed and now Richard started counting his days. One fine day he received a call from the same doctor, who apologized for his mistake, telling him that his report had got mixed up with the report of another patient with the same name . His blood report was quite normal and therefore, he would live a normal life. The news so excited Richard, but the thought of having lost everything came as a shock, which proved fatal for him and he collapsed clutching the receiver.

Death is indeed very certain, but no one can predict as to when, where, how and in what shape it may come. We are however unnecessarily afraid of it little realising the truth as echoed by William Shakespeare when he says "All that lives must die, Passing through nature to eternity."

ASSIGNMENT

- Write an original short story of a man who has been awarded death sentence after three months.

You had to catch a bus, write what you saw at the bus station and your experience there before your bus arrived
Or
A visit to a bus station

- Introduction — Why I had to undertake bus travel.
- The scene at the bus stand.
- An interesting incident.
- Settled down for the journey with a resolve.

I normally detest bus travel, not because it is uncomfortable, which it definitely is, but because it gives me a feeling of claustrophobia, that I have experienced since childhood, However last month my uncle summoned me urgently to Delhi, in connection with my long pending Visa application. Since a train ticket at such a short notice was highly improbable, I was left with no other alternative but to undertake the journey by bus. I therefore packed my bag and set forth to the bus station.

On reaching the station, I saw a huge queue at the counter where tickets were being sold. I queued up for the ticket nestling my briefcase close to me. Besides me there were several other queues, with countless passengers standing. The station was literally milling with people. Some were sitting on benches, others were perched on their luggage, while still others were lying asleep with their bags under their head, as if prepared for an eternal wait. All around there was dirt and squalor, with an occasional cow, or a dog making a detour of the place, in search of eatables thrown by passengers. How I hated myself to be amidst this squalour, but brushing aside this thought, I nudged along in my queue which was but advancing at a snails pace. There was an occasional fraying of tempers, as someone tried to jump the queue that made the nudging and jostling quite unpleasant.

It was then that a person standing a little distance from me cried out aloud, that his pocket had been picked. He immediately collared the person pushing him, accusing him of the offence. I instinctively felt for my purse and was relieved to find it intact. By now the scuffle had turned out to a free for all, with allegation and counter allegations. Fortunately a beat constable seeing the commotion arrived on the scene and took both the warring parties aside. On checking the person of the accused, the offending purse was found. While the public wanted to teach the pickpocket a lesson, the constable handled the situation with tact and led the culprit away in handcuff.

The commotion having subsided we again queued up for our tickets. I had by now advanced in my queue and in a short while I had my ticket, which I clutched in my hand and looked around for a place to rest my self. Seeing none, I placed my briefcase near a tea stall and sat on it sipping the hot tea. This relaxed me after the nerve wrecking experience of buying a ticket.

No sooner was the bus sighted, that people rushed towards it. I also collected my wits and scrambled towards it. After a lot of pushing and jostling, I found myself in the bus. So tired was I, that I thankfully sat on the first vacant seat which came my way. After about half an hour wait, the bus finally pulled out of the station. I however made a mental note, never to undertake such a long journey by bus, which left me weary well before the journey even began.

ASSIGNMENTS

- A view from a ship overlooking the harbour.
- A scene in a shopping plaza.

You had to go to the Railway Station to receive your friend. The train was one hour late. Hence you had to wait at the station. Describe what you saw and felt.

Or

The scene at the Railway Station

- Introduction — When and Why?
- Enquired from enquiry.
- Reached station.
- Scene at the station.
- An incident.
- Arrival of the train.

It was during the Christmas holidays that my friend Rohit rang up from Delhi, to inform that he was coming to Lucknow. He had to attend a marriage and wanted to know if I could receive him at the station. I enthusiastically volunteered, for the prospect of seeing my friend after a gap of five years was indeed exhilarating. Though the thought of visiting the railway station, with all the filth and dirt was daunting, but all the same there was nothing I could do about it.

The train's estimated time of arrival was seven A.M, so after confirming that it was running on time, I set forth to the railway station which was about twenty minutes drive from my residence. On reaching the station at 6.45 A.M, I was informed that the train was an hour late. Cursing the railways for their inefficiency, I trudged along to the enquiry office and indignantly questioned the clerk for the wrong information given on phone. He was quite unapologetic and vague .On prodding him, I learnt that there was a derailment at Hardoi about sixty kilometers from Lucknow, which was the cause of the delay.

Since it was inadvisable to return home, I decided to wait and looked around for a place to rest. To my dismay there was none, for the platform was milling with people. There were passengers waiting for trains, or some of them like me were waiting to receive their near and dear ones. There were still others, who with their luggage under their head were snoring away to glory. I really admired their capacity to sleep, amidst the din and cry of hawkers and vendors. A cow making a detour of the place, came heading towards me. Fearing that it would butt me, I thought it prudent to move away. It however had no such intension, for it picked up a banana peel lying before me.

I was by now feeling quite exhausted, so I took a cup of tea from the vendor close by. While I was sipping my tea, a train screeched to a halt on the platform. There was a commotion as the passengers rushed in, making it difficult for those who were disembarking. There was much shouting and confusion. In this hullabaloo, a lady who had just disembarked from the train yelled, that her chain had been snatched. Hearing her shout, a lad standing close to her broke into a run. He came rushing towards me to escape from the exit .I instinctively flung the cup of hot tea on his face. This startled him and in no time we had overpowered him. The lady profusely thanked me while the Railway Police arrested the culprit.

It was a relief to hear the announcement of the arrival of the Lucknow Mail. I took a vantage point so that I could look into the compartments. The train rolled in and to my relief, I found my friend waving out his handkerchief from one of the compartments. What a happy reunion it was, we hugged each other like long lost friends. All the din, the dirt and the clamour was lost on us, as we walked away with his baggage in tow.

ASSIGNMENTS

- You have gone to a village fair along with your friend. Describe what you saw and felt.
- A visit to a trade fair or exhibition.

A Fighter Pilot who has been believed to be killed in action returns home four years later. Write a story on what awaits him.

- Return of the pilot.
- Recalls the event that led to his capture.
- Returns home to find strangers.
- Informed of his wife's insanity.
- Happy reunion.

It was a bright Sunday morning in the month of December 1975 when squadron leader Arun Gandhi, after a period of four years in the Pakistani prison as a prisoner of war, set foot on his motherland. He was greeted at the airport by the top brass of the defence services and the diplomatic corps, with an army of newsmen trying to capture the historic moment. He strained his eyes, trying to peer through the blistering light of the flashguns, as if searching frantically for someone. The newsmen thrust the microphone before him, asking him questions which he answered almost mechanically.

It was at the press conference, that he related the sequence of events which led to the crash of his MIG 21, well inside Pakistani territory in the 1971 war. The last four years were almost hell and he had given up hope that he would ever be back home. However, here he was, thanks to God almighty. On being quizzed as to why there was nobody from his family to receive him, he was non-plussed murmuring probably they did not know.

After the welcome, he left immediately by train for his home at Lucknow. On knocking the door of his house he was greeted by an old unfamiliar gentleman, who informed him that he had purchased the house from Geeta Gandhi a couple of years ago. She and her daughter had moved out of Lucknow, to an undisclosed destination following the news of his death.

So stunned was he by this piece of news, that he stared at the gentleman with utter disbelief. Collecting his wits he trudged along to his friends house close by. It was there that Rohit informed him about Geeta, who had lost her mental balance on hearing of his death. Her parents had therefore sold the house and taken her to the mental asylum at Agra. They had also passed away last year and in all probability, Geeta would be there in Agra.

Arun and his friend set out for Agra in his car. Throughout the journey the smiling face of his wife and daughter troubled him tremendously. He had feared something bad, when there was nobody at the airport to receive him, but that events could take such a turn had never crossed his mind. The eight hours journey seemed like eternity and by dusk they had reached the mental asylum at Agra. The superintendent of the asylum was very cooperative and arranged for a special meeting with Geeta, warning however, that she was prone to get violent. Being an acknowledged psychiatrist he suggested that Arun should remind her of something touching enough to prod her memory.

With bated breath they waited for Geeta, who came supported by a maid. She had paled considerably and had a blank expression. On seeing Arun she looked at him questionably. Seeing this Arun gave her the chain, which she had lovingly presented to him. She took the chain and on opening the locket saw their snap together. Her countenance softened, as memories came rushing back to her "A...Arun," said she, tears running down her cheeks as she rushed towards him. There were tears in many an eye that was witness to this union.

ASSIGNMENT

- A man sentenced to life imprisonment returns after his sentence has been condoned. Write what awaits him on his return.
- Two men on digging a field find a pot of Gold. Write what happens thereafter.

An entertainment program organised by you on 'Teacher's Day' ends in a flop. Give an account of your feelings and your assessment as to what went wrong.

- Introduction — Preparations for the program.
- What happened on the day?
- The awkward incident.
- My assessment and reasons for the flop.
- Conclusion — Lessons learnt.

As the head of the cultural club, I decided to celebrate the teacher's day, falling on the 5th of September with a difference this year. Since we had real budding talent, it was decided to host a cultural extravaganza. The like of which the school had never seen before. The programmes finally short listed was a play which was a satire on the state of corruption, followed by a musical program by V.J. Orchestra. This was the best in town and also known to me. Since there was hardly a week left for the D-day, we began practicing in earnest staying back after school hours. To ensure smooth running of the programmes, I distributed work among all my friends and things seemed to be working well.

On the D-day I was feeling a bit nervous, but allaying all my fears we set forth with the programme in the school auditorium .The team entrusted with the reception of the teachers, were already on their job, welcoming the teachers with flowers and garlands. The students were getting restless, hence I requested them to kindly remain silent. Welcoming the teachers, I announced the start of a memorable programme for the first time in the school. This was greeted with a loud applause. The programme started with the play 'Corruption'. The curtains went up to show a politician sitting in his drawing room, with some hangers on, pressing his legs. Their dialogues were indeed juicy and in a short while, had the audience hold their sides with laughter.

Things were going along fine, till one of my team mates signaled me to come aside. The look of dismay on his face got me worried. I hastened behind the stage to learn that there was no trace of the orchestra. They had rung up to regret their participation, on account of the indisposition of their key artists. The news came as a bombshell to me, for I had not in my wildest dream anticipated such an eventuality. We had no alternative plan whatsoever .We again put our heads together and decided to approach Ashok, who was a talented singer to save the day for us. An emissary was sent to fetch him immediately. By now the play was approaching the climax. The main hero, playing the role of the politician, got up to make a small speech. He began well, but soon faltered and even prompting did not help. By now the boys were hooting and jeering and thus he had to beat a hasty retreat. The curtains were down but there was no sign of Ashok. My emissary returned with news that he had not come today. Being left with no alternative, I thought it prudent to go before the audience and apologise for this flop show.

Surprisingly, my humble apology brought an instant reaction. Our principal walked up to the stage and patted me on my shoulder, saying, "Well-done boys there is nothing to be sorry about," With a brief thanksgiving, the programme came to an abrupt end.

I was indeed feeling in the dumps and cursed myself for not having anticipated things. Later assessing the sequence of events, I realised that the programme was but doomed to fail .The extremely short time for practice and the lack of any alternate plan, was but courting disaster. I am now much wiser after the event, for not only has it has taught me more humility, but also made me more cautious and realistic.

ASSIGNMENTS

- A Fancy dress competition organised by you in your colony ends in a disaster.
- You have organised a variety entertainment in your school. Give a vivid account of your experience.

The Quarrel

- When and where?
- How the quarrel began?
- The escalation of the quarrel.
- Arrival of the police.
- Returned home.

It was a bitter cold winter morning of December last year. The sun was hiding behind the clouds, making it appear as if it was early morning. A thick fog hung heavy making the visibility quite poor indeed. The harsh cold winter wind deposited vapours on my dry face, as I strode down the foot path in Hazaratganj. I had to purchase a birthday card for my younger brother and hence, undeterred by the fog, I trudged along. Despite the harsh weather, there was a stream of vehicles on the road, for it was the peak office hour traffic.

I had to wait for quite some time at the traffic intersection, before the traffic signal allowed me to cross the road. Standing before me was a young boy, who seemed to be in a great hurry. No sooner had the traffic light turned green, he rushed out to cross the road. In the process he literally escaped being knocked down by a speeding car, which in order to avoid him screeched to a halt. This was followed by a loud bang, as another car following at its heel rammed into it from behind. Both the drivers got out and rushed towards each other menacingly. They shouted abuses at each other, accusing the other of having caused the accident. They were highly agitated and unmindful of the traffic jam they had caused. There was utter commotion as the traffic came to a standstill with cars, buses and scooters blaring their horns, trying to desperately weave their way out. In the meantime the squabble of the drivers snowballed into a free for all, as the occupants of the vehicles also joined in the melee. The lone constable at the sight did try to intervene, but beat a hasty retreat on seeing the belligerence of the warring factions.

The situation took a turn for the worse, with some bystanders joining in and soon there was a mini riot, with people scampering for cover and the shopkeepers hastily downed their shutters. The adverse climatic condition notwithstanding, the tempers continued to flare, with some miscreants pelting stones at the vehicles parked nearby. Seeing the situation go out of hand, I walked into a bank close by, to escape the fury of the mob.

The sound of sirens grew louder and louder and in a short while police reinforcements with riot gear rushed towards the site. There was a mild lathi charge before the situation was brought under control. The riotous crowd melted away, as fast as it had appeared and the streets were completely empty, as if there was a curfew in the area .The warring parties were loaded onto the police vehicles, while the fire brigade personnel's had the vehicles towed away, to clear the traffic jam.

I walked back to the parking lot some distance away to collect my scooter, for no shopping could be now possible in such a surcharged atmosphere. It was while driving back, that I could not help wondering at the foolishness of the parties. They had caused immense damage to themselves and to the public by their wrangle, which could have but been easily resolved by a mere 'sorry', or perhaps some compensation. This could have been a more civilised and decent way to behave.

ASSIGNMENTS

- You were returning from school and your bus knocked down a scooterist, Describe what happened thereafter.
- Write an account of a street quarrel that arose on account of narrow mindedness and intolerance of a group of people. How it began and what followed thereafter?

Write a story with the following ending. It was exactly as he had said it would be.

- Introduction — Description of the surrounding where and when?
- The incident.
- What happened?
- How it happened?
- My reaction — Conclusion.

I was walking down the road returning from a late night show, there was not a soul in sight. It all seemed rather strange, for never had I seen the highway so deserted. I tried to shrug off the eerie feeling that persisted, but alas! to no avail. Everything was the same that I had always seen, trees, cattle, village. What it was I could not fathom? It pieced the whole atmosphere. It made me feel so strange, one could probably take it as an instinct, intuition or gut feeling. I somehow felt that I must just disappear from the scene, which made me feel unusually different. As they say curiosity kills the cat, hence I suppose it got the better of me and I walked along, braving the danger of the unknown.

The strange feeling intensified with each step. I became suddenly aware of a physical presence. The force seemed to be like a magnet drawing me towards it. It seemed to have completely immobilized my limbs and cast a hypnotic spell over me. The clouds moved away and in the moonlight, I saw just before me a large nondescript object, which seemed to have materialised from nowhere. It was oval in shape, with several layers rotating in different direction, with beautiful coloured lights emanating from it. On the top of the circular object was a dome shaped protrusion. It seemed to be the epicenter of this object. I had seen an eyewitness account of Flying Saucers coming from outer space in the news yesterday itself, but had shrugged it off as fiction. Here was I, standing before an actual Flying Saucer.

I felt as if I was under scrutiny. I saw the lights dim a wee bit and the lower structure slide open. An escalator emerged from the hatch like opening. What followed thereafter is difficult to describe in words. A weird looking creature with a spherical head, which seemed to rotate in all directions, atop a long slender body emerged. It seemed to possess all eyes, ears and mouth, nose everything, but difficult to trace. The tentacle like arms and tubular legs completed the picture. Strange though it may seem it appeared intelligent, as it propelled toward me with considerable speed, as if in a hurry.

Before I could do anything the apparition stood before me with an object, which looked like a scanner. I felt as if I was being subjected to some scientific examination. My image appeared on a gigantic screen and I could see my internal organs pulsating. Keeping my fingers crossed, I shouted at it. The creature turned around as if suddenly disinterested and glided back into the spacecraft. With a whirring sound the escalators slid back, the lights blinked and the spaceship rose and was gone within a second.

I stood there dumbstruck. I pinched myself to make sure that I was in my senses. I rubbed my eyes and looked around, everything was there just as before, the fields, the trees, only that creature was nowhere to be seen. The eyewitness's words rang loud in my ears, for it was exactly as he had said it would be.

ASSIGNMENTS

- Write a story beginning with, 'I walked excitedly down the footpath ————————
- Write a composition beginning with, 'I was walking down the road ————————

Write about the wedding ceremony of your friend in which you took an active part.

- Introduction.
- When, Who, and How the marriage ceremony began?
- The ceremony on the arrival of the barat.
- The actual marriage.

"Marriages are made in heaven," so it is said, but they are soleminised here on earth. This is a great occasion that comes in our life but once and therefore, it calls for a celebration anywhere in the world. In our country this is a very solemn occasion, accompanied with numerous customs associated with it, making it all the more exciting and memorable. It is a wonderful mix of tradition, blended with modernity that is even admired by foreigners.

Last month my best friend Sita, who lived in my neighbourhood was married to her fiancée who was a software engineer in the United States. Since I was her best friend, I was assigned the responsibility of looking after the bride and chaperoning her at the wedding .On the appointed day since morning there was hectic activity beginning with the Haldi ceremony, wherein vermilion was applied on her followed by ladies sangeet. This over, I applied mehndi on her hands, my stint of having done a beautician course stood me in good stead .By the time this was over, it was already time for lunch. Immediately after lunch, we had to go to the market to collect her bridal wear that had been given for some last minute alterations. Thereafter we went to the bridal beauty parlour, where we spent some time. By the time they were finished, it was difficult to recognise Sita, for so striking was her beauty, that even the tinsel heroines would have had a complex.

It was now getting late, we rushed home to find the family members anxiously waiting for us. The barat was already on its way and I could hear the drum beats. We all rushed out to see the barat as it approached the gate. The bridegroom was astride on a horse bedecked with flowers. His tall figure with a golden sehra on his head, made him look like the proverbial prince. There was the 'Dwar Puja' at the gate, followed by religious ceremonies performed by the pundit. Thereafter the groom was escorted to the dais, where he was seated on a flower bedecked throne. I escorted the bride to the dais amidst showering of rose petals by the friends and relatives, who had gathered on the occasion .The Jai Mala followed, where they exchanged garlands. No sooner was it over, that people gathered around started dancing and greeting each other with joy. This was so infectious, that. I also found myself dancing in gay abandon.

The guests were invited for a sumptuous dinner, after which we too had our dinner. It was now getting late. As all the guests departed the actual ceremony began .In the Mandap the pundit lit the sacred fire, amidst chanting of hymns the bridegroom and the bride walked around the fire, making solemn promises to each other. By the time this was over it was well past midnight. I had to return home, so wishing my dear friend a very happy and successful married life, I bid her farewell.

ASSIGNMENTS

- A religious function in your neighbourhood in which you took an active part.
- A cultural function in your neighbourhood in which you took an active part.

You have just returned from a cyclone-affected area. Write an account of what you saw and what Measures are necessary for the rehabilitation of the people.

- Introduction — Recurrence of natural calamities.
- Vivid description of loss of life and property.
- The relief measures being provided by the government and voluntary agencies.
- What more needs to be done?

No matter how much man may have progressed in Science and Technology, but time and again nature has shown its supremacy over him. It is this supremacy that reminds us of a supreme power, to whom we are subservient, God the almighty. It is also partly our own undoing, for the wanton destruction of forests, green cover of vegetation and pollution cause these calamities at regular intervals. These natural catastrophes across the world, are taking a heavy toll of life and property leaving a trail of destruction in their wake.

I have just returned from Orissa, after covering the devastating cyclone that had struck it a couple of days ago. I had gone there to have a first hand account of the tragedy for 'The Daily', as a freelance reporter. The extent of destruction and human suffering I saw was unimaginable and at times belied description. I had been witness to many a disaster, but what I saw there was far beyond imagination and enough to move any normal person to grief. My visit took me to Rampur village which was the worse affected. I set out for Rampur by car in the early morning from Bhubneshwar. The road to the village was washed away, with electricity and telephone poles littered across the road. Massive trees had been uprooted and it was with great difficulty that I could reach the village by late afternoon. The place was enveloped in deadly silence, the like of which you see in a grave yard. The silence was at times broken, with the sobs and *wail* of children, huddled together in small groups besides a makeshift tent, which was their temporary shelter. Just beyond them I saw a complete village razed to the ground, with some lone survivors of families shifting the debris, in the hope of finding survivors. On the occasional spotting of a body in the debris, a painful shriek or cry would rent the air, as they gave vent to their grief.

The relief operations were in full swing and I saw the Army and the paramilitary forces, along with the administrative officials busy in removing debris, or clearing roads, They were also busy in locating and disposing of the bodies, which were at times highly decomposed. The paramedics along with doctors were providing medical aid to the injured and the ill, at temporary relief camps set up in tents. Looking above, I saw helicopters airdropping food packets to the marooned people. It was also good to see, various voluntary organisations offering food and comfort to their unfortunate brethren, in their hour of grief.

The relief measure adopted were still highly inadequate, taking into account the magnitude of the calamity, which had left more than ten thousand people dead and millions homeless. It is but a national calamity, for which besides the government and the voluntary agencies, each one of us should lend a helping hand. It is a Herculean task, to rehabilitate these people and help them to pick up their strands of life again. This can be done by collecting funds and items of daily use, which can be sent to the relief commissioner for distribution among the hapless people. It is an occasion when we must forget our squabbles and unitedly set about building the shattered lives of our unfortunate brethren of Orissa.

ASSIGNMENT

- You have just returned from an Earthquake-affected area. Write an account of what you saw and what measures are necessary for the rehabilitation of the people?

Describe a recent visit to a historical place and the impression it left on you

Or

A visit to a historical place.

- Introduction — When and How?
- Preparation for the journey and arrival on the site.
- Visit to the historical site and what I saw?
- Brief history of the monument.
- Conclusion — Impact of this monument on me.

India perhaps is amongst the few countries of the world that is blessed with a rich historical past. Some glimpses of its glorious ancient times, can be reminisced from the majestic and imposing monuments spread across the length and breadth of the country. One of these monuments, which also finds place as the wonder of the world, is the Taj Mahal at Agra. This was build by the Emperor Shah Jahan, in memory of his loving wife Mumtaz Mahal, more than three hundred years ago.

I had always wished to see this monument and hence was thrilled to learn, that our class was going on an excursion trip to Agra in the Desshera vacations. There were thirty boys in the group and after tying up with our travel agent, we set forth from Delhi by bus in the early morning. The four hours drive to Agra in the company of friends was indeed a memorable experience with lot of chorus singing, dance and music. So enthusiastic were we by the prospects of this trip, that we did not feel the strain of the journey and before we realised it, we had actually reached Agra. A quick wash at our transit house, followed by light refreshment and we were back again in the bus, for our tryst with the Taj Mahal.

Leaving the bus in the parking slot, we trudged along on foot towards the ticket counter. By the time we had got the tickets and reached the entrance, it was already late afternoon. The entrance was through a majestic gate like architecture made of red stone. From here right up to the Taj Mahal, was a passage on either side of a pond lined with fountains. The monument was surrounded with lush green grass and trees, amidst which this monument stood in awesome splendour. We slowly wound our way through the milling crowd to reach the monument, that was made of pure white marble, which sparkled in the late afternoon sunlight. On the four corner of the monument, were high minarets also made of marble .The main structure comprised the dome, beneath which lays the graves of Emperor Shah Jahan and his wife Mumtaz Mahal. The walls of the main structure and the dome had exquisite carving done on marble, with precious stones embedded in them. On seeing them closely one could not help wondering, the great mastery of the artisans who created them. Placed in the middle, were the two gravestones of marble similarly decorated, around which we moved. The actual graves lay beneath them in the basement.

The imposing structure was indeed a noble gesture of an emperor expressing his love for his beloved wife. It was however moving, to learn that these master artisan had their hands amputated, so that they could not create a similar structure elsewhere. By the time we had made a detour of the place it was late evening. Since it was the Sharad Purnima night, we decided to wait little longer to see the Taj Mahal in the moonlight.

As luck could have it there was a clear sky and as the moonlight struck it, a sigh of appreciation escaped my lips. The Taj Mahal shown like a monument bathe in milk appeared before us, as if descending from heaven. So wonderstruck was I that it left me speechless by its beauty. The sight could have inspired many a poet to pen some glorious lines about this monument. It is befittingly known as a dream in marble that symbolises true love.

ASSIGNMENTS

- You and your friends decide to visit the Red Fort at Delhi. Write about the preparations you made and what impression this monument left on you.
- Describe one frightening incident that you and your family found really nightmarish.

A Stitch in Time Saves Nine

- Introduction — Meaning of the proverb.
- Practical and sound advice.
- Proven by history.
- Conclusion – Ignore this advice To your own peril.

The meaning of this age-old proverb is quite literal. It effectively means that we must attend to things well in time, so that we can save ourselves a lot of trouble later on, if it becomes unmanageable. Just as it takes only a spark to start a fire, which if not put out in time causes great devastation. Similarly the minutest problem if not attended immediately could lead to a major catastrophe.

As one immediately attends to a small hole in one's pocket with a stitch, which if left unattended could develop into a tear, leading to nine stitches at a later date. Similarly if we postpone attending to minor day to day problems, they do not disappear, but come back to us in a much more gigantic form. A small breach in a canal, if not attended in time not only breaches the entire embankment, but also inundates large cities and villages. Kingdom's can be lost by neglecting to replace such a small thing as a nail in a horse's shoe. As most of us would have heard of the saying "For want of a nail, the shoe was lost, for want of a shoe, the horse was lost, for want of a horse, the rider was lost, for want of a rider the battle was lost, for want of the battle, the kingdom was lost." This is the most practical and sound advice, that is given by our elders including parents and teachers. However, we in our haste, tend to overlook the small details, which is the cause of major problems at a later date.

History is replete with examples validating the above saying. Had Germany got a honourable settlement after World War I, the conflagration and destruction of the World War II could have been avoided. Had the National leaders shown maturity and understanding, the partition of the country could have been avoided These are all glaring examples of what can happen to great countries, if small problems and differences are not resolved at once.

Therefore, we must attend to even minor problems immediately and not postpone action for a later date, which may be a little too late. This is a sound piece of advice that is relevant even today and would always stand us in good stead in our life. We can ignore this to our own peril.

ASSIGNMENTS

- Prevention is better than cure.
- Nip the evil in the bud.
- Unity is strength.
- Look before your leap.

The path to success
Or
Qualities required for success

- Introduction — Why some people succeed while others fail?
- Perseverance and hard work.
- Keen sharp mind with vision and ambition.
- Patience and leadership qualities.
- Positive thinking and attitude.
- Role of Destiny.
- Conclusion – Believe on doing 'Karma'.

'Nothing succeeds like success', for one who has tasted success, this comes to him naturally. Thus we find some people achieving great heights in whatever they do, while on the other hand, there are quite a few unfortunate ones who have to bear the ignominy of failure. There is, however, no mistaking the external facade of success, for behind it are qualities that are imperative for achieving it.

Success is ninety nine percent perspiration and one percent inspiration, signifying that there is no short cut to success. There are many instances where people have risen from extreme poverty to achieve great success, by sheer dint of hard work. We have such illustrious examples of Abraham Lincoln and Lal Bahadur Shastri who rose from a very humble beginning, to become the President and the Prime Minister of their respective country.

Besides perseverance, there is need for a keen and sharp mind, with a clear vision of what one wants to achieve in life. This ambition acts like a beacon of light, which impels us to strive relentlessly in the pursuit of one's goal. Thus it is not suffice that we have an ambition, but we should also be ambitious. We should have the courage of conviction, to move away from the beaten track in the pursuit of our goals.

Just as a rolling stone gathers no moss, we should also be patient to wait for the outcome of events, before rushing in without a thought of the implications. We must also be a good listener, by hearing the views of subordinates or superiors before coming to a decision. Having once taken a decision, we must lead from the front setting an example for others to emulate. We must have implicit faith in our colleagues and subordinates, to whom power and responsibility must be delegated. It was said of Napoleon, that in the thickest of battles, he slept on the horseback, for it was the general who was actually in command. Such was his faith in his generals.

The last but not the least prerequisite for success is a positive mindset, which is not unduly pessimistic. This optimistic approach enables one to see an opportunity even when the going is not good. Such a person is not easily disheartened and his perseverance does pay in the long run for, 'Life's battle does not always go, to the stronger and the fastest man, But sooner or later the man who wins Is the man who thinks he can', said H.W Longfellow.

These are all but attributes that are essential for success, but there is another essential factor over which we have no control and that is destiny fate. This is an important ingredient for success. Abraham Lincoln humbly recognised it when he said, "I claim not to have controlled events, but plainly confess that events controlled me."

Success, therefore, does not come by chance .We have to assiduously work for it with dedication and perseverance, without waiting for reward or recognition, for this is what Karma is. "Honour and shame from no condition arise. Act well your part thus all the honour lies."

ASSIGNMENTS

- 'Nothing succeeds like success'. Discuss.
- 'Success is but destined'. Give your views for or against the statement.
- Success is ninety nine percent perspiration and one percent inspiration. Discuss.

Poverty, Illiteracy and Unemployment are the major problems facing the country. Write about any one suggesting what remedies might be effective.

(ICSE 1991)

- Introduction — All major problems and are interconnected.
- Main cause – illiteracy, leading to economical and political exploitation.
- Remedies suggested, Education to be made a fundamental right.
- Quality education to be imparted and merit rewarded.
- Conclusion — Requires mass support.

Poverty, Illiteracy and Unemployment are major problems facing the country. Even after more than half a century of our independence, these problems instead of abating have further compounded, due to the ever-increasing population. There is however a strong link between them. The core issue according to me is the high level of illiteracy which is responsible for all the above ills. This is because the mature and educated citizens are very important for any country, for they are better able to appreciate their own and national issues. For "education makes the people easy to lead, but difficult to drive, easy to govern, but impossible to enslave", so said Lord Brougham.

It is this abysmally low level of illiteracy, which makes the poor and the downtrodden vulnerable to economic and political exploitation. Though adequate provisions had been made in the constitution, to ensure the empowerment and participation of the less privileged masses to bring about their emancipation. At the ground level it seems the fruits of this, have not percolated down to them. The main culprit for this being illiteracy, which deprives them of their right to claim what is lawfully theirs. Not only are they economically exploited by the landlords and traders, but politically also they fall easy prey to the mechanization of crafty politicians. Their so-called messiah treat them as vote banks for garnering power and clout for themselves, leaving them worse off. This problem can only be addressed by enlightening the masses, by imparting proper formal and non-formal education, enabling them to distinguish between good and bad. Therein lies the secret of their upliftment.

The task is indeed Herculean and requires not only financial resources, but also the political will to implement it. As a first step the government should bring out a constitutional amendment, whereby the education should be made the fundamental right for every citizen. Thereafter adequate budgetary financial provisions should be made in the corresponding five-year plan to put the necessary infrastructure in place, in the form of schools and teachers down to the village level. Adult education should also be imparted and the people should be motivated through financial assistance to become literate.

Education should not only be confined to make them literate but should also inculcate good ethical and moral values. This can be done by using modern educational tools and by appointing good qualified teachers, who can offer good role models for them to emulate. The present education that was modeled by the British for producing clerks should be immediately done away with. An education policy should be formulated, whereby the stress should be on vocational education. This would make people take up their own vocation, leading to their economic upliftment and eradication of the colossal problem of unemployment.

The government with the active support of the people can only do the above. The opposition parties should rise above party politics to pave the way for a better tomorrow for the masses. This is the only way by which we can safeguard our financial independence and take our rightful place in the world community.

ASSIGNMENTS

- Poverty and unemployment are the major problems facing the country. Write about any one suggesting what remedies might be affective.

- Unemployment is a major problem affecting the country. Suggest what remedies might be effective.

Experience is the Best Teacher

- Introduction — Leaves a lasting impression.
- Experiences are thorough.
- We should learn from experience or folklore.
- Personal experience is the best, but some times comes too late.
- Conclusion — We should learn from our, as well as experiences of others.

We have all heard of the proverb 'Once bitten twice shy'. This itself exemplifies how well we learn from our experience. Personal experiences leave an indelible impression on our minds that are more lasting and invaluable. Like a good teacher, her lessons are very thorough and we can only ignore it, to our own peril.

Experiences could be good, like helping a person in need, or it could be bad like losing money on a risky investment. However, what is important, is that we learn from them, so that we can profit from our good experience, while at the same time steer clear from those which are potentially harmful to us. Ask a child not to play with a match box for it can harm him, will probably have no impact on him, but once he has scorched his hand by the match stick, he will never in his lifetime forget this lesson. Thus we learn very meticulously from personal experience, rather than by adhering to advise of others, or by reading about them from books or periodicals.

It is however a wise man who learns from the experiences of others, like his parents, teachers or those elder to him. He also profits from books that are a virtual treasure house of knowledge and experience of others, for in the words of Francis Bacon " some books are to be tasted others swallowed and some few to be chewed and digested". The biography of great statesmen, proverbs and folklore are a veritable gold mine of knowledge, with which we can enrich ourselves. It is indeed unfortunate to find people learning from bitter experiences in their practical life, such age old truths as "all that glitters is not gold," "a bird in hand is worth two in the bush," and " Honesty is the best policy." Once experienced they are unlikely to repeat it in their lives.

We learn from everything we do, in fact life is one great journey of learning. We learn patience and forbearance when faced with adversity, courage in the face of danger and wisdom from our mistakes of omission and commission. It is however unfortunate, that some of us learn this lesson very late in life, when it is too late. Thus we find many people ignoring the simple dictum of 'health is wealth', to later regret it when their life becomes a wretch.

"Life is brief — a little hope, a little dream and then goodnight". In this short span of life we should therefore, not only learn from our own experience but should also profit from the experience of others. This would save us from many a pitfall and the unnecessary labour that goes with it, which is akin to 'inventing the wheel'.

ASSIGNMENTS

- Once bitten twice shy.
- Do we really learn from our mistakes? Discuss.

This is my own my native land or patriotism

- Introduction — Patriotism.
- Characteristics of a true patriot.
- False or pseudo patriot, with narrow nationalistic appeal.
- Much abused term in present day party politics.
- Importance of a true patriot.
- Conclusion – Be a True Patriot at heart

The word patriotism is derived from the Latin word that means ' father'. Thus the land or the country to which one belongs is called the fatherland. We owe everything to our country of birth and are happiest in serving it, as Alexander Pope says "happy the man whose wish and care, a few paternal acres abound. Content to breath his native air in his own ground".

We love our country and pride ourselves as Indian. So we are all to some extent patriots. However, a true patriot is one, who places his country first and foremost. He is ever ready to make sacrifices for his country. Since he has the welfare of the country at heart, he also criticises its wrong policies, sins of omission and commission that prevail in the society. This criticism is constructive without any self interest and motive. However, in time of crisis, as in the case of war or natural calamity, he is ready to make the supreme sacrifice.

We also have patriots of different hues, who are patriots with a selfish motive. They are pseudo or false patriots, with a narrow nationalist appeal to camouflage their real motive. They are in fact more aggressive, and flaunt their patriotism for every one to see. Their patriotism is very superficial for they prescribe to the motto "My country right or wrong". Such type of patriots operates with very narrow nationalist traits, for according to them every thing is right for the country, even its evils and negative aspects. They pose a danger for the democratic spirit of the country, for they discourage dissent. Such pseudo patriots are the precursor to authoritarian or fascist rule. We had such patriots in the fascist countries, like Germany and Italy during the Second World War. We then saw how they perpetuated crimes against humanity, in the misplaced notion of patriotism.

This is also a much used and abused word in Indian politics. As each political party claims to be more patriotic than the other. Most often this patriotism is but a facade for public consumption, while their actual interest lies in garnering votes, by raising divisive and contentious issues. Doctor Samuel Johnson describes such patriots when he said, "patriotism is the last refuge of a scoundrel".

The country grows and prospers on the strength of true patriots only. We owe our freedom to them, for whenever the country is in danger they are in the forefront to defend it, both in war and peace. As a mark of salutation to the great patriotic pilots, who laid down their lives, during the invasion of England by the Nazi air force, Mr. Winston Churchill remarked "never in the field of human conflict was so much owed by so many to so few".

We must, therefore, as a true patriot, stand for upholding all good things for the country and be ready to make sacrifices in safeguarding it. This is so for the soul of a person who feels no love for his country is dead, as Sir Walter Scot said "Breathes there the man with soul so dead. Who never to himself hath said? This is my own my native land"

ASSIGNMENTS

- 'Patriotism is the last refuge of a scoundrel' Discuss.
- A true Patriot.

Work is Worship
or
The Dignity of Labour

- Introduction — Need for work.
- Importance of work.
- Perfection requires dedication.
- The Hindu Mythology also extols 'Karma'.
- Conclusion — Virtues of work.

"An idle mind is a devil's workshop", This aptly highlights the need and role of work in our lives .Not only does it provide us a means of livelihood but helps to keep the devil (other vices) at bay. Someone rightfully remarked, "I slept and dreamt that life was beauty. I woke and found that life was duty". Thus life is work and work is worship.

Life is action and not contemplation, for man's worth is determined by his actions. It is this, which differentiates him from other creatures of the planet. It enables him to better his own quality of life, by engaging in some profession, so that the society as a whole shares the fruit of his labour. All work is dignified, for it is better than being on doles, or at somebody else's mercy. Not only does it help us in living a life of dignity, but also gives us tremendous self-confidence and self-esteem. We also observe in practical life that men do not break down from overwork, but from worry and dissipation. This is so because work generates optimism that makes life pleasant. Ordinary people have risen to great heights by excelling in their work. We have such illustrious examples of Florence Nightingale, Albert Einstein and thousands of others. They have by their sheer dint of hard work and devotion become immortal.

In this age of globalisation and severe competition, there is need for perfection in every field. Whether it is in the manufacture of a product, or the rendering of a service. We can only hope to be successful if our work measures up to the right standards. This therefore calls for sincerity, devotion and strict discipline towards our work, so that we can deliver the right product, at the best price as the fruit of our labour. Thus just as we offer prayers to the almighty God, in all humility and sincerity and wait patiently for his reward. Similarly we must do so in our work.

In the Hindu mythology, the Gita extols the virtue of 'Karma' (Deed). We must continue to do 'Karma', without expecting or waiting for reward or recognition. Work is divine and our moral duty to accomplish, for "honour and shame from no conditions arise .Act well your part, there all the honour lies." We also see the artisan's, workman and traders offering a short prayer before commencing their work .We celebrate Vishwakarma puja with great pomp and show, offering prayers to the deity of creation. This is all but a manifestation of our reverence to our work, that we regard as divine and sacred.

In the words of Rabindra Nath Tagore "God is there where the tiller is tilling the hard soil and the pathmaker is breaking the stones". Thus all work is divine and we must work hard to enjoy the fruits of our labour that indeed taste sweet. Without effort we can achieve nothing, for as William Penn said "No gain, no palm, no thorn, no throne; No gall no glory, no cross, no crown".

ASSIGNMENTS

- 'All work and no play make Jack a dull boy'. Discuss.
- Man is a tool-making animal. Discuss.
- "Honour and shame from no conditions arise. Act well your part, there all the honour lies". Discuss.

The person who influenced your life the most

- Introduction — Who has influenced and how.
- Background of his life.
- Characteristics that influenced me
  Sacrifice and devotion.
  Patriotism.
  Character and Statesmanship.
  Great visionary.
  Industrious nature, Love for children and poor.
- Conclusion – Inspiring Leader

In the journey of life we come across many people and also read about autobiographies of great men, that leaves an indelible mark in our minds. At times so great is the influence that it changes the course of our life. Thus for example the impact of Mahatma Gandhi on the young Jawaharlal Nehru, was so great that it changed the course of his life by making him join the freedom movement. I have also been profoundly influenced by the life of Pt. Jawaharlal Nehru, from what I have read about him through his autobiographies and books. The more I dwell on his life, the greater becomes my curiosity to know him better.

He was born on 14th November 1889 with the proverbial silver spoon in his mouth. His father Motilal Nehru was a wealthy lawyer, who sent him to a public school at Harrods when Jawaharlal was barely fourteen years. He subsequently joined Trinity College, from where he graduated in law. He returned to India, only to jump in the freedom struggle launched by Mahatma Gandhi. He was jailed several times and spent his youth in jail. It was then that he took to writing books like the 'Glimpses of Indian history', 'My autobiography', etc., which are till today regarded as masterpieces of literary work. The relentless struggle and the non-cooperation movement led to the Quit India resolution in 1942, that finally paved the way for India's independence. He was the unanimous choice for the Prime Minister and to him goes the credit of laying down the foundation of a strong, Democratic, Industrial and Secular country.

Some of his noble characteristics which endeared him to me were, his strong will and self-sacrifice. He could have easily led a cushy life, but he chose a thorny path for the welfare of his country. This is a tribute to a strong will, which did not deter him from his chosen path.

He was a true patriot to the core and was ever willing to make sacrifices for his country. Not only did he spend his youth in jail, but also took to wearing khadi, when the nation was in the thick of the movement against wearing of foreign spun yarns.

He was a gentleman to the core, with an impeccable character and an acclaimed world states-man, His foreign policy pronouncement of non- alignment with power blocks and the Panch Sheel for international relations, are a testimony of his foresight. India under him was intently heard at world forums, for he voiced the feelings and emotions of the under developed and developing countries boldly and truthfully.

He was a great visionary and laid the foundations of a socialistic government with emphasis on industrialisation, in the core sector. This made the country self-sufficient and today we are not only a nuclear power, but also a strong contender for a permanent seat in the Security Council.

He was a workaholic, working more than eighteen hours a day. He however still found time for children, whom he loved dearly. That is why 14th November is observed as Children's Day. His love for the poor and downtrodden was reflected in his pro poor policies, enabling them to lead a proper life.

It is these attributes of sacrifice; character, patriotism, statesmanship, industrious nature, liberal attitude and love for children that endeared him to me. Such leaders are not born everyday. Their life and its travails and how they overcome them not only inspire me, but shall continue to inspire generations, who may wonder that such a person stalked the earth in flesh and blood.

ASSIGNMENTS

- My Favourite leader.
- Mahatma Gandhi — The father of the Nation.

Choice of a Career
Or
Choice of a Profession

- Introduction — Perplexing decision.
- Opening of new vistas.
- Cardinal principles to be followed in making a choice.
- Take a decision giving due weightage to advise of parents and peers.
- Conclusion — After having taken a decision work upon it sincerely.

The dawn of the new millennium has thrown up a plethora of new career opportunities that were hitherto unknown. They have made the task of choosing a career for the youth more confusing and perplexing .The decision at times is fraught with suspense and anxiety, similar to that we see in a gambler, who with trembling solitude throws his dice. This is indeed the most unprofessional way of taking such a vital decision, that has a direct bearing on our lives.

Fortunately for us, there are vast avenues for getting career information, through Newspapers, Electronic media and the Internet. There are an equally large number of career options to choose from. For instance, in the field of Information Technology, we have new career options in the field of E-Commerce as Web designers, administrators and developers. In Science we have such new fields. like Biotechnology, Environmental Sciences, Genetic Engineering, etc. These careers are in addition to the traditional options of doctor, lawyer, engineer and a teacher.

There is however no cause for despair, for there are some basic cardinal principles that we must bear in mind while exercising our choice. The first and foremost being, that we must objectively identify our strengths and weaknesses, likes and dislikes and inborn propensities. Keeping this in mind, we should identify the careers that are best suited with respect to our disposition. It is very common to find young people, enamoured by the glamour and razzmatazz of a particular profession opting for it. Only to have their dream shattered, on discovering that it does not suit them temperamentally. They thus end up highly dissatisfied and frustrated. We therefore, see youth taking to the legal profession, on being infatuated by an eminent lawyer. After spending considerable time and money, when they set up a practice, they discover that it is not only oratory skills, but also a sharp and incisive mind that is essential for a roaring practice. They thus end up as failures and settle for anything to keep their body and soul together. The reason for their plight was, their decision being made on purely extraneous and illogical factors.

We should also give due weightage to the views of our parents, friends and peer groups. Our parents and peers can guide us by their experience. It is important that they render their advice objectively and dispassionately. It has sometimes been observed that the youth takes up a career, bowing to the wishes of his parents. Thus we see the son of an eminent doctor, taking to the medical profession, just to please his father. He may become a doctor, but in the absence of aptitude and inclination, he can never achieve his father's eminence.

As they say 'well begun is half done', for if we have taken the right option, we shall work more assiduously for realizing our dream. It does not matter if we do not get admission into the best of institutions, what matters is that after getting the requisite qualification, we excel in the field which is closest to our heart .We must remember the words of H.W. Longfellow when he says "Life's battle don't always go to the stronger and the fastest man. But soon or late the man who wins is the man who thinks he can."

ASSIGNMENTS

- Career option for youth in the new millennium.
- Youth and Career.

The philosophy of Non-violence
Or
India's greatest contribution to the civilised world

- Introduction — What is non-violence 'Ahimsa'?
- Philosophy rooted in 'Tapasya' which appealed to Indian masses.
- Criticism of this philosophy.
- Essence of the philosophy.
- Conclusion – A new path blazed by Gandhiji To achieve one's goal.

Non-violence or 'Ahimsa' according to Mahatma Gandhi "is the crux of all noble attitudes of man towards himself, towards his fellow human being, towards life and its many fold problems and finally, towards God his master" for "ends cannot justify the means and that everything in politics must be fair and honest and based upon the noble principles of non-violence and non injury". This was indeed a new philosophy, especially in politics, as till recently this concept was heard more in spiritual and religious context.

The Hindu sages in the past expounded philosophic doctrines, which are amply elaborated in the 'Upanishads'. They laid emphasis on 'Tapasya'or penance as a way to achieving progress. Thus as per this philosophy, all acquisition of knowledge, or any achievement requires restraint, self suffering, self torture and self sacrifice. It was this concept of 'Tapasya'that was present thousands of years ago and is still present in the Indian psyche, which immediately appealed to all Indians. It was the underlying reason, for the great success of this mass movement for independence, led by Gandhiji that convulsed India under him.

There were many opponents to this line of thought, who advocated more direct action even if it meant resorting to violence for achieving independence. Gandihiji however did not subscribe to their view, for according to him violence begets more violence. This philosophy was at times mistaken for cowardice, but it really required great moral and psychological courage, to fight for a cause upholding it. So immense was its appeal and so committed were his followers, that the British were in mortal fear of this semi clad Mahatma.

The essence of this philosophy was, to win the hearts of the enemy, by appealing to his natural instinct of truth and fairplay. Gandhiji often said that we should hate the sin and not the sinner. Thus we should not hate the British people, but hate their crime of subjugating millions of people and depriving them of their fundamental right to freedom. This endeared him to the masses and the struggle took the form of a mass movement leading to Satyagraha and non-cooperation. So refreshing was his approach that Nehru writes "And then came Gandhi. He was like a powerful current of fresh air that made us stretch ourselves and take deep breaths, like the beam of light that pierced the darkness and removed the scales from our eyes. He did not descend from the top, he seemed to emerge from the millions of India speaking their language ."

The culmination of the success of this philosophy was, the victory of independence from the mighty British Empire. But what mattered most was, the new path blazed by the Mahatma, in a world plagued with violence and fraud to achieve the goal. It is in fact an all pervading philosophy of life, that he prescribed for all the malady, that is eating up the vitals of our nation. To that extent we should uphold his teachings and prove ourselves worthy of his rich legacy.

ASSIGNMENTS

- The effectiveness of the philosophy of non-violence as a means of achieving goals in the present world. Discuss.
- The end justifies the means. Discuss.
- Violence is the only way of achieving one's goal. Give your views for or against the statement.

God helps those who help themselves

- Introduction — Sound, age-old logic.
- Inspiring life stories as proof.
- Fortune favours the brave.
- Importance of Karma in the Hindu mythology.
- Conclusion – Need to strive for our own betterment.

The above is an age old logic which is indisputable. We have all heard of the fable, in which a carter who on seeing his wagon stuck in the mud, prayed to 'Hercules' the god of strength to get it out for him. Hercules answered his prayer by saying, "Put your shoulder to the wheel man". The carter took his advice and lo and behold, the wagon was out of the mud. This simple fable very effectively portrays the value of self-help.

There are many true inspiring life stories of great men who were born in extreme poverty, but by sheer dint of their hard work and sincerity they rose to the highest position in their country. Names like Abraham Lincoln and Lal Bahadur Shastri are illustrious examples of what wonders can be achieved by self-help. Abraham Lincoln began his life as a woodcutter while Shastri was a schoolteacher. They however rose to become the President and the Prime Minister of their respective countries, by virtue of their labour.

We are also privy to real life 'Rags to riches' stories of great industrialist, who had literally nothing to start with. They, however, not only became wealthy, but also created an industrial empire. Examples of such men are Swaraj Paul and our own Dirubhai Ambani of the Capro and Reliance empire fame. While Swaraj Paul came as a refugee from what is now Pakistan, Dirubhai a small trader of Gujarat, had the courage to challenge the multinationals and today heads one of the largest private sector company in the country. They were able to achieve such phenomenal success due to their qualities of self-reliance, perseverance and enterprise. They are but living examples of the adage 'Fortune favours the brave'.

In the Hindu mythology also , Karma or deed is of supreme importance and it is the purpose of our life. Lord Krishna in the The Bhagwat Gita, extols the virtue of 'Karma ' to Arjun, inspiring him to wage war, for that was his Karma as a Kshetriya .The Gita also tells us that we must continue to do our karma (Duty) and not wait for reward, for it is bound to follow sooner or later.

We must therefore, pay heed to the above and continuously strive for our own betterment. We must not forget, that when even disabled people like Helen Keeler who was deaf, dumb and blind could overcome her handicaps and contribute to society, we as normal people have no reason to fail. We are reminded of what William Penn said "No pain, no palm, no thorn, no throne .No gall, no glory, no cross no crown."

ASSIGNMENTS

- Self Help.
- "No pain, no palm, no thorn, no throne .No gall, no glory, no cross no crown."
- "Fortune favours the brave". Discuss.

Your ambition in life
Or
My ambition in life

- Introduction — What is an ambition ?
- My ambition, Why is it my ambition?
- How I plan to achieve it ?
- Conclusion – Firm resolve to achieve my ambition

We are all familiar with the proverb 'Hitch your wagon to a star.' The logic behind it is simple. If we do not aspire for something great, we shall not strive for it and consequently lead a life of ignomity. The autobiographies of all great men reveal, that each of them very early in childhood had a dream, a vision of what they intended to do or become. This is distinctively apart from daydreaming, for in the words of William Shakespeare "Ambition should be made of sterner stuff". Thus it is not suffice to only dream, but one must relentlessly strive to achieve and realise this dream.

I too have a dream, an ambition of becoming a doctor. This is so because it is a noble profession, that also commands a lot of respect in the society. The white coat and the stethoscope mesmerizes me, right since my childhood .The look of concern, sense of empathy and the feeling of confidence that the doctor inspires in a patient, mitigates his suffering. He is looked upon as a messiah by the sick and the infirm. No matter how big or powerful a man might be, he invariably does fall sick and has to seek the doctor's help. There are many other professions that offer more money, power and glamour, but none commands the respect and the dignity of a doctor. All these are but transitory things, that are there today and gone tomorrow, but the status and service of a doctor does not diminish. On the other hand, if he practices his profession nobly, it increases and multiplies with the passage of time.

The road to realising my dream is not easy, nor do I expect it to be so. I would have to pass the competitive premedical examination, before I could gain entry to a medical college. I have begun preparation for the same in earnest and with God's grace I do hope to clear the test. I would like to specialise in Cardiac diseases after completing my MBBS. This is a fatal ailment that has afflicted us and is on the rise. It has now started afflicting even young people and this country would need many cardiologists to take care of them.

This is my dream which I do hope will come true. I shall leave no stone unturned to turn my ambition into reality, for I firmly believe that our triumphs and defeats are in us. H.W. Longfellow rightly echoes these sentiments when he says "Not in the clamour of crowded streets not in the shouts of plaudits of the throng. But in ourselves are triumphs and defeats."

ASSIGNMENTS

- Ambition.
- "Ambition should be made of sterner stuff". Discuss.

You go to a Hill Station write about the places you visited and what you saw during your visit
Or
A visit to a Hill Station

- Introduction — When and Where did we go?
- Where we stayed ?
- What did we do and see ?
- Our return.
- Conclusion – A delightful experience.

Last year in the summer vacations I along with my cousin, decided to visit Mussorie a hill station in the Garhwal mountains of UP, also known as the Queen of the hills. We thus boarded the Mussorie express train from Delhi and the next morning we were in Dehradun, a city on the foothill of the mountains. The taxi ride from Dehradun to Mussorie was a two hour drive, with sharp and steep turns. The deep gorges, were enough to send a chill down one's spine and so we desperately clung to our seats .

By 10 A.M. we were in Mussorie and as I stepped out of the taxi, the first thing that struck me was the cool refreshing breeze. This was a welcome change from the hot loo we had just left behind. Scampering with our baggage we set forth to the tourist lodge, which was a distance away from 'The Mall'. By the time we reached the place we were panting for breath, but were unmindful of the exhaustion.

No sooner had we got fresh, we were ready to venture out again. As my cousin was familiar with the place, we decided to go to Gun Hill top by trolley. The trolley ride was indeed memorable for the scenic beauty down below was breathtaking. Once atop the hill we set about exploring the place, which was a tourist delight. We saw tastefully done up stalls of eatables and novelty items. The spirit of merrymaking and laughter filled the air. We also joined in the fun and got ourselves photographed as Gabbar Singh, the legendry tinsel dacoit. By the time we returned to our lodge it was dark.

The next day we set out for Kempty Fall that is half an hour drive from Mussorie .The scene at the waterfall was indeed mesmerising. Small droplets of water struck us on the face, even though we were standing a distance away. The place was swarming with tourists and the children were having a whale of a time, in little pools of water besides the waterfall. Their merrymaking was so infectious, that we also joined in the fun and got drenched. Luckily we had brought our clothes, so after a quick change, we sat down for a sumptuous lunch at one of the tastefully done up restaurants .We were by now tired with exhaustion and therefore decided to return, for we had also to do packing for our departure the next morning.

I now appreciate why poets and authors get their inspiration from nature, that is in abundance on these picturesque mountains. While they have the gift of conveying their sentiments, in prose or poetry, normal mortals like me can only get moved. It was with a heavy heart that we began our journey home next morning, bidding farewell to the mountains. However, making a solemn promise, to one day again return for a longer stay in the lap of nature.

ASSIGNMENTS

- A visit to a sea beach.
- A visit to the Zoo.

The happiest day in my life
Or
The most exciting day in my life

- Introduction
- When and what happened?
- How it happened?
- What else happened?
- Conclusion – Happiest day of my life.

Life is indeed a drudgery of routine. Normally we are unable to distinguish one day from the other. There are however some days that have a special significance for us, for example our birthdays or that of our near and dear ones. We do not easily forget them but look forward to them. Besides this, there is a day, which is the happiest day of our life. It marks a turning point in our life, which we can never forget.

It was just last year when I had appeared for my ICSE examination and after a brief vacation had competed for the National Science Talent Search Examination. I had not done the science paper of the ICSE exams up to my expectations and was feeling quite dejected on this account. As the day for the announcement of results drew nearer my nervousness increased giving me sleepless nights. At time I had terrible nightmares that made my hairs stand on end. I knew my parents had great expectations from me and the thought of letting them down made me paranoid.

It was the tenth of May at about 10 a.m. my friend Mohan, rang up to inform that I had topped in the school. He had just seen the results from the internet site and had rung up to congratulate me. I was speechless, for so numb was I with apprehension, that his words did not immediately register. I was barely able to say 'Thank you' and gently put the phone down. By this time my parents and sister were crowding round me to know what the matter was. I jubilantly told them about my result. What followed was just indescribable. While my parents kissed and hugged me my friend came around to congratulate me.

I was indeed enjoying being the cynosure of all eyes and kept pinching myself to ascertain that I was not hallucinating. Just then my eyes fell on the daily newspaper which had been lying on the table, completely ignored in the commotion. No sooner had I turned the cover page when my heart skipped a beat, for Lo and Behold! staring me straight in the face was the result of the National Science Talent Search Test. With shaking fingers, I scanned the roll numbers and to my surprise I found my number. I called out to my mother and within no time the news spread throughout the neighbourhood. I had indeed become a star overnight. This was something I had just not anticipated, but it meant to me more than anything else. It was indeed a milestone towards my ambition to become a scientist.

Looking back I feel elated for what happened that fateful day which was the happiest day of my life. This day, shall always be fresh in my memory for it was the turning point in my life.

ASSIGNMENTS

- Saddest day of my life.
- The most embarrassing moment of my life.

"He who has the firm Will moulds the world to himself". Discuss.
Or
Where there is a will there is a way.

- Introduction — Man has done the impossible by sheer will power.
- Examples from everyday life.
- Meeting challenge is the essence of life.
- Examples from history.
- Conclusion — Power of our will.

Man is a creature basically six feet tall, but he has been able to conquer space and the majestic heights of the imposing mountains. He is relentlessly in the pursuit of breaking new grounds, not on account of his physical prowess, but because of his resolve and will power. We all possess this, to a lesser or greater extent. However, great souls have been known to exercise this to achieve the impossible, while lesser mortals in its absence lead an ignoble existence. This is so for men with a wavering mind and feeble will, cannot succeed in life as Victor Hugo rightly said, "People do not lack strength, they lack the will."

We all know that if we keenly desire to do something, we invariably explore ways of doing it successfully. This is akin to our own personal experience of learning cycling. We did fall and also bruised ourselves, but it did not stop us from trying again, nor did it dampen our resolve to learn cycling. Consequently we mastered the technique. Thus initial failures should not discourage us, for pursuing big and ambitious goals, as we know that there is no short cut to success. Our constant perseverance will sooner or later bear fruit and we are bound to succeed. Failure should therefore, not deter us from our chosen path, for it is but a stepping-stone to success.

It is in meeting challenges and facing our adversary that we improve ourselves. "He that wrestles with us strengthens our nerves, and sharpens our skills. Our antagonist is our helper," said Edmund Burke. Meeting challenges is the essence of life. We would not be privy to such spectacular developments, had our great predecessors, not overcome challenges posed to them by nature. There is in fact nothing impossible to achieve and Napoleon rightly said, " The word impossible exists in the dictionary of fools".

The history of mankind is replete with instances of how ordinary people achieved great things, by dint of their will power. The pioneers of aviation, the Wright brothers, had their limbs broken, but they did finally succeed in achieving their dream of flying. The result today is the development of supersonic planes, that take us around the world in a couple of hours. We have also heard of the legendary persistence of Maharana Pratap, to check the expansionist ambitions of Akbar, not by his meagre army, but because of his invincible will. These great souls have conclusively proved, that there is nothing impossible to achieve, provided one has the will to get about it. There is a Chinese proverb that says, "Great souls have will, feeble one's have only wishes."

We must therefore, not only wish and aspire for something, but also work with resolve for achieving it, for 'God helps those who help themselves". Such is the power of our will, that if we want, we can mould the world. This reminds us of what Goethe once said, "He who has the firm will moulds the world to himself".

ASSIGNMENTS

- "People do not lack strength, they lack the will". Discuss.
- "Great souls have will, feeble one's have only wishes." Discuss.

Necessity is the mother of invention.

- Introduction. — Universal truth.
- Arises from our pursuit of satisfying needs.
- Examples of how needs of communication and transportation were addressed.
- Advance made in Medical and health care.
- Conclusion — Adds spice to our lives and makes life comfortable.

There is much truth in the saying 'Necessity is the mother of invention'. Ever since the advent of man in the universe, he has been in pursuit of something to satiate his needs. It was in order to satisfy his hunger, that he took to hunting wild animals. His desire to eat wholesome food, led to the discovery of fire and food grains. The necessity of protecting his body from the scourging heat and the inclemencies of weather, led him to cover his body with fur and subsequently with fabrics, made from cotton or wool.

The journey of mankind has been a voyage in the pursuit of satisfying his needs and wants. No sooner has one need been satisfied, than it gives birth to a whole plethora of other needs. Thus what may have started of as sign language to communicate, gave rise to communication through language. This then led to recording of communication, through the evolution of alphabets. Even to day we are seeing this need being addressed through the electronic media, telephone, cellular telephone. Satellite phones and the Internet. Now we are attempting to integrate all these mediums, so that no matter where we are and what we are doing, we can always be in touch with our homes or offices. Thus we see, how our desire to do something new to meet our ever-increasing needs, has been the cause of stupendous development in the field of communication. This has been the case in all other spheres of life like transport which include road, rail, aeroplanes and a host of consumer goods. All these luxuries make the world a wonderful place to live in.

In the field of medicine and health care, it has led to discovery of newer and more effective ways of curing diseases, that were hitherto considered to be incurable. Diseases like cancer have been successfully treated by Chemotherapy and Radium treatment, while heart and other coronary diseases are now effectively treated with surgery. Even in our daily lives we observe the universal truth of this statement, when we find newer and more efficient ways of doing things.

It is this relentless endeavour to strive for satisfying our needs, that makes us discover something new which adds spice to our life. Had nature put everything to us on a platter, life would have indeed been very eventless, doing nothing and consequently, achieving nothing.

ASSIGNMENT

- The journey of mankind has been a voyage in the pursuit of satisfying his needs and wants. Discuss.

Impact of reading literature on our lives

- Introduction — Importance of reading literature.
- Impact of reading literature on our lives.
     Gives knowledge, inspires confidence, makes us better human beings
     Inculcates virtues.
- Declining tendency of reading in youth due to advent of TV, Cinema and the Internet.
- Advantage over the above.
- Conclusion — Tremendous impact on our lives.

The word literature means literally 'letters', it is on account of this that learned men are referred to as men of letters. Reading of literature is important for us, for it gives valuable insights to various facets of life. It inculcates in us the power of reasoning, as Francis Bacon said. "Read not to contradict and confute nor to believe and take for granted, nor to find talk and discourse, but to weigh and consider,"

The literary works of great authors have profoundly affected us since times immemorial The Vedas, The Ramayana, Gita, Bible and the Koran are all great literary works of noble minds, which have spread the light of wisdom since ages. While the Ramayana gives insight to human relationship, on how to treat elders, friends and colleagues. The Gita idolizes Karma (duty) that is the purpose of our lives. These provide strength and inspiration to us, in time of a dilemma. They are indeed masterpieces of art that unfold the truth of life and death, making us reverent, yet fearless. Besides this the classics of William Shakespeare, Rabindra Nath Tagore and Munshi Premchand have bequeathed to us, a wealth of knowledge on such aspects as friendship, virtues, honesty and life itself.

It provides valuable insight into the good things of life and made us aware of the negative aspects. Thus enabling us to differentiate between good or bad, virtue and evil. It makes us more humane and virtuous.

Unfortunately the youth of today, does not read literature except that from textbooks. This is due to the overpowering influence of other media, like television, cinema and the Internet of late. To that extent, he is unable to reap the fruits of wisdom, for nothing can substitute it.

Besides developing our personality and a value system, it helps us in thinking and acting logically. No matter what problems we face, we can derive strength and direction from the thoughts and actions of great sages. None of the above media touch our life so profoundly as it does.

It is therefore, without any hesitation we can say, that our lives are profoundly affected by reading literature. This is so for the inspiring thoughts of learned men broaden our vision, making us worldly-wise, for Lord Tennyson rightly said, "When Knowledge comes, wisdom lingers."

ASSIGNMENTS

- The pleasures of reading literature.
- Literature is not only to be studied but an art to be practiced. Discuss.
- "Reading maketh a Full Man; conference a Ready Man and Writing an Exact Man,"Bacon. Discuss.

Impact of fashion on students

- Introduction — What is fashion.
- Role of fashion in our lives.
- Impact on students

  Distracts them from studies and

  Vitiates the academic environment

  Creates physiological imbalance for the poor
- Conclusion — Need to strike the right balance

This is the age of fashion, which is not only confined to our dress, but also in the way we speak, behave, decorate our houses and our lifestyle in general. Fashion as described in the English dictionary is "the prevailing mode in such things as are subject to change in form of a style, as in ornaments, etiquette and especially in dress". So all pervading is its influence, that it is but natural for students to get afflicted with this symptom of modernity.

In a way it lends variety to our lives, providing an element of excitement in trying out something new. It would indeed be a drab life, if we ass were supposed to behave and dress similarly. Change is therefore not only desirable but also welcome. The hero, heroines of the tinsel world and the fashion models are the trendsetters who are the role models for our youth. They are the Icons around whom the 'fashion' revolves.

It is but natural that students, who are in their adolescence, get attracted to fashion and try to emulate their role models. This invariably distracts them from their studies and quite often they rue this throughout their lives. It does not in any way imply, that they should not be smartly dressed. They should dress and behave appropriately, so that they do not distract others as well as maintain the sanctity of the educational institution.

It has also been seen that their indulgence in fashion creates a divide among the haves and the have-nots more glaring, which at times appears vulgar. It also leads to psychological imbalance in them, as they try to ape their affluent friends. However in the absence of means they resort to unlawful and unethical acts. There are thus instances of youngsters taking to crime, just to buy a fashionable dress or suit for being in fashion.

They must therefore strike a right balance between being fashionable and what is good for them. They have all the time in the world to indulge in this luxury after having finished their education. The present time however should be devoted to studies, for it will never come back. This is because we all know that time and tide waits for none.

ASSIGNMENTS

- Fashion is the exclusive preserve of the rich. Comment.

India as you would like to see in the next twenty years

- Introduction — My vision of India.
- In terms of population.
- In terms of stature and strength.
- In terms of economic development.
- Conclusion.

India in the next two decades of the new millennium would be an emerging world power. We would be a proud self-reliant nuclear power, with a strong economy and the largest creditable working democracy. This would be the cause of envy to the outside world. The tremendous asset of technical manpower and abundance of true patriots bode well for the future of the country.

Numerically we would be the most populous country, with of one in every four inhabitants of the universe being an Indian. Thus we would have even surpassed China. This manpower would however be an asset, for it would comprise of qualified technocrats, a fair percent of English speaking people, making a positive contribution to the G.D.P of the country. Thus what Oil did to the middle east countries our enlightened computer proficient engineers and technocrats could do to us. The world would see in amazement the entrepreneurial skills of our entrepreneurs, who would have repeated the Silicon Valley success in many parts of the country and abroad.

We would also emerge as a nuclear superpower with a difference. We would be exploiting nuclear energy for peaceful purposes. This would be used for generating electricity and exploiting natural resources for the welfare of the people. A precursor to what is in store has already been made, when we successfully exploded an indigenous nuclear device in June 1999.

We have also shown to the world that we are a self-sufficient country, by withstanding the severe sanctions imposed on us, after the detonation of the nuclear device. Any ordinary country would have been unable to face up to these sanctions that would have crippled its economy. The economic reforms that had started in the last millennium would have borne fruits by then, leading to less inflation and eradication of poverty due to faster rate of development. I therefore, foresee a very bright future for the country, that has invaluable natural resources and an established industrial base, to propel it to become an economic power like Japan in the next two decades.

We have already become the envy of the international community, as regards the stability of the democratic institution is concerned. This would further prosper, so that it would reflect the rich cultural heritage of this country by the participation of all segments of the society. Thus it would be the largest working democracy in the world, where people of diverse backgrounds would live together in harmony.

The future of the country is indeed bright and this is reflected in the recent overtures that western powers are making to us. We have till now earned their respect, but we will earn their admiration too by the first two decades of the new millennium.

ASSIGNMENTS

- The India of my dreams.
- India as you see it today.

Role of newspapers in forming public opinion
Or
Influence of the press

- Introduction — Newspapers excite curiosity and impart news.
- Historical role played in forming public opinion during struggle for independence.
- More credible than other media.
- Negative role through yellow journalism.
- Conclusion.

"Newspapers always excite curiosity. No one ever lays down one without a feeling of disappointment," said Charles Lamb. It is this art of generating curiosity that compels its reader to read on. Hence the most ordinary of news can be so presented to catch the immediate attention of the reader. For example when a dog bites a man it is not news, but when a man bites a dog that is news. This is its special appeal over other media of dissipating news.

It is the most important and effective media of mass communication. Not only news, but ever since its birth it has played a pivotal role in forming and moulding public opinion. During our struggle for independence, newspapers played a stellar role in acting as mouthpieces of national leaders, to form a favourable public opinion. Even after independence, it has on many occasions acted as a crusader to raise issues that are contentious, but nevertheless require public debate. It has also helped to keep the democratic traditions alive, by offering a forceful voice of dissent, which is the lifeline for any true democracy to flourish. A free press works like a watchdog in a democracy.

Presenting news to the readers is only one facet of a newspaper for which it has many competitors. There is the Radio, Television and lately the Internet that provides instant news from across the world. What however, sets it apart from other medium is that it is more forceful and objective. Moreover there is an element of credibility in the written word, which makes the readers addict to it. The newspapers also helps the common man, to form his own opinion on diverse subjects like politics, economics and social aspects of life. It is here that the editors through their objective editorials, help in forming the public attitude of the masses. So profoundly does it affect the minds of the reader, that you can tell the paper that a person reads from the opinion he voices. The editor of a newspaper, therefore, has a very important role to play. However, unfortunately every newspaper is unconsciously or consciously coloured by its own definite policy. This is invariably because most newspapers, owe their allegiance to some business house, or a political party that have a pro or anti government leaning. There is therefore, danger for the average reader being influenced and biased, on account of this prejudiced reporting.

In the war of increasing circulation some small and regional newspapers resort to sensationalizing news, so as to increase their readership. This gives rise to what is called yellow journalism. This initially may be commercially rewarding to the media bosses, but the public has now learnt to take such reports in their stride. Invariably it lowers the credibility of such dailies and is therefore, not a wise commercial decision.

The newspapers have a stellar role to play in a democracy. They not only help in forming a public opinion on major contentious issues, but also can help the government in educating the public on its policies. They have a great responsibility and hence have to rise above commercial and other narrow-minded considerations, so as to justify the trust posed on them by the public.

ASSIGNMENTS

- Newspapers have a greater impact on the thoughts and feelings of the public than any other media.
- A free Press is necessary in a Democracy. Discuss.

Leisure its uses and abuses

- Introduction — Need of some free time (leisure).
- Importance of leisure.
- Positive contribution of leisure —
  - Improves our work
  - Promotes social interaction and social work
  - Helps in pursuing hobbies
  - Pursuing social work for greater satisfaction.
- Negative contribution being promotion of vices leading to crime.
- Conclusion – Enriches our lives.

The time we spend away from work is the time we actually spend on ourselves. This is what differentiates a man from a machine. For while a machine can work incessantly, man cannot. He does need some leisure, so that his body and mind get some rest, from the stress and strain of everyday life. This not only provides relaxation, but at times helps in his work, by bringing forth new ideas and thoughts conjectured while in leisure.

Thus if we are able to plan our leisurely hours, it would not only make us happy, but also improve our working and our life style. This would in turn have a positive bearing, on our health and family life. It is on account of this fundamental truth that makes human psychologist and progressive organisation, encourage their employees to take time off for leisure. This is done very effectively by them, either by sponsoring club membership or sending them on short vacations to exotic locations, where they can be close to nature.

It not only provides the much required change, but at times people have come back after a short vacation injecting new life into their work. Leisure could be enjoyed in different ways, for example we may go to clubs or social gatherings to improve our social interaction. While others would prefer to go to a gym or to play games. Still others would engage in catching up on their old hobby of reading books or classics. The adventurous few would take to hiking, camping, tracking, gliding etc, which lend variety and add an element of thrill to their lives. This freshens their minds and lends a variety to their lives, which would otherwise be a drudgery of routine.

Life in the cities has become so mechanical, that we are going further and further away from nature. It is important for us that we appreciate nature by going out into the countryside. Those of us who have the time should take up some sort of social work, for this will not only bring inner satisfaction but will also make us feel happy and content.

It is however, unfortunate to see that the younger generation is not putting their leisure to proper use. It is quite common to find youngsters wiling away their time in the pursuit of illusionary enjoyment, that could be in the form of engaging in vices like gambling and drugs. This is indeed a dangerous way of killing time. For if we kill time, it will sooner or later kill us. This amounts to a criminal misuse of our leisure, which we will someday regret.

A happy man is one who knows and appreciates the value of his leisurely hours. He consciously utilises this time in doing good deeds. He enriches his life by engaging in persuits that are closest to his heart for, "What is this life if full of care, we have no time to stand and stare."

ASSIGNMENTS

- Importance of leisure time occupation.
- "What is this life if full of care, we have no time to stand and stare". Discuss.

Science makes the world a better place to live.

(ICSE 1984)

- Introduction — Evolution of science.
- Effect of science on our lives in the field of:–
    - (*a*) Transportation
    - (*b*) Communication
    - (*c*) Medical
    - (*d*) Education
    - (*e*) Entertainment.
- Conclusion — Changed lifestyle by its all pervading effect.

"The unreasonable man adopts himself to the world, the unreasonable one persist in trying to adapt the world to himself. Therefore, all progress depends on the unreasonable man," says G. Bernard Shaw. Indeed it is this unreasonable man, whose persistence in unveiling the mysteries of universe, led to the giant strides made in science that today impinges on every aspect of our lives.

The last century of the millennium has seen man make, gigantic stride in the field of science and technology. He has not only been able to explore the universe, by sending manned and un-manned spacecrafts to the Moon and the Mars, but has also been able to command and control the forces of nature. Besides these achievements he has also been able to ameliorate his lot, by making life much more easier and pleasant.

Science has helped reduce considerably the time and distance involved in travelling, making the world today more accessible. We have supersonic planes that take us around the world in a couple of hours. While just a century ago it took months or years to accomplish this feat. We have also new generation of cars, trains, etc., that make travelling a real pleasure.

Gone are the days, when we waited anxiously for the news of our near and dear ones. The advent of satellite communication, cellular and trunk line communication, enable us to access our friends even across continents in a flick of a second. The world has indeed become one global village, with free flow of communication, knocking down all geographic and political boundaries.

No longer are we at the mercy of such dreadful and incurable diseases like cancer and car-diac diseases. These can be effectively cured now, while other contagious epidemics, like plague, cholera, etc., has been effectively wiped out from the face of the earth. It has helped reduce human suffering and led to an increase in the longevity of an average man's life.

Giant strides have been made in the form and quality of education. We have today large num-ber of world-class institutions that are churning out top professionals. These institutions are also catering to fundamental research and development, which are addressing hitherto unexplored areas.

Life is no longer a drab schedule of routines. We have today radio, television and the Internet. They not only provide instant news, but also have revolutionized the concept of entertainment, by making it more interactive and responsive. The Internet has indeed opened up a plethora of op-portunities for the younger generation, in the field of e-commerce and self-development.

The world today is undoubtedly a better place to live in and we owe it to science for mak-ing it even better. So all pervading is the effect, that it has not only changed our lifestyle, but also changed the way we think, talk and express ourselves. This is but a beginning.

ASSIGNMENTS

- Science a boon or a bane. Discuss.
- Mention one invention or discovery you consider most useful in man's progress and civilisation. Show how this discovery has contributed to the progress of mankind.
- Science is a good servant but a bad master.

Role of youth in nation building
Or
Challenges before the youth in nation building

- Introduction — The power of youth has been the genesis of many a revolution.
- Problems facing the nation like literacy, insanitation and other social evils.
- Role of youth in meeting social challenges by augmenting government effort in the field of :–
  Illiteracy, hygiene. superstition, child marriage, casteism, etc.
  Participation in rural upliftment and making them self reliant through cooperatives.
- Social service to be made compulsory.
- Conclusion — Imperative for their, as well as the development of the country.

The youth of today are the future citizens of tomorrow. It is therefore, imperative that they not only appreciate the problems facing the country, but also meet the challenge. The youth power has been the genesis of many a revolution around the world. They were in the forefront of the French revolution, the Communist revolution, and even our own fight for independence. Their phenomenal power if effectively mobilized, could help in nation building that is the need of the hour.

The nation even after more than fifty years of independence, has not been able to alleviate the miseries of the rural folks. The problems of illiteracy, insanitation, superstition and poverty have deprived them of the fruits of freedom .So enormous are these problems, that nothing short of a youth revolution can annihilate them. It is therefore essential that they be fired with idealism, the like of which we saw during our fight for independence.

It calls for a concentrated effort on the part of the government by involving them also in this monumental task. This has been done successfully in many European countries, where social service is but part of the curriculum. Only when the youth have acquitted themselves in this task, are they eligible for being awarded degrees and government jobs. This has had a salutary effect on the youth and the society at large.

The energies of the youth should be effectively channelised in augmenting the government efforts, in spreading literacy to the villages and slums spread across the countryside. A short interaction would not only help the rural folks, but would be an eye opener for students. Besides imparting elementary education, they can also inculcate good hygienic practices and help improve the sanitary conditions in the villages. Their interface would help remove many social evils still prevalent in the society, like superstition, evils of dowry, child marriage, casteism, etc. These dark practices are but the root cause of their backwardness.

They can play a significant role in spreading socially critical messages like 'small family, happy family','evil of alcoholism', etc. The benefits of self-reliance could be demonstrated by augmenting the government's efforts in forming and running cooperatives. This will not only make them self-reliant, but also provide gainful employment in the villages itself. This will save the cities from congestion, on account of the large-scale migration of rural folks to cities, in search of employment.

A proper orientation of youth is required, to participate in the social upliftment of the society. This will equip him to meet the challenges of his life, more practically and successfully. The government should seize this opportunity and harness this power by making social service a compulsory part of the curriculum, before awarding degrees or employment.

The youth on the other hand should rise to the occasion and take it as a challenge, rather than a humdrum assignment to be just done with it. This would only be possible, if they work with a missionary zeal, in eradicating the age-old shackles that are eating into the vitals of our country. They shall not only help the country, but shall be laying down the foundation, for their own happy and prosperous tomorrow.

ASSIGNMENTS

- Social work and the youth.
- Should social work be made compulsory for students? Discuss.

Secularism

- Introduction — What is Secularism?
- Present in our rich cultural ethos.
- A political progressive concept that delinks religion from loyalty to state.
- Relevance in India.
- Conclusion — The only progressive path for us.

Secularism is a much used and abused word in India today. Each political party is vying to prove, that it is more secular than the other, in the battle of the ballots. However, generally speaking, it is a political concept in which people of all religion, irrespective of caste or creed enjoy equal rights. There is no religion of the state and people have a fundamental right to practice the religion of their choice.

This thought is nothing new for us, as it is embedded in our cultural ethos that makes us tolerant, magnanimous and receptive to all religions. This is why we find that this country has been the birthplace of many religions like Sikhism, Jainism, and Buddhism and of course Hinduism. People over the centuries lived in peace, except for last two centuries, when foreign rulers vitiated this harmony, by their much-maligned policy of divide and rule.

The world over especially in Europe, there were countries at war with one another to prove the superiority of their religion. This was the cause of untold destruction and miseries to the people. Even within the country, the bigotry lead to internecine, quarrels and strife. The chief cause being, a religion patronised by the state. Those subjects who did not prescribe to this religion were considered as second-class citizens. It was, however, in the last century that was the period of great awakening and enlightenment, the realization dawned that all religion led to but one God. This brought forth the idea of secularism that we see today. It was also understood, that differences in religion were not incompatible with the loyalty of state. The people owing alliance to different religions could also be loyal towards their country and that religion was something very personal and distinct from politics. Since everyone enjoyed equal rights, there was no cause for strife and people could happily coexist. This was not possible in a theocratic state, where there is a state religion practised by the majority and the minorities always feel threatened.

The founders of our constitution very wisely laid out the foundation of a truly democratic and secular country that symbolises the philosophy of "unity in diversity". This concept took shape under the guidance of Mahatma Gandhi the father of the nation, which led to the blossoming of people of different religion and faith in the country. They reflect our rich cultural heritage and complement each other for their own, as well as the growth of the country. The compulsions of party politics at times bring out major differences that raise their ugly head. We have ourselves to blame for this, as they show our immaturity. We should be more nationalistic in our outlook, rather than being guided by narrow minded and selfish motives.

Secularism today is a proven and successful political belief. This is the only path by which such a large and diverse country like India can progress. In the words of Benjamin Franklin "We must indeed hang together or, most assuredly we shall all hang seperately". The true success of this belief will be, when we regard ourselves first as Indians and then as Hindus, Sikhs and Muslims.

ASSIGNMENTS

- Can Secularism succeed in India? Discuss.
- Religion in politics.
- Terrorism.

Neighbours

- Introduction — Who is a neighbour?
- Need for neighbours and their importance.
- Different types of neighbours.
- Conclusion. – Play an important role in our lives.

"Love thy neighbour, as thou love God", so says the Bible. This is an eternal saying which subscribes to the view that God is but present in our fellow countrymen. The Bible goes on further to say "God created men in his own image, in the image of God he him, male and female created he then". Thus in loving our fellow citizen, or people who are around us ,we will not only bring peace and happiness, but also bring ourselves closer to God.

Man lives in society and it is these people who are around him, who are his neighbours. Similarly in the case of countries the country immediately around us are our neighbours. It is our neighbours who make our lives happy, by helping us in our time of need and sharing our joys and sorrows. They are also at times a cause for concern, when baser instincts like jealousy, envy and hypocrisy raise their ugly heads. It is this behavioural pattern, which give rise to suspicion, distrust and a feeling of ill will towards them. Nevertheless they play an important part in our lives, for it would be difficult to envision life without them. Thus our behaviour towards them should be appropriate to their traits.

This is evidently so, for just as people are different, similarly neighbours are also of varied kinds. Shakespeare in his play the 'Merchant of Venice' figuratively describes them as "Nature hath framed strange creature in her time, some who would evermore peep from their eyes in the way of smile and other of such vinegar aspects that they would never show a teeth in way of smiling, even if nestor swears the joke be laughable". In the same way we also have neighbourly countries that act as spoil sport. They not only relish the misfortune of a next-door country, but at times through their nefarious design, work for its downfall. It is such type of neighbours whom one should be beware of. This can be assiduously done by winning their trust and confidence, rather than by re-sorting to force, which at times leads to war. We all know that "Peace hath her victories. No less renowned than war. For what can war, but endless war still breed" so said John Milton. This will not only bring peace and tranquility around us, but will also make us happy.

Neighbours thus have an important role to play in our lives. We must therefore, cultivate good neighbourly relations with them and reciprocate their love and affection. This would make us happy and the world would also become a better place to live in.

ASSIGNMENTS

- "Love thy neighbour, as thou love God,"The relevance of this philosophy today.
- Friends.
- Relatives.

Is God Dead?

- Introduction — God and reason for doubt.
- Who is God?
- What does our faith or religion tell us?
- Growth of religious fundamentalism. Cause for doubt.
- Conclusion – eternal truth.

To pose such a portentous question as the above could be only attributed to a cynic, who does not view God in the proper perspective. It could also stem from his ignorance of what God actually is. Thus to answer his query it is imperative for us to know who God actually is.

God is neither a physical nor an abstract creature, nor is he there only in temples or churches or in the idols or pilgrim spots that we so religiously visit. He is but a manifestation of all things good in life and resides in each and every living creature on earth .The Bible, therefore, says "God created man in his own image, in the image of God he him, male and female created he both". It is this eternal truth that Siddhartha set out to find, when he renounced his kingdom. Only to realise on his enlightenment, that what he had set out to seek was but present in himself. It is this path of righteousness, ahimsa and peace that gave birth to Buddhism and similarly other religions. Thus all religions lead us to salvation and ultimately to him our Lord and master.

It is this eternal pursuit of man to know God, that gave rise to spiritualism and the growth of religion. Each in its own way dwelt on the good and noble things in life, demonstrating the victory of good over evil. Thus in the Hindu Mythology, we have the great epic of Ramayana, which motivates us to emulate the noble ideals of Lord Rama. It very effectively brings out the universal truth of victory of Good over Evil. Similar is the case with other religions like Sikhism, Islamism, etc. Thus there may be hundreds of religions, but they all lead to one God and that God is omnipresent and omnipotent.

It is indeed an antithesis of the above, that we find men fighting among themselves to prove the supremacy of his religion over the other. This leads to hatred and the growth of religious fundamentalism, which is posing a grave danger to mankind. Not only does it preach hatred towards one another, but it makes us behave more akin to savages. As Charles Colton rightly said " Man will wrangle for religion, write for it, fight for it, anything but live for it."It is this skepticism that at times raises the doubt of God's existence.

The eternal truth is that, there is only one God and all religions are but a path that we should follow to achieve salvation. This will not only make our lives happier but also bring peace and prosperity to the strife torn world. Thus as long as there is life on earth, God cannot die. To have any illusions on the contrary, would be amounting to inviting disaster and doom on earth.

ASSIGNMENTS

- God and the universe.
- "Man will wrangle for religion, write for it, fight for it, anything but live for it". Discuss.
- Most of us believe in God because our parents and grand parents have brainwashed us. Give your views for or against the statement.

Fashion

- Introduction — What is fashion?
- Role of fashion in our lives.
- Advantages of fashion.
- Disadvantages of fashion.
- Need to strike the right balance.
- Conclusion – Adds flavour to our lives.

Fashion as described in the English dictionary is "the prevailing mode in such things as are subject to change in form of a style, as in ornaments, etiquette and especially in dress". This age is the age of fashion which is not only confined to our dress, but also in the way we speak, behave, decorate our houses and our lifestyle in general. So enamoured are we by the 'Me Too' concept that we adopt it, irrespective of whether it goes with our personality or not.

In a way it lends variety to our lives, providing an element of excitement in trying out something new. It would indeed be a drab life, if we all were supposed to behave and dress similarly. Change is therefore, not only desirable but also welcome. The heroes, heroines of the tinsel world and the fashion models are the trendsetters, who are the role models for our youth. They are the icons around whom the 'fashion' revolves.

It has given shape to an entirely new industry, 'The Fashion Industry'. It is estimated to be over a thousand crores. No wonder we have today large educational institutions imparting specialised fashion technology courses, example NIFT and other bodies. It has given rise to a plethora of new industries, making it an interesting career option for the youth. Besides generating jobs, it is earning valuable foreign exchange by exporting fashion garments to foreign countries. Thus offering tremendous potential for growth and improvement in our standard of living.

However, it is the exclusive preserve of the rich and influential people, for they have the means and the resources to indulge in this luxury. This creates a divide among the haves and the have-nots more glaring, which at times appears vulgar. It also leads to psychological imbalance for youth, who try to ape their affluent friends, but in the absence of means resort to unlawful and unethical acts. We have seen instances of youngsters taking to crime, just to buy a pair of fashionable shoes.

We must, therefore, strike a right balance between being fashionable and what is good for us. There is no point in senselessly copying our peers or idols , for what looks good on them, need not look good on us. It may be fashionable in America to wear short dresses, but it would be foolhardy to attempt it here. Such a person would stand out as a sore thumb and also be a subject of ridicule.

One must, therefore, be in fashion, for it adds flavour to our lives. It releases the creative urge in us on trying out a novelty and improves our lifestyles. We should however, beware of the 'herd' instinct, that impels us to emulate others without considering its suitability to us.

ASSIGNEMENTS

- Impact of Fashion on students .
- Fashion is the exclusive preserve of the rich. Comment.

Career options for the youth in the new millennium

- Introduction — Perplexing decision.
- Opening of new vistas of career options in the field of :–
  Information Technology
  Science
  Traditional careers
- Cardinal principles to be followed in making a choice.
  Inclination and aptitude
  Future career prospects
- Take a timely decision giving due weightage to advise of parents and peers.
- Conclusion — After having taken a decision work upon it sincerely.

The dawn of the new millennium has thrown up a plethora of new career opportunities that were hitherto unknown. They have made the task of choosing a career for the youth more confusing and perplexing. The decision at times is fraught with suspense and anxiety and is a vital decision, that has a direct bearing on our lives.

Fortunately for us, there are vast avenues for getting career information, through newspapers, electronic media and the Internet. There are an equally large number of career options to choose from. The new millennium shall see major advancement being made in the field of Information Technology. The advent of the Internet and associated e-commerce, shall offer immense possibilities for trade and industry. This would therefore, require manpower with specialised skills, thus creating enormous employment opportunities for the youth. For instance, the youth would have new career options as Web designers, administrators and developers beside software and hardware engineers, programmers and analysts.

In Science we have such new fields like Biotechnology, Environmental Sciences, Genetic Engineering, Nuclear medicine and a host of other fields in medicine and health like Acupuncture, Magnetic therapy, etc. These careers are in addition to the traditional options of doctor, lawyer, engineer and a teacher that would continue to attract talent.

The host of career opportunities is no cause for despair, for there are some basic cardinal principles that we must bear in mind while exercising our choice. The first and foremost being, that we must objectively identify our inclination and aptitude, strengths and weaknesses, likes and dislikes and inborn propensities. Keeping this in mind, we should identify the careers that are best suited; with respect to our disposition .We should also closely examine the future career prospects that exist for that particular branch of study, by reading and discussing extensively about it. It is very common to find young people, enamoured by the glamour and razzmatazz of a particular profession opting for it. Only to have their dream shattered, on discovering that it does not suit them temperamentally. They thus end up highly dissatisfied and frustrated.

We should also give due weightage to the views of our parents, friends and peer groups. Our parents and peers can guide us by their experience. It is important that they render their advice objectively and dispassionately. It has sometimes been observed that the youth takes up a career, bowing to the wishes of his parents. Thus we see the son of an eminent doctor, taking to the medical profession, just to please his father. He may become a doctor, but in the absence of aptitude and inclination, he can never achieve his father's eminence.

The innovative career options in the new millennium are indeed very exciting. Thus a timely decision needs to be taken for as they say 'well begun is half done'. With the right option, we shall work more assiduously for realising our dream. It does not matter if we do not get admission into the best of institutions, what matters is that after getting the requisite qualification, we excel in the field which is closest to our heart .We must remember the words of H.W. Longfellow when he says "Life's battle don't always go to the stronger and the fastest man. But soon or late the man who wins is the man who thinks he can."

ASSIGNMENTS

- Role of computers in our lives.
- Women and careers.

Relate how the reading and study of literature have enriched and refined you

- Introduction — What is literature?
- Impact of reading and literature on my life.
- Gives knowledge inspires confidence.
- Makes us better human beings.
- Conclusion — Tremendous impact on our lives.

The word literature means literally 'letters'. It is on account of this that a learned man is referred to as a man of letters. However, all writing is not literature. It is only the memorable thoughts, finely expressed in words that are called literature. The literary works of great writers that are composed in books are their priceless contribution to mankind. John Milton rightly says, "A good book is the precious lifeblood of a master spirit embalmed and treasured on purpose to a life beyond life".

The literary works of great authors have profoundly affected us since times immemorial. The Vedas, the Ramayana, Gita, Bible and the Koran are all great literary works of noble minds, which have spread the light of wisdom since ages. On being frequently prodded by my parents, I read the Ramayana and the Bhagavad Gita. Ever since I feel, I am a changed person altogether. While the Ramayana gave me insight to human relationship, on how to treat elders, friends and colleagues. The Gita idolizes Karma (duty), that is the purpose of our lives. These provide strength and inspiration to me in time of a dilemma. They are indeed masterpieces of art that unfold the truth of life and death. making us reverent, yet fearless. Besides this the classics of William Shakespeare, Rabindra Nath Tagore and Munshi Premchand have bequeathed to me, a wealth of knowledge on such aspects as friendship, virtues, honesty and life itself. This is so for "when knowledge comes wisdom lingers'. So said Lord Tennyson.

Not only has it made me more confident and knowledgeable, but also intrepid. Adversity does not scare me, for I know "Sweet are the uses of adversity which like the toad ugly and venomous, Wears yet a precious jewel on his head". Nor does death frighten me for "what is born, death is certain, and for the dead, birth is certain. Therefore, grieve not over what is unavoidable", says the Bhagavad-Gita.

It has helped me to become a better human being and transformed my personality. It has provided me valuable insight into the good things of life and made me aware of the negative aspects. This is a continuing education process, the journey of which I have just begun. There is nothing more satisfying to me, than to be in the company of a good book, for Francis Bacon aptly says, "Some books are to be tasted, others to be swallowed and some few to be chewed and digested".

I have no hesitation in proclaiming, that what I am and what I hope to be, is something that I owe to the literary works of great thinkers. I would also someday like to emulate them, maybe not in literature, but in my chosen field of work. For I know that "Lives of great men all remind us. We can make our lives sublime. And departing leaves behind us. Footprints in the sand of time."

ASSIGNMENTS

- The pleasures of reading literature.
- Impact of literature on our lives.
- Literature is not only to be studied but an art to be practiced.
- "Reading maketh a Full Man; conference a Ready Man and Writing an Exact Man", Bacon

The Place of religion in india today.

- Introduction — What is Religion ?
- Glorious role of religion in India in the past.
- Its role today — exploitation by leaders.
- Reasons for change:–
  - Personal level, we are moderate.
  - Political level, we are very aggressive.
- Cause of this dichotomy.
- Conclusion — We must be religious in the true sense of the word.

"Educate man without religion and you make them but clever devils", says Arthur Wellesley. Thus religion is not only a matter of faith but also a way of life. We all believe in God Almighty, the creator of the universe who guides our lives. God is one but he may be worshipped in the form of Jesus by Christians, Muhammad by Muslims or Ram by Hindus. It is this faith in our religion that teaches us, how to lead a good and happy life.

India has been singularly blessed on this account; it is the birthplace of Jainism, Buddhism, Sikhism and Hinduism. Most of the Saints and sages who propagated these religions were born in India. It is from here that they set out to enlighten the world. Thus culturally and spiritually our forefathers were more advanced and lived a full and happy life.

The same cannot be said of today, for religion has become a major reason for discord and unrest. Like a double-edged sword it can also incite hatred and inflame passions to such an extent, that men start behaving like beasts, baying for each other's blood. This evil facet of religion has been fanned and exploited by some religious and political leaders, for their own vested interests. It is indeed shocking to see, that in this age of enlightenment, we are still living in the dark ages, believing one religion to be superior to the other.

However, at the personal level, we find that we are being greatly influenced by the western culture. The strict moral tenets of our religion are gradually being forgotten. No longer do we find many Muslims offering Namaz five times a day, Christians going to church every Sunday or Hindus going daily to temples for offering prayer's. This is so because our outlook has become very moderate and easy going. However, at the political or social level, we are ready to exploit our religion for garnering more power. It is this contradiction in our psyche that is being exploited by the unscrupulous leaders, who sow discord among us resulting in communal strife.

The cause of this dichotomy is that we do not really understand religion. This is so as we neither have the time, nor the inclination to really know and understand our own religion. If we had really understood our own religion, things would not have come to such a pass. This is because there is no religion that preaches violence, disharmony, and disrespect for other religions. It is only we, in our ignorance, fall prey to the mechanisation of conspirators in the religious garb. This is in recent times leading to disastrous consequences. Charles Colton rightly summed up our dilemma when he said, " Men will wrangle for religion, write for it, and fight for it, anything but live for it".

The place of religion in the India of today is indeed very sensitive and politically explosive. It is however, still not too late; we should realise that we cannot wear religion on our sleeves, to be used only at will. It is something more sublime and spiritual. We must not only proclaim to be religious but we must practice it in our daily lives. This only shall lead to more love, compassion and a feeling of brotherhood, so sadly missing in the India of today.

ASSIGNMENTS

- 'Man is by his constitution a religious animal'. Provide a balanced writeup of your views on the same.
- "Educate man without religion and you make them but clever devils". Do you agree.
- "We have just enough religion to make us hate, but not enough to make us love one another". Give your views on the same.
- People these days do not really have any sense of religion and morality has decayed.

Knowledge is Power

- Introduction — Knowledge possessed by learned and the wise.
- Knowledge leads to wisdom, respect and consequently power.
- Historical facts in support.
- New era makes knowledge a premium.
- Conclusion – Essence of Power.

Knowledge is the exclusive preserve of the learned and the wise. They are thus able to use this very effectively for acquiring power for themselves or for helping others stay in power. This is so, for with knowledge comes wisdom, that is the domain of only a few. Lord Tennyson was thus right, when he said, "Knowledge comes but wisdom lingers".

Not only does knowledge make one wise, but it also makes one more articulate, humane and modest. Such people are able to explain their point of view very convincingly and dynamically, thus attracting a huge following. They have the knack of sensing people's nerves and use their oratorial skills to elicit the desired response from them. We have in this class the politicians and leaders of today, who owe their power to this art of knowledge. However, for the people with a literary or religious bent of mind, knowledge makes them modest and humane. They are thus able to rise above the ordinary, being the enlightened class or the intelligentsia to whom the ordinary people look up to. The saints, sages and learned men come in this class, around whom the society revolves. With knowledge comes respect and consequently power. Such people are able to command the respect of the masses and even the government of the day, looks unto them for their advice in solving contentious and tricky issues. It is because of this we find such people occupying positions of power, either in the bureaucracy or in the government.

This has been happening from times immemorial. The Rajas and the Emperors who ruled the country had a group of ministers or courtiers. It is through them that they wielded their power on their subjects. These people were recognised stalwarts in their respective field. They also had Rajgurus and Purohits, who advised them on religious and other delicate matters of the state. Such people were thus able to wield phenomenal power on the strength of their knowledge.

The new millennium has seen the emergence of a revolution in the field of Information Technology. This is basically a field that thrives on ideas and knowledge, which command a premium. We therefore find people with exclusive knowledge and technologies becoming more resourceful and powerful. The legendary example of Bill Gates, the chief architect of Microsoft is there before us, who has the mighty governments across the world clamouring for his attention.

There is no denying the fact that knowledge is power and this comes from extensive reading, which makes one reason the pros and the cons before taking a decision. 'Read not to contradict and confute nor to believe and take for granted, nor to find talk and discourse, but to weigh and consider', said Francis Bacon. It is this aspect of weighing and considering that sets apart a man of knowledge. He is thus able to command power, for his actions are justified and supported with reasoning. There in lies the essence of his power.

ASSIGNMENTS

- "Knowledge comes but wisdom lingers". Discuss.
- Little knowledge is dangerous. Discuss.
- Where ignorance is bliss it is folly to be wise. Discuss.

Prohibition

- Introduction — What is Prohibition?
- Is there need for prohibition? Infringement of fundamental right.
- Advantages of prohibition.
- Disadvantages of Prohibition — Loss of revenue.
- Conclusion — Best left to the individual.

The word Prohibition owes its genesis from the word 'prohibit' which means ban. In this case it is to ban the use of intoxicant beverages by the rule of law. It is a known fact that addiction to wine or liquor has led many a family to ruins, while at the same time its imposition on its citizens is seen, as an infringement of their fundamental rights. It is indeed a serious question of moral and ethics that the various state governments are trying to address.

Imposition of prohibition is desirable, as it comes as a saviour to many a family which were on their way to ruins. It has been observed that the people who are generally not well off, specially of the labour class fall easy prey to addiction. What normally starts as a minor flirtation, for overcoming weariness or frustration gradually becomes a habit. So much so that they spend their entire earnings on drinks, ruining themselves as well as their families. The state cannot be a mute witness to this state of affairs, for such people not only become a curse for their family, but also a nuisance to the society. However, not all people become drunkards. People drink for enjoyment, for overcoming weariness and for some it is a matter of aping the Jones, so as to be in fashion. Alcoholic drinks have been known to be good for health, if taken within limits as confirmed by medical experts. It is also known to provide relief to people staying in cold climatic conditions. Enforcement of prohibition is also an undue interference by the state in the private life of an individual. It is infact an infringement on his fundamental right to live freely.

Notwithstanding the above, there are many advantages which can be attributed to enforcing prohibition. Not only does it safeguard the lives of the common man, but we can save numerous lives which are sniffled out due to reckless driving of cars and motor vehicles, under the influence of liquor. It is also known to have a corrupting influence on the youth and gives rise to complicated social problems that we can do without.

However, enforcing prohibition is easier said than done. It gives rise to a plethora of other problems like bootlegging. and trafficking in illicit liquor. While the former provides encouragement to antisocial elements and makes a mockery of the law, the latter gives rise to a parallel-uncontrolled industry. This is far more dangerous, as there are numerous instances of these illicit breweries serving poisonous brew to the poor labourers, killing them in large numbers. Those that are spared death are maimed for life, either becoming blind or paralyzed. The state in turn loses considerable revenue, in the form of Excise Duty and Sales Tax. This leads to resource crunch, adversely affecting the development and social welfare activities of the state. Such is the reliance of the state on this revenue, that quite a few states had as a result of popular sentiments imposed prohibition in their state, but after some time they had to roll back the same. A specific example being, the state of Andhra Pradesh, where after a brief stint of prohibition, it was done away with.

It is of paramount importance that the public should be educated on the evils of excessive drinking. The glamour and macho illusions depicted in advertisements should be countered and its consumption in public places should be banned. After having suitably educated the public, it should be left to the discretion of the individual who should know what is best for him.

ASSIGNMENT

- Drinking of alcoholic beverages should be banned in public places. Discuss.
- The evil of Drug Abuse among students. What is the cause and suggest what remedies might be effective?

Outline of Essays
for Practice
Write Your Own Essay

Write a story begining with, It was the most wonderful sight I had ever seen ....

- What and where did you see the sight?
- What was so beautiful about it?
    - Describe what you saw, felt, heard or smelt.
    - Give some comparison of similar sights if possible.
- What happened thereafter?
    - Any specific incident related to it.
    - What you did?
- Conclusion — How it ended ?

Hobbies

- Introduction — What are hobbies?
- Need for hobbies and their importance in our lives.
    - Provides relief and recreation.
    - Oasis in a drab desert of routine.
    - Constructive work, gives a sense of satisfaction and achievement.
- Uses of hobbies in our daily lives.
    - Channalises extra energy to productive use.
    - Helps us in our old age or after retirement.
    - Sometimes blossoms as a profession in our later lives.
- Varied kinds of hobbies.
    - Stamp collection (philately).
    - Gardening, Antiques collection, photography, sports and reading, etc.
- Conclusion — It is an essence of life, giving it a new meaning,

Violence is the only means of achieving one's goals. Give your views for or against the statement.

- Introduction — Resorting to violence does not solve problems or achieves goals.
- Violence results from.
    - Anger, which leads to indiscretion ,creating obstacles.
    - Instead of building bridges, it destroys human relationships that are crucial for achieving goals.

- It leads to —

  Destruction of life and property.

  Results in changes that are irreversible and permanent.

- Goals can be achieved more effectively by —

  Discussion and building public opinion.

  Waging a battle for the human mind, rather than using muscle power. Example our own struggle for independence.

- Conclusion — Violence begets more problems than it solves. Permanent goals can be achieved by discussion, debate and understanding.

The awakening of the Indian women give your views

- Introduction — Signs of the awakening of the Indian women, with few examples.
- The position of women during medieval past, their exploitation and deprivation.
- Their emancipation in the twentieth century, by great social reformers like Vivekananda and Mahatma Gandhi.
- Discrimination even exists today in society, that is manifest in —

  The evil of dowry.

  Female infanticide and the general belief of their being a burden.

  Denial of property rights.

- Reasons for the slow pace of their awakening is on account of —

  Their docile and modest nature.

  Absence of economic independence.

  High level of illiteracy and other psychological factors.

- Need for utilising their full potential —

  By making special provisions like reservation in jobs and education.

  Steps to ensure their economic independence.

- Conclusion — Urgent need to free them from their age old shackles. They comprise nearly fifty percent of the population and their awakening augers well for the country.

Television and Cinema influence the youth more than any other media. Discuss.

- Introduction — They influence the youth because ,both are audio video media with an extensive reach and entertainment value.
- Reason for this influence

  Easily comprehendible offering instant entertainment, leaves a lasting impression on their minds.

- Positive influence on youth —

    A powerful mass communication media, which could bring to the fore socio-economic problems like, the evils of dowry, child marriage and need for family planning.

    Imparts formal and informal education.

    Promotes culture and values.

- Negative impact on youth

    Glorifies crime, sex and negative values, harmful to their impressionable minds

    Distracts them from studies and plays havoc with their career.

- Importance of Television and Cinema in our lives

    For News, Views, Knowledge and Entertainment.

- Conclusion — Need to check negative influence through effective censorship and code of conduct by mandarins of this media.

Spending millions of rupees in Space and Nuclear programs cannot be justified when the country concerned is India.

- Introduction — Do not agree with the statement.
- Importance of space and nuclear programs.

    Helps develop technology that is useful in our daily lives, for example in the field of satellite communication and energy generation.

    Unveils the mysteries of the universe, helps in exploiting our natural resources like mineral and water resources by remote sensing satellite imagery.

- Need for spending money for the above programs for —

    Putting in place an effective deterrent, for safeguarding our freedom that is priceless.

    Helps in economic development, thus improving our living standards.

- Conclusion — This is the hope for the future for any country including India.

Little knowledge is dangerous

- Introduction — Importance of knowledge in our lives.
- People with knowledge possess power and authority.
- Dangers posed by incomplete and inadequate knowledge.

    Causes personal monetary loss or loss of reputation.

    In the case of leaders and Generals, it can cause grievous loss of lives.

- Examples from everyday life.

    The inadequate knowledge of the doctor or the lawyer, can spell doom for his patient or client.

- Importance of having complete knowledge
    - Enables timely and quick decision-making.
    - Avoids dissipation of energy in trial and error or experimentation.
- Conclusion — Little knowledge on one's subject is dangerous for self and the society at large.

Money spent on the education of girls is money well spent. Give your views for or against the statement

- Introduction – Agree with the statement
    - Beneficial to the girl as well as the society.
- Advantages in educating the girl child–
    - Makes them good knowledgeable citizens of the future, leading to their emancipation.
    - Builds their self confidence and spurs them for economic independence
    - Makes an impact on their family after marriage.
    - Leads to social change and helps in the eradication of social malpractices, superstition and other evils.
- Money well spent on the education of girls for–
    - The education of a girl child addresses a future family.
    - Holds the key to our future society.
    - In view of its importance the government should subsidise their education.
- Conclusion — It is money well spent for it emancipates them, their family and the society

Benefits of reading

- Introduction — Importance of reading in our lives as —
    - Reading begets ideas and ideas rule the world.
    - Makes us refined and cultured.
- The different types of books and reading material
    - Fiction novels, books on nature, science and autobiographies
    - Magazines and newspapers.
- Benefits of reading —
    - Provides a valuable source of inspiration, giving rise to noble thoughts and ideals.
    - Treasure stove for knowledge and general awareness.
    - Source of pleasure and entertainment.

- Good and healthy hobby for students for self-development
    - Unfortunately on the wane due to the impact of television and cinema that are no substitute for reading
- Conclusion — Reading maketh a Full man (Bacon)
    - Important to cultivate this healthy hobby for our future

Television a boon or a bane

- Introduction — Most effective and fastest means of communication.
    - A Boon for mankind
- Advantages of television
    - An effective medium of entertainment and recreation
    - A potential harbinger of change in the society , through mass social and health education.
    - Valuable source of news, views and current affairs.
    - Advertisement promotes economic growth and development.
    - A powerful tool of propaganda by the government, for building public opinion
- Disadvantages of television
    - Distracts students from studies
    - Negative impact of excessive violence and sex on impressionable minds
    - Leads to less interpersonal and social interaction of people
    - Harmful effect on eyesight
- Conclusion — It is a boon for the individual and the society if judiciously used

Your first plane journey

- When, Where and How you got the opportunity?
- The scene at the airport and the procedure for check in.
- The description of the plane's interior —
    - The welcome accorded by the airhostess and the safety instructions demonstrated by her.
    - Your feeling when the plane took off.
- View of the landscape on looking out of the window.
- What you did during the journey?
    - Reading newspaper, magazines, making friends.
    - Serving of refreshments by the airhostess.
- End of the journey —
    - Announcement of reaching destination, request for putting on the safety belt.
    - Your feeling and impression on disembarking from the plane.
- A memorable journey indeed.

The generation gap is the root cause of the problems of the youth. Give your views for or against the statement

- Introduction — Agree with the statement. What is generation gap?

  It is the wide gap between the moral values, ideals, dreams, expectations of the old and the young generation.

- Reasons for the generation gap.

  It is basically a problem of change, which the older generation resists, as it is at times in conflict with their customs, values and beliefs.

  On the other hand the youth is more adaptive to change which results in misunderstanding.

- Effect of this on the youth —

  Creates family tension with the youth getting rebellious and parents feeling frustrated and angry.

  Stubbornness of both often leads to tragic consequences.

- Need to understand the phenomenon by looking into its causes —

  Parents still treat them as children and are overprotective towards them.

  Reluctance of parents to concede the independence of the youth

- Suggested remedies —

  The parents should treat youth as friends and not children.

  Motivate and encourage them.

  Accept the universal fact that change is the way of life.

  Youth will respect and regard them for their understanding.

- Conclusion — A universal and natural phenomenon effecting society worldwide.

  Requires mutual understanding and respect for the opinion of each other. This is the key to solve the above problem.

SECTION - D

Picture Composition

PICTURE COMPOSITION

Guidelines

A picture is a great stimulant .It at times makes you recall your personal experience, good or bad. Sometimes we can relate it to what we have read in the newspapers and magazines, or seen on television or films.

In the ICSE Examination you would get to write a story or a description or an account of what the picture suggests to you. Your composition may be directly about the subject or may take suggestions from it, but there must be a clear connection between the picture and the composition.

The picture may be a photograph, or an action scene or a sketch .The objective being to judge its impact on your imagination. Thus as per the question, you will have to decide whether you want to

1. Write a story on the picture.
2. Write a description of the things you see in the picture.
3. Write an account of the ideas and feelings that the picture suggests to you.

You will have to choose one of the above. However, for each of them, different approach to writing would have to be adopted. These are dwelt on in detail in the following pages, with an illustrated example based on one particular picture. The composition has been written in the three different forms so as to highlight their uniqueness.

A story based on a picture

1. Take a careful look at the picture with a view to ascertain the nuclear plot or the theme. In case it is not very evident, you may have to invent a theme bearing a direct connection with the picture .It is around this, that you will have to base your characters in the story. Thus if you see the picture of a crowd, led by a man with a clenched fist and placards, you may immediately connect it with 'strike 'or a 'protest march'. This would be the theme, while the causes would have to be imagined by you, for example it could be a workers strike or a public demonstration for a social or political cause. Similarly if you see a picture of a street or landscape flooded with water, then the theme could be 'Water logging' or 'Floods'.

2. Once having identified the theme, you can go about identifying and character sketching the key actor and the associated actors in the picture. In case the picture is based on an action sequence, you can identify yourself with the key actor and get involved in the scene, by letting loose your imagination.

3. Based on the theme you have chosen, write out a short story as to what had happened prior to the picture and what would follow, thus bringing the story to a close. A careful observation of the facial expressions, gestures, clothes could provide you valuable clues to the story.

For the illustrative example please see following page

A description based on a picture

1. Study the picture with a view to identify a specific detail.
2. Now widen the focus to take into account the other or peripheral details, given in the picture.
3. The factors or causes, which have an impact on, the details so selected.

4.   The affect of this on the other people and the general public.

5.   Conclude by summarizing the causes and their affect that you observe in the picture.

For the illustrative example please see following page.

An account based on a picture

Here you are required to give an account of what the picture suggests to you. Thus while the picture becomes the starting point for having stimulated the writer, he can now allow his thoughts and feelings to dwell on things beyond the picture. Thus in the illustrative example given, we see the starting point of picture being a flooded village, with a man and his son sitting on a thatched roof. This could be followed with your associated thoughts and suggestions, which you derive from the picture.

You could do this by dwelling on the irony of nature, where you have flood in one part of the country, whereas in another part people are suffering because of a draught .The faulty management of the water resources of the country, the large scale felling of trees and environmental degradation being the cause of this evil. This and similar other ideas could form the body of the composition.

A picture composition of this kind should have the following plan.

1.   *Introduction* — Brief description of the stimulus in the picture and its effect on you.

2.   *Body of the composition* — The different thoughts and ides from the picture, which are linked together in a logical sequence.

3.   *Conclusion* — Rounding off your thought and feelings and returning to the specific stimuli, which had triggered your imaginative adventure.

Illustrative examples

Study the picture given at page number below. Write a story or a description or an account of what the picture suggests to you. Your composition may be about the subject of the picture or may take suggestions from it, but there must be a clear connection between the picture and the composition.
                                                                              ICSE 2000

A story based on a picture

THE FLOODS

Ramu and his son had spent the last two days on the roof of their thatched hut. They were soaked to the skin, for it had rained incessantly throughout the last week. Ramu was cursing himself for his stupidity for having stayed back, when all the villagers were fleeing fearing the impending floods. He had laughed at their cowardice and had taunted them for being a quisling. How he regretted his actions and prayed fervently to God, to deliver him and his son from this tribulation.

Never in the last fifty years that he was aware of, had a flood of such magnitude happened in his village. It was on this premise, that he had scoffed of the well intentioned advise, rendered to him by his neighbours to flee, before the going got tough. Unheeding their advice he had stayed back with his son, to safeguard the little worldly possessions he had. When the floods came he was caught completely unaware and in the last moment could do nothing, but climb up to the roof of his thatched hut, along with his son. His goat and hens were swept away by the surging water before his very eyes, as he watched helplessly wringing his hands in despair. A lone cock and his pet dog Tony who managed to climb on to the roofs of the adjacent huts, were the only other survivors'. The last forty-eight hours had been hell, as he watched powerlessly livestock and valuables, being swept by the swelling water that seemed to inch up by the hour.

They were starving and thirsty. What an irony? Thought Ramu. They had not a drop to drink, with so much water around them. In anguish he cupped his palms and drank the rainwater to quench his thirst. His son followed suit and once again they sat eyes transfixed, on the horizon as if expecting deliverance.

Their prayers were answered the next morning, when the clouds drifted away to give way to bright sunshine. But the water level refused to decline. The weather conditions having improved he could see some human activity on the horizon. Gradually he could make out the silhouette of a boat emerging. This injected new life to his sagging morale. Taking out his shirt he waved frantically, so as to draw their attention. He opened his mouth to shout for help, but could barely utter a croak. To his dismay the boat drifted away oblivious to their presence. Crestfallen he slumped on the roof cursing his ill luck. The sun was now shining brightly causing blisters, thus adding to their misery. Just when everything seemed lost, he saw his son gesticulating excitedly in the opposite direction. He strained his old eyes to make out the outline of another boat, which happened to be coming in their direction. In about ten minutes the boat was alongside their hut. Ramu and his son were helped down the thatched roof, by many helping hands and given some food packets to eat. Forgetting all norms of etiquette and behaviour, they tore the food packets and literally devoured the morsels of food, without bothering to even munch them. They were so famished that they just did not care what food they were eating, what was important was that they had something to eat. Their pet dog Tony and the lone cock were also loaded on to the boat. The motorboat surveyed the village in search of survivors, but not finding any, turned back to the relief camp.

Ramu was pleased to find his colleagues and neighbours in the relief camp. God had indeed been kind, for all his relatives and friends were safe. He prayed to the Almighty, to give him the fortitude and strength to begin life afresh, for all that he possessed had been swept by the floods.

Illustrative Example. Picture in previous page

A description based on a picture

The picture is of a farmer and his son sitting on a thatched roof of their hut, which has been submerged by the surging water of the Saru River. This has been an annual phenomenon repeating every monsoon, with the onset of the rains.

The surging waters have flooded the entire village of Rampur, with all the houses and fields submerged under water. Since the village is in a low-lying area, on the banks of this river it invariably gets flooded every monsoon. This had forced the entire inhabitants to flee, but for the poor old farmer who did not have the energy to escape. His son stayed behind to keep him company and together, they along with their pet dog and a cock waited for relief to arrive. They watched in dismay their crop and valuables being swept by the water and could do nothing about it. His other livestock comprising, a goat and a few hens had been swept away. The solitary cock and his dog had the good sense of jumping on to the roof of the adjacent huts and had thus been saved, but for how long.

Floods bring havoc to the people inhabiting the low lying areas, along the banks of the rivers. These are invariably in spate in the monsoons every year. The extent of loss to public property and the personal loss of the helpless villagers is difficult to fathom. Nevertheless, they can do nothing about it, but to silently bear the agony of seeing their precious belonging being swept away before their very eyes. Floods are thus a natural calamity, which strikes them at regular intervals.

Besides causing loss of property, it causes disruption of road and rail traffic. Damages crops and bringing in its wake dreadful diseases like cholera, dysentery that take a heavy toll of human lives .The meager resources of the government, are stretched in providing relief and succor to the affected people. Relief camps are set up in the open, or in schools and colleges where the affected people live like refugees, surviving on doles of the government or the voluntary organisations, which run the camps.

Rains are indeed welcome after the scorching heat of the hot summer .We welcome the dark clouds, at the onset of the monsoon, as they promise the much awaited respite. Nevertheless for the poor farmer, living along the banks of the river, it is an ominous reminder of the impending disaster that is in store for him. It is difficult for him to rejoice, for it bring with it a bag of misfortune.

Illustrative example. Picture in previous page.

An account based on a picture

The monsoons had arrived, bringing with it the usual chaos, like water logging and floods in the low-lying areas of the villages and towns. This year too like in the previous years, the Saru river submerged large number of villages and towns. The scene was pathetic in one such village Rampur, located on the bank of this river. Here a poor old farmer, unable to escape the onslaught of the raging waters, took refugee on the top of his thatched hut. His young son stayed behind, to tend and care for him. All the villagers had fled and most of the livestock had been swept away by the floods. The only surviving pets were his pet dog Tony and a cock, who took refugee on the roof of the adjacent huts. They thus began their endless wait for relief to arrive.

This tragic scenario has been happening over the years and we have not been able to tackle this problem, which strikes us at regular intervals. It is an irony that on one hand some areas are flooded with the overflowing rivers, while at the same time there are draught like conditions in other areas of the country. We have made spectacular progress in Science and Technology, but have been unable to address this problem. The flood brings in its wake misery, destruction and enormous loss of life and property that could be avoided.

Water is a precious national resource that we have not been able to manage. This is the reason for the above paradoxical situation. Had we built dams and reservoirs in the catchment areas, we could have effectively regulated the level of river water. The excess water could have been diverted to the draught stricken areas. These dams and reservoirs could augment the generation of hydroelectric power, thus accelerating the pace of economic development.

Our callous attitude to soil conservation, reflected in the continuous felling of trees, is also responsible for floods. By denuding large tracts of forest land, we have accelerated the pace of soil erosion and consequently the rain water swiftly flows down, flooding the low lying areas.

The problem of floods, would continue to torment us and the above sight would be a regular feature in the monsoon, if we and the government do not take remedial measures. It is high time that instead of waiting for the calamity to strike, we adopt a more proactive policy by efficiently managing our water resources. This can be done by attending to the root cause of the problem as suggested above, so that that poor farmer as symbolised in the picture, does not have to suffer the repeated ravages of the floods.

Look at the cartoon given below and write an account of what it suggests to you.

ICSE 2000

Practice what you preach

The cartoon is a satire on the present social practices prevailing in the society. We hear our great leaders, elders and respected citizens proclaiming very lofty ideals and sentiments in public. However when it comes to practicing them they do just the reverse, completely oblivious of what they preached. Thus we find political leaders despising their compatriots who place their loyalties for a price, to find the very same leaders resorting to it when they stand to gain. This is the abysmally low level to which our national character has fallen.

The cartoon is but a manifestation of this national character, where we see two delegates coming out from a conference on the theme 'Save water'. Their enthusiasm reflects the resounding success of the conference. They have all the reasons to be happy for their paper on 'Need to conserve water, a precious natural resource' was greatly applauded. Their practical suggestion of individual responsibility, for conserving this valuable resource, by avoiding wastage through leaky taps and carelessness was appreciated. On coming out of the hall they find the banner put up at the venue of the seminar slightly tilted. They instruct the supervisor to set it right, completely oblivious to the fact that, just behind them water from a tap was flowing down the drain. It very aptly brings out the present style of demonstrating and proclaiming from rooftops, noble and high ideals, only to ignore them when it comes to practicing them ourselves. In other words, it is a classic example of 'darkness under the candlestick.'

We find instances of the above abounding all around us .The teacher ridicules those who take private tuitions, while at the same time indulging in this practice on the sly to rake in some additional money. The political parties deride corruption in public life and the involvement of criminals in politics, to find that they themselves are smeared with the same brush with which they are painting others. So deep rooted is this malice, that we no longer take seriously even socially relevant issues like water conservation, pollution, fuel conservation and many other critical issues. Though we pay lip service to them. This apathy is probably due to the public's observance, of the open flouting of these issues by the proponents themselves. Thus we find that even serious issues do not get the desired attention they deserve from the public, which is a cause of concern.

It seems the present society has forgotten the golden rule of "practice what you preach "or "actions speak louder than words." It is high time that we wake up to this invaluable piece of wisdom before it is too late.

Write a story or an account of description of what the picture suggest you. Your composition should be directly about the subject of the picture or may take suggestion from it, but there must be a clear connection between the picture and the composition.

ICSE 1999

THE GOOD SAMARITAN

Seema was the most talented girl of the orphanage. She had lost her parents when she was a child and had since grown up there with many boys and girls facing the same predicament. Unlike most of them, she was very lively and had a pleasing disposition, which attracted people towards her. She had a natural talent for singing, with which she used to regale her colleagues to bring them out from their depression.

One day the matron summoned them to the assembly hall in the morning and informed that one child by the name of Sweta, was suffering from a congenial heart disease. This required costly medication and a by pass surgery, that would cost a few lakh of rupees. She asked them to pray for the poor child in her hour of travail.

On learning this Seema and her friends decided to help the helpless child. They volunteered to go out in the street to sing and raise money for the girl's medication. The matron was hesitant but seeing her resolve she relented.

They began their street singing the next morning in Juhu, a rich suburban part of Mumbai, where most successful stars of the tinsel world reside. They sang the latest filmi songs with the accompaniment of the guitar played by Atul, the Basuri by Geeta and her other friends. Soon enough they had an appreciative audience, listening intently to their songs. However, by the end of the day, they were barely able to collect a few hundred rupees.

It was now approaching dusk and they were feeling quite tired .The locality in which they were staging the program also seemed to be least interested. Seema was feeling very dejected with herself, at the meagre amount they had gathered after the long arduous day. She had just concluded her song, when a fairly old and stout gentleman with dark glasses and a receding hairline approached her from behind. He had obviously been listening to her songs from a distance and was impressed. He introduced himself as Gulzar the famous film director and wanted to know if she would like to sing a song for him in his forthcoming film 'Karz'. Seema was flabbergasted at the proposal. She nodded in agreement, but if only he would help in bearing the medical expenses of the child in the orphanage.

He readily agreed giving a new lease of life to Sweta and a new life to Seema who rose to become a great singer in Hindi cinema.

Write a story or an account of description of what the picture suggest you. Your composition should be directly about the subject of the picture or may take suggestion from it, but there must be a clear connection between the picture and the composition.

ICSE 1997

THE BIRTHDAY PARTY

I was anxiously waiting to celebrate my thirteenth birthday last month, which fell on 10th October. I pestered my parents to make it a memorable one befitting a teenager. I had somehow got bored with the usual kid birthday parties. The joker caps, toys and the usual fun and games now bored me. I was now grown up and wanted to celebrate it as an adult.

Seeing my enthusiasm my parents agreed and I began preparing for the same in right earnest. I gave beautiful invitation cards to my friends. Since some lived far away, I coaxed their parents in agreeing to drop them for this special occasion.

We consciously decided to have a continental menu with chowmein, fried rice, chili chicken and chicken sweet and sour. The work of getting the cake and pastries were assigned to my father, who would collect the same on his return from office that day. My anxiety increased by the day, till the D-Day finally arrived. The day at school was quite uneventful and I waited anxiously for the school to get over. On reaching home I found every thing in order, for my mother had worked hard to arrange the furniture and prepare the food. My enthusiasm was indeed contagious, for it seemed to have rubbed on my pet dog Tommy too. Normally of a docile and lazy temperament, he appeared excited and unusually energetic, nudging close to me playfully. I locked him in the garage so that he would not be a spoilsport with my guests.

My father shortly arrived with a cake and pastries and by 7 P.M. all my friends had arrived. The party was now in full swing, with loud jazz music. Some of my friends took to dancing in gay abandon, to the beat of Vengabuys and in an hours time we were panting for breath. Being tired and famished, we helped ourselves to the delicacies. It was while we were eating, that Tommy some-how managed to sneak in. Being unaccustomed to so many guests, he barked and growled at them. I tried to shoo him away, but in vain. Suddenly he sprang at Rohit and bit him on his shank. The poor boy cried in pain, throwing his plate at him. I was livid with anger and hit him with a stick lying nearby, thus forcing him to flee.

Gone was the merrymaking as we all crowded around Rohit, who was writhing in pain. My mother bandaged his wound, reassuring him of no complication for Tommy was duely vaccinated. However, as a precautionary measure, we took him in our car to the nursing home nearby. There he was administrated first aid, after which we dropped him home.

By the time we returned it was just about midnight. It was indeed a hectic day and a memorable one as that for "All well that ends well."

Write a story or an account of description of what the picture suggest you. Your composition should be directly about the subject of the picture or may take suggestion from it, but there must be a clear connection between the picture and the composition.

UNIQUE LOVE

At dusk sitting on the steps of the temple after a tough days work, my attention was drawn to a commotion along the pathway leading to the temple. I finished the prasad and walked towards the place with curiosity, to discover that there was a dead monkey, with a small baby snuggling close to it. The little baby was oblivious of the fact, that his mother was no more. The people around were at loggerhead as to what to do with the dead monkey, for it would shortly start decomposing, giving rise to a stink.

I looked at the little monkey, who appeared dismayed as to why people were surrounding him. He huddled closer to his mother as if to seek protection. I was really touched to see the baby and my heart went out to it. I suddenly was reminded of my past, when I had also lost my parents in a tragic accident. My uncle had treated me worse than an animal. One day I had no choice, but to leave the village and go to the city to take up work as a labourer at a construction site. I brushed aside these thoughts as the municipal van came to halt in front of the body. The body of the dead monkey was loaded and the baby climbed on to the van. It was immediately picked up and thrown on to the road. In a flash the van disappeared. The little baby monkey ran after it for some distance but in vain.

As the vehicle disappeared, the crowd also thinned out. I looked around and saw the little one sitting on the path, as if in mourning. I could read the agony in his eyes and instantaneously decided, that I would look after this baby, till he was able to fend for himself. As I went close stretching my hands towards him, he looked up at me as if trying to read my thoughts and placed his little paws in my hand .We had no language to share, but sensed that we needed each other.

It has been two years now and we are more than a family. I named him Bhola as it suited him so much. He became my companion through thick and thin. Wherever I went Bola would accompany me and attend to my needs .He was loved by everyone and nobody feared him. We shared whatever he received .He would get me some fresh fruits from the orchard, or the temple and I would provide him bread. Most of the time he spent in the temple, where people showered him with love and affection. The Hindus regarded him as the incarnation of the Lord Hanuman.

I wonder what I would have done without Bhola. He would wait for me everyday accompanying me back home, sitting comfortably on my shoulders. We would have a nice sumptuous meal, after which I would lie down to rest, while Bhola   played with my hairs .I would close my eyes in deep slumber and he would not move till my nap was over. Before we wound off for the day, we would go for a short stroll. Sometimes I wonder as to why we call them animals, for they are better than human beings .We had no language, but the bond of love was indeed strong.

Write a story or an account of description of what the picture suggest you. Your composition should be directly about the subject of the picture or may take suggestion from it, but there must be a clear connection between the picture and the composition.

ICSE 1991

FLYING

"Flying Officer Amrish Sharma please report to the commanders office immediately,"the intercom buzzed. It was the voice of the second in command with an air of urgency. Amrish who was sipping his tea in his office, got up with a start .He gulped the remainder of his tea and dashed towards the commander's office. Knocking the door he entered the office to find the entire squadron waiting anxiously for him. Saluting the Wing Commander he nodded his head to his colleagues. The Commander gestured him to sit down and after clearing his throat began. "Well gentleman we have an emergency. Orders have come for our squadron to be on red alert. We have been assigned the task of neutralizing the enemy post at peak no. 4050, from where the enemy is targeting the civilian areas of Kargil". What followed was a detailed briefing on how it was all to be done, with the commander explaining the strategy on the sand model before him. When it was over he looked around questioningly "Any Questions". Getting an affirmative nod he said "Well good luck then, get cracking immediately,"and the meeting was over.

Amrish walked towards his Avro fondly looking at it. He had been flying this for quite some time now, on routine reconnoiter flights, but it was indeed a long time since he was flying this on a real mission. A pang of jealousy crossed his heart, when he saw his colleagues preparing themselves to be on stand by, in their supersonic MIG 21 fighters. He had always wanted to fly these jets, but was   destined to fly these winged aircraft, which are akin to Dinosaurs in modern aviation. It had made him feel inferior to the fighter pilots, but here was an opportunity for him to finally show them his mettle.

Brushing aside these thoughts, he set about with the task at hand. As per plan he had to make a reconnoiter of the site and give precise location to the artillery gun fire, to neutralize the enemy post. In the event this failed, the fighter pilots were to go in action and bomb the location. The last option was fraught with danger, for it could lead to escalation of conflict, which was to be avoided. The Commander had reposed a lot of faith in him and he felt a great sense of responsibility. He looked up at the sky offering a short prayer, as he boarded the plane . On receiving the signal he pulled the throttle, the plane raced on the tarmac and in a flash he was airborne. He headed towards peak 4050. Flying close to the site, he started relaying the location of the enemy artillery gun to his commander. Soon enough there was the boom of artillery fire, as the guns on the Indian side opened up. Their target was, however, not accurate. Amrish continued to give direction, pinpointing their accuracy and soon their precision improved. The result of their fire was very devastating, which he recorded with the automatic camera. The strafing bullets of antiaircraft gunfire jolted him and he took the plane to a greater height to escape the enemy attack. The action lasted for about half an hour, after which the adversary fire subsided, indicating their obliteration.

He returned to base to receive a standing ovation from his colleagues'. He found in their eyes a new respect for him. Gone was his complex, he had proved that he was as good a fighter than any of them.

Write a story or an account of description of what the picture suggest you. Your composition should be directly about the subject of the picture or may take suggestion from it, but there must be a clear connection between the picture and the composition.

ICSE 1984

STRUGGLE

It was a cold winter morning in the month of November. The sweet fragrance of the morning breeze and the twittering of the birds, awakened Shyam to another day in his life. On hearing a loud cluttering sound, he peeped out of the window to see a small boy around eight years old, relentlessly pulling a cart with all his strength that he could muster. He was scantily dressed, walking barefoot in the chilly weather.

The sight made him somber and anguished .He was reminded of something that he had long since forgotten. It took him down memory lane to a similar morning eighteen years ago. He desperately tried to control the tears that brimmed in his eyes, trying to fight them back. Leaning against the window, he could not help as old memories came flooding back to him .How happy was he with his parents and his elder brother, when the cruel hands of fate snatched his parents in a road accident. Since he and his brother were very young to manage the fields, their paternal uncle took over the management of the fields.

As days passed by, they were treated more like servants and were not even given enough to eat. They had to slog long hours in the field, for the measly morsels that were given. The last straw came, when Mohan his elder brother overheard his cousin conspiring with his ruffian friends, for getting rid of them. The earth slipped from under his feet, as he rushed home bundling his belonging, literally dragging him out of sleep. In the cover of night they sneaked out of the village, traversing the sugarcane fields, walking throughout the night till their legs gave way.

Being extremely tired and hungry, they rested under a tree in a thicket along the road. On day break, they sought refugee in a temple on the outskirts of the city. The prasad they had, was just enough to keep their body and soul together, after which Mohan set out in search   of work. He did find one as a cart puller, for the local merchant and was entrusted with the work of carrying food grains to the godown. He worked very hard, but their cup of misery was not full yet, He was struck with Tuberculosis and hence had to abandon work. It was then that Shyam could no longer remain a mute spectator. He picked up the cart at the tender age of eight and set about the task that his brother had undertaken .The merchant was initially hesitant, but seeing his resolve and determination he gave in. Thus while boys of his age went to school, he was pulling the cart day in and day out .His hard work and perseverance were in vain, for he could not save his elder brother, but was able to win the confidence and favour of the merchant. Soon enough this bore fruit, and he became his partner in business.

God had indeed been kind, for he the days of struggle were finally over .He now had a house and sufficient money to take care of his needs. He, however, had a soft corner for these little boys, who have the self respect to work and not to beg for a living. He looked up at the sky, as if in thanksgiving to the Lord, who had at long last been so benevolent. He prayed to Him to shower similar kindness on this young lad, who God knows under what circumstances, was engaged in a work far beyond his age and capacity.

Write a story or an account of description of what the picture suggest you. Your composition should be directly about the subject of the picture or may take suggestion from it, but there must be a clear connection between the picture and the composition.

REUNION

It was an agonizing wait at the railway platform on a bright Sunday morning. The initial euphoria of receiving my old friend had indeed evaporated into thin air, as I waited exasperatedly for the Bombay Mail to steam in. This was the third announcement of the train getting late for another one hour, which stretched my patience to the limit.

The long wait of two hours in the waiting room had stiffened my legs. I paced up and down the platform trying to bring back the circulation, stifling a yarn in between to overcome my boredom. I had poured over the morning newspaper in great detail, had a cup of tea and done everything conceivable to keep from falling asleep.

It suddenly dawned on me as to how I would recognise Venkatesh, whom I would be seeing after a gap of over fifteen years. I distinctly remember him to be a tall, thin, fair complexion boy, with a jovial smiling face. The pranks that we indulged at school would even now make me smile occasionally. Since he belonged to Medak (a district in Tamil Nadu) we had pet named him Medhak (frog). No sooner would he enter the class, the boys would start croaking welcome. He good-naturedly returned the croak that left us rolling with laughter. At times the teachers would also join in the fun that he reciprocated with equal fervour. On passing out from school we had drifted away. While I had joined the engineering college at Delhi and settled here itself, Venkat had gone for higher education to the United States, after which he had settled down in Bombay, establishing his own business. We had however, kept in touch with an occasional letter or phone. It was therefore a pleasant surprise yesterday morning, when he rang to tell me, that he was coming to Delhi today on a business assignment and enquired if I could receive him. I was happy at the prospect of meeting him and had therefore rushed through my morning routine, to be in time to receive him.

Cursing the railways and their sloppiness, I gave vent to my frustration on a stray dog that had come sniffing upto me. The public announcement system cracked to life, announcing the arrival of the train heralding my endless wait. The train steamed in and being its last destination all the passengers disembarked. There was just no sign of Venkat. It was when I was about to give up my search, that I noticed a tall obese man with a receding hairline walk towards me, with a briefcase in hand. This just couldn't be Venkatesh. I brushed aside the thought, walking past him in the other direction. Suddenly my ears stood on end when I heard a familiar croak. Looking at the direction from where it came, I found it emanating from the obese man I had just walked past.

There was no mistaking the sound. I rushed to him with open arms and soon we were locked in a tight embrace. The humdrum of the surroundings was lost on us, as we hugged and thumped each other in gay abandon. This was to the amusement of people around, who were witness to this strange reunion. My weariness, frustration and disgust were now behind me, as we merrily made our way out of the station.

Write a story or an account of description of what the picture suggest you. Your composition should be directly about the subject of the picture or may take suggestion from it, but there must be a clear connection between the picture and the composition.

FOOD POISONING

It was a long agonising wait outside the emergency ward of the civil hospital. Sitting on the bench, I felt pangs of despair on hearing no news of my brother, who had been wheeled into the intensive care unit. Like me there were other members of my neighbourhood, each with a somber expression reflecting anxiety. It was indeed an anticlimax to the grand celebration we had yesterday, when there was an entertaining cultural programme in our locality followed by a sumptuous dinner. The youth of our neighbourhood were in the forefront in organising and managing the programme, which was a grand success. This had created tremendous goodwill and a spirit of camaraderie, as people of different caste and creed hugged and wished each other Holi Mubarak.

It was only early in the morning that my younger brother Atul started complaining of severe pain in his stomach. Within half an hour it grew from bad to worse and he lost consciousness. I and my father rushed him to the hospital, in an ambulance that I had called in the meantime. On reaching the hospital we found a number of people from our locality, each with a similar tale to tell. There was something wrong with the dinner that had led to food poisoning. Some people were being wheeled in the wards, followed by their relatives. Finding the atmosphere in the hospital suffocating and depressing. I sat on the bench for a breath of fresh air, surveying the pathetic sight.

My next door neighbour Mr. Gulam Mohammed sitting next to me patted me, asking me not to worry, for all would be right soon .The conversation soon veered around to what could have gone wrong. It was probably the ice-cream or the panner dish which was the culprit. After some discussion we concluded that it was the paneer vegetable, as I had not taken the same while my brother had. They all nodded in agreement. It was then I saw my father walking towards me with a look of relief on his face. God was kind, Atul was out of danger. There was a sigh of relief all around. We enquired about the fate of our other neighbours, to find that they were all out of danger. The worse was indeed over. They were all safe and would be discharged by evening. We returned home to get fresh and bring food and clothing for Atul.

ASSIGNMENTS

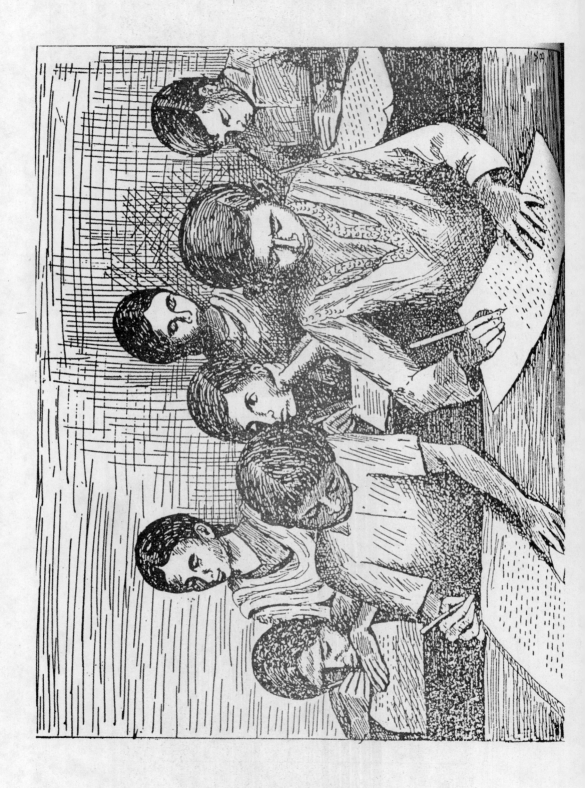

Letters Writing

GUIDELINES FOR LETTER WRITING

Writing letters is one of the most important form of communication and plays a vital role in our lives. Over the years there has been a revolution in the field of communication, like the telephone, wireless, cell phones, fax and of late the E-Mail, which are, must faster. Leaving aside the fax and the E-Mail, which lack permanence a letter is a permanent record, which we can always refer to later. It has a personal touch and projects the personality of the writer. We must therefore exercise proper care in learning this art, for it plays an important part in fostering good relations with people and business organizations.

We can broadly classify letters into:

1. Personal Letters
2. Formal / Business / Official letters

They differ in format and tone

Letter writing has a maximum of 10 marks in the ICSE examination which are allocated as follows

Proper layout	Subject Matter	Expression
2 ½ marks	2 ½ marks	5 Marks.

Proper Layout

This is a format in which a letter is written. It is different for personal and formal letters and are given later. Care should be taken to adhere to the proper format.

Subject Matter

Since the letter is written to communicate something .You are judged on how effectively you have covered the subject. Hence your composition should be brief yet relevant to the subject.

Expression

The letter tests your skill in expression and thus carries a high weight age of marks. It would be helpful to keep the following in mind while writing the same.

1. As in all composition write to a plan.
2. Give an interesting introduction and concluding sentence.
3. Follow a logical or chronological order by dividing the letter into paragraphs to mark change in subject matter.

Use direct and simple language,. Avoid high flown or vague language.

Personal Letters

These are letters written to friends, colleagues, neighbours, acquaintances and relations i.e. (persons known to us.). Their style is therefore simple, natural and with an informal tone, with a touch of witticism to make it intimate. The tone is conversational in form, with spontaneity.

The usual subject of such letters could be exchanging news, views, extending invitation, congratulations, sympathy, expressing grief or sympathy, apology, etc. Besides taking care to observe the basic rules of writing composition like grammar, punctuation and spelling, we must ensure that it has a proper layout and content.

Layout Of A Personal Letter

A letter in general has six parts, they are:

1. **The address of the writer** at the top right hand corner of the page. Each part of the address should be in a separate line, with the name of the city and the pincode no. coming last. The format being block type, with or without punctuation marks. A typical address would look like

101, Golf link Apartments,

90 , Park Road ,

Lucknow- 226001.

10thOctober, 2007

2. **Date.** The date on which the letter was written should be below the writers address, after leaving a space of one line as shown above. The month should be written in full, and not abbreviated as 10/10/2007, or Oct 10, 2007. The 'th' should be written on the line, and not as 10th .There is a comma after the month, followed by a full stop after the year.

3. **The salutation or greeting** is written on the left hand side of the page, below the writers address and date. It is followed by a comma. The salutation would depend on your relationship or closeness to the person you are writing. The different form of salutations along with their subscription are given at serial number 5.

4. **The body of the letter** comprises

   a. **The opening statement** that sets the tone of the letter. The letter could be in response to a previous letter, or refer to particular subject, or be general in nature. A few examples of such opening statements could be

      Hope this letter finds you in the best of health and spirits.

      It has been a long time since I wrote to you.

      Thank you very much for the ......

      I am sorry to hear that ....

      I would like to congratulate you ....

      I would like to apologise for ...., etc

   b. **The subject matter.** Like any other composition, it must be written to a plan, and enumerated in the form of paragraphs.

   c. **The concluding sentence** which gently sums up the subject, and leaves a loving impression on the reader. A few examples of such sentences are as given below

      Kindly give my regards to Uncle and Auntie.

      I am looking forward to meeting you .

      Wishing you a speedy recovery.

      Looking forward to hearing from you, etc

5. **The Subscription or courteous leave taking.** This is written after the concluding sentence on the right hand side of the page followed by a comma. It is a polite leave taking,

and has different forms, depending on the person you are addressing the letter. A few salutations and subscriptions are as given below.

To whom the letter is	Salutation (greeting)	Subscription (ending)
Father Mother	Dear Father, or My dear Dad, Dear Mother, or My dear Mummy,	Yours affectionately, or Your affectionate son, or Your loving son , etc
Brother /Sister	Dear brother, Dear sister,	Your loving brother, / sister, or Yours loving,
Uncle/ Aunt	Dear Uncle, /Aunt,	Your affectionate nephew, / niece, Or Yours affectionately,
Grandparents	Dear Grandpa / Grandma	Your affectionate grandson,/ granddaughter,
Close friend Acquaintance	My dear Arti, Dear Mr. Sharma, Dear Ms Arti	Yours sincerely, or Your friend, Yours sincerely, or Yours truly,

6.   **The Signature and name of the writer** comes below the subscription. Here you can write your first name.

Illustrated examples of some letters given in subsequent pages

Formal / Business / Official Letters

They are formal letters written to government agencies or company official's .The tone of such letters should be formal and not sound too personal and intimate. It should be concise, with statement of relevant facts and be to the point. Under this category are the following types of letters:

1.   Letter of application
2.   Letter to a newspaper
3.   Letter of complaint
4.   Letter of apology
5.   Letter of persuasion

The   Layout Of A Formal Letter

1.   **The address of the writer and date** is written at the top right hand corner of the page, same as in case of personal letters.

2.   **Name and address of the Receiver.** This is written immediately after the address of the sender and the date, but on the left hand side of the letter. A few examples of such letters addressed to officials, business firms, and an unknown addressee are as

given below.

The Managing Director Reliance Industries Limited 70, Nariman Point Mumbai -400001	Messrs Lekhraj and Company Ltd 90, Park Road Lucknow 226001
The Advertiser/s Box No. 1001 The Times of India Hazratganj Lucknow - 226001	

3. **The salutation or greeting** is written on the left hand side of the page below the name and address of the addressee. This is followed by a comma. The salutation varies depending on the person you are addressing the letter to. It could be a man or a lady or a business firm. The different forms of salutations along with the subscription are given at serial number 6.

4. **Business heading** The subject of the letter is written in brief between the salutation and the first paragraph. It may be underlined

5. **The body of the letter** comprises
   a. **The opening statement** which should either be in response to an earlier communication, or have a reference to the subject of the letter. A few examples of such opening statements could be
      This has reference to your letter dated ….
      Thank you for your letter dated ….
      I would like to apply for …., etc
   b. **The subject matter.** It must be written to a plan and enumerated in the form of paragraphs, maintaining the formal tone throughout the letter.
   c. **The concluding sentence** is a gentle request and varies depending on the topic of the letter. Few examples of such sentences are
      I shall be looking forward to a positive reply ….
      I shall be grateful if my application is considered favourably, etc

6. **The Subscription or courteous leave taking**. This is written after the concluding sentence on the right hand side of the page followed by a comma. A few salutations and subscriptions are as given below.

To whom the letter is addressed	Salutation (greeting)	Subscription (ending)
Business/Govt. official	Dear Sir, or Dear Madam,	Yours faithfully, or Yours truly,
Business firm	Dear Sirs,	Yours faithfully, or Yours truly,
College Principal Or Teacher	Sir, or Madam,	Yours obediently, or Your obedient pupil,
News paper Editor	Sir,	Yours faithfully, or Yours,

7. The Signature and name of the writer comes below the subscription followed by the designation (if relevant)

8. The address or superscription on the envelope in which the letter is to be sent.

Salient Features of a Letter of Application

It has all the characteristic features of an official letter. However since the objective of this letter is to project one's suitability for the assignment in question. It must cover the following parameters:

1. Refer to the advertisement or brief reference to the post applied for.
2. Qualification and experience beginning from the present or most recent, to the past.
3. Refer to testimonials and Curriculum vitae, which must be enclosed .
4. Give an assurance of earnestness if appointed.

Illustrated examples given in subsequent pages.

Salient Features of a Letter to a Newspaper (or Editor)

It has all the characteristic features of an official letter except for the salutation and the superscription, which are Sir, and Yours faithfully, respectively. It however differs in certain aspects like:

1. It should be addressed to the Editor.
2. The tone should be formal with a clear and forceful approach, leading the reader to your point of view.

Illustrated examples given in subsequent pages.

Salient Features of a Letter of Complaint

It has all the characteristic features of an official letter. We should avoid making immediate strong demands or holding out a threat of dire consequences. It should be strongly worded but reasonable. The brief outline of the body copy could be as follows:

1. Reference to complaint.
2. Causes of complaint and its effect on you and the surrounding.
3. Request for action.

Illustrated examples given in subsequent pages.

Salient Features of a Letter of Apology

It has all the characteristic features of an official letter. Since the essence of the letter is an apology, it must besides expressing this, also offer an explanation as to why it arose. There must also be some assurance about steps being taken, to set the matter right. A brief outline of the body copy of such a letter is as under:

1. Reference to the complaint
2. Give a plausible explanation with facts.
3. Inform about action being taken
4. Conclude with a formal apology.

Illustrated examples given in subsequent pages.

Salient Features of a Letter of Persuasion
/Patronage or Help

It has all the characteristic features of an official letter except for the tone, which is more persuasive in nature .The purpose being to convince the reader to your point of view. Hence the need for logical arguments, substantiating your point of view, backed with data and facts .A brief outline of the body copy of such a letter could be

1. State the purpose of your letter.
2. The availability of present facilities and amenities, that is inadequate.
3. Need for change, with plausible arguments and facts.
4. Likely benefits that would accrue if the change were made.
5. Conclude with reiterating your proposal and its likely benefits.

Illustrated examples given in subsequent pages.

ILLUSTRATED EXAMPLES OF PERSONAL LETTERS

Your mother has won the National Award for *Meritorious Teachers.* **Write a letter to a friend giving details of the award, the award ceremony and the celebrations that followed.**

(ICSE 2004)
Z 20 HAUZ KHAS
New Delhi-110029

15 May, 2004

My dear Rohan,

Hope this letter finds you in the best of health and spirits. I could not reply to your letter earlier, for I had gone to Delhi for a week. I had accompanied my mother who had won this year's National Award for 'Meritorious Teachers'. This award was bestowed on her, on account of the excellent marks obtained by her students, in the secondary examination .

Like in previous years, the ceremony was held in the Vigyan Bhawan in South Delhi. This is a majestic complex, with a huge auditorium , surrounded with plush green lawns having innumerable water fountains. The venue of the award ceremony was the auditorium. It had plush interiors, with wood paneled walls, thickly carpeted floors, and push back seats brightly upholstered. The dais was aesthetically designed, with huge chandeliers and spot lights. Facing the dais were a battery of press photographers and TV cameramen, getting ready to record the historic moment. The recipients of the awards were seated to the left of the dais, while the VIP's were seated to the right. The honorable Prime Minister Dr. Manmohan Singh was seated in the front row, with members of his cabinet and other dignitaries.

The hall was packed to capacity, and at precisely 11 AM the President Shri A. P. J. Kalam arrived in great style, escorted by his body guards. The spectators rose with respect, as he was led to the dais by the honourable Prime Minister. The Minister of Human Resources Shri Arjun Singh read out his welcome speech. This was followed by a cultural program of dance and music. Thereafter the actual award ceremony commenced. Each teachers was called to the dais, to receive the award from the President. The award comprised of a shawl, a gold plated memento, and a certificate. It was indeed a great moment for my mother, when her name was called out. She received the award, amidst thunderous applause from the audience. It was a proud moment for all of us, for she was the lone recipient of this honour from Lucknow.

The award ceremony was followed by a sumptuous lunch, hosted in the sprawling lawns of the complex. Here I had the golden opportunity of meeting many great personalities, with whom I got myself photographed. I shall show you these photographs on your next visit to Lucknow.

It was indeed a great event, which I shall never forget for a long time to come. I wish you had been there to share this experience. How are your studies going on? Please give my regards to uncle and aunty , and reply to my letter at the earliest.

Your loving friend,
Siddhant

ASSIGNMENTS

1.   Write a letter to your friend who is discouraged by his failure in the examination .
2.   You have been selected for the best student award in your school . Write a letter to a friend giving details of the award, the award ceremony and the celebrations that followed.

You wish to become a journalist while your parents want you to become a doctor. Write a letter to your mother giving reasons why you should be allowed to pursue your ambition.

(ICSE 2003)

1/153, Vijay Khand,
Gomti Nagar,
Lucknow-226010

20 th May, 2003.

My dear Mummy,

I was overjoyed to receive your long awaited letter yesterday. Reading it made me forget my homesickness for a while, and bought forth pleasant memories. My studies are going on at an even pace. Next year, as you rightly pointed out in your letter, we shall have to choose from the elective subjects of Maths, Biology or Arts.

I sincerely value your advice, for taking up Biology for pursuing a career in Medicine. There is indeed no doubt that a doctor's profession is very noble, but I somehow do not have any inclination or aptitude for Biology. I find it boring especially the dissection part is quite nauseating. It is on account of this, I did not score good marks in this subject. in the school examination.

On the other hand in English language and literature I scored good marks. I got the highest marks in English language because of which I have been nominated as the editor of our school magazine which is to come out shortly. I have contributed a number of articles in this magazine. Besides this. a number of my articles have been published in the local edition of the 'Times of India'. This has encouraged me to pursue a career in journalism, which I find very interesting and challenging.

Journalism as a profession, is also very noble and respectable. They are the fourth estate, that serve as a watchdog in a democracy, safeguarding our freedom. Being a journalist, gives one an opportunity to serve the nation, by highlighting important social and national issues, besides protecting the common men: from exploitation and injustice.

There is ample scope for growth in this profession, with tremendous potential in the print and electronic media. It also offers good opportunity to show one's creativity, and hence there is greater job satisfaction. Moreover journalists have easy access to the high and mighty bureaucrats and politicians. They are respected for their views and make a valuable contribution to the society. Their significance can be gauged from the fact that, many great men including Mahatma Gandhi, Dr Radha Krishnan, began their career as a journalist.

I would therefore seek your blessings, in pursuing this career, for which I have a natural liking. Please give my regards to daddy, and love to my dear brother Rohit.

Your affectionate son
Siddhant.

ASSIGNMENTS

1. You have been selected to participate in the National youth festival to be held in another city. The dates however clash with your final school exams you are however keen on going. Write a letter to your parents stating the pros and the cons and seeking their advice

2. You borrowed a book from a friend and lost it in a bus Write a letter to your friend telling him about the loss and how you will make amends for it

You were held up in the countryside one night due to a railway accident .Write a letter to your friend narrating the incident.

(ICSE 2002)

1/153, Vijay Khand,
Gomti Nagar,
Lucknow-226010.

30 th June, 2002.

Dear Mohan .

It has been a long time since I last wrote to you .I could not even reply to your letter as I was busy preparing for my AIIMS examinations for which I had to go to Delhi last month.

You must have read about the train accident that took place on the Lucknow Mail on the 20 th of June. I was traveling in this train, when somewhere between Lucknow and Kanpur at about 11 .30 PM there was a loud bang, and I was thrown down from my berth. There was pitch darkness all around with people screaming and shouting .I was relieved to find myself in one piece, collecting my bag I crept slowly towards the exit. There was a virtual stampede as everyone was trying to rush out. Once out of the compartment, I walked up toward the engine. What I saw sent a chill down my spine. Two bogies had derailed and were completely smashed because of the speed of the train. People trapped in the compartment were crying in pain. With the help of a few villagers from the countryside, we began to rescue people .The rescue team, police and the ambulances arrived after about an hour's time, because of the inaccessibility of the site of the accident. They rushed the injured to the nearest hospital in Unnao.

The railway officials requested us to wait till daybreak for a relief train for our onward journey .I had therefore no option but to spend the night out in the countryside .It was nevertheless a unique experience which I shall never forget . "Adversity indeed brings with it strange bedfellows". I found absolute strangers helping and showing concern for each other. The farmers from the nearby villages brought us food and milk. Soon we had a small kitchen running just next to the tracks, as they served us hot tea and biscuits. I was indeed moved by their social consciousness and generosity for absolute strangers. With daybreak came the relief train and I was able to continue my onward journey.

It was indeed a nightmarish experience that I shall never forget .The only silver lining was the kind gesture of the villagers, who even today uphold the noble traditions for which India is so well known .I am now eagerly waiting for the results that are expected next month. Give my regards to uncle and auntie

Your loving friend ,
Siddhant

ASSIGNMENTS

1. While returning home you met with an accident . Write a letter to your friend describing what happened and what you learnt from that experience.

You have just returned from the holiday at a hill station. Write a letter to your friend mentioning what you found most interesting about the place and give two reasons to explain why you consider it an ideal place for a vacation.

(ICSE –2001)

1/153,Vijay Khand ,
Gomti Nagar,
Lucknow-226010
15 th May, 2001,

My dear Arun.

It has been quite some time since I last wrote to you .The last month was indeed very hectic, for our first term examination was in full swing., after which our summer vacations commenced. I along with my friend Rohit, decided to go to Mussorie, for a short vacation .I have just returned from there yesterday, and am still to recover from the exhilarating experience of the place.

Mussorie is a hill station in the Garhwal mountains of Uttaranchal, also known as the Queen of the hills. It is near Dehradun, the capital of this state ,which is located on the foothill of the Himalayas.The taxi ride from Dehradun to Mussorie is a two hour drive, with sharp and steep turns. The deep gorges , sent a chill down our spine and we desperately clung to our seats.

As I stepped out of the taxi, the first thing that struck me was the cool refreshing breeze. This was a welcome change, from the hot loo we had just left behind. Scampering with our baggage, we set forth to the tourist lodge, which was a distance away from 'the Mall'.

We visited the Gun Hill top,which is the highest mountain peak there, by trolley .The trolley ride was indeed memorable, for the scenic beauty down below was breathtaking. Once atop the hill ,we set about exploring the place, which was a tourist delight. There were tastefully done up stalls of eatables and novelty items .The spirit of merrymaking and laughter filled the air .We also joined in the fun and got ourselves photographed as Gabbar Singh, the legendry tinsel dacoit

The next day we set out for Kempty Fall, that is half an hour drive from Mussorie .The scene at the waterfall was indeed mesmerizing. Small droplets of water struck us on the face, even though we were standing a distance away .The place was swarming with tourists and the children were having a whale of a time, in little pools of water beside the waterfall. Their merriment was so infectious, that we also could not resist getting drenched. Luckily we had brought our clothes, so after a quick change we sat down for a sumptuous lunch at one of the tastefully done up restaurants. The next day we visited Dhanaulti, that is 30 kilometers from Mussorie. This place is famous, for its mountains covered with pine tree and the virgin natural beauty.

Mussorie is an ideal place for a vacation, because of its salubrious climate, which is very pleasant in summers.The mountains and the natural beauty ,which is in abundance, is indeed a tourist delight. The picturesque surroundings ,gives a feeling of being in the lap of nature .It rejuvenates us, by providing a welcome change to the humdrum of daily chores.

You must also plan a visit to this place and I am sure you will enjoy it. Give my love to Anil and regards to uncle and auntie.

Your friend
Siddhant

ASSIGNMENTS

1. You have just returned from the holiday away from home . Write a letter to your mother mentioning what you found most interesting about the place.
2. Write a letter to your friend describing an amusing article you have read in the newspaper. State what you found amusing and Why?

You have just received a birthday gift from your uncle from abroad. Write a letter thanking him for the gift and your reasons why you like the gift.

(ICSE 2000)

> 1/153, Vijay Khand,
> Gomti Nagar,
> Lucknow.
>
> 10 th October 2000

Dear Uncle,

  Thanks a lot for the wonderful gift sent by you. I received it just in the nick of time on my birthday itself. It was indeed very thoughtful of you to have remembered my birthday. We all missed you, Aunty and Tanya that day.

  In the evening I had a small party at home, where some of my school friends had come over and we thoroughly enjoyed ourselves. My Papa gave me a new sports bicycle, which I had set my heart on for quite some time. However, the beautiful watch that you sent me was really marvellous. I had long wished to change my watch that had become old. Your present was as if in answer to my prayer. Its stopwatch feature shall help me in preparing for the cycling competition at school. Till now I had not been able to time my speed properly, in the absence of an accurate timing device. With this I shall be able to precisely gauze my performance, for I intend to win the race. I propose to take part in the five hundred metre cycle race to be held early next month and hence this would really come in handy.

  Thanks again for your thoughtful present, which shall always remind me of you. Please give my love to Tanya and regards to Aunty.

> Yours affectionate nephew,
>
> Rohit.

ASSIGNMENTS

1. Write a letter to your father requesting him to send some money so as to enable you to go on an educational tour with your friends.
2. You have received a birthday card from your friend. Write to him thanking him for the same.

You are incharge of a group, which is to go camping next month. Your friend who is unwell at present will join in later. Write a letter to same friend informing him/ her where all the members have to meet, how you will travel to your destination, and what things you should carry with you and how you will return home.

(ICSE 1999)

1/153 Vijay Khand,
Gomti Nagar,
Lucknow,
10 th September. 2000

My dear Shruti,

I received your letter yesterday and was unhappy to learn that you are down with jaundice, since last week. I hope that you would recover soon, so as to join us at the summer camp which is being held at Kempty falls in Mussoorie from 15th May to 30 th May.

The venue of the camp chosen this year is very picturesque .It is located in the Garhwal hills and is famous for the waterfall. People from far of places come to see this waterfall, which is a major tourist attraction. There will be ample opportunity for hiking and mountaineering which we all are anxiously looking forward to. You will be happy to know that I have been made the in-charge of the camping group.

We shall board Doon Express at 7 p.m., from Charbagh railway station in Lucknow on 14th May. Thus we should assemble at the station by 6 p.m. At this time of the year the weather there will be pretty cold. You should therefore carry with you, some light woolen garments along with camping gear, like torch, matches, rope, binocular and camera, etc. In your case, you should also bring medicines that have been prescribed by your doctor.

We would be returning by the same train and will reach Lucknow on 1 st June at 7a.m. So please inform your parents to receive you at the station. I hope that our program is clear to you. In case of any doubt, please do write to me. You must also seek your doctor's advice, before confirming your participation in the camp.

Wishing you a speedy recovery.

Your loving friend,
Rohit

ASSIGNMENTS

1. You have recently joined a new boarding school. Write a letter to a friend telling him or her of what you like or dislike about your new school.
2. Write a letter to your father telling him of what you like or dislike about your hostel.
3. Write a letter to your friend inviting him or her to join you for a trek to Mussorie. You must highlight the special features of the trek and the things that should be brought by him / her.

You have been embarrassed by an incident involving a group of friends. Write a letter to your mother relating the incident. Express your feelings and how you intend to overcome the impact of the incident.

(ICSE 1996)

J. K. Hostel,
Hauz Khas,
New Delhi-110011.

10 th October. 2000

My dear Mummy,

I am sorry for not having written to you for quite some time. It was not on account of my being busy, but I had indeed been upset of late. Last weekend was indeed very embarrassing for me, but now things are back to normal and there is no cause for worry.

It so happened that last Sunday I and my hostel friends decided to go for a picnic to Kukrail, a picnic spot on the outskirts of the city. We therefore packed some eatables and set forth in the early morning on our bicycles. We had a fantastic day with a lot of merrymaking, fun and games and were thoroughly exhausted. With the onset of dusk, we decided to call it a day, and packed up for the return journey. Unfortunately for me, my bicycle chain broke on the way. Being left with no alternative, I loaded the bicycle on a rickshaw and proceeded to Uncle Sharma's house, which was close by. I spent the night at his place.

On returning to my hostel the next morning, I was hauled up by my friends, and then the warden, for my carelessness in not informing them of my whereabouts, I had caused them tremendous embarrassment, as my friends were unable to offer an appropriate explanation for my absence. They were severely reprimanded by the warden. Thereafter they began a massive manhunt for me. They rang up my local guardian, and all friends and acquaintances. On getting no news of me, they passed a sleepless night. Had I not returned in the morning, they were contemplating to lodge an FIR with the local police. I had indeed blundered, and felt guilty for my lapse. It just did not strike me, that my absence would spell so much of trouble. I felt very ashamed and apologised, for the inconvenience I had unknowingly caused to them.

As punishment I have been denied gate pass for the next three months. Hence I would be unable to spend Deepawali at uncle's place. All the same I am happy for my friends have forgiven me for the embarrassment, that I had caused to them, and things are now back to normal.

Please do not worry about me. Give my love to Rohit and regards to Daddy. I shall soon be writing to them soon.

Your affectionate son,

Siddhant

There is an unexpected happening; you are unable to go to the airport to receive your friend who is arriving from abroad. Write a letter to your friend explaining your problem and request him to help you out.

(ICSE 1994)

I / 153, Vijay Khand,
Gomti Nagar,
Lucknow –226910.

10 th October, 2000.

My dear Arun

    I have been trying to contact you on phone, but have not been able to get across. Probably your phone is out of order. There is an immediate problem, and I would need your help. You would remember Rohit Sharma, who was our batch mate in ICSE. He is coming from America tomorrow, for spending his winter vacations with us. I had to go to the airport to receive him and had everything lined up.

    Unfortunately for me, I have just received a fax message of my uncle's illness from Calcutta. I have to therefore rush to Calcutta by the evening train today. Thus I would be unable to receive Rohit, who is coming by the Indian Airlines flight No 432, which lands at the Indira Gandhi International Airport at around 6 AM tomorrow.

    I would request you to receive him at the airport and bring him home. My mother shall be waiting for him. Please explain the situation to him, for I shall return in a day or two. In the meantime, you can give him company, so that he does not get bored.

    I am sorry for the above inconvenience, but I do hope you shall take care of him till I return. Please do let me know if I could get anything for you from Calcutta, besides the Rassagullas which you are so fond of.

Thanks

Your friend.

Siddhant.

Write a letter of condolence to your friend who has lost his father.

I/ 153, Vijay Khand,
Gomti Nagar,
Lucknow,

10th, October, 2000.

My dear Arun,

It was indeed shocking to learn of the untimely passing away of your father. He seemed so lively and happy, when I last met him at your place. It is unbelievable to think that he is no more with us. Your loss is indeed irreparable, for nothing in the world could fill the vacuum created by his untimely demise.

I am deeply grieved and would like to offer my sincerest sympathies, on your great bereavement. I have no words to express my profound anguish and sorrow on this great loss.

It is in such trying times that one despairs, but death is the ultimate truth, which we have to accept. It is inevitable and we have no choice but to reconcile to this fact of life. The Bhagwat Gita also says, "For what is born death is certain, and for the dead birth is certain. Therefore grieve not over that which is unavoidable". So please do not lose heart, his memory will always guide and inspire us

May God give you the forbearance, to bear this loss manfully and may his great soul rest in peace.

Your friend,
S.Singh

ASSIGNMENTS

1. Write a letter of condolence to a friend whose grandfather has just died.
2. In the last summer vacation you had spent a week with your friend who stays in a hill station. Write a letter thanking him for his hospitality and how you enjoyed the stay.

Write a letter to your friend telling him of an incident in which you played a heroic role.

B 24, Mahanagar,
Lucknow,

30th October, 2000

My dear Rita,

I was happy to receive your letter last week and to know that you are doing well in school. The events of the last week, however, were very hectic, which was a major reason for my delay in replying to your letter. I have yet to recover from the incident that took place last Saturday night.

That night I was alone with my mother, as my father had gone out of station on an official assignment. We were watching the television, when all of a sudden three young ruffians forced their entry through the main door. They held us at gunpoint and demanded the keys of the locker from my mother. While she was in the process of locating the keys, I got an opportunity in knocking the pistol out of his hand and began shouting for help. This was something they had not anticipated and were completely taken off guard. They took to their heels, but not before I had laid my hands on the leg of one of the desperadoes. I clung with all my might, as he made a desperate effort to free himself.

It was however my lucky day, for by now our neighbours had also come to my rescue. The desperado was overpowered and handed over to the police, who arrived shortly thereafter. I had indeed become a hero overnight, with press correspondents crowding around me for an interview, that was splashed in the newspapers the next morning. I also learn that I have been chosen for the bravery award ,conferred on children on the Republic Day.

This is great news for me and I thank God for delivering us from this ordeal unscathed. I wish you could also come with me to Delhi, and share my moment of glory, when I receive the award from the President of India on the coming Republic Day. Give my regards to uncle and aunty.

Your friend,

Rahul.

ASSIGNMENTS

1. Write a letter to a foreign pen friend who has asked you to describe one of your festivals.
2. A friend living abroad has written to you asking for information about a particular school in your city, which he or she intends to join. Write a letter giving details of the institution, which you consider may be useful to your friend.

ICSE 1997

You made an appointment with a friend but unfortunately you could not keep it. Write a letter of apology to him explaining fully what prevented you from keeping the appointment.

1/53, Vijay Khand,
Gomti Nagar,
Lucknow.

10th October, 2000

My dear Arun,

I am extremely sorry, for not being able to keep the appointment with you yesterday. I had indeed looked forward to seeing the evening show of the movie "The lost world" at the Plaza with you. However, circumstances did not permit me to keep this appointment and I could not even inform you of the same. I am sure you must be annoyed and angry with me, but I could not help it.

Immediately on returning home from school, I found my parents waiting anxiously for me. They had just received an urgent call from Delhi, informing them that my grand mother was critically ill. I immediately had to change and off we sped to Delhi by car. The next few days were indeed tense with anxiety. I found myself busy with all odd errands. With God's grace, her condition improved within a week and we returned back yesterday evening.

I hope you will appreciate, that under the circumstances, it was not possible for me to have kept the appointment with you. Do accept my sincere apology for the same.

Yours friend,

S.S. Singh

ASSIGNMENT

1. Write a letter of apology to your friend for having forgotten a dinner engagement. Explain the circumstances and give a reasonable excuse.

Write a letter to your friend telling him/her about a film which you have recently seen.

1/153, Vijay Khand,
Gomti Nagar,
Lucknow.

15th October, 1999.

My dear Shweta,

    I received your letter last week but was unable to reply, as I was busy with my half yearly exams. As my exams were over my friends and I thought of going to a movie. We decided to see the 'The lost world', a movie on the dinosaurs made by Stephan Steinberg, which had just been released. We bought the tickets and reached the theatre in the nick of time. We had barely taken our seats, when the movie began.

    It was a splendid movie and was about the inhabitance of dinosaurs in an unknown island, discovered far away from the continents. A team of scientists were sent there to study the environment and the behaviour of the dinosaurs. The news of this discovery caught the world by surprise. A team of hunters also set forth to the island, to capture the dinosaurs, to exhibit them in the cities for raking in a fortune.

    Initially the hunters were able to capture a few dinosaurs, however, soon the tide turned against them, when the dinosaurs took their revenge. The dinosaurs were so enraged by the hunters, that they killed most of them and forced them to flee. The lucky ones that survived, decided to flee with their catch. On the other hand the team of scientists showed utmost concern for the dinosaurs, at times endangering their own lives. The dinosaurs mistook them for the hunters and turned their ire on them. Left with no alternative they also had to flee. In order to call for help, they had to reach a communication post that was right in the middle of the island. They were lucky enough to find the solar power radio working and sent across their distress call. While the dinosaurs were closing in on them, they were heroically picked up by a rescue helicopter and returned safely home. The hunters in the meantime had been successful in fleeing with one dinosaur and its baby. The ship that actually brought the dinosaurs to New York came crashing ashore, as the dinosaurs had eaten all the hunter crewmembers. The dinosaur now roamed around the streets of New York crushing everything from car to buses like matchboxes looking for its baby. Every one was at their wits end, when it suddenly dawned on the scientist that the only way to end the devastation, was to return the baby dinosaurs to its mother. They located the baby dinosaur and cleverly placed it in a cage on a ship. The dinosaurs came looking for it and was eventually caged in the ship, that set sail on its return voyage for releasing the dinosaurs in their natural habitat.

    It was a movie full of imagination, very well conceived with a good script and screenplay. It took us thousand of years back when the dinosaurs roamed the earth. In a very subtle but effective manner it portrayed the evil of civilization and explicitly brought out what could happen if the dinosaurs were to return in the present world. The movie was made marvellous, with excellent sound effects and photographic techniques. It left a deep impression in my mind. You should also see this movie, which I am sure you will like.

    So best of luck for your exams and convey my regards to aunty and uncle.

Your friend,

Soumya

ASSIGNMENT

1.   You have won a price in the interschool mono acting competition. Write a letter to your friend describing your feelings before, during and after the performance.   *ICSE 1991*

ILLUSTRATED EXAMPLES OF OFFICIAL LETTERS

Your school had contributed a large sum of money to the Prime Minister's Relief Fund to help the victims of an earthquake. You visited the place recently and were shocked to see the poor living conditions of the victims. Write a letter to the Officer In-Charge of the Prime Minister's Relief Fund, drawing his attention to the plight of the people in the affected area.

(ICSE 2004)

St. Francis College.
Shahnazaf Road.
Lucknow- 226001.

23 rd May, 2004

Officer Incharge,
Bahadur Shah Zafar Marg,
New Delhi.

Subject : Inadequate relief to victims of earthquake

Dear Sir,

In response to the call of the honourable Prime Minister, our school St Francis College had contributed Rs. 10 lakhs, to the Prime Minister Relief Fund for the earthquake victims of Gujarat. This had been sent to you by cheque number. 9865 dated 10 March 2003, drawn on State Bank of India. Having contributed to this noble cause we had felt, that the money would have provided some help, to our ill fated brethren in Gujarat.

I was however shocked to see the plight of the people, when I visited Bhuj last week, on a personal visit. It is now over three years since the calamity struck this place, but I still found people living in cracked and damaged buildings. In Lalganj locality located 15 km to the south of Bhuj, I found rubble strewn all over the place . The narrow roads had been encroached upon by the people, who were afraid to live in their damaged houses. There was acute scarcity of water. The living conditions of the people were deplorable, with chocked drains , and sewage water flowing on the road.

I was informed by the local residents, that some development work had been done, in the more affluent parts of the town. However, this place has yet to receive the attention of the administration.

I would request you, to kindly draw the attention of the authorities concerned, to the plight of people in Lalganj, Bhuj. We shall be courting another disaster in the form of an epidemic, unless immediate steps are taken to rectify the situation there.

I felt it my bounden duty to inform you of the state of affairs in Lalganj . I hope you will ensure, that these people do not suffer on account of administrative neglect. They should get their due share of relief, which the people of the country have so generously contributed.

Your's faithfully,
Siddhant Singh.

ASSIGNMENTS

1. Write a letter to the commissioner of police requesting him to stop the loud music being played by some antisocial elements in your locality. This is disturbing students preparing for their annual examination .

2. Write a latter to the Railway Station Manager complaining about a booking clerk who has been very rude to you.

Write a letter to the Chief Minister of your state drawing his attention to the urgent need for a government hospital in your district.

(ICSE 2001)

A 20,Shastri Nagar,
Barabanki,
Uttar Pradesh,

10 th April 2001.

The Chief Minister,
Government of Uttar Pradesh,
Lucknow.

Subject : Urgent need for a government hospital in Barabanki

Dear Sir,

This is to draw your kind attention, to the poor health care facilities available to the citizens of Barabanki district, for want of a government hospital. At present there is only one primary health centre in the district, with a skeletal staff of doctors and paramedics. This is highly inadequate, to cater to the requirement of the entire district.

The district comprises of eight tehsils, with a population of more than ten lakhs, spread over one hundred square kilometers. In case of ailment, the poor villagers have to either go to the nearest government hospital at Lucknow, or be at the mercy of private nursing homes, which fleece them for ordinary ailments. The fees charged by them are exorbitant, while the facilities offered are quite elementary. This often leads to greater complication at a later date, for want of timely diagnosis. They lack infrastructure like CT Scan and Ultrasound that are essential for proper treatment.

The abysmal low level of health care facilities, result in many valuable lives being lost, for want of timely medical care .A government hospital, would be able to cater to the inhabitants of the town, and the surrounding villages. It would besides providing basic health care amenities, also help in the economic development of the district and its poor peasants.

There is thus an urgent need for a government hospital in Barabanki district, to safeguard the health of its residents, and also help in the economic development. I sincerely hope, you will accede to my request, for which I shall be obliged.

Yours truly,
O.P.Singh.

ASSIGNMENTS

1. Your school would like to participate in a quiz program telecast by Doordarshan Kendra. As the secretary of the cultural club of your school write a letter to the Station Director seeking his permission.

2. Write a letter to the Mayor of your city ,objecting to the construction of a market near your house located in a residential locality .

You are incharge of the welfare club of your school. Write a letter to the district magistrate requesting him to inaugurate a special project that the club is to launch soon. Inform him of the details of the inauguration ceremony, the nature of the project and what you expect to achieve.

(ICSE 1996)

Captain,
Literary Club,
Public School,
Lucknow.

15th September, 1999.

District Magistrate,
Lucknow.

Subject – Request for inaugurating 'Jagrit', project of our school.

Dear Sir,

It gives me great pleasure to inform, that the literary club of our school is launching a special project called, Jagriti, that shall be managed by the students. Under the project, the students of the school from eighth class onwards, shall voluntarily provide free education to the poor children of the surrounding slums. Our principal has kindly consented, to make available a few classrooms after school hours, so that we can go ahead with the project. We shall also be providing them free educational aids, like stationery and some refreshments, so that they are motivated to join our programme.

The objective of the special project, which was the brainchild of our benevolent principal, is to educate the underprivileged children of the surrounding slums. They have no means of acquiring education and often take to antisocial activities, that are harmful to them as well as the society. This will besides educating them, help them mould their lives in becoming good citizens, thus fulfilling the objective of 'Jagriti'.

We intend to commence this project from the 2nd of October, as a mark of respect to Mahatama Gandhi with a small ceremony in our school at 10 A.M. There would be a cultural programme presented by the school students and a painting competition by the new students of 'Jagriti'. We would request you, to kindly spare some time from your busy schedule and inaugurate this special project in our school, that would ameliorate the lot of poor children. Your esteemed presence and blessings would inspire us in this noble cause.

We look forward for your confirmation.

Thanking you,

Yours faithfully,

S P Singh,

ASSIGNMENTS

1. Write a letter to the mayor of your city requesting him to act as a judge for a debating competition to be held at your school. Give the necessary details regarding the conduct of the competition.

2. Write a letter to the manager of Indian Airlines for reservation of air tickets for a college tour.

ILLUSTRATED EXAMPLES OF LETTER OF APPLICATION

Read the following advertisement.

WANTED

Suitable young sales assistant-on a part time basis-to market garments for a leading fashion designer. Apply to the Manager, New Creations ,147, Lajpat Nagar, New Delhi-110024. Write an application in response to this advertisement.

(ICSE 2002)

1/153, Vijay Khand,
Gomti Nagar,
Lucknow-226010
30 th June, 2002.

Manager,
New Creations,
147,Lajpat Nagar,
New Delhi- 110024.

Subject – Application for Sales Assistant.

Dear Sir

Kindly refer to your advertisement in 'The Times of India' dated 10 th June 2002, inviting applications for Sales Assistant. I would request you to consider my application for the same.

I am appearing for the ICSE examinations from Boys High School Lucknow, and am 16 years of age. Marketing is my natural choice, for I am extrovert by nature, and like meeting and talking to people. In the last summer vacations, I had the opportunity to work for UNICEF, promoting their greeting cards in the city of Lucknow .I was able to generate good sales for their greeting card, by soliciting institutional business from reputed business houses in the city.

The above part time assignment, would supplement my family income, and also give me an excellent exposure to the garment and fashion industry. This experience would be very useful to me in making a career of it, after finishing college.

I assure you that with my good interpersonal skills, and positive attitude to work, I will be able to meet your expectations. I shall be obliged, if you would give me an opportunity to work for your prestigious organisation.

Your's faithfully,
Siddhant Singh

ASSIGNMENTS

1. Write an application to the managing Director of a company for the post of a sales executive in his company.
2. Write an application to the Editor of a local daily for the post of a proofreader in his office.

Write an application to the principal of a school in answer to their advertisement for an English teacher. Give details of your education and experience.

1/153, Gomti Nagar,
Lucknow.- 226010
12th November, ,2000.

The Principal,
Boys High School.
Dehradun.

Subject : Application for English teacher.

Dear Sir,

In response to your advertisement in 'The Hindustan Times' dated 10th November 2000, I would like to submit my application for the post of an English Teacher, in your prestigious school. I would request you to kindly consider my application for the same.

I have done M.A. in English, followed by B.Ed. from Lucknow University. This was after completing my schooling from St Thomas School. Thereafter since 1982 I have been teaching in various reputed schools in Lucknow. Thus I have a cumulative experience of more than fourteen years teaching English, Geography and other subjects, from class V1 to class X. Presently I am teaching English to ICSE students of Boys High School, Lucknow for the last eight and half years

Besides being the subject teacher, my responsibilities include the school magazine, organising extracurricular activities like Debates, Dramatics, Quiz and excursion visits of students. The school besides emphasising on excellence in education, lays equal stress on co-curricular activities. The results of the last academic year were excellent, with most of the students securing A grade in English.

I am forty years of age and have good health .My present employer would also have no objection to my taking up the new assignment, for better future prospects.

I am confident of coming up to your expectations, and am enclosing my Curriculum Vitae for your kind perusal. Given an opportunity, it will be my sincere endeavour to prove my worth, by putting my heart and soul to a profession I am deeply committed to.

Awaiting a favourable reply.

Yours truly,
Jayant Joshi

ASSIGNMENT

1.   Write a letter to a business firm in answer to their advertisement for a shorthand typist.

ILLUSTRATED EXAMPLES OF LETTER TO THE EDITOR

As the secretary of your school dramatics club write a letter to the editor of a daily newspaper giving him details of a play to be staged its date, time and venue and ask him to give it as much publicity as possible.

(ICSE 1985)

Secretary,
Dramatic's Club,
Public School ,
Lucknow-226001
6 th October, 2000.

The Editor
The Daily,
Lucknow.

Subject : Request for giving publicity

Sir,

I am pleased to inform, that our school dramatics club is staging a play titled 'Corruption', in the Ravindralaya on the 10th of October at 6 PM. The play dwells on the evil of corruption and its effect on the common man. It vividly portrays the plight of middle class youth, and their disillusionment with the society, plagued by this vice. It   subtly conveys a social message, that will stir the conscience of the common man, and also serve as bacon of light for the youth so aggrieved.

It has been scripted by the renown playwright Mr. Muzaffar Ali, with screen play and direction by the famous dramatist Mr. Gulzar .The students of the club have put in tremendous hard work for the last over one month, in perfecting the play. We are sure that the general public will appreciate our effort, for it deals with issues which are closest to their heart.

In order to make the play a success, we would request you to kindly give wide publicity to the play, through your august newspaper in the events column. The tickets for the play have been priced very nominally, so that it is within the reach of the common man. The proceeds of the play shall be donated to the Prime Ministers. Relief fund.

We look forward to your help, by giving good exposure to this maiden endeavour of our club. This will boost our morale   and help us in contributing for a noble cause.

Thanking You,

Yours truly,
Siddhant Singh

ASSIGNMENTS

1. Write a letter to the editor of a daily newspaper appealing for help to the cyclone victims of Orissa.

2. Write a letter to the editor of a daily newspaper, commenting about the deterioration in the quality of films being presently exhibited.

A newspaper has published an inaccurate account of a theft in your house. Write a letter to the editor of what actually happened.

(ICSE 1995)

A124, Nehru Apartments,
Gomti Nagar,
Lucknow.
15 th October, 1999.

The Editor,
The Daily,
M.G. Road,
New Delhi-110001.

Subject : Inaccurate account of a theft in my house by your newspaper

Sir,

I was deeply pained to read the press report in your paper captioned 'Thieves loot black money' that appeared on the 11th of October. The news report filed by your correspondent is not only incorrect, but far from the truth. There are various glaring anomalies in his report that I would like to bring to your kind notice.

The serious allegation of black money amounting to Rs. Ten lakhs being looted   is a travesty of the truth. The exact loss reported in the FIR No. 194 lodged with the police was Rs 10000 only, while valuables amounting to Rs. One lakhs had been stolen. Moreover being a service employee, I have been a regular Income Tax payee. There is therefore no question of my having access to black money as mentioned in the report.

Besides this, there are other anomalies, like making the case of an ordinary theft seem like a dacoity. This is indeed sensationalising the news that is highly erroneous and misleading.

The fact however was that I was sleeping in my bedroom, on the first floor of my house that fateful night. The burglars probably scaled the boundary wall and broke open the window of my study on the ground floor. They thereafter ransacked my study and drawing room, decamping with some cash and valuables stated above. I discovered the theft early next morning. There was no scuffle and gunshots as stated in your paper. The report is highly malevolent, with an intent to harm my reputation, and has caused me grievous mental agony. A paper of your repute ought to avoid such misleading and malicious report based on hearsay.

I would request you to kindly publish a correction, stating the bare facts, so that the harm inadvertently done by your paper is set right.

Thanking You,

Yours faithfully,
Sharad Saxena.

ASSIGNMENT

- Write a letter to the editor of a daily newspaper, complaining about the frequent failure of electric supply in your locality.

Write a letter to the editor of a local daily about the bad condition of roads and drains in your city requesting him to publish the same so as to bring it to the notice of the appropriate authorities.

90,Vijay Khand,
Gomti Nagar,
Lucknow-226010.
1 st June, 2000.

Sir,

Subject : Bad condition of roads and drains in Lucknow.

I would like to draw the attention of the authorities through the column of your daily, to the pitiable conditions of roads in the city. Leaving aside the main thoroughfares, the condition of the road in the bylines and the colonies are indeed very pathetic, It is quite common to find big pot-holes right in the middle of the road, which are in a state of disrepair. It is very difficult to drive during the day, while venturing out at night is to court disaster. The absence of street lighting makes these potholes a virtual deathtrap. It has accounted for innumerable accidents in the recent past, some of which have been fatal.

The drainage system is even worse, as most of the drains are lying choked. This was exposed the other day, when the pre monsoon showers proved hollow the claim of the civic authorities, of being prepared for the monsoons. In this mild shower, most of the localities, including the posh markets were flooded with water. The unauthorized encroachment of land by vendors and influential people, have played havoc with the drainage system of the city. One shudders to think, what could happen with the advent of monsoons beginning early next month.

There is however still time to set things right, before it is too late. The road repairs and the cleaning of the drains should be taken up concurrently, without any delay. Wherever required, the encroachment of public land that is impairing drainage, should be immediately demolished .The encroachment of land should also be made a cognizable offence under law, with strict penalties to discourage people from it. This would not only make the city roads wide and decongest the traffic, but would also make the city clean and beautiful.

I would therefore request the civic authorities, to kindly take heed to this serious civic problem, that is playing havoc with the lives and property of the common man.

Yours truly,
Siddhant Singh

ASSIGNMENT
- Write a letter to the editor of a daily newspaper focusing on the increasing incidents of thefts and robberies in your locality and suggest some preventive measures.

ILLUSTRATED EXAMPLES OF A LETTER OF COMPLAINT

While on a business trip you had to spend a week at a large hotel. However the poor facilities and the rude behaviour of the hotel staff made your stay very unpleasant. Write a letter of complaint to the manager of the hotel expressing your feeling of annoyance and suggesting what could be done to improve the standard of the hotel.

(ICSE 1989)

24, Mall Avenue,
M.G.Road,
Lucknow–226001
23 rd May, 2000.

The Manager,
Skylark Hotel,
Bombay.

Subject : Poor facilities in your hotel.

Dear Sir,

I had come on a business trip to Bombay and had checked in your hotel on 3rd April 1999 in room no.106. I found the overall service of the hotel quite poor, that belied your claim of offering three star facilities. I had brought this to your notice on a number of occasions, during my one-week stay in your hotel, but there was hardly any   improvement.

The room given to me was humid with poor ventilation. The sheets were dirty and quite shabby. When I requested room service to change them, they were brusque in telling me that the sheets had been changed in the morning. I had to remind them daily to change the sheets, that poorly reflects on the quality of housekeeping .The room service was atrocious and required several reminders before what was ordered finally arrived.

The quality of food was not in keeping with the star status, though it was priced accordingly. On a few occasions I had to return the food, as it did not seem fit for eating. The staff at the reception counter was insensitive to the needs of guests. I would have to remind the operator a number of times, before I could get my number. With all these shortcomings, one would have expected a reasonable tariff. On the contrary the tariff charged for the single room was Rs.2,500.00 per day, which is unreasonable taking into account the amenities available.

I would therefore request you to kindly investigate the shortcomings, so that guests are not put through the ordeal that I had to face .I would also suggest that you should take immediate steps to improve the housekeeping, catering and room service in your hotel. There seems to be an immediate need for training the existing staff, on matters of etiquette. You should also pay personal attention to the guests, so as to   make their stay comfortable. This will improve the goodwill of your hotel and justify your claim of a three star hotel offering five star amenities.

Yours truly,
S. Sharma

ASSIGNMENT

- Write a letter to the railway Station Master complaining about the untidy conditions of waiting rooms in the railway stations. Suggest what improvements can be done.

A travel agency has sent your tickets for the wrong date. Show your dissatisfaction, the inconvenience caused and ask them to put the mistake right. Enclose the tickets.

20, Vivek Khand,
Gomti Nagar,
Lucknow-226010.
5 th September, 2000.

The Proprietor,
Sky Travels,
10, M.G.Road,
Lucknow-226001.

Subject : Wrong tickets sent by your agency.

Dear Sir,

I am pained to inform you that my travel plans have been jeapordised on account of carelessness shown by your staff booking the tickets. I had requested your manager Mr. Sharma to book a two-tier AC ticket for Delhi by Satabdi Express, for 9th September. Today to my horror, I was delivered a ticket for the 11 th of September that is of no use to me.

I have to be in Delhi on 10 th mornings to attend a seminar in which I am presenting a paper. It was on account of this, I had booked my ticket a week in advance, as I did not want to risk getting a waitlisted ticket. I am hereby returning the ticket, and would like you to immediately arrange for a confirmed ticket, for 9 th by Shatabdi Express or any other suitable train. I shall expect an immediate response, confirming the status of my ticket by today evening. This is imperative, for I have to confirm my travel plan to my host. Besides I have to make other necessary arrangements that I am unable to do now.

Meanwhile you should investigate as to how this happened, and ensure that it does not recur in future. This would be in your own business interest, so that clients like me do not suffer inconvenience on account of lapses at your end.

Yours truly,
Shantanu Sharma.

ASSIGNMENT

- Write a letter to the General Manager of a furniture showroom complaining that the furniture delivered to you was damaged in transit .Show your dissatisfaction and ask him to attend to it immediately.

There has been a serious theft in your house and you feel the police are not making sufficient efforts to arrest the thieves. Write a letter to the Director General of Police complaining of the inefficiency of the local police requesting him to take necessary action.

(ICSE- 1991)

A124, Nehru Nagar,
Lucknow-226010.
18 th October 1999.

Director General of Police,
U. P. Police,
Lucknow-226010.

Subject : No progress made against my FIR Number GN 104

Dear Sir,

I would like to draw your kind attention to the extremely tardy progress made by the Nehru Nagar Police station regarding my FIR Number GN 104 dated 11 October 1999, regarding a theft that took place in my house on the intervening night of 10 th / 11 th October 1999. I had gone to Delhi to attend a wedding with my family, the previous night. The next day I received a phone call from my friend Mr. S. P. Saigal informing about the theft . I rushed back to learn that the local police took an hour's time to come to the scene. By this time, a sizeable crowd had gathered in front of my house.

Despite the insistence of my friend, the inspector Mr. S.K.Sharma was unable to summon the dog squad, that could have given some vital clues, for catching the culprit. However nothing much was done, except for waiting for me to return and record my statement. In this theft I have lost cash amounting to Rs 10000 besides   valuables amounting to Rupees two lakhs. It is now over a week but nothing substantial like questioning the people whom I suspect, or taking the fingerprints has been done. The pace at which the investigation is in progress, there is just no hope of catching the thieves.

It is indeed very surprising to note, that despite the tremendous advances made in criminology, our police is still adopting primitive methods of investigation. There are no preventive measures taken, to tackle this menace, that has become a frequent occurrence in our colony. There is no police patrolling and rounding up some suspicious character, that hang around the dhabas that abound in this residential colony.

I would request you to kindly instruct the officers to expedite the investigation, so that the culprit can be brought to book, for which I shall be obliged.

Thanking you,

Yours truly,
Sharad Singh.

ASSIGNMENT

1.   Write a letter to the Station Director of Doordarshan complaining about the poor quality of T V programs being shown.

Your Immediate neighbour has a habit of playing the music system loudly at night, which disturbs you specially during the examination days. Write to him of your complaint suggesting steps that he could take to solve this problem.

A124, Nehru Nagar,
Lucknow.
18 th October,1999.

Dear Mr Sharma

I would like to draw your kind attention to a problem, which has been disturbing me for quite some time. I had initially thought that it could be some occasion for celebration, but its persistence has caused me tremendous annoyance. This is with reference to your habit of playing the music system loudly at night. The sound of blaring music, late at night causes tremendous discomfort to me and the people around.

Since we are living in very close proximity to each other, the high-pitched music cause distraction that at times becomes excruciating. I am also a great fan of music, and love to spend my leisurely hours hearing it. The problem however arises, when it is heard at volumes loud enough to cause uneasiness to others especially during late night. I and my younger brother are unable to sleep at night, because of the loud drumbeats. This has now started telling on my performance at school. I was unable to concentrate on my studies, during the examinations last month, which caused me tremendous pain and apprehension. Your habit of listening to loud music at night has become a predicament for the neighbourhood, who are also equally aggrieved .

I have no intention of coming in the way of your love for music, but would request you, to kindly keep the volume of the sound system low. This shall help me to concentrate on my studies. The late night partying could he held indoors, so that the ambience of the night is not disturbed. This would enable us to sleep in peace. I would indeed be grateful if you could take note of my suggestion, and take appropriate steps, so that this problem is resolved at the earliest.

Yours sincerely,
Sharad Singh

ASSIGNMENT

1. Write a letter to your immediate neighbour who runs a workshop in his house. The noise of the machine and generators disturbs you especially during the night. Complain to him and ask him to take steps to solve the problem.

Write a letter to the local police complaining of a theft that took place in your neighbouring flat.

(ICSE- 2000)

124, Nehru Apartments,
Gomti Nagar,
Lucknow.
15 th October, 1999.

The Superintendent of Police,
Police Station,
Gomti Nagar.

Subject : Theft in my neighbouring flat

Dear Sir,

I would like to draw your kind attention to a theft that took place in my neighbouring flat number 123 Nehru Apartments, on the intervening night of 10 th / 11 th October. The owner of the flat Mr. R.N. Gupta, a close friend of mine had gone to Delhi to attend a wedding with his family, the previous night. In the morning when I came out of my flat for my usual morning walk, I found the main door of his flat ajar with a broken lock flung on the floor. Fearing the worst I informed the local police station of the incident, and also my friend at Delhi. The local police took an hour's time to come to the scene. By that time a sizeable crowd had gathered in front of the flat.

Despite my insistence, the inspector Mr. S.K.Sharma, was unable to summon the dog squad, that could have given some vital clues for catching the culprit. However nothing much was done, except for waiting for the family to return and record their statements. Mr. Gupta informed that the valuables amounting to rupees two lakhs have been stolen. The pace at which the investigation is in progress, there is no hope of catching the thief.

It is indeed very surprising to note, that despite the tremendous advances made in criminology, our police is still adopting ancient methods of investigation. There is also no preventive measure taken, to tackle this menace that has become a frequent occurrence. I would therefore request you to kindly have this theft investigated. Appropriate measures must also be taken to ensure the safety of the inhabitants of these apartments.

Yours truly,

Sudhanshu Saxena.

ASSIGNMENT

1.   Write a letter to the Inspector General of Police complaining about the anti social activities of some misguided elements in your area.

ILLUSTRATED EXAMPLES OF LETTER OF APOLOGY

You are the manager of a reputed firm. A consignment sent by you to one of your regular customers was returned with a letter complaining of the inferior quality of goods. Write a letter of apology, explaining the causes and your plans for replacement

(ICSE 2003)

Kapoor Industries
Nariman point,
Mumbai.- 400010
20 th July,2003.

Mr A.B. Mishra
Manager Housekeeping
Taj Hotel,
Lucknow.

Subject : Your complaint on the quality of linen supplied.

Dear Sir,

We are in receipt of your letter ref. TH/123 dated. 30 June 2003, drawing our attention to the quality of linen supplied to you last month. Our Quality Control department has examined the above consignment sent by you, specially taking note of your complaint, regarding the colour and coarseness of material supplied.

We agree that the quality of linen supplied, is not in absolute conformity to the sample enclosed with the order. There has obviously been some mistake, in dispatching the same. However, the colour of the linen is the same as we have been supplying to you over the years. The stains on some pieces, could have been on account of the consignment getting wet, while in transit.

We thank you for drawing our attention to this lapse, which we sincerely regret. I have personally taken up the matter with the concerned staff, and have instructed them to send fresh stocks, confirming to your specifications. In order to avoid damage in transit, we shall be packing the consignment in plastic sheets, rather then gunny bags. The consignment shall be sent tomorrow, and would reach you in about a week's time.

May I apologise once again for the above lapse, and the inconvenience it may have caused you, I would like to assure you, that we shall take remedial measures to ensure that it does not happen in future. We greatly value your patronage, and would look forward to a long and fruitful association.

Yours truly,
Sharad Singh
MANAGER

ASSIGNMENTS

1. You are the manager of a hotel. A customer has complained about the quality of food served to guests at his sons birthday party. Write a letter of apology.

Write a letter to your friend apologising for your bad behaviour. Explain what the circumstances were that had caused you to act in the way you did and make amends for what you had done. *(ICSE 1984)*

Vijay Khand,
Gomti Nagar,
Lucknow.
10th Oct., 2000

My dear Anil,

I am indeed very sorry for what happened yesterday. Believe me, I had no intention of hurting your feelings, when I had snapped back at you during recess.

Actually I was feeling very upset, on my being reprimanded by my class teacher, for not having completed my project work. It was while I was brooding over this and feeling sorry for myself, when you had come along thumping my shoulder, with your gracious offer for accompanying you to the canteen. It was in this frame of mind, that I had snapped back at you. I felt angry, thinking you were insensitive to my feelings. It was only later that I realised, that your offer was well intentioned and anticipated to draw me out of my dumps.

You had acted like a true friend, but I had misunderstood your intent. It has been years since we have known each other and I would not like this small incidence to come in the way of our friendship.

Please do forgive me for this lapse and join me for a small party at the canteen today. This would bring me tremendous joy and strengthen our friendship further.

Your friend,
S. Sharma

ASSIGNMENTS

1. You have been unable to keep an appointment with your friend the following Sunday. Write a letter of apology to him.
2. Write a letter to the principal of your school giving an explanation of your misbehaviour and offering a satisfactory apology.

Suppose you are the Sales Manager of a showroom selling cars. A customer had booked a car for which he had deposited advance and had been assured delivery in ten days time. The supply got delayed on account of partial shutdown of factory for preventive maintenance. The annoyed customer rang up after two weeks. Write a letter apologising for the delay.

Bharat Automobiles,
M.G.Road,
Lucknow-226001
10 th Sept. 2000.

Mr. K.K.Sharma,
12, Butler Palace,
Lucknow-226001.

Subject : Delivery of your car.

Dear Sir,

Thanks for your phone call today, drawing my attention to our promise of delivering your car last Saturday. I am however sorry to inform you, that there has been a delay in giving delivery of the vehicle, for which I would like to apologise.

Normally we are in a position to deliver a car within ten days of the date of booking. However last week our manufacturer informed, that they were slowing down dispatches, due to partial shutdown of their factory for carrying out preventive maintenance. This would be over in a week's time from now. Unfortunately due to oversight, our sales staff did not inform you of this development, which is regretted.

I have now personally checked with the manufacturer, who has assured commencement of dispatches from next week onwards. We are therefore expecting a consignment in ten days time, taking into account the transit time of three days. I shall ensure that you get delivery of your vehicle from this consignment itself.

May I apologise once again for our oversight, and for the inconvenience that it may have caused you. I would like to assure you that we shall immediately contact you on receipt of the consignment, and would request you to kindly bear with us till then.

Yours truly,
S K Singh.
Sales Manager.

ILLUSTRATED EXAMPLES OF A LETTERS OF PERSUATION

Write a letter to the director of tourism of your state informing him of the problem faced by tourists who visits your city. Suggest some measures to promote tourism in your city.

(ICSE 1993)

A124, Nehru Apartments,
Gomtinagar,
Lucknow.
15 th October, 1999.

Director of Tourism,
Government of Uttar Pradesh,
Lucknow .

Subject : Problems faced by   tourist visiting   Lucknow.

Dear Sir,

I wish to bring to your kind notice, the tremendous inconvenience faced by the tourist visiting the historic city of Lucknow. Their problem begins from the moment they disembark at the railway station or the airport. There are no information centers there to get information about hotels, transport and sightseeing places in the city. They are left to the mercy of unscrupulous touts and guides who fleece them. They are tricked by the owners of small hotels, that abound around the railway station, and made to part with huge sums of money for ordinary amenities.

The auto rickshaws charge exorbitant fares, as they are unmetered. The rickshaw pullers resort to cheating and create unpleasant scenes. The guides at the historical sites like the Imambara and the Residency also take them for a ride, charging more than the normal rate. Being inadequately trained, they are discourteous with the tourist, causing unpleasantness and ill will.

These incidents sully the fair reputation of the city, known for its courtesy and culture. It leaves a   bad impression on the mind of the tourists. I would therefore request you to take immediate steps to redress the problem before it is too late. There is immediate need for a   tourist information counter in the railway station, and the airport, where complete information on hotels, tourist sites and road maps, are available. Special tourist buses should ply during fixed hours, in the morning and afternoon, for the benefit of passengers. Prepaid auto and taxi service should be operated. Proper trained guides should only be allowed at the historical sites, with fixed remuneration for their services.

If these measures are taken, Lucknow could attract good tourist traffic, for the city has a vast tourist potential that remains unexploited. An effective advertisement campaign, using the print and the electronic media could help augment the flow of tourist traffic, which could be a boon to the economy of the city. I hope you will take immediate steps, to make the tourists stay in the city, a pleasant experience, and consider the suggestions made favourably.

Thanking You,

Yours truly,
Amit Sharma

ASSIGNMENT

1.   Write a letter to the Municipal Corporator asking for providing more amenities like playing fields and parks for people in your locality.

Your club plans to hold a youth festival in the city. As president of the club write a letter to the Managing Director of any well known companys giving details of how you intend to organise the festival and requesting him to sponsor it.   *(ICSE 1997)*

56, Sector-A,
Gomti Nagar,
Lucknow
10th, May, 2000.

Mr. Anil Ambani,
Managing Director,
Good Luck Industries,
Lucknow.

Dear Sir,

You shall be happy to learn that the Jagriti Youth Club of Lucknow is planning to hold a youth festival in the Ravindralaya from the 10th to the 17th of December. This programme shall be dedicated to our brave Army Jawans who laid down their lives in Kargil. The proceeds of the festival shall be donated to the Kargil Fund, for the rehabilitation of the widows and children of the martyrs.

During the festival teams from all over the state shall be participating. There will be dramatics, musical concerts, for which we have invited eminent judges like Lachu Maharaj and Muzarraf Ali. They have consented for the same. In order to make the programme interesting,we have also invited a few special guests to perform at the festival. A few of them have already confirmed their participation. We are expecting a good response from the general public, in view of the star attractions.

A festival of this magnitude has never been held in the city till date. The budgeted expense for the same, would work out to Rs. 10 lakhs on a conservative estimate. This is because most artists are performing voluntarily, to show their solidarity with the valiant jawans.

We would like your help in this noble cause and would request you to kindly sponsor the show, to cover the budgeted expenses. This shall also give you tremendous publicity mileage and generate excellent goodwill for your products. We are sure, you would also like to participate in this great cause and shall look forward to your confirmation by this week end.

Thanking you,

Yours truly,
XYZ,
President,
Jagriti Youth Club,
Lucknow.

ASSIGNMENT

1. Write a letter to the mayor of your city requesting him to open an amusement park in the city for the benefit of children.

Write a letter to the manager of your local bus depot, pointing out that there are very few buses on your route in the morning and these are invariably late thereby causing inconvenience to many daily passengers.

(ICSE 1998)

45,Vijay Khand
Gomti Nagar ,
Lucknow -226010
9 th July 1998,

The Depot Manager,
Local Bus Depot,
Lucknow .

Dear Sir,

Subject : Inadequate number of buses in Route no 1

I would like to draw your kind attention, to the plight of daily commuters travelling in the city buses on route number one, which operates from the airport to Chinhat .The buses are very inadequate and are invariably late, especially in the peak morning hours.

As you are aware, this is the only mode of transport, for the residents of the colonies around the airport to the city, which is twelve kilometers, away. The number of buses plying on this route, is incommensurate to the population of the colonies. This results in the buses being perpetually overcrowded .The situation in the morning is really very pathetic, for it is the peak traffic time .The office goers and the college students can be seen lined up for hours at the bus stops, waiting for buses to come which invariably are late. The few buses that do come are over crowded. The plight of lady commuters is inexplicable .The antisocial elements like the pickpockets have a field day. There is hardly any day when such instances of pick pocketing are not reported.

May I request you, to kindly monitor the punctuality of the buses in the morning, so as to provide immediate succor to the aggrieved public. In addition to this, I would request you to kindly review the adequacy of the buses plying on this route, taking into account the number of commuters. This will go a long way in easing the difficulties of the daily commuters.

Yours truly,
K. K. Singh.

Write a letter to the principal of your school expressing your wish to continue studying in the same school after class X. Your letter should make clear what course /stream you wish to follow and why you have decided to choose that course

(ICSE 1999)

2/34 Virat Khand,
Gomti Nagar,
Lucknow-226010
10th May, 2000.

The Principal
Boys High School
Hazratganj
Lucknow

Subject : Re-admission to class XI Science stream

Sir,

I am a student of class X C of your school and have given my ICSE Board exams in March 2000. In view of the new session commencing from next month, I would like to seek readmission in class XI Science stream with Mathematics.

In the last five years that I have been in the school, I have found the environment very conducive for learning. The teaching faculty is one of the best, with very good and cooperative staff. There is also a very good mix of academics, with extracurricular activities. I would like to continue studies in this school itself. The reason for my opting for the science stream is the penchant for the subject, which is also my hobby. I have scored good marks in the half yearly and the pre board exam. The copy of my report card is   enclosed for your kind perusal.

My choice of subjects is also in line with my ambition of becoming a top-notch computer engineer. I plan to join IIT after completing my ISC. This is for I see a bright future in the realm of Information Technology, where there is tremendous potential for growth. The academic environment of the school shall enable me to realise my dream.

It is my sincere desire that I pursue further studies in my almamater. I would therefore request you to kindly grant me admission in class XI in the Science stream with Mathematics in this prestigious school, for which I shall be thankful.

Your obediently,
Siddhant Singh.

Write a letter to the principal of your school expressing your wish to continue studying in the same school after class X. Your letter should make clear what course (stream) you wish to follow and why you have decided to choose that course.

Om Nagar
Ajmeri Gate
Delhi - 110016

The Principal,
Holy High School,
Daryaganj,
Delhi.

Sub.: An application for the admission in the Science stream.

Sir,

I am a student of class X-C of your school. I offer my services as ......

....

....

....

....

....

....

....

....

....

....

Yours faithfully,
....

Recent Letters

Many area near your school have been affected by floods. You are the President of your school social service club. Write a letter to the Mayor of your town / city telling him / her what you plan to do for the relief of the victims, suggest ways in which you can combine with other organizations bringing about better distribution of relief items.
                                                                        (ICSE 2012)

President,
Social Service Club,
City School,
Lucknow.
2 March 2012.

Mr L. R. Gupta.
Mayor,
Lucknow.
Dear Sir,

Subject : Volunteering help for the flood affected people of Gomtinagar.

The flood situation in the city has become very grave with water now entering low lying areas of Gomtinagar and Arjunganj, which are around my school. Our social service club has decided to help the district administration in providing relief to the flood affected families.

We have appealed to the students, to contribute for this noble cause, both in cash and kind. The cash so collected would be donated to the flood relief fund, while the clothes; utensils medicines and food, would be distributed to the flood victims.

In order to ensure speedy relief, we have formed three teams, who would coordinate with the other agencies engaged in the work. While the first team would lend a helping hand to the Red Cross, doctors and paramedic staff in the inoculation drive, to prevent the out break of an epidemic. The second team would help the Swam Sewak Dal in the distribution of clothes and other relief material. The third team would help other voluntary organizations and NGO's, in the preparation and distribution of food packets, water and milk.

Besides this, we would also be happy to provide any other help that you may suggest. This is the least we can do for our less fortunate brothers, in their hour of travail.

S. K Singh
President.

You were taken by your school to visit a place of historical interest. Write a letter to your classmate who was unable to go on the trip, telling him / her about the trip, why it was important and what you gained from the experience.

(ICSE 2012)

2 March 2012

Dear Amit,

I hope this letter finds you in the best of health and spirits. It is now over a week since you fell ill. How is you health now? Do not worry about studies, for nothing much happened last week. This was for last Sunday our class teacher took us for an outing to Fatehpur Sikri, a town perched atop a rocky ridge just 37 kilometers from Agra. The one and half-hour drive in our school bus was very entertaining, as we all sang and danced to the amusement of our teachers.

While on our way, the guide Mr. Salim informed that Fatehpur Sikri was built by Emperor Akbar in 1569. This was in gratitude to the Sufi saint Shaikh Salim Chistii, who prophesied that he would soon have a heir to the throne. As a mark of faith and his recent victories, he named the new city Fatehpur Sikri. Compared to our city Agra, the city seemed quite deserted. There were huge monuments, all built with red sandstone, having a natural blend of Hindu and Islamic architectural design.

The first enclosure of the palace was a vast courtyard called the Diwan- e –Aam, where the Emperor gave public audience. Beyond this was a huge second enclosure the Diwan-e Khas, or the hall of private audience. This astonishing chamber had massive curved pillars, richly ornamented with exquisite carvings and fretwork. Toward the east was Jodhabai's palace, where Akbar's Queen Jodhabai lived. It was the largest of all the palaces in the complex with traditional Hindu and Islamic carvings on the walls. The blue tiled roof was the only splash of colour in the entire complex. Besides these monuments there was the Mariam's Palace, Panch Mahal, Salim Chisti's tomb and the gigantic Buland Darwaza, which were a delight to watch.

It was sad to see the ghost city, which four centuries ago was the capital of Emperor Akbar, who just abandoned it after fourteen years of founding it. The reason cited by historians being the lack of water supply in the area.

I could not help marvel at the great despotic power of the Emperor, who built such massive palaces and a city, only to fulfill a sudden whim and just abandoned it.

The visit was indeed very interesting and educative. It would always remind me of the importance of planning for the future. This is for only Emperors can get away with such historic blunders

Wishing you a speedy recovery.

Your friend,
Siddhant.

Write a letter to the local Municipal Corporation malaria epidemic in your city. State the causes and sugg problem.

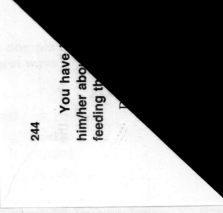

244

You have

him/her abo

feeding th

The Mayor
Lucknow Municipal Corporation,
Lalbagh,
Lucknow.
226001

Subject- Outbreak of malaria epidemic in the city of Lucknow.

Dear Sir

The onset of monsoon has aggravated the problem of water logging in the city of Lucknow. One has to wade through knee-deep water to reach office or school when it rains.

This problem is more acute in the old city areas of Lucknow like Chowk, Daliganj and Thakurganj. The drainage system here is in shambles, causing great hardships to the residents of these localities. The stagnant water in the choked drains and low lying areas, is the breeding ground for mosquitoes, that has resulted in the outbreak of malaria which is now spreading fast.

There is immediate need to clear the choked drains and pump out the stagnant water form the low-lying areas. To curtail the spread of the epidemic spraying of disinfectants and fogging is immediately required in these localities.

Besides this, there is an urgent need to organize special health camps, so that people afflicted with the disease get prompt medical aid.

I am sure you will appreciate the gravity of the situation and take immediate steps to save valuable lives.

Thanking You

Your's sincerely

Sunil Sharma

...just acquired an unusual pet. Write a letter to your friend telling ...t it. Give details about the care you have to take in looking after and ...e pet.

(ICSE 2011)

Dear Amit,

Thanks for the wonderful birthday card you sent me. It was indeed very thoughtful of you to remember it. This year I celebrated my birthday differently, instead of the usual party and cake cutting, I went with my friends for a picnic to Sahid Smarak, which is on the banks of the river Gomti. After the boat ride on the river, we sat down on the bank savouring the sceneric beauty. Just then I noticed a brown coloured tortoise, the size of a small plate crawling towards us. We all crowded around it, but unmindful of our glare, it painstakingly made its way toward the crumbs of left over sandwiches.

Scooping the creature in the empty paper lunch box, I decided to take it home as a pet. The idea did not initially appeal to my parents, but seeing my enthusiasm they finally acceded to my request. I made a small shelter of twigs and leaves for him in one corner of the kitchen garden. 'Sandy' (as I call him) made himself comfortable in his new surroundings. To escape the summer heat he crawled into a shallow pool of water near his new abode.

It was great fun playing with him in the evening. He crawls out of the pit on seeing me wave a loaf of bread. After finishing it he hides himself under the shell. The sight of a leafy shoot only gets him to stick his neck out. It is amusing to play this game of hide and seek, after which I guide him back to his shelter.

I am sure you will also like him when you visit us this summer vacation. Give my regards to Uncle and Auntie

Your loving friend

Sunil.

Your class was taken to visit an old age home where you spent half a day with the residents. Write a letter to a friend telling him/her what you saw, how you felt and in what way you have changed since the visit.   (*ICSE 2010*)

Dear Siddhant,

Last Saturday my class teacher took us to 'Cheshire Homes' an old age home in Lucknow. We all were quite apprehensive about visiting such a place, instead of the zoo or a picnic spot that would have been more fun. However since nothing could be done, I packed some magazines, and books along with my tiffin and set out to school.

The home was about half an hour's drive from school on Raibareilly road .A driveway led to a moderate size whitewashed building with a porch. On one side of the driveway was an immaculately maintained lawn.

At the home we were greeted by the warden who offered to take us around. He informed that there were 25 inmates in the home, most of them over 80 years old. Some were from very good families, but had been forsaken by their families, as they could not look after them.

As we entered the common room the somber silence was shattered by the excited voices from about a dozen seniors, some of them playing cards around a table with utter disinterest. Others were drooling on chairs before a television. On seeing us they threw down their cards and called out to us. One elderly lady bend with age, clutching a stick came up to me, wanting to know my name and interests. She was so overjoyed when I gave her the books and magazines, that she called her husband. They thanked me profusely kissing my forehead showering me with blessings. The warmth and affection moved me to tears.

We then went around to the cafeteria and the lawn, talking to many seniors. Their face lighted up on seeing us. They gave us chocolates, while others shook our hand warmly and lovingly patted us on our back. Some even thanked us for visiting them. So great was their sense of isolation and neglect.

I returned from the visit with an indelible impression in my mind. How could anyone be so cruel, in keeping one's parents away from the family they so lovingly nurtured? The thought troubles me no end. I now have a new found respect for my grandparents and try to make them happy and comfortable. This is the least I can do for them in their sunset years.

Your loving friend

Rohan

Write a letter to the Director of a Television Channel complaining about the quality of the programmes telecast. Suggest ways to improve the programmes.

(ICSE 2010)

20. Vidhan Sabha Marg.
Lucknow. U. P.
226010
20th March 2010

Director DD 1
Doordarshan,
10,Janpath,
New Delhi.110001

Subject- Improving the quality of programmes telecast

Dear Sir,

I am an old patron of the programmes telecast by your channel. I enjoy viewing the Rangoli, and serials like Jalsa and Udaan. However of late I find the quality of some programmes like 'Kabhi Sas Kabhi bahu', 'Samachar' and the 'Regional News' not up to the mark.

The serial Kabhi Sas Kabhi Bahu has now dragged on for over three years. The story line has been too stretched to now make it boring. The newsreaders' lack emotion while reading the news in 'Samachar',. making even 'breaking news' appear to be ordinary. As for the Regional News the coverage is primarily political, with social and cultural news being sidelined. To cite an instance, the marriage of 101 couples by a social organization in Lucknow last month, did not find a place in the regional news telecast.

In order to keep the interest of the viewers alive, I would suggest that the duration of the serials be time bound, so that it does not lose focus. Moreover serials on social issues like 'evil of child marriage', 'family planning' and 'female infanticide' should be telecast. The 'Samachar' should be made more interesting, by not only showing the news but also making the viewer experience it. As regards the 'Regional News' it should be more broad based, making it regional in the true sense.

I hope you will give due thought to my above suggestions and take steps to retain the interest of loyal viewers like me.

Yours faithfully
Siddarth Singh

You have recently read a book which has greatly impressed you. Write a letter to your cousin telling him / her why you were impressed. Advise him / her to read the book.
(ICSE 2009)

19, Park Road,
Lucknow.
226001

15 th May 2009

Dear Mohit,

It has been quite some time since I last wrote to you. I was busy with my exams last month and hence could not reply to your letter. Last week I read a book "Adventures of Huckleberry Finn." by Mark Twain, which I had brought from the school library. It is a real life story of a young boy named Huck Finn, who at the age of fourteen, is torn between what he is taught to do by the upright town people, and what he wants to do. He is tormented by his abusive father, and therefore after much deliberation leaves Hannibal, Missouri, an American city .on the banks of the river Mississippi to see life on his own. Jim a runaway slave who is his man Friday accompanies him in this adventurous escapade.

Huck helps Jim to escape from the clutches of his cruel master. In those days a slave was treated more like an animal, and had no rights what so ever. A deadly fate awaited them if they were caught. Huck took pity on Jim, and agreed to help him to go to Ohio, away from the charge of his evil owner. They escaped on a homespun raft and sailed down the river Mississippi .On their journey they meet a variety of people, some good and considerate, while others bad, narrow-minded and selfish.

The author in his typical lucid yet humourous style tells the behaviour of people in that era, through the eyes and words of a teenager. He pokes fun of the religious folks, show the stupidity of feuds, ridicules lawyers, shows the true colours of con men, picks on doctors, and generally mock almost everyone, including fourteen-year-old boys.

It is a classic like his other famous novel Tom Sawyer and is worth reading. The story line is so real, that you get hooked on to it and will not rest till you have finished it. I suggest you should also read this book for it enhances your ability to see the humourous side of life, by observing the actions and behaviour of ordinary people around us.

Give my live to uncle and aunty and love to your little sister Asha.

Your friend,

Siddhant.

You are the President of the school Nature Club. Write a letter to a well-known Social Worker or Environmentalist inviting him / her to be the Chief Guest at the Annual Function of the Club. Give some details about your Club and the Annual Function.

(ICSE 2009)

Nature Club,
St Peters School,
23, Mall Road,
Nainital,
Uttarakhand.
15 th May, 2009.

Mr. Sunderlal Bahuguna,
Mall Road,
Nainital.

Subject – Request for being the Chief Guest

Dear Sir

We are organizing an annual function of 'Nature Club' in our school on the 15th of April 2009. The three hour program shall begin from 10 AM.

On this occasion the members of the club shall enact few skits and plays, highlighting the need to preserve the environment. We shall also initiate a tree plantation drive by the students in the school, campus.

We shall be honoured if you could grace this occasion as the Chief Guest. Your esteemed presence and enlightened words on the Chipko movement, would inspire the students and boost their morale for the noble cause.

Thanking you,
Your's Sincerely,
Siddhant Singh.
President

Write a letter to a friend who was absent from school on a day when a really comical incident took place. Describe the incident, say what was so funny about it and what you learnt from it. *(ICSE 2008)*

Dear Amit

I was surprised not to see you in school yesterday. Hope you are hale and hearty. We had a really comical incident yesterday, which you missed. Mr. Johnson our Chemistry teacher, had given us a salt for identification in the Chemistry practical period. While I was busy setting up the apparatus, our friend Mohit began heating the salt in a test tube to observe its reaction. While heating his pen slipped from the table and fell on the floor. He bent to pick up his pen and in the process brought his head close to the burner. Before I could react his hair above his forehead caught fire. I rushed to his rescue, and was able to douse the small flame with my handkerchief. He looked stunned and bewildered, but thankfully was unharmed. In the commotion that followed, Mr. Johnson rushed to our table and asked me to take him to the dispensary. I escorted him to the dispensary, where after applying a cream on his forehead he was discharged.

We returned to the classroom. As we walked in all the boys burst out laughing, seeing the vacant space on his head in place of his curly locks .He indeed looked funny but sportingly bore the embarrassment with a grin.

He was indeed lucky to have escaped unscathed from the incident, that was basically due to his carelessness. It however highlighted the importance of precautions we must take, in doing Chemistry practical, which Mr. Johnson frequently emphasizes. Henceforth, I have resolved to be careful and observe all precautions in carrying out my work. This shall not only save me from embarrassment, but also from bodily harm.

Your loving friend,

Siddhant

Traffic jams in your city/town are getting worse day after day. Write a letter to the Deputy Commissioner of Police (traffic) complaining about the problem and offering suggestions for improvement.

(ICSE 2008)

1/153, Vijay Khand,
Gomtinagar,
Lucknow,
12 March, 2008

Deputy Commissioner of Police (Traffic),
12, Ashok Marg,
Lucknow,
226001

Subject-Frequent traffic jams on the main thoroughfares of Lucknow

Dear Sir,

I would like to draw your kind attention to the frequent traffic jams on the main thoroughfares in Lucknow. With the increase in the population of the city, and the corresponding increase in vehicular traffic, this problem is aggravating day by day.

The problem becomes very serious during peak traffic hours in the morning and evening i.e.10 A.M. to 11A.M. and 5 P.M. to 6 P.M. respectively. This is the time when people come to office and return home. Traffic snarls are very serious in Charbagh, Vidhan Sabha Marg and Ashok Marg route right up to Nishatganj. These routes also become jammed in the afternoon from 1 P.M. to 2 P.M. when school buses and vans ferry school going children home.

To surmount the problem, I would suggest that commercial vehicles including intercity buses should not be allowed on these routes during the above peak hours. Slow moving transport like thelas, tongas should also be restricted for they restrict traffic movement on the bridges

I am sure with the above measures the traffic on these routes would be considerably decongested. This would not only reduce traffic jams in the city but also make life easy for the citizens of Lucknow.

Thanking You,
Yours Sincerely,
Siddhant Singh

One of your grandparents has completed one hundred years of age. Write a letter congratulating him/her, expressing gratitude, praise and admiration for the way he/he has lived his/her life.

(ICSE 2007)

110, Sector D,
Aliganj
Lucknow-226024.
10 th April, 2007.

Dear Grand Pa.

Many, many happy returns of the day. I would like to congratulate you, on your centenary birthday. This is a very important occasion. for me, and I have informed all my friends about it.

I am very proud of you, for at your age, while others look for crutches, you are hale and hearty. This is because of regular exercises, and eating good and healthy food. I am grateful for your advise on the above. You would be pleased to know that I go out for a morning walk, and do regular exercises in the morning and evening .

Being a self made man, your life has indeed been a great struggle, from which you emerged victorious. I draw inspiration from the countless incidents narrated by you, while serving in the British army, during the Second World War .

I look forward to meeting you very soon. I pray to God for your good health and many many years of happiness.

Your loving Grandson,
Siddhant.

A company has been marketing spurious medicines behind claims that its product could be effective in preventing the avian flu or other forms of influenza. Write a letter to the Drug Controller General of the Directorate of Health Services, examining the claim of the company and explaining the harm these kind of claims could cause.

(ICSE 2007)

1/153,Vijay Khand,
Gomti Nagar,
Lucknow.

10 th April, 2007.

Drug Controller General,
Directorate of Health Services,
10, Lodi Road ,
New Delhi- 110001

Subject : Spurious medicines being marketed by X Y Z pharma.

Dear Sir,

I would like to draw your immediate attention, to the misleading claims being made by XYZ Pharma, about a drug which they claim to be effective in   preventing Avian flu, or other forms of influenza. They are marketing this drug in the name of 'Xeon', and have launched a massive campaign in the media, to promote the sale of this medicine.

I became a victim of their propaganda, and purchased this medicines last month, in the wake of the Avian flu scare, that had gripped the city. To my horror, I found myself stricken with influenza, and had to seek immediate medical attention from Dr V. K. Narayan, my family doctor. I later learnt from him, that the claim made by the company, are highly exaggerated. This is for, there is presently no drug that can actually prevent Avian flu. There could be thousands of other innocent people like me, who have fallen victim to this spurious drug. It could lead to serious after affects, putting the health of people in jeopardy.

I would request you to have the matter investigated, and restrain the company from marketing such spurious medicines by making false claims.

Your's sincerely,

K.P.SINGH

Your cousin is missing from home. Write a letter to the Superintendent of Police of your locality, requesting him to trace your cousin. Give all relevant details that may help the police department. *(ICSE 2006)*

1/153 Vijay Khand,
Gomtinagar
Lucknow-226010.
1st May, 2006.

Superintendent of Police,
Gomtinagar,
Lucknow .

Subject : Missing report of my cousin Anurag Singh

Dear Sir

My cousin Anurag Singh son of Shri Atul Kumar Singh has not returned home since 3rd April 2006. He had gone to attend coaching class in the evening, and has since not returned .He has been staying with me for the last two years, and is a student of class X in St Thomas College, Gomtinagar, Lucknow .

I have made all enquiries from his friends and relatives, but have not been able to locate him. He is lean and slim, 5 ft 5 inches in height, and fair in complexion He was wearing white shirt and blue jeans . I am enclosing his latest photograph, to help identify him. I would be grateful, if you could kindly help me in finding him, for which I shall be obliged .

Your's truly,
Raunaq Singh.

Recently you went to a restaurant for dinner and there you saw your favourite sports star. You had an opportunity of spending some moments with him or her. In a letter to your friend, give a brief account of your memorable meeting with the sports star.

(ICSE 2006)

> 90, Aliganj,
> Lucknow-226024.
> 1 st May, 2006.

Dear Arjit,

It has been quite sometime since I last wrote to you . This was for I was busy in preparing for my exams, that ended last week. To celebrate the occasion, my parents took me to Oudhyana Restaurant, in the Taj Residency hotel .

While I was savouring the delicacies served before me, I noticed an unusual flurry of activity in the table just next to me .To my surprise, I saw Sachin Tendulkar and his wife being escorted to this table by the hotel staff. My heart leaped with joy, as I saw him settle on the chair facing me. After the waiters had taken his order, I caught his attention and excusing myself, I walked up to him in a trance. This was like a dream come true, and made me speechless for a second. However gaining composure, I wished him and his wife good evening, and introduced myself .I told him how I adored him, and loved his game . He blushed modestly, and invited me to be seated. For the next couple of minutes we spoke of mundane things about cricket .He encouraged me to work hard ,and practice continuously, for this can only improve my game . He also wanted to know the places of tourist interest in and around Lucknow, which I graciously provided .

The waiters in the mean time had started serving the dishes. Realizing that this dream was about to end. I took out a ten rupee note from my pocket, and asked him to autograph it. He smiled and with a flourish penned "To Alankrit with love Sachin".

I have since then framed this note, and hung it in my study room. It reminds me of the few precious moments I shared with Sachin, the great cricket maestro .I shall show you the same when you come to Lucknow.

Rest is all fine. Give my regards to Uncle and Aunty and love to Ronnie .

> Your loving friend
> Alankrit

Write a letter to the Director of the Archaeological Survey of India complain-ing about the damage caused to a historical monument in your city due to negligence. Suggest steps that the civic authorities should take to preserve the monument.
(ICSE 2005)

153,Gomti Nagar,
Lucknow- 226010.
10 May, 2005.

Director,
Archaeological Survey of India,
Hew Delhi-100001.

Subject : Precarious condition of historical monument at Lucknow.

Dear Sir,

I would like to draw your attention to the precarious condition of 'The Residency 'a his-toric monument at Lucknow that symbolizes our freedom struggle.

This monument on the banks of the river Gomti, is known for the significant role it played, during the first war of Independence, against the British empire. Unfortunately, this heritage is being slowly but surly eroded. In the absence of proper security arrangements, people are inscribing their names and messages on the walls, that not only disfigure but also endanger the monument. The lush green lawns are   littered with polythene bags and eatables, giving the place an unpleasant look. The absence of proper drinking water in the complex, makes the visit   antagonizing. This is further compounded by numerous self designated guides, who thrust themselves on the hapless tourists, fleecing them at times.

I would therefore request you, to take immediate steps for preserving this national heritage, by improving security arrangements. The civic authorities should also be instructed, to make proper arrangements for drinking water in the complex. Registered guides should only be al-lowed to operate in the complex.

These measures would go a long way in safeguarding this important monument, and also make it a memorable visit for the tourist.

Yours sincerely,
Sudhanshu Sharma

Proverbs, Idioms, Synonymous words and Confusing Words

PROVERBS

Proverbs are the distilled wisdom of sages handed down to us from time immemorial. They provide us with valuable insight to life and provoke us to think .We can use these maxims or adages to support our arguments and add depth and colour to our composition. An appropriate proverb used in your composition or speech, adds a volume of meaning and makes it instantly appealing. They are no doubt the gems of wisdom and we are giving below some of the most common proverbs in alphabetical order.

A

A bad workman quarrels with his tools. (*an inefficient person complains about the circum-stances*)

A bird in hand is worth two in the bush.

A burnt child dreads the fire.

A drowning man clutches at a straw.

A friend in need is a friend indeed. (*a true friend is the one who can be depended upon in trouble*)

A good beginning is half the battle won.

A little learning is a dangerous thing.

A man is known by the company he keeps. (*we can know the character of a person by observ-ing the type of friends he has*)

A man who can control his mind can control his destiny.

A penny saved is a penny earned.

A rolling stone gathers no moss. (*an unsteady person will never make good*)

A stitch in time saves nine.

A thing of beauty is a joy forever.

Adversity often leads to prosperity.

After the storm comes the calm.

All fingers are no same.

All is fair in love and war.

All is well that ends well.

All seems yellow to the jaundiced eye.

All that glitters is not gold. (*appearances are deceptive*)

All work and no play make Jack a dull boy.

An empty vessel makes the most noise.

An idle mind is the devil's workshop.

Art is long, life is short.

As you make your bed you must lie on it.

As you sow so shall you reap.

B

Bad news travels fast.

Barking dogs seldom bite.

Beggars cannot be choosers.

Better alone than in bad company.

Better late than never.

Better safe than sorry.

Birds of a feather flock together.

Blood is thicker than water.

Books and friends should be few and good.

Brevity is the soul of wit.

Catch at the shadow and lose the substance.

Charity begins at home.

Children are what you make them.

Cleanliness is next to Godliness.

Coming events cast their shadows before.

Comparisons are odious.

Courtesy costs nothing, but gains much.

Crime never pays.

Cut your coat according to your cloth.

Dead men tell no tales.

Die is cast. (*Decision has been made*)

Do not put all your eggs in one basket.

Don't count your chicken before they are hatched.

Don't cut off your nose to spite your face.

Don't kill the goose that lays the golden egg.

Early bird catches the worm.

Early to bed, early to rise makes a man healthy, wealthy and wise.

Easier said than done.

East or west home is best.

Every cloud has a silver lining.

Every dog has his day.

Everybody's business is nobody's business.

Everyman for himself and God for us all.

Everything is fair in love and war.

Example is better than precept.

Experience is the best teacher.

Extremes are dangerous.

F

Failures are the pillars of success.

Familiarity breeds contempt.

Flies are easier caught with honey than with vinegar.

Forbidden fruit is the sweetest.

Forewarned is forearmed.

Fortune favours the brave.

G

Give a dog a bad name and hang him.

Give the devil his due.

God helps those who help themselves.

Great mind think alike.

Great talkers are little doers.

H

Half a loaf is better than no bread.

Haste makes waste.

He knows most who speaks last.

He laughs best who laughs last.

He who spits against the wind spits against his own face.

Honesty is the best policy.

I

If wishes were horses, beggars might ride.

If you wish for peace, prepare for war.

It is better to be late than never.

It is easier to pull down than to build.

It is never too late to mend.

It is no use carrying coal to Newcastle.

It is no use crying over spilt milk.

It never rains but it pours. (When events happen in quick succession)

It takes two to make a quarrel.

J

Jack-of-all-trades master of none.

L

Laugh and the world laughs with you weep and you weep alone.

Let bygones be bygones.

Let sleeping dogs lie.

Little knowledge is dangerous.

Live and let live.

Look before you leap.

Lost time is never found.

Love is blind.

M

Make a mountain of a molehill.

Make hay while the sun shines.

Man is not a prisoner of his fate but of his own mind.

Man proposes God disposes.

Many drops make the mighty ocean.

Misfortune never comes alone.

Money makes the mare go.

Much cry and little wool.

N

Necessity is the mother of invention.

Never look a gift horse in the mouth.

Never say die.

Nip the evil in the bud.

No man is indispensable

No pain no gain.

No smoke without fire.

Nothing succeeds like success.

O

One good turn deserves another.

One man's meat is another man's poison.

One swallow does not make a summer.

Out of sight out of mind.

Out of the frying pan to the fire.

P

Pen is mightier than the sword.

Penny-wise pound-foolish.

Pour oil on troubled waters. (Try to calm a quarrel with soothing words)

Power corrupts and absolute power corrupts absolutely.

Practice makes perfect.

Prevention is better than cure.

Pride goes before a fall.

R

Reckless youth makes rueful age.

Religion is opium for the masses.

Rome was not built in a day.

Rumour is a great traveller.

S

Seeing is believing.

Self-help is the best help.

Set a thief to catch a thief.

Slow and steady wins the race.

Small beginnings make great endings.

Something is better than nothing.

Sound mind dwells in sound body.

Spare the rod and spoil the child.

Speech is silver silence is golden.

Still waters run deep.

Stoop to conquer.

Strike the iron while it is hot.

T

The more the merrier

The proof of the pudding is in the eating. (*the real taste is in the practical, not the theoretical aspect*)

The saucepan should not call the kettle black.

The wearer knows where the shoe pinches.

There are two sides to every question.

There is many a slip between the cup and the lip.

There is no smoke without fire.

They also serve who stand and wait.

Think before you ink.

Those who live in glass houses should not throw stones.

Time and tide waits for none.

Time cures more than the doctor.

Time is a great healer.

Time is money.

Tit for tat.

To err is human to forgive is divine.

Too many cooks spoil the broth.

Truth is evergreen.

Two heads are better than one.

Two is a company three is none.

U

Uneasy lies the head that wears the crown.

United we stand divided we fall.

Unity is strength.

V

Variety is the spice of life.

Virtue is its own reward.

Virtue thrives in adversity.

W

Waste not, want not.

What can't be cured must be endured.

What is done cannot be undone.

What is sport to the cat is death to the rat.

When the cat is away the mouse is at play.

Where there is a will there is a way.

While in Rome do as Romans do.

Who will bell the cat?

Wine and wenches empty man's purses.

Y

You can take a horse to the water but you cannot make him drink.

You cannot shoe a running horse.

You cannot teach old dogs new tricks.

Youth and age will never agree.

Z

Zeal without knowledge is a runaway horse.

IDIOMS

A

An apple of discord (*A cause of dispute*):

Kashmir is an *apple of discord* between India and Pakistan.

The apple of the eye (*Someone very precious*):

His son was *the apple of his eye.*

With open arms (*With great love and enthusiasm*):

His friends welcomed him *with open arms.*

All and sundry (*Everybody without discrimination*):

We do not share our secrets with *all and sundry.*

To keep someone at arms length (*Avoid being too friendly*):

He kept him *at arms length* because of his dubious character.

To come of age (*To attain twenty one years of age*):

He shall *come of age* this month.

To have an axe to grind (*To have a personal favour to obtain*):

The political parties have an *axe to grind* in keeping this contentious issue alive.

Much ado about nothing (*A lot of fuss over some insignificant matter*):

The opposition parties are raising *much ado about nothing* on this issue.

All agog (*Thrilled, excited*):

He was *all agog* on hearing the good news.

B

With one's back to the wall (*In a difficult situation*):

They were fighting the battle *with their back to the wall.*

To make a clean breast of (*To confess one's mistakes*):

The thief made a *clean breast of* his crime in court.

To burn one's fingers (*To get into trouble*):

He *burnt his fingers* by meddling in his friends family matter.

To breed bad blood (*To create hatred among people*):

The communal leaders *breed bad blood* among the people in the name of religion.

To bring to book (*To bring to justice*):

All corrupt officials should be *brought to book.*

To be in the good books of (*In favour with*):

Ram is *in the good books of* his teacher.

To burn the midnight oil (*To study hard late into the night*):

A student should *burn the midnight oil* if he has to succeed in life.

A bolt from the blue (*A complete surprise*):

The unexpected news came as a *bolt from the blue.*

To nip in the bud (*To stop something in the very beginning*):

Bad habits should be *nipped in the bud.*

To bury the hatchet (*To forget the past quarrel*):

They agreed to *bury the hatchet* and work together in future.

To bear the bunt of (*To face the difficulty*):

The manager had to *bear the bunt of* the unions wrath.

Not to bat an eyelid (*Not to show any sign of embarrassment*):

He was so shameless, that he did *not bat an eyelid* on being caught lying.

To back the wrong horse (*To support the wrong person*):

He was bound to fail, for he had *backed the wrong horse.*

To let the cat out of the bag (*To tell a secret*):

He decided it was time *to let the cat out of the bag.*

Out of the band box (*Neat, spick and span*):

His suit appeared out *of the band box.*

Lock stock and barrel (*Completely*).

They decide to shift their office *lock stock and barrel.*

To have all one's eggs in one basket (*To risk everything on one source*):

We must not put *all our eggs in one basket* in the present environment.

To beard the lion in his own den (*To confront one's enemy on his own home ground*).

The army decided *to beard the lion in has own den by attacking militant hideouts.*

To blow hot and cold (*To be unreliable*):

The religious leaders *blow hot and cold* on the achievements of the government.

To know on which side one's bread is buttered (*To know what course to follow to benefit one*):

He is a shrewd person who *knows which side his bread is buttered.*

Like a bull in a china shop (*Extremely clumsy*):

Taking him to the exhibition is *like taking a bull to a china shop*

Break the back of something (*Finish the hardest part of the work*):

Their defeat at Kargil *broke the back* of the militants.

Take a bull by the horn (*Face a difficulty or danger boldly*).

If you want to solve the problem you must *take the bull by the horn.*

Get too big for one's boot (*Become very self important or conceited*).

After being promoted he is *getting too big for his boots.*

C

To cook accounts (*To prepare false accounts*):

The tax authorities caught him for *cooking up accounts.*

A cat and dogs life (*A life full of quarrel*):

The husband and wife are leading *a cat and dogs life.*

To rain cats and dogs (*To rain heavily*):

It *rained cats and dogs* last night.

To call a spade a spade (*To be frank*):

He did not hesitate in *calling a spade a spade*.

A cat on hot bricks (*Uneasy*):

He behaved like a *cat on hot bricks* at the party.

Cheek by jowl (*Side by side*):

Politicians and criminals work *cheek by jowl*.

A nail in one's coffin (*Something that will ruin one's plan*):

The massacre was *a nail in the coffin* of the British empire in India.

To take up the cudgels for (*To defend enthusiastically*):

He *took up the cudgels for* his subordinate at the meeting.

A skeleton in a cupboard (*A source of shame*):

The political party has a number of *skeletons in their cupboard*.

Keep one's chin up (*Remain cheerful in difficult circumstances*):

His parents advised him to *keep his chin up* and face the problem as it comes.

Let the cat out of the bag (*Reveal a secret by mistake*):

My friend *let the cat out of the bag* by mentioning to my father about the lottery ticket I had purchased.

D

Day in and day out (*Everyday*):

We are *day in and day out* taught good manners in school.

To throw dust in someone's eye (*To mislead someone*):

Tall claims made by companies in their advertisements is like throwing dust in customers eyes.

Between the devil and the deep sea (*Between two equally dangerous situations*):

Aladdin found himself *between the devil and the deep sea*.

In the doldrums (*Miserable*):

The economy is in a state of *doldrums*.

The sword of Damocles (*Imminent danger*):

His impeachment by the Senate hung like *the sword of Damocles* on his head:

Go to the dogs (*Be ruined*):

His business has *gone to the dogs*.

Lead a dogs life (*A life of misery*):

He is *leading a dogs life* as he has lost his job.

E

To keep an eye on (*To keep a watch on*):

The policeman *kept an eye* on the suspicious man.

To see eye to eye (*To agree with*):

The two friends could not *see eye to eye* on this matter.

To turn a deaf ear to (*To refuse to listen*):

He *turned a deaf ear* to his parents advise.

To elbow one's way through (*To push forward*)

I *elbowed my way* to get into the bus.

To eat one's word (*To apologise*)

The proud king had *to eat his words* on being defeated

To move heaven and earth (*To make every possible effort*):

He *moved heaven and earth* to get justice.

To eyewash (*To deceive*)

It was an *eyewash* to convince the party.

Ill at ease (*Uncomfortable, Uneasy*)

He was *ill at ease* throughout the party.

Turn a deaf ear to (*To refuse to listen*)

He *turned a deaf ear to* our warning and hence is in trouble.

F

To feather one's own nest (*To serve one's own interest*)

The minister was accused of *feathering his own nest.*

To fall flat (*To meet with cold reception*)

His suggestion of going to court *fell flat.*

In the face of (*In spite of*)

He succeeded in life *in the face of* many hardships.

To drag one's feet (*To act in slow and hesitant manner*)

The management was *dragging its feet* on implementing the new wages.

To foot the bill (*To pay the bill*)

His father had to *foot the bill* for the lavish birthday party.

A fair weather friend (*A friend in prosperity only*)

We should beware of *fair weather friends.*

To ruffle one's feathers (*To annoy one*)

This incident *ruffled his feathers.*

To set the Thames on fire (*To do something remarkable*)

His achievements were akin to *setting the Thames on fire.*

To put one's best foot forward (*Do ones best*)

We are expected *to put our best foot forward* in the presence of guests.

To catch some one on the wrong foot (*Catch someone doing wrong*)

He was *caught on the wrong foot* as Ravi found him cheating.

Have something at one's fingertips (*Know all the details of something*):

His mastery on his subject is complete, for he has everything *on his fingertips.*

To keep a straight face (*To remain unexpressive*)

Even though he was caught lying he *kept a straight face.*

G

To get even with (*To take revenge*)

He *got even with* his enemy when he brought about his ruin.

To grease one's palm (*To bribe*)

He had to *grease the babu's palm* to get his work done.

To throw down the gauntlet (*To challenge*)

The defending champion *threw down the gauntlet* at him.

To go astray (*To wander from the right path*)

In the absence of proper guidance there was no stopping him *to go astray.*

The gift of the gab (*Ability to speak*)

The leader had *the gift of the gab* and the public was listening to him intently.

A good Samaritan (*A kind hearted helpful person*)

He was a *good Samaritan* for the orphans of the city .

A greenhorn (*An inexperienced person*)

He was *a greenhorn* in politics.

H

Hand and glove with (*On very intimate terms*)

The police are *hand in glove with* the criminal.

With a high hand (*Oppressively*)

He ruled the country *with a high hand.*

From hand to mouth (*Barely making ends meet*)

The poor farmers lead a *hand to mouth* existence.

Head and shoulder above (*Much superior*)

He is *head and shoulder* over other students in his class.

To keep one's head (*To remain calm*)

The manager *kept his head* in the face of grave provocation

Make (someone's) hair stand on end (*Terrify someone*)

The horror film *made my hairs stand on end.*

Fall into the hands of (*Be caught*)

He *fell into the hands of* the enemy and was captured.

Heart and soul (*Completely*)

He put his *heart and soul* in completing the assignment.

Learn by heart (*To memorise something*)

He has *learnt the lesson by heart.*

Take to heart (*Become very sad. Upset*)

You must not *take his unkind remark to heart.*

Take heart (*Become encouraged*)

The soldiers *took heart* on learning that reinforcement was arriving.

Take to one's heel (*Run away*)

The thieves *took to their heels* on seeing the police.

Hall mark (*Evidence of excellence*)

This was the *hallmark* of his career when he became the governor.

To win hands down (*To win easily*)

He *won the competition hands down* for there was no strong contender.

A hard nut to crack (*A person hard to tackle*)

He convinced him though he was a *hard nut to crack*

To hit the nail on the head (*To guess rightly*)

He *hit the nail on the head* by calling him a coward.

Achilles heel (*A weak spot in a mans character*)

His short temper was his *Achilles heel.*

High and mighty (*Arrogant*)

The official behaved in a *high and mighty* manner.

To hit below the belt (*To be unfair*)

By calling him names behind his back was like *hitting him below the belt.*

Straight from the horses mouth (*Direct information from reliable sources*)

He heard the news from the *horses mouth* and hence it is true.

Put the cart before the horse (*Reverse the logical order of things*)

Making education a fundamental right is like *putting the cart before the horse* without proper infrastructure.

I

The ins and outs of (*The details of*)

The teacher knew the *ins and outs* of the subject.

To break the ice (*To begin the conversation*)

He *broke the ice* by introducing himself.

To iron out (*To smoothen*)

They *ironed out* their difference.

To know something inside out (*To know thoroughly*)

He knew the place *inside out.*

To skate on thin ice (*To say /do something dangerous*)

He was *skating on thin ice* when he volunteered to go to the expedition.

To have too many irons in the fire (*To try to do too many things at the same time*)

He failed because he *had too many irons in the fire* and hence could not concentrate.

The lion's share (*The largest share*)

He got the *lions share* of the loot.

J

To get the jitters (*To get nervous*)

He *got the jitters* on being questioned by the police.

To hit the jackpot (*To win a big prize*)

He became rich overnight as he *hit the jackpot.*

A jack of all trades (*A person who can do many different kind of work*)

He is a *jack of all trades.*

Jam packed (*Full to capacity*):

The hall was *jam packed* .

K

To kowtow with someone (*To behave in a slavish manner*)

The honest man refused *to kowtow with anyone.*

Next of kin (*Nearest relative*)

The railways announced compensation to the *next of kin.*

Killer instinct (*A ruthless nature*)

The Indians lacked the *killer instinct* to win the match.

Dressed to kill (*To dress impressively*)

She was *dressed to kill* at the party.

To keep body and soul together (*To manage to exist somehow*)

The poor people barely are able *to keep their body and soul together.*

To keep the pot boiling (*To keep thing going*)

He asked him *to keep the pot boiling* till he returned from the hospital.

Keyed up (*Roused, excited*)

He was all *keyed up* till the interview was over.

L

To win laurels (*To win glory*)

He *won laurels* for his school at the interschool athelatic championships.

To toe the line (*To follow instructions exactly*)

The press decided *to toe the line* of the government during the emergency.

To laugh in one's sleeve (*To be secretly amused*)

He was *laughing in his sleeves* when he saw his opponents quibbling among themselves.

The long and the short (*The substance of*)

The *long and the short* of the story is that honesty is the best policy.

Pull (someone's) leg (*Make fun of someone*)

He got angry for his friend kept *pulling his leg.*

There's many a slip 'twixt the cup and the lip (*Thing can go wrong anytime*)

He thinks he will win the election but *there is many a slip 'twixt the cup and the lip.*

M

To make a mountain out of a molehill (*To exaggerate an unimportant matter*)

The newspapers have a habit of *making a mountain out of a molehill.*

A man of letters (*A scholar*)

He is a *man of letters.*

Made to order (*Made to individual requirement*)

His dress was *made to order.*

To make or mar (*To succeed or fail*)

The youth can *make or mar* their future.

To steal a march upon (*To gain an advantage over*)

By launching their popular programme the star channel *stole a march* over their rivals.

To put words in one's mouth (*To tell one what to say*)

The judge restrained the lawyer from *putting words in the mouth* of the witness.

N

In a nutshell (*Briefly*)

He told him the incident *in a nutshell.*

To get on one's nerves (*To make one irritated*)

The crafty boy *gets on my nerves.*

To save one's neck (*To save one's life*)

He told a lie *to save his neck.*

To lead someone by the nose (*To make one do whatever one wants*)

She *led her husband by the nose.*

Null and void (*Invalid*)

The court struck down the order as *null and void.*

To pay through the nose (*To pay an excessive price*)

The five star hotel makes you *pay through the nose.*

Tooth and nail (*Fiercely*)

They fought *tooth and nail* till the last man.

O

The order of the day (*The current fashion*)

Corruption has become the *order of the day.*

A tall order (*An unreasonable demand*)

Accepting the unions demand was a *tall order* for the management.

One track mind (*A mind preoccupied with one subject*)

He refuses to be serious for he has a *one track mind.*

On and off (*At intervals*)

It has been snowing *on and off* for several days.

A tall order (*A difficult request*)

It was indeed a *tall order* to achieve the target.

Out of the woods (*Free from troubles*)

The economy is still not *out of the woods.*

P

Part and parcel (*An essential element*)

Good manners are a *part and parcel* of our personality.

To pass the buck (*To evade responsibility*)

The officer *passed the buck* for the mistake to his senior.

To play second fiddle (*To take subordinate position*)
Circumstances compelled him *to play second fiddle* to his leader.

To praise to the skies (*To praise excessively*)
His teacher *praised to the skies* his academic achievements.

To hold the purse strings (*To have control over the finance*)
The finance manager *holds the purse strings*.

Packed like sardines (*Packed closely together*)
In the buses people are *packed like sardines*.

To pay someone in his own coin (*To retaliate*)
He decided to *pay him in his own coin* by declining his invitation.

A bitter pill to swallow (*A disagreeable experience to undergo*)
The rebuke from his boss was a *difficult pill to swallow*.

From pillar to post (*From one place to another*)
He ran *from pillar to post* to get justice.

To wash ones dirty linen in public (*To discuss one's grievances publicly*)
The political leaders are in the habit of *washing their dirty linen in public*.

To put a spoke in a persons wheel (*To thaw a persons plan*)

Q

To be in a quandary (*To be perplexed*)
The strike having failed the workers were *in quandary*.

To queer a person's pitch (*To spoil a person's chances*)
He tried *to queer his opponents pitch* by spreading false rumours.

To be quits (*To be on even terms*)
They decided *to be quits* by paying their past dues.

R

On the rocks (*In extreme difficulties*)
His marriage is *on the rocks*.

To rule the roost (*To have full power*)
The militants are *ruling the roost* in the mountains.

To smell a rat (*To have a doubt*)
The policemen *smelled a rat* when they found the diary missing.

To rub shoulders with (*To be in close contact with*)
He *rubs shoulders* with the rich and the powerful.

At random (*Without any purpose*)
He selected a few boys *at random*.

The rank and file (*The average person*)
The *rank and file* of the party workers were with him.

To rise like a phoenix (*To rise with a new vigour*)
The Congress party *rose like a phoenix* after his martyrdom .

In a rut (*Decay, dying*)

After his death the organisation was *in a rut*.

Rat race (*Fierce unending competition*)

There is a *rat race* to reach the top in the corporate world.

S

At sixes and sevens (*In disorder*)

We found his room *at sixes and sevens*

Not worth one's salt (*Incompetent*)

He is a worthless person *not worth his salt*.

Side by side (*Standing close together*)

They stood *side by side* at the farewell party.

Sheet anchor (*Main support*)

His mother played a *sheet anchor* role in his life.

To take the wind out of a person's sail (*To frustrate a persons effort*)

The economic liberlisation policy of the government *took the wind out* of the opposition's sail.

To roll up one's sleeve (*To get ready for a fight*)

He is for ever ready *to roll up his sleeves* to prove his point.

On the sly (*Secretly*)

They got married *on the sly*.

Spick and span (*Smart*)

His office was *spick and span*.

To stoop to conquer (*To humiliate oneself to succeed ultimately*)

In our lives we have at times *to stoop to conquer*.

A cock and bull story (*A lie*)

Do not believe his *cock and bull story*.

To spin a yarn (*To tell a tale*)

He was too good at *spinning a yarn* when caught.

To start from scratch (*To start from the beginning*)

The cyclone victims had *to start their lives from scratch*.

For a song (*Very cheaply*)

He sold his property *for a song* .

To leave no stone unturned (*To take every possible measure*)

He did not *leave any stone unturned* to get himself transferred.

Give the cold shoulder (*Show distaste for his company*)

His friends *gave him a cold shoulder* for his behaviour.

To put one's shoulder to the wheel (*To work hard at a task*)

They decided *to put their shoulders to the wheel* and finish the incomplete task.

Separate the sheep from the goats (*Distinguish good people from bad people*)

A good manager is able to *distinguish the sheep from the goat*.

A wolf in sheep's clothing (*An apparently harmless person who is really an enemy*)

Do not be taken in by his sweet tongue for he is a *wolf in sheep's clothing.*

Pull one's socks up (*Make an effort to improve one's performance*)

His teacher advised him *to pull up his socks* failing which he would fail in the exams.

Have something up one's sleeve (*Have some secret for use when needed*)

The opposition parties brought in a no confidence motion for they *had something up their sleeves.*

T

To take one to task (*To rebuke*)

The principal *took him to task* for coming late to school.

On tenterhooks (*In suspense*)

Till the exams were over I was *on tenterhooks.*

A Herculean task (*A very difficult task*)

Eradication of poverty is *a Herculean task* for any government.

To stem the tide (*To meet a force well*)

His spirited campaign *stemmed the tide* and saved his party from defeat.

Thick skinned (*Insensitive*)

The politicians are *thick skinned* people.

To take a back seat (*To occupy a subordinate position*)

In the bedlam the main issue *took a back seat.*

To take French leave (*To be absent without permission*)

He was away on *French leave* and hence was punished.

To throw the baby out with the bathwater (*To throw away a useful thing along with the useless*)

Privatisation of all industries is like *to throw out the baby with the bathwater.*

To throw a spanner in the works (*To disturb a plan*)

Raising of contentious issues is like *throwing a spanner in the works* of the ruling party.

Topsy turvy (*Upside down*)

His world turned *topsy turvy* on his fathers death.

Under someone's thumb (*Controlled by someone*)

She is completely *under her husband's thumb.*

To play one's trump card (*To make one's most powerful move*)

He decided *to play his trump card* and had them floored.

Be on one's toe (*To be ready or prepared for action*)

They were all *on their toes* on hearing their master coming .

To hold one's tongue (*Be silent say nothing*)

With great difficulty I managed *to hold my tongue.*

Armed to the teeth (*Completely armed*)

The soldiers were *armed to the teeth.*

Put one's card on the table (*Be honest and open about one's intentions*)

He decided to *put his cards on the table* so that they could come to an agreement.

U

In unison (*Together*)

They sang in *unison*.

Underway (*To progress*)

The preparation for the concert is *underway*.

Up in arms (*Rebellious*)

The workers were *up in arms* fighting for their rights.

Upwardly mobile (*Aspiring to advance in life*)

The youth leaders are *upwardly mobile* class.

V

In vogue (*In fashion*)

This dress is *in vogue* today.

Vested interest (*Personal interest*)

He had a *vested interest* in awarding the contract to the firm.

A voice in the wilderness (*No listener for a message*)

His opinion was *a voice in the wilderness* .

W

To hold water (*To be sound in reason*)

These arguments will not *hold water* in a court of law.

To be worth its weight in gold (*To be precious*)

An honest person is *worth his weight in gold*.

To run amuck /wild (*To grow undisciplined*)

The soldiers *ran amuck* leading to mutiny .

To win the day (*To be victorious*)

His bravery *won the day* for them

Forty winks (*A short nap*)

The writing on the wall (*A warning to someone to take immediate heed*)

His defeat at the election was a *writing on the wall* after the civic election six months ago.

Keep the wolf from the door (*Have enough money to avoid hunger and need*)

They earn so little that it is difficult to *keep the wolf from the door.*

Y

Yeoman service (*Useful help*)

Mother Teresa did a *yeoman service* for the poor and the sick.

Yes man (*A submissive man*)

The manager was a *yes man* to the top management.

Young Turk (*Young person eager for radical change in the established order*)

The *young Turks* demanded a change in the leadership of the party.

Year in and year out (*Throughout the year*)

We hear of heinous crimes *year in and year out.*

Z

Zero hour (*The crucial moment*)

He raised the question at the *zero hour.*

Zero –in –on (*To focus one's attention on*)

They *zeroed in on* the militants .

Zebra crossing (*Striped street crossing*)

We must cross the road at the *zebra crossing.*

SYNONYMOUS WORDS AND PHRASES

While writing composition that may be in the form of an essay or a letter we should avoid using the same words again and again. Repetition of the words and phrases makes the composition appear monotonous and uninteresting. There are several words or phrases which can express the idea more explicitly. We are giving below some commonly used words with their synonymous which will be useful, but you must add on them as you improve your vocabulary, so as to embellish your composition.

Word	Synonymous
Actual	Genuine, true, real, authentic.
Affectionate	Loving, fond, tender, doting, dear.
Angry	Annoyed, cross, vexed, indignant, upset.
Bad	Vile, wicked, depraved, evil, defective, deleterious, unwholesome.
Beautiful	Lovely charming, attractive, pretty, comely, graceful, fair.
Begin	Start, commence, initiate, set about.
Cheat	Deceive, delude, dupe, trick, bluff, defraud, swindle, outwit, mislead.
Crowd	Multitude, throng, gathering, mob, concourse.
Cruel	Ruthless, brutal, inhuman, merciless, barbarous, unfeeling.
Definitely	Surely, undoubtedly, positively, unmistakably.
Desire	Crave for, long for, wish, yearn for.
Die	Pass away, breathe one's last, expire, depart from this world.
Ever	Perpetually, forever, always, eternally, continually.
Examine	Scrutinise, go through, analyse, explore, probe, inspect, investigate, scan.
Extremely	Greatly, exceedingly, highly, vastly, preeminently.
Faithless	Disloyal, untrustworthy, traitorous, treacherous, false, insincere,
Feeble	Faint, weak, languid, frail. Infirm.
Great	Grand, distinguish, eminent, august, illustrious, renowned, famous, celebrated.
Horrible	Dreadful, monstrous, hideous, ghastly, awful, terrific, appalling.
Inquire	Investigate, enquire, look into the matter, study.
Insufficient	Lacking, not enough, deficient, running short of, inadequate
Jolly	Cheerful, blithe, merry, gay, jovial, festive, joyous.
Kill	Slay, destroy, massacre, slaughter, butcher, assassinate, exterminate.
Lift	Hoist, raise, elevate, exalt.
Little	Tiny, minute, small, diminutive, small, trivial, inconsiderable.
Mad	Insane, demented, lunatic, deranged, maniacal.
Make	Create, produce, cause, mould, fashion, construct, fabricate.
Nervous	Ill at ease, uncomfortable, anxious, shaky, agitated, timid, timorous.
Noise	Tumult, din, row, outcry, clamour, hue and cry, pandemonium, uproar.
Outdated	Old, obsolete, outfashioned, primitive, antiquated.
Obstruct	Block, hinder, bar, check, prevent, thwart, blockade, impede.
Persuade	Prevail on, convince, urge, incite, coax.

Plentiful	Numerous, abundant, innumerable, copious, profuse,
Quick	Brisk, nimble, rapid, fast, prompt, swift, adroit, speedy.
Reject	Discard, disqualify, throw out, cast away, abandon.
Request	Entreat, ask, solicit, beseech, beg.
Scold	Rebuke, admonish, reprimand, upbraid, censure, reprove, chide, to take to task.
Surprised	Astonished, amazed, wonderstruck, dumbfounded, astounded, stupefied.
Teach	Instruct, educate, enlighten, train, inculcate, tutor.
Thow away	Dispose of, get rid of, remove, cast away.
Urgent	Imperative, insistent, pressing, important.
Violent	Fierce, raging, furious, raving, turbulent, impetuous, vehement.
Well bred	Refined, cultured, gentlemanly, civil, polished, polite, and courteous.
Yield	Succumb, surrender, submit, capitulate.
Zenith	Climax, culmination, summit, pinnacle, apex.

WORDS LIKELY TO BE CONFUSED

Accept	*to receive favourably*
	He decided to accept the invitation.
Except	*excluding*
	Everyone was present at the party except Ram.
Adapt	*to adjust properly*
	He has adapted himself to the changed circumstances.
Adopt	*to take over or accept as one's own*
	They decided to adopt a child.
Adept	*thoroughly proficient*
	He is adept at playing the guitar.
Advise (v)	His father *advised* him to work hard.
Advice (n)	He turned a deaf ear to my *advice*.
Affect	*To influence*
	This incident will *affect* his business.
Effect	This incident will have a negative effect on him.
Altar	*A place of offering*
	The priest knelt before the *altar*.
Alter	*To change*
	The management refused to *alter* the decision.
All ready	*Quite prepared*
	He was *all ready* for the show.
Already	*Before now*
	I have already done the work.
Assay	*Attempted*
	Many explorers had *assayed* to climb the Mount Everest.
Essay	*Write up. Composition*
	She wrote a good *essay* on life.
Allusion	*Reference*
	There is no *allusion* in this passage to the Hindu mythology.
Illusion	*Deception*
	Some people revel in *illusions* of grandeur.
Amiable	*Lovable*
	His *amiable* nature won him many friends.
Amicable	*Friendly*
	They reached an *amicable* settlement.
Antique	*Old fashioned*
	He is fond of *antique* furniture.

Antic	*Absurd or silly action*
	They laughed at the clown's *antics*.
Assent	*Consent*
	The governor gave his *assent* on the bill.
Ascend	*To move upwards, to rise*
	The aeroplane made a steep *ascend*.
Bale	*Bundle*
	He sold few *bales* of cotton.
Bail	*Security*
	The prisoner was released on *bail*.
Birth	*To be born*
	She gave *birth* to a son.
Berth	*A sleeping place in a ship or a train*
	He got a *berth* reserved in the train.
Bare	*Without cover*
	He walked *bare foot*.
Bear (v)	*To carry*
	Your labour will *bear* fruit one day.
Bear (n)	*To endure*
	He could not *bear* the pain.
Born	*Give birth to*
	I was *born* on 10th October.
Borne	*Endured*
	The poor mother had *borne* many hardships.
Bore	*Weary of*
	He was *bored* with the speech.
Boar	A boar is a wild animal
Canvas	*A kind of rough cloth*
	The players used *canvas* shoes.
Canvass	*To solicit votes*
	The political parties *canvass* for votes for their candidates
Causal	*Accidental*
	It was a *casual* remark.
Casual	*Due to, or referring to a cause*
	There is no *causal* connection between health and longevity of life.
Compliment	*An expression of praise*
	Give my *compliments* to your brother.
Complement	*That which completes*
	The couple *complement* one another.
Canon	*Rule*
	You must not act against the *canons* of morality.

Cannon	*A large gun*
	The soldiers fired the *cannon*.
Censor (n)	*An official empowered to delete parts of a book or a film.*
Censor (v)	*To make deletions or changes*
	The news was *censored*.
Censure	*To criticise adversely.*
	The opposition censured the government.
Censer	*A vessel in which incense is burnt*
	The priest held up the *censer* during prayers.
Confident	*Sure*
	I am *confident* of his success.
Confidant	*A trusted person*
	Ram is his *confidant* for he trusts him fully
Census	*Official count of population*
	A *census* is conducted every ten years.
Senses	*Consciousness of*
	He lost his *senses*
Check	*Examined*
	I have *checked* the agreement.
Cheque	*Written order to a bank to pay*
	He wrote a *cheque*.
Caste	He is a Brahmin by *caste*.
Cast	He was *cast* out from his community.
Deathly	*Like death*
	He looked *deathly* pale.
Deadly	*Fatal*
	The bullet caused a *deadly* wound.
Decent	*Respectable*
	He was given a *decent* farewell.
Descent	I. *Origin*
	He was of royal *descent*.
	II. *Coming down*
	His fortunes are on the *descent*.
Dissent	*Differ or disagree*
	The opposition *dissented* on the bill.
Device (n)	*A contrivance*
	He thought of a clever *device*.
Devise (v)	*Plan*
	Can you *devise* a way out.
Defer	*Postpone*
	The examinations were *deferred* for a week.

Differ	*Disagree*
	I *differ* with you on this matter.
Deference	*Regard*
	He treats his teacher with *deference*.
Difference	Find the *difference* between the two sums.
Dairy	He brought milk from the *dairy*.
Diary	He records everything in his *diary*.
Dose	*Quantity of medicine*
	He took his *dose* of medicines.
Doze	The old man *dozed* off to sleep.
Dual	*Double*
	He had a *dual* role in the film.
Duel	*Combat between two people.*
	He challenged him to fight a *duel*.
Die	All living things *die*.
Dye	She *dyed* her hair.
Extinguish	*Put out*
	He *extinguished* the fire.
Distinguish	*Find the difference*
	Distinguish between these two words.
Eminent	*Famous*
	He is an *eminent* doctor.
Imminent	*Likely to happen very soon*
	War is *imminent*.
Exhausting	*Tiring*
	It was an *exhausting* day.
Exhaustive	*Comprehensive, complete*
	He had written an *exhaustive* book on Indian history.
Expedient	*Advantageous, suitable*
	It is *expedient* that he should go.
Expeditious	*Quick, doing speedily*
	An *expeditious* mechanic will take at least one hour to complete the work.
Facility	*Advantage, use*
	He was given the best of *facility*.
Felicity	*Intense happiness*
	Only the virtuous can enjoy true *felicity*.
Fain	*To be glad*
	I would *fain* to have helped you.
Feign	*To pretend*
	He *feigned* illness.
Feet	He touched his *feet*.

Feat	*Deed of skill*
	The acrobat was applauded for the difficult *feat*.
Fair	His dealings are *fair* (honest).
	He has a *fair* complexion (light in colour).
	I went to see the village *fair*.
Fare	*Passage money*
	What is the train *fare* to Delhi?
Floor	He dropped his hat on the *floor*.
Flour	*Powdered grain*
	Bread is made from wheat *flour*.
Gait	*Manner of walking*
	He walked with a particular *gait*.
Gate	The peon opened the *gate*.
Gaol	*Jail*
	The criminal was sent to the *gaol*.
Goal	*Aim, object*
	He achieved his *goal* in life.
Hair	He has long *hair*
Hare	Wild rabbit
	The *hare* and the tortoise had a race.
Heir	He is the *heir* to the throne.
Hale	*Healthy*
	My father is *hale* and hearty.
Hail	He *hails* from Bihar.
	She *hailed* a taxi (called).
Heal	*Cure*
	The doctor *healed* his wounds.
Heel	He injured his *heel* while playing.
Hole	There was a *hole* in the wall.
Whole	The *whole* class was punished.
Horde	*Large gangs*
	They were attacked by *hordes* of villagers.
Hoard	*Store secretly*
	It is illegal to *hoard* essential commodities.
Ingenuous	*Frank, artless*
	He is liked for his *ingenuous* nature.
Ingenious	*Skilful*
	He is very *ingenious* in his work.
Knotty	*Difficult*
	The government is faced with a number of *knotty* problems.

Naughty	*Ill behaved.*	
	He is a *naughty* boy.	
Later	I met him *later.*	
Latter	He offered me mangoes and apples, but I preferred the *latter.*	
Lessen	*To reduce*	
	This cream will *lessen* your pain.	
Lessons	Learn your *lessons* well.	
Loath	*Unwilling*	
	He is *loath* to go with me.	
Loathe (v)	*Dislike*	
	I *loathe* practical jokes.	
Lightning	*Electric discharge in clouds*	
	He was struck by *lightning.*	
Lightening	*Making less heavy*	
	The teacher earned the gratitude of the students by *lightening* the burden of home work.	
Lighting	He is *lighting* the fire.	
Lose	He wanted to *lose* weight.	
Loose	We should wear *loose* clothes.	
Mail	The postman delivers the *mail.*	
Male	The *male* sheep is called ram.	
Mane	*Long hair on the neck of an animal*	
	The horse has a long *mane.*	
Main	The *main* door was open	
Medal	I have won a gold *medal.*	
Meddle	*Interfere*	
	He warned him not to *meddle* in his affairs.	
Metal	Gold is a precious *metal.*	
Mettle	*Ability or courage*	
	This challenge will prove his *mettle.*	
Night	The moon shines at *night.*	
Knight	*A chivalrous soldier*	
	Don Quixote imaginel himself so be a *knight.*	
Pair	I brought a *pair* of socks.	
Pear	*A fruit*	
	Pear is a delicious fruit.	
Persecute	*To worry, to harass*	
	The Nazis *persecuted* the Jews.	
Prosecute	*To bring before a court*	
	Trespassers will be *prosecuted.*	

Precede	*Go before*
	This lesson *precedes* the one you are reading.
Proceed	*Go on*
	Let us *proceed* on our journey.
Principal	He is the *principal* of our college.
Principle	*Rule of conduct*
	He is a man of *principle*.
Patrol	The police *patrol* at night caught the thief.
Petrol	The price of *petrol* has been hiked.
Pray	We *pray* to God.
Prey	*Victim.*
	He fell a *prey* to his evil design.
Practice (n)	*Repetitive*
	Practice makes perfect.
Practise (v)	*Do act upon*
	We must *practise* what we preach.
Prophecy (n)	*Foretelling*
	His *prophecy* was true.
Prophesy (v)	*Foretold*
	He *prophesied* the fall of Moscow.
Preposition	'On' is a *preposition*.
Proposition	*Subject for debate*
	The *proposition* to be discussed is whether war is an evil.
Price	The *price* of this book is very high.
Prize	He won the first *prize*.
Quite	*Altogether*
	This is *quite* different from the original.
Quiet	*Silent*
	The teacher ordered the children to keep *quiet*.
Quire	24 sheets of paper.
Choir	*Body of singers*
	The song was sung by the village *choir*.
Coir	*Coconut fibres*
	Give me one metre of *coir* matting.
Rain	*It rained today.*
Reign	*Ruling period*
	Akbar had a long *reign*.
Rein	*The means of control*
	The rider held on to the *reins* of the horse.
Re-dress	*Dress again*
	The doctor *redressed* his wound.
Redress	*Set right*

	He pleaded with the court to *redress* his grievance
Reverend	*Worthy of respect*
	The *reverend* preacher was respected by all.
Reverent	*Expressing respect*
	Reverent study of the Gita will make you a better man.
Revered	*Held in great respect*
	He *revered* his father.
Ring	I heard the phone *ring*.
Wring	If you *wring* the wet cloth all water will come out.
Right	Turn to your *right*.
Rite	*Ceremonies*
	The priest conducted the religious *rites*.
Write	*Write* an essay on school life.
Wright	*Maker*
	Shakespeare was a great play *wright*.
Route	*Path*
	The bus took a different *route*.
Root	This plant has long *roots*.
Route	*Complete defeated*
	The Army was *routed* in battle.
Sale	This book is for *sale*.
Sail	The ship set *sail* on its long voyage.
Spacious	*Roomy*
	It was a *spacious* room.
Specious	*Appearing to be correct*
	It is a *specious* argument.
Sole	*Only*
	He was her *sole* companion.
Soul	The *soul* is immortal.
Soar	*Rise high*
	The bird *soared* up in the sky.
Sore	*Painful*
	I have a *sore* throat.
Strait	*A narrow passage of water between two land masses*
	Palk *strait* separates India from Sri Lanka.
Straight	He ordered us to stand *straight*
Stationary	*Not moving*
	The sun is *stationary*.
Stationery	*Writing material*
	He has a *stationery* shop.
Statue	*An image*

Gandhiji's *statue* is garlanded on 2nd October.

Statute   *Written*

The *statute* is no longer in force.

Tale   *Story*

He had an interesting *tale* to tell.

Tail   The dog had a short *tail*.

Throne   The king sat on the *throne*.

Thrown   He was *thrown* out from the team.

Team   He was in the football *team*.

Teems   *Abound*

The tank *teems* with fishes.

Urban   *Pertaining to town and cities*

He comes from an *urban* area.

Urbane   *Courteous, refined in manners*

His *urbane* manners won him many friends.

Usurer   *Money lender*

Shylock was a *usurer*.

Usher   *One who shows people to their seats*

Mr. Ram works as an usher in the theatre.

Unanimous   *All of the same opinion*

They were *unanimous* in their decision.

Anonymous   *Without the name of the writer*

He received an *anonymous* letter.

Vacation   *A period of holiday*

He went out during the summer *vacations*.

Vocation   *Occupation*

What is his *vocation* in life?

Vane   *Weathercock*

The *vane* showed us the direction of the wind.

Vain   *Uselessly*

They tried in *vain* to win the match.

Vein   *Blood vessels*

The *vein* carries the blood from the heart.

Veracity   *Truthfulness*

I have full faith on the *veracity* of his statement.

Verocity   *Greed*

The hungry children fell to eating with *verocity*.

Veil   *Covering for the face*

She peeped at her husband through her *veil*

Vale   *Valley*

The *vale* of Kashmir is indeed beautiful.

Wail	*Cries of lament, sorrow*
	She wailed on hearing the tragic news.
Wane	*Decrease*
	The moon is now on the *wane*.
Waste	Do not *waste* your pocket money.
Waist	She had a *delicate* waist.
Wander	Do not *wander* about on the street.
Wonder	I *wonder* why he did not come.
Weather	The match was cancelled due to bad *weather*.
Whether	*If*
	I asked him *whether* he was happy.
Wither	*Decay*
	The flower has *withered*.
Wet	I got *wet* in the rain.
Whet	*Stimulated*
	The sight of food *whetted* my appetite.
Yoke	The farmer put the *yoke* on the necks of the bullocks.
Yolk	The *yolk* of the egg was yellow.
Wreck	*Destroyed*
	The ship was *wrecked* in the sea.
Wreak	*Give. Play to*
	He is determined to *wreak* vengeance on his enemies.
Wreath (n)	Garland of flowers
	Wreaths were placed at his bier.
Wreathe (v)	*Encircled*
	Flames *wreathed* the ship on all sides.

Comprehension and Summary Writing

COMPREHENSION AND SUMMARY WRITING

Comprehension is derived from the word comprehend which means 'the power to understand'. It is therefore basically an exercise to test a person's understanding and grasp of the language. In this exercise, we are to read a given passage which may be of six to seven hundred words or more and then answer questions pertaining to it. The quality of our answers, forms the basis of assessment and evaluation. It is increasingly being adopted in various competitive examinations at state or national level like NIFT, NID, TOEFL. and other competitive examinations, to test a person's comprehension skill. It is therefore imperative to bone one's reading skills, by developing a good reading habit, and developing comprehension skill, for grasping the main points, or the essence of the passage in the shortest possible time. This is crucial especially for doing well in a competitive examination.

How to go about it.

It is usually not difficult to get a general idea of what the passage is all about, but this is not sufficient. To comprehend the contents of the passage, means to understand thoroughly, what the author intends to convey through the medium of words.

There are no specific rules as to how one should go about it, but at the same time a good vocabulary and extensive reading habit stands one in good stead. While the former helps in understanding the difficult words, the latter aids in grasping what the author implicitly or explicitly wants to communicate. This is so, for writers sometimes use phrases and ways of expression, that carry a wider and deeper meaning, than the words themselves convey literally.

Both these assets have to be assiduously cultivated, by reading literary works of good writers, or even newspaper editorials. What is of paramount importance, is that, one should be able to reach down to the inherent idea of the passage, difficult words notwithstanding. This is so, for difficult words used in the passage, can be quite often comprehended contextually.

It would be helpful to follow the following steps while attempting an exercise in comprehension.

Suggested steps while attempting an exercise in comprehension

1. First read the passage once and the questions that follow it, to get a general idea of the theme .

2. Read the passage again slowly and carefully. In case you encounter difficult words, underline them. Usually such difficult words are used contextually, and if one is able to grasp the inherent idea in the passage, these words won't be hard to comprehend.

3. Read the passage once again and locate the answers to the questions in the passage. You can underline or jot down keywords, which answers the question.

4. Make sure that you understand the question. Try to rephrase it in more simple terms at the same time absorbing all it's implications. Most often writing out the answers without fully absorbing what is actually being asked, leads to incorrect answers.

5. Mark the central idea of each passage in the left or right margin of the paper or just underline the key words .This would come in handy, for writing the summary.

6. Develop a holistic overview of the passage with the help of these interconnected ideas.

7. Answer the questions in your own words without lifting any words from the passage. Avoid lifting words from the passage as far as possible. In the event it is unavoidable, you may lift a word or two enclosing it between quotes.

8. While answering the questions keep to the facts given in the passage. Do not add any extraneous element on your own, unless specifically asked for. Write correct relevant answers with no ambiguity and without beating about the bush.

9. Answer the question in the same tense it has been asked.

10. After having written out the answer cross check by again referring to the question to confirm that your answer is relevant and complete.

Do's

• Read the passage once, and the questions that follow, to get a general idea of the subject it deals with.

• Read the passage again this time more thoroughly, underlining or noting the main points (or keywords) on the left or right margin.

• Take a holistic overview of the passage.

• Write the answers to the questions in your own words.

• Be brief and to the point in your answers.

• Use simple and direct language, avoid ambiguity.

Don'ts

• Do not begin writing answers before reading the passage twice, and comprehending what it conveys.

• Do not lift sentences from the passage while answering the questions.

• Do not beat about the bush while answering question.

• Do not give your comments unless specifically asked for.

• Do not explain or elaborate on a point with your own comments. Keep close to the passage.

Meaning of a word or phrases

While explaining the meaning of a words or phrases, you must explain them in relation to their context as well as to their general meaning (refer to solved examples).

Writing a summary

The final question could be either to write a summary on the passage, or to logically explain a given situation. In either case you would be required to summarise the passage, or relevant portions of the passage, that would require skills of condensation and restatements. It would thus be helpful to know what a summary actually is.

What is a SUMMARY ?

A summary is a brief restatement of the contents of an essay, chapter, book, or any other written work. In our case it is a passage, and hence should focus on the central idea of the passage.

When writing a summary it would be helpful to follow these steps:

1. Read the passage to identify the writer's purpose.

2. Identify the main ideas and analyze the structure.

3. Outline the passage. Underlining the main idea/thought.

4. Write one-sentence summaries for each stage of thought. Use your own words. If you must use the author's words, enclose them within quotes..

5. Write first draft 4 to 5 words in each line for ease in counting.

6. Eliminate repetitions, details, and personal opinions.

7. Insert transitional expressions and phrases to avoid choppiness.

8. Check against the original for completeness, accuracy, and balance.

9. Proofread for grammatical errors.

10. Write out the final copy.

To summarise we must keep in mind the following. .

Do's

- Concentrate on main ideas.
- Be objective. The summary should reflect the content of the original passage only.
- The summary has to be complete. It has to reflect the entire content of the original passage, not a part of it.
- It should be brief, complete, accurate, objective, and in your own words

Don'ts

- Do not give examples, and other minor details.
- Do not include your ideas on the topic.
- Do not plagiarize. Use your own words, or enclose the original words within quotes.
- Do not leave out important parts to make the summary short.

ILLUSTRATIVE EXAMPLES

Read the following passage carefully and answer the questions that follow:

The saving of certain wild animals from extinction has for many years been a problem for zoologists and other specialists; but more recently the problem has become so acute, and has received so much publicity, that most people are now concerned about it. This may at first seem strange because one of the most <u>gratifying</u> developments of the last few years has been the passing of strict laws to protect wild animals and the <u>consequent</u> decline in the hunting of big–game for sport. Why is it, then that some rare wild animals are still threatened with extinction and even some of the less rare ones are rapidly <u>declining</u> in number?

One reason is the 'march of civilization'. When an area is wholly cleared of vegetation to make room for new towns, factory sites or hydroelectric plants, the natural home of several species is destroyed. The displaced must either migrate to another area or perish. Even the clearing of land for a road or an airfield may involve 'pushing back' the jungle, and the smaller the area in which wild animals compete for a living the smaller the number that can hope to survive.

Civilization brings, too, swift and easy transport and so assists those who are determined to break the various protective laws. Thieves can elude the game wardens, shoot an elephant for its tusks, a rhinoceros for its horn, or a deer for its meat and be miles away from the <u>site</u> of the crime before the dead or dying victim is even discovered.

It is sad to <u>reflect</u> that civilization, which can bring so many benefits to people who have previously known only hunger and misery, brings also facilities for the heartless criminals who, for the material gain, will slaughter some harmless animals and threaten the disappearance of its kind from the earth forever.

(*a*) Answer the following questions briefly in your own words:

(*i*)   "This may at first seem strange". To what does the word 'this' refer?

(*ii*)   Why does the author think that 'this' may seem strange?

(*iii*) How does modern transport threaten the survival of wild animals?

(*iv*)   What is the sad reflection that the author makes in the last paragraph of the passage?

(*b*)   In not more than 60 words of your own, mention ways in which the 'march of civiliza-tion' threatens to make certain rare wild animals extinct.

ILLUSTRATIVE ANSWERS

(*i*)   The word 'this' as used in the passage by the author refers to the growing   extinction of rare wild animals

Key word being 'wild animals from extinction'

(*ii*)   The author thinks this increasing rate of extinction of wild animals to be   strange, for people are generally more aware and concerned about this problem. Moreover stringent laws have been made to protect the wild animals, thereby resulting in the sharp decline of game hunting. Inspite of these severe measures their growing extinction is indeed strange.

Key word being 'people are now concerned' and 'strict laws to protect wild animals'

(*iii*) The modern transport systems, like the roads and airports for plying motor vehicles and aeroplanes, involves clearing of large tracts of land. This destroys the natural habitat of the wild animals, and encroaches upon the forestland, forcing them to migrate to other areas, that may not be very hospitable. As the forestland gets reduced, they find it increas-ingly difficulty to grow and thrive. This overcrowding, results in making them compete for the scarce resources available, and consequently results in the survival of the fittest, leaving a large number to perish.

Keywords being 'clearing of land ', 'pushing back the jungle', and ' compete for a living'

(*iv*)   The sad reflection the author makes is the irony, that while the advancement in science and technology brings numerous benefits to people it also helps unscrupulous criminals to slaughter innocent animals. They kill animals, using highly sophisticated weapons and escape   by traveling in fast automobiles. Thereby misusing the advancement made in society for their material gains, unmindful of their extinction from the face of the earth.

Keywords being 'civilisation brings many benefits to people', 'facilities for heartless criminals',

(*c*)   In not more than 60 words of your own, mention ways in which the 'march of civilization' threatens to make certain rare wild animals extinct.

The advancement of civilisation, threatens to make rare wild animals extinct. The growth of cities, factories and construction of roads and airports, reduces the forestland available to animals forcing them to migrate. This overcrowding makes them compete for the scarce natural resources, consequently only few survive. Furthermore the fast means of transport, enable poachers to kill these animals and escape.

Identify the main ideas

The advancement of civilisation threatens to make certain rare wild animals extinct.

Outline the   passage

Growth of cities–construction of roads, airfields – destroys their natural home – reduction in forestland available for animals,–leads to overcrowding with lesser number surviving – scientific advancements helps poachers .

ILLUSTARTIVE EXAMPLE 11

More than 150 years ago after the death of John Dalton, whose atomic theory is the basis of chemistry, scientist has established the cause of his colour blindness.

Dalton could not distinguish red from green .In 1794 English chemist was the first to describe colour blindness which became known as Daltonism. The word is still used in French, Spanish and Russian.

Scientist from London and Cambridge have examined DNA from fragments of Dalton's eyes preserved at his request by the Manchester Literary and Philosophical Society, and have shown that he lacked the gene for making the green pigment in the retina.

Dalton who lived from 1766 to 1844 gave instructions for his eyes to be examined after death. He had believed that that the vitreous humour, the clear substance in the inner chamber of the eyes must in his case be tinted blue so that it absorbed red light.

At the autopsy no such blue tint was found. But from Dalton's perception of how he perceived light, historians have concluded that he must have lacked the pigment in the retina that is sensitive to red light.

That is now showing to be wrong after work by a team led by Dr David Hut of the Institute of Ophthalmology of London University and Dr John Mollon, from Cambridge University.

Dalton's Daltonism was no great handicap for him. He did not discover it until his 20's and once turned it to his advantage. As Quaker, he had resisted being presented to William IV because he refused to wear court dress. When he was given a honarary degree at Oxford in 1832, however it was suggested that he should meet the king in the university's robes. But they were scarlet, a colour that Quaker could not wear. Dalton announced that to him the robes appeared not scarlet but gray. He was duly presented to the king.

(*a*) Answer the following questions in your own words

 (*i*)   Why is the science of Chemistry indebted to Dalton

 (*ii*) How did the Daltonism come into existence?

 (*iii*) What was Dalton's own theory about his blindness?

 (*iv*) How could the scientists study Dalton's ailment many years after his death?

 (*v*)   How did his handicap once proved advantageous to him?

(*b*) In not more than 60 words of your own, state what you understand by Daltonism and the past and present views about it.

Illustrative Answers (*a*)

 (*i*)   The science of Chemistry is indebted to Dalton because his atomic theory forms the basis of chemistry.

Keyword being 'atomic theory'

 (*ii*) The term Daltonism came into existence after the name of the great scientist Dalton. Dalton could not distinguish between red and green, and thus was the first scientist to describe colour blindness.

Keywords being 'first to describe colour blindness'

 (*iii*) Dalton's own theory about his colour blindness was that the vitreous humour, which is the clear substance in the inner chamber of his eyes, must be tinted blue. This absorbed the red light making him unable to perceive colour.

Keywords being 'vitreous humour' 'tinted blue'

(*iv*) The scientists could study Dalton's ailment many years after his death, because the Manchester Literary and Philosophical Society had preserved his eyes. This had been done on Dalton's own request.

Keywords being 'preserved by the Manchester Literary and Philosophical Society'

(*v*) His handicap once prove advantageous, for as a Quaker, he was opposed to wearing the scarlet dress which is a must for anyone being presented to the king. After getting his honarary degree from Oxford, he agreed to meet the king wearing these university robes. He did so because the robes looked gray to him and not scarlet, because of his colour blindness.

Keywords being 'resisted being presented to William IV', 'But they were scarlet, a colour that Quaker could not wear', 'to him the robes appeared not scarlet but gray'.

(*b*) Daltonism is the phenomenon of colour blindness first described by Dalton. According to him the vitreous humour in his eyes could be tinted blue, making it absorb red light. Historians concluded from his description that his retina lacked the pigment sensitive to red light. Modern tests however reveal, that he lacked the genes for making the green pigment in the retina.

UNSOLVED EXERCISES
Exercise 1
Read the extract given below and answer the questions that follow

One evening some of Napoleon's soldiers were having a drink together when a young Frenchman brought a friend to their table. He explained that his friend was a Swede and knew no French: but he admired Napoleon so much that he wanted to join the French army and fight for him.

The soldiers looked up and saw a tall young man with blue eyes, they liked him at once. They explained that his new friends, would help him if any difficulty *arose* about the language.

The officers saw that he was the right sort of man for them, and he became one of Napoleon's soldiers, He fought bravely in many battles, and gained their respect. His knowledge of French remained very weak, because he was not good at learning languages.

Several years later they heard that Napoleon himself was coming to inspect them, and the Swede was warned that the great man would *probably* ask him some questions. He looked very anxious.

It was well known that Napoleon always asked the same three question and usually in the same order. The first question was "How old are you?" The second was, "How long have you been in my army?" And the third was "Did you serve in either of my last two *campaigns*."

The Swede could not possibly remember all these words and so he learnt the answers in the proper order. His friend gave him a lot of practice.

For many days, the, practice continued. The Swede used to walk about, saying to himself, "Twenty-three, Sir, Three years, Sir, Both, Sir!" Before the day of the inspection, his friends were satisfied. He knew his words. There ought to be no trouble.

Napoleon arrived standing in front of the motionless line of soldiers .He looked at them with great satisfaction. Then he began to walk along the lines, smiling sometimes in a friendly way, and saying a few words here and there. The Swede stood quite still except that his lips moved slightly. He was still practicing.

Napoleon suddenly caught sight of the tall soldier and realised at once that he had never seen him before. He stopped in front of him and asked his questions. Unfortunately this time the great man began with the second question.

"How many years have you been in my army?" He demanded

"Twenty-three, Sir," said the Swede clearly and well. Napoleon was surprised. He looked at the tall man and asked, "How old are you, then?"

"Three years, Sir," said the Swede bravely. Napoleon was *astonished* and angry.

"Either you are mad, or I am," he declared. "Both, Sir!" cried the Swede proudly.

(*a*) Five words are given below. Give the meaning of each as used in the passage. One-word answers or short phrases will be accepted.

  (*i*)   arose

  (*ii*) anxious

  (*iii*) compaign

  (*iv*) probably

(*v*) astonished

(b) Answer the following questions in your own words:

  (*i*)   Give a brief description of the newcomer. Why did he want to join the particular army?

  (*ii*) Give two positive and one negative character of the Swede?

  (*iii*) What caused the Swede some anxiety?

  (*iv*) Why did the Swede learn the answers only?

  (*v*)   How did the Swede practice?

(*c*) In not more than 60 words of your own, state what happened when Napoleon's arrived

Exercise 2

Beethoven was born on 16th December 1770 in Bonn, Germany. His father was a musician in the local court .His first teachers were his father and the court organist.

In 1787, Beethoven visited Vienna capital of Austria and had some lessons from Mozart, a noted Austrian composer. From 1792 he lived there <u>permanently</u>. In Vienna, Beethoven won fame as a pianist, and studied composition under Haydn and Albrechtsberger at about 29, Beethoven began to suffer from deafness, which later became total. Increasing deafness separated him from the world around him. He became suspicious of even his closest friends. His illness made him <u>irritable</u>. However, his musical <u>output</u> continued.

Beethoven's life was complicated by insecure financial situation and the insulting behaviour of his narrow-minded brother. None of his housekeepers could stand his temper for long. He had conflicts with his audiences, and bitter quarrels with persons who commissioned music from him. Memories of his love for Josephine the countess Von Deym that was ignored by her, accompanied Beethoven throughout his life.

In his early period, Beethoven composed in the classical style of Mozart and Haydn. Later, he abandoned classical styles and became the major <u>forerunner</u> of nineteenth century, romantic music. Among his piano musical compositions, ' Moonlight', 'Waldstein'and 'Appassionata' are well known.

Beethoven enthusiastically defended the ideal of the French revolution and of English par- liamentarianism. He believed <u>passionately</u> in liberty, and tried to express his beliefs through his music.

In the later years of his life from 1815 to his death when he was totally deaf Beethoven entered the 'Missa Solemnis'– one of the most moving of religious compositions. His 9th and last symphony (a long series piece of music for an orchestra of many instruments) he celebrated the ideal of human brotherhood.

Beethoven can truly be called the Shakespeare of music. His music is even today a part of our lives. He was the greatest musician, perhaps the greatest artist that ever lived.

Beethoven passed away in 1827.

(a) Five words are given below. Give the meaning of each word as used in the passage. One- word answers or short phrases will be accepted.

  (i) Permanently

  (ii) Irritable

  (iii) Output

  (iv) Forerunner

  (v) Passionately

(b) Answer the following questions briefly in your own words :

  (i) What evidence is mentioned in the passage to show that Beethoven was exposed to music from the early childhood?

  (ii) What might have led him to settle down in Vienna?

  (iii) What impact did his deafness have on him?

  (iv) Mention the factors that made his life complicated and miserable?

  (v) What were his political views?

(c) In not more than 60 words of your own, justify how Beethoven could truly be called the Shakespeare of music.

Exercise 3

The 'pull of gravity 'does thousand of useful jobs for us. It keeps railway trains on the tracks; it produces waterfalls from which electric power can be generated, and so on, but from the point of view of space travel, it is a very great nuisance, because it tries to prevent us from leaving the earth. If we could <u>insulate </u>ourselves from the pull of gravity by simply making some kind of an- tigravity screen, the greatest problem of space travel would be solved. HG Wells had this idea in his story , 'The first men in the moon'. The cabin of his space ship was fitted with roller blinds of, 'cavort', <u>mythical</u> substances with the power of cutting off gravity. By rolling down the appropri- ate blind, the space ship would be guided in the right direction. Such ideas, however belongs to science fiction.

In the world of reality the only way of overcoming gravity is by means of a bigger push in the opposite direction, Although the push need not to act all the time. With a gun, for example, a very large push acts on the shell for the short time that it is in the barrel. The speed attained by the shell then enables it to travel to a height or distance. The largest gun that has ever been made is the Paris gun. {Known as Big Bertha}. It could send a shell 75 miles, and the Germans used it to bombard Paris in the first world war. No such gun is likely to be put into action again. Long gun barrels are difficult to make and wear out easily.

Also the atmosphere exerts so much resistance at higher speeds, that the gun's range is severely reduced by it. But for the atmosphere, the shells from Big Bertha would have travelled twice as far? Jules Verne (a Novelist) used a gun to send his travellers round the moon in his story 'From the Earth to the Moon.' He was aware of the difficulty of making a long barrel, and so he used the vertical shaft sunk in the ground from which the shell could be fired. Even if this ideas worked (and it is doubtful that it would) the atmosphere would very <u>effectively</u> prevent anything fired from the earth's surface for reaching the moon. The air resistance would be so great, that the shell would be destroyed even before it <u>emerged</u> from the barrel. Such a detail, however, need not spoil a good story, nor need the fact that the occupants of the shell would certainly have been crushed to death, by the initial impact of the firing.

Where a gun fails, the rocket <u>succeeds</u>. Troubles of air resistance can be avoided with a rocket by arranging for the greatest speed to be reached only after it has risen above the denser atmosphere. As a weapon of war, the rocket has now succeeded the long range gun. Its range can exceed from one side of the globe to the other.

(a) Five words are given below. Give the meaning of each as used in the passage. One-word answers or short phrases will be accepted
   (i) <u>nsulate</u>
   (ii) <u>mythical</u>
   (iii) severely
   (iv) emerged
   (v) succeeds

(b) Answer the following questions as briefly as possible in your own words
   (i) Give one example to show how the pull of gravity serves a useful purpose in our lives?
   (ii) Why is the pull of gravity a nuisance in space travel ? How can it be overcome to facilitate space travel?
   (iii) What is the only way of overcoming the force of gravity in real life? Illustrate your answer with reference to the firing of a gun ?
   (iv) How does the atmosphere affect the range of the gun ?
   (v) How does the rocket succeed in space travel while the gun fails?

(c) In not more than 60 words of your own state the problem posed by the pull of gravity on space travel and how iit can be overcome ?

Exercise 4

When James learnt from his hostess that there was not another house within three miles, that she could accommodate him with a bed, and his horse with lodging and oats, he thanked Heaven for his good fortune in stumbling upon this homely <u>habitation</u>, and determined to pass the night under the protection of the old cottage, who gave him to understand that her husband, who was a farmer, had gone to the next town to dispose off his merchandise, and in all probability would not return till next morning. James sounded the old woman with a thousand artful <u>interrogations</u> and she answered with such appearance of truth and simplicity that he concluded that his person was quite secure, and after he had his supper, desired she would conduct him into the chamber where she proposed he should take his rest. He seemed extremely satisfied with his lodging, which in reality exceeded his <u>expectations</u>, and his kindly landlady, cautioning him against letting the candle approach the straw took her leave, land locked the door on the outside.

James whose experiences taught him to be suspicious and ever on his guard against the treachery of his fellow creatures, could have dispensed with this instance of her care in confining her guest to his chamber and began to be seized with strange fancies, when he observed there was no bolt on the inside of the door, by which he might secure himself from intrusion. Consequently, he began to take a survey of every object in the apartment, and, in the course of his enquiry, had the <u>mortification</u> to find the dead body of a man, still warm.

Such a discovery could not fail to fill our hero with horror for he concluded that he himself would undergo the same fate before morning. In the first moments of his fear he ran to the window, with a view to escape by that outlet, but found his flight <u>effectually</u> obstructed by strong bars. Then his heart began to palpitate and his knees to totter; his mind filled with thoughts of death and he immediately resolved to take measures for his own safety.

He undressed the corpse that lay bleeding amidst the straw and deposited it on the bed in the attitude of a person who sleeps at his ease; then he extinguished the light, took possession of the place from whence the body had been removed, and, holding a loaded pistol in each hand waited expectantly. About midnight the door was softly opened; he saw the shadow of the two men <u>stalking</u> towards the bed. When they reached it one of them thrust a dagger into the heart of the corpse. The stroke was repeated and the assassins concluding the work was effectually done retired for the present with a design to rob the deceased at their leisure.

(a) Five words are given below. Give the meaning of each as used in the passage. One-word answers or short phrases will be accepted

    (i) habitation

    (ii) interrogations

    (iii) mortification

    (iv) stalking

    (v) effectually

(b) Answer the following questions as briefly as possible in your own words.

    (i) What information did James received from the old woman that led him to believe that the cottage would be a suitable place for him to spend the night. ?

    (ii) What did the old woman say about her husband?

    (iii) Why did James feel that he would be safe in the cottage?

    (iv) What observations caused James to feel uneasy as soon as he was alone in the chamber?

    (v) Mention what four steps James took to ensure his safety?

(c) Describe how James reacted on discovering the dead body and the actions he took for his safety?

(Your answer should not exceed 60 words.)

Exercise 5

Read carefully the passage given and answer the questions (a) (b) and (c) that follow, in your own words.

According to the Freudian theory, and that of many others whose writings have preceded his by hundred or even thousands of years, dreams do not reveal anything about the future. Instead they tell us something about our present unresolved and unconscious complexes, and may lead us back to the early years of our lives, when, according to psychoanalytic theory, the ground was being prepared for these later defects. There are three main hypotheses in this general theory. The first is that the dream is not a meaningless jumble of images and ideas, accidentally thrown together, but rather that the dream as a whole, and every element in it, are meaningful. The second point that Freud makes is that dreams are always in some sense, a wish *fulfillment;* in other words, they have a purpose, and this purpose is the satisfaction of some desire or drive, usually of an unconscious *character.*

Thirdly, Freud believes that these desires and wishes, having being *repressed* from consciousness because they are unacceptable to socialised mind of the dreamer, are not allowed to emerge even into the dream without a disguise so heavy that they are unrecognisable. Freud's argument of the meaningfulness of dreams is directly connected with his general theory that all our acts are meaningfully determined. A theory which embraces habits, mispronunciations, gestures, lapses, emotions and so forth. These reveal the influence of an unconscious self, which sometimes influences our behaviour. This doctrine, too, was widely accepted hundreds of years before Freud was born, though, he was an extremely effective popularizer of the theory.

Let us now turn to the second part of Freud's doctrine, namely the view that a dream is always a wish fulfillment. This is linked up with his general theory of personality. Roughly speaking, Freud recognised three main parts of personality; one, which he call the id, is a kind of reservoir of unconscious drives and impulses; this reservoir as it were, provides the dynamic energy for most of our activities. Opposed to it we have the so–called superego, which is partly conscious and which is the repository of social morality. Intervening between the two, and trying to resolve their opposition, is the *ego*; that is the conscious part of our personality. In religious language we might liken the id to the concept of original sin and that of superego to the concept of conscience. Classical scholars will have no trouble remembering the striking anticipation of the Freudian doctrine in Socrates' story –"As I said in the beginning of this tale, I divided each soul into three – two horses and a character, and one of the horses was upright and temperate and the other wild and insolent." This part of Freud theory, too, is then by no means novel and original, but has been part of educated thought for over two thousand years.

The link up between Freud's theory of personality and his theory of dream interpretation is a very simple one; the forces of the id are constantly trying to gain control of the ego and to force themselves into consciousness. During the individual's sleeping life the superego is less watchful and consequently some of the desires start up in the id and are allowed to escape in the *form* of dreams. However, the superego may nod, but is not quite asleep, and consequently these wish-fulfilling thoughts require to be heavily disguised. This disguise is stage managed by what Freud calls the dream work. Accordingly it is necessary to distinguish between the *manifest* dream, that is the dream as experienced, and the latent dream, that is the thoughts, the wishes and the desires expressed in dream with their disguises removed. The task of the interpreter, therefore, is to explain the manifest dream in terms of the latent dream.

(*a*) Five words are given below. Give the meaning of each word as used in the passage. One-word answers or short phrases will be accepted.

    (1) Hypothesis

    (2) Repressed

    (3) Manifest

    (4) Reservoir

    (5) Form.

(*b*) Answer the following questions as briefly as possible in your own words-

    (1) How are dreams meaningful according to Freud?

    (2) What connection is there between Freud's views of sleep and those of personality and behaviour?

(3) What does Socrates story illustrate?

(4) What does the author mean by 'latent' dream?

(5) In not more than 60 words of your own explain the main features of Freud's theory of dream.

Exercise 6

Read carefully the passage given and answer the question (a) (b) and (c) that follow, in your own words.

Since times immemorial terrorist acts have included assassination seizing hostages and a variety of atrocities that only fiendish minds can devise. Terrorist gives immediate explanation for their violence. They declare that the society is sick and cannot be cured by half measures of reform and that as the state itself uses violence it can be overcome only by violence. They also *assert* the righteousness of their cause justifies any action that they may take.

Contemporary terrorism involves a group of individuals who are product of affluent industrialized society. They seek to destroy this society in the name of some revolutionary concept. Examples of such group would include The Italian Red Brigade, the German Border Meinhof Gang, the Indian Naxalite movement et al. Another group of terrorist comprises those espousing more traditional political causes – the unification of Ireland, the homeland for Palestinians, the establishment of Khalistan, majority *rule* in South Africa. Acts of international terrorism are committed to terrorise nations and government into *compliance*.

International terrorism is distinguished by three characteristics. First it embodies a criminal *act*. Second it is politically motivated and their violence is directed against innocent people. Finally international terrorism *transcends* national boundaries through the choice of targets, the commission of the act in foreign country and an effort to influence the policies of a foreign government.

One of the factors, which can be considered as a cause of terrorism, is that most of the nations are undergoing a process of drastic socio economic changes and as a result there are groups who feel deprived and resort to terrorism as a form of protest. Another factor is the ethnicity explosion. When a group feels insecure it searches for a strong identity and this results often in fundamentalism .The principal manifestation of this occurs in areas that have multiple culture or *races*.

What does the future hold for terrorism? International terrorism has been rising in frequency at a dramatic rate. Indications are that it is almost certain to increase as it seems to pay – political blackmail and get results and punishment for convicted terrorist are light while free publicity is acquired on a massive *scale*.

Terrorism has entered the mainstream of world politics and would become a new form of warfare. With the availability of small and inexpensive means of destruction a handful of men would have an enormous impact upon states and societies. It is not unrealistic to envision some countries preferring to arm and use terrorist to pursue their foreign policy objectives rather than through direct involvement in a conflict with another state .

The world as a whole is weary of a nuclear holocaust and restraining rational voices make the superpowers aware of the self-destructive nature of such a war. But there is a real danger that the world might explode with a million mutinies, which will destroy mankind just as surely.

To counteract the growth of terrorism and the inhuman meaningless killing of innocents, peace loving governments all over the world must *crack down* on this menace and condemn all terrorist acts as criminal acts. What is more the terrorist cause must not pay; political blackmail must not get results. While every effort must be made for peaceful results there must be no <u>flinching</u> from using force when necessary. Punishment for convicted terrorist must not be light. Most of all the publicity which terrorist receives on such a massive scale must never be given. If the terrorist acts are neither acknowledged or flaunted abroad with great fanfare their balloons will be pricked and their causes dead.

Finally it is essential that anti terrorist strategies are taken up on an international scale. It is essential to have good intelligence on terrorist and their plans. This most effective weapon must be kept secret to be effective. It is also essential to develop tools for handling a terrorist situation including special units for hostage rescue or other missions and clear legislative authority. The fight against terrorism must be undertaken by a strong united world because it is a *fight for humanity*.

(*a*) Five words are given below. Give the meaning of each word as used in the passage. One -word answers or short phrases will be accepted.

(*i*)   Assert

(*ii*) Transcends

(*iii*) Compliance

(*iv*) Crackdown

(*v*)   Flinching

(*b*) Answer the following questions as briefly as possible in your own words.

(*i*)   How do terrorist justify their acts?

(*ii*) What types of terrorism are found in modern times?

(*iii*) What features are common to international terrorism?

(*iv*) What does the author think to be a cause of terrorism?

(*v*)   What future for the world does he predict if terrorism is not restrained ?

(*c*) In not more than 60 words of your own, state the measures recommended by the author for counteracting terrorism?

Exercise 7

Read carefully the passage given and answer the question (*a*) (*b*) and (*c*) that follow, in your own words.

It is generally accepted that the experiences of the child in his first years largely determine his character and, later, personality. Every experience teaches the child something and the *effects are cumulative*. 'Upbringing' normally used to refer to the training and the treatment of the child within the home. The ideal and practices of child rearing vary from culture to culture. Early upbringing in the home is naturally affected both by the culture pattern of the community and by the parents capabilities and their aims. It depends, also, on the innate abilities of the child. Wide differences of innate intelligence and temperament exist even in children of some family. Intelligent parents realise that the particular setting of each family is unique and there can be no rigid general rules, the first necessity in successful upbringing being a *secure* emotional background with parents who are united in their attitude to their children.

The beginnings of discipline are in the nursery. Even the youngest baby is taught by gradual stages to wait for food, to sleep and wake at regular intervals and so on. If the child feels the world around him is warm and friendly one, he slowly accepts its rhythm and accustoms himself to *conforming* to its demand. Learning to wait for thing, particularly for food, is a very important element in upbringing, and is achieved successfully only if too great demands are not made and the child can understand them.

A good mother knows that if his energies are not given an outlet, her child's continuing development may be *warped*. An example of this is the young child's need to play with mud and sand and water. A child must be allowed to enjoy these 'messy' but tactile stages of discovery before he is ready to go on the less physical pleasures of toys and books. Similarly, throughout life, each stage depends on the satisfactory completion of the one before. Where one stage of child development has been left out, or not sufficiently experienced, the child may have to go back and capture the experience of it. A *good* home makes this possible, for example, by providing the opportunity for the child to play with a clockwork car or toy railway train up to any age if he still needs to do so. This principal, in fact, underlies all psychological treatment of children in difficulties with their development, and is the basis of work in the child clinics.

Every parent watches eagerly the child's acquisition of each new skill–the first spoken words, the first independent steps, or the beginning of reading and writing. It is often tempting to hurry the child beyond his natural learning rate, but this can set up dangerous feelings of failure and stages of anxiety in the child. This might happen at any stage. A baby might be forced to use a toilet too early, a young child might be encouraged to learn to read before he knows the meaning of the words he reads .On the other *hand*, though, if a child is left alone too much, or without any learning opportunities, he loses his natural zest for life and his desire to find out new things for himself.

Learning together is a fruitful source of a healthy relationship between children and parents. By playing together, parents learn more about their children and children learn more from their parents. Toys and games, which both parents and children can share, are an important means of achieving this cooperation. Building block toys, jigsaw puzzles and cross words are good examples.

Parents vary greatly in their degree of strictness or indulgence towards their children. Some may be especially strict in money matters; others are severe over time of coming home at night, punctuality for meals or personal hygiene. In general the controls imposed represent the needs of the parents and the values of the community as much as the child's own happiness and well-being.

As regards the development of moral standards in the growing child consistency is very important in parental teaching. To forbid a thing one day and excuse it the next is no foundation for morality also, parents should realise that 'example is better than *precept*'. If they are hypocritical and do not practice what they preach their children may grow confused and emotionally insecure when they grow old enough to think for themselves, and realise they have been to some extent, deceived. A sudden awareness of a marked difference between their parents' ethics and their morals can be a dangerous disillusion.

(*a*) Five words are given below. Give the meaning of each word as used in the passage. One-word answers or short phrases will be accepted

(1)   Warped

(2)   Tactile

(3)   Conforming

(4)   Precept

(5)   Ethics

(*b*)   Answer the following questions as briefly as possible in your own words:

(*a*)   What factors influence the upbringing of a child?

(*b*)   How can learning to wait for thing be successfully taught to a child? Suggest a reason why this is an important lesson to be learnt ?

(*c*)   Why is it necessary for each stage of development to be satisfactorily completed ?

(*d*)   Why is it important for parents to share learning activities with their children?

(*e*)   What according to the author is the role of parents in imparting moral standards to their children?

(*c*)   In not more than 60 words of your own, outline the major principles of bringing up a child as given in the passage?

Exercise 8

Read carefully the passage given and answer the question (*a*) (*b*) and (*c*) that follow, in your own words

The weather had improved; a *brisk* wind from the southwest had driven off the fog. Mr. Cronch, to please himself had walked into the city. He had fifteen pounds in his pocket, and looked into the shop windows. He *still* wore his large black hat and the beggars avoided him. They took him to be a Jewish moneylender, or else a Baptist minister. Beggars are <u>shrewd</u> judges of character. They have to decide quickly. Their income depends on it .To beg from the wrong man means loss of time – perhaps prison.

Mr. Cronch went down a narrow street where some offices were. One of this was the office of a moneylender. A gentleman who looked <u>worn</u> out of sickness and trouble, came out of the door. A woman, his wife who carried a baby in her arms, waited for him in the street. The gentleman shook his head. Evidently the security he had offered was not good enough.

There arose a little conversation between them. "I could go to the mother's", the woman said. "If I had the money, I could go with you," the man observed. "The change would do me good, and I might get work in Bristol." "Baby will be easier in a few months," the woman said. "mother will not mind taking us, but you will have to stay here," "I can't let you go," the man said he made a curious sound in his throat.

Mr. Cronch stood near the pavement. Who would have noticed Mr. Cronch? The couple paid no heed to him. But presently they turned to where he stood. for Mr. Cronch had spoken. " Lie thee down oddity!" He had said aloud. The gentleman smiled he could do nothing else. The baby held out her arms to Mr. Cronch she wanted his hat. Mr. Cronch took two five-pound notes from his wallet and gave them to the woman, and then he walked away.

For his own pleasure he had walked out of the city into the poor part of the town. He walked slowly along and looked at the vegetables in the green grocer's shop. He wondered that people could buy such old stuff. If he offered anything like this at the Westminister market, he would never find a purchaser. He remembered the <u>lordly</u> freedom of the wild heath. Their nature might be cruel, but life and death joined hands in the dance .The sun could shine and when darkness came it was the darkness of God . The town was different.

Mr. Cronch went down a <u>dingy</u> court. Clothes were hung from house to house, and barefooted children played in the gutter. The air was heavy with human odour and factory stench. Then Mr. Cronch came across something worse than misery.

A man sat leaning against a wall, with half his face eaten away. His eyes were gone; he cried to everyone whose footsteps he heard, to lead him to the river. When Mr. Cronch came by he cried out the more. Mr. Cronch stopped. "Lie thee down oddity." he said angrily, "Lead me to the river," the man begged "Come," said Mr. Cronch and led the man to the river .A policeman who knew the man's wish followed him. At the <u>brink</u> of the river the man said. "I am afraid, only give me one little push, and I shall die." "Certainly." Said Mr. Cronch and pushed him into the river. The man sank.

The police officer came to demand Mr. Cronch's name and address; he had made a note of what had happened. "You will appear at court charged with murder," he said." But now you can go!"

Adopted from; 'Lie thee down oddity!'
BY Powys

(*a*) Five words are given below. Give the meaning of each word as used in the passage. One-word answers or short phrases will be accepted

(*i*) shrewd

(*ii*) worn

(*iii*) lordly

(*iv*) dingy

(*v*) brink

(*b*) Answer the following questions as briefly as possible in your own words:

(i) What reasons are forwarded by the writer for saying "Beggars are shrewd judges of character"?

(ii) After Mr. Cronch said,'Lie thee Down Oddity' , what impact did his words have on the man and the baby?

(iii) How did Mr. Cronch react after seeing the wild heath?

(iv) What picture is formed of Mr. Cronch's character from the passage?

(v) Explain in the context of the passage, what is meant by 'Oddity.'?

(*c*) In not more than 60 words write about Mr. Cronch's encounter with the beggar and the police officer.

Exercise 9

One of the main reasons why wrong ideas and useless practices can grow up is ignorance. Among <u>primitive</u> tribes today as was the case too in pre-historic times, there is hardly any scientific knowledge, everything is mysterious. The sun rises and sets and the moon changes; but people have no idea why, or what are the relations of the heavenly bodies to the earth. No one knows anything about the natural causes of rain or drought, storms or earthquakes, famine or disease. Thus everything is put down to <u>mysterious</u> influences by magic or by good and bad spirits. Such ideas cannot very well be called <u>superstitious</u> so long as no better explanation is available. But reason may show that they are false; and finally when scientific knowledge demonstrates the way things really work, the ideas of magic or spirit-influence can be seen to be mere superstitions.

So, as science progresses, superstition ought to grow less. On the whole, that is true. But it is surprising how superstitions linger on. If we are tempted to look down on savage tribes and other nations for holding such ideas, we should remember that even today, among the most civilized nations, a great many equally stupid superstitions exist and are believed in by a great many people. It is worth making a list of the superstitions which you know about. Some people will not sit down thirteen at table; other will not light three cigarettes from one match or do not like to start anything important on a Friday, or refuse to walk under a ladder; many people buy charms and talismans because they think they will bring them luck. Perhaps you yourself are inclined to believe in some of these ideas! Try to find out if there is really anything in any of them, and what reasons there may be for people believing in them.

Probably the most terrible example of superstition is the belief in witchcraft. In western Europe, during the sixteenth and seventeenth centuries, over three-quarters of a million people were killed, mostly after being tortured, because they were found guilty of witchcraft something for which today we can find no scientific evidence. When people give reasons for <u>persecuting</u> others, we ought to be very sure that their reasons are not merely superstitions, or based on false principles.

In addition, even in civilized nations today, many actions take place and laws are made on the basis of principles which are just as much unproved <u>assumptions</u> as were many of those of the philosophies of the middle ages. For instance, it is often held as a principle that white people are by nature superior to people of other colours. This is rather like the 'principle of perfection' we have just mentioned. In the same sort of way, the ancient Greeks believed themselves to be by nature superior to the barbarians of Northern and Western Europe. The only way to see if there is anything in such a principle is to make scientific studies of number of whites and blacks and brown people under different conditions of life and education and find what they can and cannot achieve.

(*a*) Five words are given below. Give the meaning of each word as used in the passage. One-word answers or short phrases will be accepted.

    (*i*) primitive

    (*ii*) mysterious

    (*iii*) superstitious

    (*iv*) Persecuting

    (*v*) Assumptions

(*b*) Answer the following questions as briefly as possible in your own words.

    (*i*) What reasons are given for natural changes by the primitive tribes ?

    (*ii*) What are superstitions according to the writer?

    (*iii*) What are some of the most common superstitions existing today in civilised society?

    (*iv*) Why do people buy charms and talismans?

    (*v*) What is the 'principle of perfection' according to the writer?

(*c*) In not more than 60 words of your own mention some common superstitious beliefs and how we can overcome them.

Exercise 10

Read the following passage carefully and answer the questions that follow.

We must not think of Aristotle as a kind of private tutor to the heir to the Macedonian Empire. The Greeks had ideas of a different kind. Aristotle was allowed to set up a school of his own at Mieza, near Pellas, in the province of Emathia. Here, in the Grove of the Nymphs, Alexander and the sons of various nobles pondered the teachings of Aristotle. The boys would gather round the great stone chair of the master, or walk with him in the shady path about the temple of learning.

One and all had an admiration for their teacher that amounted to worship, but Alexander never allowed his veneration of the wisdom and knowledge of Aristotle to become slavish. One morning Aristotle asked a pupil whose rank was more than <u>patrician,</u> "What wilt thou do when, in the ordinary course of events, thou ascendest the throne of thine ancestor, and becomest king ?" The youth modestly replied that in every crisis he would seek the advice of his old master and abide by it. Another prince, also questioned, replied in like manner. The same question was put to the young Alexander, who responded, " I cannot tell, nor can any man, what the morrow will bring forth. When the time comes, ask me that question again, and I will answer thee according to the circumstances."

Philip rendered every honour possible to the teacher of his son. The tyrant had at some previous time seen fit to lay waste Stagira. To mark his admiration for the philosopher, he caused the city to be rebuilt, and recalled from <u>banishment</u> its former citizens, some of whom were living in slavery, and all in great misery. It was a magnificent gesture and worthy of a great king, though we must remember that in ancient Greece a city was often no larger than a small town of today.

Aristotle <u>implanted</u> in the young Alexander a love of Homer which lasted him all his life. In other ways, too, teachings were such that Philip exclaimed to Alexander in a transport of generous admiration, "Verily, not in vain have we honoured. Aristotle and rebuilt his native town, for a man is deserving of the highest reward who has given thee such doctrine of the, duties and the functions of kings!"

Alexander's admiration and affection for his master lasted long after he had ceased to be a pupil. "To my father," he avowed, " I owe my life, to Aristotle the knowledge how to live worthily." When the latter was engaged in his biological researches, Alexander placed the services of a thousand men at his disposal. They were to help in observing and reporting on the habits and <u>characteristics</u> of birds, beasts and fishes. Alexander was also extremely generous in money gifts.

Many valuable manuscripts were thus placed within the reach of the man who otherwise would not have been able to afford them.

When Alexander set out for Asia, Aristotle returned to Athens, then the cultural centre not only of Greece but of the world. Here, at the age of fifty, he opened a school. This was called the Lyceum, from its nearness to the temple of Apollo Lyceius. Pupils flocked to it in order to benefit by the teachings of one who was now, by common consent, the foremost philosopher of the age. The word "Lyceum" still survives though few of those who use it connect it with the site of a heathen temple. Those who frequented the Lyceum soon became known as the <u>peripatetic</u> philosophers, possibly from their habit of walking up and down as they conversed.

The teachings of Aristotle covered a wide range. His was a philosophy founded on facts, for he possessed the exact and scientific mind that characterizes the best type of physicians. Indeed, he first intended to follow his father's profession and had already gained some experience in dissection and other branches of medical study when he abandoned the idea. To the end the study of biology was his favourite pursuit.

(*a*) Five words are given below. Give the meaning of each word as used in the passage. One-word answers or short phrases will be accepted.

(*i*)   patrician,

(*ii*) banishment

(*iii*) implanted

(*iv*) characteristics

(*v*)   peripatetic

(*b*) Answer the following questions as briefly as possible in your own words:

(*i*)   How did Philip show his veneration for Aristotle ?

(*ii*) What was the essence of Aristotle's teachings to Alexander ?

(*iii*) How did Alexander help Aristotle in his biological researches ?

(*iv*) Who became peripatetic philosophers and how ? .

(*v*)   What helped Aristotle the most in his philosophy which was founded on facts ?

(*c*) In not more than 60 words of your own mention how Alexander expressed his admiration and affection for his master.

Exercise 11

When Joan was twelve ,she declared that she had heard a voice from God, and from then on she vowed that she would remain a virgin and lead a holy life. During the next few years she continued to hear voices, and to see visions, and she became convinced that it was her mission in life to save her country and crown the true king in Rheims Cathedral.

It seemed a wild and fantastic notion to her companions and her parents. Her father said he would drown her rather than let her yield to such ideas. But Joan had made up her mind, and nothing would stop her. In 1428, when she was sixteen, she bearded in his castle Robert de Baudricourt, who held Vaucouleurs for the dauphin, and demanded an escort to Chinon. Robert was flabbergasted. He was not the man to be impressed by the story that the apparitions of St. Michael, St. Catherine and St. Margaret had entrusted to a peasant maid the task of freeing France from foreign invaders.

But Joan was convinced of the genuineness of her inspiration and no initial failure would daunt her. This time she won over certain of Baudricourt's followers, with the result that he was prevailed upon to give her the escort she demanded. In January , 1429, dressed as a man, and with six followers, the maid set out for Chinon.

For the moment her difficulties were over. Charles, in utter despair, and ready to jump at the vaguest hope, received her with open arms. After a private conversation with her, in which she reassured him as to his legitimacy, and convinced him of her own divine mission by a revelation which she ever afterwards kept secret, he publicly declared his confidence in her. In spite of the blusterings of the gross and incompetent La Tremouille, he announced that provided she would submit herself to examination by theologians at Poitiers, he would give her command of a force to relieve Orleans, which was then being besieged by the English in their efforts to penetrate south of the Loire.

She went to Poitiers, satisfied the theologians, and Charles fulfilled his promise. On April 28, Joan, in white armour, wearing a sword with five crosses, which she had previously declared would be found in the church of St. Catherine de Fierbois and which was so found, with an army of 4,000 men, accompanied by the Duke of Alencon and escorted by procession of priests, arrived before Orleans, and joined the commander of the garrison, the Bastard of Orleans, after wards Count of Dunois.

What followed is one of the most astounding stories of the history of war. The French had been cowed by the continued success of the English. Their spirit was broken, and two hundred of the invaders could strike terror into the hearts of a thousand Frenchmen. The coming of the maid transformed them. With her inspiring figure to lead them, confident of her divine destiny, they suddenly became new men. They sallied forth from the town, attacked the English, stormed the "bastille" of the Augustines; and then, after a week of increasing triumph, came the final victory, with the capture of the Tourelles, the towers commanding the bridge across the river, held by the English. This was Joan's greatest exploit. The Tourelles seemed impregnable, but she planted the first scaling ladder, and led assault after assault, rallying her men to deeds of heroic valour that would have seemed incredible ten days before. Only when she fell with an arrow through her shoulder did she leave the front of the attack. But not for long. She had her wound dressed, and came back to her place, and when Dunois was in favour of retiring, saying the Tourelles could not be won that day, she spurred him on to one last, glorious effort. It was successful. The French entered the Tourelles, with the maid's banner borne aloft in triumph.

(a) Five words are given below. Give the meaning of each word as used in the passage. One-word answers or short phrases will be accepted.

(i)   flabbergasted

(ii)   prevailed

(iii) blusterings

(iv)   theologians

(v)   impregnable

(b) Answer the following questions as briefly as possible in your own words:

(i)   What made Jeanne realise that she was destined to save her country ?

(ii) How did Jeanne convince Baudricourt of her determination in saving her country ?

(iii) What condition did Charles lay down before helping Jeanne ?

(iv) What change was seen in the French when Jeanne led the assault ?

(v)   What was Joan's greatest exploit ? .

(c) In not more than 60 words of your own mention how Joan (Jeanine de Arc) freed France from foreign invaders.

SECTION - I

Grammar

AGREEMENT OF VERB WITH THE SUBJECT

In a grammatically correct sentence the verb must agree with the subject and should be in the same number and person.

1. When two or more singular nouns or pronouns are joined by 'and' the verb is plural, e.g.

    (a) Gold and diamond *are* precious metals.

    (b) Hate and jealousy *are* human emotions.

    (c) *Are* you brother and sister at home?

2. If the two subject suggest one idea then the verb is singular, e.g.

    (a) Bread and butter *is* for breakfast.

    (b) Honour and glory *is* his reward.

3. If two singular nouns refer to the same person or thing the verb is singular, e.g.

    (a) My friend and guide *has* come.

    (b) The novelist and poet *is* dead.

4. When two or more singular subjects are connected by or, nor, either,...or, neither,....nor, the verb is singular e.g.

    (a) No nook *or* corner *was* left untouched.

    (b) Either the cat or the dog *has* been hit.

    (c) Neither praise nor blame *seem* to effect him.

Exception to the rule:-

However when one of the subjects joined by '*or*', or '*nor*' is plural, the verb is plural e.g.

    (a) Neither the Chairman nor the Directors *are* interested.

    (b) Either Shyam or his brothers *are* to be blamed.

5. When two subjects joined by 'or', or 'nor', are of different persons the verb agrees with the nearer e.g.

    (a) Either he or I *am* mistaken.

    (b) Neither you nor he *is* to blame.

    It is advisable however to avoid such sentences construction and write them as

    (a) He is mistaken or else I am.

    (b) He is not to blame nor are you.

6. 'Either', 'neither',' each', 'everyone', 'many', must be followed by a singular verb

    (a) Each of these substances *is* found in the state.

    (b) Neither of the two man *was* strong.

    (c) Many a man *has* succumbed to the temptation.

    d.   Everyone *was* called for the interview.

7. A collective noun takes a singular verb when the collection is thought of as one whole e.g.

    (a) The committee *has* sent its report.

    (b) The house *has* elected the Chairman.

If the collective noun implies the individuals of the collection then the verb is plural e.g.

The members of the committee *are* divided on one point.

8.   When a plural noun which is also a proper noun for some single object, or a collective unit it is followed by a singular verb e.g.

   (a) Gulliver's travel *was* written by Swift.

   (b) The United State of America *has* a big army.

9.   When a plural noun denotes some specific quantity or amount as a whole the verb is generally singular.

   (a) Ten kilometer *is* a long distance.

   (b) One hundred paise *is* equal to one rupee.

10. When two nouns are joined by 'with' or 'as well as' the verb agrees with the first noun e.g.

   (a) Iron *as well as* coal *is* found in Bihar.

   (b) The gangster *with* all his men *was* killed.

11. As a general rule the verb agrees in number with the subject of the verb i.e. if the subject is singular, verb is also singular e.g.

   (a) The quality of the mango *is* good (the subject being quality).

   (b) Many of his books *were* destroyed (subject being books).

12. Some nouns are plural in form but singular in meaning hence they take a singular verb e.g.

   (a) The news *is* very good.

   (b) The wages of sin *is* death.

13. None though properly singular in form but plural in meaning takes a plural verb e.g.

   None *are* so deaf as those who will not hear.

EXERCISE

Use the appropriate word given in brackets to complete the sentence

   1.   The jury _____ divided in their opinion. (is/are)

   2.   No news _____ good news. (is /are)

   3.   The man and the women _____ absconded. (have/has)

   4.   The three musketeers _____ written by Dumas. (is /was)

   5.   None but the brave _____ the honour. (deserves/deserve)

   6.   Either of the applicants _____ suitable. (was/were)

   7.   The quality of the clothes _____ not good. (was/were)

   8.   Neither food nor water _____ found there. (was/were)

   9.   Bread and butter _____ his only food. (is /are)

   10. All possible means _____ been tried. (have /has)

ANSWER

1 is, 2 is, 3 have, 4 is, 5 deserves, 6 was, 7was, 8 was, 9 is, 10 have

ACTIVE AND PASSIVE VOICE

A verb is in the Active Voice when its form shows that the person or thing denoted by the subject does something or is the doer of the action e.g.

Ram helps Hari. (Ram the subject does something)

A verb is in the Passive Voice when its form shows, that something is done to the person or thing denoted by the subject e.g.

Hari is helped by Ram i.e. something is done to Hari (the person denoted by the subject). The verb helped is then in the passive voice.

It will be noticed that when the verb is changed from active voice to passive voice the object of the transitive verb in the active voice i.e. Hari becomes the subject of the verb in the passive voice.

Passive Voice is generally preferred when active forms would involve use of a vague pronoun or noun like

My pen has been stolen.   (passive voice)

Somebody has stolen my pen.   (active voice)

Thus pronoun like somebody, they, we, etc, need not be used in the passive voice sentence.

Rules for Conversion from Active Voice to Passive Voice

1. Object of Transitive Verb becomes the subject of the verb in the passive voice i.e. in the above example

    Ram helps Hari (Hari the object of the Transitive verb in active voice becomes the subject of the verb helped in passive voice. This is possible only in transitive verb because an intransitive verb has no object e.g.

    (a) Ram helps willingly. (There is no object)

2. If the transitive verb has two objects any of the two objects can become the subject in the passive voice. e.g..

    (a) Active voice:-   I taught Ram History.

    (b) Passive voice:-   History was taught to Ram by me.

    Or Ram was taught History by me.

3. The preposition verb should not be dropped when changing from active voice to   passive voice.

    (a) Active voice:-   They laughed *at* the Joker.

    (b) Passive voice:- The joker was laughed *at* by them.

4. To change the auxiliary verb from active voice to passive voice add 'be' along with the past participle of the verb.

    (a) Active voice:-   Ram can do the work.

    (b) Passive voice:- The work can *be* done by Ram.

5. To change imperative sentences 'let …be' is used. If the sentence is to remain as imperative, otherwise 'should be' is used.

(a) Active voice:-   Close the door.

(b) Passive voice: - Let the door be closed.
    or The door should be closed.

6. When in an imperative sentence a transitive verb is used, then it is change to passive voice in the following manner.

(a) Active voice:-   Get out.

(b) Passive voice:-   You are ordered to get out.

EXERCISE 1

Change from Active Voice to Passive Voice

1. One should keep ones promise.

2. Give the order.

3. Someone has picked my pocket.

4. The enemy has defeated our Army.

5. I opened the door.

6. He taught me to read German.

7. We must listen to his words .

8. We admire the brave.

9. We expect good news.

10. Do you understand my meaning?

11. I saw him opening the box.

12. Subject him to severe punishment .

13. Did you never hear that name ?

14. He will be greatly surprised if they chose him.

15. They chose him leader .

EXERCISE 2

Rewrite the sentences as per instruction given.

1. Who has broken the jug? (Begin By whom..........)

2. Show the right path. (end ...shown).

3. Avoid easy solutions. (end........avoided).

4. All desire wealth and some acquire it. (Begin Wealth..........).

5. Why should I be suspected by you. (End ...suspect me).

6. Without effort nothing can be gain. (End...gain nothing).

7. Who taught you such tricks as these? (Begin...By whom...........).

8. Alas! We shall hear his voice no more. (Begin....Alas! His voice........).

9. Do you not understand my meaning? (End....understood).

10. Summon the fire brigade. (End..............summoned).

ANSWER

EXERCISE 1

1. Promises should be kept.
2. Let the order be given.
3. My pocket has been picked.
4. Our army has been defeated.
5. The door was opened by me.
6. I was taught by him to read German.
7. His words must be listen to.
8. The brave are admired by us.
9. Good news is expected
10. Is my meaning understood?
11. He was seen opening the box.
12. Let him be subjected to severe punishment.
13. Was that name never heard?
14. He will be greatly surprised if he is chosen.
15. He was chosen leader.

EXERCISE 2

1. By whom was the jug broken?
2. Let the right path be shown.
3. Easy solutions should be avoided.
4. Wealth is desired by all and acquired by some.
5. Why should you suspect me?
6. Without effort one can gain nothing .
7. By whom were you taught such tricks as these?
8. Alas! His voice shall no more be heard by us.
9. Is my meaning understood?
10. Let the fire brigade be summoned .

TENSE

PRESENT TENSE

Simple Present Tense is used :-

1. To express a habitual action as
   I get up at 5 AM everyday.
2. To express a universal truth or fact e.g.
   Honey is sweet.
   Fortune favours the brave.
3. To express an action taking place in the immediate present.
   Here comes the bus.
   There she goes.

4.   To indicate the present period.

    He works in this office.

5.   To express a future fixed action.

    The train starts at 5 pm.

    We go to the bank next week.

6.   In a vivid narrative as a substitute for a simple past.

    Ram rushes forward and kicks the ball.

7.   In Time clauses, when it is introduced by conjunction of time such as when, while, until, till, after, as soon as, no sooner, then, etc.

    I shall wait *till* you come.

    When you reach home I shall meet you.

8.   In Conditional Clauses

    If it rains we shall get wet.

    Unless he studies, he will not pass.

    We will wait, until she comes back.

9.   To introduce a quotation

    Shakespeare says "frailty thy name is women"

10. In exclamatory sentences beginning with here, there.

    Here comes Sohan!

Present Continuous Tense is used

1.   For an action going on at the time of speaking.

    The boys *are playing* football.

2.   For a temporary solution which may not actually happening at the time of   speaking.

    I *am reading* Tom Sawyer. (Not reading at the movement).

3.   For an action planned in the near future.

    I *am going* to the circus tonight.

4.   For a repeated, or habitual action used with an adverb like always, continually, constantly, very, etc.

    He is always *helping* the weak.

Present Perfect Tense is used

1.   To indicate completed action in the immediate past.

    He has *just returned* from office.

2.   To express past action whose time is not defined.

    Have you read this book.

    Mr. Ram *has been* to US(A)

3.   To express a past action the effect of which still continue

    I *have cut* my finger.

    I *have finished* my work.

4. To denote an action beginning at sometime in the past and continuing up to the present move-
    ment.

    I *have known* him for a long time.

    We *have lived* here for 10 years.

    Also used with since and for. 'Since' means from that point, to the time of speaking. While
    'for' is used for a period of time.

    He has been ill *since* last week.

    I have lived here *for* two years.

Present Perfect Continuous Tense is used :-

1. For an action which began at sometime in the past and still continue.

    They *have been playing* since 4 o' clock.

2. For an unfinished action

    We *have been building* the house

3. For drawing conclusions

    Her eyes are red, she *has been crying*.

PAST TENSE

Simple Past Tense is used :-

1. To indicate an action completed, occurring with an adverb of time.

    I *read* the letter yesterday

    or Without an adverb of time. The time being implied

    I didn't sleep well.

    Who left the door open?

2. For past habits or repeated actions.

    He always carries a bag.

3. To denote an action which continue for sometime in the past.

    We *studied* chemistry for two years.

Past Continuous Tense is used :-

1. To denote an action going on sometime in the past

    He *was listening* to the radio all day.

    She *was weeping* bitterly

2. With an adverb 'all' emphasizing continuity or with 'still'

    It was *raining all* night.

    It was *still raining* when I woke up

3. For persistent habits in the past used with always, continually

    He was *always grumbling*

4. Used in making polite enquiries

    I *was wondering* if you could help me.

Past Perfect Tense is used :-

1. To describe an action completed in the past.

    Mahatma Gandhi *died* on 30 Jan 1948.

2. However if two actions happened in the past it may be necessary to show which happened
    earlier. The simple past is used in one clause and the past perfect in the other .

    The patient *had died* when the doctor *arrived*.

3. With verb to show unfulfilled hopes and wishes. Thus verbs like expect, hope, suppose, thinks, wants, etc is used to describe things we hoped to do but could not do .

   I *had thought* to send him a letter but could not send it.

Past Perfect Continuous is used :-

1. For an action that began before a certain time in the past and continued up to that time as

   At that time he *had been editing* the newspaper for two years.

2. Can be used for drawing conclusions.

   Her eyes were red, it was obvious she *had been crying* all day.

FUTURE TENSE

Simple Future Tense is used :-

1. For an action that has still to take place.

   I *shall see* him tomorrow.

2. Some other ways of expressing the future by using 'will', 'shall', 'be going to'

   I *will see* him tomorrow. or I *shall see* him tomorrow.

   I *am going* to see him tomorrow.

3. By using 'going to' to describe the speakers intention to do something in fairly immediate future.

   I *am going to* think about it.

   He *is going to* be a Doctor when he grows up.

Future Continuous Tense is used :-

1. To represent an action as going on at some time in the future as

   The guests *will be arriving* anytime from now.

2. For future events that are planned

   He *will be meeting* us next month.

   I *shall be seeing* the President tonight.

3. In the interrogative form this tense is used to ask a polite question.

   Will you be doing it in our absence?

Future Perfect Tense is used to indicate the completion of an action in a certain time in the future.

   I *will have* returned by the year 2010.

   Before you come, he *will have* slept.

Future Perfect Continuous Tense is used to indicate an action that is in progress over a period of time and will end in the future as

   By next June we *shall have been* living here for four years.

SEQUENCE OF TENSES

It is the principle according to which, the tense of the verb in the subordinate clause, follows the tense of the verb in the principal clause, as per the following rules:-

Rule no. 1

A Past Tense in the principal clause is followed by a past tense in the subordinate clause e.g.

Principal Clause	Subordinate Clause
He saw	that the clock had stopped.
She replied	that she felt better

There are however three exceptions to this rule

Exception 1

The principal clause in the past tense may be followed by a present tense in the subordinate clause when it expresses a universal truth.

Newton *discovered* that the force of gravity *makes* apples fall.

He *said* honesty *is* always the best policy.

Exception 2

When subordinate clause is followed by 'then'. In this case even if the principal clause is in the past tense, it may be followed by any tense i.e. Present , Future or Past as required by the sense of the subordinate clause.

He *liked* you better than he *likes* me.

He *valued* his friendship more than he *values* mine.

Exception 3

When the subordinate clause denotes place, reason or comparison, it may be in any tense, even if there is a past tense in the principal clause

He *succeeded* because he *is* hardworking.

Ram *was* smart but his brother *is* smarter.

Rule no. 2

If principal clause is in Present or Future tense, the tense of the verb in the subordinate clause can be Past, Present or Future depending on the sense conveyed.

She *says* that she *went* home.

She *will say* that her friends have *deserted* her.

There is however one exception.

When a subordinate clause expresses a purpose, condition or time, its verb is always in the present tense, even if the verb in principal clause is in present or future tense.

I *shall nurse* him so that he *can live*.

We *shall leave* when the meeting *is* over.

Rule no. 3

When the subordinate clause is introduced by a conjunction 'lest'. It is always followed by 'should'.

Ram studies *lest* he *should* fail.

Rule no. 4

When the subordinate clause is introduced by 'as though' or 'as if'. The present tense is generally used to indicate present time and the past perfect to denote past time as

He pretends *as if* he *were* mad.

They laughed *as though* they *were* crazy.

Rule no. 5

In conditional sentences the tense of the verb in the principal clause is future and the verb in the subordinate clause is present.

Unless Shyam *apologizes,* he *will be* punished.

Point to note

Before attempting to write the answers to the question, it would be advisable to first read the passage, without attempting to put in any word and get the sense of the time involved. That is whether the time specified is in the present, past or future tense. You would occasionally find a clue in the passage, which would determine the tense of the sentence / passage. eg

    a)   He (play)————here for a long time now.

    b)   She (spoke)————about this for a long time now.

In both the above sentences, you will observe that the word 'now' tells us that the timing is in the present tense, while the word 'long time' indicates the use of the continuous tense. Thus we see that the 'playing' and 'speaking' had begun earlier, and is still continuing to the present, as indicated by "now". This indicates that the sentence is in the present perfect tense and the right form of the verb to be used here would be *'has been studying'*, or *'has been speaking'*. Thus you should be keenly aware of such clues, that would help you in sensing the timing, so as to use the proper tense in writing out your answer. Quite often you would also find more than one correct answer, provided the sequence of tense is maintained.

EXERCISE 1

Complete each of the following sentences with a suitable form of the word given in brackets

    1.   So long as the rain _____ I stayed art home. (continues / continued)

    2.   He went were he _____ find work. (could / would)

    3.   He walked as though he _____ slightly lame. (was /were)

    4.   I studied hard in order that I _____ succeed. (should/ might)

    5.   I would not attempt it if you _____ me. (ask / asked)

    6.   Now that we _____ safe we stopped to take breath. (feel / felt)

    7.   You _____ go only if you have permission. (can / could)

    8.   I wished that I _____ come earlier. (could / would)

    9.   She boasted as if she_____ everything.(known/ knew)

   10.   Run fast least you _____ miss that bus.(would/ should)

EXERCISE 2

Complete each of the following sentences with a suitable form of the word given in brackets

    1.   He went where he _____ find work. (can or could).

    2.   He behaves as one _____ expect him to do. (may or might).

    3.   As he _____ not there, I spoke to his brother. (to be).

    4.   Whenever we _____ ,we talk of old times. (to meet)

    5.   I would die before I _____ .(to lie).

6. I would not attempt it, if you _____ me. (to ask)

7. He ran because he _____ in a hurry. (is)

8. He has always _____ faithful to me. (be).

9. A man of high character never _____ his word. (break).

10. He had _____ (play) the piano since 6 O'clock this morning.
    He had just _____.(stop).

EXERCISE 3

Complete each of the following sentences with a suitable form of the word given in brackets

1. Did you _____(know) any English when you first _____(arrive) here?

2. This bicycle has _____ (be) in our family for fourteen years.

3. All the boys _____ (assemble) in the class before the teacher_____.(come)

4. I _____ (work) in this office for a number of years before I _____(force) to resign.

5. He _____(feel) weak for he had not _____ (not eat) anything for many hours.

6. When the train _____ (arrive) at the platform, all the people _____(be) impatient.

7. The little boy _____ (forget) to buy what his father had _____ (ask) him to.

8. "You see", he _____(say), and _____ (go) to open the door.

9. What have you _____(do)? _____ (look) for you for ages.

10. Look, some strange bird _____ (fly) over us.

11. They were ———at the thought of meeting a tiger. (terror)

12. The purpose of the filter is to ——— the drinking water. (pure)

13. Having listened to all the evidence the jury ———————to consider the verdict. (retire).

14. He was ——— by a sudden noise. (awake)

15. He has no ——— of the case. (know)

EXERCISE 4

In the following passage fill in each of the numbered blanks with the correct form of word given in brackets. Do not copy the passage but write in correct serial order the word appropriate to the blank space)

Football ___ (1) (be) considered a fascinating and fast moving sport. Over the years it has gained in popularity. I am myself a great football fan. Last year I _____ (2) (be) watching a thrilling match at the local stadium a group of spectators including myself _____(3) (be) about to leave the stand just before the end of the game. We were half way down the stairs when suddenly a goal was scored. And there was a great cheer from the spectators. If there _____(4) (not be) a goal the crowd _____(5) (not cheer). If the crowd _____(6) (not cheer) we _____ (7) (not run) back up the stairs to se what had happened. Unfortunately while _____ (8) (run) back we _____(9) (crash) into the rest of the spectators, on their way down and there _____ (10) (be) this frightful accident!

ANSWERS

EXERCISE I

1. continued 2. could 3. was 4. might 5. asked 6. felt 7. can 8. could 9. knew

10. should

EXERCISE 2

1.could 2.may 3. was 4.meet 5.lie 6. asked 7.was 8. been 9.breaks 10.been playing / stopped.

EXERCISE 3

1. know / arrived 2. been 3. had assembled / came 4.had worked / was forced 5. felt / eaten 6.arrived / were 7.forgot / asked 8. said/ went 9. been doing / have been looking 10. are flying11. terrorized 12. purify 13. retired 14. awakened 15. knowledge

EXERCISE 4

1. is 2. was 3. were 4. had not been 5. would not have cheered 6. had not cheered 7. would not have run 8. running 9. crashed 10. was

DIRECT AND INDIRECT SPEECH

We can report the words of a speaker in two ways

1. In Direct speech: We may quote his actual words in inverted commas by placing a comma before the remark e.g.

> Hari said, "I am very tired now".

2. In Indirect speech we may report what he said without quoting his exact words e.g.

Hari said that he was very tired then.

You would note the following important changes made in changing direct speech to indirect speech in the above examples

1. Use of conjunction 'that' before the indirect statement.
2. Pronoun changed from 'I' to 'he'.
3. Verb 'am' changed to 'was'.
4. Adverb 'now' changed to 'then'.

Rules For Changing Direct Speech To Indirect Speech.

Rule 1- Use of conjunction 'that' before the indirect statement except in case of imperative sentences and exclamatory sentences e.g.

> Hari said *that* he was very tired then.

It is often omitted incase of verbs such as says, think, agree, promise, mention, notice, etc.

Rule 2- Change in pronouns of first and second person in Direct speech to third person in Indirect speech taking into account the gender of the subject. Thus

I, you	(singular)	becomes	he, she
My, your	(singular)	becomes	his, her
We, you	(plural)	becomes	they
Our, your	(plural)	becomes	their

e.g. Ram said "I am very busy".

Ram said that he was very busy.

Note:

(a) In changing pronouns their relation with the reporter and his bearer are indicated rather than with the original speaker. e.g..

Direct speech :-	He said to me, "I don't like you".
Indirect speech :-	He said he didn't like me.
Direct speech :-	She said to him, "I don't like you".
Indirect speech :-	She said she didn't like him.
Direct speech :-	I said to him, "I don't like you".
Indirect speech :-	I said I didn't like him.

(b) If the pronoun he or she stands for different persons then the name of the person refer to can be inserted in brackets after the pronoun.

> Sita said to Richa " I like your dress".
>
> Sita told Richa that she (Sita) liked her (Richa's) dress

Rule 3

If reporting verb is in Present or Future Tense, the tense of the verb in the reported speech is not changed e.g.

> He says "I *am* busy".
>
> He says that he *is* busy.
>
> He will say "I *was* busy."
>
> He will say that he *was* busy

Rule 4

If reporting verb is in the Past Tense, the tense of the verb in the reported speech is also changed into one of the forms of the past tense Thus the verb changes as per norms given below .

Shall becomes *should*	*Come* becomes *came*
Will becomes *would*	*Is coming* becomes *was coming*
May becomes *might*	*Has come* becomes *had come*
Can becomes *could*	*Has been coming* becomes *had been coming*
Is, am, are becomes *was, were*	

The Present Simple Tense becomes Past Simple Tense

> He said " *I play* football every evening".
>
> He said *he played* football every evening.

Present Continuous becomes Past Continuous

> He said " I *am playing* football".
>
> He said he *was playing* football.

Present Perfect becomes Past Prefect

> He said " I *have played* football for two years".
>
> He said he *had played* football for two years.

Present Perfect Continuous becomes Past Perfect Continuous

        He said " I *have been playing* football for two years.

        He said he *had been playing* football for two years.

Future becomes Conditional

        He said " I *shall play* football next year".

        He said he *would play* football next year.

Future Perfect becomes Conditional Perfect

        He said "I *shall have played* football for two years next June".

        He said he *would have played* football for two years next June.

Exceptions To The Above Rules

(a) If reported speech expresses **universal truth or habitual fact** the tense of the verb in the reported speech is not changed into the corresponding past.

        He said, " Earth goes round the Sun".

        He said that Earth goes round the Sun.

        "German is easy to learn", he said.

        He said German is/ was easy to learn.

(b) The reporting verb 'say' is changed into 'tell' if it is followed by a verb.

        Direct Speech :- "We shall go on a picnic" he said to me.

        Indirect Speech :- He told me they would go on a picnic.

        Direct Speech :- The teacher said to the boys, "You should do your work regularly".

        Indirect Speech:- The teacher told the boys that they should do their work regularly.

Rule 5 – Words expressing nearness in time or place are changed into words expressing distance.

Now becomes then	Come becomes go
Here becomes there	Today becomes that day
Thus becomes so	Yesterday becomes the previous day
This becomes that	Tonight becomes that night
These becomes those	Last night becomes the previous night
Hither becomes thither	Tomorrow becomes the next day
Hence becomes thence	Ago becomes before

Exception If 'this, here, now, etc' refers to some object, place or time that is present to the speaker, then no change in adjective or adverb is made in the reported speech. e.g.

        Ram said, "Here is the pen I have been looking for".

        Ram said that here was the pen he had been looking for.

(I) Changing Assertive Sentences

        Assertive sentence in the indirect speech are introduced by the conjunction   'that'

        He said to Ram, "You are a good boy".

        He told Ram that he was a good boy.

(II) Changing Interrogative Sentences.

In reporting questions the indirect speech is introduced by such verbs as asked, enquired, wonder, wanted to know.

(a) If the answer to the question is either yes or no, we use 'whether' or 'if'.

He said, "Will you listen to such a man"?

He asked them whether they would listen to such a man.

(b) In negative statement we use 'do' and 'did'. The same is used in negative indirect questions.

"Don't you like to play football" Hari asked Ram.

Ram asked Hari if he didn't like to play football.

(III) Changing Imperative Sentences

In reporting an imperative sentences like a command or request. The reporting verb 'say' or 'tell' is changed to a verb expressing a command, advice or request e.g.

Word used in Commands: -	order, bid, warn
Word used in Request:-	request, implore
Word used in Proposal: -	advise, proposed, suggest
Word used in Prohibit: -	forbid,
Word used in Entreaty:-	entreat, pray, beg.

(a) 'that ' is commonly not used

(b) The imperative mood is changed into the infinitive.

(c) Rules for change of pronoun must be observed. e.g.

He said to me, " Please give me your book".

He requested me to give him my book.

"Call the first witness", said the judge.

The judge commanded them to call the first witness.

He shouted, "let me go".

He shouted to them to let him go.

Note: When 'let' in direct speech expresses a proposal or a suggestion we use 'should' and change reporting verb to 'propose' or 'suggest'.

He said to me "let us have tea".

He suggested to me that we should have tea.

When let does not express a proposal it should be changed to 'might' or any other verb according to the sense.

He said, "let me have some food".

He wished that he might have some food.

IV) Changing Exclamatory Sentences .

When the Direct Speech is introduced by some verb expressing exclamation or wish as , exclaim, cry, wish, confess, etc

All interjections are omitted, but their force is kept by suitable adverbs or expressive words as given below.

Hurrah! expresses joy	Bravo! expresses approval
Hush! expresses attention	Pooh! expresses contempt
Alas! expresses grief , sorrow	Ugh! expresses disgust.
What! Or Oh! expresses scorn	

The conjunction 'that' is used after the reporting verb e.g.

"Alas ! Sohan has failed in his exams," said Rohan .

Rohan exclaimed with sorrow *that* Sohan had failed in his exams.

Exclamatory words 'what or 'how' are changed into very, highly, greatly according to the sense e.g.

"What a nice day it is," she said.

She exclaimed that it was a very nice day .

The teacher said, "Bravo ! you have done very well."

The teacher applauded us saying that we had done *very* well.

Rani said "How cleaver I am."

Rani exclaimed that she was *very* cleaver.

"So help me Heavens !" he cried. " I will never steal again."

He called upon heavens to witness his resolve never to steal again.

The soldier said, "Curse on the traitor."

The soldiers *bitterly* cursed the traitor.

EXERCISE 1

In each of the following sentences A is complete but B is incomplete. Complete B making it as similar as possible in meaning to sentence A

1. The teacher said "lets go on a picnic tomorrow."

    The teacher proposed _____

2. He said, "Let me go, I'm already late".

    He asked _____.

3. They said, "shall we have a holiday tomorrow" ?

    They asked _____

4. The beggar said to him, "Give me something to eat."

    The beggar implored _____

5. "Do you really come from China", said the Prince.

    The Prince asked _____

6. "Do you write a good hand", he said.

    He asked _____

7. He said, "My God I am ruined".

    He exclaimed _____

8. He said "What a pity you did not come"?
   He exclaimed _____

9. "Are their enough papers left Anil," asked the teacher.
   The teacher asked Anil _____-

10. Hari asked me whether I played cricket.
    Write in Direct Speech _____

11. He said that he would go as soon as it was possible
    Write in Direct Speech _____

12. He said, "friends we should remain calm."
    He said that _____

13. " Would you mind closing the window",she said.
    She asked _____

14. He said "Ugh! He is such a rascal."
    He exclaimed _____

15. "When does the next train come ?" I asked.
    I asked _____

EXERCISE 2

Rewrite the sentence in indirect speech.

1. Sita said "Virtue is own reward ."

2. He said " My pen is lost ".

3. He said to him " You are stupid ".

4. The teacher said" I am busy now."

5. He said, "It may rain tomorrow."

6. He said ," Last night I met a lion."

7. The leader said, "I will fight now or never."

8. He said to us, "Are you going today?"

9. He said to me, "Give me your pencil."

10. He said to the students , "Do not make noise."

EXERCISE 3

Rewrite the sentence in indirect speech.

1. He said to the servant, "Leave my house at once.".

2. "What a terrible storm it is!"

3. She said," Alas; how foolish I have been!"

4. He said," How I wish they would come!"

5. He said," Farewell my countrymen,"

6. He said, "Bravo ! You have done well".

7. He said ,"Alas! I am undone ."

8. He said to him ," Please wait here till I return."
9. The rebel said to the King ," Pardon my fault, Sir".
10. She said to us , "Let us have some music."

ANSWERS

EXERCISE 1

1. The teacher proposed that they should go on a picnic the following day.
2. He asked me to let him go, as he was already late.
3. They asked if the would have a holiday the next day.
4. The beggar implored him to give him something to eat
5. The Prince asked whether I really came from China.
6. He asked whether I wrote a good hand.
7. He exclaimed sadly that he was ruined.
8. He exclaimed that it was a great pity, I had not come .
9. The teacher asked Anil whether there were enough papers left.
10. Hari said , "Do you play cricket."
11. He said, " I shall go as soon as it is possible."
12. He said that they should remain calm.
13. She asked if I would mind closing the window.
14. He exclaimed with disgust that he was such a rascal.
15. I asked when the next train would come.

EXERCISE 2

1. Sita said that virtue is own reward.
2. He said that his pen was lost.
3. He told me that I was stupid
4. The teacher said that he was busy then.
5. He said that it might rain the next day.
6. He said that he had met a lion the previous night.
7. The leader said that he would fight now or never.
8. He enquired of us whether we were going away that day.
9. He asked me to give him my pencil.
10. He forbade the students not to make noise.

EXERCISE 3

1. He ordered the servant, to leave the house at once.
2. He exclaimed that it was a terrible storm.
3. She confessed with regret, that she had been very foolish.
4. He exclaimed that he wished they would come.
5. He bade farewell to his countrymen.
6. He applauded him, saying that he had done well.
7. He exclaimed with sorrow, that he was undone .
8. He requested him to wait there, till he returned.
9. The rebel begged the king, to pardon his fault.
10. She suggested to us, that we should have some music.

TYPES OF SENTENCES

Sentences are of three types, **Simple, Compound and Complex Sentences**.

SIMPLE SENTENCE is one which has only one subject and one predicate.

He (Subject) was an honest man. (Predicate)

COMPOUND SENTENCE is one made up of two or more Principal or Main Clauses.

The moon was bright and we could see our way.

The above are two sentences joined by the conjunction 'and'. Each has a subject and a predicate of its own. Hence each part is what we call a 'clause'

COMPLEX SENTENCE also consists of two parts .One being the Principal or main clause while the other being a dependent or Subordinate clause.   (which cannot stand by itself)

They rested when evening came. Principal Clause They rested - makes sense .

Subordinate clause When evening came - cannot stand by itself and make sense .

SYNTHESIS OF SENTENCES

The combining of two or more sentences into one new sentence is called Synthesis

Combining Two Or More Simple Sentence Into A Single Simple Sentence.

A Simple sentence has *one finite verb*. Thus when combining two or more sentence into one simple sentence we must use only finite verb and do away with the others. We can combine two or more sentence into one simple sentence as follow

1. **By using a Participle** (A participle is that form of verb which partakes the nature of both a verb, and an adjective)

   (a) When two actions occur simultaneously we use present participle to join two sentences. e.g.

   They went away. They were crying

   They went away crying.

   (b) When one action occurs after the other we use present participle to combine the two sentences.

   He started early. He arrived there at noon.

   Starting early he arrived there at noon.

   He jumped up. He ran away.

   Jumping up he ran away.

   (c) When one action follows the first action we use the perfect participle

   I lost my license. I applied for a new one.

   Having lost my license, I applied for a new one.

   (d) If one of the two sentences has a passive verb we use past participle to join them.

   I saw few trees. The trees were laden with fruits.

   I saw few trees laden with fruits.

2. By using a Noun or a Phrase in Apposition

This is my friend. His name is Ram.

This is my friend Ram.

Einstein was a great scientist. He made many inventions.

Einstein, a great scientist , made many inventions.

3. By using a Preposition with a Noun or Gerund.

(A Gerund is that form of the verb which ends in – ing and has the force of a Noun and a Verb e.g. swimming, believing, hearing, receiving, etc.)

He is poor. He is honest

In spite of *being* poor he is honest.

Her husband died. She heard the news. She fainted.

On *hearing* the news of her husband's death she fainted.

4. By using an Adjective

Marco Polo made many discoveries. The discoveries were wonderful.

Marco Polo made *many wonderful* discoveries.

5. By using an Adverb or Adverbial Phrase.

The bus was crowded. That was unusual.

The bus was *unusually* crowded.

He deserved to succeed. He failed

He failed *undeservedly*.

The sunset. The boys had not finished the game.

The boys had not finished the game by sunset.

6. By using an Infinitive that is often followed by to.

He is very fat. He cannot run.

He is too fat *to run*.

I have some duties . I must perform them.

I have some duties *to* perform.

7. By using an Absolute Phrase.

The police arrived . The crowd disappeared.

The police having arrived, the crowd disappeared.

The weather was pleasant . We went for a picnic.

The weather being pleasant, we went for a picnic.

EXERCISE 1

1. He hurt his foot. He stopped.
2. I was walking along the street one day. I saw a dead snake.
3. The magician took pity on the mouse. He turned it into a cat.
4. He was weary of failure. He emigrated to Africa.
5. I was returning home. I saw a man he looked very ill. He was lying by the road side.

6. Jawaharlal Nehru died in 1964. He was the first Prime Minister of India.
7. The word of command will be given. You will then fire.
8. The judge gave his decision. The court listened silently.
9. He amused us very much. He sang a funny song.
10. It was a very hot day. I could not do my work satisfactorily.
11. The King died. His eldest son came to the throne.
12. His father was dead. He had to support his widowed mother.
13. I will speak the truth. I am not afraid of the consequences.
14. He must apologize. He will not escape punishment otherwise.
15. He cannot afford a car. He is too poor
16. He wants to earn his livelihood. He works hard for that reason.
17. He is very honourable. He will not break his word.
18. I accept your answer. I do it without reserve.
19. He was obstinate. He refused to listen to advice.
20. He persevered, He was not deterred by obstacles.

ANSWER

1. Having hurt his foot he stopped.
2. While walking along the street one day I saw a dead snake.
3. Taking pity on the mouse the magician turned it into a cat.
4. Being weary of failure he emigrated to Africa.
5. Returning home I saw a man looking ill lying by the roadside.
6. Jawahar Lal Nehru the first Prime Minister of India died in 1964.
7. At the word of command you will fire.
8. The court listened silently to the decision given by the judge.
9. He amused us very much by singing a funny song.
10. It being a very hot day. I could not do my work satisfactorily.
11. The King having died, his eldest son came to the throne.
12. His father being dead, he had to support his widowed mother.
13. I will not be afraid to speak the truth.
14. He must apologize to escape punishment.
15. He is too poor to afford a car.
16. He works hard to earn his livelihood
17. He is honourable enough not to break his word.
18. I unreservedly accept your answer.
19. He obstinately refused to listen to advice.
20. He persevered indomitably

(B) Combination Of Two Or More Simple Sentences Into One Single Compound Sentence
Simple sentences may be combined to form combined sentences by the use of **coordinative conjunctions.** These are of four kinds

    (1)   **Cumulative conjunction** like and, both, and not only,…but also, not less then, as well as etc. These merely add one statement to another e.g.

        Simple :-   He is a fool. He is knave.

        Compound:-   He is a fool and a knave. or

He is both a fool and a knave. or He is a fool as well as a knave
or He is not only a fool but also a knave.

(2) **Adversative conjunction** which express opposition or contrast between two
statement like- but, still, yet, never the less, however, etc. e.g.

Simple :-   He is poor. He is happy

Compound:-   He is poor, still he is happy.

Simple :-   He failed in the examination. He persevered.

Compound:-   He failed in the examination nevertheless he
                        persevered.

(3) **Alternative conjunctions** which express a choice between two alternatives by
using, either…. or, neither…nor, for, therefore, etc.

Simple :-   He is obstinate. He was punished.

Compound:-   He was obstinate, therefore he was punished.

Simple :-   He is not a fool. He is not a knave.

Compound:-   He is neither a fool, nor a knave.

(4) **Illative conjunctions**

Join sentences in which one statement is inferred from the other by using
therefore, so, for, yet. e.g.

Simple :-   He is weak . He cannot run fast.

Compound:-   He is weak so he cannot run fast.

Simple :-   He was caught stealing . He was punished.

Compound:-   He was caught stealing, therefore he was
                        punished.

EXERCISE

1. He does well. He is nervous at the start.
2. It is raining heavily. I will take an umbrella with me.
3. I am in the right. You are in the wrong.
4. He was fined. He was sent to prison.
5. We must hasten. The robbers will overtake us.
6. The train was wrecked. No one was hurt.
7. Ram is ill. He still attend school.
8. I shall not oppose your plan. I cannot approve it.
9. He is a rich man. He did not earn his wealth. He does not appreciate the value of
    money. He squanders it.
10. The storm abated. The Sun shone. The ship wrecked mariners could see no sign of
    land.

ANSWER

1. He does well *only* he is nervous at the start.
2. It is raining heavily *so* I will take an umbrella with me.
3. I am in the right *but* you are in the wrong.
4. He was *not only* fined *but* also sent to prison.

5. We must hasten *or* the robbers will overtake us.

6. The train was wrecked *but* no one was hurt.

7. Ram is ill *yet* he still attend school.

8. I shall not oppose your plan, however I cannot approve of it.

9. He is a rich man *and* as he did not earn his wealth, he does not appreciate the value of money *and* squanders it.

10. The storm *having* abated, the Sun shone, *but* the ship wrecked mariners could see no sign of land.

(C) Combination Of Two Or More Simple Sentences Into A Complex Sentence.

Simple sentences can be combined into a complex sentence by using –Noun clause, Adjective clause, Adverb clause.

(a) **Using Noun clause** – A Noun clause is a group of words which contain a subject and a predicate of its own and does the work of a Noun e.g.

> I except that I shall get a prize.

Expect what? That I shall get a prize. This is a noun clause that does the work of a noun.

Simple ;-   He will be late . That is certain.

Complex:-   It is certain that he will be late.

Simple ;-   He may be innocent. I do not know.

Complex:-   I do not know whether he is innocent.

(b) **Using Adjective Clause**— An adjective clause is a group of words which contain a subject and a predicate and does the work of an adjective.

> The pen which has a red cap is mine.

What type of pen? Which has a red cap, describes the pen and hence does the work of an adjective.

Thus two or more simple sentences may be combined into one complex sentence by introducing adjective clauses using who, whom, whose, or which, where and why. e.g.

Simple :-   She keeps her ornaments in the safe. This is the safe.

Complex :-This is the safe where she keeps her ornaments.

Simple :- My father met her son. He is now in America.

Complex:- My father met her son who is now in America.

c. **Using Adverb Clauses** An adverb clause is a group of words which contain a subject and a predicate of its own and does the work of an adverb e.g.

> He finished first though he began late.

(though he began late) is an Adverb clause .

Thus two or more simple sentences may be combined into one complex sentence by introducing adverb clauses and using subordinating conjunctions like if, since, because, unless when, whose, through, which, until, before, as, that, e.g.

Simple :-   I waited for my friend. I waited till he arrived.

Complex:-   I waited for my friend until he came.

Simple :-   You are strong. I am equally strong.

Complex:-   I am as strong as you are.

Simple:-   You will pass. Work hard.

Complex:-   You will pass if you work hard.

EXERCISE 1

Join the sentences without using 'and' or 'but'.

1.   He is wrong. I am sure of it.
2.   He said some thing. I did not hear.
3.   I am very sorry. I cannot adequately express my sorrow.
4.   We have been deceived. That is the truth.
5.   This is the school. I was taught there.
6.   You put it somewhere. Show me the place.
7.   The theft was committed last night. The man has been caught.
8.   You are not keeping your good health lately. Can you tell me the reason?
9.   His mother must be very tired. She had no sleep last night.
10. I will get ready. Do not go till then.
11. It was very hot last night. I could not sleep.
12. You have tears. Prepare to shed them now.
13. The lion is stronger. The fox is weaker.
14. He is being victimized. He still keeps a level head.
15. He saw me. He ran away then.

EXERCISE 2

Join the following sentences to make one complete sentence without using 'and', 'but' or 'so'

1.   He may slay me. I will trust him .
2.   He is not an idler. He is not a gambler.
3.   Ali is guilty. Hari is guilty no less .
4.   He is mad. He feigns madness.
5.   He was found guilty. He was hanged
6.   He is not a liar. He is not a coward .
7.   I have no food. I have no money .
8.   Do your work properly. Leave my service .
9.   Give him some water to drink. He will die of thirst.
10. You must work hard. You will fail in the examination .

EXERCISE 3

Join the following sentences to make one complete sentence without using 'and', 'but' or 'so'

1.   He does not know anything. He pretends ignorance .
2.   Ravi and Rani were lovers. Their parents hated each other
3.   Forgive us . We forgive our enemies .
4.   The new teacher is young. He is good looking .

5. He refused to believe the beggar .He had a frown on his face .
6. He has failed many times. He still hopes to succeed .
7. I speak the truth. I am not afraid of it.
8. He has five children. He must provide for them .
9. He is going to Paris, He will start business there .
10. Health is very important. It must not be neglected .

EXERCISE 4

Do as directed.

1. He works hard. His aim is to gets a scholarship. (Use that)
2. Honesty is the best policy. Have you never heard it. (Use that)
3. He may betray me. I will trust him. (Use though)
4. You snore loudly. I cannot sleep. (Use since)
5. He is short tempered. I like him all the same. (Begin Inspite)
6. You must pass the exams. Your future depend on it. (Use since)
7. The man is a crook . We met him in the market. (Use whom)
8. Gandhi ji was a leader. He was also a great philosopher. (Use besides)
9. You will succeed. You must work hard. (Use unless)
10. My friend is not a judge. He is not a lawyer. (Use neither)

ANSWER

EXERCISE 1

1. I am sure that he is wrong.
2. I did not hear what he said.
3. I cannot adequately express how sorry I am.
4. That we have been deceived is the truth.
5. This is the school where I was taught.
6. Show me the place where you put it.
7. The man who committed the theft last night has been caught.
8. Can you tell me the reason why you are not keeping good health lately.
9. His mother must be tired as she had no sleep last night.
10. Do not go till I get ready.
11. As it was very hot last night I could not sleep.
12. If you have tears prepare to shed them now.
13. The lion is stronger than the fox is.
14. Though he is being victimized, he keeps a level head.
15. When he saw me, he ran away.

EXERCISE 2

1. He may slay me yet I will trust him .
2. He is neither an idler nor a gambler .

3.   Hari no less than Ali is guilty.
4.   Either he is mad or he feigns madness
5.   He was found guilty. Therefore he was hanged
6.   He is neither a liar nor a coward
7.   I have neither food .nor money
8.   Either you work properly or .leave my service.
9.   Give him some water to drink else h e will die of thirst
10.   You must work hard otherwise you will fail in the examination.

EXERCISE 3

1.   Either he is pretending ignorance or he does not know anything,
2.   The parents of Ravi and Rani who were lovers hated each other.
3.   Forgive us as we forgive our enemies .
4.   Besides being young the new teacher .is good looking.
5.   The frown on his face showed that he refused to believe the beggar.
6.   In spite of many failures he still hopes to succeed.
7.   I am not afraid to speak the truth.
8.   He has five children to provide for .
9.   He is going to Paris to start business there .
10.   Health is very important to be   neglected.

EXERCISE 4

1.   He works hard so that he gets a scholarship.
2.   Have you never heard that honesty is the best policy .
3.   Though he may betray me I will trust him.
4.   Since you snore loudly, I cannot sleep
5.   Inspite of the fact that he is short tempered , I like him.
6.   Since your future depends on it, you must pass the exams.
7.   The man whom we met in the market is a crook.
8.   Besides being a leader Gandhi ji was also a great philosopher.
9.   Unless you work hard you will not succeed.
10.   My friend is neither a judge nor a lawyer.

TRANSFORMATION OF SENTENCES 1

The transformation of a sentence is the conversion of the sentence from one grammatical form to
another without changing its meaning. It provides a variety to our expression and makes the sentence more varied and interesting. This can be done as follows
1) In Sentence Containing The Adverb 'too'
    The news is too good to be true.

The news is so good that it cannot be true.

It is never too late to mend .

It is never so late that one cannot mend.

(2) Interchange The Degree Of Comparison.

By changing the degree of comparison of an adjective or an adverb in a sentence without changing its meaning.

Positive Degree :-	No other metal is as *useful* as iron.
Comparative Degree :-	Iron is *more useful* than any other metal.
Superlative degree :-	Iron is the *most useful* of all metals.
Positive Degree:-	Swati is not so *cleaver* as some other girls of her class.
Comparative Degree:-	Some girls of the class are *cleverer* than Swati.
Superlative Degree:-	Swati is not one of the *cleverest* girls in the class.

(3) Interchange Of Voice From Active To Passive And Vice Versa.

Active Voice :-	Brutus stabbed Caesar
Passive Voice :-	Caesar was stabbed by Brutus.
Active Voice :-	One should keep one's promise.
Passive Voice :-	Promises should be kept.
Active Voice :-	I shall be obliged to go.
Passive Voice :-	Circumstance will oblige me to go.

(4) Interchanging Affirmative Sentences Into Negative Sentences And Vice Versa.

Affirmative :-	He is greater than me.
Negative :-	I am not so great as him.
Affirmative :-	I was doubtful whether it was you .
Negative :-	I was not sure that it was you.
Affirmative :-	He is the cleverest boy in the class.
Negative :-	No other boy in the class is as cleaver as he.

(5) Interchanging Interrogative Sentences To Affirmative Sentences And Vice Versa.

Interrogative :-	Why waste time in listening.
Assertive ;-	It is foolish to waste time in listening.
Interrogative :-	Can anyone bear such an insult.
Assertive ;-	No one can bear such an insult.
Interrogative :-	Who does not love his country ?
Assertive ;-	Everyone loves his country.

(6) Interchanging Exclamatory Sentence To Assertive And Vice Versa.

Exclamatory :-	If only I was young again!
Assertive :-	I wish I was young again.
Exclamatory :-	Alas ! poor is dead.
Assertive :-	It is very sad that poor Harish is dead.
Exclamatory :-	What would I not give to see you happy.
Assertive :-	I would give anything to see you happy.

(7) Interchanging One Part Of Speech To Another.

He fought bravely

He put up a brave fight.

He showed generosity even to his enemies.

He was generous even to his enemies.

EXERCISE 1

1. He speaks too fast to be understood. (Begin He speaks so fast.....)
2. My heart is too full for words. (Begin My heart is.......)
3. The mangoes are so costly that you cannot buy them. (Use too)
4. Akbar was one of the greatest kings. (Use greater)
5. Do not insult the weak.(Begin Let ....)
6. Only a millionaire can afford such extravaganza. (Begin None.......)
7. Everybody will admit that he did his best. (Begin Nobody.........)
8. Where there is smoke there is fire (Begin There is..........)
9. Ah, what a sight was there! (End ....sight)
10. He was dismissed for negligence. (Use negligent)

ANSWER

1. He speaks so fast that he cannot be understood.
2. My heart is so full that I cannot express my feelings.
3. The mangoes are too costly for you to buy.
4. Akbar was greater than most other kings.
5. Let not the weak be insulted.
6. None but a millionaire can afford such extravaganza
7. Nobody will deny that he did his best.
8. There is no smoke without fire.
9. There was a wonderful sight.
10. Being negligent, he was dismissed.

TRANSFORMATION OF SENTENCES 2

1. Conversion Of Simple Sentences To Compound (Double) Sentences by enlarging a word or a phrase into a coordinate clause e.g..

Simple :-   The teacher punished the boy for indiscipline.

Compound :-   The boy was undisciplined and so the teacher punished him.

Simple :-   In spite of his riches ,he is unhappy

Compound : -   He is very rich but still he is unhappy.

2. Conversion Of Compound (Double) Sentences To Simple Sentences by substituting a Participle for a Finite Verb

Compound :-   He finished his work and went to bed.

Simple : -   Having finished his work he went to bed.

By substituting a Preposition for a Clause.

Compound : -   You must hurry up or you will miss the bus.

Simple :-   You must hurry up so as not to miss the bus.

3. Conversion Of Simple Sentence To Complex Sentence by expanding a word or a phrase into a subordinate clause, which may be a Noun, Adjective or Adverb clause e.g.

Simple :-   He confessed his crime.

Complex :-   He confessed *that he was guilty.*

Simple :-   His silence proves his guilt.

Complex :-   The fact *that he is silent* proves his guilt.

Simple :-   On the arrival of the train the bus will leave.

Complex :-   The bus will leave *as soon as the train arrives.*

4. Conversion Of Complex Sentence To Simple Sentence by changing the Noun, Adjective or Adverb clause as given below.

Changing Noun Clause

Complex :-   Tell me where you live.

Simple :-   Tell me your *address*

Complex :-   He said *that he was innocent*

Simple :- He declared his *innocence.*

Changing Adjective Clause.

Complex :-   Time *which is once* lost is lost forever.

Simple :- Time *once* lost is lost forever.

Complex:-   He died in the village *where he was born.*

Simple :-   He died in his *native* village .

Changing Adverb Clause

Complex :-   He was *so tired that he could* not stand

Simple :- He was *too tired* to stand .

Complex :-   You have succeeded *better than you hoped.*

Simple :- You have succeeded *beyond your hopes.*

5. Conversion Of Compound Sentence To Complex Sentence by changing one of the coordinate clauses .

Compound :-   Waste not , want not.

Complex :-   If you do not waste , you will not want.

Compound :-   Do as I tell you , or you will be punished.

Complex :-   Unless you do as I tell you, you will be punished.

 6. Conversion Of Complex Sentence To Compound Sentence by changing the subordinate clause to a coordinate clause.

Complex :-   We can prove that the Earth is round.

Compound :-   The Earth is round and we can prove it.

Complex :-   If you do not work hard you will not pass.

Compound :-   You must work hard or you will not pass.

EXERCISE

1. Being occupied with important matters, he had no time to see us. (Begin He was)
2. In the event of such a thing happening, I shall resign. (Begin Let.......)
3. He neither returned the gods nor paid the bill. (Begin Besides.......)
4. He escaped several times but was finally caught. (Begin In spite.....)
5. With your permission I will go away. (Begin If.......)
6. Industry will keep you from want. (Begin If.......)
7. I convinced him of his mistake. (Use mistaken)
8. You or I must go away. (Begin If.........)
9. It is surprising that he did not succeed. (Begin He ....)
10. I know what you told him. (Begin You told ....)
11. If I am right you must be wrong. (Begin Either ....)
12. But for the accident , they should have had a good picnic. (Begin If. .)
13. Nobody will deny that he is honest. (Begin Everyone ....)
14. Only a fool would believe you. (Use nobody)
15. We sow so that we may reap. (End ....sow)

ANSWER

1. He was occupied with important matters, and therefore had no time to see us.
2. Let such a thing happen and then I shall resign.
3. Besides not returning the goods, he did not pay the bill.
4. In spite of his escaping several times he was finally caught.
5. If you permit me I will go away.
6. If you are industrious you will be kept from want.
7. I convinced him that he was mistaken.
8. If you do not go away, I must.
9. He did not succeed, and this is surprising.
10. You told him something, and I know it.
11. Either I am right, or you are.
12. If the accident had not happened they would have had a good picnic.
13. Everyone will agree that he is honest.
14. Nobody but a fool would believe you.
15. We desire to reap therefore we sow.

MISCELLANEOUS EXERCISES

Rewrite the following sentences according to the instructions given after each. Make other changes that may be necessary but do not change the meaning of each sentence

EXERCISE 1

1. He is too old to learn things. (Replace too with so)
2. I will never again make the mistake of opening the door to a stranger
    (Begin   Never again .....)

3. I am certain you have made a mistake. (Begin   You have ......)
4. I have found the book I had lost. (Begin   I had lost ....)
5. As Caesar loved me, I weep for him. (Begin   Caesar loved ....)
6. As he was ambitious I killed him. (Begin He was ambitious ....)
7. I could answer if I chose. (Begin   I can answer ....)
8. Unless we run we shall miss the bus.(Begin We must run   ....)
9. If I am right you must be wrong. (Begin   Either ....)
10. A man like him should succeed. (Begin   Such a man ....)

EXERCISE 2

1. While there is life there is hope. (Begin Life and ....)
2. If I make a promise I keep it . (Begin   I make .....)
3. As you sow ,so you will reap . (Begin You will ....)
4. To escape punishment you must confess your fault. (Begin Either you confess ....)
5. I am not so rich as he. (Begin   He is ....)
6. He is the richest man in the city. (Begin   No one ....)
7. Blood is thicker than water. (Begin   Is not ....)
8. This tree is too high for me to climb. (Replace too with so)
9. This plane flew straight from Banglore to Delhi. (Rewrite using flight.)
10. This is the greatest discovery that the world has ever known. (Begin Never has.........)

EXERCISE 3

1. It is better to starve than beg. (Rewrite using starving)
2. Sachin is one of the best players of the team. (Use better)
3. Waste not, want not. (Begin If you do ....)
4. One should keep one's promise. (Begin Promises ......)
5. A senseless man repeats his mistake. (Rewrite using sensible)
6. Unfortunately he failed in the first attempt. (Use succeed)
7. Business without adequate investment is of no use. (Begin No business....)
8. Running is the healthiest exercise. (Begin No other ......)
9. He was happy to leave the house. (Rewrite using happily)
10. This should be of the greatest value to mankind.(Begin Nothing ....)

ANSWERS TO MISCELLANEOUS EXERCISES

EXERCISE 1

1. He is so old that he cannot learn things.
2. Never again will I ever make the mistake of opening the door to a stranger.
3. You have made a mistake and of this I am certain.
4. I had lost the book ,but I have found it .
5. Caesar loved me and so I weep for him.

6. He was ambitious and therefore I killed him.
7. I can answer, but I don't chose to.
8. We must run or we shall miss the bus.
9. Either I am right or you are.
10. Such a man as he should succeed.

EXERCISE 2

1. Life and hope are inseparable.
2. I make a promise only to keep it.
3. You will but reap the fruits of your sowing.
4. Either you confess your fault or you will be punished.
5. He is richer than I.
6. No one in the city is as rich as he.
7. Is not blood thicker than water.
8. This tree is so high that I cannot climb it .
9. This flight is straight from Banglore to Delhi.
10. Never has the world known a greater discovery .

EXERCISE 3

1. Starving is better than begging.
2. Only a few players of our team are better than Sachin,
3. If you do not want, do not waste.
4. Promises should be kept.
5. A sensible man never repeats his mistake.
6. Unfortunately he did not succeed in the first attempt.
7. No business can succeed without adequate investment .
8. No other exercise is as healthy as running.
9. He left the house happily.
10. Nothing should be of such great value as this to mankind.

ADJECTIVE

An adjective describes the person place or object which are noun or a pronoun refers to. It describes the quality, quantity, size and origin of the person, place or object.

Adjectives change in form to show comparisons are called degree of comparison and are used when more than two things are compared. They are

1. Positive degree being the simplest form of comparison.
2. Comparative degree is the higher degree of quality
3. Superlative degree is the highest degree of quality

Formation Of Comparative And Superlative Degree Of Comparisons. The positive degree can be changed to comparative and superlative degree as follows:

1. By adding 'er' for comparative and 'est' for superlative

Positive	Comparative	Superlative
Sweet	Sweeter	Sweetest
Similarly for small, Tall, Kind. Bold, Claver, Kind, Young, Great		

2. When positive degree ends in 'e' by adding 'r' and 'st'

Positive	Comparative	Superlative
Brave	Braver	Bravest
Similarly for fine, white, large, able, noble, wise		

3. When positive ends in 'y' preceded by an consonant then 'y' is changed to 'i' before adding 'er' or 'est'.

Positive	Comparative	Superlative
Happy	Happier	Happiest
Similarly for easy, heavy, merry, wealthy.		

4. When the positive is of one syllable ending in a single consonant preceed by a short vowel the consonant is doubled before adding 'er' and 'est'.

Positive	Comparative	Superlative
Big	Bigger	Biggest
Similarly for red, hot, thin, sad, fat.		

5. When positive is of more than two syllables then comparative and superlative are form by adding more and most to the positive.

Positive	Comparative	Superlative
Beautiful	More beautiful	Most beautiful
Similarly for difficult, industrious, courageous, useful, hopeless, boring, modern, recent, foolish, famous, Certain etc.		

6. Some adjectives take either 'er' , 'est' or 'more' and 'most'. These are Polite, simple, feeble, gentle, nervous, cruel, common, handsome, pleasant, stupid etc.

7. There are still other adjectives which change form by irregular comparisons like

Positive	Comparative	Superlative
Good	better	Best
Bad/ evil	Worse	Worst
Little	Less/ Lesser	Least
Much/Many	More	Most
Late	Later	Latest / last
Far	Farther	Farthest
In	Inner	Inmost / Inner most
Up	Upper	Upper most / up most

Correct Use Of Adjectives

1. **Later or latest** :- refers to time. Later being the opposite of earlier eg.

    (a)   Ram came to the class later than me.

    (b)   Tell me the latest news.

2. **Latter and last**:- refers to position or order. Latter is the opposite of former e.g..

    (a)   The latter part of the movie was boring.

    (b)   He came last in the race.

3. **Elder and eldest** :-used only for persons not animals or thing, and are confined to the members of the same family e.g.

    (a)   Ram is my elder brother.

    (b)   Hari is my eldest son.

4. **Older and Oldest** :-used for persons and things. Older is followed by than e.g.

    (a)   He is older than I am.

    (b)   This is the oldest tree in our village.

5. **Farther and further**:- Farther means more distance while further means additional e.g.

    (a)   His house is at the farther end of the street.

    (b)   She received no further reply

6. **Nearest and Next**:- nearest means the shortest distance away while next refers to the sequence of things coming one after the another. E.g.

    (a)   Where is the nearest bank?

    (b)   My friend lives in the next house.

7. **Neither and Either**:- refers to two persons or things. Sometimes means both of the two things are not involved e.g.

    (a) Nobody can persuade either friends to quarrel.

    (b) Neither answer is correct.

8. Each and every Each refers to individual members of the group while every is used when talking about all of them e.g.

    Each visitor was garlanded.

    Every village in our state is electrified.

EXERCISE

Write the correct words in the blanks-

1. The majority of the members accepted the _____ proposal (latter, later).
2. Is there no _____ news than last week? (latter, later)
3. The chairman accepted the _____ proposal. (latter, later)
4. I have an _____ sister. (elder. older)
5. She is the _____ of the two sisters. (elder. older)
6. He is the _____ member of the house (Oldest, eldest)
7. Of the two brothers Ram is the. (Oldest, eldest)
8. I cannot walk any _____. (farther, further)
9. No _____ reason is given. (farther, further)
10. Did you hear the _____ news. (latest , last)
11. Today is the _____ day of the school. (latest , last)
12. His house is _____ to mine. (next, nearest)
13. The _____ police station is two km away. (next, nearest)
14. _____ boy is supposed to show his homework. (each, every)
15. They came here _____ day. (each, every)

ANSWER

1. latter 2. later 3. latter 4. elder 5. older 6. oldest 7. eldest 8. further 9. farther 10. latest 11. last 12. next 13. nearest 14. Each 15. every

Transformation Of Sentences By Changing The Degree Of Comparison Of The Adjective
The following should be noted while transforming sentences
1. When comparing two things the comparative degree of adjective is used
    He is taller of the two brothers .
2. When two objects are compared by a comparative degree of adjective it is followed by 'than'. The thing that is compared, must be excluded from the class of things with which it is compared, by using the word 'other'
    Iron is more useful than any other metal. and not
    Iron is more useful than any metal (for iron is itself a metal)
    Shakespeare is greater than any other author.
3. When comparison is made by using a superlative degree, the thing or class of thing must be included in the comparison. eg
    Ganga is the holiest of all rivers (not all other rivers)

She is the cleverest of all pupils.(not all other pupils)

4. The comparative degree is always followed by 'than' but comparatives ending in 'or' are followed by the preposition 'to' instead of 'than' eg

He is *junior to* all his colleagues.

Hari is *inferior to* Ram in intelligence.

Similarly for other words like superior ,prior, anterior, posterior, senior etc

5. The second form of comparison must correspond in construction with the first. eg

The population of UP is greater than that of any other state in India.   and not

The population of UP is greater than any other state in India

(for what is compared is the population and not the state)

Transformation Of Sentences

By changing the degree of comparison of an adjective without changing the meaning of the sentence.

Positive:-   He is as wise as Solomon.

Comparative :-   Solomon was not wiser than he is .

Positive:-   Birds do not fly as fast as the aeroplane .

Comparative :-   The aeroplane flies faster than birds .

Positive:-   No other metal is as costly as gold

Comparative:-   No other metal is   costlier than gold

Superlative:-   Gold is the costliest of all metals.

Positive:-   Very few cities in India are as big as Mumbai.

Comparative:-   Mumbai is bigger than most other cities in India

Superlative:-   Mumbai is one of the biggest cities in India.

EXERCISE

Rewrite the sentences according to the instruction given after each .Make other changes that may be necessary, but do not change the meaning of the sentence.

1. Very few doctors in the hospital are as dedicated as he is.(Begin He is ..)
2. Silver is more plentiful than gold. (Begin Gold is….)
3. Akbar was one of the greatest of Indian Kings. (Begin Very few…)
4. The pen is mightier than the sword. (Begin The sword is…..)
5. A wise enemy is better than a foolish friend. (Begin A foolish friend…..)
6. I get up earlier than she does .(End ….as I do)
7. Lead is heaviest of all metals (Use heavy)
8. He is not the best boy in the class . (Begin He is……)
9. I know him quite as well as you do . (Begin You do not …)
10. Very few cities are as large as Delhi. (Begin Delhi is bigger….)

ANSWER

1. He is the most dedicated doctor in the hospital.
2. Gold is less plentiful than silver.

3. Very few Indian Kings were as great as Akbar.
4. The sword is not as mighty as the pen.
5. A foolish friend is not so good as a wise enemy.
6. She does not get up earlier as I do.
7. No other metal is as heavy as lead.
8. He is not better than most other boys in the class.
9. You do not know him better than I do.
10. Delhi is bigger than most other cities

CONDITIONAL SENTENCES

Conditional sentences or suppositions are often expressed by conditional clauses. These are of three types-

Type I Probable/likely condition.

This is used to describe condition which may or may not be fulfilled.

If clause	Main clause
Likely condition to be satisfied All present tense used	Likely outcome Use will/shall or will be/shall be

Few example   in all Present Tense

	If clause	Main clause
Simple present :-	If you work hard	you will succeed
Present continuous:-	If you are hard working	you will succeed
Present perfect:-	If you work hard	you will be successful
Present perfect continuous:-	If you have been working all day	you will need rest

In all the above cases, if the condition in the conditional clause takes place, the action stated in the main clause will take place. Thus it relates to a future event.

Exceptions to the above

1. If there is an **order or instruction** in the main clause, we use the Imperative Tense in place of Future Tense e.g.

    If you don't want to be punished, do it at once.

    If you need any help, come to me.

2. If it expresses a universal truth, a fact, or a habitual action, then the tense in both the clauses is the same e.g.

    If you heat water, it boils.

    If we work hard, we succeed.

    Note: 'If' can be replaced by 'when' in the above sentences.

    Use of 'when'

    If we are sure of a particular event to happen, we use 'when'. e.g.

    When I go there, I'll take your letter with me.

Type II Improbable/unlikely/imaginary conditions

If clause	Main clause
Condition is hypothetical or imaginary	unlikely to be fulfilled
Simple Past tense used	Use would/should
was/were	would be/ should be

In Type II conditional sentences, the 'if' clause is followed by a past tense, hence we use 'was' or 'were'. The main clause is normally formed with 'would'. However 'should' can be used instead of would after 'I' and 'we'.

>If he was taller, he would become a soldier.

Use of were/was :- 'were' is more formal and used preferably in purely imaginary statements e.g.

>If I were a bird, I would fly.

Use 'were to' emphasise the suppositional nature of the condition   e.g.

>If I were to become a Minister, I would serve the public honestly.

Use of could, might and ought in the main clause shows ability, possibility, and duty e.g.

>If she was here, she could help us (shows ability).

>If she was here she might help us (shows possibility).

>If she was here she ought to/should help us (shows duty).

Type III   Impossible condition

If clause	Main clause
Impossible condition	Condition cannot be fulfilled
Past Perfect tense had /had been	Use would/should/ should have been

Here the verb in the 'If' clause is in Past Perfect Tense, as the time is past. The verb in main clause is in perfect conditional, as the condition cannot be fulfilled, for the action in the 'if' clause did not take place. e.g.

>If you had worked hard, you would have passed.

>If we had been ill, we would not have come.

>If I had won the match, I would have been happy.

Use of 'would be', 'should be' in main clause.

When there is a past action in the 'if' clause, and   present action in the main clause, we use past perfect tense in 'if' clause, and would be /should be in main clause e.g.

>If I had being driving slowly, I *would be* hale and hearty now.

Replacing' if ' by 'unless', 'but for', 'provided', 'suppose'

1.   Replacing by 'Unless'

>If + Negative verb = Unless + Affirmative verb eg

>If he doesn't come soon, he will repent.

Unless he comes soon, he will repent.

If he does not apologise, he will be punished.

Unless he apologises, he will be punished.

2.   Replacing by 'But for'

But for = if it were not for / if it had not been for. e.g.

If there was no rain, we would have come earlier.

But for the rain, we would have come earlier.

3.   Replacing by 'Otherwise'

If you don't work hard, you won't succeed.

Work hard *otherwise* you won't succeed.

4.   Replacing with 'provided'. Provided used mainly with permission.

If you finish your work today, you can have leave tomorrow.

   Provided you finish your work today, you can have leave tomorrow.

5.   Replacing with suppose/supposing = what if

   If we missed the bus, what shall we do?

Suppose we missed the bus, what shall we do?

Inverted variations.

These occur in all the three conditional types of sentences when 'if' is left out and 'should', 'were' and 'had' are placed before the subject. eg

   If he were to hear of this, he would be happy.

Type I   Should he hear of this, he would be happy.

Type II   Were he to hear of this, he would be happy.

Type 111 Had I won the match , I would have been happy

EXERCISE

1.   If you are honest, people _____ (vote)for you.
2.   If I had done my homework ,I _____(punish)by the teacher .
3.   If you_____(go) out in the rain you might have caught cold.
4.   He might have succeeded if he _____ (accept) our help.
5.   If he does not hurry he won't catch the train.(Begin Unless…..)
6.   If it were not for his help ,I would have died. (Begin But for….)
7.   If I _____ (know) that you were coming ,I would have stayed home.
8.   If you _____(will/ would) invite her she will come .
9.   If Lata were to sing I _____ (would / will) come
10. If I had asked you ,you _____ come

ANSWER

1.   If you are honest, people <u>will vote</u> for you.
2.   If I had done my homework ,I <u>would not have been punished</u> by the teacher ..

3. If you <u>had gone</u>   out in the rain you might have caught cold.
4. He might have succeeded if he <u>had accepted</u>   our help.
5. *Unless* he hurries he won't catch the train
6. *But for* his help, I would have died.
7. If I <u>had known</u> that you were coming ,I would have stayed home .
8. If you   <u>would</u> invite   her she will come.
9. If Lata were to sing I <u>would</u> come
10. If I had asked you ,you <u>would have come</u>.

PREPOSITION

What is a preposition?

A preposition is a word placed before a Noun or a pronoun to show in what relation the person or thing denoted by it stands in regard to some thing . Liberally meaning 'Placed before .'

Thus we see that a preposition joins a noun to another noun, pronoun or an adjective or to a verb example :-

Rita is fond of *chocolates.*

Sometimes the preposition may be placed after *its* object.

The policeman ran *quickly* toward the car.

The thief succeeded in *escaping*

Omission of Preposition.

Preposition omitted	Before noun indicating place or time	We did it last month (omit in) Wait a minute (omit for) I cannot walk a yard (omit for)

Preposition at the end

When object of preposition is that	Here is the document that you asked for.
When the object is an interrogative pronoun	What are you looking for? (or at)
That is the boy I was speaking of ?	
What are you thinking of?	

Kinds of preposition
Simple preposition

on	up	from	since	after
till	with	off	by	for
to	at	out	over	off
to	through	under	during	

Compound Prepositions

ahead	until	among	amidst	outside
along	inside	above	upon	without
away	underneath	within	throughout	beneath
between	before	around	amongst	unto
into	below	about	beyond	
~~across~~				

EXERCISE 1

Fill in the blanks with an appropriate word:-

1. _____ a Ford he has a Maruti car

2. He despaired _____ success.

3. He is true _____ his King

4. He is very different _____ his brother .

5. He inspires respect _____ his friends

6. Dogs have antipathy _____ cats

7. One is sure _____ what one sees

8. Though he was not well he calmly went _____ his business.

9. While cleaning his gun it went _____ killing his friend.

10. This plan will remain a secret _____ you and me

EXERCISE 2

Fill in the blanks with an appropriate word:-

1. No guests are allowed _____ the night.

2. He was _____ himself with anger when his sister teased him

3. When I go to my hometown I always look _____ my childhood friends.

4. If you are ever in the city you are welcome to look _____ at my office.

5. Her plan differs _____ mine in many ways

6. She differs _____ me in every matter that comes up for discussion.

7. He promised to look _____ his uncle went he went to England.

8. He promised to look _____ his old parents when he went to stay with them.

9. If you look _____ the telescope distant stars appear very near.

10. The manager promised to look _____ their complaint.

EXERCISE 3

Fill in the blanks with an appropriate word:-

1. The minister agreed _____ the proposal of ensuring strict enforcement of law.

2. The neighbors complained _____ his unruly behaviour

3. He felt sad on parting _____ his friend

4.   He began to listen ——————— sounds indicating the presence of some animal.

5.   The cottage industry is threatened ——————— ruin because of the rapid industrialisation .

6.   His enemy threatened ———ruin him.

7.   We looked forward ——————— the pleasure of his company soon.

8.   Despite being a better team we won ——————— them in the match.

9.   It was a difficult task getting permission to go on an excursion, but Ram finally won ——————— his parents

10.   My parents frown ——————— the type of music I usually hear.

ANSWERS

EXERCISE 1

1. Besides 2. of 3. to 4. from 5. in 6. to 7. of 8. about 9. off 10. between

EXERCISE 2

1. during 2. with 3. for 4. in 5. from 6. with 7. up 8. after 9. through 10. into

EXERCISE 3

1. to 2. about 3. from 4. for 5. with 6. to 7. to 8. against 9. over 10. on

Listening (Aural) and Speaking (Oral) Skills.

LISTENING SKILLS

What does it mean to really listen? How is it different to hearing?

Listening and hearing are not the same. Hearing is the first stage of listening. Hearing occurs when our ears pick up sound waves that are then transported to the brain. This stage is our sense of hearing which need not be an active process.

Listening on the other hand is an active communication process. To really listen we must be an active participant in the communication process. In active listening, the meaning and evaluation of a message must take place before a listener can respond to the speaker. Therefore, the listener is also actively working while the speaker is talking. This is possible because the speed of our thought is two to three times faster than the speed of speech.

Real listening is an active process that has three basic steps.

1. **Hearing what is being said :** Hearing means just listening enough to catch what the speaker is saying. For example, you were listening to a report on tigers, and the speaker mentioned that no two tigers are alike. If you can repeat the fact, then you have heard what has been said.

2. **Understanding what is being said :** This happens when you take what you have heard and understand it in your own way. Let's go back to that report on tigers. When you hear that no two tigers are alike. You might think, "Maybe this means that the pattern of stripes is different for each tiger."

3. **Judging what is being said :** Having understood what the speaker has said, think whether it makes sense. Do you believe what you have heard? You might think, "How could the stripes be different for every tiger? But then the fingerprints of every person is different. Well this seems believable."

It is here that real active listening has taken place.

Benefits of being an active listener.

Being an active listener pays rich dividends in your academic life.

* It enables you to understand and grasp what is being taught in school and college,.
* You are able to understand and respond to questions in class.
* It makes you learn more about people and enlarge your circle of friends.
* It improves your communication skills, thereby avoiding misunderstanding or confusion.
* If you listen to others you earn their respect. They could be your parents, teachers or your peers.

How to improve our listening skills?

Some people are good listeners while others are not. Each of us are blessed with the same faculties, However some use it while others don't. This skill like any other can be cultivated by observing a few fundamental rules and their constant practice.

FUNDAMENTAL RULES FOR BEING A GOOD LISTENER.

* **Quieting the mind :** To be a good listener you have to concentrate on the message, by eliminating internal and external distractions.

  Examples of external distraction:

  Classmates arriving late, or shuffling of papers by others.

Noise from outside classroom

Weather being too hot or cold.

Examples of internal distraction:

Concern over argument with friend from the night before

Worry about project / homework.

Physiological needs like hunger, thirst etc.

- **Give your full attention to the speaker:** Don't look out of the window or at what else is going on in the room.
- **Make sure your mind is focused :** It can be easy to let your mind wander if you think you know what the person is going to say next, but you might be wrong! If you feel your mind wandering, change the position of your body and try to concentrate on the speaker's words.
- **Listen for main ideas.:** The main ideas are the most important points the speaker wants to get across. Jot them down in your own words.
- **Maintain eye contact with the instructor.** You may look down to write your notes, but maintaining proper eye contact with the speaker keeps you focused and involved in the lecture.
- **Focus on the content, not delivery.** Do not be distracted by the accent, tone or mannerism of the speaker, focus your mind on what is being said.
- **Avoid emotional involvement.** When you are too emotionally involved in listening, you tend to hear what you want to hear- not what is actually being said. Try to remain objective and open-minded.
- **Hear the speaker out.**

Don't jump to conclusions.

Don't stop listening because of an emotional response to a word or topic.

Don't give up because the subject is difficult.

- **Be alert for other verbal and nonverbal cues.**

Change in the tone of voice .

Body language of the speaker..

- **Treat listening as a challenging mental task.** Listening to an academic lecture is not a passive act. You need to concentrate on what is said, so that you can process the information into your notes.
- **Stay active by asking mental questions.** Active listening keeps you on your toes. You can ask yourself What key point is the speaker making? How does this fit with what I know?

SPECIMEN PAPER FOR LISTENING SKILLS IN ENGLISH LANGUAGE

Paper 1   Duration 30 minutes

Name _____

Class _____

Roll No _____

Note for the candidate

A passage will be read aloud by the examiner twice. During the reading you may make brief notes on the rough paper you have bee given.

At the end of the second reading you will answer the questions in ink by ticking or encircling the appropriate answer.

The duration of assessment is 30 minutes which includes the time taken for the two readings and answering the questions.

The intended marks for the questions are given in brackets.

SPECIMEN PASSAGES FOR LISTENING SKILLS

Few passages for reading are given below. The examiner shall read out the passage twice, the first time at normal speed and the second time at a slower speed. During the reading of the passage the candidate can take brief notes. At the end of the second reading, the candidate has to tick mark or circle the most appropriate answer from the multiple choice options given at a, b, and c

The Questions and the suggested answers are given after the passages

PASSAGES FOR READING

1. TSUNAMI

Tsunami is a Japanese word with the English translation 'harbour wave' represented by two characters, the first character 'tsu' means harbour, while the second character 'nami' means wave. In the past Tsunami were referred to as ' tidal waves' by the general public and as 'seismic waves' by the scientific community. The term tidal wave is a misnomer, although tsunami's impacts upon the coastline is dependent upon the tidal level at the time the tsunami strikes, tsunami are unrelated to the tides. Tides result from the imbalanced extraterrestrial gravitational influences of the moon, sun and other planets .The term 'seismic sea wave' is also misleading. 'Seismic' implies an earthquake related generation mechanism, but a tsunami can also be caused by a non-seismic event such as a landslide or a meteorite impact.

Tsunami can be generated when the sea floor abruptly deforms and vertically displaces the overlying water Tectonic earthquakes are a particular kind of earthquakes that are associated with the earth's crustal deformation, when these earthquakes occur beneath the sea, the water above the deformed area is displaced from its equilibrium position. Waves are formed as the displaced water mass, which acts under the influence of gravity, attempts to regain its equilibrium. When large areas of sea floor elevate or subside, a tsunami can be created. Large vertical movements of the earth's crust can occur at plate boundaries. Plates interact along these boundaries called faults.

A tsunami can be generated by any disturbance that displaces a large water mass from its equilibrium position. In the case of earthquake related tsunami the water column is disturbed by the uplift or subsidence of the sea floor. Submarine landslides which often accompany large earthquakes as well as collapse of volcanic edifices, can also disturb the overlying water column, as sediment and rock slump down slope and are distributed across the sea floor. Similarly a violent submarine volcanic eruption, can create an impulsive force that uplifts the water column and generates a tsunami. Conversely submarine landslides and cosmic body impacts disturb the water from above, as momentum from falling debris is transferred to the water into which the debris falls.

What happens to the tsunami as it approaches land? As the tsunami leaves the deep water of the open sea and travels to the shallow water near the coast, it transforms. A tsunami travels at a speed that is related to the water depth – hence as the water depth decreases the tsunami slows.

The tsunami's energy flux that is dependent on the wave speed and the wave height remains nearly constant. Consequently as the tsunami speed diminishes as it travels into the shallower water its height grows. Because of the shoaling effect, a tsunami imperceptible at sea, may grow to be several meters or more in height near the coast. When it finally reaches the coast, a tsunami may appear as a rapidly rising or falling tide, a series of breaking water, or even a bore.

2. HUMANOID ROBOT

The Honda Motors Corporation introduced a new version of its humanoid robot that can jog, find its way around obstacles and respond to human touch. Developers of the robot that looks like a child in astronaut suit and is named Asimo, say the new model is a significant advance over earlier versions and bring them closer to a bipedal machine that can move on its own, through homes and offices and interact naturally with human beings.

But despite the technological advances, Honda has not made much progress in just what the robot might be used for. " We want to develop something that is useful to people. We want to think more about how, as we get along." Said Takabonu ho a Managing Director and the head of the company's research and development division.

The robot 4 ft and 3 inches tall, demonstrated its form on Wednesday. It walked onto a wide stage and then after a few steps, drew its arms closer to its sides and lifted its knees high as it broke into a jog, hydraulic muscles whirring loudly.

Perfecting the running motion was a technological challenge, the robots developer said, because the rapid arm movement tended to throw the robot off balance. To counteract these forces engineers installed a new joint in the robot's hips.

Asimo also received new joints in its wrists and hand, to make it more adapt at picking up small objects, and one in the neck allowing it to tip its head to the side.

Androids like Asimo are becoming increasingly common in robot happy Japan. Honda introduced its first walking robot in 1996. Sony is making its humanoid robot and a robotic dog called Albo. Toyota unveiled its humanoid robot in March.

Honda executives have said that they envision an era when robots will work as aids for the elderly or perform dangerous tasks. Robot technology may also some day have application in auto assembly plants. But Honda concedes that the day when humanoid robots will be available in showrooms alongside Civic sedan is still a long way off.

Honda has been renting out earlier versions of its robots as guides in museums or to entertain at company events. For this the company charges a million yen a day.

The car manufacturer will not say how much it has invested and spent in developing the robots. Japanese press reports have put the figure in the tens of millions of dollars.

3. MOODS

Moods say experts are emotions that tend to become fixed, influencing one's outlook for hour's days or even weeks. That's great if your mood is a pleasant one, but a problem if you are sad, anxious, angry or simply lethargic.

Perhaps the best way to deal with such moods is to talk them out, sometimes though there is no one to listen. Modern pharmacology offers an abundance of tranquilizers, anti-depressant and anti- anxiety drugs. What people don't realize, however is that scientists have discovered the effectiveness of several non-drug approaches to pry you loose from an unwanted mood. These can be as good as prescription drugs and have added benefits of being non-toxic and non – addictive. So in moments of bad mood try one of these antidotes instead of rushing to the chemist. Of all self help techniques; aerobic exercises seem to be the most effective cure for a bad mood. Aerobic exercises such us running cycling or brisk walking, swimming or other repetitive activities, boot the heart beat rate, increasing circulation of blood and improve the body's utilization of oxygen. Just for 20 minutes, three to five times a week is just that you need.

"Colours are nutrients to the mind, as vitamins are to the body." Says Patricia, a New York colour psychologist. She suggests to keep away from red to diffuse irritability and anger. Avoid wearing colours that make you feel down- black or dark blue. Go for warm, bright and active colours that lighten your mood. Neutral colours such as soft shades of blue have a soothing, calming effect and alleviate anxiety and tension.

There is a reported basic link between food and mood. Carbohydrates eaten alone stimulate the brain's production of serotinin, responsible for making us feel calm and relaxed. It is a sort of comfort food with a tranquilizing. Eating protein tends to sustain alertness and mental energy. The best proteins are shellfish, chicken, etc.

A strong connection has been found between high caffeine intake, and increased depression, irritability and anxiety. People are often depressed when their thoughts are negative and distorted. If you avoid being critical of yourself and think positive thoughts, you're actually more likely to feel happy. It is important to lift oneself out of one's own self defeating moods and to take an interest in someone else.

4. DECISION–MAKING

Decision-making is a very vital part of our lives. This is because what we are today is largely a result of the decisions we take in the past. Similarly, whatever happens tomorrow, will be a result of the decisions we take in the present.

It is not possible to reverse the wrong decisions we have taken in the past, but it is possible to train ourselves into a good decision maker for the future. If we don't, we will end up doing what we have always done and thus get what we have always got. Philosopher Walter Kaufman called this Decidophobia.

All sort of decisions big or small, relevant or irreverent, conscious or unconscious, punctuate our lives. Sometimes, we don't even realize we are taking a decision. Those who avoid taking a decision, leave everything to chance and float about life with a 'what will be, will be ' attitude.

To enhance our decision-making, we must first of all gather as much information as possible about the issue, before we take our decision. We might be heading for a failure, if our decisions are based on half-baked information.

If you have set a guiding principle for your life, decision-making becomes a lot easier. For example, if you value integrity and honesty and consider them to be of vital importance, you will never waiver.

Sometimes decisions are very difficult to make, especially when the odds seem to be against us. In this case giving yourself a little time to decide wouldn't be a bad idea at all. Circumstances change with time and then it may be easier to see which action is more preferable to the others.

Being clear about you goal can facilitate decision-making. If we know exactly what we want to be or what we want to do in the next five years, or even ten, we will decide to undertake actions which will lead us to our goals. So outline you short and long term goals in black and white.

Action is vital consequence of decision-making. It is necessary follow-up. Only when we act, we will get a feedback of whether our decision has been correct or not, and then we can proceed in a more focused way. So it is essential to move from the world of thought to the arena of action.

5. MARTIN LUTHER KING

Martin Luther King, one of the greatest man to walk on this earth, started the defence force, with which the American Blacks got their right and gained freedom from the distressing racial discrimination.

Martin was born on January 15,1929. His family lived in the outskirts of Atlanta. The fact that he could not pray with White children, or that he had to offer a seat in the bus to a White, disturbed him. When he was eight year old his father a Baptist pastor, told the family a sad story. 'Bessie Smith, a great singer met with an accident . An ambulance rushed her to the nearest hospital, but she was not admitted because she was black. The ambulance took her from one hospital to another, but she could not find a place for herself because these hospitals were only for the Whites. She died for want of blood.' From that day, Martin Luther King dreamt of becoming a liberator of the Blacks.

King completed his studies at More House College, and then earned a doctor's degree in theology at Boston University. In 1935 King married Alabama Saprano Coretta Scott. That very year he became a pastor and preached his first sermon in the Baptist Church of Atlanta. As a young man, he was greatly impressed by Mahatma Gandhi's success in the political field and the power of Ahimsa. King decided to follow the path of non-violence and get millions of Black their due. He felt that the Blacks had immensely contributed towards the building of America, and there was no reason why they should not be treated with respect.

King drew national attention in 1956. Since the Blacks were not permitted to sit in the same buses as the Whites, he led a boycott of public buses in Montgomery. A year later, after many arrests and threats, the US Supreme Court gave a ruling that racial segregation of public transport was unlawful. The victory taught the Blacks the power of non-violence. After 1957 King began visiting various places to deliver lectures. Soon he became a powerful orator, drawing the attention of the people the world over.

King continued the fight, a peaceful fight, demanding the rights of the Blacks. In 1964 he was awarded the Noble Peace Prize. In 1967, King led many peaceful demonstrations against the Vietnam War and in 1968 he declared a Poor People's Campaign. On April 4, of that very year, while planning a demonstration of striking sanitation workers, he was shot dead by an assassin.

QUESTIONS ON PASSAGES FOR LISTENING SKILLS

Attempt answering these questions only after listening to the given passage twice.

Encircle the most appropriate answer

1. Tsunami

Q.1. Why is 'tidal wave' for a tsunami a misnomer?   (1)

    (*a*) Tidal wave impacts upon the coastline.

    (*b*) Tsunami results from imbalance extra terrestrial gravitational influence.

    (*c*) Tsunami are unrelated to the tides.

Q.2.   How are tides caused?   (1)

(*a*) Tides are caused from imbalance extra terrestrial gravitational influence of the moon, sun and other planets.

(*b*) Tides are caused by the earth's gravitational influence.

(*c*) The rotation of the earth on its axis causes tides.

Q.3.   Tsunami's are caused when :   (1)

(*a*) Large areas of the sea floor elevates or subsides because of an earthquake.

(*b*) Large areas of the sea floor elevates or subsides because of an earthquake, sub marine landslide or submarine volcanic eruption.

(*c*) The sea level abruptly deforms and vertically rises.

Q.4   What are Tectonic earthquakes?   (1)

(a) They are earthquakes only under the sea.

(*b*) Tectonic earthquakes are earthquakes that are associated with earth's crustal deformation.

(*c*) They are earthquakes only on the land.

Q.5   How are earthquakes caused ?   (1)

(*a*) Earthquakes are caused by vertical movements of the earth crust at the plate boundaries called faults.

(*b*) Earthquakes are caused by friction at the plate boundaries called faults.

(*c*) Earthquakes are caused by submarine volcanic eruptions.

Q.6.   What happens when a violent submarine volcanic eruption takes place?   (1)

(*a*) Tidal waves are formed.

(*b*) A tsunami can take place

(*c*) An earthquake can take place

Q.7   The speed of the tsunami :   (1)

(*a*) Increases as the water depth decreases

(*b*) Remains constant as the water depth decreases.

(*c*) Decreases as the water depth decreases.

Q.8.   The tsunami may grows to several meters in height because   (1)

(*a*) Its speed increases in shallow water and its height grows.

(*b*) As it speed decreases in shallow water its height grows.

(*c*) Its wave speed and wave height remain constant.

Q.9.   The shoaling effect makes the tsunami: (1)

(*a*) Imperceptible at sea.

(*b*) Violent at sea .

(*c*) Causes high tidal waves at sea.

Q.10. What happens to the tsunami as it approaches land?   (1)

(*a*) It speed increases and its height increases.

(*b*) Its speed decreases and height increases.

(*c*) Its speed remains constant and hence its height increases.

2. Humanoid Robot

Encircle the most appropriate answer.

Q.1. Why is the new version of robots developed by Honda Motors called humanoid?   (1)

(a) Because it can work like humans.

(b) Because it can jog , find its way around obstacles and respond to human touch.

(c) Because it was developed by humans beings.

Q.2. Why is Asimo closer to a bipedal machine?   (1)

(a) Because it can move on wheels.

(b) Because it can jog and lift small objects.

(c) Because it can move on its own in homes offices and interact with people.

Q.3. According to the developer what is Asimo's important flaw?   (1)

(a) It's usefulness to people has not been identified.

(b) It cannot replace human beings.

(c) It cannot work on its own without external help.

Q.4. What human activity did Asimo demonstrate?   (1)

(a) It jogged for few steps.

(b) It responded to human touch and instruction.

(c) It walked few steps drew it's arm to its sides, lifted its knees and jogged.

Q.5. Why was the running motion a challenge to developers ?   (1)

(a) The rapid leg movement threw the robot off balance.

(b) The rapid arm movement threw the robot off balance.

(c) The jogging movement threw the robot off balance.

Q.6. How did the developers overcome the challenge?   (1)

(a) They installed a new joint in the robot's hips?

(b) They installed a new joint in the robot's legs?

(c) They installed a new joint in the robot's arms?

Q.7. The new joints in the robot's wrist and hands enabled Asimo to :   (1)

(a) Help it in jogging.

(b) Help in maintain its balance.

c) Pick up small objects.

Q.8. Humanoid robots can in future work as :   (1)

(a) Work as household help for humans.

(b) Aids for elderly or perform dangerous tasks.

(c) Replace costly human labour.

Q.9.   To what use has Honda been renting out its robots?   (1)

(a) To work in auto ancillary units.

(b) To perform dangerous tasks.

(c) To act as guides in museums and entertain at company's events.

Q.10. According to press reports the car manufacturer has invested. (1)

(a) Tens of millions of dollars.

(b) Millions of dollars.

(c) Undisclosed amount spent on the project.

3. Moods

Encircle the most appropriate answer.

Q.1. Moods are a problem when : (1)

(a) They are happy and pleasant.

(b) They are for a short duration.

(c) They are sad , anxious, angry or lethargic.

Q.2. What is the best way to deal with bad moods? (1)

(a) To talk them out with friends and relatives.

(b) Brood over them.

(c) Do introspection to find its cause.

Q.3. How can one pry loose from an unwanted mood? (1)

(a) Use of tranquilizers and anti depressants.

(b) Get abundant sleep.

(c) Aerobic exercises are most effective.

Q.4. How does it get you out of the unwanted mood? (1)

(a) By decreasing heart beat thereby decreasing anxiety.

(b) By increasing heart beat, thereby increasing blood circulation and oxygen utilization.

(c) By inducing sleep thereby relaxing the mind.

Q.5. How else can one overcome a bad mood? (1)

(a) By reading an interesting novel.

(b) By watching a good movie.

(c) Colours can have a soothing effect on one's mood.

Q.6. Colours that add to gloom are : (1)

(a) Black or dark blue.

(b) Red

(c) Green and yellow.

Q.7. Colours that lighten one's mood are (1)

(a) Grey and blue.

(b) Red.

(c) Warm, bright and active colours.

Q.8. What type of food helps overcoming a bad mood?

(a) Carbohydrates and proteins.

(b) Fats, and vegetables

(c) Fast food.

Q.9. Depression, anxiety and irritability increases with :   (1)

    (*a*) Increase in protein intake.

    (*b*) Increase in caffeine intake.

    (*c*) Increase in carbohydrate intake.

Q.10. One can feel happy by :   (1)

    (*a*) By avoiding being critical of other people.

    (*b*) By doing introspection and meditation.

    (*c*) Avoiding being critical of oneself and thinking positive thoughts.

4. Decision Making

Encircle the most appropriate answer

Q.1. What is Decidophobia?   (1)

    (*a*) Taking decisions for the future.

    (*b*) Being afraid of taking decisions

    (*c*) Taking decisions in the light of past experience.

Q.2. The course of our lives is largely determined by :   (1)

    (*a*) The decisions we take in the present.

    (*b*) The decisions we take in the past.

    (*c*) The decisions we take for the future.

Q.3. People who avoid taking decisions :   (1)

    (*a*) Plan their future.

    (*b*) Go about life happily.

    (*c*) Leave everything to chance.

Q.4. What should be your first step towards decision making?   (1)

    (*a*) List out alternate course of action.

    (*b*) Refer to past experience.

    (*c*) Gather maximum information about the issue.

Q.5. How does decision making become easy?   (1)

    (*a*) Relating to past experience.

    (*b*) A good value system.

    (*c*) Relating to one's ambition in life.

Q.6. What does the author suggest, when decision are difficult to make?   (1)

    (*a*) Consider all alternative course of action.

    (*b*) Gather information on the issue.

    (*c*) Give your self time to ponder.

Q.7. Why would such a course of action help in decision making?   (1)

    (*a*) You may not be required to take any decision.

    (*b*) Circumstances may change with time.

    (*c*) You would have more information on the issue.

Q.8. What according to the author facilitates decision making?   (1)

    (*a*) Out lining your short and long term goals.

(b) Having a clear value system.

(c) Having an important goal in life.

Q.9. Decision making is futile if it is not: (1)

(a) Planned to meet long and short term goals.

(b) If not in line with one's value system.

(c) Followed by action.

Q.10. How does the author advise one to proceed in a more focused way?   (1)

(a) Move from the world of inaction to action.

(b) Move from the world of thought to the arena of action.

(c) Keep one's short and long term goals in mind.

5. Martin Luther King

Encircle the most appropriate answer

Q.1. Martin Luther King got for American Blacks :   (1)

(a) Right to travel in public transport.

(b) Right to contribute to America's development.

(c) Freedom from racial discrimination.

Q.2. What disturbed Martin Luther King?   (1)

(a) He had to offer a seat in the bus to a White.

(b) He could not play with White children.

(c) Being a Black he had no civil rights.

Q.3. What did Martin Luther King dream of as a child?   (1)

(a) Becoming a leader of the Blacks.

(b) Becoming a liberator of the Blacks.

(c) Becoming a pastor of the Blacks.

Q.4. After completing his doctor's in theology Martin Luther King became :   (1)

(a) A liberator.

(b) A pastor.

(c) A leader.

Q.5. Martin Luther King was greatly impressed by :   (1)

(a) The non-violence movement Ahimsa.

(b) Mahatma Gandhi.

(c) Abraham Lincoln.

Q.6. Why did he lead a public boycott of public transport?   (1)

(a) Because Blacks had to offer a seat to the Whites.

(b) Because Blacks were not permitted to sit in the same buses as the Whites.

(c) Because Blacks were not allowed to travel in buses.

Q.7. What was his first victory?   (1)

(a) The Supreme Court ruling allowing Blacks to use public transport.

(b) The Supreme Court's ruling giving equal rights to Blacks.

(c) The Supreme Court's ruling making racial segregation in public transport unlawful.

Q.8.   For his great contribution he was awarded :   (1)
       (a) The Liberators Award.
       (b) The Noble Peace Prize.
       (c) A medal of honour.

Q.9.   For which skill was Martin Luther King known?   (1)
       (a) Leadership skill.
       (b) Organizational skill.
       (c) Oratorical skill.

Q.10. He was shot dead by an assassin while :   (1)
       (a) Leading a demonstration of workers.
       (b) Planning a demonstration of striking sanitation workers.
       (c) Planning a peaceful march of workers.

SUGGESTED ANSWERS TO QUESTIONS ON THE PASSAGES.

Tsunami

Q.1. (c)   Q.2. (a)   Q.3. (b)   Q.4. (b)   Q.5. (a)   Q.6. (b)   Q.7. (c)   Q.8. (b)
Q.9 (a)   Q.10. (b)

Humanoid Robots

Q.1 (b)   Q.2. (c)   Q.3. (a)   Q.4. (c)   Q.5. (b)   Q.6. (a)   Q.7. (c)   Q.8. (b)
Q.9 (c)   Q.10. (a)

Moods

Q.1. (c)   Q.2. (a)   Q.3. (c)   Q.4. (b)   Q.5. (c)   Q.6. (a)   Q.7. (c)   Q.8. (a)
Q.9. (b)   Q.10. (c)

Decision Making

Q.1. (b)   Q.2. (a)   Q.3. (c)   Q.4. (c)   Q.5. (b)   Q.6. (c)   Q.7. (b)   Q.8. (a)
Q.9 (c)   Q.10. (b)

Martin Luther King

Q.1. (c)   Q.2. (a)   Q.3. (b)   Q.4. (b)   Q.5. (b)   Q.6. (b)   Q.7. (c)   Q.8. (b)
Q.9. (c)   Q.10. (b)

SPEAKING (ORAL) SKILLS

By speaking we communicate our thoughts and ideas to others. It is an important attribute for succeeding in modern society. This is for, no matter how brilliant or hard working you are, unless you are able to communicate your thoughts and ideas effectively, success will always elude you. It is therefore imperative to strengthen your speaking / communication skills to achieve success in life. Like other skills, it is slightly more complicated than it seems, for it involves more than just pronouncing words. Normally we find ourselves in three kinds of speaking situations. interactive, partially interactive, and non-interactive speaking situations.

- **Interactive speaking situation** include face-to-face conversations or telephone calls, in which we alternately listen and speak and have a chance to ask for clarification or repetition.
- **Partially interactive speaking situation** are when giving a speech to a live audience, the audience does not interrupt the speech. The speaker nevertheless can see the audience and judge from the expression on their faces and body language whether he or she is being understood. This is followed by a discussion wherein the audience seeks answers to their queries from the speaker.
- **Totally non-interactive speaking situation** such as recording a speech for a radio broadcast .

We are required to follow the partially interactive speaking situation for the internal assessment of ICSE examination. This requires the students to select one topic from the five topics, prepare his presentation in an hour's time and speak on it for about two minutes. The student may refer to brief notes in the course of the presentation, but reading or excessive dependence on notes would be penalized. This is followed by a discussion on the same with the examiner, who would ask few questions on the presentation.

The subject for presentation may include narrating an experience, providing a description, giving direction how to make or operate something, expressing an opinion, giving a report, relating an anecdote, or commenting on a current event.

How to speak effectively?

Our speech is effective when it is clear, unambiguous, logical and last but not the least voiced confidently.

• Clear

Clarity in speaking your thoughts, which is easy to comprehend catches the attention of the listener.

• Unambiguous

It should convey the precise thought that you want to convey without any ambiguity.

• Logical

A thought that is supported by logic and reason catches the immediate attention of the listener. Having aroused his interest, it is easy to hold his attention.

• Voiced confidently

Last but not the least, whatever you say must be voiced confidently. The secret of voicing your thought confidently lies in being your natural self. Unwanted stress causes tension in the body which tightens the muscles of the throat, thereby constricting breathing. This affects the sound of your voice and conveys nervousness and lack of confidence.

POWER OF SPEECH

If you have difficulty in communicating your ideas in English, practice speaking on any given subject in a group. Cultivate the habit of reading newspapers editorials, listening to discussions on current issues on TV .This will gradually boost your confidence.

To begin with observe the following

- Keep your sentences short.
- Use simple words.
- Jot down in few words, the idea you want to communicate.
- After speaking take feedback from your friends and well wishers.

Our Speech basically has two important components.

1. Voice
2. Delivery

1. Voice

We are all born with a certain type or quality of voice and can do nothing about it. However we can always try to improve it by speaking in front of a mirror or by speaking to a group. Try to instill confidence in your voice without speaking too loudly. Do not be apologetic about your voice, if you feel that it lacks authority Remember that an orator like Mahatma Gandhi, drew attention not because of the quality of his voice, but because of what he said, and how he said it.

2. Delivery

You would have observed that good orators modulate their voice while speaking. This is for while writing we use full stop, comma, exclamation mark and paragraphs. These are however not available to us while speaking. Good orators therefore alter the pitch, speed and also pause at appropriate intervals, to make their communication effective.

Therefore do not ramble on and on in a monotonous tone, Organise your ideas and present them in an appropriate manner, by raising your voice to highlight important words or phrases.

Conquer these five before speaking.

There are five important things that one must conquer.

➢ **Fear**

it is quite common for one to freeze for the first time while speaking publicly. It is therefore very important to overcome this fear. One can do so by constant practice. Try to speak on any given subject with your friends or relatives. You can also do it alone, by speaking on a given subject in front of a mirror. Evaluate your tone, body language, facial expression, while you speak.

➢ **Negative Thinking**

Avoid negative thinking. Think positively on the subject.

➢ **Anxiety**

We get anxious when we are fearful. Therefore try to listen to your voice to smoothen out the rough edges. The best way to conquer this anxiety, is to introduce   yourself to an imaginary audience, by speaking aloud for at least two minutes on any subject.

➢ **Overconfidence**

Academic excellence does not in any way have an impact on your presentation skills.

➤ **Knowledge and Preparation**

'Knowledge is power' said Francis Bacon. This is amply true if you want to conquer your fear and anxiety. Good knowledge and adequate preparation on relevant issues provide a perfect solution to all the above problems.

In the internal assessment the examiners will assess you on the following parameters which are enumerated after the syllabus for internal assessment . They are:-

A. **Fluency of language :** This is the ability to speak fluently and with ease. It includes the operational command on the language with natural flow of thoughts using correct grammar, and pronunciation.

B. **Subject matter:** To speak effectively on a subject it is important that the points raised by you are relevant and logical. This requires good knowledge of the subject. Since you have to choose one topic from the four or five topics. Select a topic with which you are familiar and can speak confidently on it for two minutes and also answer questions of the examiner. The one hour time you have to prepare your presentation should be used to note down all the relevant points on the subject on a piece of paper. In the course of your deliberation you would need to add or eliminate few points

C. **Organisation or structure:** our presentation like an essay also has three parts – The introduction, body , and conclusion, therefore divide the relevant points noted above under these three heads.

1. **Introduction:-** The beginning of your presentation is the most important part. It is here you establish a rapport with the audience and catch their attention. You should start the presentation by:

   • Greeting the teacher / audience

   • Introduce yourself

   • State the topic of your presentation.

Your presentation should ideally begin as follows:-

Good Morning / Afternoon. Respected Teacher and friends.

Let me introduce myself. My name is Siddhant Singh of Class X C

The subject of my presentation is _____ or

I would like to speak to you on _____or

The theme of my presentation is _____

This could be followed by stating your objective, purpose or aim.

You can make your introduction interesting by using any of the following strategies :-

   ➤ **By using quotes of great philosophers** or simple proverbs. Thus for example if the topic is: 'Should the Film Censor Board be abolished?,' you could start with a quote like, 'Hidden apples are always sweet'.

   ➤ **By defining the subject:** Topics like advertising, corporal punishment, child labour could be begun by defining their meaning.

   ➤ **By posing a question:** You can also begin by asking a provocative question. The answer to the question is obvious but would draw the immediate attention of the audience. Thus if you were to make a presentation on 'Cigarette smoking is injurious to health,' you could very well begin by posing a question. " Would you spend money everyday for a dose of poison?"

➢ **By making a shocking statement:** You could begin your presentation on a topic like 'corruption' by stating, 'Every man has a price.'

➢ **By quoting facts, figures :** On a topic like 'The importance of Education in India' You could begin by stating 'Even after 64 years of independence over 30 percent of the people are still illiterate."

➢ **By narrating a short story** relating your personal experience

➢ **By making a strong opening statement** like

'School examinations should be abolished, or

'Environmental pollution is a threat to the entire human race.'

2. **Body:-** The body should logically develop the topic based on objective stated in the beginning. Sequence your ideas by organizing the points noted by you.The few possibilities for sequencing ideas are :-

- Logically
- In chronological order
- From general to specific
- From known to unknown
- Cause to effect
- Problem to solution.

Link the ideas by ensuring smooth transition from one point to another.

3. **Conclusion:** Concluding you presentation is very important for this is the final impression you leave on the audience. It should sum up the topic briefly reiterating the important points and your opinion on the same.

Finally thank the teacher and the audience for listening to you.

D. **Vocabulary:** This plays an important role in giving a presentation. A good vocabulary gives you the ability of using appropriate words conveying the precise thought.

E. **Delivery:** Good orators modulate their voice while speaking. Vary your vocal pace, tone and volume of your voice and also pause at intervals. This would improve the quality of the presentation, for a monotonous presentation is dull and puts the audience to sleep.

F. **Understanding :** This is reflected in the emphasis you give to the important points, by raising your voice, changing your tone or by appropriate gestures.

G. **Gestures / Body language:** The body betrays your inner feeling and emotions, It reveals your inner self, and hence a good body language gives an extra punch to your presentation. You can have a good body language by:

- **Smiling:** It has been scientifically proved, that the more you smile, the more positive reaction you get from others. Smiling reflects your pleasant disposition and is comforting to people around you.

- **Eye contact:** Maintain eye contact with the teacher / audience This is for the eyes, are the most revealing and accurate of all human communication signals. Punctuate words with gestures – Gestures should complement your words. Thus you can tell, how big the fish was, and show them with your arms.

- **Posture:** While standing stand straight but relaxed, with your arms besides you. Do not slouch, lean against the table or shuffle your feet.

Do's for a positive body language is

- Be natural and relaxed.
- Don't forget to smile
- Maintain eye contact
- Make appropriate gesture.

Don't

- Lose eye contact with the teacher. audience.
- Look at notes while speaking.
- Look at the roof or the floor.
- Sway back and forth while speaking.
- Put your hands in the pocket.

It is but natural that initially you would be nervous, however this should not prevent you from practicing. Select a topic and after jotting down the points speak for about two minutes on the same in front of a mirro. Critically analyse your presentation on all the parameters given above, including your body language, Your parents, friends can also help you in this exercise and with practice you would overcome your nervousness and gain confidence.

EXAMPLES OF AN ORAL PRESENTATION

1. EXPRESSING AN OPINION

Good Morning Respected Teacher and friends.

Let me introduce myself. My name is Sunil Kumar of Class X A. I would like to express my opinion on an age old saying " Failure is but a stepping stone to success."

'Success doesn't mean the absence of failure, it means winning the war not every battle.' Behind every success story, there is also a story of great failure. Unfortunately while we are aware of the great achievements, we do not know the failure, toil and tears, that are behind each success.

We should therefore take failure in our stride, for it is but another step that takes us closer to our goal. If we fail again, it means there is one more road we should not take. It thus gives us valuable experience and as we all know ' Experience is a great teacher.'

Failure makes us humble and in our grief we find the courage and faith to overcome the set-back. It makes us more down to earth, practical and realistic. Giving us an opportunity to reassess our objective, plan, and the future course of action, in the light of mistakes we have made.

However turning a stumbling block to a stepping-stone, requires one to overcome the fear of failure and doubt. These usually arise when we fail and affect us psychologically and even physically. The only possible way to overcome this, is to have a firm belief and conviction in our work and avoid committing the same mistake again. A strong will and burning desire to succeed is a sure passport to success.

History is replete with examples of great failures that eventually became great success stories. We know of Abraham Lincoln, who failed in business, had a nervous breakdown, lost a Congressial and senatorial race and even failed to become the Vice President, but ultimately was elected the President Of USA. Walt Disney faced many rejections from editors of newspapers, who said he had no talent. While working in a mouse infected shed he saw a mouse, that inspired him to make a cartoon of Mickey Mouse and the rest is history. The Wright brothers were also ridiculed for trying to make a machine fly. In the face of countless failures, they eventually made their famous flight, paving the way for aeroplanes. All of them however had one thing in common – A firm will and desire to succeed. They took defeat as a detour and not as a dead end.

Failing does not make you a failure. Giving up, accepting your failure and refusing to try again does. We should therefore use failure as driving force to propel us towards our goal, rather than deviate from it. This is possible only when we have a positive approach, a strong self-belief and commitment towards our work.

Failure is indeed a stepping-stone to success. We must not treat it as an obstacle, that deter us from our goal, but as a learning experience that pave the way for future success, This is for in the words of H. W. Longfellow

"Life's battle don't always go,

To the stronger or faster man.

But sooner or later the man who wins .

Is the man who thinks he can."

Thank you.

EXERCISE FOR PRACTICE

Few essay topics given in the book with slight modification can be referred to.

1. Hobbies are a waste of time. Refer table of Contents (Section B) Sl No 14
2. Should capital punishment be abolished. Refer table of Contents (Section B) Sl No 20
3. A stitch in time saves nine. Refer table of Contents (Section B) Sl No 81
4. Experience is the best teacher. Refer table of Contents (Section B) Sl No 84
5. Work is worship. Refer table of Contents (Section B) Sl No 86
6. God helps those who help themselves. Refer table of Contents (Section B) Sl No 90
7. Where there is a will there is a way. Refer table of Contents (Section B) Sl No 94
8. Necessity is the mother of invention. Refer table of Contents (Section B) Sl No 95
9. Knowledge is power. Refer table of Contents (Section B) Sl No 110.
10. Are we happier than our forefathers.
11. Genius are born not made.
12. Examinations are a necessary evil.

2. NARRATING AN EXPERIENCE

Good Morning, Respected Teacher and friends.

Let me introduce myself. My name is Sunil Kumar of Class X A. I would like to relate an experience, which I had while I was in class V.

Nature has always fascinated and astonished me. The transformation of an ugly caterpillar to a beautiful butterfly that Mrs. Johnson my Science teacher taught in class seemed quite unbelievable. I decided to see it for myself, for ' Seeing is believing.'

That evening I searched the garden for a caterpillar, the object of my study. After an extensive search I came across a cocoon the size of a small pea, stuck to a twig on the green hedge of the garden. Carefully I plucked the twig and placed it on the window shelf of my study. Everyday before going to school I would look for any change in the cocoon. One day after returning from school I observed a small opening in the cocoon. Excitedly, I sat and watched for several hours as the small wriggly creature struggled to force its body through the small opening. After some time it stopped making any progress. It appeared to have got stuck in the cocoon.

Taking pity on the small creature, I decided to help it free itself. With a small scissor I cut open the cocoon, making the butterfly emerge easily from the cocoon, on the glass plate placed below. I watched keenly to see the butterfly fly. But there was something strange. The creature seemed quite unlike the beautiful butterfly I saw in the garden. It had a swollen body and shriveled wings. Days passed, but the butterfly refused to fly and died shortly afterwards.

Disappointed with my experiment, I asked Mrs. Johnson. She patiently listened to me. After I had finished recounting my experiment, she smiled and said "Son, your untimely help has cost the butterfly her life. This is for the creature's struggle to get through the small opening of the cocoon is nature's way of forcing fluids from the body of the butterfly into its wings. This makes it strong enough to fly."

I felt guilty and sorry for the little butterfly, for in my eagerness to help, I had inadvertently killed it. However I had learnt an important lesson. We often have to struggle in life, this makes us strong, for 'Triumph's do not come without effort.'

Thank You.

EXERCISE FOR PRACTICE

1. Narrate an incident that you found very amusing. Refer table of Contents (Section B) Sl No 65
2. Narrate an experience of an encounter that changed your life.
3. Narrate an experience that you found very frightening.
4. Narrate an experience that showed appearances could be deceptive.
5. Narrate an experience that taught you a lesson.

3. PRESENTING A REPORT

Good Morning Teachers and friends.

Let me introduce myself. My name is Sunil Kumar of Class X A. I am here to report on the acute problem of water logging in the city of Lucknow.

The heavy rains this monsoon, has exposed the grave problem of water logging in the city. This is despite the Municipal Corporation spending a substantial amount, in providing civic amentias to the residents of the city. The problem this year is very grave, several localities including the posh Hazratganj market, have knee-deep water after every thundershower.

Other localities like Gomtinagar and Aliganj are also badly affected. When asked a resident of Gomtinagar said, "We are living in perpetual fear of water entering our homes after every short spell of rain. The dug up roads and the encroachment on public land have choked the drains."

The situation in low-lying areas is far worse. These localities like Daliganj and Arjunganj and parts of old Lucknow, have been inundated with the rising water of the river Gomti. The river is already flowing above the danger mark. With the meteorological department predicting more rains in the coming days, the situation is bound to aggravate further. The administration has already shifted affected people to relief camps, that have been set up in schools and other public buildings. In the absence of a bundh in the low lying areas, this has now become an annual feature

The Mayor, Mr. Dinesh Sharma blames the Jal Sansathan for digging up roads to lay the sewer lines. This has blocked the drains, leading to the sorry state of affairs. The Jal Sansthan in turn blames the government, for not releasing funds in time, to enable it to complete the work before the onset of monsoon. The blame game continues with each passing the buck to the other.

The callousness of the authorities is indeed alarming.The unhygienic conditions prevailing in the city due to water logging, is an open invitation for epidemics like malaria, cholera and other deadly diseases, that could cost many dear lives. There is an urgent need to address this problem immediately.

EXERCISE FOR PRACTICE

1. Give a report on a national calamity that took place in the country. Refer table of Contents (Section B) Sl No 79.
2. Give a report on the inter school cultural festival held in you school.
3. Give a report on the 'Teachers day' function in you school.
4. Give a report on the Annual day function held in you school.

4. GIVING A DISCRIPTION OF A FESTIVAL

Good Morning, Respected Teachers and friends

Let me introduce myself. My name is Sunil Kumar of Class X A. I am here to describe how we celebrate the festival of Holi.

Holi is the festival of colours. It is celebrated with enthusiasm and gaiety on the full moon day, in the month of Phalgun, which is the month of March as per the Gregorian calendar. People of different states with different traditions celebrate this festival. What makes Holi so unique and special, is the spirit of gaiety which remains the same throughout the country.

Holi can also be called the festival of Spring, for it marks the arrival of spring, the season of hope and joy, after the gloomy winter months. Nature also seems to rejoice, as fields are laden with food grains that promise a good harvest. The garden is filled with flowers that bloom, colouring the surroundings and filling fragrance in the air.

The entire country wears a festive look.The markets are abuzz with activity, as shoppers flock to purchase colourful gulal, abeer and pichkaris. These can be seen in the shops on the roadside. Besides these, shops of sweets and clothes do brisk sales. Housewives cook gujiya, mathri and papri for the family, and, guests

The festival has various legends associated with it. The foremost is the legend of the demon King Hiranyakashyap, who demanded everybody in his kingdom to worship him, but his pious son Prahlad became a devotee of Lord Vishnu. Hiranyakashyap wanted to kill him. He asked his sister Holika to enter a blazing fire with Prahlad in her lap, for Holika had a boon which made her immune to fire. Story goes that Prahlad was saved by the Lord himself, for his extreme devotion, while the evil minded Holika was burnt to ashes. This was for her boon worked only when she entered the fire alone.

Since then people light a bonfire called Holika, on the eve of Holi and celebrate the victory of good over evil.

Another popular legend behind it is that the naughty and mischievous Lord Krishna, started the trend of playing colours. He applied colour on his beloved Radha, to make her look like him. The trend soon gained popularity amongst the masses. The Holi celebrations at Mathura, Vrindavan - the places associated with the birth and childhood of Radha and Krishna are known for their gaiety.

The next day after Holika Dahan is the day of great excitement. People form groups called tolis and move around applying gulal and abeer on each other, and exchanging greetings. They sing and dance on the rhythm of the dholak and eat mouthwatering delicacies. Children spray colours on one another with their pichkaris and throw water on passers by.

After a fun filled and exciting day, people meet friends and relatives in the evening and exchange sweets and greetings. The spirit of Holi encourages the feeling of brotherhood, with even enemies becoming friends. People of all communities and religions participate in this joyous and colouful festival, that strengthens the secular fabric of the country.

EXERCISE FOR PRACTICE

1. Give a description of Deepawali celebration in the country.
2. Describe a recent outing with your friends.
3. Describe a school excursion

5. COMMENTING ON A CURRENT EVENT

Good Morning Respected Teacher and friends.

Let me introduce myself. My name is Sunil Kumar of Class X A. I would like to comment on a current event that took place in the country between 19 Feb and 2 April 2011. This was the 2011 ICC Cricket World Cup. It was the tenth Cricket World Cup which was co-hosted by India, Sri Lanka and Bangladesh.

The one-day cricket matches of 50 overs' was accorded international status, with fourteen national cricket teams competing in the tournament. It was a mega event which had millions of people across the globe glued to their TV sets in the course of the tournament. The popularity of the event could be gauged by the fact that the broadcasting rights was sold for US$ 2 billion. It was also for the first time that the tournament was broadcasted in High Definition format, covered by 27 cameras, including new low 45-degree field cameras. Other technological advances included the use of Umpire Decision Review System.

The promotion campaign 'Entertainment ka Baap', and official song 'De Ghuma Ke', composed by Shankar- Ehsaan incorporating Indian rhythms and rock, drove the audience crazy. 'Stumpy' the young elephant was the mascot of the tournament.

The glittering opening ceremony was held on 17 February 2011 at Bangabandhu National Stadium Dhaka, with the first match played on 19 February 2011 between India and Bangladesh at the Sher-e-Bangla National Stadium in Mirpur Dhaka. Thereafter matches were played in India at Banglore, Chennai, New Delhi, Nagpur, Ahmedabad, Mumbai, and Mohali. In Sri Lanka matches were played at Colombo, Kandy, and Hambantota. In Bangladesh at Dhaka and Chittagong.

All the matches were full of suspense and some had a nail biting finish, especially the Semi final match between India and Pakistan at Mohali on 30 March, which India won by 29 runs. The second Semi finals between Sri Lanka and New Zealand played at Colombo on 29 March, was won by Sri Lanka. The nerve wrecking final match between India and Sri Lanka played at Wankhede Stadium Mumbai on 2 April 2011 was won by India, defeating Sri Lanka by 6 wickets. India thus became the first nation to win the Cricket World Cup final on home soil. It also won 3 million US $ and the coveted ICC Cricket World Cup Trophy. All rounder Yuvraj Singh was declared the man of the tournament, for his sterling performance with the bat and the ball.

It was after more than two decades that India under the captainship of Mahinder Singh Dhoni, won the Cup for the country and restored our national pride.

EXERCISE FOR PRACTICE

1. Comment on Anna Hazare's campaign against corruption.
2. Comment on any national or international event that you find interesting.

6. GIVING DIRECTION TO OPEN AN E MAIL
ACCOUNT AND SEND E MAIL

Good morning Respected Teachers and friends :

Let me introduce myself. My name is Sunil Kumar of Class X A. I would like to talk to you on. How to open an e-mail account and send an e mail on yahoo.com.

To open an e mail account you require the following

A computer with an internet connection. Thereafter you can proceed as follows:-

1. Start the computer.

2. Click on the Internet Explorer icon on the desktop.Type www.yahoo.com and press Enter key to open the yahoo site.

3. In the dialogue box click SIGN IN to yahoo.

4. Type you yahoo ID in the dialogue box, say siddhant and your password (The password should contain letters, at least one numeral and one special character like $, etc). Thereafter click SIGN IN . A message on the screen informs, this ID is not taken Are you trying to register for a new account.

    Click Register for a new account.

5. A new dialogue box opens on the computer monitor.

    Fill in your name, sex, date of Birth, your e mail Id and the password you have chosen above. Reconfirm the password. Answer secret questions to help you retrieve your password, in case you forget.

    Thereafter click CREATE MY ACCOUNT

6. CONGRADULATION message appears on the screen

Now click CONTINUE button to open the yahoo mail page.

Sending the e mail

1. On the Yahoo page click the compose new mail button.

2. Type the e mail address and the subject in the dialogue box.

3. Thereafter type the message.

4. Now click the 'SEND' option.

5. Message has been sent appears on the screen.

EXERCISE FOR PRACTICE

1. How to open a Saving bank account in a bank.

2. How to bake a cake / bread.

3. How to defrost a refrigerator.

SECTION - K

Solved Question Papers

SOLVED QUESTION PAPER FOR ICSE 1999 EXAMINATION
ENGLISH – Paper 1
(Two hours)

Answer to this paper must be written on the paper provided separately.
*You will **NOT** be allowed to write in the first 15 minutes.*
This time is to be spent in reading the question paper.

*Attempt all the **four** questions*
The intended marks for questions or parts of questions are given in [ ].
You are advised to spend not more than 35 minutes in answering Question no. 1 and 20 minutes in answering Question no. 2

*Attempt all **four** questions.*

Question 1

(Do not spend more than 35 minutes on this question).

Write a composition (**350 – 400 words**) on any one of the following   [25]

(*a*) River and lakes are always interesting and commercially important to people who live near them. Describe some of the ways in which people living close to a lake or a river use it to their advantage commercially and also for their relaxation and amusement all through the year.

(*b*) "Cigarettes smoking in public places should not be allowed". Argue either **for** or **against** this statement.

(*c*) Of all the subjects you are studying at present, which one do you think would be most useful to you in future and why?

(*d*) Write a story beginning "I do not believe in Ghosts ...."

(*e*) Study the picture given below. Write a story or a description or an account of what the picture suggests to you. Your composition must be about the subject of the picture or may

take suggestions from it. But there must be a clear connection between the picture and your composition.

Question 2

(Do not spend more than 20 minutes on this question).

Select **one** of the following: [10]

(a) You are in charge of a group, which is to go camping next month. Your friend, who is unwell at present, will join later. Write a letter to the same friend informing him /her when and where all the members have to meet, how you will travel to your destination, what things you should carry with you and how you will return home.

OR

(b) Write a letter to the principal of your school expressing your wish to continue studying in the same school after Class-X. Your letter should make clear what course or stream (Commerce, Science or Humanities) you wish to follow and why you have decided to choose that course.

Question 3

Read the following passage carefully and answer the questions (a), (b) and (c) that follow:

[25]

The beaver had made a dam two hundred yards long and it had formed out of the quickly flowing stream, a wide stretch of water about twenty feet deep .The dam was so firm and broad that it was easy for me to walk along it. After hundred and fifty yards I came to a 'beaver's castle' a great heap of logs, skillfully fitted together, the lower part covered with earth and plants. The upper logs were put loosely together so that air could pass through to the interior.

In the late autumn before land and water are covered with snow and ice, the beaver has to make its dwelling frost proof. It collects young trees and gnaws the stem in a double cone until the tree falls. Then the long stems are gnawed into small sections, the thin twigs bitten off and the logs dragged to the dwelling. There the timber is piled on the 'castle', sometimes to a ten or a dozen feet .Mud is brought from the bottom of the lake and packed between the logs with the animal's clever forepaws .The interior is lined with the finest wood shavings. In this tall shelter the beaver remains high and dry, and protected from frost throughout the winter.

The only access to the dwelling is under the water, and even the forest wolves are unable to pull the building apart.

The water is the beaver's element. On land it moves slowly and awkwardly. Thus it is *vital* for the beaver to have water in which it can swim, and where Nature has not provided this condition for it, it has created it with its dam.

The beaver's activities change whole landscapes. With the dam for instance on which I was standing, beavers had turned a whole wooded valley into a lake, trees that had stood there had been killed by the water and had disappeared. Aquatic game had settled there. Ducks swam past us and great must have been the number of fish, as swamps of trout had swam past me in the clear stream. Wide stretches of meadows had come into existence on the banks, with flat landing places to which well-beaten beaver tracks lead. Many years of building, gnawing and dragging must have gone to the completion of this immense work, creating a new region for the beavers to live in .

(a) Four words are given below. Give the meaning of each as used in the passage. A one word answer or a short phrase will be accepted.   [2]

   (i)   Gnaws
   (ii) Access
   (iii) Vital
   (iv) Aquatic

(b) Answer the following questions as briefly as possible and in **your own words**
   (i)   What evidence in the passage suggests that beavers build fairly strong dams?   [3]
   (ii) How does a beaver ensure that its 'castle 'is well ventilated?   [2]
   (iii) How does a beaver fell a tree?   [2]
   (iv) Why do beavers build dams?   [2]
   (v)   Quote a sentence from the passage that tells us that beavers just love being in or near water?   [1]
   (vi) Mention two changes that may be brought about in the landscape by the activity of the beavers.   [3]

(c) In **not more than 60 words** describe a beaver's 'castle' and write how the animal makes it frost proof.   [10]

Question 4

(a) Rewrite the following sentences correctly according to the instruction given after each. Make other changes that may be necessary, but do not change the meaning of each sentence.   [10]

   (i)   He is fortunate to have won the prize.
          (Begin: Fortunately ....)
   (ii)   It was quite dark. They came back home.
          (Rewrite as one sentence without using 'and')
   (iii) As soon as the newspaper reaches the stands it is sold out.
          (Begin: No sooner ...)
   (iv)   Mohan was too slow to catch the thief.
          (Rewrite using "So .... that.")
   (v)   The assignment will be completed by me within a month.
          (Begin : I will....)
   (vi)   Cleopatra is the most famous Egyptian queen.
          (Begin: No other......)
   (vii) It is sad that you are leaving the town.
          (Begin : How.....)
   (viii) The son arrived after his mother had died.
          (Begin : It was after ......)
   (ix)   My father goes for a walk every morning.
          (Rewrite using 'fail')
   (x)   The judge punished the guilty.
          (Begin : The guilty......)

(b) In each of the following sentences there is a blank space which can be filled in by a single word. Fill in each blank with the word which is appropriate. (Do not write the sentences)   [5]

   (i)   The teacher was pleased .... the performance of the student.

    (*ii*)   He slept .... eight o'clock.

    (*iii*)   The cat sprang .... the table.

    (*iv*)   I shall return .... an hour.

    (*v*)   He will be dropped .... the team if he does not make a big score.

(*c*) Fill in the following blank spaces with a suitable form of the word given in the brackets: [5]

When we .... (1) (visit) the volcano, it was in a state of eruption. We .... (2) (stand) near the summit on an irregular plane. It .... (3) (heap) up with stones and cinders and enormous rocks which .... (4) (hurl) from the volcano in terrible confusion. We .... (5) (rush) to a specially built shelter nearby.

Answers

1. (*a*) Refer to Contents Section B Sl No. 61

   (*b*) Refer to Contents Section B Sl No. 06

   (*c*) Refer to Contents Section B Sl No. 08

   (*d*) Refer to Contents Section B Sl No. 59

2. (*a*) Refer to Contents Section E Sl No. 06

   (*b*) Refer to Contents Section E Sl No. 32

3. (*a*) (*i*)   Gnaw — bite or chew steadily

      (*ii*)   Access — approachability

      (*iii*) Vital — essential, important

      (*iv*) Aquatic — living or growing in water

  (*b*) (*i*)   The beaver build fairly strong and broad dams, that the author could walk and even stand on them, as he surveyed the landscape.

      (*ii*)   The beaver build their castle with the heap of logs, covering the lower part with plant and earth and setting the upper logs loosely, so that air can pass through which would help in ventilation.

      (*iii*) The beaver nibble closely at the stem of the young trees in a double cone as a result of which the tree falls.

      (*iv*) The beaver loves being in or near water, for while it moves slowly and awkwardly on land, it swims effortlessly in water. Thus where nature has not made water available to it in its vicinity, it builds dams to collect water.

      (*v*)   'The water is the beavers elements.'

      (*vi*) The two changes that may be brought about in the landscape by the activity of the beavers are (*a*) Wooded valleys are converted into lakes (*b*) Wide stretches of meadows come into existence.

  (*c*) Beaver's castle is a heap of logs .The lower part is covered with mud and plants while the upper logs are loosely fitted for proper ventilation. They gnaw the stems of trees into small sections, which are then piled on the castle, packed with mud. The interior is lined with fine wood shavings to make it frost proof.

4. (a) (i)   Fortunately he has won the prize.

   (ii)   It was quite dark when they came back home.

   (iii)   No sooner does the newspaper reach the stands, it is sold out.

   (iv)   Mohan was so slow that he could not catch the thief.

   (v)   I will complete the assignment within a month.

   (vi)   No other Egyptian queen is as famous as Cleopatra.

   (vii)   How sad to know that you are leaving town.

   (viii)   It was after his mother's death that the son arrived.

   (ix)   My father never fails to go for a walk every morning.

   (x)   The guilty was punished by the judge.

(b) (i) With   (ii) At   (iii) On   (iv) Within   (v) From

(c)   1. Visited   2. Stood   3. was halped   4. Hurled   5. Rushed

QUESTION PAPER FOR ICSE 2000 EXAMINATION

ENGLISH

Paper 1

(Two hours)

Answer to this paper must be written on the paper, provided separately

*You will **NOT** be allowed to write in the first 15 minutes.*

This time is to be spent in reading the question paper.

*Attempt all the **four** questions*

The intended marks for questions or parts of questions are given in [ ].

You are advised to spend not more than 35 minutes in answering Question no. 1 and 20 minutes in answering Question no. 2.

Question 1

(Do **not** spend more than 35 minutes on this question).   [25]

Write a composition (**350 – 400 words**) on any **one** of the following.

(*a*) You have been on a plane journey recently, while going through a cloud the plane developed engine trouble. Describe what took place in the plane and how you were saved.

(*b*) One of your parents has influenced you considerably. Give details of the influence.

(*c*) Which in your opinion is more important – a healthy body or a healthy mind? Give relevant arguments to support your opinion.

(*d*) Look at the cartoon given below and write an account of what it suggests to you.

(e) Study the picture given below. Write a story or a description or an account of what the picture suggests to you. Your composition must be about the subject of the picture or may take suggestions from it. But there must be a clear connection between the picture and your composition.

Question 2

(Do not spend more than 20 minutes on this question).

Select one of the following: [10]

(a) You have received a birthday gift from your uncle from abroad. Write a letter thanking him for the gift and give your reasons why you like his gift.

OR

(b) Write a letter to the local police complaining of a theft that took place last night in your neighbours flat.

Question 3

Read the following passage carefully and answer the questions (a), (b) and (c) that follow:

Cameron Mounger and I have been friends since we were teenagers. Both of us liked music, and several years after we left school, Cam, as we called him, became a disc jockey.

Recently he told me a story about the day he was down to his last dollar. It was the day his luck and his life changed.

The story begins in the year 1970 when Cam was an announcer and a disc jockey at a radio station in Texas and attained celebrity status. He met many countrymusic stars, and enjoyed flying to Nashville, the center of country music, in the company plane with the station owner.

One night Cam was in Nashville for a show. After it was over an acquaintance invited him back stage with all the stars. "I didn't have any paper for autographs, so I took out a dollar note,"Cam told me "Before the night was over, I had <u>virtually</u> every stars autograph, I guarded that dollar note and carried it with me always. I knew I would treasure it forever."

Then the radio station where he was working was put up for sale and many employees found themselves without a job. Cam landed part time work at another station and planned to hang on to his job long enough for a full time position to open up.

That winter was extremely cold in Texas. The heater in Cam's old car <u>emitted</u> a hint of warm air, the windscreen defroster didn't work at all. Life was hard and Cam was broke. With the help of a friend who worked at the local supermarket he occasionally got food that was spoilt and was being thrown away. "This kept me and wife eating, but we still had no cash."

One morning as Cam left the radio station he saw an old man sitting in an old yellow car in the car park. Cam waived to him and drove away. When he came back to work that night, he noticed the car again, parked at the same place. After a couple of days it <u>dawned</u> on him that the car had not moved .The fellow in it always waived <u>cordially</u> to Cam as he came and went. What was the man doing sitting in the car for three days in the terrible cold and snow?

Cam discovered the answer the next morning. This time the man rolled down the window. He introduced himself and said he had been in his car for days with no money or food, Cam recalled. He had come from out of town to take a job. But he arrived three days early and couldn't go to work right away.

Very <u>reluctantly</u> he asked if he might borrow a dollar for a snack to get him by until the next day, when he would start work and get a salary advance. I didn't have a dollar to lend him. I barely had petrol to get home .I explained my situation and walked to my car, wishing I could have helped him.

Then Cam remembered the dollar which the country music stars at Nashville had signed. He wrested with his conscience a minute or two, pulled out his wallet and studied the note one last time. Then he walked back to the man and gave it to him. "Somebody has written all over this,"the man said, but he didn't notice that the writing was dozens of autographs. He took the note.

"That very morning when I went back home trying not to think about what I had done, things began to happen." Cam told me. "The telephone rang, a recording company wanted me to do an ad that paid $500. It sounded like a million. In the next few days more opportunities came to me out of nowhere. Good things kept coming steadily, and soon I was back on my feet."

The rest as they say, is history. Things improved dramatically for Cam. His wife had a baby. Cam opened a successful car repair shop and built a nice home. And it all started that morning in the car park when he parted with his last dollar.

Cam never saw the man in the old yellow car again. Sometimes he wanders if the man was a beggar or an angel.

It doesn't matter. What matters is that it was a test — and Cam had passed.

(*a*) Five words or phrases are given below. Give the meaning of each word as given in the passage .One word answer or short phrases will be accepted.

   (*i*)   Virtually

  (*ii*)   Emitted

 (*iii*)   Dawned

      (*iv*) Cordially

      (*v*) Reluctantly   [5]

(*b*) Answer the following questions **brefly in your own words**:

      (*i*) What was Cam's first occupation in life? What did he do in the end for a living?   [2]

      (*ii*) How did he get signatures of singing stars?   [2]

      (*iii*) On what did Cam get the autographs? Why?   [2]

      (*iv*) How did he lose his full time work?   [1]

      (*v*) How did the man in the yellow car attract Cam's attention?   [2]

      (*vi*) Why did the man in the yellow car ask for a loan of one dollar?   [1]

(*c*) In **not more than 60 words,** explain how Cam's life changed when he made his greatest sacrifice.   [10]

Question 4

(*a*) Rewrite the following sentences correctly according to the instruction given after each. Make other change that may be necessary but do not change the meaning of each sentence.   [5]

      (*i*) Waste not, want not

          (Begin with: **If**..)

      (*ii*) I accept your offer

          (Use: **acceptable**)

      (*iii*) It is normal for a child to eat four times a day.

          (Use: **normally**)

      (*iv*) I caught a train and went to Calcutta.

          (Use: **having**)

      (*v*) One should keep one's promises.

          (Begin with: **Promise**..)

(*b*) Complete each of the following sentences using the appropriate form of verb given in brackets: [5]

      (*i*) I have just .... my work. (do)

      (*ii*) Yesterday Mr. Anthony .... out of town. (go)

      (*iii*) I told him that we .... them of our intention a year ago. (inform)

      (*iv*) He .... in this office since October. (work)

      (*v*) I showed the teacher what I .... (write)

(*c*) Fill in each blank with a suitable word (Do **NOT** write the sentences):   [5]

      (*i*) It has been a long time .... I saw her.

      (*ii*) Anita received an invitation .... dinner.

      (*iii*) Good food is necessary .... good health.

      (*iv*) Can you cure me .... this ailment?

      (*v*) He is too miserly to part .... money.

(*d*) Join each of the following pair of sentences **without** using '*and*' or '*but*'

      1. They are very old.   [5]

         They cannot run.

2. John was a philosopher.

   He was a poet.

3. Pollution levels, are increasing.

   Many children are getting sick.

4. Hurry up.

   You will be late.

5. Social service is demanding.

   It has its own rewards.

Answers

1. (*a*) Refer to Contents Section B Sl No. 57

   (*b*) Refer to Contents Section B Sl No. 58

   (*c*) Refer to Contents Section B Sl No. 05

2 (*a*) Refer to Contents Section E Sl No. 05

   (*b*) Refer to Contents Section E Sl No. 25

3. (*a*) (*i*) Virtually – Practically, almost

   (*ii*) Emitted – Give out

   (*iii*) Dawned – Understand, become evident

   (*iv*) Cordially – Warmly, friendly

   (*v*) Reluctantly – Unwilling, disinclined

(*b*) (*i*) Cameron Mounger called Cam by his friends, was an announcer and Disc jockey at a radio station in Texas where he was a celebrity.

   In the end he opened a successful car repair shop for a living.

   (*ii*) On one of his official tours to Nashville for a show, he was invited backstage by one of his acquaintances, when the show was over. Here he met all the singing stars and thus got an opportunity to take their signatures.

   (*iii*) He took their signatures on a dollar note, as he did not have any paper for taking their autographs.

   (*iv*) He lost his full time work because the radio station where he worked was put up for sale.

   (*v*) The old man in the yellow car drew Cam's attention, because he would always wave out to him affectionately, whenever he would pass by .His car remained parked in the same place and this recurred continuously for three days.

   (*vi*) The man in the yellow car said that he had come from town to take up a job, but had arrived three days earlier. Very hesitatingly he requested Cam to lend him a dollar for a day so that he could buy a snack. He would return it the next day, when he would start work and get his salary advance.

(*c*) Cam was poor and down to his last dollar. After he made his great sacrifice, he got a call for doing an advertisement for $500 from a recording company. Thereafter he got similar opportunities without effort and was able to fend for himself. He became a father and opened a successful car repair shop besides building a home for himself.

4. (a)   (i)   If you do not want anything do not waste it.

      (ii)   Your offer is acceptable to me.

      (iii)   Normally a child eats four times a day.

      (iv)   Having caught the train I went to Calcutta.

      (v)   Promises should be kept.

  (b)   (i)   I have just <u>done</u> my work.

      (ii)   Yesterday Mr. Anthony <u>went</u> out of town.

      (iii)   I told him that we <u>had informed</u> them of our intention a year ago.

      (iv)   He <u>worked</u> in this office since October.

      (v)   I showed the teacher what I <u>wrote.</u>

  (c)   (i)   Since

      (ii)   For

      (iii)   For

      (iv)   Of

      (v)   With

  (d)   1.   Since they are very old, they cannot run.

      2.   John was a philosopher as well as a poet.

      3.   Many children are falling sick due to the increasing level of pollution.

      4.   Hurry up else you will be late.

      5.   Though social service is demanding, it has its own reward.

QUESTION PAPER FOR ICSE 2001 EXAMINATION
Paper 1
(Two hours)

Answer to this paper must be written on the paper provided separately

*You will **NOT** be allowed to write in the first 15 minutes*
This time is to be spent in reading the question paper

---

*Attempt all the **four** questions*
The intended marks for question or part of question are given in [ ]
You are advised to spend not more than 35 minutes in answering question no 1and 20 minutes in answering Question no 2

---

*Attempt all **four** questions*

Question 1.

(Do not spend more than **35** minutes on this question)

Write a composition (**350 – 400 words**) on any **one** of the following: -   [25]

(*a*)   Describe a weekly market scene in your area. State why you like or do not like the scene.

(*b*)   Democracy is the best form of government. Give your views either for or against this statement.

(*c*)   Imagine that your sister is going to get married. You have to shoulder the responsibilities for the wedding reception. How would you handle the situation?

(*d*)   There are three kinds of people in this world – the Wills, the Won'ts and the Can'ts. The first accomplish everything, the second oppose everything, and the third fail in everything. By giving reasons or referring to some incidents, state in which category you fall.

(*e*)   Study the picture given below. Write a story, or a description or an account of what the picture suggests to you. There has to be a clear connection between the picture and the composition.

Question 2

(Do not spend more than 20 minutes on this question.)

Select one of the following: -   [10]

(a)   You have just returned from the holiday at a hill station. Write a letter to your friend mentioning what you found most exciting about the place and give two reasons to explain why you consider it an ideal place for a vacation.

(b)   Write a letter to the Chief Minister of your state drawing his attention to the urgent need for a government hospital in your district.

Question 3

Read the following passage carefully and then answer the questions (a), (b) and (c) that follow.

Crewman Fredrick Persson was on deck, helping, to bring the Swedish cargo ship 'Carman' into Bristol docks, when a rope coiled around his right hand suddenly jerked tight, all but severing his four fingers.

He was rushed to the special reconstructive surgery unit at a local hospital, where doctors decided two of his fingers were too badly <u>mangled</u> to be saved. In a delicate eight hour operation using the most sophisticated microsurgery techniques, plastic surgeon Donald Sammut succeeded in reattaching the others. "I am happy to have even two fingers left," the young Swede said gratefully as he came out of the surgery.

His relief was short-lived. Within 48 hours the fingers started to go black. "A blockage of blood was building up,"explains Sammut.

Modern surgery could do no more, so Sammut resorted to one of the medicine's oldest aids; the leech. Over the next two days, he fastened a <u>succession</u> of black slippery creatures to Persson's fingers. They sucked out surplus blood, freeing veins to reconnect naturally so that circulation was restored. A fortnight later, in November 1993, Persson flew home.

Leeches come in around 650 species, from 1.5 centimetre long slivers to specimens that reach a jumbo 45 centimetres when fully extended and are found in many parts of the world. These annelids – not all bloodsucking – breathe through the skin, have two hearts and go for months between meals. Some have suckers at each end of their body. They are making an astonishing comeback in medicine. In recent years Hirudo medicinalis, the leech used for medical purposes, has performed its quiet miracles for thousands of surgical patients and accident victims around the world.

When the leech bites into the flesh with its 300 sharp teeth, leaving an inverted Y shaped mark, it injects a powerful anaesthetic; and the patient feels no pain. As it starts sucking the leech <u>secretes</u> a coctail of substances that act as an anti –coagulant, to ensure the blood's purity and keeps it flowing. Even though the leech may suck for 30 minutes, "bleeding" may continue for several hours or so, clearing the most challenging blockage.

Ear reconnections are <u>notoriously</u> difficult because the ear's blood vessels are so small, measuring no more than half a millimetre in diameter. When five years old Guy Condelli had his right ear bitten off by a dog, surgeons reattached it in a 12-hour operation. But three days later it turned blue, than purple.

The surgeon leading the medical team Joseph Upton, who had used leeches to help heal wounds of war victims in Vietnam, decided to try them in Guy's case. Over six days, 12 were attached to Guy's ears, one by one until they dropped off, swollen and sated. By the last day of his treatment blood was circulating throughout his ear, and the following day its colour was back to normal.

Surgeon Peter Mahaffey helped pioneer the modern use of leeches in Britain –against opposition from colleagues reluctant to take a " backward" step – when stitching back a finger in 1979. Now he always keeps a jar of them in his plastic surgery unit. Mahaffey's leeches along with those used for Fredrick Persson's fingers and Guy Condelli's ear, come from Britains only leech breeding farm founded and run by Dr Roy Sawyer in South Wales.

Sawyer first encountered leeches as a boy in Swamplands of South Carolina, USA. "Often when swimming, I'd find leeches on me, I considered them as natural, if unwelcome, as mosquitoes."

At school, he became <u>fascinated</u> by the leech's role in medicine. "Historically, leeches were employed as a mild form of blood - letting for the early stages of inflammatory diseases," he says. "For centuries bleeding was almost the only surgical treatment, apart from amputation.

(a) Five words from the passage are given below. Give a word or phrase that can replace them in the passage.

    (i) mangled

    (i) succession

    (ii) secretes

    (iii) notoriously

    (iv) fascinated   [5]

(b) Answer the following questions in your own words: -

    (i) How was Fredrick Persson cured when his fingers turned blue?   [2]

    (ii) State why, after a leech bite, bleeding continues for several hours?   [2]

    (iii) How were the leeches used for Guy Condelli's ear?   [2]

    (iv) What happens when leeches bite?   [2]

    (iv) Quote the sentence which shows what leeches were used for by medical experts.

                                                                   [2]

(c) In not more than 60 words of your own state Sawyer's connection with leeches   [10]

Question 4

(a) Rewrite the following sentences correctly according to the instructions given after each. Make other changes that may be necessary, but do not change the meaning of the sentence.   [5]

    (i) Suresh suddenly thought of a splendid idea.

       (End:................. to Suresh.)

    (ii) Raunak missed the bus because he was late.

       (Use:.................... catch.)

    (iii) Sheena returned one week ago.

       (Begin: It has.............)

    (iv) "I am sorry for insulting you", said Lakshmi to Madhu.

       (Begin: Lakshmi apologised...........)

    (v) He could not complete the race as he had injured his foot.

       (Use prevented.)

(b) Fill in the blanks with suitable words.   [5]

    (i) The car battery has run_____; it needs recharging.

    (ii) How can you put _____ with his unpleasant manners?

    (iii) We had agreed to meet at the cinema at 7.30, but he never turned _____.

    (iv) You must reach the place_____ sunset.

    (v) Cholera has broken _____ in our village.

(c) Complete each of the following sentences with a suitable form of the word given in brackets: -   [5]

    (i) It _____(rain) heavily all night in Delhi.

    (ii) Children are not _____ (permit) to attend the function.

    (iii) Shanaque said that he _____ (will) give an early reply.

   (*iv*) Sophia will be_____ (punish) if she does not do her work

   (*v*) He is poor at _____ (memory) lengthy poems.

 (d) Join the following sentences to make one complete sentence without using *and* or *but*.   [5]

   (*i*) Rahil is a clever boy. The other boys are not so clever.

   (*ii*) It rained heavily. We could not have the tournament.

   (*iii*) You must study diligently. You will miss your grade otherwise.

   (*iv*) The air- hostess was injured. She helped the victims.

   (*v*) The supervisor was out of the hall. The students made a lot of noise.

Answers

1. (*a*) Refer to Contents Section B Sl No. 56

  (*b*) Refer to Contents Section B Sl No. 28

  (*c*) Refer to Contents Section B Sl No. 78

  (*d*) Refer to Contents Section B Sl No. 04

2. (*a*) Refer to Contents Section E Sl No. 04

  (*b*) Refer to Contents Section E Sl No. 14

3. (*a*)

  (*i*) crushed, smashed

  (*ii*) series

  (*iii*) produces, gives out

  (*iv*) dreadfully, well known to be

  (*v*) delighted, attracted

 (*b*)

 (*i*) Fredrick Persson's finger turned blue after the microsurgery, due to a blockage of blood in the veins. Dr Donald Sammat fastened one after the other, a number of black slippery leeches, to Persson's fingers. The leeches sucked out the surplus blood, thereby freeing the veins to reconnect naturally, so that circulation was restored and he was cured.

 (*ii*) As the leech starts sucking blood, it produces a mixture of fluids that act as an anti-coagulant. This ensures the blood's purity, and keep it flowing freely for several hours, rather than coagulating as in the normal course.

 (*iii*) For over a period of six days, twelve leeches were attached to Guy Condelli's ear one after another, until they dropped off bloated and satisfied with blood. This was because, ear reconnections are very difficult, on account of extremely small diameter of ear blood vessels.

 (*iv*) When the leech bites into the flesh with its 300 sharp teeth, it leaves an inverted Y shaped mark. The victim does not feel the pain, because it simultaneously injects a powerful an-aesthetics.

 (*v*) "Historically leeches were employed as a mild form of blood letting for the early stages of inflammatory diseases,".

(*c*) Doctor Roy Sawyer owned the only leech-breeding farm in Britain and supplied them for medicine. He first encountered leeches, as a boy in the Swamplands of South Carolina, USA. While swimming, he often found them on himself .He considered them natural and annoying as mosquitoes. Later at school, he was fascinated by their role in medicine and bred them.

4.

(a)

    (i)   A splendid idea suddenly occurred to Suresh.

    (ii)   Raunak could not catch the bus, as he was late.

    (iii) It has been a week since Sheena returned.

    (iv) Lakshmi apologised to Madhu for insulting her.

    (v)   An injured foot prevented him from completing the race.

(b)

    (i)   down

    (ii)   up

    (iii) up

    (iv) before

    (v)   out

(c)

    (i)   rained

    (ii)   permitted

    (iii) would

    (iv) punished

    (v)   memorising

(d)

    (i)   Rahil is the cleverest of all the boys.

    (ii)   We could not have the tournament as it rained heavily.

    (iii) If you do not study diligently you will miss your grade

    (iv) Though the airhostess was injured, she helped the victims.

    (v)   The students made a lot of noise when the supervisor was out of the class.

QUESTION PAPER FOR ICSE 2002 EXAMINATION
Paper 1
(Two hours)

Answer to this paper must be written on the paper [provided separately]

*You will **NOT** be allowed to write in the first 15 minutes*
This time is to be spent in reading the question paper

---

*Attempt all the **four** questions*
The intended marks for question or part of question are given in []
You are advised to spend not more than 35 minutes in answering question no 1 and 20 minutes in answering Question no 2

Question 1

(Do not spend more than **35** minutes on this question)

Write a composition (**350-400 words**) on any **one** of the following.   [25]

(a)   'Society is influenced more by show than by substance'. Relate an incident from your experience, which brings out the truth of this statement.

(b)   Men and Women should have equal rights. Give your views for or against the statement.

(c)   It was a long awaited climax to your period of training for the parachute Regiment –the day of the first jump! Describe how you prepared yourself for the parachute drop, the drop itself, and your feeling after the event.

(d)   You have just interviewed a famous person at his /her residence. Write an account of the whole experience. You may include the following points.

Preparation for the interview – description of the person's home –A brief description of his / her achievements – What happened during the interview –his / her behaviour – general impressions.

(e)   Study the picture given below. Write a story or a description or an account of what the picture suggests to you. Your composition must be about the subject of the picture or may take suggestions from it. But there must be a clear connection between the picture and your composition.

Question 2

(Do not spend more than 20 minutes on this question.   [10]

(a) You were held up in the countryside one night due to a railway accident .Write a letter to your friend narrating the incident.

(b) Read the following advertisement.

WANTED

Suitable young sales assistant–on a part time basis-to market garments for a leading fashion designer–Apply to the manager, New Creations ,147, Lajpat Nagar, New Delhi-110024.

Write an application in response to this advertisement.

Question 3

Read the following passage carefully and answer the questions that follow:

The saving of certain wild animals from extinction has for many years been a problem for zoologists and other specialists; but more recently the problem has become so acute, and has received so much publicity, that most people are now concerned about it. This may at first seem strange because one of the most <u>gratifying</u> developments of the last few years has been the passing of strict laws to protect wild animals and the <u>consequent</u> decline in the hunting of big - game for sport. Why is it, then that some rare wild animals are still threatened with extinction and even some of the less rare ones are rapidly <u>declining</u> in number?

One reason is the 'march of civilization'. When an area is wholly cleared of vegetation to make room for new towns, factory sites or hydroelectric plants, the natural home of several species is destroyed. The displaced must either migrate to another area or perish. Even the clearing of land for a road or an airfield may involve 'pushing back' the jungle, and the smaller the area in which wild animals compete for a living the smaller the number that can hope to survive.

Civilization brings, too, swift and easy transport and so assists those who are determined to break the various protective laws. Thieves can elude the game wardens, shoot an elephant for its tusks, a rhinoceros for its horn, or a deer for its meat and be miles away from the <u>site</u> of the crime before the dead or dying victim is even discovered.

It is sad to <u>reflect</u> that civilization, which can bring so many benefits to people who have previously known only hunger and misery, brings also facilities for the heartless criminals who, for the material gain, will slaughter some harmless animals and threaten the disappearance of its kind from the earth forever.

(a) Five words are given below. Give the meaning of each word as used in the passage. One -word answers or short phrases will be accepted.   [5]

(i)   Gratifying

(ii) Consequent

(iii) Declining

(iv) Site

(v)   Reflect

(b) Answer the following questions briefly in your own words:

(i)   "This may at first seem strange". To what does the word 'this' refer?   [2]

(ii) Why does the author think that 'this' may seem strange?   [2]

(iii) How does modern transport threaten the survival of wild animals? [2]

(iv) Using single sentence for each, give the meaning of: [2]

    (1) 'pushing back' the jungle

    (2) compete for a living.

(v) What is the sad reflection that the author makes in the last paragraph of the passage? [2]

(c) In not more than 60 words of your own, mention ways in which the 'march of civilization' threatens to make certain rare wild animals extinct. [10]

Question 4.

(a) Rewrite the following sentences correctly according to the instructions given after each.

Make other changes that may be necessary, but do not change the meaning of the sentence.

(i) John has probably forgotten the date of examination.

    (Begin; In....)

(ii) Very few countries are as large as India.

    (Use; 'larger'.)

(iii) The sergeant asked; 'Did you have any training before'?

    (Rewrite using; 'whether' or 'if')

(iv) If you don't come, I will not go out.

    (Begin: Only...)

(v) He sold his house to a wealthy diamond magnate.

    (Rewrite using 'bought' instead of 'sold') [5]

(b) Complete each of the blanks (1-5) using the appropriate form of the verbs given in brackets:

The falcons were obviously in a heat of fury when the ravens (1)_____ (come) scouting along the cliff. The falcons (2)_____ (attempt) to drive away the ravens. The ravens, however, (3)_____ (fly) unconcerned to and fro. Only at the last split second of each falcon's drive, (4)_____ (do) the ravens turn over sideways to present that remarkable beak which (5)_____ - (can) transfix the falcon were it to continue its wild drive. [5]

(c) Fill in the blanks with appropriate words:-

(i) He was let off _____ a fine.

(ii) The Principal called _____ a written application.

(iii) Where did you come _____ this word?

(iv) How did this topic come _____?

(v) The Chairman assured the Committee that he would look _____ the matter.

[5]

(d) The following words have different meanings though spelt in the same way. Use each of them in two separate sentences to illustrate this.

(i) Present

(ii) Swallow

(*iii*) Bank

(*iv*) Match

(*v*) Scale.   [5]

Answers

1.

(*a*) Refer to Contents Section B Sl No. 53

(*b*) Refer to Contents Section B Sl No. 03

(*c*) Refer to Contents Section B Sl No. 54

(*d*) Refer to Contents Section B Sl No. 55

Picture composition

"Charity begins at home" Rohit had ingrained this virtue from his father the late Shri Rajapati Shastri the great freedom fighter .So unlike his counterparts he chose to set up an NGO for providing medical facilities to the people of his village in Banda district .His decision surprised his friends and colleagues, who were either planning to go abroad for better prospects, or trying to join some prestigious hospitals in the metropolitan cities. They tried to dissuade him but all in vain.

The initial going was rough but Rohit remain undaunted. Seeing his missionary zeal ,the gram panchayat was inspired and pledged full support to him in his noble endeavour. They donated a piece of land in the village and helped him set up a dispensary. In about a year's time, he had a small ten bed hospital running in the village .The villagers were overjoyed, they no longer had to trudge thirty kilometers to the nearest primary center for medical help. The charitable hospital not only provided medicines, but also gave free medicines to the poor and needy peasants.

The good work done by him soon caught the attention of philanthropic organisations like the Red Cross, and the District Lions club. They donated generous amounts to him to carry on the good work. They also donated an ambulance van to his hospital, to enable him to reach out to the other villages in the interior, that had remained beyond the reach of the primary health centers of the government.

With the onset of monsoons, the villages were cut off from the district headquarters due to floods. One day the gram pradhan informed him that there was an outbreak of cholera in the village Panki, ten kilometers down south. Rohit immediately put on his Gandhi cap, and taking a few volunteers with him reached the village in his ambulance. The seriously ill patients were carried to the ambulance on stretchers .The not so serious ones were brought by him in a wheel chair. They made several trips to the village and by evening, he had thirty serious cases of cholera to attend to. He sought help from the local villagers, and also sent an SOS to the district hospital. Soon the government machinery went into action, and a team of doctors and medical staff were rushed to his hospital. His relentless efforts finally bore fruit, and in about a week's time all the patients were discharged from the hospital.

He received accolades from all quarters including the government for his good work .The government of India awarded him the Mahatma Gandhi award for social upliftment, and sanctioned sizeable grants to enable him to establish a chain of such hospitals in the villages .The trail blazed by him today inspires many a medical graduate to follow in his footsteps, rather than to migrate abroad, or live a mundane life in the cities.

2.

(*a*) Refer to Contents Section E Sl No. 03

(*b*) Refer to Contents Section E Sl No. 16

3.

   (*a*)

   (*i*)   Satisfying

   (*ii*)   Resultant, event that follows another

   (*iii*) Decreasing in number

   (*iv*)   Place of incident

   (*v*)   Mediate, consult with oneself

   (*b*)

    (*i*) The word 'this' as used in the passage by the author, refers to the growing extinction of rare wild animals.

    (*ii*) The author thinks this increasing rate of extinction of wild animals to be strange, for people are generally more aware and concerned about this problem. Moreover, stringent laws have been made to protect the wild animals thereby resulting in the sharp decline of game hunting. Inspite of these severe measures, their growing extinction is indeed strange.

    (*iii*) The modern transport systems, like the roads and airports for plying motor vehicles and aeroplanes involves clearing of large tracts of land. This destroys the natural habitat of the wild animals, and encroaches upon the forestland, forcing them to migrate to other areas that may not be very hospitable. As the forestland gets reduced, they find it increasingly difficulty to grow and thrive. This overcrowding results in making them compete for the scarce resources available, and consequently results in the survival of the fittest, leaving a large number to perish.

    (*iv*) Using single sentence for each, give the meaning of

       'Pushing back' the jungle

    The ever-increasing expansion of the towns and the cities, results in ' pushing back' the jungle.

       Compete for a living.

    The poor are finding it increasingly difficult to compete for a living, in this age of cut-throat competition and rising inflation.

    (*v*) The sad reflection the author makes is the irony, that while the advancement in science and technology brings numerous benefits to people, it also helps unscrupulous criminals to slaughter innocent animals. They kill animals, using highly sophisticated weapons, and escape by travelling in fast automobiles. Thereby misusing the advancement made in society for their material gains, unmindful of their extinction from the face of the earth.

   (*c*) In not more than 60 words of your own, mention ways in which the 'march of civilization' threatens to make certain rare wild animals extinct.

The advancement of civilisation, threatens to make rare wild animals extinct. The growth of cities, factories and construction of roads and airports, reduces the forestland available to animals, forcing them to migrate. This overcrowding, makes them compete for the scarce naturals resources, consequently only few survive. Furthermore the fast means of transport, enable poachers to kill these animals and escape.

4.

(*a*)

(*i*)   In all probability John has forgotten the date of the examination.

(*ii*)   Very few countries are larger than India

(*iii*)   The sergeant enquired whether he had any previous training

(*iv*)   Only if you come will I go out

(*v*)   A wealthy diamond magnate brought his house.

(*b*) Complete each of the blanks (1-5) using the appropriate form of the verbs given in brackets:

The falcons were obviously in a heat of fury when the ravens (1) <u>came</u> scouting along the cliff. The falcons (2) <u>attempt</u> to drive away the ravens. The ravens, however, (3) *flew* unconcerned to and fro. Only at the last split second of each falcon's drive, (4) *did* the ravens turn over sideways to present that remarkable beak which (5) *could* transfix the falcon were it to continue its wild drive

(*c*)   Fill in the blanks with appropriate words:

(*i*)   He was let off <u>with</u> a fine.

(*ii*)   The Principal called <u>for</u> a written application.

(*iii*)   Where did you come <u>across</u> this word?

(*iv*)   How did this topic come up ?

(*v*)   The Chairman assured the Committee that he would look <u>into</u> the matter.

(*d*) The following words have different meanings though spelt in the same way. Use each of them in two separate sentences to illustrate this.

(*i*)   Present

His father gave him a beautiful watch as his birthday present.

The teacher marked him absent, as he was not present in the class.

(*ii*)   Swallow

He was in such a great hurry, that he could barely swallow the food given to him by his mother.

He watched in delight, the flock of swallows that flew past on the beach.

(*iii*)   Bank

My father brought money from the bank, to buy a new bicycle for me.

We must not bank on fair weather friends for they are bound to leave us in time of need.

(*iv*)   Match

He prepared rigorously for the inter school football match which was to start next month.

People are finding it easier to find a match for their wards, from the matrimonial advertisements in the newspapers.

(*v*)   Scale.

Tenzing was the first Indian to scale the Mount Everest.

The scale of competition has increased many folds in the last few years

QUESTION PAPER FOR ICSE 2003 EXAMINATION
Paper 1
(Two hours)
Answers to this paper must be written on the paper provided separately.
*You will **NOT** be allowed to write during the first 15 minutes.*
This time is to be spent in reading the question paper.
The time given at the head of this paper is the time allowed for writing the answers.

---

*Attempt all **four** questions.*
The intended marks for questions or parts of questions are given in brackets [].
You are advised to spend not more than 35 minutes in answering Question 1 and 20 minutes on answering Question 2.

Question 1

*(Do not spend more than **35** minutes on this question.)*

Write a composition **(350 - 400 words)** on any **one** of the following: -   [25]

(*a*) While on a picnic you and your friends decide to go sailing. Unfortunately, your boat capsizes in a violent storm. However, all of you manage to swim to safety. Give a vivid account of the incident.

(*b*) Looking back at the last ten years' of your life, describe the events that have been significant in shaping your personality.

(*c*) Animals should not be used for drug development or medical research. Express your views either *for* or *against this* statement.

(*d*) Write a short story to illustrate the proverb 'Knowledge is Power'.

(*e*) Study the picture given below. Write a story or a description or an account of what it suggests to you. Your composition may be about the subject of the picture or may take suggestions from it; but there must be a clear connection between the picture and your composition.

Question 2.

(Do not spend more than 20 minutes on this question.)

Select **one** of the following: [10]

(a) You wish to become a journalist while your parents want you to become a doctor. Write a letter to your mother giving reasons why you should be allowed to pursue your ambition.

(b) You are the manager of a reputed firm. A consignment sent by you to one of your regular customers was returned with a letter complaining of the inferior quality of goods. Write a letter of apology, explaining the causes and your plans for replacement.

Question 3.

Read the following passage carefully and answer the questions that follow:

An important reason for ants' success is their ability to talk not with words but with tastes and smells. Their vocabulary is made up of a mixture of substances they produce in various parts of their bodies and Emit via their glands. The so-called pheromones are signals that other Ants can smell and taste. The messages they communicate set off a specific kind of behaviour: fetching food for instance or looking after the brood or feeding the queen. Furthermore, ant-talk is not limited to food. Ants use a hundred, different scents to communicate a hundred different messages. With such a sophisticated *array* of messenger fragrances, ants organize complicated tasks with close-lo-perfect efficiency.

Every ant is a specialist with a vocation of its own. The queen has one of the biggest workloads laying eggs round the clock. Despite the presence of a queen, an ant colony is not a monarchy. The word 'queen' is actually a misnomer. "She doesn't reign over the others," says Holldober. "She's a machine for laying eggs." From morning till night she produces her daughters, the sterile workers of the colony. Males don't have to do much and the queen only produces them when reproduction time is approaching. Their main job is to fertilize the winged females. After that they die.

Messengers don't have much free time either. When you see a handful of ants scurrying around in the kitchen, without any apparent purpose, it doesn't mean they've lost their bearings. They're scouts *foraging* for food. Once they've found something edible, they report back to base, depositing their chemical spores on the way. "Food located, please, collect," is the taste and smell message for the other members back at the nest.

Very, soon, long chains of worker ants begin scurrying back and forth. From their nest *ferrying* food which they hand over to ants who specialize in housekeeping. The duties of these ants include keeping the nest in good order and cleaning and feeding the queen.

Jet ants settle in hollow trees where they build papery structures to live in. In these trees they keep herds of greenflies which they actually milk in the same way we milk cows. It's a model partnership. To satisfy their need for amino acids, the greenflies have to ingest large quantities of sap. As a result, surplus sugar forms in their bodies, which they excrete through their rear ends. This so-called honeydew is the jet ants' main source of nourishment. In return, the ants see to it that the green flies don't get stuck fast in their own honey and also protect their herds from marauding *predators* such as ladybirds. "It's a form of dairy farming," says Holldober.

Dairying is only one of the many *ingenious* ideas ants have come up with in the course of evolution. Small red wood ants, for example, regulate the temperature in their high-rise anthills by sunbathing on warm spring days and then scuttling back to the nest double quick to give off the warmth they've soaked up.

An ant colony, Moldable says, is an almost perfectly organized network of equal status elements complementing one another in all they do. Ants will do anything as long as it's in the service of the common weal. "Maybe socialism does work after all under certain circumstances," Holldobler grins. "Karl Marx just had the wrong species in mind."

(*a*) Five words are given below; Give the meaning of each word as used in the passage.

One word answers or short phrases will be, accepted.

(i)   Array
(ii) Foraging
(iii) Ferrying
(iv) Predators
(v)   Ingenious   [5]

(b) Answer briefly the following questions in your own words:
   (i)   What is meant by 'misnomer'? Why is the word 'queen' a misnomer?   [2]
   (ii) When do the chains of worker ants move about in a hurry?   [2]
   (iii) What is referred to as 'milk' from the greenflies?   [2]
   (iv) What do the greenflies receive in return for giving milk to the ants?   [2]
   (v)   What does Ḥölldobler wish to communicate by the following sentence:
         "Karl Marx just had the wrong species in mind."   [2]

(c) In not more than 60 words *of* your own, state how the ants work in a well-
     organized manner.   [10]

Question 4.

(a) Rewrite the following sentences according to the instructions given after each. Make, other
     changes that may be necessary but do not change the meaning of each sentence.   [5]

   (i)   Had I not helped her, she would not have succeeded. (Begin: But. ....)
   (ii) His unexpected victory surprised everybody in the school. (Begin: His unexpected victory
         took.......)
   (iii) If he apologises he will be pardoned. (Use unless instead of if)
   (iv) Nobody in our city can run as fast as Usha. (Begin, Usha)
   (v)   Joe requested his friend to wait there till he returned.   (End..... till I return.)

(b) Fill in the blanks with appropriate words: [5]
   (i)   The outgoing Manager will hand............charge to his successor.
   (ii)   Her request for a transfer was turned ....
   (iii) A man is known ....the company he keeps.
   (iv)   Not all of us are alive......... the threat arising from global warming.
   (v)   You must reach home ...... sunset.
   (vi)   The five players quarrelled .... themselves.
   (vii) We have lived in this village ... ten years.
   (viii) He found himself .... pressure to grant the request.
   (ix)   He proved himself equal ..... the task.
   (x)   He was unwilling to take ..... the challenge.

(c) In the following passage fill in each of the numbered blanks with the correct form of the word
     given in brackets. Do not copy the passage, but write in correct serial order the word or phrase
     appropriate to the blank space.   [5]

Example: 0 *lived*

Once there 0 ....(live) a monk who (1)....... (decide) to make his followers always laugh. People
flocked to him to listen to his jokes and (2)..........   (return) home laughing. The monk
would make fun of himself and of others, (3)....................(make) sure that there (4) ....(be)
not a single gloomy face in the crowd. After some years when he (5).............   (die) and
yet cheerful, his followers asked him how he (6)..................(manage) to be happy even on his
deathbed. He did not reply but made a last wish that he should be cremated with his clothes on.
He wished that he should be kept on the funeral pyre with, the same clothes he (7)..................
(wear). His wishes were carried out_ and to every one's surprise, when the pyre was (8).......... .
(light) it was found that the old monk had (9) .... (hide) firecrackers under his clothes. Even
on his cremation pyre, he (10)........ (entertain) people.

(d) Join the following sentences to make one complete sentence without using 'and', 'but' or 'so':
                                                                                                    [5]
   (i)   He found the book at last. It was in the library.
   (ii) She received the message. Immediately she went to meet her brother.
   (iii) Tom may run fast. He cannot catch the train.
   (iv) I saw men at work on a new building. It was to be a factory.
   (v)   Suresh did not come to school. He did not send in an application.

Answers

1.

(a) Refer to Contents Section B Sl No. 50

(b) Refer to Contents Section B Sl No. 51

(c) Refer to Contents Section B Sl No. 02

(d) Refer to Contents Section B Sl No. 52

(e) **PICTURE STORY**

"Mummy, the train is late by an hour" I yelled, hearing the announcement being made on the public address system. I slackened my pace, and held back the luggage trolley, which I was vigorously pushing. I was indeed disappointed at having to wait an hour on the railway platform, amidst all dirt and confusion, that one usually finds on a railway platform.

I had anxiously looked forward to this day, when we were to go to Kanya Kumari, to spend our summer vacations. We were to catch the Rajadhani Express train, which would take us right up to Trivandrum, from where we would take a local train for Kanya Kumari. A week before the journey, we had meticulously packed our returned luggage, taking all essential clothing, bedding and some edibles. By the time the packing was over, we had   packed all the items in a big suitcase, while my clothes were packed in two small briefcases. I was given the exclusive responsibility to take care of my baggage. Reaching the station I pulled a luggage trolley, and put my. briefcases on it. My father called a porter, and placed the big suitcase on his head, and slung the bedding on his shoulder. My mother clutched the handbag containing eatables, while my father carried the cold water bottle, and hung the camera on his shoulder. Thus merrily we trudged, towards the entrance of the railway station.

My mother sighed in disappointment on hearing the announcement, and casually asked my father to check the departure time of the train on the ticket. The very mention of 'ticket' made my father's mouth fall open. He seemed to be dumb struck for a moment. He searched his trouser pockets and purse, but there was no trace of the tickets. He had obviously forgotten to put them in his wallet I.

All pandemonium broke loose, as my father and mother accused each other for the lapse. Placing the luggage on the railway platform, he rushed back home to collect the tickets. It was indeed a long and antagonizing wait, that stretched, to about fifty minutes. All the while I was anxiously pacing up and down the platform. watching the minute hand on the big clock tick by.

My heart beat increased, with the announcement of the arrival of the Rajdhani Express. Just then I saw my father rushing toward us, waving the tickets, that he had finally found.

I hugged my mother with joy. We finally headed towards the compartment, as the train screeched to a halt. The journey to Trivandrum was exhilarating, especially the sceneric beauty along the sea coast in Kerala. The journey was memorable and we visited all the important tourist spots around Kanya Kumari. After a brief sojourn at a beach resort in Kovallum, we returned home, with pleasant memories of our vacation.

2.

   (a)   Refer to Contents Section E Sl No. 02
   (b)   Refer to Contents Section E Sl No. 26

3.

(a)

(i) Array- series of

(ii) Foraging- making intrusion, inroad.

(iii) Ferrying- convey, pass to and fro.

(iv) Predators- animals preying upon others.

(v) Ingenious- clever at contriving.

(b)

(i) By misnomer we mean contrary to the general belief. The word "Queen " is a misnomer. for though an ant colony has a queen. She does not rule over the other ants like a monarch. She however has no work. except to lay eggs round the clock that produce the sterile daughters.

(ii) When ants sent scouting for food, find something edible, they report back to the nest through smell and taste messages. To help other ants locate the food, they deposit chemical spores from their bodies on the way. The worker ants pick up the scent, and come to collect the food, forming long chains. They move about in a hurry, going to and fro from the nest, carrying the food, which they give to other ants that specialise in housekeeping. This goes on, till the food that has been located, is transported safely to the nest.

(iii) The surplus sugar excreted by the greenflies, is the main source of nourishment for the jet ants. This surplus sugar is referred to as the honey dew, or the 'milk' from the greenflies, in the above passage.

(iv) The greenflies receive protection from its enemies, like the ladybird, by living in the papery nests, built by the Jet ants in the hollow of trees. Furthermore the jet ants consume the excess sugar produced by the greenflies, thereby ensuring that they do not get stuck in the honey they produce.

(v) Holldober makes a sarcastic comment on Karl Marx, and his much professed ideals of Socialism. According to him, while socialism has failed miserably in the human species, as is evident from the collapse of the USSR and east European countries, it works very successfully in an ants colony. This is for in an ant's colony, all ants enjoy equal status, unlike humans. Obviously Karl Marx philosophy was more suited to the ant species, rather than the human being, for whom it was propounded.

(c)

Every	ant	has	a	specific
vocation	The	queen	lays	eggs
that	produce	the	sterile	workers
The	messenger	ants	scout	for
food	They	communicate	and	guide
other	ants	to	it	through
smell	and	taste	messages	Housekeep-
ing				
ants	take	care	of	the
Queen	and	keep	the	nest
clean	All	ants	have	equal
status	and	complement	each	other
in	a	well	organised	manner

4.

(a)

(i) But for my help she would not have succeeded.

(ii) His unexpected victory took everybody by surprise.

(iii) Unless he apologises he will not be pardoned.

(*iv*)   Usha runs the fastest in our city.

(*v*)   Joe said to his friend " wait here till I return."

(*b*)

(*i*)   Over

(*ii*)   Down

(*iii*)   By

(*iv*)   To

(*v*)   Before

(*vi*)   Among

(*vii*)   For

(*viii*)   Under

(*ix*)   To

(*x*)   Up

(*c*)

0. lived

1. decided

2. returned

3. making

4. was

5. was dying

6. managed

7. was wearing

8. lit

9. hidden

10. entertained

(*d*)

(*i*)   He at last found the book in the library.

(*ii*)   Immediately on receiving the message. She went to meet her brother.

(*iii*)   Tom cannot catch the train no matter how fast he runs.

(*iv*)   I saw men at work on the new building that was to be a factory.

(*v*)   Suresh did not send in an application for not being able to come to school.

Paper 1

(Two hours)

Answers to this paper must be written on the paper provided separately.

*You will **NOT** be allowed to write during the first 15 minutes.*

This time is to be spent in reading the question paper.

The time given at the head of this paper is the time allowed for writing the answers.

---

*Attempt all **four** questions.*

The intended marks for questions or parts of questions are given in brackets [].

You are advised to spend not more than 35 minutes in answering Question 1 and

20 minutes on answering Question 2.

Question 1

*(Do not spend more than **35** minutes on this question.)*

Write a composition (**350 - 400 words**) on any **one** of the following:- [25]

(a) You have lived in your ancestral house since birth. The house is to be sold so that flats may be built. Narrate the circumstances that led to this decision and describe your feelings about moving out of the house.

(b) Write about two deeds you have done, one of which gave you immense joy and satisfaction, while the other was a cause of deep regret.

(c) 'Teenagers today are more worldly-wise than their parents.' Express your views for or against the statement.

(d) Write a short story which illustrates the truth of the statement.
   'Self- help is the best help.'

(e) Study the picture given below. Write a story or a description or an account of what it suggests to you. Your composition may be about the subject of the picture or may take suggestions from it; however, there must be a clear connection between the picture and your composition.

Question 2

(Do not spend more than 20 minutes on this question.)

Select **one** of the following:-   [10]

- (*a*) Your mother has won the National Award for *Meritorious Teachers*. Write a letter **to a friend giving details of the award, the award ceremony and the celebrations that followed**.

- (*b*) Your school had contributed a large sum of money to the Prime Minister's Relief Fund to help the victims of an earthquake. You visited the place recently and were shocked to see the poor living conditions of the victims. Write a letter to the Officer In-Charge of the Prime Minister's Relief Fund, drawing his attention to the plight of the people in the affected area.

Question 3

Read the following passage carefully and answer the questions that follow:-

From the edge of a steep ridge, I peered down into the Redstone Valley. Like many summer days in north-west Alaska, the morning had begun bright and wind-swept, but now a dark cloud was drifting in from the east. I decided to move on. Camp was still three kilometers down the hill.

It had been eighteen years since I had first come to this vast untamed wilderness. Still there was the <u>lure</u> of the place - the chance to live, move and breathe. Settled in Ambler, a small village in the Kobuk Valley, I'd found life among the Inupiat Eskimos as rich and textured as the Arctic landscape around us. However, even a bright summer day could mean trouble.

As I slung my pack onto my shoulders, a big Arctic mosquito thudded against my cheek. There had been a few of them through the day, but it was early in the season - the ice had melted just two weeks before and I'd scarcely noticed the mosquitoes. But now as I wound down the ridge, the last breeze faded, and they were on me. Rising in clouds from the soggy Tundra, they pelted against my face. I looked for the repellent in my pack, but in vain.

I was flailing away, nailing five or six at a whack, but there were thousands mobbing me now. They were diving in nose-first, piercing me right through my clothes, dozens at a time. Four hands wouldn't have been enough. Years of Alaskan experience had taught me what to do in a situation like this. I turned up my collar, cinched my pack straps tight and sprinted. When I saw my tent, I was still going strong. So were the mosquitoes. They trailed me in a whining veil. Each time I slowed down, the attack resumed. Pausing just long enough to unzip the screen door, I dived through to safety. It took me fifteen minutes to hunt down the hundred or so that entered the tent with me.

After I'd cornered the last one, I took stock and tried to relax. My hands and neck were <u>smeared</u> with blood, and every centimeter of the exposed skin was punctured. Outside, the insistent wail was nearly deafening. Mosquitoes settled over the tent, making a strange pattern on the nylon mesh. Not until later that night, when a cold rain swept in and scattered the mob, did I stick my own itching nose outside again. Local <u>legend</u> has it that an animal, or human being for that matter, caught in one of these mosquito attacks, can be sucked dry.

Blood thirsty though they are, the big Arctic mosquitoes are frail creatures. These infamous' Alaska state birds', averaging a little over half a centimeter in length, can't even withstand a substantial breeze. They'd wither under bright sunlight. Too hot or too cold, too much or too little rain, they run for cover. They spend most of their brief lives hiding under leaves, waiting for the right feeding condition . A still humid cloudy evening is perfect.

The upper Kobuk Eskimos know how to handle mosquitoes. As soon as the river is clear of ice, many Ambler people load up their boats and head for the chilly, wind-swept coast to spend the summer. Of course, they also fish and hunt seals, but it's no coincidence that this annual migration sidesteps the worst of the mosquito season.

(*a*) Five words are given below. Give the meaning of each word as used in the passage. One word answers or short phrases will be accepted. [5]

    (*i*) peered

    (*ii*) lure

    (*iii*) soggy

    (*iv*) smeared

    (*v*) legend.

(*b*) Answer the following questions briefly in your own words:-

    (*i*) Why did the author feel that he should move on? [2]

    (*ii*) Where did the author come from? Why did he come to this particular place? [2]

    (*iii*) Why did the author consider the Arctic mosquitoes 'frail creatures'? [2]

    (*iv*) According to the author:-

        (1) Why was a 'still, humid, cloudy evening perfect' and for whom? [2]

        (2) In which season was the mosquito menace at its peak?

    (*v*) Why did the Ambler people head for the chilly wind-swept coast? [2]

(*c*) In not more than 60 words of your own, describe how the mosquitoes came upon the author and how he managed to escape from them. [10]

Question 4

(*a*) Rewrite the following sentences according to the instructions given after each. Make other changes that may be necessary but do not change the meaning of each sentence

    (*i*) The thieves stole everything from the merchant and left him for dead.
    (Begin: Having.............)

    (*ii*) Prema consulted her parents before accepting the job offer.
    (Begin: Prema did not................)

    (*iii*) The driver lost his job because of rash driving.
    (Begin: If the driver.....................)

    (*iv*) Very few doctors in the hospital are as dedicated as he is.
    (Begin: He is ....)

    (*v*) The Principal dealt with the miscreants firmly.
    (Begin: The Principal was..............) [5]

(*b*) Fill in the blanks with appropriate words:-

    (*i*) He may turn _____ when we least expect him.

    (*ii*) The jewel was sold _____ thrice its cost price.

    (*iii*) They took _____ the company with all its liabilities.

    (*iv*) The new Manager gets_____ well with his colleagues.

    (*v*) Please contact me _____ 9 a.m. and 10 a.m.

    (*vi*) Priya was knocked _____ by a speeding car.

    (*vii*) Pursued by his enemies, he swam _____ the river to safety.

    (*viii*) They drove him _____ the city in their new car.

    (*ix*) _____ other things, they found an old sword near the ruins of the building.

    (*x*) He flew _____ a rage when he was challenged. [5]

(*c*) In the following passage fill in each of the numbered blanks with the correct form of the word given in brackets. Do not copy the passage, but write in correct serial order the word or phrase appropriate to the blank space.

Example: (0) *went*

I (0) (go) into the Administrative Block and (1)_____(be) then (2)_____ (lead) into the office of the Superintendent. He was (3)_____ (sit) there, reading the newspaper. The large desk in front of him was (4)_____ (pile) high with a great assortment of papers, most of which looked official and scientific, a heap of them partially (5)_____ (cover) the telephone. As the Superintendent (6)_____(stand) up, I (7) _____(see) that he was an immensely tall man. He (8)_____ (come) towards me and (9)_____ (stare) at me, (10)_____ (breathe) heavily through his nose. [5]

(*d*) Join the following sentences to make one complete sentence without using 'and', 'but' or 'so'

[5]

    (*i*) He got married suddenly. This took everyone by surprise.

    (*ii*) He completed the work on time. There were many obstacles.

    (*iii*) Ritu's plan is perfect. She wants everyone to realise this.

    (*iv*) Sophia is a quiet girl. She is an introvert.

    (*v*) I met Sheila's mother. She works in a school nearby.

Answers

1 (*a*)

    (*a*)   Refer to Contents Section B Sl No. 48

    (*b*)   Refer to Contents Section B Sl No. 49

    (*c*)   Refer to Contents Section B Sl No. 01

    (*d*)   Refer to Contents Section B Sl No. 52

(*e*) Picture Composition

The picture of an axe falling on a tree in full bloom, reflects our callous attitude towards trees, that are an important natural resource of the country. Trees not only provide food, fodder, and timber but also help in containing environmental pollution. Their importance in maintaining the ecological balance and the climatic conditions of the region are also well known. In spite of these well known facts, man's unquenchable thirst for land, makes him cut trees, thereby denuding large tracts of land. This greed if not effectively checked would spell our doom.

As we all know trees cleanse the atmosphere by using carbon dioxide and releasing life giving oxygen. They thus help in sustaining life on the earth. They also help in preserving moisture in the atmosphere, which has a profound effect on the climate of the region. Thus regions with good forest cover, are blessed with more rainfall, like the north eastern region and the hills of the country. They also prevent soil erosion in the mountainous region, thereby helping in maintaining the ecological balance of that particular area. Trees in the forest help in protecting wild life, that would otherwise become extinct. Besides food and fodder for cattle, they also provide us many useful products like rubber, sandalwood and medicinal herbs, that are obtained from their bark and roots.

The Government of India appreciating the important role of trees for national development has formulated a comprehensive forest policy. This policy has been designed to conserve this important natural heritage and aims at having a minimum of one third of country under forest cover. Ideally the area under forest cover should be 60% in the hills and 20% in the plains. To effectively implement this policy massive afforestation programs have been launched. Under this program, the forest department with the help of NGO's has planted trees along roads, canals and railway lines. The general public has also been exhorted to plant trees, for which free seedlings are made available. Under the Van Mahotsav Program, the government encourages citizens to plant a tree for every child in the countryside. The objective being, to make people realise the importance of trees as an important national asset.

We are therefore much indebted to trees, for besides helping sustain life on earth, they also provide us many important products of daily use. We should therefore stop the mindless felling of trees for our materialistic gains, and help the government in conserving this important natural resource.

2.

(*a*) Refer to Contents Section E Sl No. 01

(*b*) Refer to Contents Section E Sl No. 13

3.

(*a*)

    (*i*)   peered – looked closely and intently

    (*ii*)   lure – attract, entice

    (*iii*)   Soggy – humid, damp, heavy.

    (*iv*)   Smeared – smudge, covered with dust.

    (*v*)   Legand – old story, myth.

(*b*)

(*i*)

    The author felt that he should move on, for though it was a bright and breezy summer day, dark clouds were drifting in from the east. The author also knew, that such conditions in the Artic region, could spell trouble. Moreover, as his camp was three kilometers down the hill, he hastened towards it.

(*ii*)

    The author came from Ambler, a small village in the Kobuk valley. He had settled and lived there for the last 18 years. He had come to this particular place, being charmed with its natural beauty, that had not been spoiled by civilisation .The vast expanse of greenery made him live, move and breathe freely.

(*iii*)

    The author considered the Arctic mosquitoes frail creatures, for these blood sucking creatures were easily swept away by a slightest breeze. They also perished under bright sunlight. They could not withstand too hot or too cold climatic conditions or too little or too much of rainfall. They could only survive and thrive in a still and humid climate. Their inability to survive in slightly adverse climatic conditions, makes the author refer to them as frail creatures.

(*iv*)

    (1)   A still, humid cloudy evening was perfect for the Arctic mosquitoes. This was because in such climatic conditions, there was no wind, less sunshine, because of the clouds, and an average temperature. Such conditions were therefore ideal for the Arctic mosquitoes, to thrive and feed on their prey, for they could not survive in too hot, or cold climate, or even a slight breeze.

    (2)   The mosquito menace was at its peak during the summer season. This was the time when the ice in the river melted, and the weather was not so cold as in the winter .

(*v*)

    The Ambler people living in the upper Kobuk region, headed for the chilly windswept coastal region, to spend the summer. They did so to protect themselves from the onslaught of these blood sucking mosquitoes that thrive in the Kobuk region during the summers. Here they took to fishing and hunting for seals

(*b*)

    One bright, calm summer day, the author was attacked by a swarm of mosquitoes, that then thrive in Alaska. Unable to ward them off with his hands, he ran toward his camp three kilometers downhill being trailed by them. Unzipping the screen door, he dived into the tent. He managed to escape after killing hundred mosquitoes that came trailing him.

4 (*a*)   (*i*)   Having stolen everything from the merchant, the thieves left him for dead.

           (*ii*)   Prerna did not accept the job offer, until she consulted her parents.

           (*iii*)   If the driver had not driven rashly he would have not lost his job.

           (*iv*)   He is one of the few dedicated doctors in the hospital.

           (*v*)   The Principal was firm in dealing with the miscreants.

(*b*)

Fill in the blanks with appropriate words:-

   (*i*)   He may turn <u>up</u> when we least expect him.
   (*ii*)   The jewel was sold <u>at</u> thrice its cost price.
   (*iii*) They took <u>over</u> the company with all its liabilities.
   (*iv*)   The new Manager gets <u>along</u> well with his colleagues.
   (*v*)   Please contact me <u>between</u> 9 a.m. and 10 a.m.
   (*vi*)   Priya was knocked <u>down</u> by a speeding car.
   (*vii*) Pursued by his enemies, he swam <u>across</u> the river to safety.
   (*viii*) They drove him <u>around</u> the city in their new car.
   (*ix*)   <u>Among</u> other things, they found an old sword near the ruins of the building.
   (*x*)   He flew <u>into</u> a rage when he was challenged.

(*c*)

   (1) was
   (2) led
   (3) sitting
   (4) piled
   (5) covered
   (6) stood
   (7) saw
   (8) came
   (9) stared
   (10) breathing

(*d*)

   (*i*)   His getting married suddenly took everyone by surprise.
   (*ii*)   Inspite of many obstacles he completed the work on time.
   (*iii*) Ritu wants everyone to realise that her plan is perfect.
   (*iv*)   Sophia being a quiet girl, is an introvert.
   (*v*)   I met Shiela's mother who works in a school nearby.

Answers to this Paper must be written on the paper provided separately.
*You will **not** be allowed to write during the first 15 minutes. .*
This time is to be spent in reading the question paper.
The time given at the head of this Paper is the time allowed for writing the answers

---

*Attempt all **four** questions.*
The intended marks for questions or parts of questions are given in brackets [ ].
You are advised to spend not more than 35 minutes in answering Question 1
and 20 minutes in answering Question 2.

Question 1

*(Do not spend more than **35** minutes on this question.)*

Write a composition **(350 - 400 words)** on any **one** of the following:-

(a) Imagine a situation in which a character from your favourite book comes alive. Write an imaginary account of a day spent with this character.

(b) 'The commercialization of festivals has eroded their real significance.'

Express your views either for or against this statement.

(c) You have returned to your city after spending five years in a foreign country. The city has changed during your absence. Describe the changes that have affected the life of people in the city. Give your personal views regarding the changes.

(d) Write an original short story that concludes with the sentence, 'After it was allover, I realised that every cloud has a silver lining.'

(e) Study the picture and poem given below. Write a story or a description or an account of what it suggests to you. Your composition may be about the subject of the picture or may take suggestions from it; however, there must be a clear connection between the picture and your composition.

What Makes a Dad?

God took the strength of a mountain,
The Majesty of a tree,
The warmth of a summer sun,
The calm of a quiet sea,
The generous soul of nature,
The comforting arm of night,
The wisdom of the ages,
The power of the eagle's flight,
The joy of a morning in spring,
The faith of a mustard seed,
The patience of eternity,
The depth of a family need,
Then God combined these qualities,
When there was nothing more to add,
He knew his masterpiece was complete,
And so, He called it...Dad

Question 2

(Do not spend more than 20 minutes on this question.)

Select one of the following:-   [10]

(a) Write a letter to the Director of the Archaeological Survey of India complaining about the damage caused to a historical monument in your city due to negligence. Suggest steps that the civic authorities should take to preserve the monument.

(b) Your pen-friend from Japan plans to visit your school and attend classes and activities for the duration of a month. Write a letter briefing him/her on your school routine. Give any other information that you think your friend may need.

Question 3

"*Read the following passage carefully and answer the questions that follow:-*

The story of Robinson Crusoe, few people know, is based on a real life incident. The son of a cobbler, Alexander Selkirk was a wayward young man, with little respect for authority. Abject conditions at sea and the cruelty of the captains made the sailors miserable in those days. It was not surprising that Alexander became rebellious and malevolent when he became a sailor.

In 1704, he was Sailing Master on a ship; when it anchored for repairs near the desolate island of Juan Fernandez about 650 kilometres west of Chile. They were looking for gold, which they often got by plundering other ships. In the days that followed, Alexander hatched a conspiracy. He *instigated* the other sailors to leave the ship and remain on the island. They would declare a mutiny. Perhaps, Alexander reasoned, that the Captain would accept their demands if he believed that his men would refuse to sail otherwise. Unfortunately for Alexander, the crew played the Judas. The Captain, getting to know of Alexander's part in the planned mutiny, left him behind on the island as he was a bad influence on the men. He was provided with a few necessities, among them, a copy of the Bible.

Alexander, **marooned** on an island populated only by wild cats and goats became adept at hunting and his food soon comprised of fish, turtles and meat. He also made clothes with goat skin. Although a cobbler's son, he could not make shoes. Running barefoot after goats had hardened the soles of his feet. He read the Bible again and again and slowly took to reading it aloud. He spoke and sang to the cats and learnt to milk goats.

Once, during his stay on the island, a Spanish ship anchored near the island and the crew rowed in. Alexander was petrified and hid in the thick foliage. In those days Spain and England were at daggers drawn. Fortunately the Spaniards left after a brief fest.

In February, 1709, two English ships sailed in to collect fresh water and shoot goats. Alexander rushed to them for succour. He looked strange with his *unkempt* hair, beard and goat skin clothes. His rescuers understood him with great difficulty . His speech had changed a great deal . His vocabulary had shrunk and he had to grope for words .They did however manage to understand his story finally.

Alexander took a job as a sailor on one of the ships and reached London in 1711. He returned home with a large fortune. However, he ran out of his fortune in two years and had to return to sea. Alexander's adventure became well-known.

Eight years later, Daniel Defoe gave the story a new shape with many twists, calling it *The Adventures of Robinson Crusoe*. It was now the story of a man who was shipwrecked on an island and lived alone for an unbelievable twenty eight years.

(a) Three words from the passage are given below. Give the meaning of each word as used in the passage. One word answers or short phrases will be accepted.

(i) instigated

(ii) marooned

(iii) unkempt

(b) Answer the following questions briefly in your own words:-

(i) Explain the phrase, 'with little respect for authority'.   [2]

(ii) Why did Alexander become reckless and malevolent when he became a sailor?   [2]

(ii) What was the conspiracy that Alexander hatched? Why did he do so?   [2]

(iv) How did the *crew play the Judas?* [2]
(v) Why was Alexander petrified when the crew of the Spanish ship rowed in? [2]
(vi) Mention two points of difference between Alexander's actual story and Defoe's version. [2]
(c) In about 60 words of your own, give an account of Alexander's adventure on the island. [8]
(d) Give a title to your summary in 3(c). Give a reason to justify your choice. [2]

Question 4
(a) In the following passage, fill in each of the numbered blanks with the 1 correct form of the word given in brackets. Do not -copy the passage, but write in correct serial order the word or phrase appropriate to the blank space.
Example: (0) *returned.*
After Christopher Columbus (0) ....(return) from his famous voyage across the Atlantic, the King of Spain (1).............(wish) to celebrate the great event and do honour to the man who (2)............ (make) himself a national hero. He (3).......... (do) so by holding a banquet in honour of the explorer. To this banquet he (4).......................(invite) many of the nobles of the King's Court. Some *of* them (5).............(be) jealous of the success Columbus (6) ....
(achieve). One of them sat next to Columbus. He turned towards Columbus and said, "Of course you (7)................ (be) a brave man but it doesn't take much intelligence to do what you have done. After all, anyone can take a ship and sail on and on till he (8)............(reach) land." [4]

(b) Fill in the blanks with appropriate words:-
(i) The safari parks of South Africa abound............................... wild animals.
(ii) The young man excels................................... both music and dance.
(iii) She is a diligent student, worthy... praise.
(iv) I saw ....his plan and realized that he was going to cheat us.
(v) I was.................... the impression that the meeting had been cancelled.
(vi) Always be true.......................... yourself.
(vii) The villagers lodged a complaint....................... the corrupt officials.
(viii) I can rely.................... my sister for help. [4]
(c) Explain the difference in meaning between the pairs of sentences given below:-
(i) (1) She must have repainted the car.
(2) She must have the car, repainted.
(ii) (1) "The girl," said the boy, "was ugly."
(2) The girl said the boy was ugly. [4]
(d) Rewrite the following sentences according to the instructions given after each. Make other changes that may be necessary; but do not change the meaning of each sentence
(i) Jasdeep has probably forgotten his mother's birthday. (Begin: In ..)
(ii) Mr. Sharma advised the children not to go out in the cold. (End with : "..............." said Mr. Sharma)
(iii) For more information please contact the secretary of the club. (Begin: Should ....)
(iv) He could not take part in the singing competition as he had a sore throat. (Use: prevented)
(v) Ritika returned to school a week ago. (Begin: It has been................)
(vi) She was beautiful and humble. (Begin: Not only... ...)
(vii) Both the players are not adequately prepared for the tournament. (Begin: Neither....................)

(viii)   A fragrant flower is the loveliest creation of nature.

(Begin: No other ....)   [8]

ANSWERS

1.   (a) Refer to contents Section B. S.N. 62

(b) Refer to contents (Recent Essays) Section A Sl N 19

(c) Refer to contents (Recent Essays) Section A Sl N 20

2.   (a) Refer to contents (Recent letters) Section F Sl No. 15

3.

(a) Three words from the passage are given below. Give the meaning of each word as used in the passage. One word answers or short phrases will be accepted.

(i)   instigated

Bring about , prompt , initiate

(ii) marooned

Stranded , deserted , abandoned

(iii) unkempt

disheveled , untidy

(i)   Alexander Selkirk was very rebellious and strong headed by nature. He therefore never liked to confirm to any sort of discipline, that was enforced by people in authority. It was because of this, he had little respect for authority.

(ii) Alexander Selkirk became reckless and malevolent on becoming a sailor because of his rebellious nature.. The miserable conditions under which the sailors lived, and the cruelty shown by their captain emboldened him to revolt ..This was because he did not like to confirm to any strict discipline.

(iii) In 1704 Alexander Selkirk while working as a sailing master of a ship that anchored near a desolate island Juan Fernandez hatched a conspiracy. He motivated the other sailors to declare a mutiny, by leaving the ship and remaining on the island, thus refusing the captain's order for sailing. He did this for he thought that such an action would force the captain to accept their demands and make the life of the sailors a little comfortable while sailing.

(iv) The crew like Judas, who had betrayed Lord Christ, informed the captain about the conspiracy, and the key role played by Alexander Selkirk. Since the captain felt that Alexander was a bad influence on his man, he left him behind on the island, with few necessities including a copy of the Bible.

(vii) Alexander was petrified when the crew of this Spanish ship rowed into the island, for in those days Spain and England were sworn enemies . He hid himself in the thick foliage, for being an Englishman ,they would have taken him prisoner . Fortunately for him the Spaniards after taking a brief rest left the island .

(viii) **Mention two points of difference between Alexander's actual story and Defoe's version.**

While Alexander was intentionally left on the desolate island as a punishment for instigating the sailors of the ship to mutiny. . Robinson Crusoe 's story was of a man who had reached the island on being ship wrecked .

While Alexander stayed alone in the island for barely five years . Daniel Dofoe version of the story had Robinson Crusoe staying on the desolate island for twenty eight years.

(c) In about 60 words of your own, give an account of Alexander's adventure on the island.

On being marooned in the island Alexander became an expert hunter. His food comprised of fish, turtle, meat and milk .He wore goat skin and read the Bible . Once a hostile Spanish ship anchor neatly .He hid himself till they departed. After five years two English ships sailed in .. Alexander sought their help relating his story of misery.

(d) Give a title to your summary in 3(c). Give a reason to justify your choice.

TITLE THE CASTAWAY

This title is more apt for Alexander was indeed 'a castaway ' by the captain of the ship. This was a punishment for his role in instigating the sailors to stage a mutiny

Question 4

Example: (0) *returned.*

1. wished
2. had made
3. did
4. invited
5. were
6. had achieved
7. are
8. reaches

(b) Fill in the blanks with appropriate words:-

(i)   The safari parks of South Africa abound <u>with</u> wild animals.

(ii)   The young man excels <u>in</u> both music and dance.

(iii)   She is a diligent student, worthy <u>of</u> praise.

(iv)   I saw <u>through</u> his plan and realized that he was going to cheat us.

(v)   I was <u>under</u> the impression that the meeting had been cancelled.

(vi)   Always be true <u>to</u> yourself.

(vii) The villagers lodged a complaint <u>against</u> the corrupt offi cials.

(viii) I can rely <u>upon</u> my sister for help.

(c) Explain the difference in meaning between the pairs of sentences given below:-

(i)   In the first sentence suggest that the girl must have repainted the car herself, whereas the second sentence implies that the car is old and the girl must get it repainted.

(ii)   In the first sentence the boy is commenting that the girl was ugly. While the second sentence has the girl stating that the boy was ugly..

(*d*) (*i*)   In all probability Jasdeep has forgotten his mother's birthday.

(*ii*)   " Do not go out in the cold, children" said Mr.Sharma.

(*iii*) Should you need any more information please contact the secretary of the club.

(*iv*) His sour throat prevented him from taking part in the singing competition.

(*v*)   It has been a week since Ritika returned to school.

(*vi*) Not only was she beautiful but was humble too.

(*vii*) Neither of the players are adequately prepared for the tournament.

(*viii*) No other creation of nature is lovelier than a fragrant flower.

Paper 1
(Two Hours)

Answers to this Paper must be written on the paper provided separately,
*You will **not** be allowed to write during the first 15 minutes.*
This time is to be spent in reading the question paper.
The time given at the head of this Paper is the time allowed for writing the answers.

---

*Attempt all **four** questions*
The intended marks for questions, or parts of questions are given in brackets [ ].
You are advised to spend not more than 35 minutes in answering Question 1
and 20 minutes in answering Question 2

Question 1

*(Do not spend more than **35** minutes on this question.)* [25]

Write a composition **(350 - 400 words)** on *any one* of the following:

(a) You are a spectator at a cricket match. Trouble erupts suddenly in the stadium and you witness a riot among the crowd. Give a vivid description of the scene.

(b) India has always believed in the value of the family. Discuss the changes, both good and bad, that have resulted from the break-up of the traditional Indian joint family.

(c) *The Computer will soon replace the Book.* Express your views either for or against this statement.

(d) Write a short story which illustrates the truth of the statement, *Rumour is a great traveller.*

(e) Study the picture given below. Write a story or a description or an account of what it suggests to you. Your composition may be about the subject of the picture or may take suggestions from it: however, there must be a clear connection between the picture and your composition.

Question 2

(Do not spend more than 20 minute on this question.)

Select one of the following:

(a) Recently you went to a restaurant for dinner and there you saw your favorite sports star. You had an opportunity of spending some moments with him or her. In a letter to your friend, give a brief account of your memorable meeting with the sports star.

(b) Your cousin is missing from home. Write a letter to the Superintendent of Police of your locality, requesting him to trace your cousin. Give all relevant details that may help the police department.

Question 3

Read the following passage carefully and answer the questions that follow:

There came to our town some years ago a showman who owned an institution called the Gaiety Land. Overnight, our Gymkhana Grounds became *resplendent* with banners and streamers and coloured lamps. From all over the district, crowds poured into the show. Within a week of opening, in gate money, they collected five hundred rupees a day. Gaiety land provided us with all sorts of fun and gambling and side shows. For a couple of annas, in each booth, we could watch anything from performing parrots to crack motor cyclists. In addition to this, there were lotteries and shooting galleries, where, for an anna, you always stood a chance of winning a hundred rupees.

There was a particular corner of the show which was in great favour. Here, for a ticket costing eight annas, you could be lucky enough to acquire a variety of articles-pin cushions, sewing machines or even a road engine. One evening, they drew a ticket, number 1005, and I happened to own the other half of the ticket. Glancing down the list of articles, they declared that I had become the owner of a road engine.

I looked *stunned*. People gathered around and gazed at me as if I were some sort of a curious animal. Some people muttered and giggled, "Fancy anyone becoming the owner of a road engine!"

It was not the sort of prize one could carry home at short notice. I asked the showman if he could help me to transport it. He merely pointed at a notice whichb decreed that all the winners should remove their prizes immediately after the draw and by their own effort. However, they had to make an exception in my case. They agreed to keep the engine at the Gymkhana Grounds till the end of the season, and then, I would have to make my own arrangements to take it out. When I asked the showman if he could find me a driver, he just smiled and said, "The fellow who, brought it here had to be paid a hundred rupees for the job and five rupees a day. I sent him away and made up my mind that if no one was going to draw it, I would just leave it to its fate."

"Can't I sell it to some municipality ?" I asked innocently, He burst into a laugh. "As a showman I have enough trouble with municipal people. I would rather keep out of the way."

My friends and relatives poured in, to congratulate me on my latest *acquisition*. No one knew precisely how much a road engine would fetch; all the same they felt that there was a lot of money in it. " Even if you sell it as scrap iron, you can make a few thousands." Some of my friends declared. Everyday I made a trip to the Gymkhana grounds to have a look at my engine. I grew very found of it. I loved its shining brass parts. I stood near it and patted it affectionately, hovered about it, and returned home everyday only at the close of the show. I thought al my troubles were coming to an end. How ignorant I was! How little did I guess that my troubles had just begun!

(a) Three words from the passage are given below. Give the meaning of each word as used in the passage. One word answer or short phrases will be accepted.

     (i)   resplendent

     (ii)   stunned

     (iii)   acquisition

(b)   (i)   Which two sentences in the first paragraph show that Gaiety Land was popular?

     (ii)   Give three reasons for the popularity of *Gaiety Land*.

     (iii)   What is meant by *'it was not the sort of prize one could carry home at short notice"*?

     (iv)   What was the showman's response to the narrator asking for help to transport the road engine?

     (v)   Why was the showman ready to leave the road engine to its fate?

(c)   In not more than 60 words, describe the reactions of the public, friends and relatives towards the narrator on his winning the road engine. How did he treat his proud possession?

(d)   Give a title to your summary in 3(c). State a reason to justify your choice.

Question 4

(a) In the following passage, fill in each of the numbered blanks with the correct form of the word given in brackets. Do not copy the passage, but write in correct serial order the word or phrase appropriate to the blank space.

Example:

(0) giving

Mid-afternoon while (0)_____ (give) my report to Mrs. Biggs, I (1)_____(hear) a loud thumping (2)_____ (come) from the direction of her store room. "what (3)——————— (be) all that noise downstairs?" I asked. "Probably a rat. I don't hear anything," she replied. I ran down stairs and (4) _____ (open) the store room door. There was Mr.Biggs (5)——(look) very dusty and very disgruntled he wanted to know why Mr, Biggs (6)_____(shut)him up for hours. He had gone into the store room in search of a walking stick and Mrs. Biggs, (7) _____ (see) the door open, had promptly (8)_____(bolt) it.

(b) Fill in the blanks with appropriate words:

    (i)   He refused to put................ with their interference in his affairs.

    (ii)   She has been going................ the script for days.

    (iii)   It is our duty to protest............injustice.

    (iv)   He soon became accustomed .... the harsh weather.

    (v)   Dilip went out.................his way to help the poor.

    (vi)   He was able to put ....his ideas so cleverly that he impressed everyone.

    (vii)   He persists ....teasing the other children in the class.

   (viii)   I have been waiting for you..............four o'clock.

(c)   Join the following sentences to make one complete sentences without using and, but or so :

    (i)   Sahil composed a wonderful song. It became a hit.

    (ii)   Rani reached the spot. We were to meet there.

    (iii)   Dick met me. I gave him the document.

    (iv)   Shenaz was very upset. I wanted to help her out.

(d)   Rewrite the following sentences according to the instructions given after each. Make other changes that may be necessary, but do not change the meaning of each sentence:

    (i)   As soon as the chief guest arrived, the band started playing.

         (Begin: No sooner............)

    (ii)   He went to the library and to the bank.

         (Begin: Not only........)

    (iii)   Though he is very poor, he helps others in need.

         (Begin: Inspite................)

    (iv)   He does not intend to leave the Company.

         (Use; Intention)

    (v)   "Do you want some more ice cream or slice of cake?" asked my aunt.

         (Begin: My aunt asked............)

    (vi)   They are painting a mural on the front wall.

         (Begin. A mural ....)

    (vii)   Tansen was the best singer in Akbar's court.

         (Use: Better.......)

   (viii)   You remembered to buy a loaf of bread, didn't you?

         (Begin: You didn't ....)

ANSWERS

1.

   (a) Refer to contents Section A (Recent Essays) Sl No. 18

   (b) Refer to contents Section A (Recent Essays) Sl No. 17

   (c) Refer to contents Section F (Recent Essays) Sl No. 16

2.

   (a) Refer to contents Section F (Recent letters) Sl No. 14

   (b) Refer to contents Section F (Recent letters) Sl No. 13

3.

   (a)

      (i) resplendent - glittering, dazzling .

      (ii) stunned - astonished, bewildered, surprised.

      (iii) acquisition - achievemer ttainment.

(b) (i) The two sentences in the first paragraph which show that Gaiety land was popular are, From all over the district, crowds poured into the show. Within a week of opening, in gate money, they collected five hundred rupees a day.

(ii) Gaiety Land became popular because : Firstly it provided all sorts of fun like watching performing parrots, or crack motor cyclist do feats for a couple of annas. Secondly there were shooting galleries where for an anna you could win a prize of Rs 100. Lastly there was a popular lottery in which by paying just eight annas, you could win a variety of prizes,.ranging from a pin cushion to a road engine.

(iii) The road engine which the narrator had won in the lucky draw was very big and bulky. Thus unlike other prizes in the lucky draw, it could not be carried home, without making elaborate arrangements. Hence it could not be taken by the narrator at a short notice.

(iv) The showman's response to the narrator's request for help in transporting the road engine home, was very discouraging and unhelpful. He drew his attention to a notice, which stated that all winners had to remove the prizes immediately after the draw, by their own effort. He however agreed to keep the road engine in the Gymkhana Grounds till the end of the season, after which the narrator would have to make his own arrangement to take it away.

(v) The showman was ready to leave the road engine to its fate, if nobody won it in the lucky draw. This was for, it was a costly prize to keep and maintain. The driver who had brought the road engine to the ground, had too be paid Rs 100 for bringing it. Thereafter he had to be paid Rs 5 per day as wages. This compelled the showman to send away the driver, and leave the road engine to its fate, if it was not won in the lucky draw.

(c)

the	reaction	of	the	public
on	the	narrator	winning	the
road	engine	was	very	amusing
his	friends	and	relatives	congratulated
him	for	even	at	scrap
value	the	road	engine	would
fetch	few	thousand	rupees	he
treated	his	proud	possession	affectionately
hovering	around	it	everyday,	till
the	show	ended	he	loved
the	shining	parts	and	became
fond	of	the	road	engine

(c) Give a title to your summary in 3(c). State a reason to justify your choice.

Title of the passage.

WORRISOME PRIZE

This title is apt for winning the road engine as a prize caused a lot of worry for the narrator. He felt no joy on winning the road engine as a prize in the lucky draw.

4.

(a) (1) heard

(2) coming

(3) is

       (4) opened
       (5) looking
       (6) had shut
       (7) seeing
       (8) bolted.

(b) (i)   He refused to put.........up....... with their interference in his affairs.

    (ii)   She has been going.........over....... the script for days.

   (iii)   It is our duty to protest...against ....injustice.

   (iv)   He soon became accustomed ...to......... the harsh weather.

    (v)   Dilip went out......of...........his way to help the poor.

   (vi)   He was able to put ....across...........his ideas so cleverly that he impressed everyone.

  (vii)   He persits ...on...........teasing the other children in the class.

 (viii)   I have been waiting for you...since...........four o'clock.

(c) (i)   Sahil composed a wonderful song that became a hit.

   (ii)   Rani reached the spot where we were to meet.

  (iii)   When Dick met me I gave him the document.

  (iv)   I wanted to help Shenaz as she was very upset.

(d) (1)   No sooner did the chief guest arrived, the band started playing.

    (2)   Not only did he go to the library, but he also went to the bank.

    (3)   Inspite of being very poor, he helps others in need.

    (4)   He has no intention of leaving the company.

    (5)   My Aunt asked me whether I would have some more ice cream or a slice of cake.

    (6)   A mural is being painted by them on the front wall.

    (7)   There was no better singer than Tansen in Akbar's court.

    (8)   You didn't forget to buy a loaf of bread.

QUESTION PAPER FOR ICSE 2007

ENGLISH

Paper 1

(Two Hours)

Answers to this paper must be written on the paper provided separately.

*You will **not** be allowed to write during the first 15 minutes.*

This time is to be spent in reading the question paper.

The time given at the head of this Paper is the time allowed /or writing the answers.

*Attempt **four** questions.*

The intended marks for questions or parts of questions are given in brackets [ ].

You are advised to spend not more than 35 minutes in answering Question 1 and 20 minutes in answering Question 2.

Question 1

*(Do not spend more than **35** minutes on this question.)*

Write a composition **(350 - 400 words)** on any **one** of the following:

(a) Recall a remarkable event of social importance in your city or locality. Give a little of its background, the event as it occurred, and its impact on the lives of people.

(b) Cinema both entertains and educates the masses. Express your views, either for or against this statement.

(c) Siblings often grow up side by side in families; yet have very different life experiences. If you have one or more siblings and feel that your lives have differed significantly, write an essay explaining the reasons and the effects of such differences.

(d) Relate an incident or write a short story which has as its central idea 'advice not taken'.

(e) Study the picture given below. Write a story or a description or an account of what it suggests to you. Your composition may be about the subject of the picture or may take suggestions from it; however, there must be a clear connection between the picture and your composition.

Question 2

(Do not spend more than 20 minutes on this question.)

Select one of the following:

(a) One of your grandparents has completed one hundred years of age. Write a letter congratulating him/her, expressing gratitude, praise and admiration for the way he/she has lived his/her life.

(b) A company has been marketing spurious medicines behind claims that its product could be effective in preventing the avian flu or other forms of influenza. Write a letter to the Drug Controller General of the Directorate of Health Services, examining the claim of the company and explaining the harm these kinds of claim could cause.

Question 3

Read the following passage carefully and answer the questions that follow:

The boy was idling in the market-place on the look-out for mischief. All at once he saw it beckoning him. Workmen had been slating the church spire. And their ladders stretched invitingly from earth to steeple.

All children like scrambling up to high places to see if the world looks any different from an apple tree or a stable loft. Over and above his love for climbing, Michael had a longing to do things that had never been done before. As he gazed at the spire, crowned by a golden ball and weather-vane, an idea crept into his mind - he would be the first person in Flushing to stand on the golden ball beneath the weather-vane! He glanced around. No one was looking; Michael began to swarm up the ladder. At the top of the tower there rose a slated spire crowned by a golden ball and weather-vane. At last Michael found himself squatting on top of the ball, holding on by the vane.

Presently he heard workmen moving below. He did not peer over or speak. He was not going to be hauled down before Flushing had seen him. The voices died away and Michael sat resting.

At last he felt ready to *startle* the town. He pulled himself to his feet and keeping tight hold of the weather-vane, managed to stand on top of the ball. It was well that he had a cool head and iron nerves.

Someone must have cast a *casual* glance up at the vane and seeing his little figure, cried out. In a minute or two Michael was delighted to see the market-place full of people who had rushed out of their shops and houses to gaze the dizzy sight. It was splendid to have all those eyes and hearts glued upon you!

But Michael did not intend to stay there until he was fetched down, to be handed over to his father and cuffed before the crowd. After a while he prepared to descend of his own free will.

He leaned over the ball. The ladder had gone. The workmen had taken it away!

A sudden feeling of sickness and giddiness came over Michael. He mastered it.

To wait for rescue was a humiliating end to his escapade. He would come down alone, even if it cost him his life.

The spire at the base of the ball was only half slated, and Michael saw some hope of gaining a foothold on the old part. He clasped his arms round the top of the ball and let his body swing down; he was just able to feel the first slate with his toes. Those toes were shod with iron toe-caps, for Michael was hard on his shoes. Michael kicked with his armoured toes till the slate crashed and then he got a foothold on the wooden laths beneath.

He rested for a minute, with aching arms and a stiff body. He must change his grip on the ball, which was too big to slide his arms down; he must get clear of it, and somehow *grasp* the spire beneath. One false move and he would be hurled on to the cobbles below.

Slowly he began to slide his hands together at the top of the ball, and then downward over its bulging face. Every inch was packed with peril; every inch pushed him backward towards death. It seemed to him that he would be too weak to hold when the time came for him to grasp the spire.

But at last, the steady, deadly creeping of his fingers brought him to a point where he could bend forward. With a sudden snatch he caught the base of the ball.

The next moment he was kicking out a stairway in the old tiles and swarming swiftly down. He reached the foot of the spire, lifted the trapdoor of the tower, ran down the steps, and was caught by his father in the organ loft.

(a) Three italicised words from the passage are given below. Give the meaning of each word as used in the passage. One-word answers or short phrases will be accepted:

    (i)   startle

    (ii) casual

    (iii) grasp

(b)   Answer the following questions briefly in your own words:

    (i)   What was Michael doing in the market-place? What attracted his attention?

    (ii)   What did Michael long to do? What did he plan to do to accomplish this?

    (iii) How did Michael display 'a cool head and iron nerves'?

    (iv) Which sight filled Michael's heart with delight and why?

    (v) Why did Michael not wait for rescue?

    (vi) Use the word 'face' in a sentence of your own such that it has a different meaning from that it carries in the passage.

(c) With close reference to the last five paragraphs of the extract and in not more than 60 words, trace. Michael's descent from the top of the ball to the foot of the spire.

(d) Give a title to your summary in 3(c). State a reason to justify your choice.

Question 4

(a) In the following passage, fill in each of the numbered blanks with the correct form of the word given in brackets. Do not copy the passage, but write in correct serial order the word or phrase appropriate to the blank space.

Example:

(0) am convinced.

I (0) _____ (convince) that my father (1) (remember) by all those who value integrity. He (2) _____ (be) a man of learning and also saw to it that he (3) _____ (teach) his pupils, with passion and patience. He at times (4) _____ (use) to lose his temper, but that was because he always (5) _____ (want) his pupils to learn and learn well. As a person, he was honest and simple. His greatness (6) _____ (lie) in the fact that he (7) _____ (have) a pure heart, devoid of malice. Such a man is always valued and (8) _____ (be) very rare to find.

(b) Fill in the blanks with appropriate words:

    (i) Truth always prevails———————————the long run.

    (ii) Sujata stood ———————————— the river and saw the ship pass by.

    (iii) She took some money ———————————her father to buy a video game.

    (iv) Shilpa gave me a rare gift ———————————my birthday.

    (v) Deepak was very upset ———————————— me.

    (vi) Michelle is longing ———————————meet me.

    (vii) It has been a long time ———————————I met my sister.

    (viii) The worker asked ———————————his wages.

(c) Join the following sentences to make one complete sentence without using *and, but.* or *so:*

   (i)   John gave me the novel. John wanted me to review it.

   (ii) Debjani received my note. She sent her reply within a week.

   (iii) Raja is a great footballer. He is also popular.

   (iv) Jennifer saw that I was confused. She came to my rescue.

(d)   Rewrite the following sentences according to the instructions given after each. Make other changes that may be necessary, but do not change the meaning of each sentence:

   (i)   Anne paid a heavy price for her recklessness.
          (Begin: It.....................)

   (ii)   No sooner had Ram narrated the story than he was praised.
          (Begin: Hardly ....)

   (iii) Tanuja is a very friendly girl and is always cheerful.
          (Begin: Besides ....)

   (iv)   They had to put off the garden party because of the heavy rain.
          (Begin: The heavy ....)

   (v)   Margaret said to me, "Please do not forget to meet me tomorrow".
          (Begin: I was ....)

   (vi)   Inspite of my warning Dev, he ignored me.
          (Begin: Though ....)

   (vii) The business talks failed because neither side was willing to compromise.
          (Begin: Since ....)

   (viii) They were very afraid and so they could not speak.
          (Begin: Being......................)

ANSWERS

1. (a)   Refer to contents Section A (Recent Essays) Sl. No. 15

    (b)   Refer to contents Section A (Recent Essays) Sl. No. 13

    (c)   Refer to contents Section F (Recent Essays) Sl. No. 14

2. (a)   Refer to contents Section F (Recent Letters) Sl. No. 11

    (b)   Refer to contents Section F (Recent Letters) Sl. No. 12

3.

(a) (i)   Surprise , alarm

     (ii) Informal, relaxed

     (iii) Clutch, take hold of

(b)

     (i)   Michael was idling in the marketplace, wanting to do some mischief.

           A ladder put up by the workmen, slating the church spire, attracted his attention .

     (ii) Michael longed to do something that had never been done before.

To accomplish this desire he planned to be the first person in the town of Flushing to stand on the golden ball, beneath the weather-wane above the church spire.

(iii) Michael displayed that he had a cool head and iron nerves, by standing on the golden ball located on top of the spire of the church. Standing precariously on the ball, at such a great height , was only possible because of his cool head and iron nerves.

(iv) On seeing his little figure perched precariously on the golden ball atop the spire of the church, a large crowd gathered in the marketplace. The sight of such a large crowd watching his feat filled Michael's heart with delight.

He was filled with joy, for he had climbed on top of the golden ball atop the spire of the church, a feat that had never been done before by anyone in Flushing .

(v) Michael did not wait for being rescued, because he knew that he had done mischief, and would thus be handed over to his father, to be scolded in front of the huge crowd .This would be a humiliating experience, for his great feat of climbing atop the golden ball .

(vi) He was unable to *face* the debtors for he had defaulted in the repayment of loans taken from them.

(c)

Michael	decided	to	descend	on
his	own	to	escape	humiliation.
He	clasped	the	golden	ball
got	a	foothold	on	the
spire	below	it,	and	then
on	the	wooden	laths.	Sliding
his	arms	over	the	ball
he	let	go	clasping	its
base.	Sliding	down	the	spire
he	lifted	the	trapdoor	and
ran	down	the	steps	into
the	arms	of	his	father.

(d) **Title – DEADLY MISCHIEF**
The mischievous act of Michael was very deadly and dangerous, and could have cost him his life.

4.
(a)
1. is remembered
2. was
3. taught
4. used
5. wanted
6. lay
7. had
8. is

(b)

1. in
2. beside
3. from
4. on
5. with
6. to
7. since
8. for

(c)

1. John gave me the novel which he wanted me to review.
2. On receiving my note Debjani sent her reply within a week.
3. Raja being a great footballer is also very popular.
4. Jennifer on seeing me confused came to my rescue.

(d)

1. It was a heavy price that Anne had to pay for her recklessness.

2. Hardly had Ram finished narrating the story when they started to praise him.

3. Besides being friendly, Tanuja is also a very cheerful girl.

4. The heavy rain made them put off the garden party.

5. I was requested by Margaret not to forget to meet her the day after.

6. Though I had warned Dev, yet he ignored me.

7. Since neither side was willing to compromise, the business talks failed.

8. Being afraid they could not speak.

QUESTION PAPER FOR ICSE 2008

ENGLISH

Paper 1

(Two hours)

Answers to this paper must be written on the paper provided separately.
*You will **not** be allowed to write during the first 15 minutes.*
This time is to be spent in reading the question paper.
The time given at the head of this Paper is the time allowed /or writing the answers.

*Attempt **four** questions.*
The intended marks for questions or parts of questions are given in brackets [ ].
You are advised to spend not more than 35 minutes in answering Question 1 and
20 minutes in answering Question 2.

Question 1

*(Do not spend more than **35** minutes on this question.)* [25]

Write a composition **(350 - 400 words)** on any **one** of the following:-

(a) Write a short story in which a little girl, her twin brother and the school bully are the main characters.

(b) "No other subject taught in school is as important as Moral Science". Express your views either for or against this statement.

(c) Elements of Western Culture have had a very influential role on cultures of the world. How are these elements different from those of Indian culture? What according to you, should we as Indians adopt from the West to make life more meaningful.

(d) A village fair is very different from a city one. It is usually held annually and is connected with a religious festival or harvest. The purpose of such fairs is usually trade and to exhibit and sell village handicrafts. Describe one such fair.

(e) Study the picture given below. Write a story or a description or an account of what it suggests to you. Your composition may be about the subject of the picture or you may take suggestions from it; however, there must be a clear connection between the picture and your composition.

Question 2

(Do not spend more than 20 minutes on this question.)

Select one of the following:- [10]

(a) Write a letter to a friend who was absent from school on a day when a really comical incident took place. Describe the incident, say what was so funny about it and what you learnt from it.

(b) Traffic jams in your city / town are getting worse day after day. Write a letter to the Deputy

Commissioner of Police (Traffic) complaining about the problem and offering suggestions for improvement.

Question 3

Read the following passage carefully and answer the questions that follow: -

Sita went to her grandfather and sat down beside him.

'When you are Cungry: tell me,' she said, 'and I will make the bread.'

'Is your grandmother asleep?'

'Yes. But she will wake soon. The pain is deep.'

The old man stared across the river, at the dark green of the forest, at the leaden sky, and said, 'If she is not better by morning, I will take her to the hospital in Shahganj. They will know how to make her well. You may be on your own for two or three days. You have been on your own before.'

Sita nodded <u>gravely</u> she had been alone before; but not in the middle of the rains with the river so high. But she knew that someone must stay behind. She wanted Grandmother to get well and she knew that only Grandfather could take the small boat across the river when the current was so strong.

Sita was not afraid of being left alone but she did not like the look of the river.

That evening it began to rain again. Big pellets of rain were scarring the surface of the river. But it was warm rain and Sita could move about in it. She was not afraid of getting wet, she rather liked it. In the previous month, when the monsoon shower had arrived, washing the dusty leaves of the tree and bringing up the good smell of the earth, she had exulted in it, had run about shouting for joy. She was used to it now, even a little tired of the rain, but she did not mind getting wet. It was <u>steamy</u> indoors and her thin dress would soon dry in the heat from the kitchen fire.

She walked about barefooted, barelegged. She was very sure on her feet. Her toes had grown accustomed to gripping all kinds of rocks, slippery or sharp, and though thin, she was surprisingly strong.

Black hair, streaming across her face. Black eyes. Slim brown arms. A scar on her thigh: when she was small, visiting her mother's village, a hyena had entered the house where she was sleeping, fastened on to her leg and tried to drag her away but her screams had roused the villagers and the hyena had run off.

She moved about in the pouring rain, chasing the hens into a shelter behind the hut. A harmless brown snake, flooded out of its hole, was moving across the open ground. Sita took a stick, picked the snake up with it, and dropped it behind a cluster of rocks. She had no quarrel with snake. They kept down the rats and the frogs. She wondered how the rats had first come to the island - probably in someone's boat or in a sack of grain.

She disliked the huge black scorpions who left their waterlogged dwellings and tried to take shelter in the hut. It was so easy to step on one and the sting could be very painful. She had been bitten by a scorpion the previous monsoon and for a day and a night she had known fever and great pain. Sita had never killed living creatures but now, whenever she found a scorpion, she crushed it with a rock! When, finally, she went indoors, she was hungry. She ate some <u>parched</u> gram and warmed up some goat's milk.

Grandmother woke once and asked for water and Grandfather held the brass tumbler to her lips.

The roof was leaking and a small puddle formed on the floor. Grandfather kept the kerosene lamps alight. They did not need the light but somehow it made them feel safer.

It rained all night.

(a)   Three words from the passage are given below. Give the meaning of each word as used in the passage. One word answers or short phrases will be accepted.

    (i) gravely

   (ii) steamy

   (iii) parched   **[3]**

(b) Answer the following questions briefly in your words.
   (i) Why was Sita willing to stay alone?   [3]
  (ii) What had made Sita like the first monsoon shower?   [2]
 (iii) Why did Sita have a scar on her thigh?   [2]
 (iv) Which word in the passage tells us that Sita did not need to fear the snake?   [1]
  (v) Why did she think snakes were useful?   [1]
 (vi) What did Sita do with the snake?   [1]
(vii) The passage tells us that Sita never killed living creatures. Why did she crush
    scorpions with a rock?   [1]
(viii) Why did they keep the lamps alight?   [1]
(c) What kind of a girl was Sita? Describe her in 60 words.   [8]
(d) Give a title to your summary in 3 (c). State a reason to justify your choice.   [2]

Question 4
(a) In the following passage, fill in each of the numbered blanks with the correct form of the word
   given in brackets. Do not copy the passage, but write in correct serial order the word or phrase
   appropriate to the blank space.
   Example: (0) was. There (0) (be) some confusion in the doorway. A man (1) _____(get) into
   the compartment (2) ——————— (stammer) an apology. Then the door (3) ———————
   (bang) and the world was (4) ____ (shut) out again. I (5) ——————— (return) to my berth.
   The guard (6) ——————— (blow) his whistle and we (7)———— (move)   off. Once
   again 1(8)——————— (has) a game to play.   [4]

(b) Fill in the blanks with appropriate words:-
   (i) The elderly man prepared himself for a life_____ retirement.
  (ii) Do you take his word ——————— mine?
 (iii) Rohini is very concerned ——————— her father's health.
 (iv) Altaf had many books and papers scattered all——— the room.
  (v) The Phoenix is a legendary bird that rises ——— its ashes.
 (vi) The police pulled the briefcase from ——————— the table.
(vii) The mob rushed onto the pavement, everyone seemed angry _____everyone else.
(viii) The old woman looked ——————— the cupboard, searching for the photograph.   [4]

(c) Join the following sentences to make one complete sentence without using *and*, *but* or *so*.
   (i) The heart attack was mild. Mr. Bose stayed in bed for three weeks.
  (ii) The men went out to see if anyone was missing. The women stayed behind to care for
    the injured
 (iii) Her mother warned her not to talk to strangers. She told her not to accept gifts from people
    she did not know.
 (iv) Everyone was drenched wet by now. The rain had come down harder   [4]

(d) Re-write the following sentences according to the instructions given after each.
    Make other changes that may be necessary, but do not change the meaning of each
    sentence.
   (i) "Have you walked alone, this long distance today?" he asked Sumita.
    (Begin: He asked Sumita if……………..   )
  (ii) The detective interrogated the suspect closely for over three hours.
    (Begin: The suspect.———————   )
 (iii) I suddenly realized that the room was too small for the three of us to share. (Begin: I
    suddenly realized that the room was so……….   )
 (iv) In spite of all/her efforts, Susan did not succeed.
                              (Begin: Despite……………   )

(v)   As soon as the bell rang, the children rushed out of class.

       (Begin: No sooner.................   )

(vi)   Sachin stood first in class and he also excelled at debate.

       (Begin: Not only ....   )

(vii) She was the only person capable of being House Captain.

       (Use: capability)

(viii) Rohan was the tallest boy in the basketball team.

       (Rewrite using: taller)   [8]

Answer

1.   (b) Refer to contents Section A (Recent Essays) Sl. No. 11

      (c) Refer to contents Section A (Recent Essays) Sl. No. 12

      (d) Refer to contents Section B Sl. No. 56

2.   (a) Refer to contents Section F (Recent Letters) Sl. No. 09

      (b) Refer to contents Section F (Recent Letters) Sl. No. 10

3.

  (a)
       (i)   Gravely – grimly, sternly
       (ii)   Steamy – humid, moist.
       (iii) Parched- dry
  (b)
       (i) Sita's grandmother was seriously ill and in great pain. Her grandfather suggested that if she was not better by morning he would take her to the hospital in Shahganj. They would thus be away for 2 to 3 days during which Sita would have to stay alone as she had on previous occasions.

       (ii) Sita liked the monsoon showers as they washed the dusty leaves of the trees making the surroundings greener. These showers also brought out the good earthy smell of the dry earth.

       (iii) Sita as a little girl had gone to visit her mother's village. While sleeping a hyena had entered the house and seizing her thighs had tried to drag her away. However her screams had awakened the villagers and the hyena had fled. The injury mark on healing had left a scar on her thigh.

       (iv) The word in the passage that tells us that Sita did not need to fear the snakes was 'Harmless'

       (v) She thought snakes to be useful for they checked the growing number of frogs and rats by feeding on them.

       (vi) She picked it up with a stick and dropped it behind a cluster of rocks.

       (vii) The passage tells us that that Sita never killed living creatures. Why did she crush scorpions with a rock?

Though Sita never killed living creatures, she disliked the scorpions. This was for a scorpion had bitten her the previous monsoon. She had suffered great pain and fever for a day. Thus whenever she found a scorpion she crushed it with a rock.

       (viii) They kept the lamp alight for Sita's grandmother was ill and could require attention anytime. Furthermore the roof of their hut was leaking due to the continuous downpour of rain throughout the night and the light from the lamp made them feel safe.

(c)

Sita	lived	in	an	island
with	her	grandparents.	Being	brave
she	occasionally	stayed	alone	in
their	absence.	She	loved	getting
wet	in	the	rain.	She
never	killed	living	creatures	except
scorpions.	Though	thin	she	was
strong	had	black	hair	end
eyes,	slim	brown	arms	and
a	scar	on	her	thigh
due	to	hyena	bite	when
she	was	a	little	girl.

(D) Title is **Sita the brave girl**

This is an apt title for the passage, because she is a brave girl, who. lives on an island with her grandparents amidst the vagaries of nature.

4.

(a)   (0) was, (1) was getting, (2) stammering, (3) banged, (4) shut, (5) returned, (6) blew, (7) moved, (8) had.

(b)   (1) of, (2) or, (3) about, (4) over, (5) from, (6) under, (7) at / with, (8) in.

(c)

   (i)   The heart attack being mild, Mr. Bose stayed in bed for three weeks.

   (ii) The men went out to see if anyone was missing while the women stayed behind to care for the injured.

   (iii) Her mother warned her not to talk to strangers, neither to accept gifts from people she did not know.

   (iv) With the rain coming down harder, everyone was drenched wet by now.

(d)

   (i)   He asked Sumita if she had walked alone the long distance that day.

   (ii) The suspect was closely interrogated by the detective for over three hours.

   (iii) I suddenly realized that the room was so small making it difficult for the three of us to share it.

   (iv) Despite all her effort Susan did not succeed.

   (v)   No sooner had the bell rung the children rushed out of class.

   (vi) Not only did Sachin stand first in class, but he also excelled in debate.

   (vii) She was the only person who had the capability of being the House Captain.

   (viii) No other boy was taller than Rohan in the basketball team.

QUESTION PAPER FOR ICSE 2009

ENGLISH

Paper 1

(Two hours)

Answers to this paper must be written on the paper provided separately.
*You will **not** be allowed to write during the first 15 minutes.*
This time is to be spent in reading the question paper.
The time given at the head of this Paper is the time allowed /or writing the answers.

Attempt *four* questions.

The intended marks for questions or parts of questions are given in brackets [ ].
You are advised to spend not more than 35 minutes in answering Question 1 and
20 minutes in answering Question 2.

Question 1

(Do not spend more than **35** minutes on this question)

Write a composition **(350 -400 words)** on any **one** of the following:- (25)

(a) Recall a time in your life when you were certain about something but were later proved terribly wrong.

(b) Write a short story entitled 'Escaped'.

(c) "The use of mobile phones has lowered active social life and has become an addiction." Express your views either for or against this statement.

(d) The waiting room at a railway station presents a wonderful opportunity to observe human behaviour. Describe an experience when you were early for a train and had to spend some time in the waiting room with different kinds of people.

(e) Study the picture given below. Write a story or a description or an account of what it suggests to you. Your composition may be about the subject of the picture or may take suggestions from it; however, there must be a clear connection between the picture and your composition.

Question 2

(Do not spend more than 20 minutes on this question. Select one of the following:- (10)

(a) You have recently read a book which has greatly impressed you. Write a letter to your cousin telling him / her why you were impressed. Advise him / her to read the book.

(b) You are the President of the school Nature Club. Write a letter to a well-known Social Worker or Environmentalist inviting him / her to be the Chief Guest at the Annual Function of the Club. Give some details about your Club and the Annual Function.

Question 3

Read the following passage carefully and answer the questions that follow: -

At school everybody seemed to' be overwhelmed by the thought of the examinations. It was weeks since anybody had seen a smile on Shankar's face. Somu had become brisk and businesslike. The Pea took time to grasp jokes and seldom made any either. And as for Rajam, he came to school at the stroke of the first bell, took down everything the teacher said, and left at the stroke of the last bell, hardly uttering a dozen words to anybody. Mani was beginning to look worried and took every opportunity to take Shankar aside and have his doubts (that arose from time to time as he plodded through his texts) cleared. He dogged the steps of the school clerk. There was a general belief in the school that the clerk was omniscient and knew all the question papers of all the classes.

One day Mani went to the clerk's house and laid a neat bundle containing fresh brinjals at his feet. The clerk was pleased and took Mani in and seated him on a stool.

The clerk looked extremely **amiable** and Mani felt that he could ask anything at that moment and get it. The clerk was murmuring something about his cat, a lank ill-fed thing, that was nestling close to him. Most of what he was saying did not enter Mani's head. He was waiting feverishly to open the topic of question papers. The clerk had meanwhile passed from cats to eye-flies; but it made little difference to Mani, who was waiting for the other to pause for breath to launch his attack. 'You must never let these eye-flies buzz near your eyes. All cases of eyesore can be traced to it. When you get eyesore the only thing you can do is to take a slice of raw onion ... .'

Mani realized that the other would not stop, and butted in, 'There is only a week more for the examinations, sir .... '

The clerk was slightly puzzled: 'Yes. Indeed, a week more ... You must take care to choose only the juicy variety, the large juicy variety, not the small onion ... " Sir,' Mani interrupted, ignoring the juicy variety, 'I am much worried about my examination.' He tried to look pathetic.

"1 am glad. If you read well, you will pass,' said the Oracle.

'You see, sir, I am so worried, I don't sleep at nights, thinking of the examination ... If you could possibly tell me something important ... I have such a lot to study. I don't want to study unnecessary things that may not be necessary for the examination. He meandered thus. The clerk understood what he was driving at, but said, 'Just read all your portions and you will pass.' Mani realized that diplomacy was not his line. He asked bluntly, 'Please tell me, sir, what questions are we getting for our examination?'

The clerk denied having any knowledge of the question papers. Mani flattered him by asking, if he did not know the questions, who else would. By just a little more of the same judicious flattery the clerk was moved to give what Mani believed to be 'valuable hints'. In spite of the fact that he did not know what the First Form texts were the clerk ventured to advise, 'You must pay particular attention to Geography. Maybe you will have to practice map-drawing a lot. And in Arithmetic make it a point to solve at least five problems every day, and you will be able to tackle Arithmetic as easily as you swallow plantains.'.

'And what about English?' ... L .

'Oh, don't worry about that." Have you read all your lessons?' 'Yes, sir,' Mani replied without conviction.

'It is all right then. You must read all the important lessons again, and if you have time, yet again, and that will be ample.'

These answers satisfied Mani greatly. On his way home, he smiled to himself and said that the four annas he had invested on brinjals was not after all a waste.

(a)   Give the meanings of the following words as used in the passage. One word answers or short phrases will be accepted plodded amiable conviction.   (3)

(b)   Answer the following questions briefly in your own words.

  (i)   What effect did the coming examinations have on: Shankar, Somu, The Pea and Rajam?   (4)

  (ii) Which word in the passage describes the clerk as all knowing?   (1)

  (iii) Why did Mani give the clerk fresh brinjals?   (2)

  (iv) What did the clerk believe was the reason for eyesore? What was the remedy?   (2)

  (v)   Why did Mani try to look pathetic?   (1)

  (vi) Why did Mani ask the question bluntly?   (2)

(c)   What did Mani really want to know? What valuable hints was he given? Write your answer in not more than 60 words.   (8)

(d)   Give a title to your summary in 3(c). State a reason to justify your choice._____(2)

Question 4

(a)   In the following passage, fill in each of the numbered blanks with the correct form of the word given in brackets. Do not copy the passage, but write in correct serial order the word or phrase, appropriate to the blank space.

Example: (0) spoke.

As she (0)_____(speak) I (I) _____(rise) and (2) _____ (go) to the centre blackboard, I (3) ——————— (find) the _____chalk (4) _____   (write) in block letters the title of the book. Then I (5) _____(put) the chalk down and went to (6) _____(sit), beside her, to (7) _____(hold) her hand. The day had barely (8) _____ . (begin).   [4]

(b)   Fill in the blanks with appropriate words:-

  (i)   I prevailed' _____him to join the gymnasium.
  (ii)   The curious child eagerly begged_____an answer to the riddle.
  (iii) He was bent _____coming first in the examinations.
  (iv)   The theory exam was followed _____a group discussion.
  (v)   I ran_____ my teacher at the show last night.
  (vi)   She is extremely anxious _____an interview next week.
  (vii) What a contrast _____the two siblings!
  (viii) The brothers fought _____.. their father's property.   [4]

(c)   Join the following sentences to make one complete sentence without using and, but or/ so: [4]

  (i)   Swarna asked me a question. I was unable to answer it.
  (ii)   You helped Tania. She will always be grateful.
  (iii) I heard you won a prize. I am extremely delighted.
  (iv)   There was heavy traffic. We reached the stadium on time.

(d) Re-write the following sentences according to the instructions given after each. Make other changes that may be necessary, but do not change the meaning of each sentence.

(8)

(*i*)   Study hard now or you will regret it. (Begin: Unless)

(*ii*)   The boy asked, 'Why are you lying on the road in this manner?'

(Begin: The boy asked why he)

(*iii*) Megha is too tall to crawl under the table. (Begin: Megha is so ….)

(*iv*)   He arrived in school on time even though he stopped for a bite on the way. (Use in spite of instead of even though) .

(*v*)   She opened the kitchen door and a cockroach ran out. (End with 'cockroach',)

(*vi*)   Arjun was a better speaker than his brother. (Begin: His brother)

(*vii*) Asha missed her examination because of her illness. (Begin: Her illness)

(*viii*) As soon as the curtain came down the applause rang out. (Begin: No sooner)

Answer

1. (*a*) Refer to contents Section A (Recent Essays) Sl. No. 08

(*b*) Short Story

(*c*) Refer To contents Section A (Recent Essays) Sl. No. 09

(*d*) Refer to contents Section A (Recent Letters) Sl. No. 10

2   (*a*) Refer to contents Section F (Recent Letters) Sl. No. 07

(*b*) Refer to contents Section F (Recent Letters) Sl. No. 08

3

(*a*) plodded - Slog, labour.

amiable - agreeable, friendly.

conviction – confidence, certainty

(*b*)

(*i*) The coming examinations made Shanker very serious and unsmiling, while Somu became more alert and businesslike. The Pea took time to grasp jokes and seldom cracked any himself. Rajam on the other hand was very punctual in attending classes, taking down everything the teacher said, and left school without speaking to anyone.

(*ii*) Omniscient.

(*iii*) Mani gave fresh brinjals to the clerk, because he firmly believed that the school clerk knew the question coming in the examinations. He therefore tried to bribe him with fresh brinjals so as to please him. and obtain from him valuable hints of questions coming in the school examinations.

(*iv*) The clerk believed that eyesores are caused by eye flies buzzing near the eyes. The remedy for eyesores according to him was to take a slice of raw onion, the large juicy variety and squeeze it near one's eyes.

(*v*) Mani tried to look pathetic, so that the clerk would take pity on him, and give him valuable hints of questions coming in the examinations.

(vi) Mani told the clerk that he was very worried, and could not sleep at night thinking of the coming examinations. He pleaded that since there was so much to study, it would be helpful if the clerk told him some important questions, that were to come in the examination. The clerk understood, but replied "read all your portions and you will pass." Realising that he was not getting the desired result diplomatically, he bluntly asked the clerk to tell him the questions that were to come in the examination.

(c) Write your answer in not more than 60 words.

Mani	wanted	to	know	the
questions	that	were	coming	in
the	examination	from	the	school
clerk	The	valuable	hints	given
by	him	were	to	pay
attention	to	Geography	particularly	map
drawing.	Solve	at	least	five
problems	a	day	in	Mathematics.
Read	all	important	lessons	in
English	few	times	if	time
permits.	This	would	enable	him
to	pass	the	school	examinations.

(e) Title

PASSING EXAMINATIONS

The hints given by the clerk in fact are broadly for anyone sitting for any examination.

4.

(a)

Example:

0 spoke. 1. rose 2 went 3 found 4 and wrote 5 put 6 sit 7 hold 8 begun.

(b)   Fill in the blanks with appropriate words:-

(i) upon (ii) for (iii) on (iv) by (v) into (vi) of/ about (vii)   between (viii) over

(c)

(i)   Swarna asked me a question, which I was unable to answer.

(ii) Tania will always be grateful for the help you gave her.

(iii) I am extremely delighted on hearing that you won a prize.

(iv) Despite the heavy traffic we reached the stadium in time.

(d)

(i)   Unless you study hard now you will regret it later.

(ii) The boy asked why he lay on the road in such a manner.

(iii) Megha is so tall that she cannot crawl under the table.

(iv) Inspite of stopping for a bite on the way, he arrived to school in time.

(v) As she opened the kitchen door, out ran a cockroach.

(vi) His brother is not a better speaker than Arjun.

(vii) Her illness made Asha miss her examination.

(viii) No sooner had the curtain come down the applause rang out.

QUESTION PAPER FOR ICSE 2010

ENGLISH

Paper 1

(Two hours)

Answers to this paper must be written on the paper provided separately.
*You will **not** be allowed to write during the first **15** minutes.*
This time is to be spent in reading the question paper.
The time given at the head of this Paper is the time allowed for writing the answers.

---

*Attempt **all four** questions.*
The intended marks for questions or parts of questions are given in brackets [ ].
*You are advised to spend not more than **35** minutes in answering Question 1 and **20** minutes in answering **Question 2**.*

Question 1

(Do not spend more than **35** minutes on this question)

Write a composition (**350 -400** words) on any **one** of the following:-   [25]

(a) Think of a time when you achieved a personal goal. Say why the goal was important to you and how you achieved it. Describe how you felt on achieving it.

(b) "More lessons are learnt on the sports field than in the classroom". Express your views either for or against this statement.

(c) A school carnival or fete is a great occasion for fun with friends. Describe one such event in your school.

(d) Write an original story, beginning with the following line: The water was cold, I took a deep breath and jumped.

(e) Study the picture given below. Write a story or a description or an account of what it suggests to you. Your composition may be about the subject of the picture or you may take suggestions from it; however, there must be a clear connection between the picture and your composition.

Question 2

(Do not spend more than 20 minutes on this question. Select one of the following:-   [10]

(a) Your class was taken to visit an Old Age Home where you spent half a day with the residents. Write a letter to a friend telling him/her what you saw, how you felt and in what way you have changed since the visit.

(b) Write a letter to the Director of a television channel complaining about the quality of the programmes telecast. Suggest ways to improve the programmes.

Question 3

Read the following passage carefully and answer the questions that follow:

They pass me everyday, on their way to school - boys and girls from the surrounding villages and the outskirts of the hill station. There are no school buses plying for these children: they walk.

For many of them, it's a very long walk to school.

Ranbir, who is ten, has to climb the mountain from his village, four miles distant and two thousand feet below the town level. He comes in all weathers, wearing the same pair of cheap shoes until they have almost fallen apart.

Ranbir is a cheerful soul. He waves to me whenever he sees me at my window. Sometimes he brings me cucumbers from his father's field. I pay him for the cucumbers; he uses the money for books or for small things needed at home.

Many of the children are like Ranbir - poor, but slightly better off than what their parents were at the same age. They cannot attend the expensive residential and private schools that abound here, but must go to the government-aided schools with only basic facilities. Not many of their parents managed to go to school.

They spent their lives working in the fields or delivering milk in the hill station.

The lucky ones got into the army. Perhaps Ranbir will do something different when he grows up. He has yet to see a train but he sees planes flying over the mountains almost every day.

"How far can a plane go?" he asks.

"All over the world," I tell him. "Thousands of miles in a day. You can go almost anywhere."

"I'll go round the world one day," he vows. "I'll buy a plane and go everywhere!"

And may be he will. He has a determined chin and a defiant look in his eye. Up to a few years ago, very few girls in the hills or in the villages of India went to school. They helped in the home until they were old enough to be married, which wasn't very old. But there are now just as many girls as there are boys going to school.

Bindra is something of an extrovert - confident fourteen year old who chatters away as she hurries down the road with her companions. Her father is a forest guard and knows me quite well: I meet him on my walks through the deodar woods behind Landour. And I had grown used to seeing Bindra almost every day.

When she did not put in an appearance for a week, I asked her brother if anything was wrong.

"Oh, nothing," he says, "she is helping my mother cut grass."

"Soon the monsoon will end and the grass will dry up. So we cut it now and store it for the cows in winter."

"And why aren't you cutting grass too?"

"Oh, I have a cricket match today," he says, and hurries away to join his team-mates. Unlike his sister, he puts pleasure before work!

Cricket, once the game of the elite has become the game of the masses. On any holiday, in any part of this vast country, groups of boys can be seen making their way to the nearest field, or open patch of land, with bat, ball and any other cricketing gear that they can cobble together. Watching some of them play; I am amazed at the quality of talent, at the finesse with which they bat or bowl. Some of the local teams are as good, if not better, than any from the private schools, where there are better facilities. But boys from these poor or lower middle-class families will never get the exposure that is necessary to bring them to the attention of those who select state or national teams. They will never get near enough to the men of influence and power. They must continue to play for the love of the game, or watch their more fortunate heroes' exploits on television.

(a) Give the meanings of the following words as used in the passage.
   One word answers or short phrases will be accepted.
   (i) defiant
   (ii) elite
   (iii) exposure [3]

(b) Answer the following questions briefly in your own words.

    (*i*)   In what way are the children" better off than their parents?   [2]
    (*ii*)   What was Ranbir's ambition?   [2]
    (*iii*)   How has the fate of girls changed?   [2]
    (*iv*)   In what way was her brother different from Bindra?   [2]
    (*v*)   Why is the narrator amazed? .   [2]
    (*vi*)   Why does the author call the heroes on television 'fortunate'?   [2}

(c)   In not more than 60 words, relate what difficulties the children face in their daily lives. How does the author feel about it?   [8]

(d)   Give a title to your summary in 3(c). State a reason to justify your choice.   [2]

Question 4

(a)   In the following passage, fill in each of the numbered blanks with the correct form of the word given in brackets. Do not copy the passage, but write in correct serial order the word or phrase, appropriate to the blank space.   [4]

Example: (0) given.

But just when I had almost (0)_____ (give) up-hope, I was (1) _____ (strike) with a brilliant idea: my birthday was due fairly soon, and if I (2)_____ (deal) with the family skillfully, I (3) _____ (feel) sure, I could not only get a boat but a lot of other equipment as well. I (4) _____ (suggest) to the family that, instead of (5) _____ (let) them choose my presents, I (6) _____ (may) tell them the things that I(7)_____ (want) most. In this way they could be sure of not (8)_____ (disappoint) me.

(b)   Fill in the blanks with appropriate words:-   [4]

    (*i*)   I refrained _____ telling Reeta the truth.
    (*ii*)   The leader counted _____ the cooperation of his colleagues.
    (*iii*)   The public was cautioned _____ pickpockets.
    (*iv*)   Janaki escorted her daughter to the cinema theatre as she was anxious _____ her safety.
    (*v*)   Their path was beset _____ difficulties yet they succeeded.
    (*vi*)   The mouse crept stealthily _____ the cheese·
    (*vii*)   It was good _____ you to invite Sheila for the picnic.
    (*viii*)   Smoking _____ public places is now banned.

(c)   Join the following sentences to make one complete sentence without using and, but or/ so: [4]

(4)   (*i*)   You will surely be late. Hurry up!
    (*ii*)   The trekkers got lost due to the heavy fog. They had misplaced their map as well.
    (*iii*)   She has to apologize. He will not meet her again if she does not do so.
    (*iv*)   I wear this expensive outfit very sparingly. I bought it last month.

(d)   Re-write the following sentences according to the instructions given after each. Make other changes that may be necessary, but do not change the. meaning of each sentence.

    (*i*)   Unless Ria takes care of her health, she will not be able to look after her family.
         (Begin: Ria must ......)
    (*ii*)   His arrogance was the cause of his losing the election.
         (Rewrite the sentence using "arrogant")
    (*iii*)   If you are not a member you cannot borrow books.
         (Begin: Only ....)
    (*iv*)   It is a pity our vacation is not longer.
         (Begin: I wish ....)

(v) Raju did not complete the exercise on time.
(Rewrite the sentence adding a question tag)

(vi) Rohan was so terrified of being left alone in the house that he started screaming.
(Begin: So ....   )

(vii) The teacher asked, "How many of you think the answer is correct?"
(Rewrite the sentence using indirect speech)

(viii) Sunil is the fastest runner in the school.
(End: .... as Sunil.)

Answer

1. (a) Refer to contents Section A (Recent Essays) Sl. No. 05

   (b) Refer to contents Section A (Recent Essays) Sl. No. 06

   (c) Refer To contents Section A (Recent Essays) Sl. No. 07

2. (a) Refer to contents Section F (Recent Letters) Sl. No. 05

   (b) Refer to contents Section F (Recent Letters) Sl. No. 06

3.

(a) Give the meanings of the following words as used in the passage.
   (i) rebellious
   (ii) privileged
   (iii) experience

(b)

(i) The children were better of than their parents, in the same age. This was for at that time only few of them went to school. Most of them spent their time working in the fields, or delivering milk in the hill station. However now most of the children went to school and also played cricket and other games in the holidays.

(ii) Ranbir's ambition in life when he grew up, was to buy a plane and go everywhere. He also desired to go around the world one day.

(iii) How has the fate of girls changed?
The fate of the girls had changed over the years,. for a few years back, very few of them went to school. Most of them helped their mother in the household work, and were married off at a very young age. However now equal number of girls and boys went to school .

(iv) In what way was her brother different from Bindra?
Bindra's brother was different form her because he put "pleasure before work." While Bindra along with her studies, helped her mother in cutting grass for the cows to eat in winter. Her brother was busy playing cricket, and hurried to join the team for a cricket match, scheduled that day.

(v) Cricket 'the game of the elite, had now become the game of the masses. On a holiday group of boys would play cricket in an open patch of land , with their bat, ball and improvised cricket gear. The narrator was amazed at the quality of talent, and the finesse with which they batted and bowled. Some of the local team were as good, if not better than the team from the private schools which had better facilities.

(iv) The author calls the cricket players heroes on television 'fortunate' , because coming form a better family background, they had better facilities and exposure to improve their game. Being superior placed, they were able to catch the attention of people with power and influence, to get selected in state and national teams whose matches were telecast, making them heroes. On the other hand equally talented poor boys, played cricket only for the love of the game.

(c)

Life	of	children	in	the
hills	is	difficult.	Most	children
have	to	walk	long	distances
to	reach	school.	Being	poor
they	wore	cheap	shoes	until
they	were	worn	out.	The
girls	besides	going	to	school
also	helped	in	household	work.
The	boys	played	cricket	with
amazing	talent	in	the	open
fields.	with	no	amenities.	The
author	feels	sad	for	them._____

(d)

Title HEROES OF THE HILL

The children of the hills are indeed heroes. This is for despite the hardships of life, they study and play with no facilities and amenities, compared to other children.

4.

(a)

1. struck 2. would deal 3. felt 4. would suggest 5. letting 6. might 7. wanted 8. disappointing

(b)

1. from 2. on 3. against 4. about 5. with 6. towards 7. of 8. in

(c)

(i)   If you do not hurry, you will surely be late.
(ii) The trekkers having misplaced their map got lost due to the heavy fog.
(iii) Unless she apologises, he will not meet her again.
(iv) I wear very sparingly this expensive outfit, which I brought last month.

(d)

(i)   Ria must take care of her health, failing which she shall not be able to look after her family.
(ii)   His arrogant behavior made him lose the election.
(iii) Only members can borrow books.
(iv)   I wish our vacations were longer.
(v)   Did Raju complete the exercise on time?
(vi)   So terrified was Rohan on being left alone in the house that he started screaming.
(vii) The teacher wanted to know how many of the students though the answer to be correct.
(viii) No other runner in the school is as fast as Sunil.

QUESTION PAPER FOR ICSE 2011

ENGLISH

Paper 1

(Two hours)

Answers to this paper must be written on the paper provided separately.
*You will **not** be allowed to write during the first **15** minutes.*
This time is to be spent in reading the question paper.
The time given at the head of this Paper is the time allowed for writing the answers.

---

*Attempt **all four** questions.*
The intended marks for questions or parts of questions are given in brackets [ ].
*You are advised to spend not more than **35** minutes in answering Question 1 and **20** minutes in answering **Question 2**.*

Question 1

(Do not spend more than **35** minutes on this question)

Write a composition **(350 -400 words)** on any **one** of the following:-   (25)

(a) "Private tuitions are a necessary evil." Give your views either *for* or *against* this statement.

(b) Write an original story entitled: Lost and Found

(c) Relate a special incident or experience in your life which you still recall with happiness.

(d) Children's Day is celebrated in your school every year. Write what you particularly liked about this year's celebration. What did you learn from the efforts of those who planned and organised the function? How did you express your gratitude to them?

(e) Study the picture given below. Write a story or a description or an account of what it suggests to you. Your composition may be about the subject of the picture or you may take suggestions from it; however, there must be a clear connection between the picture and your composition.

Question 2

(Do not spend more than 20 minutes on this question. Select one of the following:-   (10)

(a) Write a letter to the local Municipal Corporation complaining about the malaria epidemic in your city. State the causes and suggest ways to deal with the problem.

(b) You have just acquired an *unusual* pet. Write a letter to your friend telling him / her about it. Give details about the care you have to take in looking after and feeding the pet.

Question 3

Read the following passage carefully and answer the questions that follow:

I rested for a moment at the door of Anand Bhavan, on Market Road, where coffee drinkers and tiffin eaters at their tables sat transfixed uttering low moans on seeing me. I wanted to assure them,

'Don't fear, I am not out to trouble you. Eat your tiffin in peace, don't mind me. You...nearest to me, hugging the cash box, you are craven with fear, afraid even to breathe. Go on, count the cash, if that's your pleasure. I just want to watch, that's all. If my tail trails down to the street, if I am blocking your threshold: it is because, I'm told, I'm eleven feet tip to tail. I can't help it. I'm not out to kill.... I'm too full —found a green pasture teeming with food on the way. Won't need any for several days to come, won't stir, not until I feel hungry again. Tigers attack only when they feel hungry, unlike human beings who slaughter one another without purpose or hunger ... '

To the great delight of children, schools were being hurriedly closed. Children of all ages and sizes were running helter-skelter screaming joyously, 'No school, no school. Tiger, tiger!' They were shouting and laughing· and even enjoyed being scared. They seemed to welcome me. I felt like joining them, and bounded away from the restaurant door and trotted along with them, at which they gleefully cried, 'The tiger is coming to eat us; let us get back to the school!'

I followed them through their school gate while they ran up and shut themselves in the school hall securely. I ascended the steps of the school, saw an open door at the far end of a veranda, and walked in. It happened to be the headmaster's room, I believe, as I noticed a very dignified man jumping on his table and heaving himself up into an attic. I walked in and flung myself on the cool floor, having a partiality for cool stone floors, with my head under the large desk-which gave me the feeling of being back in the Mempi cave ...

As I drowsed, I was aware of cautious steps and hushed voices all around. I was in no mood to bother about anything. All I wanted was a little moment of sleep; the daylight was dazzling. In half sleep I heard the doors of the room being shut and bolted and locked. I didn't care. I slept.

While I slept a great deal of consultation was going on. I learnt about it later through my master, who was in the crowd — the crowd which had gathered after making sure that I had been properly locked up — and was watching. The headmaster seems to have remarked some days later, 'Never dreamt in my wildest mood that I'd have to yield my place to a tiger ...' A wag had retorted, 'Might be one way of maintaining better discipline among the boys.'

'Now that this brute is safely locked up, we must decide,' began a teacher. At this moment my master pushed his way through the crowds and admonished, 'Never use the words "beast" or "brute". They're ugly words coined by humans in their arrogance. The human being thinks all other creatures are "beasts". Awful word!'.

(a) Give the meaning of each of the following words or phrases as used in the passage. One
     word answers or short phrases will be accepted.   [3]
     (i) transfixed
     (ii) helter-skelter
     (iii) admonished
(b) Answer the following questions briefly in your own words.
     (i) What reassurance did the tiger give the coffee drinkers?   [2]
     (ii) In what way are tigers different from human beings?   [2]
     (iii) Why were the children delighted?   [2]
     (iv) What did the headmaster say some days later?   [2]
     (v) What was the wag's response ?   [2]
     (vi) Which sentences tell us that the tiger's owner had great respect for the tiger? [2]
(c) (i) In not more than 60 words describe the tiger's activities from the time it followed the
          school children till it slept.
     (ii) Give a title to your summary in 3 (c). Give a reason to justify your choice.

Question 4
(a)   Fill in each of the numbered blanks with the correct form of the word given in brackets. Do
      not copy the passage, but write in correct serial order the word or phrase appropriate to the
      blank space.   [4]

Example:

(0) We were not _____(allow) to talk during the lecture.

Answer: allowed.

The children (1)_____ (sit) In a neat circle and (2)_____ (begin) (3) _____ (copy) their multiplication tables. Most (4) _____ (scratch) in the dirt with sticks they had _____(5) (bring) for that purpose. The more fortunate (6) _____ (has) slate boards that they (7) _____ _ (write) on with sticks (8) _____ (dip) in a mixture of mud and water.

(b) Fill in the blanks with appropriate words: [4]

  (i)   He congratulated me _____ my great achievement.

  (ii) The poor man is afflicted _____arthritis.

  (iii) She is blind_____ the faults of her husband.

  (iv) The boss had many complaints _____ Shyam.

  (v)   You must prepare _____ the examination.

  (vi) She is not aware _____ the danger.

  (vii) Ravi was accurate _____his calculations.

  (viii) They hid the money _____ the carpet.

(c) Join the following sentences to make one complete sentence without using *and, but* or *so*. [4]

  (i)   The minister was wise. The king did not trust him.

  (ii) We reached the port. The storm came on.

  (iii) One should not borrow money. One should not lend money.

  (iv) She will win the prize. She deserves it.

(d) Re-write the following sentences according to the instructions given after each. Make other changes that may be necessary, but do not change the meaning of each sentence. [8]

  (i)   This horse is better trained than yours.
        (Begin: Your ....)

  (ii) The children will sit out in the garden if the weather is cool.
        (Begin: The children won't .... :)

  (iii) The thief ran so fast that the police could not catch him.
        (Rewrite using: too.)

  (iv) Her attitude often annoys me.
        (Rewrite using: annoyance ....)

  (v)   The child disappeared as soon as the bus stopped.
        (Begin: Hardly ....)

  (vi) There is no success without effort.
        (Begin: Whenever ....)

  (vii) "Please teach me to cycle" she asked her brother.
        (Rewrite in indirect *form)*

  (viii) The peasants regarded him as a thief and called him a villain.
        (End:.................... the peasants)

Answer

1. (a) Refer to contents Section A (Recent Essays) Sl. No. 03

    (b) Story entitled Lost & Found

    (c) Refer to contents Section A (Recent Essays) Sl. No. 05

    (d) Refer to contents Section A (Recent Essays) Sl. No. 04

2. (a) Refer to contents Section F (Recent Letters) Sl. No. 03

    (b) Refer to contents Section F (Recent Letters) Sl. No. 04

3.

(a) (*i*) Transfixed - spellbound, root to the spot.

(*ii*) Helter- skelter - haphazard, disorganised

(*iii*) Admonished - reprimand, scold.

(b) (*i*) The coffee drinkers sat rooted to their seats on seeing the tiger blocking the entrance of the restaurant. The tiger however reassured them, that they need not fear him, for he had a good meal on the way. This meal would last him several days and hence he was not out to kill. He requested them to go about their work unmindful of him, for he just wanted to watch them.

(*ii*) Tigers are different from human beings, for they attack and kill only if they are hungry. On the other hand human beings kill and slaughter one another without any reason. Thus while tigers kill to satisfy their hunger, humans kill for no such purpose.

(*iii*) As the news of the tiger roaming the street of the town spread, the schools closed hurriedly. This delighted the children and they ran about joyously screaming' No school, no school, Tiger, tiger!'

(*iv*) The head master who had jumped on his table in fright, and had pulled himself up into the attic on seeing the tiger walk into his room. He remarked some days later that he had never dreamt in his wildest frame of mind giving up his position to a tiger some day.

(*v*) The wags response to the head masters comment was, probably making way for the tiger, as headmaster was one way of enforcing better discipline among the boys of the school.

(*vi*) 'Never use the words "beast" or "brute". They're ugly words coined by humans in their arrogance. The human being thinks all other creatures are "beasts". Awful word!'.

(c)

(*i*) The tiger joyously trotted after the children through the school gate .He walked into the headmaster's room at the end of the verandah. The headmaster jumped on his table in fright and pulled himself into the attic. The tiger than flung himself on the cool stone floor with his head under the large desk and drowsed off to sleep.

(*ii*) Headmaster's Nightmare
The sight of the tiger walking into his room was indeed a nightmare for the headmaster, which he would never forget throughout his life.

4

(a)

1. sat	2. began	3. copying	4. scratched	5. brought
6. had	7. wrote	8. dipped		

(b)

1. for	2. with	3. to	4 . against	5. for
6 . of	7. in	8. under		

(c)

(*i*) Though the minister was wise the king did not trust him.

(*ii*) As we reached the port the storm came on.

(*iii*) One should neither borrow nor lend money.

(*iv*) She deserves to win the prize.

(d)

    (*i*) Your horse is not better trained than this one.

   (*ii*) The children won't sit out in the garden if the weather is not cool.

  (*iii*) The thief ran too fast for the police to catch him.

  (*iv*) Her attitude often cause me annoyance.

   (*v*) Hardly had the bus stopped when the child disappeared.

  (*vi*) Whenever there is success ,it is not without effort.

 (*vii*) She requested her brother to teach her to cycle.

(*viii*) He was regarded as a thief and called a villain by the peasants

QUESTION PAPER FOR ICSE 2012

ENGLISH

Paper 1

(Two hours)

Answers to this paper must be written on the paper provided separately.
*You will **not** be allowed to write during the first **15** minutes.*
This time is to be spent in reading the question paper.
The time given at the head of this Paper is the time allowed for writing the answers.

---

*Attempt **all four** questions.*
The intended marks for questions or parts of questions are given in brackets [ ].
*You are advised to spend not more than 35 minutes in answering Question 1 and **20** minutes in answering **Question 2**.*

Question 1

(Do not spend more than **35** minutes on this question)

Write a composition (**350 -400** words) on any one of the following:-   [25]

(a) Write an original short story that begins with the word: It wasn't going to be easy she knew…. But somehow she had to confront him. she took a deep breath, and walked into the room.

(b) 'Money causes more harm than good.' Express your views either for or against the statement.

(c) People play a very important role in our lives. Describe in vivid detail any one person and show how he / she has been a very special influence in your life.

(d) Modes of communication are constantly changing, What are some of these changes? Say which one change you like best and why?

(e) Study the picture given below. Write a story or a description or an account of what it suggests to you. Your composition may be about the subject of the picture or you may take suggestions from it, however there must be a clear connection between the picture and the composition.

Question 2

(Do not spend more than 20 minutes on this question. Select one of the following:-   (10)

(a) Many area near your school have been affected by floods. You are the President of your school social service club. Write a letter to the Mayor of your town / city telling him / her what you plan to do for the relief of the victims, suggest ways in which you can combine with other organizations bringing about better distribution of relief items.

(b) You were taken by your school to visit a place of historical interest. Write a letter to your classmate who was unable to go on the trip, telling him / her about the trip, why it was important and what you gained from the experience.

Question 3

Read the following passage carefully and answer the questions that follow:

It as a dull autumn day and Jill Pole was crying behind the gym. She as crying because they had been bullying her. This is not going to be a school story so I shall say as little as possible about Jill's school, which is not a very pleasant subject. It was co educational a school for both boys and girls, what used to be called a "mixed" school, some said it was not nearly so mixed as the minds of the people who ran it. These people had the idea that boys and girls should be allowed to do what they liked. And unfortunately what ten or fifteen of the biggest boys and girls liked best was bullying the others. All sorts of things, horrid things, went on which at an ordinary school, would have been found out and stopped in half a term, but at this school they weren't. Or even if they were, the people who did them were not expelled or punished. The Head said they were interesting psychological cases and sent for them and talked to them for hours. And if they knew the right sort of things to say to the Head, the main result was that you became rather a favourite than otherwise.

That was why Jill Pole was crying on that dull autumn day on the damp little path which ran between the back of the gym and the shrubbery. And she hadn't nearly finished her cry when a boy came around the corner of the gym whistling, with his hands in his pocket. He nearly ran into her.

" Can't you look where you're going?" said Jill Pole.

" All right," said the boy, "you needn't start……"and then he noticed her face, "I say, Jill," he said. "what's up?"

Jill only made faces: the sort you make when you're trying to say something but find that if you speak you'll start crying again. "It's Them; I suppose ….as usual," said the boy grimly, digging his hands further into his pocket.

Jill nodded. There was no need for her to say anything, even if she could have said it. They both knew.

" Now look here," said the boy, "it's no use…"

He meant well, but he did talk rather like someone beginning a lecture. Jill suddenly flew into a temper. (which is quite a likely thing to happen if you have interrupted in a cry.)

"Oh, go away and mind your business," she said." Nobody asked you to come **barging** in, did they? And you're a nice person to start telling us what we all ought to do, aren't you? I suppose you mean we ought to spend all our time sucking up to Them, and currying favour, and dancing attendance on Them like you do."

" Oh, Lord." said the boy, sitting down on the grassy bank at the edge of the shrubbery, and very quickly getting up again because the grass was soaking wet .His name unfortunately was Eustace Scrubb, but he wasn't a bad sort.

" Jill!" he said , " is that fair?"

"I d-don't know and I don't care ," sobbed Jill..

Eustace saw that she wasn't quite herself yet and very sensibly offered her a peppermint. He had one too. Presently Jill began to see things in a clearer light.

"I'm sorry Eustace ," she said presently.

(a) Give the meaning of the following word as used in the passage. One word answers or phrases will be accepted. 					(3)

    (i) Bullying

    (ii) Expelled

(*iii*) Barging.
(b) Answer the following questions in your own words.
     i. Why was Jill crying?   (2)
     ii. Why do you think she was crying behind the gym?   (2)
     iii. Who is the Them referred to?   (2)
     iv. Why did Jill fly into a temper?   (2)
     v. Which sentences tells us that Jill and Eustace Scrubb had suffered similarly? (2)
     vi. When did Jill begin to see things differently?   (2)
(c)
     i. What kind of school did the children go to ? Write your answer in not more than 60 words.   (8)
     ii. Give a title to your summary in 3 (c).Give a reason to justify your choice   [2]

Question 4

(*a*) Fill in each of the numbered blanks with the correct form of words given in brackets. Do not copy the passage, but write in correct serial order the word or phrases appropriate to the blank space.   (4)

Example My guide _____(tell) me if I wanted to meet these people I would have to walk two miles.

Answer told.

We finally (1) _____(reach) a village where I (2) _____ (meet) a lady whose age [3] _____(can) not immediately make out. My translator(4) _____(find) it difficult to interpret the lady's words because her dialect was quite different. She (5) _____(is) a dark skinned and dark haired lady. She must have been around seventy years old but there was no gray in her hair .She obviously could not afford to dye her hair. So what was her secret? Nobody (6) _____ (know). It must have been a 'secret' common to all for not one person in the whole village (7) _____(has) a trace of gray hair! I (8) _____(think) about it for a long time.

(*b*) Fill in the blanks with appropriate words: [4]
    (*i*) He was touched _____ pity hen he herd the tale.
    (*ii*) The poor man is afflicted _____arthritis.
    (*iii*) The mother prevented the child_____ going out in the rain.
    (*iv*) The baby crawled _____ the table and hid there.
    (*v*) Once up a time a great King ruled _____ these villages and towns.
    (*vi*) She is smarter _____ the two.
    (*vii*) Shiela insists _____wearing that dress, although her mother thinks it is too short for her.
    (*viii*) The teacher complained _____ him when she met his mother in the market.

(*c*) Join the following sentences to make one complete sentence without using *and, but* or *so*.   [4]

    (*i*) He lived in the city for many years. He could not find his way about.
    (*ii*) She complained that her brother did not know anything. Her brother claimed that he knew everything.
    (*iii*) The coffee isn't strong. It won't keep us awake.
    (*iv*) I finished my homework. I switched on the TV.

(*d*) Rewrite the following sentences according to the instructions given after each. Make other changes that may be necessary but do not change the meaning of each sentence.   [8]
    (*i*) My mother left a month ago.
      (Begin : It has _____)
    (*ii*) Anil was wrong to lose his temper.
      (Begin: Anil ought_____)

    (*iii*) As soon as the Chief Guest had seated himself the play began.
          (Begin: No sooner _____)
    (*iv*) Rajiv said to Arjun "Is this the book you were reading yesterday."
          (Begin: Rajiv asked Arjun If_____)
    (*v*) Only a foolish person would be taken in by this trick.
          (Begin: None_____)
    (*vi*) Everybody has heard of Gandhiji.
          (Begin: ho_____)
    (*vii*) He will issue the cheque only when he hears from the head office.
          (Begin: On _____)
    (*viii*) Father will send you a message if his flight is cancelled.
          (Begin: Should_____)

Answer

1.   (*a*) Story
      (*b*) Refer to contents Section A (Recent Essays) Sl. No. 01
      (*c*) Refer to contents Section B Sl. No. 59
      (*d*) Refer to contents Section A (Recent Essays) Sl. No. 02

2.   (*a*) Refer to contents Section E (Recent Letters) Sl. No. 01
      (*b*) Refer to contents Section E (Recent Letters) Sl. No. 02

3.
(a)
    (*i*) harassment
    (*ii*) debarred / excluded
    (*iii*) collide against

(b)
    (*i*) Jill Pole was crying behind the gym because some of the bigger boys and girls of her school, which was a co educational one had been harassing her. This made her upset and being unable to control her emotion she started to cry.

    (*ii*) She was crying behind the gym, for she did want anyone to see her anguish. She did not want to share her feelings with anyone and hence she chose to let loose her emotion behind the gym, where no one was present.

    (*iii*) Who is the Them referred to?
         In this passage, 'Them' is referred to the ten to fifteen big boys and girls in her coeducational school who liked to bully other students of the school.

    (*iv*) Jill lost her temper when Eustace Scrubb her fellow student came whistling merrily round the corner of the gym nearly collided with her. Instead of sympathizing with her he began to what appeared to Jill, give her a lecture. This annoyed Jill and she told him to get lost.

    (*v*) "It's Them; I suppose ….as usual," said the boy grimly, digging his hands further into his pocket.
         Jill nodded. There was no need for her to say anything, even if she could have said it. They both knew.

    (*vi*) Jill lost her temper when Eustace Scrubb instead of sympathizing with her, tried to lecture her. Though he meant well but Jill was in no mood to listen. Sensing this Scrubb who was a decent boy instead of being offended by her outburst, offered her a peppermint, taking one himself. This small gesture of understanding and empathy, made Jill see the brighter side of life and get over her grief.

(c)

(i)

The	children	went	to	a
coeducational	school	that	was	run
by	people	who	believed	that
boys	and	girls	should	be
allowed	to	interact	freely.	Unfortunately
big	students	liked	to	bully
Others.	They	did	horrid	things
which	would	have	been	stopped
in	an	ordinary	school.	Here
however	the	Head	perceived	them
as	psychological	Cases,	spoke	to
them	making	them	his	favourites.

Give a title to your summary in 3 (c).Give a reason to justify your choice (

(ii) School of Bully's

The entire school was in fear of these 10 to 15 big boys and girls who harassed all the students and did horrid things that are unacceptable in any ordinary school. However instead of being reprimanded, they were encouraged in their wayward behaviour by the head of the school.

4.

(a)

1. reached   2. met   3. could   4. found   5. was   6. knew   7. had   8. thought.

(b)

1. with   2. for   3. from   4. under   5. over   6. of   7. on   8. about.

(c)

(i) Although he lived in the city for many years yet he could not find his way about.

(ii) She complained that her brother did not know anything, while he claimed to know everything.

(iii) The coffee is not strong enough to keeo us awake.

(iv) Having finished my homework, I switched on the TV.

(d)

(i) It has been a month since my mother left.

(ii) Anil ought not to have lost his temper.

(iii) No sooner had the chief Guest seated himself, the play began.

(iv). Rajiv asked Arjun if this was the book he was reading the day before.

(v) None but a foolish person would be taken in by this trick.

(vi) Who hasn't heard of Gandhiji.

(vii) On hearing from the head office he will issue the cheque.

(viii) Should his flight be delayed father will send you a message.

QUESTION PAPER FOR ICSE 2013

ENGLISH

Paper 1

(Two hours)

Answers to this paper must be written on the paper provided separately.
*You will **not** be allowed to write during the first **15** minutes.*
This time is to be spent in reading the question paper.
The time given at the head of this Paper is the time allowed for writing the answers.

*Attempt **all four** questions.*
The intended marks for questions or parts of questions are given in brackets [ ].
*You are advised to spend not more than **35** minutes in answering Question 1 and **20** minutes in answering **Question 2**.*

Question 1

*(Do not spend more than **35** minutes on this question)*

Write a composition (**350 -400** words) on any one of the following:-   [25]

(*a*) Write an original short story that begins with the words: "In the background I could hear an awful commotion, men's voices raised and women screaming."

(*b*) 'Boarding schools are far better than day schools for the all-round education of a child'. Express your view either for or against this statement.

(*c*) You were on a school trip and were on your way back to the hotel late one night when your school bus, full of children, broke down in a lonely area. Describe what you saw and experienced as you looked around. How was the problem solved?

(*d*) Teaching someone else how to do something can be a rewarding experience. Think of a skill that you have helped someone to develop Perhaps you taught someone how to swim or to bake a cake, or helped someone learn how to study more effectively. Narrate the events that made up the process of teaching the skill, and say what made the experience important and memorable for you.

(*e*) Study the picture given below. Write a story or a description or an account of what it suggests to you. Your composition may be about the subject of the picture or you may take suggestions from it; however, there must be a clear connection between the picture and your composition.

Question 2

(Do not spend more than 20 minutes on this question.

Select one of the following:- (10)

(a) You will soon have to make a decision about the subjects that you wish to study in classes XI and XII.

Write a letter to your Grandfather telling him about the subjects that you plan to take up. Be sure to explain the reason for your choice and how you think these subjects would help you in the future.

(b) The children in your neighbourhood are forced to play on the street for want of a proper play area. Write a letter to the Editor of a popular newspaper, pointing out the need for a playground in your neighbourhood.

Give reasons why you think a play area is necessary and point out how it would benefit everyone who lives in that area.

Question 3

Read the following passage carefully and answer the questions that follow:

There were other boys in Manjari village, but Bisnu was the only one who went to school. His mother would not have fussed if he had stayed at home and worked in the fields. That was what the other boys did; all except lazy Chittru, who preferred fishing in the stream or helping himself to the fruit off other people's trees. But Bisnu went to school. He went because he wanted to. No one could force him to go; and no one could stop him from going He had set his heart on receiving a good schooling. He wanted to read and write as well as anyone in the big world and so he walked to school every day.

A colony of langoors lived in the forest. They fed on oak leaves, acorns, and other green things, and usually remained in the trees, coming down to the ground only to play or sun themselves. They were beautiful, supple-limbed animals, with black faces and silver-grey coats and long, sensitive tails. They leapt from tree to tree with great **agility**. The young ones wrestled on the grass like boys.

A dignified community, the langoors did not have the cheekiness or dishonest habits of the red monkeys of the plains; they did not approach dogs or humans. But they had grown used to Bisnu's comings and goings and did not fear him. Some of the older ones would watch him quietly, a little puzzled. They did not go near the town; because the boys threw stones at them. And anyway, the forest gave them all the food they required.

Coming from another direction was a second path, and at the junction of the two paths Sarru was waiting for him. Sarru came from a small village about three miles from Bisnu's and closer to the town.

They **hailed** each other, and walked along. They often met at this spot, keeping each other company for the remaining two miles.

'There was a panther in our village last night,' said Sarru.

This information interested but did not excite Bisnu. Panthers were common enough in the hills and did not usually present a problem except during the winter months, when their natural prey was scarce.

'Did you lose any animals?' asked Bisnu.

'No. It tried to get into the cowshed but the dogs set up the alarm. We drove it off.'

'It must be the same one which came around last winter. We lost a calf and two dogs in our village.'

'Wasn't that the one the shikaris wounded? I hope it hasn't become a cattle-lifter.'

'It could be the same. It has a bullet in its leg. These hunters are the people who cause all the trouble. They think it's easy to shoot a panther. It would be better if they missed altogether, but they usually wound it.'

'And then the panther's too slow to catch the barking-deer and starts on our own animals.'

'We're lucky it didn't become a man-eater. Do you remember the man-eater six years ago? I was very small then. My father told me all about it. Ten people were killed in our valley alone.'

'What happened to it?'

'I don't know. Some say it poisoned itself when it ate the headman of the village.

Bisnu laughed. No one liked that old **villain**. They linked arms and scrambled up the stony path to school.

(*a*) Give the meaning of each of the following words as used in the passage. One word answers or short phrases will be accepted.   [3]

    (*i*) agility

    (*ii*) hailed

    (*iii*) villain

(*b*) Answer the following questions briefly in your own words.

    (*i*) How was Chittru different from other boys?   [2]

    (*ii*) What was Bisnu's ambition?   [2]

    (*iii*) What information did Sarru give Bisnu?   [2]

    (*iv*) How did the information affect Bisnu?   [2]

    (*v*) Why did the panther become a cattle-lifter?   [2]

    (*vi*) What joke does Sarru make?   [2]

(*c*)

    (*i*) In not more than 60 words describe what the narrator tells us about the behaviour of the langoors.   [8]

    (*ii*) Give a title to your summary in 3 (c). Give a reason to justify your choice.   [2]

Question 4

(*a*) Fill in each of the numbered blanks with the correct form of the word given in brackets. Do not copy the passage, but write in correct serial order the word or phrase appropriate to the blank space.

Example:

(0) A woman _____ (wait) at an airport one night, with several long hours before her flight.

Answer: was waiting.

She (1)_____ (hunt) for a book in the airport shops, (2)_____ (buy) a bag of cookies and found a place to sit. She (3)_____ (engross) in her book but happened to see that the man sitting beside her, bold as could be, grabbed a cookie or two from the bag in between, which she tried to ignore to avoid a scene. So she (4)_____ (munch) the cookies and watched the clock, as the gutsy thief diminished her stock. She (5)_____ (get) more irritated as the minutes ticked by, thinking, "If I wasn't so nice, I (6)_____ (black) his eye." With each cookie she took, he took one too. When only one was left, she wondered what he would do. With a smile on his face, and a nervous laugh, he (7)_____ (take) the last cookie and broke it in half. He offered her half, as he ate the other. She had never known she could be so angry and turned to gather her belongings. As she reached for her baggage, she gasped with surprise, there was her bag of cookies, in front of her eyes. If mine are here, she moaned in despair, the others were his and he (8)_____ (try) to share.

[4]

(b)   Fill in the blanks with an appropriate word:

    (i)   She takes a lot of trouble_____ her work.

    (ii)   Our English friends have taken_____ Indian food quite quickly.

    (iii)   He got an A+_____ the Mathematics test.

    (iv)   He jumped _____the river to save his friend from drowning.

    (v)   Always be prepared _____a surprise test.

    (vi)   She hid _____the cupboard and gave everyone a fright.

    (vii)   She is fond _____pets.

    (viii)   The brothers quarrelled _____themselves for their father's property.   [4]

(c)   Join the following sentences to make one complete sentence without using and, but or so.

    (i)   We had better get ready now. We may not have time to' reach the airport.

    (ii)   Mr. Liew has been sick. He has been so since he came back from Japan.

    (iii)   The debating teams were very happy. Both were declared joint-champions.

    (iv)   He escaped from the prison. He looked for a place where he could hide.   [4]

(d)   Re-write the following sentences according to the instructions given after each. Make other changes that may be necessary, but do not change the meaning of each sentence.

    (i)   These windows need cleaning again.
       (Begin: These windows will ....)

    (ii)   My mother said I could go with you only if I returned home by five 0' clock.
       (Use: as long as)

    (iii)   It doesn't matter which chemical you put into the mixture first, the results will be the same.
       (Use: difference)

    (iv)   Who does this pen belong to?
       (Begin: Do you know ....)

    (v)   Heavy rain has caused the cancellation of the outdoor garden party.
       (Begin: Due ....)

    (vi)   I've never seen so many people in this building before.
       (Begin: This is ....)

    (vii)   If we light the fire, the rescuers will see us.
       (Begin: We will ....)

    (viii)   Only a few books were remaining on the shelf when we left.
       (Begin: Most...............)

Answer

1.

(b)   **'Boarding schools are far better than day schools for the all-round education of a child'. Express your view either for or against this statement.**

    ●   **Introduction-**'The battle of Waterloo was won in the playing fields of Eton.' Boarding schools provide an unequaled academic environment, because of greater interaction between the students and teachers facilitating mentoring.

    ●   Give an opportunity to mingle with students of different background leading to friendship, tolerance and trust

- Emphasis on extra curricular activities nurtures their creative talent, making them independent
- Helps mould character inculcating virtues of self disciplines, open-mindedness, perseverance and hard work
- Prepares them for the academic rigors and social challenges of college life.
- The tough and hectic, life compared to the easy going life at home, inculcates virtues of time management.
- **Conclusion-** Long queue of parents, desirous of admitting their wards in boarding schools, despite the high cost is ample proof of the crucial role they play, in moulding the future of children.

'The battle of Waterloo was won in the playing fields of Eton.' Eton being a famous boarding school in England, that trained boys for career in the military and civil services. The superior character of the young men from this school, tipped the balance in favour of the British during wars. Indeed many leaders emerged from the hallow portals of such boarding schools, to guide the destiny of their nation often creating history. It is an undisputed fact that boarding school are far better then day schools for the all round development and education of a child.

Boarding schools provide an unequaled academic environment, because of greater interaction between the students and teachers. This interface unlike day schools is not just limited to 6 – 8 hours. The small class size enables teachers to give individual attention to each student. Thus even less academically endowed students fare well. This interaction fosters better mentoring of the students, as it takes into account their special skills and attributes. This helps the students to hone the specific talent, which stands them in good stead later in life.

The residential campus environment provides a unique opportunity to mingle with students of different communities, religion and culture. This not only leads to greater understanding of others, but also evolves a spirit of camaraderie, friendship, tolerance and trust between them, that endures for a lifetime.

Besides studies there is extra emphasis on extra curricular activities like sports, music, dramatics, painting through different club activities. This nurtures their creative talent, making them more innovative and confident.. It is this ability to think independently, that makes them more outgoing and successful in life.

Living and studying in a group also help in moulding their character. They inculcate important virtues of self disciplines, open-mindedness, perseverance and hard work that makes them emerge as leaders in future. A fact borne out by the number of leaders both political and military, coming from such boarding schools.

The campus life also prepares them for the academic rigors and social challenges they are to face in college life. Being adaptive by nature, they are better able to assimilate knowledge and also interact with students coming from diverse backgrounds. Being accustomed to staying away from home, they are not prone to home sickness and hence adopt to the new environment comfortably.

Life here is indeed more tough and hectic, compared to the easy going life at home, where they live under the perpetual protective care of parents. This inculcates the importance of time management. A virtue that is important in facing the challenge of adult life. This makes them more independent and accomplished then their counterparts in the professional as well as social life.

The long queue of parents, desirous of admitting their wards in boarding schools, is ample proof of the important and crucial role they play, in moulding the future of children. This is despite the high cost and the pain of seeing their loved ones staying away from them.

(c) **You were on a school trip and were on your way back to the hotel late onenight when your school bus, full of children, broke down in a lonely area. Describe what you saw and experienced as you looked around. How was the problem solved?**

- **Introduction-** The bus axle broke in the middle of a jungle while returning from Dudhwa National Park.
- A sudden fear crept into my heart on peering out of the window.
- Our class teacher warned us not to go out.
- Peered out of the bus window. Pulled back on hearing the alarm call of a languor.
- Saw a herd of 'Neel gais' darting fearfully across the road. Danger seemed to be lurking nearby.
- A strange feeling of being a bait crept through me.
- **Conclusion-** Fortunately nothing happened and we were back in our hotel. I however did not forget to say a brief prayer, before I dosed off to sleep.

'Clank, clank,' followed by the screeching of the tyres, jolted me out of my slumber. Rubbing my eyes, I peered out of the bus window to see pitch darkness all around. "What happened?" As if in answer to my query the lights came on and the driver's cabin door opened. The conductor and guide, a short stout man, with a receding hairline emerged, gesticulating with his hand and uttering, "Axle toot gaya." We groaned in disgust and slumped back in our seat.

Peering down at my wristwatch, I realized that we had barely traveled an hour from Dudhwa National Park and were about another hour's journey to our hotel in Lakhimpur. Thus probably we were in the middle of the jungle. A sudden fear crept into my heart. I anxiously peered out of the window, straining my eyes to survey the surroundings. In the dim moonlight I could see nothing but tall sal and sesam trees, their leaves rustling in the mild breeze. This too seemed quite loud, in the sudden silence that had enveloped us.

"Well boys," the voice of our class teacher Mr Johnson broke the stillness. "The bus axle has broken and they are trying to call for another bus, that will ferry us to the hotel. However this shall take two to three hours. Please stay inside the bus, for we are in a dense forest area. Do not, I repeat do not venture out under any circumstances." Hearing this few students who had scampered out of their seats, hoping to straighten their legs outside, slumped back in their seat. My worst fears being confirmed, I stretched my legs, trying to make myself as comfortable as possible.

After some time, unable to bear the stuffiness inside the bus, I slid the window pane and stuck my neck out to catch some fresh air. An earthy fragrance of an unusual variety wafted in the air, which seemed quite refreshing. The occasional hooting of an owl and chirping of birds, livened the otherwise grave atmosphere.

This unusual calm was suddenly broken by a loud alarm call of a languor, that echoed through out the jungle. Just then I felt two strong hands on my shoulders pushing me back to my seat, simultaneously slamming the window shut. Mr Johnson stood glowering at me "Stupid we are in the jungle, the alarm call you just heard, could in all probability herald the presence of a tiger in the vicinity."

This heightened my anxiety. I started peering through the closed window panes of the bus. Trying to get a glimpse of the elusive animal, who had not put in an appearance on our forest trek through out the day. Minutes ticked by but nothing happened. Suddenly the calm was broken by what seemed to be a herd, trampling the dry leaves. In the head light of the bus I saw a herd of Neel gais' darting across the road. Seeing the fear stricken animals from so close quarters made me a bit nervous. Danger indeed seemed to be lurking nearby.

A strange feeling crept through me. I had read stories of Jim Corbet and how he killed man-eaters using a goat as a bait. I could now imagine how the goat may have felt, waiting for the tiger to pounce on it. Unfortunately here we were the bait and the tiger the hunter.

Fortunately nothing happened. After an hour or so a new bus arrived and under the watchful eyes of the teacher and conductor, we were herded into it. By midnight we were back in our hotel. I however did not forget to say a brief prayer, before I dosed off to sleep.

(*d*) **Teaching someone else how to do something can be a rewarding experience. Think of a skill that you have helped someone to develop. Perhaps you taught someone how to swim or to bake a cake, or helped someone learn how to study more effectively. Narrate the events that made up the process of teaching the skill, and say what made the experience important and memorable for you.**

- **Introduction-** The board exams had just got over. Met little Rahul and his mother.
- His mother looked quite perplexed and sought my help in helping Rahul out in his studies.
- Rahul was obedient but very careless, because of severe emotional problems
- Instead of scolding and reprimanding him, I motivated him with chocolates for not making mistakes.
- **Conclusion-** He later topped the ISCE board examination. Basically needed someone to believe in him.

The board exams had just got over. I heaved a sigh of relief, as I walked out of the examination hall, thinking of the thing I had missed while preparing for the examination. Just then, I noticed little Rahul my neighbours son coming out from the Principal's office, clutching his mother hand. He looked quite distraught and avoided looking at me. I found this quite unusual, for normally he would greet me very cheerfully as ' Amit Bhaiya'

His mother looked quite perplexed and worried. Acknowledging my greeting she thrust Rahul's report card in my hand. The red circles in Math's and English required him to appear in the supplementary examination, for getting promoted to class V. "Amit can you help him in his studies," she entreated. Taken aback by her sudden request I fumbled, "me". "Yes Amit, he likes you and moreover your exams are now over, surely you can spare an hour for him daily." Rahul looked entreating at me and I simply did not have the courage to say no.

Returning home I cursed myself for having ruined my summer vacation, that I had so fondly looked forward to. Little did I know that I was going to experience an altogether different experience, that would last a lifetime.

I found Rahul to be obedient, but very careless. Initially I would scold him and even twist his ears, Gradually I discovered that he had severe emotional problems, because of his parents being separated. His working mother hardly had time for him. The long hours in the crèche after school, bore adversely on him.

I decided to change track. Instead of scolding and reprimanding him, I made him redo the exercise, gently pointing out the mistakes he had made. To further motivate him, I would announce a reward of a chocolate, for each exercise he did without making any mistake. Gradually I found that the lessons he previously found boring, became enjoyable to him. Each time I explained a new concept, his eyes would light up and I could feel a strange sense of accomplishment.

After his supplementary exams were over, his mother came to me with tears in her eyes. He had done extremely well, and had also started behaving well at home. A couple of years later, I learnt that he had topped in the ISCE board examination. I found the small part that I had played in his growth, very rewarding. He basically needed someone to believe in him.

2.

You will soon have to make a decision about the subjects that you wish to study in classes XI and XII.

Write a letter to your Grandfather telling him about the subjects that yoplan to take up. Be sure to explain the reason for your choice and how you think these subjects would help you in the future.

B/103, Silverline Apartments,
Faizabad Road,
Lucknow,
226010.
10 th May 2013

Dear Grandpa,

It was really refreshing talking to you on phone yesterday. I appreciate your concern for me and the interest you showed in the subjects I should choose for my XI and XII class. Out of the three streams i.e. Maths, Biology and Commerce, I plan to take up the first.

In this stream I shall have to study Physics, Chemistry, Mathematics and English. Out of the two optional subjects Computer and Hindi, I plan to choose Computers. Besides having a natural inclination for these subjects. I find them quite interesting, logical and even challenging. Moreover they open up many career options in the field of engineering and scientific research.

Fortunately my college has very good and experienced faculty in all these subjects. I am sure with their guidance, I shall be able to do well not only in the ISC board examination, but also crack the tough IIT competitive examination.

This would pave the way in realizing my dream of becoming an IITian, for which I seek your blessing. Please give my regards to Grandma

Your affectionate grandson
Siddhant.

(b) The children in your neighbourhood are forced to play on the street for want of a proper play area. Write a letter to the Editor of a popular newspaper, pointing out the need for a playground in your neighbourhood.

Give reasons why you think a play area is necessary and point out how it would benefit everyone who lives in that area.

B –103, Nehru Enclave,
Gomtinagar,
226010.
10th May 2013

The Editor,
The Daily,
MG Road,
Lucknow,
226001.

Subject : *Need for a play area for children in Shakti Nagar.*

Dear Sir,

I would like to draw the attention of the authorities, through the column of your prestigious daily, for the need of a play area for the children of Shakti Nagar colony Lucknow.

The colony in ward No IV has about two thousand residents, but unfortunately there is no playground for children. The nearest playfield is in Sharda Nagar, which is five kilometers away. The children are therefore forced to play on the streets. This besides obstructing the traffic, also endangers their life.

A play area in the colony would make the children happy and healthy. It would also help nurture and develop future sporting talent, that the country desperately needs.

The clean open space would be a boon for the residents, specially senior citizens for strolling in the morning and evening. It would keep them physically fit and healthy.

There is ample space in the colony for such a playfield. The authorities need to only clean up the garbage dumping yard, just opposite the petrol pump. This is a sore spot in the area. It would not only clean up the locality, but also meet a long standing demand of the residents of the area.

I therefore appeal to the concerned authorities to kindly take note of this serious problem, that besides endangering the lives of children, also poses a health hazard for the residents of the colony

Thanking you,

Yours faithfully,

Amit Sharma.

3.

(*a*) Give the meaning of each of the following words as used in the passage. One word answers or short phrases will be accepted.   [3]

   (*i*) nimbleness

   (*ii*) greeted

   (*iii*) bad character

(*b*) Answer the following questions briefly in your own words.

   (*i*) How was Chittru different from other boys?

   The other boys in the village worked in the fields. Chittru was different. He was lazy and preferred to fish in the stream, or eat the fruits from the trees of other people.

   (*ii*) What was Bisnu's ambition?

   Bisnu's ambition was to be able to read and write as well as anyone in the world. He therefore set his heart on receiving a good schooling. He walked everyday to school, l that was five miles away from his village.

   (*iii*) What information did Sarru give Bisnu?

   Sarru informed Bisnu about a leapord that had come to their village the previous night. Fortunately it did not kill any animal, as the dogs had set off the alarm before it could enter the cowshed. The villagers then chased it away.

   (*iv*) How did the information affect Bisnu?

   The information interested but did not excite Bisnu . This was for seeing a panther in the hills is quite common. They do not pose much of a problem, except during the winters when there is shortage of their natural prey.

(v) Why did the panther become a cattle-lifter?

Sarru and Bisnu agreed that the panther could have become a cattle lifter on being wounded by the shikaris. These people create most of the problem because they often wound the animal, making them slow in catching their natural prey like the barking deer. Hence in order to survive, they kill domestic animal and become cattle –lifter.

(vi) What joke does Sarru make?

When Bisnu enquired from Sarru about a panther that had killed 10 people in the valley 6 years ago. Sarru jokingly told him that he did not exactly know for he was very young. However according to some people in the village, it poisoned itself when it ate the headman of the village, who was disliked by everyone.

(c) (i) The langoors were a dignified community, that lived in the forest feeding on its vegetation. They remained in the trees, coming down only to play or sun themselves. While the adults leapt from tree to tree with great agility, the young ones wrestled on the grass. Unlike the red monkeys of the plains they did not approach dogs or humans.

(ii) TITLE

Dignified Langoors

They behaved in a very dignified manner, showing no cheekiness or dishonest habits like their brethren in the plains

4.

(a) 1. hunted.   2 brought   3. was engrossed.   4. munched.
     5. was getting.   6. would have blackened.   7. took.   8. had been trying.

(b) 1. over/in 2 to 3 in 4 into 5 for 6 inside 7 of 8 among

(c) (i) We should better get ready now for we may not have time to reach the airport.

(ii) Ever since Mr Liew returned from Japan he has been sick.

(iii) Both the debating teams were very happy on being declared joint champions.

(iv) Having escaped from prison, he looked for a place to hide

(d) (i) These windows will need to be cleaned again.

(ii) My mother said that I could go with you as long as I returned home by five o' clock.

(iii) It doesn't make any difference which chemical you put into the mixture first, the results will be the same.

(iv) Do you know the owner of this pen.

(v) Due to heavy rains the outdoor garden party was cancelled.

(vi) This is the first time I have seen so many people in the building.

(vii) We will light the fire, so that the rescuers will see us.

(viii) Most of the books had been removed from the shelf when we left.

NOTES

NOTES